Yona Sabar

A Jewish Neo-Aramaic Dictionary

Semitica Viva

Herausgegeben von Otto Jastrow

Band 28

2002
Harrassowitz Verlag · Wiesbaden

Yona Sabar

A Jewish Neo-Aramaic Dictionary

Dialects of Amidya, Dihok, Nerwa and Zakho, northwestern Iraq

Based on old and new manuscripts, oral and written bible translations, folkloric texts, and diverse spoken registers, with an introduction to grammar and semantics, and an index of Talmudic words which have reflexes in Jewish Neo-Aramaic

2002
Harrassowitz Verlag · Wiesbaden

Printed with a subsidy of American Academy for Jewish Research; Iranian Jewish Cultural Organization of California; Memorial Foundation for Jewish Culture; UCLA Council on Research (the Academic Senate); UCLA International Studies and Overseas Programm (Faculty Research); UCLA Center for Medieval and Renaissance Studies (GSR).

Die Deutsche Bibliothek – CIP-Einheitsaufnahme
Ein Titeldatensatz für diese Publikation ist bei Der Deutschen Bibliothek erhältlich

Die Deutsche Bibliothek – CIP Cataloguing-in-Publication-Data
A catalogue record for this publication is available from Die Deutsche Bibliothek

e-mail: cip@dbf.ddb.de

Printing and binding: Memminger MedienCentrum AG
Printed in Germany

ISSN 0931-2811
ISBN 3-447-04557-4

This dictionary is dedicated to the blessed memory

of my mother Miriam Sabar

who taught me Jewish Aramaic

as my mother tongue

תנצב"ה והויא מנוחתה בגן עדן

LIST OF CONTENTS

Acknowledgments

I am grateful to the following organizations for their support of my work:

American Academy for Jewish Research
Iranian Jewish Cultural Organization of California
Memorial Foundation for Jewish Culture
UCLA Council on Research, the Academic Senate
UCLA International Studies and Overseas Program, Faculty Research
UCLA Center for Medieval and Renaissance Studies (GSR)

During the many years that I worked on this dictionary, I discussed innumerable linguistic issues with my colleagues. Foremost among them is Simon Hopkins, who very patiently read the entire Introduction and made important and useful comments. Shelomoh Morag (ז"ל), Hans Jakob Polotsky (ז"ל), and Franz Rosenthal, all encouraged and inspired me at various stages of this work. Kasia Szpakowska, and Michael Fishbein, were most helpful, knowledgeable and patient in guiding me through technical computer-related problems. Others whose diverse help is much appreciated are Werner Arnold, Eliezer Chammou, Michael Chyet, Herbert Davidson, Gideon Goldenberg, Wolfhart Heinrichs, Robert Hoberman, Massood Haroonian, David Hirsch, Ralph Jaeckel, Vyacheslav Ivanov, Olga Kapeliuk, Wolf Leslau, Antonio Loprieno, Hezi Mutzafi, Amnon Netzer, Edward Odisho, Estiphan Panoussi, Fabrizio Pennachietti, Nahid Pirnazar, Marc Saperstein, Stanislav Segert, Michael Sokoloff, Yaffa Israeli, and Hossein Ziai. I am also grateful to Otto Jastrow, Editor of Semitica Viva, for including the dictionary in this series, and Michael Langfeld of the Otto Harrassowitz Verlag for his kind help and cooperation with all the details of the publication. Last but not least, my wife Stephanie, and my sons Ariel and Ilan (יצ"ו), were gracious and helpful whenever I needed moral or other support. Finally, to all the "last Mohican" informants, who had already passed away, and who provided me with many oral and written texts, and answered many of my questions about obscure meanings of words and points of grammar, I say: **הויא מנוחתוכון בגן עדן, אמן** May your (eternal) resting (place) be in Paradise, Amen!

Y.S.

Foreword

This dictionary is an effort to document the vocabulary of Jewish Neo-Aramaic in all its written and oral registers. The documentation includes: (a) context references, whenever possible, to all words in the written sources, and most of the oral ones; (b) cognates in older Eastern Aramaic, especially Syriac and Babylonian (Talmudic) Jewish Aramaic; (c) in the case of the numerous loanwords, the source of each, be it Arabic, Hebrew, Kurdish, Persian, Turkish etc.

Jewish Neo-Aramaic was used by Jewish communities in the remote and inaccessible areas of Kurdistan, presumably a residue (which includes also many neighboring Christian dialects) of older Aramaic dialects from Talmudic times and before. However, the oldest known manuscripts in Jewish Neo-Aramaic are only from 1647–1670 C.E., yet reflect older strata, with an established orthography and literary style.

In the early 1950s, practically all the Jewish communities of Iraqi Kurdistan, with the rest of the Jews of Iraq, emigrated en masse to Israel and the Jewish Neo-Aramaic dialects spoken by them have been almost entirely superseded by Hebrew. Therefore, it is my hope that this volume will be followed by dictionaries of the other Jewish Neo-Aramaic dialects of Iraq and Iran before they become totally extinct. Finally, I would like to consider this dictionary a linguistic monument to all the communities of Jewish Neo-Aramaic speech who used this language not only for everyday communication, but also for their literary and religious thoughts and sentiments.

Yona Sabar
Department of Near Eastern Languages and Cultures,
University of California, Los Angeles (UCLA)
October 2001; חוה"מ סוכות תשס"ב

Introduction

I. Jewish Neo-Aramaic: General Character and History

1. Jewish Neo-Aramaic (JNA) dialects belong to a large group of North-Eastern Neo-Aramaic (NENA) dialects which were spoken until our times by most Jews and Christians throughout Kurdistan (politically divided today by Iraq, Iran, Turkey and Syria). These dialects are related to older Eastern Aramaic/Syriac dialects, known to us mostly through classical literary works which once prevailed in a much larger area (the most famous for Jewish Aramaic being the Babylonian Talmud, and Targum Onkelos and Jonathan, which, however, are of mixed East-West origin). However, it should be emphasized that the modern dialects do not seem to be the direct descendants of the classical literary dialects.[1] A much smaller residue of old Western Aramaic (Syria-Palestine) is represented by three Christian and Muslim mountain villages north of Damascus, the largest being Ma'lula (**Maᶜlūla**)[2]. An important group among the Christian Neo-Aramaic (ChNA) dialects is that of Tur Abdin (known as Turoyo, **Ṭūrōyo**) in Turkey, which stands geographically between the Eastern Neo-Aramaic dialects and the Western Neo-Aramaic of Syria (the Ma'lula group), but which is structurally much closer to the former.[3] Modern Aramaic also includes Modern Mandaic, spoken by Mandeans (Gnostics) in Ahwaz (**ʾahwāz**) ,[4] Iran, and parts of Iraq until recently, and although of Eastern origin, typologically it is not related to NENA.[5] Note that Ma'lula, Turoyo, and Mandaic do not include any Jewish dialects.

2. With the Islamic conquest in the seventh century, Aramaic in the towns of Lower Iraq was very quickly superseded by Arabic as a spoken language and eventually as culture language as well. However, the remote and almost inaccessible areas of Kurdistan remained virtually free of Arabic influence, thus enabling the original Aramaic dialects to survive there until modern times. After the collapse of the Ottoman empire, followed by the rise of national governments in Iraq, Iran, Syria, and Turkey, the beginning of motorized transportation, and urbanization of rural areas, the national languages, Arabic, Persian, and Turkish, began to gradually encroach upon Neo-Aramaic. The decline of Neo-Aramaic has been critically accelerated by the emigration of the Kurdistani Jews to Israel, where their Neo-Aramaic has been gradually replaced by Hebrew, and the emigration of the Christian Neo-Aramaic speakers first to large cities such as Baghdad, Teheran, and then, especially after the recent Gulf War, to Europe, America, Canada, Australia, and South America.

3. According to Ben-Jacob's monograph on Kurdish Jews (1981), there were throughout Kurdistan at various times about two hundred villages and towns in which Jews lived, mostly with Christian and Muslim Kurds, but occasionally only by themselves. The numbers were very small, in some settlements only a few families, the largest having no more than a few hundred families (at least in our times). It is estimated that the total number of Kurdistani Jews ca. 1950, before their emigration to Israel, was about 25,000 persons. However, due to frequent

---

[1]For some typological similarities see Khan 4.

[2]On which see Arnold 1989-91; Arnold forthcoming.

[3]Hob89:4, 6; Jastrow 1990a:90; Khan 2.

[4]Macuch1965, 1993; cf. Hob89 4; Khan 2.

[5]On some shared grammatical and lexical features of NENA dialects, see Fox 1994; for a good comparative summary work of all groups, see Jastrow 1997.

tribal wars and the general instability of life in Kurdistan, the Jewish population, as well as others, rose and fell continuosly. Documents, travellers' reports and manuscripts suggest that some places had a large Jewish population in the past, e.g., Nerwa, Amidya (**ᶜamídya**, official Ar **ᶜamādīya**), Arbil (Z **ʾárwil**, K **hawlar**, official Ar **ʾirbīl**)[6], but are known to have had only a few families in our time; and vice versa, a place with a large, relatively speaking, Jewish population in our time, e.g., my hometown of Zakho (**zāxo**), whose Jewish population numbered about 315 families in 1950[7]) is hardly mentioned in historical sources.[8]

4. In addition to the geographical division of Neo-Aramaic dialects into groups according to the various parts of Kurdistan (southern, northern, central, eastern), there also existed , as is especially noticeable in places with large Jewish population, such as Zakho in Iraqi Kurdistan and Urmia in Iranian Kurdistan, a subdivision into Christian and Jewish dialects (similar to the division of the Arabic dialects of Baghdad and Mosul into Christian, Jewish and Muslim)[9]. These divisions and subdivisions were quite distinctive from one another in part of their phonology, morphology, syntax and vocabulary, to the point of reducing mutual intelligibility among the speakers of dialects distant from each other to almost zero. It is necessary to mention that due to the rugged topography of Kurdistan, both Neo-Aramaic and Kurdish until modern times were very rich in dialects.[10] It will not be an exaggeration to say that every village and little town has its own Kurdish and Neo-Aramaic dialect or at least certain peculiar linguistic features. The village of Arodhin (**ʾarādi n**), for example, had only two Jewish families and they seem to have had their own dialect!

---

[6]Khan 1.

[7]Yona .1989:36; Sabar, forthcoming; on a folkloristic-Historical character of the Jews of Zaklho, see Gavish.

[8]Out of 533 localities and rivers listed in B.-Z. Eshel, *Jewish Settlements in Babylonia during Talmudic Times*, only a few are known from more recent times, e.g., #40 = אקרא דסליקוס = כרכא דבי סלוך = כרכוך Karkuk; #45 ארבל(י) Arbil; #389 נציבין Nusaybin [=Z **nıṣṣēbin**]; #485 כרדו/קרדו 'CordyeneEshel, *Jewish Settlements in Babylonia during Talmudic Times*, only a few are known from more recent times, e.g., #40 = אקרא דסליקוס = כרכא דבי סלוך כרכוך Karkuk; #45 ארבל(י) Arbil; #389 נציבין Nusaybin [=Z **nıṣṣēbin**]; #485 כרדו/קרדו 'CordyeneEshel, *Jewish Settlements in Babylonia during Talmudic Times*, only a few are known from more recent times, e.g., #40 אקרא דסליקוס = כרכא דבי סלוך = כרכוך Karkuk; #45 ארבל(י) Arbil; #389 נציבין Nusaybin [=Z **nıṣṣēbin**]; #485 כרדו/קרדו 'Cordyene' = **Gzīra** or **Jazīrat Ibn-ᶜUmar** =T **Cizre** (see below n. 121). = **Gzīra** or **Jazīrat Ibn-ᶜUmar** =T **Cizre** (see below n. 121). = **Gzīra** or **Jazīrat Ibn-ᶜUmar** =T **Cizre** (see below n. 121).

[9]Blanc; Jastrow 1989.

[10]As expected, also Talmudic Aramaic reflects and mentions various local dialects; see details at Epstein 14-17; cf. e.g., ההיא בת מחוזא דהות נסיבה לנהרדעא; אתו לקמיה דרב נחמן; שמעא לקלא דבת מחוזא היא (כתובות נד/א) 'A woman of Mahoza was married to a man from Neharde'a; they came before Rabbi Nahman, and (after) hearing her pronunciation, (he realized) that she was from Mahoza.

5. The Jewish dialects can be provisionally divided into four major groups (with some major localities in parentheses): (1) North-West Iraqi Kurdistan (Zakho, Dihok, Nerwa); (2) South-East Iraqi Kurdistan (Arbil, Koy Sanjaq; Rawanduz) (3) Iranian-Turkish Azerbaijan (Urmia, Bashqala, Salamas, Sablagh); (4) Iranian Kurdistan (Saqqiz, Bijar, Sena, Kerend) . The first group, generally speaking, seems to be the most conservative (see below), with many more Aramaic, 'Semitic', features, including substantial Arabic influence, some of it through Kurdish, followed by the second, while the third and fourth are the most 'non-Semitic', heavily influenced by Kurdish, Persian and Azeri Turkish, some or all of which were spoken by the local Jews as well[11] . Christian Neo-Aramaic (ChNA) dialects are divided, generally speaking, along the same lines and show similar spheres of influence from the neighboring languages, i.e., Arabic, Persian, Kurdish, and Turkish dialects. Kurdish, an Iranian, non-Semitic language has two major groups of dialects, Kurmanji in the northwest (which has the greatest effect on our group), and Sorani in the southeast (with little effect, if any, on our group). There is no doubt that Kurdish has had the most substantial impact on all the NENA dialects, Jewish or Christian.[12] Almost all NENA speakers spoke Kurdish as well, and some spoke only Kurdish, e.g. Sherwan.[13] There is no doubt that many loanwords from Arabic, Persian or Turkish entered JNA through Kurdish. However, in Iraq, especially in modern times when the contacts with Mosul and Baghdad became more intensive, many NENA speakers spoke Arabic (Anatolian, Syrian, Iraqi dialects) as well, and often shifted from NENA to Arabic altogether.[14]Some Kurdish Jews in Iraqi Kurdistan, for example in the village of Sindor, spoke Arabic as their everyday language, as well as in the towns of Aqra, Karkuk, and Arbil.[15] However, even the old literary JNA texts of Nerwa (copied in1647-1670 CE) show much lexical and literary influence and perhaps even knowledge of literary Arabic, as may be suggested by 'bookish' Arabic words and sentences in which almost every word is Arabic or derived from Arabic, e.g. **xlıqle ʾilāha ʿinsān umzōyınne bmanṭiq ublisān** 'God created man and embellished him with speech and language.'[16]

6. It is difficult at this point of research to speak of 'proto' JNA, or to identify which linguistic features unite all JNA dialects, distiguishing them from ChNA in general.[17] The only

---

[11]Hopkins 1993: 64.

[12]Chyet 1995, 1997; Garbell 1965b; Hopkins 1991:790; Hopkins 1999: 321-27; Kapeliuk 1999:12-15; Khan 9.

[13]Hopkins 1993: 64.

[14]Cf. Khan 10-11, including influence on grammar.

[15]Jastrow 1990b.

[16]Sabar 1966:340; cf. Koran 55:3-4; Mengozzi 26-28 on 'Learned Multilingualism' on ChNA. Arabic loanwords are attested already in Ge'onic Aramaic/OS, e.g., כַּבָּזָא, כבאזא/OS ܟܒܙܐ < Ar خبّاز; see SokBA 550).

[17]See, however, Goldenberg 2000 on some early NA grammatical features, such as the coupla paradigms, neutralization of gender in the plural, the participles replacing the finite verbal forms, the use of the infinitive in compound tenses, which are more or less typical to almost

safe feature unique to all JNA vs. ChNA is the mostly religious-cultural Hebrew lexical element in all Jewish dialects (and Jewish languages in general). These elements, absorbed during many centuries in exile, include mostly Judaic terms and concepts, but surprisingly some everyday secular words as well. Of course, after the emigration to Israel, JNA has absorbed hundreds of loanwords from Israeli Hebrew (not included in our JNA Dictionary) (=JNAD), and eventually JNA will be totally superseded by it.[18] Similarly, ChNA may be distinguished from JNA by the loanwords of Christian religious-cultural character from classical-liturgical Syriac. As expected, also Biblical proper names used by Jews and Christians have different pronunciations, e.g. JNA **+rāḥel** 'Rachel' (H רחל) , **+rıfqa** 'Rebecca' (H רבקה), **+avrāham** 'Abraham' = ChNA **rāxīl, rapqa , orāham**. One can speak of differences between JNA vs. ChNA mostly in a certain locality, such as Zakho, Koy Sanjaq, or Urmia, but less so as a whole.[19] While JNA and ChNA in Zakho were mutually intelligible and quite similar, in Urmia and Koy Sanjaq they were quite different.[20]. Generally speaking, however, ChNA seems more conservative, especially in the vocabulary, than JNA, e.g. retention of diphthongs (e.g. **bayta** 'house', **layle** 'night'; **mawta** 'death', **kawda** 'liver')[21], and older vocabulary (e.g. **ʾimāma** 'day', **ṣapra** 'morning', **šlāma** 'greetings', **ṭāwa** 'good'). However, some caution is necessary, since a word known as 'typical' ChNA in one place may be quite common in JNA in another place or time (as I have learned from my studies of old Nerwa texts in which I found 'typical' ChNA words, such as **dıx** 'how', **yāma** 'sea', **ʾilāna** 'tree', **p-r-x** 'to fly' **ṭıllaṯ** 'three', f., **mdīta** 'city'[22], **zūze** 'money' (so well known from the Passover song **Ḥad-Gadyā** is replaced by **pāre** < T/K,[23] but in JNA of Kerend (4th group) **zuze** is the regular word for 'money'. The Jewish dialect in each place was quite different and almost unintelligible for a Jew visiting from one place to another. There was no JNA koine that Jews from various localities could use among themselves. Hopkins mentions that even within Iran, Jews from Azerbaijan found it very difficult to understand Jews from the

all dialects of NENA; Hob85, Hob91, for reconstructing some common words and forms.

[18]Sabar 1975.

[19]Hob89:8; Sabar 1995; Hopkins 1993:65.

[20]See examples in Mutz :13, e.g., **xa béta rā́ba** (Ch.)/**xa belá ruwwá** (J.) 'a big house'. Mutzafi assumes that a possible explanation for the 'deep gap' between the two may be that the Jews and the Christians came from different regions and kept most of the original features, even after living very closely in Koy Sanjak itself for centuries. An interesting example of the inter-religious differences is in a reconstructed actual text from Z (PolU 431), in which Jews converse with Christians, using various Christian forms and words: **xōni hōle zwīna** 'My brother has bought...' = JNA **ʾaxōni wēle zwīna**; but the Christians make no adjustment to the Jewish dialect, using typical ChNA forms and words: **bʾalāha** 'by God', **diyyōxun** 'yours', **ṭıllas** 'three', **xammıš** 'five' (f.), **ʿınnābe** 'teeth'; **mdafōye** 'lose (teeth)'.

[21]Hob93:117; but see below, VI, §15.7.

[22]Cf. Hob93:121-22; some of these words are also known from JNA in Iranian Kurdistan.

[23]Sabar 1983:164; Sabar 1988:101; in a folktale from Zakho (PolU 1) **zūza** (quite rare) means 'tax, tribute'.

adjacent Kurdistan region, and they had to resort to Persian instead, not to mention Jews from more distant areas.[24]

6. The vocabulary in the dictionary belongs entirely to the North-West group, which, in addition to Zakho proper (Z), includes the immediately neighboring dialects of Nerwa (N, spoken) and old Nerwa Texts (NT), Amidya (Am), Dihok (D), Arodhen (Arodh), Gzira (Gz). As expected, there is much vocabulary common not only to all members of this group, but to other groups as well.[25] As mentioned, this group, as a whole, is the most conservative. Yet, there are exceptions in vocabulary, i.e., other groups may retain a native Aramaic word, while our group has a loanword, e.g., 'male', 'sea' are **ʾurza** (K), **baḥḥar** (Ar) in Z, but **dexra**, **yama** in the 3rd group.[26] The following are some distinctive phonological and morphological features that demonstrate the conservative character of our group.

7. One such feature is the pronunciation of ancient interdentals **d̠** and **t̠**, which even in our group have various pronunciations: Respectively, **d̠** and **t̠** in D, **d** and **t̠** in Am, **d** and **s** in spoken N (but most probably **d̠** and **t̠** in NT), **z** and **s** in Z. Outside of this group, both of them may be pronounced as lateral **l** (e.g.,**ʾila** < **ʾid̠a** 'hand', **bela** <**bēt̠a** 'house'.[27]

8. NT, Am and D have two sets of 3rd person pronouns, one of which is much closer to older Aramaic forms, i.e., **ʾāhu(n)** 'he', **ʾāhi(n)** 'she' , **ʾahnun** 'they, c.' Z, however, has only the other set: **ʾāwa, ʾāya, ʾāni**. Outside our group just: **o** 'he, she', **oni** 'they'.[28]

9. The 3rd m. and f. suffixed pronouns in NT are **-e(h), -a(h)**, (e.g. מנאה = **mınnah** 'from her'; אביה = **ʾıbbeh**), which in some neighboring Christian dialects have become **-eḥ, -aḥ**. e.g., **mınnaḥ**, but Z has just: **-e, -a**.[29] However, outside our group, these pronouns are:

---

[24]Hopkins 1993: 65-66. Note that Christian Neo-Aramaic words or variants, used by Jewish speakers when quoting proverbs or folksongs originating in Christian dialects are included in JNAD and indicated as such (e.g., תורא **tawra** 'ox'; שלאמא **šlāma**; צפארה **ṣpāre** 'morning'; ממכאנה **mamkāne** 'breasts'; כליא **xılya** 'milk'; כמא **kımma** 'mouth'; בייא **bayya** 'house'.

[25]For the purpose of comparison, to find out what is common and what is different in form and semantic nuances, I have included in square brackets at the end of the entry many linguistically interesting examples from the Jewish dialects of the other groups, especially from Garbell (1965)'s glossary, and the very recent works of Khan, Israeli, Mutzafi (all references clearly indicated).

[26]Sabar 1983:166, 168.

[27]Cohen 950; Khan 7, 8; Israeli 18; Kapeliuk 1997: 540-42 sees the **d̠/t̠** > **l** as an Irano-Aramaic Sprachbund; cf. Mutz 31ff.; but for **l** > **d̠**, see already in TA (and OS and even before?) in certain forms of the root אזל 'to go': אזדא/אזלא; אזדו/אזלו, and סרגל/ סרגד (ܣܪܓܠ) 'to trace a line'; for more details see Epstein 58; Friedman, passim.

[28]Israeli 29; Khan 8; on the development of the latter sets from the first and their relation to older Aramaic forms, see Hob90:84-87.

[29]Sara 1974:64; Sabar 1995:34.

-ev, -av;[30] cf. also NT occasional אבוה **ʾıbbuh** = Z **ʾıbbu** 'in them'.

10. Our group, and especially Z itself, has a clearer gender distinction of all singular pronouns, whereas in other dialects and groups the gender (and even number) difference is either vague or does not exist at all, e.g., Z: **ʾaw** (m.), **ʾay** (f.) 'this', **ʾan** 'these (c.)', but NT **ʾadya** 'this' (c.)'; Am: **ʾayya** 'this (c.).' Outside the group, one pronoun serves all: **o** 'he, she, that (c.), those (c.)'.[31]

11. Also, while our group uses forms of the demonstrative pronouns, whose relation to classical Syriac/Aramaic forms is quite obvious, the other groups use a Kurdish suffix **-ake**, e.g., **ʾaw** <**haw**] **bēṯa** vs. **belake** 'the house'.[32]

12. The ordinal numbers in our group are normally made of the cardinal number preceded by the Aramaic possessive particle **d**, whereas in the other groups the Kurdish suffix **-min** is often used: **yarxa dʾarba** vs. **yarxa dʾarbamin** 'the fourth month'.[33]

13. There are, in addition to lexical differences, some important phonological and morphological differences within our group as well and they will be discussed later, in the Chapters on Phonology and Morphology. Here it is enough to mention just the following characteristic innovations: The 2nd and 3rd suffixed plural personal pronouns are **-ōxun, -ōhun** in Z, D, and Am[34], but **-ēxun, -ēhun** in NT. NT and Am have preterite verbal forms with 'sandwiched' 1st and 2nd objective pronouns, e.g. **qṭīl-ın-ne** 'He killed me (m.)', **qṭīl-ıt-te** 'He killed you (m. sg.)'[35], which in Z would be respectively paraphrased: **qam qāṭıl-li, qam qāṭıl-lox**. However, the 3d person is used in Z as well: **qṭīl-ā-le** 'He killed her', etc. NT, as expected, preserving some archaic grammatical features that are rare or even unattested in the more recent dialect, e.g. **māṯe** (מאתה; cf. OA מְאתַי) 'two hundred' (vs. the common **tarteʾma**); מאן, מן **man** (cf. OA מן, מאן) 'who?' vs. the common **mani**; **rurwa** < רברבא 'big' > Z **⁺ruwwa**, Am **⁺ʾurwa**; נהתא **nhaṯa/nahṯa** (?) 'ear' > Z **nāsa**; **n-ʾ-h** to light, to dawn (OA נגה); **nʾahta** dawn. In Am/ Arodh/NT **ā** › **ō** occasionally.[36] Lexically, of course, there is a lot in common, but there are some words typical to each dialect, e.g., Z **n-p-q** 'to go out', **bāš** 'good', **ṯāli** 'for me', vs. NT, Am, Arodh **p-l-ṭ, šapīra, ṭlāṯi**.[37] It seems that NT and Gzira have the pl. of R_3**y** end with **-i**, like the sound verb, e.g.,: **šāti, dāri, yāʾi**, whereas in Z the m.sg. and pl. have coalesced: **šāte, dāre, yāʾe**. Note also Gz **raxúqa,**

---

[30]Khan 8; Israeli 29

[31]Israeli 32; Khan 8.

[32]Khan 10; Israeli 79.

[33]Khan 10, Israeli 84, with other variants.

[34]Hob89:195.

[35]Cf. Hob89:36: **ptix-án-noxun** 'You (pl.) opened me (f.)'.

[36]Cf. below VI, §15.4.

[37]Sabar 1988:99.

raxúqta 'distant' vs. Z/NT **raḥūqa, raḥuqta; ṣoráya** 'Christian', ⁺**nūra** 'fire' vs Z **sōrāya, nūra; zōna** (< OA זבנא) 'time' vs. Z **zūna**.[38]

[38]For details on all these see below.

II. The Sources for the Dictionary

The Neo-Aramaic lexicon represented in the JNAD includes words from oral and written texts of the first group, i.e., Zakho and its immediate vicinity (see I, §5, above) as were used by the Jewish communities in these localities until their en masse emigration to Israel ca. 1950.[39] More specifically:

1. The dialect of Zakho (Z), known to me as my mother tongue and recorded by me on index cards during the last thirty years or so, is represented in all its registers, including: spoken ones (everyday speech, oral, published and unpublished, folk literature (see III below and Bibliograpphy), recorded-oral and written Bible translations, ritual literature, baby talk, women's talk, cryptic lingo, etc.). The Bible translations, orally transmitted from generation to generation, are significant for they preserve many archaic words which had disappeared from the spoken register, a lucky strike for an historical study of colloquial languages that, relatively, have little written records. These translations also reflect how the community of Kurdish Jews understood the Bible, and, paradoxically, vice versa: thanks to the Hebrew original, we know today, almost fifty years after their last functional use, what these archaic JNA words more or less meant. The distance in time and the old age of the informants affect even spoken registers; whenever I was not sure about the meaning or pronunciation, or the correct plural form, etc., I would ask a few informants, and at times they would come up with very similar answers, but at others, they couldn't recall the meaning or the form at all, or would give just some vague answer.

2. The large corpus of Nerwa Texts (NT), found in manuscripts from 1647-1670 CE, and most probably reflecting strata of some 100-200 years before[40], includes extensive Midrashic (homiletic) literature, Bible commentaries, and hymns. Most of it has been published, but some, mostly hymns, is still unpublished (=NTU). NT are very important for diachronical study of JNA and NA in general, and serve as an important link between modern dialects and older ones, since most of the modern dialects have very little written material. Also, they are the only extensive literary texts, showing a tradition of at least a few hundred years, which seems to have reached its peak in the *yeshivot* established by the famous family of Barazani rabbis in Amidya (and probably the neighboring Nerwa) and elswhere. NT are also distinguished for their relatively consistent spelling system for JNA.

3. Amidya (Am) texts include the texts published by Hoberman (Hob89, Hob97), the Passover Haggadah by Avidani (AvidH), Bible translations (Sabar 1983a, 1983c, 1988a) and Amidya words in Brauer (1947, 1993), Rivlin's works, and some unpublished manuscripts (AmU). Many texts in Rivlin's work (RivSh, etc.), even when called 'Zakho', seem to reflect

---

[39]Note that loanwords from Israeli Hebrew and Palestinian Arabic, such as **mits** 'juice', **mxonat kvisa** 'washing machine', **nāmūsīye** 'bed', **ʿattāla** 'porter', that entered JNA after the emigration to Israel are usually not included; on which see Sabar 1975b.

[40]As suggested by some (archaic?) spellings: in some manuscripts there are many cases of final **-h**, e.g. ביתוה **bēṯuh** 'their house', but in others normally ביתו; or לילי, תרי 'night, two', respectively for לילה, תרה; for more details see Sabar 1976a: Chapter IV.

Amidya/Nerwa dialects alternating with Z, e.g., בַּאבֵּיכון/בַּאבוכון **bābēxun/bābōxun** (RivSh134-5) 'your father'; אִמֵּינִי **ʾımmēni** (as in Z) 'with us'/מִנֵּיכון **mınnēxun** 'with you' (as in Am)(both ibid.:132; **mın** in the sense of 'with,' and the morpheme **-ēxun** do not exist in Z; see. I, §13 above). This being the case in Rivlin and other late traditional texts, where forms from various dialects co-exist due to (mis)copying, misprints, or inconsitent dialect adjustment etc., we found it necessary to give the reference mostly to the written or published source, i.e., Rivlin: Shirat (=RivSh); Avidani: Haggadah (=AvidH), etc., in their abbreviated form, rather than by attribution to a particular dialect (Am, D, N, Z etc.). This, of course, excludes the spoken registers which I have collected from oral sources.

4. Dihok texts include selected Bible translations published in Sabar 1983a, 1988a, 1990a, 1993, 1994 (=BT1-BT5) and words from selections of unpublished Bible translations in PolG.

5. Arodhen texts include just a sample in Sabar 1988a (=BT2) , and a few words from my and Hezi Mutzafi's collection (private communication).

6. Gzira texts include only texts recorded in Israel (See Nakano), which include many Israeli Hebrew (e.g., **mits** 'juice') and Palestinian Arabic words (**aywa** 'yes') - all usually ignored in JNAD. Also some transcriptions seem to be influenced by Japanese, e.g., **kutléni** for **kutréni** 'both of us' (Nakano 1970 , 167, twice); **xazlu** for **xazru** 'near them'; **jaġíla** for **jġíla** 'busy'; **xzí** for **xwazí** 'would that' (all ibid. 195), and perhaps **millíʾta** for **mıllıta** 'nation' (ibid. 198); **ṣoráya** (emphatic) = Z **sōrāya** (plain) 'Christian'. Some seem 'instant' creations, e.g., **kanáfta** 'wing' (< H כנף, Gz73 58, 77).

III. Jewish Neo-Aramaic Studies

The discovery and study of NA is relatively young. The study of ChNA dialects is only about one hundred and thirty years old. ChNA dialects have been documented in several grammars, old (Noeldeke 1868; Maclean 1895, and others) and more recent (O. Jastrow, Krotkoff, Sara, and others), and dictionaries (Maclean 1901, Oraham 1943, and others), glossaries, chrestomathies, etc. The study of JNA is even younger, beginning in earnest with Duval (1883), but becoming more intensive only after the emigration of Kurdish Jews to Palestine-Israel in the 1920s and the 1950s, thus making the study of their dialects more accessible to scholars, such as Rivlin, Garbell, Polotsky, and others.[41] These scholars also were quite aware that these dialects would be soon on the verge of extinction to be superseded by Israeli Hebrew, making the task of recording them very urgent. At present there are several scholars in Israel and abroad, such as Goldenberg, Hoberman, Hopkins, Israeli, Kapeliuk, Khan, Mutzafi, and Sabar, dedicating much time and energy to the study of JNA in general, or to the comparsion of JNA with ChNA, or to the description of one specific JNA dialect or another. One should also mention that, in recent years some caring native speakers, having realized that their spoken language is about to die, and especially being now aware that it is not so-called 'Kurdit' 'Kurdish' (as popularly called in Israel), but rather Aramit 'Aramaic,' a sister of Hebrew and a quasi-holy Jewish language, they have resorted to 'preserving' it by publishing translations of religious material from Hebrew (e.g., AlfH, AlfM), a cook-book with the original food names (ShiKC), and two dictionaries (Shilo 1995; Yona 1999). Both of these dictionaries are basically a valiant labor of love. Shilo's is an effort to translate every word and even the explanations and conjugations of Hebrew words in A. Even-Shoshan's Hebrew dictionary (א, אבן-שושן, *מלון חדש*; many editions, e.g., Jerusalem, 1955), often inventing words or idiosyncratic suffixes to match the sounds and meaning of the Hebrew source[42]. These dictionaries also include many words from Israeli Hebrew, mistakenly assumed by the authors to be JNA. Yona's is more serious and more systematic, but he, too, mostly translates from a Hebrew dictionary and includes his own translations of Hebrew proverbs, and religious quotations[43] for pedagogical reasons, including words and terms that were never used in Kurdistan.[44] Many of these words were included probably unintentionally, because the distance in time of over forty years since they had left Kurdistan made it difficult for the authors to remember which words were actualluy used in Kurdistan and which became

[41]For a recent exhaustive bibliography on JNA see Hopkins 1993.

[42]E.g., in the letter Tav, every real or invented NA word is prefixed with **ta** [='for' (?)] to make it sound more like the Hebrew word it translates, i.e., H תִּיכוֹנִי 'middle' = NA תַּפַּלְגָא (Shilo 915)[= {**ta**}**palga**]; H תַּלְיָן 'executioner' = NA תַּמְתַלְתְיָנָא (921) [= {**ta**}**mtaltyāna**; incidentally, even **mtaltyāna** is not a real word, as the word for 'excecutioner' is **jállad** < Ar]; H תָּמִיר 'tall' = NA תַּרוֹמָנָא (927) [= {**ta**}**rōmāna**].

[43]According to the author (p. 21): מן התנ"ך, מספרות חז"ל, ומספרות אחרת 'from the Bible, Rabinical literature, and other literature'.

[44]E.g., קֶשׁ, (ע) ת = מְזֻמָּן (Yona 403) [< En 'cash', common in Israeli Hebrew] is assumed to be an adjective (ת = תואר) from Arabic (ע)! Also the Hebrew transcription misleadingly suggests **qeš** (and betrays its Israeli pronunciation; see below V, §2.5) instead of the expected **keš**. The word for 'cash' in Z was **nıqdi** (Ar).

known only in Israel.[45] It is hoped that most recent studies, such as the fine monograph by Khan and the Ph.D. Dissertations of Yaffa Israeli and Hezi Mutzafi, and other studies in the future will enable scholars to form a comprehensive and comparative view of JNA Dialects in our time and in past centuries . IT is my sincere hope that this dictionary of an important and most conservative group of spoken and written JNA dialects will serve this purpose as well.

---

[45]Therefore, I made it a point not to utilize these two dictionaries, fearing that if I found there a word that was not known to me before, it would not be a real word but rather invented or imagined. For this and other reasons I tried to give the contextual written source for most words of JNAD, especially when there was any doubt about meaning, pronunciation, etc.

IV. The Vocabulary of JNA and Its Relations to Other Languages

1. As expected, most of the native words are more or less reflexes of older classical (Eastern) Aramaic/Syriac dialects (OA/OS) in form and meaning, and for many words the same meaning, if not the exact same sound, survived without a change for centuries, e.g., Z **šarqiᶜa**, OS **šarqūᶜā**, still mean exactly the same in both: 'a resounding slap on the face;' **xwīṣa** f. 'crushed pieces of bread soaked in hot butter and sprinkled with sugar' < OA/OS חביצא m. 'dish of flour, honey, and oil.[46] The word **qāša** '(Christian) priest' is derived from OA/OS **qaššā**, which is a late sporadic contracted reflex of the common form **qaššīša**; **bıltīta** 'worm in wood' has not changed much from TA בּוּלְטִיתָא 'worm-eaten (wood)'[47]. However, there are also quite a few words which show clear phonological, morphological and semantic innovations, at least when compared with words listed in OA/OS dictionaries. As is obvious to any scholar of NA, just as the morphology cannot be considered a direct descendant of classical literary (Eastern) OA/OS (see I, §2 above), neither can the vocabulary. It is quite probable that some words existed only in the spoken registers of OA/OS. The available dictionaries basically document only the literary/written registers that have survived from classical times.[48] For example, the root **ṭ-p-r** 'to burn', **ṭapparīṯa** 'excessive heat', well known in JNA, is not listed in any OA/OS dictionaries, may be related to Akkadian **tipāru** 'torch', and perhaps existed in some spoken register of OA/OS (marked *OA in JNAD).[49] Similarly, the root **s-y-l** 'to fuck' (probably due to its vulgarity, used mainly in curses) is not attested in OA dictionaries, but seems to be an obvious Aramaic cognate of H סלל/סוּל/סלסל 'commit lewdness'.[50] In some cases, a common NA (Z) root appears to be very rare in OA/OS, e.g., **x-r-ʾ** 'to wash thoroughly (with a rubbing sponge)' seems to be a metathesised reflex of *OA **r-ḥ-ᶜ** (רחע, cognate of H רחץ, Ar رحض),

rarely attested in an OA dialect, including the Samaritan, in which it is reflected as **r-ᶜ-y**, and recently in Western NA.[51] Other examples: **g-r-š** 'to pull, drag' is common in NA and in OS, but Babylonian Aramaic has only גרש, pa. 'to divorce' (SokBA 305); the meaning 'drag' is well attested, however, in the Jewish Palestinian Aramaic (SokPA 137); NA **x-p-q** 'to embrace' = OA/OS **ḥ-b-q** + OS **ᶜ-p-q**; NA **dehna** 'fat' = Targumic דַּהֲנָא (M. Jastrow 281); but OA/OS

---

[46]Cf. SokBA 426 האי חביצא דאית ביה פירורין כזית 'a **ḥaviṣa** dish which has olive sized [bread] pieces', showing that the 'receipe' of this dish didn't change much. Cf. also Ar. خبيص 'medley'.

[47]See M. Jastrow 146: בּוּלטיתא; Arukh: בולטיתא, בלטיתא; מלטיתא; OS ܒܠܛܝܬܐ.

[48]Cf. Sokoloff's observation and conclusion: "Many Jewish Babylonian Aramaic words occurring even in the printed editions are absent from the lexica" (SokBA 16, n. 35). OS/OA lexica consulted forJNAD are (see Bibliography): Aruch Completum; Brockelmann; M. Jastrow; Levy; Payne-Smith; and especially Sokoloff, which used the database of the Comprehensive Aramaic Lexicon Project, co-ordinated by S.A. Kaufman, which is now available online.

[49]For another possible etymology, see below VIII, §17.5

[50]See M. Jastrow 995: סולל < סוּל to sport; (euphem.) to commit lewdness (women with children or with other women).

[51]See Greenfield 1991: 592-3; Fassberg 288-90; and below VIII, §17.1.

דוּהֲנָא (SokBA 315); **dūka** ~ **dukṯa** 'place' = OA/OS/Mand דוּכְּתָא; Targ דוכא; pl. **dūkāne** ~ **dukawāṯa** = OA pl. דוּכָּאתָא ~ דוּכְּתֵי ~ דוּכְּוָאתָא (SokBA 318); **dıdwa** (m.), **dıdūṯa** (f.), 'fly'; pl. **dıdwe** = OA דֵּידְבָא ; pl. דֵּידְבָתָא; NA **darāša** (< **qaṭṭāla** formation) one who publicly expounds Scripture, a darshan = OA **daršānā** (< **qaṭlānā** formation; NA **xaḏāra** 'peddler' = OS ܚܕܘܪܐ/OA הָדוֹרָא (< **qātōlā** formation); **xıšbōna** 'account' = OA/OS; חוּשְׁבָּנָא;[52] **yaqūra** 'heavy' = OA/OS יַקִּירָא dear, heavy, expensive; כאוא, כהוא **kāwa**, **kahwa** (NT2), air-hole, little window = Mand כאוא; OA/OS כַּוְּותָא/BA כַּוָּה*; Ar كوّة f.; pl. כוואתא **kawāṯa** (NT3), כהויה **kahwe** (NT2), כַּוַאוֵוי **kawāwe** (Z; Sa83c 38, Am) = OA/OS pl. כַּוֵּי. In some cases the NA word has cognates, or similar sounding words, in several contact languages, and it is not sure which one was the lending source, if any.[53]

2. While many loanwords from Arabic, Kurdish, Persian, Turkish, Hebrew, and other languages are more or less expected reflexes in form and meaning, there are quite a few local innovations and variations as well. Again, some of these probably existed in the spoken registers of the original languages, and, therefore, are not listed in the dictionaries. Moreover, some Kurdish (Kurmanji) and Iraqi Arabic words which I knew as a child (ca. 1950), are missing, or at least I could not find them (in spite of a thorough search) in the specific dictionaries, e.g., **ḥınd-ıl-ḥōt** 'see-saw'; some were found by a trial and error, e.g., **jalal** 'brook' < Ar **šallāl**; **qahwāna** 'music record'[54] < IrAr **qawāna** (cf. K **qawān** 'cylinder'); **qānaqīne** 'vessels or things no longer in use' < JAB **qalāqīl**; **rōṭa** 'log' (only in Dozy); **xızna** 'linen' (only in O. Jastrow 1990b). In some cases it is difficult to decide whether a word is native Aramaic or a loanword, e.g., ⁺**marra** 'spade' may be inherited from OA/OS (originally Ak > Gr) or reborrowed from K/Ar; similarly, **ṭ-l-q** 'to divorce'; **t-r-k** 'to leave behind'; **t-k-l** 'to trust', **tuklāna** 'trust' - all show a root common to Arabic and Aramaic. The middle and final **k** sound would suggest Arabic, but there are OA roots with **k** in these positions (but of different status altogether), e.g., **r-k-x** 'be soft'; **x-š-k** 'be dark' (see below VI, §§2, 9). As mentioned, many Arabic words are borrowed through Kurdish (or Persian, Turkish) as indicated by their pronunciation, e.g., **ᶜızzıta** 'honor' (< K **ᶜızzat** < Ar **ᶜızza**), which has also a direct Ar doublet **ᶜızze**. In some rare cases, a NA word may be traced equally to OA and Kurdish due to coalescence in form and meaning, e.g., **ču** 'no' < OA שום/K **č u**; **ž** 'on, from, because', an allegro form of **rıš/ž** 'on, over' < OA רישא/K **ž**;[55] Finally, even Hebrew loanwords may undergo semantic and other changes, e.g., **šamaᶜti** 'an obedient woman' (< שמעתי 'I heard'); **ᶜaṣamōṯ** 'obstinate, rigid,' (< עצמות 'bones'); **pēqīyaᶜ** 'impudent' (< H פִּקֵּחַ 'smart, alert'?). The

---

[52]The NA form suggests an OA/OS form, which is not listed in the proper dictionaries (e.g., SokBA 443), except by M. Jastrow 441, which mentions in parenthesis a 'Ms. חֶשְׁבּוֹנָא'. Perhaps from H חֶשְׁבּוֹן? See, however, BA שָׁלְטָנָא ~ שִׁלְטוֹנָא 'ruler'.

[53]See below VIII, §17.5.

[54]The insertion of **h** in NA is probably due to a folk etymology, associating it with **qahwa** 'coffee', and indeed the first records were played in Kurdistan only in a **qahwaxāna**, 'coffe-house'.

[55]Cf. MacKenzie I 197.

general European words are mostly borrowed through neighboring languages, e.g., +**warwar** < 'revolver' (< IrAr/K).

3. A thorough grammar of this north-western group of JNA is a separate work, to be published hopefully in the future. The following grammatical observations are not meant to be a comprehensive grammar, but rather an introduction to the lexicon included in this dictionary, pointing out some general grammatical and semantic tendencies, as well as some interesting exceptions and aberrations, thus providing the user of the dictionary with some necessary comparative information to refer to when needed. This introduction is also meant to serve scholars in comparative studies of classical Syriac/Aramaic and Semitic languages in general, as well as the present day contact languages of the area.

V. Observations on Orthography[56]

1. The Hebrew spelling adopted for all entries in JNAD for words from the spoken registers follows closely that of NT (from 1647-1670 CE)[57], which may be considered 'classical' JNA. Written JNA, like other traditional Jewish languages (Judeo-Arabic, Yiddish, Ladino), is written in the Hebrew alphabet. The spelling is similar to Hebrew and Aramaic plene spelling (כתיב מלא), but with some important differences, such as almost regularly using the א to indicate **ā** in medial position.[58] In contrast to ChNA, which usually has an etymological historical spelling based on Syriac orthography,[59] the spelling in JNA is quite phonetic, e.g., כמשא **xamša** <OA חמשא 'five'; שואא **šōʾa** <OA שבעא 'seven' (=ChNA ܚܡܫܐ, ܫܒܥܐ). The following are some typical features of the spelling system.

2. CONSONANTS. Regular Hebrew letters are used to indicate identical sounds (in traditional **mizraḥi**='Near Eastern'/'Arabic' pronunciation) in both languages, i.e., ו=**w**; ח=**ḥ**; ט=**ṭ**; צ=**ṣ**; ק=**q**. There is no graphic distinction in NT between fricative and plosive pronunciation of ב(ג)דכפת, e.g., כשכא **xiška** 'darkness'; תלתה **talṯe** 'two years ago'. However, **ġ**,when representing Ar غ, is usually marked as ג', (ג with גרש) but just ג in H words, e.g., מג'ארא **maġāra** cave (Ar), but מנהג **minhaġ** 'Jewish custom, law' (H). The other fricative consonants are only rarely marked: אאב'אהי **ʾavāhi** 'settled area' (K); כ'ספא/כֿספא (with גרש, נקודה) **xispa** 'clay', מלכֿא **milxa** 'salt' vs מלכא **malka** 'king'. However, in more recent texts some scribes may add a dot over every fricative בדכפת,[60] and some are very inconsistent (especially in texts published by Rivlin). Avidani (originally of Amidya but lived many years in Israel) often uses ס (=s /ṯ?) instead of the expected ת **ṯ**, probably influenced by Z spelling and pronunciation and lack of **ṯ** in Israeli Hebrew, e.g., גנסא 'garden'; בסר 'after', מוסיליה 'he brought', אידאסוך 'your hands' (AmU1 79a).

2.1. Note also the following diacritical signs: גֿ indicates either **j** or **č**, and occasionally even **ž**; but normally ז' indicates **ž**, which some scribes indicate by ש with a dot on the top of the middle tooth, e.g., **žān** 'birth pang' may be spelled: ז'אן, גֿאן, שֿאן.[61] Finally, צֿ indicates **ẓ** (Ar ض/ظ). In some mss. ד may be used for צֿ, e.g., ד-י-ע (D) ⁺**ḏ-y-ᶜ** (?), but normally צֿ-י-ע **ẓ-y-ᶜ** 'to get lost'.

---

[56]For all the examples quoted here and the rest of the Introduction, usually only partial necessary information is given; for a fuller picture, including references, attested variants, etymology, language of origin, etc., see the relevant entries in the Dictionary (JNAD).

[57]For details see Sabar 1976a: Chapter IV.

[58]See below n. 66.

[59]For details on the ChNA orthography see Hoberman 1996.

[60]However, גֿ indicates **č** or **j**; see below V, §2.1, and VI, §1.

[61]To be exact, a dot is placed on the middle 'tooth' of the ש.

2.2. There is no graphic indication of doubling, e.g., גלא **gılla** 'grass'; טפה **ṭappe** 'ball'; כפא **kaffa** 'palm of hand'. Rivlin has occasionally two letters for doubling in forms such as קאטללה **qāṭıl-le** 'he kills him', מיררה **mır-re** 'he said' (RivSh 231-2).

2.3. Medial consonantal **w/y** or diphthongs may be written with one or two וו/יי, e.g., ארגוון/ארגואן **ʾarjawan** 'crimson'; דאיים/דאים **dāyım** 'always'; איכר/אייכר **ʾaykar** 'then, that time'.

2.4. Some scribes tend to use prosthetic aleph quite profusely, usually ignored in JNAD; e.g., **tre** 'two' may be spelled אתרי **ıtre**; (א)טלהא **(ı)ṭlāha** 'three', (אי)טלמתא **(ı)ṭlımṯa** 'loaf' (BT1, D); cf. Socin 161, 165: **empılle** 'he fell'; **erkūlu** 'they rode', etc. However, in a few words the א has become a permanent part of the word: **ʾıšta** 'six'; **ʾıšti** 'sixty'; **ʾıxre** 'excrement'; 'pillar' is **stūna** in Z, but אסתונא **ʾıstūna** in NT(cf. same scribe). An interesting case is the word for child, which is **yāla** in Z and in NA in general and is assumed to be from OA ילדא **yaldā** › ***yāḏlā**[62] › **yāla**; however, in NT the spellings איאלא **ʾ(ı)yāla**, pl. אייאלה **ʾ(ı)yāle**,[63] seem to support that the א is not prosthetic but rather etymological, probably < Ar عيال 'children'[64]

2.5. Traditional texts published in Israel, such as AvidH, often adjust the JNA spelling according to modern Hebrew, i.e., using ג' for **j**, ח for **x**, צ' for **č**, and even ק for **k**,[65] e.g., דוּמַיִק **dūmāyık** 'eventually' (AlfH 65), פתקי/פתכי **pıtk/qe** (?) 'notes' (RivSh 124-5). Occasionally, the spelling is affected by traditional H: שַׂרְדַאר **sardar** 'chief' , as a translation of H שַׂר (BT1, D); שְׂעַארֶי **saʿāre** 'barley' =H שְׂעוֹרִים (BT4, D); שׂפאתי **sıppāṯi** 'my lips' (ZU 73a); עֵינָא **ʾēna** 'eye', שׁוֹעָא **šōʾa** 'seven' (RivSh 123, 129).

2.6. In NT (and rarely in Am, but not in Z; see Hob97: 316) the letters ב (**v**) and ו (**w**) may interchange, especially in K loanwords, e.g., שובאן/שוואן **šuv/wān** 'shepherd' (Z **šıvāna**); כונאב/כונאו **xunav/w** 'dew' (Z **xunaf**); היבי/היוי **hīv/wi** 'hope' (Z **hīvi**); סהוה **sahwe** (cf. AvidH 31, RivSh 160 סַהְוֵי)[66] 'fear' (Z **sahve**); and in native words: נוקבא/נוקוא **nuqv/wa** 'female' (Z only **nuqwa, nuqqūsa**); רביכותא/רויכותא **rv/wīxuṯa** 'space' (Z only **rwīxūṯa**) ; כוכביה/כוכויה **kuxv/we** 'stars' (Z only **kuxwe**); see also Z **yāwi** 'they give' (< OA יהבין), but

---

[62]Cf. Z root **y-z-l** ‹ **y-ḏ-l** ‹ **y-l-ḏ** (OA ילד) .

[63]And in Sa83c 38, Am; cf. Mengozzi: **ʾyāla**; Mutzafi 2000b:240 suggests OA עול [cf. עולא, עילא 'infant, foal'] or Ar عيال (?).

[64]As already suggested by Noeldeke; see Kapeliuk 1997: 536, n. 26.

[65]Cf n. 40 above.

[66]No **sahve** (סהבה) was attested in Am/NT. The word may be from Ar سهوة 'distraction', but see K **sehev, saw** < P **sahim** 'awe'; MacD 221 **saham**; Garbell 329 **sahm** 'dread'.

Am יָבִיא[67] **yāvi** (AvidH 5)'; however, both NT and Z have **v** in סיבותא **sēvūṯa** 'old age', instead of the expected (i.e., in Z) ***sēwūṯa**. A reverse case

2.7. Velarized or emphatic words (see below VI, §10) often have alternate spellings, when possible, with ת/ט, ס/צ, e.g., תשטה/טשתה/טַשְׁטֵי **⁺tašte**[68] 'basin'; ט-ר-ס/ת-ר-צ **⁺t-r-s** 'to fix, to heal'; ס-ב-ח/צ-ב-ח **⁺s-b-ḥ** 'to praise'; ר-ס-מ/ר-צ-מ **⁺r-s-m** 'to inscribe'; מרתבה/מרטבי **⁺martabe** 'high rank'; צְרֵי/סוּרֵי **⁺surre** 'secrets' (AvidH 9, 12). Less learned scribes may have very 'phonetic' spellings, e.g., יִצְרַאֵל, normally ישראל, **⁺yisrāʾel** 'Israel' (BT, D); מריטא **⁺maritta** (< **marirta**) 'bitter' (f.) (BaBin 103); צלוצא **⁺ṣlōṣa** (< צלותא) 'prayer'; נצוצא **⁺naṣūṣa** (< נצותא **naṣūṯa**) 'war';(RivSh 173, 281); רפצא **⁺rapṣa** 'big' (< רבתא) (AvidH 52; cf. רבצא, AlfM 51); מליצה **⁺mlīṣa** 'full' (< מליתא) (AlfH 69); מוֹצְצְלֵי **⁺mōṣiṣle** 'he listened' (< מוצתלי>OA צוּת)(AlfH 61); קטליטון **qaṭlēṭun** 'you kill' (<תון-). Occasionally, de-emphatization, is suggested: שרטה/שרתי **šarṭ/te** 'conditions' (< Ar شرط); קצתא/קסתא/קיצטא **qiṣ/st/ṭa** 'story' (< P/K < Ar قصة). The traditional spelling is usually silent regarding other emphatic or potentially emphatic consonants, i.e., **⁺b, ⁺č, ⁺d, ⁺l, ⁺m, ⁺p, ⁺r**. A rare spelling, מררו (NT2) **⁺mirru** (normally just מרו) may indicate an effort to do that, but see above, V, §2.2.

3. Particles and Word Boundaries. The possessive-relative particle ד **d** is often suffixed, rather than prefixed, e.g., ביתד חכומא **bēṯid ḥakōma** 'house-of the king'; at times, redundantly, both: נוייד דדוגלא **nūyid (d)dugla** 'prophet of falsehood'. Later scribes often use ת- **-t** instead (not necessarily reflecting devoiced ד, but perhaps by influence of H/Ar f. construct **-t**: שַׁאתִית **šātit** 'year of'; מכדיית **mxiḏyit** 'from the breast of'; קצרת דידה **qaṣrit dīdah** 'her palaces' (NTU1 43a); cf. also לאת (common in RivSh, PolG [always from D], but unknown in Z, oral or written) **lāt** 'no' (< **la+d** ?), e.g., לַאת וֵילַא **lat wēla** 'she was not' (PolG); **lat kīʾin** 'I do not know' (PolUR 22).

3.1. The present particle is usually written as ג **g** even when pronounced (at least in Z), due to assimilation, as **k / q**: גשאקל **kšāqil** 'he takes'; גכרהי **(k)karhi** 'they detest'; גקאים **(q)qāyim** 'he gets up'. At times it is suffixed to the negation particle: לג דאאר **lag dāʾir** 'he doesn't/will not return'; לַג זוֹנַך **lag zōnax** 'we will not buy' (RivSh 125); לך תארץ **lak tāriṣ** 'he doesn't/will not heal'. Note also: גִיגַאלֵינַא **g(i)gālēna** 'I reveal', אִגַאִיתִין **i(g)-gāʾētin**[69] 'you act proud' (RivSh 221, 245).

3.2. The future particle is usually written as ב **b** even when, due to assimilation, it is pronounced **m/p** (again at least in Z) : במאית **(m)māyiṯ** 'he dies'; בפאיש **(p)pāyiš** 'he remains'. The variant בד **bid** may occasionally be prefixed: בְדְאַוִת **bid-ʾāwit** 'he will make' (RivSh 288).

---

[67]The final א is due to a Hebrew influence; cf. H homograph יביא 'he will bring'.

[68]The upper cross usually indicates an emphatic pronunciation of the entire word.

[69]For the indication of vowels by vowel letters and vowel signs, see below V, § 5ff.

3.3. The negation particle may occasionally be prefixed, especially in the following verbs (pronounced as one unit, with acccent on **lá**-): למצה **lá-mṣe** 'he can't'; לגבן **lá-gbın** 'I don't want'; לפיש **lá-pīš** 'no more' (NT5 385). Cf. also K/P נא/נ- **na-**: נא חקאנא/נחקאנא **na-ḥaqqāna** 'unjust, not right'.

3.4. The copula אילה , אילא, etc. in NT is commonly independent, but in other texts it is usually suffixed (in a syncopated form): יָקוּרֵילֵי **yaqūre-le** 'it is heavy' (AvidH 62); אַוָלֵי **ʾāwa-le** 'it is he' (AlfH 79); אאנילו **ʾānī-lu** 'it is they'; in Am 3rd person copula may be fronted: **la kıs mōṣıl** 'it (f.) is near Mosul' (Hob89 176).[70]

3.5. As seen from the preceding sections, word boundaries, especially of particles, are not always fixed, and may fluctuate quite arbitrarily (less so in good manuscripts such as the NT), e.g., ולגנאהי **wal-gnāhe** 'they sigh', בַּאדִּתְּכוֹר **ba-dı-txōr** 'well-please-remember!' (BaBin 148); וְנְתִיבַא **wın-tīva** 'I am sitting' (RivSh 273); פרחתואבא **farḥıtwa-ba** 'You would have enjoyed it', מבשליבו **mbašlī-bu** 'they cook in them' (NT5 387, 409); זליבה **zılle-ba** 'walked in it' (NT6 135); גמהימנכבוך גמיקנכבוך ... דמאינככבוך **gımhēmınax-box gımyaqınax-box... dım'enxax-box** 'we believe in Thee (and) we trust in Thee... (but we can't) look at Thee (out of awe)' (NTU4 157a); כְּזִימַא **xzī-ma** 'see what', יכאניות **yıkkān-īwıt** 'Thou art unique' (NTU4 156b); מניות **mani-wıt** 'who you are' (ibid. 158a); but קִים לֵיה **qım-le** 'he got up', תְּרֵי אְסַר **tre-ʾsar** 'twelve' (RivSh 224-5, 272). Note also גנעדן **gan-ʿēdı n** 'Garden of Eden'; אֵינְיוֹמַא **ʾēn-yōma** 'eye of day'='the sun (dial)'; אַנְגֻורֵי **ʾan-gūre** 'those-men'; אַנְתֵילוּ **ʾan-ṯēlu** 'that-came', but אַן כִּיכְלִיוַא **ʾan kıxlīwa** 'those who were eating' (PolG); cf. strange boundaries in Socin (159): **ís-alīḏi** [< **isa lʾīḏi**], **brāti qamyāwínna** ... 'Come to (shake) my hand, I have given my daughter (to your son).' An example of blended words: סרֿאסת **sar-rast** 'straight ahead'.

4. As in other Semitic languages, the orthography of words not vocalised with diacritical points, as usual in NT, in spite of the prolific use of vowel letters, or even because of them, creates many homographs, e.g., פאלא may stand for **paʾla** '(her) laborer'; **peʾla** '(her) radish'/'wave'; **fāla** '(her)big portion'/'luck'. Similarly, כשכא = (1) **xıška** 'darkness'; (2) **xaška** 'it (f.) becomes dark'; (3) **xašxa** 'it fits'; (4) **kaška** 'lump of dried milk'; (5) **kašxa** 'show-off dress'; ארכה = (1) **ʾarxe** 'guests'; (2) 'his guest(s)'; (3) **ʾırxe** 'mill'; משותתא = **mšuttıta/mšuttatta** 'exiled' (p.p m./f.). Spellings of certain verbal forms may stand for conjugation II (< פַּעֵל) or IV (< אפעל), e.g.: מכלוצה 'to save' may stand for **maxlōṣe** (IV, as in Z) or **mxalōṣe** (II, Am, NT); in less known or unknown verbs the decision is made based on other forms, if attested, e.g., מויקרה **muyqırre** 'he honored' indicates IV (whereas * מיוקרה ***myōqırre** would suggest II).

5. VOWELS. Vowel letters אהו"י are profusely used to indicate the basic short and long

---

[70]Cf. Z **wın tīwa** 'I am sitting' (but see below V, §3.5); **wıt tīwa** 'you are sitting'; **wēle tīwa** 'he is sitting'; and the reverse, **tīwa wın**, etc., is also acceptable; however, the shorter form **-le** is always suffixed in Z: **yaqūra-le** 'it is heavy', but not ***le-yaqūra** (which actually would mean 'it is not heavy' < **lēwe yaqūra**).

vowels[71] as follows. (1) In final position: א-= -a, ה(י)- = -e. ו- = o/u; י- = i/e, e.g., כמארא [OA חמרא] **xmāra** 'donkey'; כמארה [OA חמרי] **xmāre** 'donkeys'; כאלו **kālo** 'bride', עיקו **ʿēqu** 'trouble'; שרקי **šarqi** 'east(ern)'; לילה/לילי **lēle** 'night', תרה/תרי **tre** 'two'. (2) In medial position: -א- = ā; -ו- = (long/short) o/u; -י- = (mostly long/some short) e/i/ı, e.g., כתאוא **kṯāwa** 'letter'[72]; כודא **kōda** 'liver', כורא **kūra** 'kiln'; גובתא **gubta** 'cheese'; קטילא, קטלתא/ קטילתא **qṭīla** , **qṭılta** 'killed' (p.p. m., f.); מרא/מירא **mırra** 'she said'; מידא **mēḏa** 'table'; **did** 'of'.

5.1. At times, י, א may be added in closed syllables to indicate the quality of short vowels, e.g., כַאלְוֵוי (also כַלְוֵוי) **kalwe** 'dogs' (PolG; RivP 211), כַאלְתָא (also כַלְתָא) **kalṯa** 'daughter-in-law', כִיכְלַא **kıxla** 'eye-dye'; כִיפְנַא **kıpna** 'hunger' (PolG); especially so in case of ambiguity, such as גיזאן/גיזין **gēzın** 'I (m.) go'/ **gēzan** 'I (f.) go'; ואנוא **wánwa** 'I (f.) was' (NTU1 43b); ספאר (NT5 408) **sáfar** 'journey' (Ar), vs. ספר **sēfa/ır** 'Torah scroll' (H); or due to Arabic influence (?): בג'דאד **báġdad** 'Baghdad', ארגואן/ארגוון **ʾarjáwan** 'crimson' (final short unaccented vowel in NA, but long and accented in Ar: بغـداد, ارجـوان); חאשך/חָשַך **ḥášak** 'far from you, far be it' (Ar حشاك). In some cases a vowel letter (and/or vowel sign) may even indicate a vowel-less or murmured consonant, e.g., מִיגֻונְדִרו **mgundırru** 'they rolled' (PolG); רַאצַאת **rāṣt** 'right' (K), רַאנַג **rang** 'color' (PolG).

5.2. These tendencies are more or less consistent in NT, but in later JNA texts there are many variations, such as י- , and even יא-, א- used for -e ,. e.g., טורַני...טַפַייא **ṭūrāne...ṭappāye** 'mountains...hills', סוּסֶא **sūse** 'horse', מִדְרַשֵי אִלַייא **mıdrāše ʾılāye** 'heavenly schools' (RivSh 197, 203, 200); רִיפְיֵיא **rıpye** 'slack' (pl., PolG).

5.3. Note also that final ה- in (archaic?) pronominal suffixes may stand in NT for consonantal **-h**, i.e., כמארה = **xmāre(h)** 'his donkey' (as well as **xmāre** 'donkeys'); לבו/לבוה **lıbbu(h)** 'their heart'; מנא/מנאה **mınna(h)** 'from her.'

5.4. The common interchange of almost identical vowels **ı, ü** is reflected by the various spellings of the same word and often by the same scribe, e.g., עטמא/עיטמא/עוטמא **ʿı/üṭma** 'leg'; פמא/פימא/פומא **pı/ümma** 'mouth'; דמאה/דומאה **düm'e** 'tears'; מוחוב/מוחיב/מוחב **muḥı/üb** 'lover'; פוהום/פִיהוֹם **fühom** 'understanding'; תוכריא/תכוריא **tüxırya/tıxürya** 'memory'. Some vowel variations seem to indicate older traditions, e.g., נוביא suggests **nuvya** 'prophet' (Sa83c

---

[71] This description is of the normal spelling in NT, and of the vowel sounds as I know them from Z, and other adjacent JNA dialects (See above, II). Needless to say, there are many exceptions, and some important ones will be discussed in the following sections.

[72] The use of vowel letters, including א for medial **ā(a)** vowel is common in Babylonian Aramaic, especially in manuscripts and non standardized editions, e.g. אינאשא **ʾināša** 'man', באתי **bāte** 'houses' (SokBA 120, 208), and many more; cf. examples quoted in Morag: 44: גמארא, באעי , חיוארא. Even spellings which avoid two successive א א in final position, e.g., אראה for אראא 'land') are related to this tradition, e.g., בַנָאָה (m.) 'builder' (SokBA 222).

20, Am), but Z **nūya**; NT נווייא, נבייא **nw/vīya**;[73] בקרתא **baqarta** (Z, NT), but **bıqurta** (בִּיקֻורְתָא, +PolG; cf. בוקארא < OS; H בַּקָּרַת), 'question, request (for advice)'; pl. **baqaryāṯa** (Z); בקורייתא **bı/uquryāṯa** (Babin 105; PolG); קֻורֶנְיַיאתַא/קֻירְונְיַיתַא **qurınyāṯa/qırunyāθa** 'corners' (PolG).

5.5. In addition to vowel letters, vowel points (נקודות) are very rarely used in NT, and mostly to distinguish between otherwise homographs: טִלָּא **ṭılla** 'shade' vs. the ubiquitous טלא **ṭla** 'for'; שֵׁאְתַא **šeʾṯa** 'hour' vs. שאתא **šāta** 'year'; or a rare word: מְשַׁמֵר/מְשַׁאמִיר **mıšāmır** 'sexually unfaithful, deserter' (NT3). However, in later traditional texts, vowel points are used in addition to, or instead of, the vowel letters, usually quite erratically, with no distinction between צירי/סגול, פתח/קמץ, שורוק/קבוץ, and occasionally even חולם; שווא often stands for **a/ı**, and many other inconsistencies, e.g., הַיָא/הָיָא **hayya** 'quickly' (AvidH 9); מֻאורַכְלֵי/מואורַכְלֵי **muʾuraxle** 'he helped us cross' (ibid. 42-43); טֻורֵית **ṭūrıt** 'mountain of', דֻוכַא **dūka** 'place' (BT1, D:טז); דוהון **dōhun** 'their' (BT, D); סִיתֻונַא/אִסְתֻונַא/אִסְתוּנַא **ıstūna/stūna** 'pillar' (RivSh180; PolG:D); מִיגִ׳יד **m(ı)jīd** [Z **mjīd**] 'except' (AvidH 67), מַרְטְבֵי **marṭabe** 'rank' (BT1, D:טז), חָכּוֹמַא **ḥakōma** 'king' (BT2, D:82; PolG:D); שְׁפִירַא (RivSh 118) **špīra/šapīra** (?) 'good'.[74]

5.5.1. This applies to H loanwords as well: בַּרַכַא **barāxa** 'blessing', בְּרָכוֹת **bırāxōṯ** 'blessings' (AvidH 6, 71); אָדָם/אַדַם **ʾádam/ʾadám** (?) 'Adam' (RivSh119); שָׁלִיחַ/שַׁלִיחַ **šālīyaḥ** '(God's) messenger' (AvidH 31).

5.6. Some vocalizations seem to indicate a variant or remnant of older tradition, e.g., שִׁבַּת **šıbbaṯ** 'Sabbath', מְשִׁיחַ **mišīyaḥ** 'Messiah'; מִצּוֹיֵי **mıṣṣōye** 'matzahs'; מָרוּר **mārūr** 'bitter herbs' (AlfH 23);[75] קם/קים **qam/qim** conversive particle; שושא/שֵׁישַׁא **šū/īša** 'glass' (RivSh 265); אִרבוֹשֵׁב **ʾırbōšeb** 'Wednesday', אַרוֹתַא **ʾarōta** 'Friday' (RivSh198- 201; cf. Khan 561 **ʾarota**) (but Z normally **ʾırōta, ʾarbōšıb, šūša, qam, māšīyaḥ, maṣṣōye**).

5.7. Hebrew words, as a rule, keep their original spelling, especially in NT and in the work of learned scribes, except when a morpheme is affixed: נשמה **nıšāma** 'soul', but נשאמוך **nıšām-ox** 'your soul'; מדראשיה **mıdrāš-e** 'schools'; מלאאכה **malʾāx-e** 'angels'; תוֹרִית **tōr-ıt** 'Torah of'; but at times also without any suffix, e.g., פאסוק/פסוק **pāsuq** 'verse'; כוונה/כוונא **kawwāna** 'concentration in prayer'; דיין/דייאנא **dayyāna/dáyyan** 'judge'; צָארוֹת **ṣārōṯ** 'troubles'; סם המות/סמאמות **sam-(h)ammāweṯ** 'deadly poison'; ענין/עניאן **ʿınyan** 'interest, care'; רבאבות **rıvāvōṯ** 'myriads' (RivSh 195).

---

[73] Cf. MacD 209:**nwīya**; Garbell 322:**niwya**.

[74] In present day dialects (Khan 581; MUTZ 230): **špira**. The pronunciation of all these vowels reflects the 'Sephardic' pronunciation of traditional Hebrew, e.g. (all according to Z), שְׁכִינָה **šaxīna** 'Divine presence, Shekhina'; צַעַר **ṣāʿar** 'sorrow'; חָכָם **ḥāxa/ām** 'Hakham'; בֵּית **bēs** '(letter) beth'; סְעֻדָּה **sıʿoza** 'festive meal'.

[75] The pronunciation of some of these Hebrew words is known also from JAB.

5.8. Hebrew may affect the vowel spelling of certain words that are homophonous in JNA and H: יונה/יונא **yōna** 'dove', קומה/קומא **qōma** 'stature'; מה/מא **ma** 'what?'; note also איו **ʾaw** 'that' (BT, D; BaBin 149); אָהוּא **ʾāhu** 'he' (=H הוּא, AvidH 20); יָבִיא **yāvi** 'they give' (like H יָבִיא 'he brings', AvidH 5); אַרְיֵה/אַרְיָא **ʾarya** 'lion' (H אַרְיֵה).[76]

[76]For more details see Sabar1999a.

VI. Observations on Phonology

1. CONSONANTS. The stock of consonants in Z (and Gzira) is: **ʾ ʿ b č d f g ġ h ḥ j k l m n p q r s ṣ š t ṭ (ḍ) v w x y z ž**; Am has also **ṯ**; D and (most probably) NT, have **ḏ** and **ṯ**. Emphatic consonants indicated by a dot under the letter, other than those listed here, e.g., **ḷ**, tend to be phonemic occasionally (see below IV, §10.2). The general relations of JNA consonants to cognates in OA/OS and other contact Semitic and non-Semitic languages is as follows (in alphabetical order and their order in JNAD):

א **ʾ** =OA ג/ע/א רפה, e.g., אראא **ʾarʾa** 'land' < OA ארעא; שראאה **šrāʾa** 'lamp' < OA שרגא.

ב, בּ **b** = OA ב קשה: בנאתא **bnāṯa** 'daughters'; ראבא **rāba** 'much, many' (OA רַבָּא); occasionally **b > p** (due to assimilation): רפתא **rapṯa** (OA רבתא); **s-p-r** 'to hope' (OA סבר)[77].

ב (בֿ/ב') **v** attested mostly in Kurdish and Hebrew loanwords: שבאנא/שב'אן **šavān(a)** 'shepherd' (K); עבירה **ʾavēra** 'transgression' (H). However, in later texts, ב (= **v/w** ?) is alternately used with ו (=**w/v** ?) also in native words, probably influenced by Israeli Hebrew in which ו and ב = **v**, e.g., גֵיבֵיד/גֵיבֵת = **gēvid/t** 'he makes' (RivSh 274; OA עבד; Z **ʾ-w-z**); גַנָבֵי **ganāve** (Z **ganāwe**),'thieves'; יָבִיא **yāvi** 'they give' (AvidH 5; OA יהב; Z **yāwi**); רְבֵילָךְ **rvēlax** 'you grew up' (ibid. 27), and even לֵיבֵיתוּן **lēvētun** 'you are not' (RivSh 126; OA הוי; Z **lēwētun**), but also כַשְׁוַא **xašwa** 'she thinks'; אֻרְוַא **ʾurw**'big' (RivSh 136-7); see also ו.

ג, גּ **g** = OA plosive ג (ג קשה): גומלא **gumla** 'camel'; fricative ג (ג רפה) = (**ġ**), attested in Hebrew loanwords: מנהג **mınhaġ** 'custom'; see also א; ג'.

ג̇ **j** (rarely **ž**; v. ז') attested mostly in Arabic loanwords: ג̇נא **jınna** 'demon'; see also V, §2 above.

ג̇ [ג̃] **č** attested mostly in Kurdish/Persian/Turkish loanwords: ג̇איי **čāy(i)** 'tea' (K/P); ג̇קמק **čaqmaq** 'lighter' (T); but also native ג̇ירי **čēri** 'autumn' (< OA תשרי); איג̇א **ʾıčʾa** 'nine' (< OA תשעא). See also V/2 above.

ג', גּ **ġ** attested mostly in Arabic loanwords with غ: מג'ארא **maġāra** 'cave'; see also ג, א. In more recent texts, the apostrophy is often omitted, e.g., גְגַדְאִי **gġadʾi** 'they bind' (BaBin).

ד , ד **d** = OA ד קשה: דמא **dımma** 'blood'.

ד, ד̇ **ḏ** (**ḍ/ẓ**)= OA ד רפה : אידא **ʾiḏa** 'hand'. In D and Am texts, ד̇ seems also to indicate **ḍ/ẓ**:, e.g., ד̇ילִים **ẓılım** (here, and in the next examples, ד̇ = **ẓ** as in Z?) 'oppression' (Ar ظُلم);

---

[77]See more below VI, §8.

דֵיעְתַלַא **ẓeʿta-la** 'it is lost' (RivP #102, Ar ضيع); קָאדֵיוָא **qāẓēwa** 'he provided' (Avidh 42, Ar قضي). Other scribes may use ד for both **d** and **ḏ**. See also צ̇, ז.

ה **h** = OA (and H) ה.

ו **w** = OA (and H) ו, Ar و, as well as OA ב רפה (and rarely, in diphtongs, פ רפה) > **w**: ורידא **warīḏa** 'vein'; וכיל **wakil** 'agent' (Ar); כתאוא **kṯāwa** (OA כתבא) 'letter'; נושא **nōša** (OA נַפְשָׁא) 'self'; מצוה **miṣwa** 'religious duty' (H). See also ב/ב̇.

ז **z** = OA ז, and in Z of OA ד רפה: אזא **ʾizza** 'goat' (OA עזא); איזא **ʾīza** 'hand' (Z); occasionally also **ẓ**: קְזֵילֵי **qẓēle** (Z!) 'he provided' (AlfH 42). See also צ̇, ד/ד̇.

ז' (ז̇) **ž** mostly in Kurdish loanwords: באז'ר **bāžir** 'city'; may interchange with ש̈ (and ג̇): ז'אן/ שאן̈ **žān** 'pain' (see above V, §2.1); cf. also ש-ג'-ל/ז'-ג'-ל **š/ž-ġ-l** 'to work' (Ar شغل).

ח **ḥ** attested mostly in Arabic and Hebrew loanwords or roots: חראמא **ḥarāma** 'forbidden; nonkosher' (Ar); חכומא **ḥakōma** 'king'; חכם **ḥāxām** 'sage, rabbi' (H); occasionally in native words (conditioned by adjacent **q**): רחוקא **raḥūqa** 'distant'; נ-ח-ק **n-ḥ-q** (D **n-q-ḥ**) 'to touch'. See כ, כ̇.

ט **ṭ** = OA ט: ט-מ-ר **ṭ-m-r** 'to bury'; טופרא **ṭupra** 'nail'; occasionally (in emphatic neighborhood) **ṭ** < **t** (see above V, §2.7 and below VI, §10), and vice versa: **ṭ** > **t** (see below VI, §10.3; cf. ad ס below); also **ṭ** ~ **ḍ** (mostly in **ṭ/ḍ-b-l** 'to have a ritual bath'; **ṭ/ḍabanja** 'revolver').

י **y** = OA י: יומא **yōma** 'day'; ירקא **yirqa** 'greenery'.

כ, ך **k** = OA כ קשה: כלבא **kalba** 'dog'; כיפא **kēpa** 'stone'.

כ, כ̇/כ' **x** = OA ח (**ḥ**), כ רפה (**x**); Ar خ (**x**): כמשא **xamša** 'five' (OA חמשא); א-כ-ל **ʾ-x-l** 'to eat'; כברא **xabra** 'word' (Ar خبر); מלאאכ̇ת שינא **malʾāxit šēna** 'angels of peace' (NT5 387).

ל **l** = OA ל: לכמא **laxma** 'bread'; מלכא **milxa** 'salt'.

מ **m** = OA מ: מטרא **miṭra** 'rain'; אמרא **ʾamra** 'wool'.

נ **n** = OA נ: נושא **nōša** 'self' (OA נפשא); תמניא **tmanya** 'eight'.

ס **s** = OA ס (שׂ), and in Z also OA ת רפה: ספיקא **spīqa** 'empty'; ביסא **bēsa** (Z) 'house'; see ת, ת̇; צ̇.

ע ᶜ mostly in Arabic and Hebrew loanwords: עג̈ב ᶜ**ajab** 'wonder'; עיבור ᶜ**ıbbur** 'calendar'.

פ, פּ **p** = OA פ רפה/קשה: פמא **pımma** 'mouth'; מלפאנא **malpāna** 'teacher'; see ו.

פ, פ̇ **f** mostly attested in Arabic and Hebrew loanwords and roots: פקיר **faqir** 'poor'; כפא **kaffa** 'palm'; פ-ה-מ **f-h-m** 'to understand' (Ar); הפטרה **hafṭāra** 'haftara' (H).

צ **ṣ** = OA צ (and H/Ar ص): ציוא **ṣīwa** 'tree'; צליוא **ṣlīwa** 'crucified'; צחתא **ṣaḥḥıta** 'health'; ציצית **ṣīṣi(t̲)** 'prayer shawl'. Occasionally **ṣ** › **s** (cf. above ad ט).

צ̇ **ẓ** = mostly attested in Arabic (Kurdish, Turkish) loanwords with ظ/ض: צ̇אלם **ẓālım** 'oppressor'; צ̇עיף **ẓaᶜif** 'weak'. See ז, ד̇.

ק **q** = OA ק: קלמא **qalma** 'louse'; ק-י-מ **q-y-m** 'to get up'.

ר **r** = OA ר: מרירא **marīra** 'bitter'; רומאנא **romāna** 'high'.

ש, שׁ **š** = OA ש: שמינא **šamīna** 'fat'; שמשא **šımša** 'sun'.

ש̇ (in good mss. the dot is on the middle tooth) **ž** interchanges with ז̇ or ג̇; mostly in K loanwords: דִשְׁמְנֵי **dıšmıne** 'enemies' (BaBin 108) ש̈אן **žān** pain (AvidH 50; RivSh 117 mistakenly reads it **šān**, connecting it with Ar شان); cf. also cases of **š** › **ž**: **xıš/žbōna** 'acount' (OA חשבונא) **š/ž-ġ-l** 'to work' (Ar شغل).

ת, תּ **t** = OA ת קשה: תלמידא **talmīd̲a** 'disciple'; תלגא **talga** 'snow'; see also ט **ṭ**.

ת, ת̇ **t̲** = OA (and H) ת רפה and Ar ث: מותא **mōt̲a** 'death'; ביתא **bēt̲a** 'house'. In more recent texts, influenced by Israeli Hebrew (which doesn't have **t̲**) or by Z, scribes often oscillate between ת and ס: שַׁבְּתָא/שַׁבְּסָא **šıbt̲/sa** 'Sabbath' (RivSh 197-8); and even in a Z text: אָתֵי לִימְכַסוֹסֵי **ʾāse** (< OA אתי) **lımxassōse** (< OA חדת) 'become renewed' (AlfH 63); see ס.

2. Reflexes of בגדכפת. Normally, OA fricative ב > **w**[78]: **šwāwa** (OA שבבא) 'neighbor'; **ʾōda** (< *ᶜ**awda** <OA עַבְדָא) 'slave'; **kt̲ūta** (< ***kt̲īwtā** <OA כתיבתא) 'written'; fricative ג > **ʾ**: **šrāʾa** (OA שרגא) 'lamp'; fricative פ > (mostly coalesced with) **p**: **ʾıpra** (OA עפרא) 'dust'; fricative דכת are usually retained (except that **d̲** > **z** and **t̲** > **s** in Z,[79] and **d̲** > **d** in Am); e.g., **k-t̲-w** כתב 'to write'; **b-x-y** בכי 'to cry'. However, there are many exceptions (i.e., not

[78]Cf. TA in Epstein 18:אווד = אבד 'be lost'; SokBA 76 אווק = חפק/אבק 'to embrace'

[79]Perhaps a recent phenomenon; see above V, §2; in a text copied by A. Socin in 1870 from a Jew of Zakho there are a few examples of **d̲** (an error?) instead of the usual **z**; see Sabar forthcoming b.

retained or reversed), and especially in verbal roots there is usually a levelling, e.g., the root of all the forms (verbal and nominal) of OA רכב 'to ride' > NA **r-k-w**; חשך > **x-š-k** 'be dark'[80]; גחך > ***g-x-x** > **g-x-k** 'to laugh';[81] H loan כשוף **xiššūf** 'sorcery' (and **xišūfkar** 'sorcerer'); רגש > **r-ʾ-š** 'to notice, awake'; and the H (< JAB?) loan root **ṭ-b-l** 'to have a ritual bath'; **ṭabīla** 'a ritual bath'[82]. Similarly, **k-w-n** II < **kawwāna** (H) 'to intend' (=H צָדָה, BT2); 'to stare, examine' (**mkōwinne bāš bid dē xamsa** 'He stared long at this lass,' PolG); **v-k-š** 'to request' a H loanword in Israeli JNA[83]. Occasionally, a fricative is maintained in one dialect but not in the other, e.g., Am (Hob89 196) **p-t-x** = Z **p-s-x** 'to open'. See also above IV, §2 , and below VI, §9. Note also the reflexes of OA פדנא 'plow' > **biṯāna** (NT2)/**piṯāna** (NT3)/**bizāna** (< **biḏāna**) (Z). The root **b-z-r** (Z, PolG) 'to scatter, sprinkle' seems to be derived from OA בזר (H פזר), but attested in NT3 as בדר (only once, בדרה **bḏirre** 'he scattered') which exists in OA/OS as well; but ביזירה **bizīre** spices (NT5). However, some cases, such as כוזא **kōza** 'pile' < K/P کوز **kūz**, but כודא **kōḏa** (?)(pl כוֹדֵי **kōḏe** =H צִבּוּרִים חֲמָרִים,) in PolG, seem to be hyper-corrections. An interesting case is **ʾiḏwa** (NT/D אִידְוַא/אדוא) '(casting) lot'; according to M. Jastrow 1043 the OA variants are עַדְבָא/עַדְוָוא/עִדְוָא, which supports the NA version, but SokBA 844 has only (!) עַדְבָא; some dialecteal differences may be due to borrowing or influence of a contact language, e.g., **lubna, lubinṯa** brick; cf. Ar لَبِنَة/لِبْن but OA לְבֵינְתָא; OS ܠܒܢܬܐ; Mand ליבתא; pl. **lūne** (לונה, NT1; NT5 404);[84] cf. OA לִיבְנֵי, OS ܠܒܢܐ; but Z **lubne**.

2.1. Residue of the old allophones remains in a few cases: **kalba** 'dog', pl. **kalwe**; **bēṯa** 'house', pl. **bāte**; **zwāna** 'to buy', **mzabōne** 'to sell'; **palga** 'half'; **mpalōʾe** 'to share, divide'; **xšāwa** 'to think', **mxašbōne** 'to calculate', denomanitavie from **xižbōna** 'account'.

2.2. There is also some new distribution of fricative ~ plosive alternants (all Z): **ʾidyo** 'today' vs. **ʾizlal** 'tonight'; **badla** 'shift' vs. **bazil-mbinoke** 'early morning shift'; **ʾīs** 'there is' vs. **ʾitli** 'I have'; **mīsa** 'dead' vs. **mitle** 'he died'; **q-f-y** (< Ar/OA/OS?) 'to surface at river's bank (drowned people, logs), to anchor', but **qapya** / **qāfōya** driftwood; **q-p-y** (< OS) II 'to collect, search and find (things)'.

2.3. In Z **v** is maintained in K and H loanwords: **zvāra** 'to walk around' (K); **kāvōz** 'honor' (H); but in Am **v** > **w** even in loanwords, i.e., **zwāra, kawod**; **niwīn** (NT נוין)

---

[80]Interestingly enough, the reflex of √ חשך in Mutz 239 is **x-š-x** (!) (~ **x-š-k-n**).

[81]The change seems to be due to dissimilation: ***gxixle** > **gxikle** 'he laughed'; cf. OA לחך > NA **l-k-x** 'to lick'; Israeli H: הכחיש **hikxiš** < **hixxiš** 'he denied'; see Sabar 1999b.

[82]For more details about בגדכפ"ת in NA see Kapeliuk 1997; cf. Mutz 29-33.

[83]In H. **b ~ v** according to certain rules, (i.e., בִּקֵּשׁ, but לְבַקֵּשׁ, יְבַקֵּשׁ, מְבַקֵּשׁ); for more details see Sabar 1975:496.

[84]Cf. MacD 144 **lyūnā**, sg.

'bedding' (Z **lıvīne** < K); **xunaw** 'dew' (Z **xunaf**< K); **lıġāw** (NT לג'או) 'bridle' (Z **lıġāva** < K; cf. Ar لجام); **nawūʾa** נוואה (NTU4 161a, but otherwise נבואה, H) 'prophecy.'

2.4. **ṯ** appears as **h** in ***tlāha** 'three', and as **l** in **xalunta** (NT) 'sister' (< ***xaṯunta** ‹ **xāṯa**).

2.5. OS/OA fricative פ in a few rare cases is reflected as a vowel (***af** › **aw** › **o**, like fricative ב): **nōša** 'self' < נפשא **nafšā**; **rušta** 'shovel' < OS ܪܰܦܫܐ; **dōqa** 'baking pan' < OA/OS **ṭafqā**; in Am this occurs in Ar loanwords as well: **tawsir** (Z **tafsir** < Ar تفسير) 'translation'; **tawtiš** (Z **taftiš** < Ar تفتيش) 'inspection' (Hob97 316, 319).[85]

2.6. Fricative פ **f** is retained in Ar/K (in contrast to ChNA in which > **p**) and H words and roots: **fahōma** 'intelligent' (Ar فهم); **ʾāfırra** 'fodder' (K); **hafṭāra** 'Prophetic portion read on Sabbath' (H הפטרה); occasional exceptions such as **ṣūpa** 'hall' < T **sofa** 'hall' < Ar **ṣuffa** 'stone bench' are probably borrowed from ChNA; cf. MacD 263: **ṣūpā** 'ante-room'.

2.7. Doubling of fricatives in native or loanwords is rare but possible: **ʾaxxa** 'here' (OA); **mxaṯṯōṯe** 'to renew'; **kaffa** 'palm' (Ar); **šıvva** 'fresh branch' (K).

3. Gutturals (Laryngeals and pharyngeals): ע ח ה א. Already in Talmudic (or even Targumic) Aramaic there are clear indications of the weakening or mixing of the gutturals, e.g., אידא/עידא 'holiday' (=Z **ʾēza**); אפצא/עפצא 'gallnut' (=Z **ʿapṣa**); אטמא/עטמא 'thigh'; אצר/עצר 'to press, wring out'; אקר/עקר 'to uproot'; דהנא/דחנא 'oil' (=Z **dehna**); הילולא(OA)/ܚܠܘܠܐ (OS)'wedding feast' (Am **x/h/ḥılūla**); אובא/עובא/חובא 'bossom' (Z **ʿubba**) ;[86] and confusion of אמרא/חמרא/עמרא 'donkey'/'wine'/'lamb'/'wool', respectively.[87] In our group, as in NENA in

---

[85]Cf. Mutz 216 **nūṭa** 'oil' < OA ניפטא; Kapeliuk 1997: 530, n. 9.

[86]See the commentators remarks on לא יכניס אדם את ראשו לתוך אובו ויקרא את שמע (תוספתא ברכות) in N. Braverman, "An Examination of the Nature of the Vienna and Erfurt Manuscripts of the Tosefta," (in Hebrew) in Language Studies V-VI, ed. M. Bar-Asher, Jerusalem, 1992:165; the word is traced to Biblical H. (חֻבִּי 'my bosom', Job 31:33) and has a cognate in Akkadian as well; see ibid , n. 92. Z has **ʿubba** which may be native or a direct loan from Ar عُبّ.

[87]B. 'Eruvin 53b: בני גליל דלא דייקי לישנא...אמר להו: אמר למאן אמר למאן? אמרו ליה:גלילאה שוטה, חמר למירכב, או חמר למשתי, עמר למילבש, או אימר לאתכסאה; cf. B. Talmud Megillah 24b, and P. Talmud Berakhot 2-4 regarding the people of Haifa, Tiv'on, and Beth-She'an who mixed their alephs with 'Ayins and vice versa: אין מורידין לפני התיבה לא אנשי בית שאן ולא אנשי בית חיפה ולא אנשי טבעונין מפני שקורין לאלפין עיינין ולעיינין אלפין; on these and other weakened consonants in TA (and some examples are well known from NA), see Epstein 17-19: להמא/לחמא 'bread' [=Z **laxma**]; אזל/עזל 'spin' [=Z **ʾzl**]; אטמא/עטמא 'thigh' [=Z **ʿıṭma**]; ארבלא/ערבלא 'sieve' [=Z **ʾırbāla**]; SokBA: ארבא/ערבא 'lamb' (=Z **ʾırba**); אבד/עבד 'to make' (=D

general, normally, OA/OS **ḥ** › **x**; **ᶜ** › **ᵓ** (see above). However, in our group **ḥ** and **ᶜ** occasionally are retained in native words as well (especially near emphatic and back consonants, and some perhaps by influence of Ar/H): (a) with **ḥ** : **ḥuqqa** 'rung' (OA/OS **ḥawqā**), **pısḥa** 'Passover', **tıḥāla** (!) 'spleen' (OA/OS טְחָלָא/Ar طحال), **r-ḥ-q** 'to be far', **raḥūqa** 'far' (but Gz **raxúqa**), **p-š-ḥ** 'to wide open (legs in obscene way)', **r-ḥ-m** 'to show mercy', **ḥ-z-q** 'to be strong'; **n-ḥ-q** (Z)/**n-q-ḥ** (D) 'to touch' (OS نقر 'to peck')); **š-ṭ-ḥ** 'to lie down' (vs. **š-ṭ-x** 'to spread out')[88]; (b) with **ᶜ**: **ᶜutma** 'thigh'; **ᶜapṣa** 'gallnut' (OA/OS), **šarqīᶜa** 'a resounding slap on the face' (OS, cf. above IV, §1), **waᶜda** 'time' (OS/Ar), **ᶜ-r-ṭ** 'to fart with sound' (OS), **ṣ-ᶜ-r** 'to curse'; **l-ᶜ-ṭ** 'lick' (OA לעט; but Ar لطع); **ṣ-r-ᶜ** 'to go mad' (Ar).[89]

3.1. **ḥ** and **ᶜ** usually are retained in Ar and H loanwords: **ḥammāla** 'porter', **⁺ᶜabra** 'raft'; **⁺rāḥel** 'Rachel', **ᶜaġāla** 'purification' (H הגעלה). However, there is at times weakening of even Ar **ᶜ** ; **xıleᵓta** 'gift' (Ar خلعة); **maᵓmōre** 'to build' (Ar عمر); **n-f-ᵓ** 'be useful' (but **manfaᶜa** 'benefit'); **maᵓōne** 'helping (in general)' (but **ᶜyāna** 'helping (only God:man)') (Ar √ عون); **ᵓjāba** 'to want, to wish' (but **mᶜajōbe** 'wondering') (Ar √ عجب).[90]

3.2. Cases of **h** › **ḥ** (often in emphatic environment): **ṭaḥra** 'noon heat' (OA טהרא) ; **q-ḥ-y** 'set on edge (teeth)' (OA קהי); **q-ḥ-r** 'grieve' (Ar قهر, but IrAr **q-h/ḥ-r**) ; **jah/ḥannam** 'hell'; **čıḥıl** 'uncouth' (Ar جاهل) and within the group: Z **ḥınnar** 'art, skill' vs. NT הנר **hınnar** (K/P); Z **ṣıhyon** vs. Am **⁺sıḥyon** ‹ **ṣiyyōn** (ציון) 'Zion'; Z **hīl** 'until' vs. Am/D **ḥīl**; NT באבה **babeh** 'his father' vs ChNA **bābeḥ**, etc.[91]

3.2.1. Cases of **ḥ** › **h**: **ṣehwa** (Z) ''thirst' (OA/NT צחוא **ṣeḥwa**); similarly, **ṣ-h-y** 'to be thirsty'; מהרום **mahrum** (NT) 'forbidden' (Ar محروم); **h-j-m** (NT, but Z **ḥ-j-m**) 'to

---

ᵓ-w-d̲); באי/בעי 'to want' (NT באי; Z **ᵓ-b-y**), etc. Cf. already Biblical H פתאם/פתע.

[88]Individual verbs may retain the **ḥ** in one dialect (group), but not in the other, e.g., Z **g-x-k** 'laugh', **xōla** 'rope' = respectively, **g-ḥ-k**, **ḥola** in Khan 553, 570; Z **r-ḥ-m** 'to have mercy' is **⁺r-h-m** 'have pity' K/T < Ar in Garbell 291, and **rxima** 'beloved', **raxmana** 'lover', **raxmanula** 'love', in Garbell 328.

[89]On the interaction of the pharyngeal with emphatic consonants see below, IV, §10; cf. Mutz : 26-29 (much more common there due to a much stronger Kurdish influence; cf. Khan 563-4 **ᶜamra** 'wool'; **ᶜaqla** 'leg'; **ᶜipra** 'dust', etc., but all begin with **ᵓ** in Z); for even **y** › **ᶜ**, see Khan 574 **maᶜe** 'water' (= Z **⁺māya**) and occasionally the opposite: **ᵓaṣli** 'original' (< Ar), **ᵓilaj** 'treatment', **ᵓādat** 'custom' (Khan 561-3) - all begin with **ᶜ** in Z; cf. also Khan 573 **lóᵓa** 'inside' = Z **lᶜōya**.

[90]I do not know of Ar **ḥ** › **x** in Z, but see Mutz 238/Khan 585 **xml** 'stand, wait' < Ar حمل.

[91]See Sabar 1995:34; Sara: 64.

calm' (Ar حجم); **žaḥır** (Z < K)/**žahar** (Am) (Sa83c 32); **ḥ-r-d-f** 'to collapse, push down' < Ar هدف?

3.2.2. Cases of **h** › **ḥ** › **x**: **r-x-ṭ** (NT) 'run' (< OA רהט); חלולא/הלולא/כלולא **x/h/ḥılūla** 'wedding feast' (Am) (AvidH 6; Br47 99, 118; Br93 414); מכלתא (OS ܡܚܠܐ; OA מהולתא) 'fine sieve'.[92] An interesting case is **šıxāṭa** (Z < IrAr) 'match box', but Am **šıḥḥāṭa** (Hob97 318 < SyAr).[93]

3.3. Cases of **ʾ** › **ᶜ** (including some Ar words via K): **⁺ᶜarnūwa** 'hare' (OA ארנבא) ;**ᶜarmōta** 'pomegranate' (ChNA ܥܪܡܘܛܐ); **ʾ-b-y** (Z)/**ᶜ-b-y** (NT, AM, OA עבי) 'to swell'; **ᶜınjāṣe** 'prunes' (OA אגסין/עוגסין' pears'; Ar **ʾ/ᶜinjāṣ** 'pear; plum'; **g-r-ʾ/ᶜ-l** 'be grimy, soiled' (OA גאל/געל); **ᶜálquš** 'Alqosh' (town);[94] **qúrᶜan** 'Koran' (K < Ar); **ᶜıns** 'people'/**ᶜınsān** 'human being' (Ar انسان); **ᶜınglēzi** 'English'; and perhaps **ʾ-l-q** (Am < Ar √ ألق)/**ᶜ-l-q** (Z) 'to shine, to light'.

3.4. Cases of **ḥ** › **ᶜ** in some H/Ar loanwords: **taᶜbūla** 'trick' (H תחבולה); **gazrūwaᶜ** 'rude' (H גס רוח); **pēqīyaᶜ** 'impudent' (< H פִּקֵּחַ?); **qīyaᶜ** 'grime' (< H כִּיחַ?); **šarḥ/šarᶜ** 'Bible translation in JNA' (< Ar شرح).

3.5. NA **ᶜ/ʾ** may also originate from an OA **ġ**: **šrāʾa** 'candle' (OA שרגא); **narʾa** 'axe' (OA נרגא); **peʾla** 'radish' (OS ܦܓܠܐ); **š-ʾ-r** 'to kindle (fire)' (OA שגר); **n-ʾ-s** 'bite, sting' (< OA נגס); **raᶜ/ʾōla** (NT רעולא; BT, D ראולא **raʾōla**, OS ܪܓܘܠܐ) 'rivulet'; **lᶜōya** 'inside' (OA לגו).

3.6. In baby talk there are cases of **q** › **ᶜ** (like OA ארקא > ארעא?): **ᶜūna** 'buttocks' (K **qūn**); **ᶜıto** 'shorty, tiny' (< K **qito**); **ᶜāᶜe** < Ar/P **qaqqa** 'kaka', child's excrement (cf. Steingass: ققّا).

3.7. One of the most interesting phonological features is the dialectal insertion (of Kurdish origin?) of **ʾ** or **h** to break a long vowel (often itself resulting from the degimantion of a long consonant): **taneʾṯa** (BT, D:תְּנֵיאְתָא) 'letter' (OA תניתא, Z **tanēsa**); **daʾpa** (Z)[95] 'board' (NT **dāpa**, Arodh **dappa** ,OA **dappā**); **ṭapeʾṯa** (Am) 'hill' (D **ṭappēṯa**, OS **ṭappāyā** hillside'); **kahwa** (NT כהוא) 'air hole' (OA **kawwā**; Z **kāwa**); **sahma** (Am) 'poison' (Z **sāma** < OA **sammā**); **behra** (Z) 'well' (OA **bērā**); **ṣıhyon/ṣıyyon** (archaic in Z < OS <

---

[92]See Epstein 18: מהולתא; cf. Ar منخل; JNAD:נ-כ-ל 'to seive'.

[93]Cf. H-OA √לחלח ~ √ לכלך 'to moisten; to soil'.

[94]Cf. similar change in TA locality names, in Eshel 29, 251, e.g., אקרא/עקרא 'Aqra'(< חקרא 'fortress'; cf. M. Jastrow: חקרא; and present day town of **ᶜaqra**, not becessary identical, since there were several localities with that name; see Eshel ##36-43).

[95]Cf. Mutzafi 2001 198 **daᶜba** (!) 'beast' < Ar دابّة **dābba**.

H ציון) 'Zion'; **tıhna** (NT תהנא) 'smoke' (Z **tınna**); **sehrāne/sērāne** 'communal picnic' (K < Ar سيران 'trip'); ⁺**bıč'a** 'bastard' (< * ⁺**bı'ča** < K **bīča**); and perhaps **n a ḥṯa** (?)(NT נהתא) /**nāsa** (Z) 'ear'; **mıs/zta** (Z)/**m'ısta** מאיסתא (NT), pl. **mızze**, 'hair'; **jōqa** (Z, NT)/**ju'qa** (?) (גׄואקא, AmU2 10a).For even some more unusual cases, including insertion of א even before double consonants, in a manuscript from Amidya[96]: יואמא **yo'ma** (?) 'day'; יואשא **yō'ša** (?) 'dry land'; נוניאתא **nuni'ṯa** 'fish' (sg.); שאמיה **šı'me** (< **šımme**) 'sky'; נדארו **ndı'ru** (< **nḏırru**) 'they vowed'.[97] However, the same manuscript omits normally retained א (< etymological ע) : שמיליה **šmēle** 'he heard' (OA שמע); טויליה **ṭwēle** 'he fell asleep' (OA טבע) ; גודתו **gōdıttu** 'you make them' (OA עבד); cf. below VI, §3.9.

3.7.1. Some of these may be due to contamination: **pe'la** 'wave' < K **pēl**, contaminated with **pe'la** 'radish' (cf. above IV, §3.5); **ṭwe'le** (Z) 'happy is...' (< OA טובא ל-; NT טוילה **ṭwēle**), due to **ṭwe'le** 'he fell asleep' (OS ܛܒܥ ܒܫܢܬܐ 'sank in sleep, be in deep slumber');[98] **dehna** 'loan' (< Ar دين) due to **dehna** 'oil'.

3.8. There are words with **ḥ** or **ʿ** whose origin is obscure, e.g., **ḥ-ṭ-ḥ-ṭ** 'to be excited amorously'; **ḥabbōre** 'smart woman'; **ʿ-j-q** 'to be elated'; **ʿ-y-č** 'to smear'.

3.9. Written texts reflect many cases of reduction of vowelless **'** > zero especially in verbs: שמילו **šmēlu** 'they heard'; פלילי **plēle** 'he divided' (< **ple'le** < OA פליג לה); **zdēṯa** 'fear' (< **zde'ṯa**); but occasionally also cases of disappearance of voweled **'**: שַׁמַך (RivSh 174) **šam(m)ax** < **šam'ax** 'we hear'; קריתא/קריאתא **qarēṯa/qare'ṯa** 'pumpkin' (NT6 136); תאנא/תינא **te'na/tēna** 'fig' (Sa83c:17, Am); גמארי **gmāre** 'it aches' (OA מרע) (Sa83c:20, Z); occasionally also vowelless **h**: **bēna** < **behna** 'a while' (Socin 165).

3.10. Varia: אכא/הכא **'/haxxa** 'here' (RivSh 131); **'ayam~hayəm** 'time' (Ar أيام);[99] **'/hafsāra** 'bridle'; **h/'ēxal** 'sanctuary'; **drā'e/drāye** 'arms' (RivSh 169); **y/'ısrā'el** 'Israel'; **šımmāhe/-ye-/'e** 'names'; **gōyim/gōhim** 'Gentiles'; **lahta/lāta/la'ta** 'candle's flame' (< להט/להב?);[100] for doubling of pharyngeals, see below, VI, 4.1.

4. DOUBLING. Old doubling in some common formations is not retained: **qaṭāla**

---

[96]See Sabar 1981b:131 (note 12).

[97]Cf. also Gz **milli'ta** 'nation', Nakano 1970 198.

[98]Cf. however, BA טות in connection with בת 'to sleep'; Ar طوى 'fold up, roll over'.

[99]For interdialectal **'** > **h**, cf. e.g., : Z **'ēma** (< OA) 'which', **'arzan** (< K) 'cheap', **'īwan** (< Ar/P) 'portico' = respectively: **hema, harzan, haywan** in Khan 569.

[100]See ל-ה-י (< *__l-h-w__ <OA להב) **l-h-y** 'shine, gleam'; cf. פ-ל-ה-י, להיבה, להווגׄיתא, להום (?).

'killer' (OA **qaṭṭālā**); **ganāwa** 'thief';[101] **ʾatīqa** 'old (thing)'; **paṭīra** 'unleavened bread'; **tanūra** 'oven'; **skīna** 'knife' (OA **sakkīna**); but: **dıbbōra** 'wasp'; **šıppōla** 'hem'; **ṣırrōpa** 'frost-bite'. In loanwords from Ar it may be retained (in newer loans ?) or not (in older, naturalized, ones ?): **ḥadāda** 'ironsmith'; **ṣafāra** 'coppersmith'; but **ḥammāla** 'porter'[102]; **ṭarrāḥa** 'logger'; **ṭayyarči** 'pilot'; an interesting case is ⁺**rızza** 'rice' (OS/Ar) vs. ⁺**rıza** (Ar رضى) 'wish'.

4.1. New doubling due to probable "minimality constraints"[103] on typical NA word structure: **šímma** 'name' (OA שְׁמָא); **dímma** 'blood'; even in H loanwords: **šáṭṭar** 'document' (H שְׁטָר); **pıddōma** 'stopper' < OA פְּדָמָא; **šátti-ʿérev** 'cross' (H שְׁתִי וערב 'warp and woof'); **šaqqīṯa** 'channel' (OS **šāqīṯā**); **maʿassēr** 'tithe' (H); **baḥḥar** (Ar **baḥr**) 'sea'; ⁺**saʿʿa** 'hour' (Ar ساعة); **mıṣṣır** 'Egypt' (Ar **miṣr**); **faqqa** 'Muslim clergy' (Ar فقهاء/فقيه). See also above VI, §2.7.

5. LIQUID CONSONANTS. **l, m, n, r** may interchange: **šınšılta/šılšılta** 'chain, dynasty'; **brōne/bnōne** 'sons'; **yıbbum** (Z, H)/**yıbbun** (NT יבון) 'levirate marriage'; **šınšılta** 'large family' < OA **šalšelta** 'chain; dynasty'; **balsam/balsan** 'balsam'; **lıvīne** (Z)/**nıwīn** (NT נוין) 'bedding'; and in verbs: **m/n/labōle** 'to carry'; **m/npāla** 'to fall'; **nābēn** ‹ **mā bēn** 'between'; **mār** (regular)/**māl** (rare) 'say!'; **ʾīman** (regular)/**ʾīmal** (rare) 'when' (Sa83c 16, Am); **d-n-d-l/d-l-d-l** 'to dangle'; **kutrēni** (Z)/**kutlēni** (Gz) 'both of us' (Nakano 1970 167, twice; perhaps a trascription influenced by his Japanese?); מעדר כילותא **maʿḍar xēlūṯa** (rare) ‹ **maḥẓar xērūṯa** (< Ar محضر خير) 'recommendation' (ZU 73b; **xırše** (regular, OA חרש) /**lıxše** (PolG, OA לחש?) 'sorcery'; **l-k-z** (regular)/**n-g-z** (PolG) 'to push by elbow, to nudge'; ⁺**qırrām** (Z)/**qul/rzum** (NT, Am, D < Ar قُلزُم < Gr?) 'reed'; **sarnīʾa** (NT)/ **sırn/moʾta** (BaBin/PolG < P?) 'grape skin'.[104]

5.1. They are inserted sometimes for dissimilation of a geminate: **š-n-d-l** 'to pamper, coax' (< OA **šaddil**); **g-m-b-l** 'to shape into a ball' < OA **gabbil**; but also **sārıṭlāna** 'crab' OA **sarṭānā**; **ʾırjāla** 'lifetime' < Ar **ʾajal**; **ʿanfarim** 'bravo!' (< IrAr **ʾāfarim**), **reškāsa** 'testicles' <**ʾeškāṯa**.[105]

5.2. Nunation: There are many cases in which a non-etymological **n** is suffixed (sometimes

[101]Cf. Mutz : 22: **ganāwa** 'thief', but **zaqqāra** 'weaver'; **rakkāwa** 'rider' (both not geminated in Z); cf. also **dukka** 'place', but Z **dūka**.

[102]For cases of dissimilation (outside of our group) see Khan 570, 571 ⁺**ḥambāla** (= Z/Ar **ḥammāla**) 'porter', **kalba/kalla** (=Z/IrAr **kalla**) 'block of sugar'

[103]On this and other explanations for the new doubling see Hoberman forthcoming.

[104]Cf. TA, Epstein 19: תליסר = תריסר 'twelve', נהמא = להמא 'bread', ריגלי/ניגרי 'feet', כלמי 'lice' (cf. H כנם; NA קלמי), etc.; Eshel 252: ארדיכל/אדריכל, etc.

[105]Cf. Mutzafi 2000a: 316 **sarıṭlāna** 'crab'; **lpa** 'to bake'; Epstein 19: שנתא/שתא 'year'

optionally): **ʾāhu(n)** 'he'; **ʾāhi(n)** 'she'; **ʾiṯ(ın)** 'there is'; **mīr(ın)** 'was said'; **ʾaraq(in)** 'arack'; **hešta(n)** 'yet'; **ʾīman** 'when' (OA **ʾēmaṯ**); **hālan** (< הלא) 'lo, behold' (=H הרי, הלא) .

6. METATHESIS. Words may show metathesis when compared with OA/OS or a contact language: **xmāṭa** 'needle' (OA מחטא); **lumla** 'utterance' (OA מְמַלָּא speech?); **xmōṭe** 'nasal mucus' (Ar مخاط; OA חוטמא); **kabʾa** 'anklebone' (Ar كعب); **xaffıkṯa** 'trap' (Ar فخّ); **qulfa** (NT)/**qufla** (Z) 'lock' (Ar قفل) ; **darāje** (Am)/**jarāde** (Z) 'stairs' (Ar دراج) ; **ḥāxām/xāḥām** 'rabbi, sage' (H חכם) .[106]

6.1. Dialectal or alternate metathesis is common in certain verbs: **b-ʾ-y** (NT)/**ʾ-b-y** (Z) 'to want' (OA בעי); **y-z-l** (Z)/**y-ḏ-l** (NT < OA ילד **y-l-d**) 'to give birth'; **y-q-ḏ** (NT)/**q-y-z** (Z) 'to burn'; **w-y-š** (Z)/**y-w-š** (NT) 'to dry' (OA יבש); **š-ʿ-b-z** (Z)/**š-ʿ-ḏ-b** (NT< H/OA שעבד) 'to enslave' (); **l-y-p/y-l-p** 'to study' (OA אלף); **y-r-m/r-y-m** 'to rise'; **y-ʾ-l/ʾ-y-l** 'to enter' (OA **ʿ-y-l** ע-י-ל < **ʿ-l-l** ע-ל-ל); **b-y-l/y-b-l** 'to carry' (OA יבל); **s-w-y** 'to age' < OA סיב; **x-r-ʾ** 'to wash well' < *OA רחע; **š-ṭ-y** 'to float' < OA שיט; **ṭ-m-ʾ** 'to taste' (OA טעם); **ṭ-m-ʿ** 'to overlay' < Ar طعّم; **d-q-r** (NT < OA דקר) /**d-r-q** (Am)/**d-q-š** (!) (Z) 'to gore'; **n-d-y** (OA, Z, NT)/**n-y-d** (D) 'to jump'; **t-w-n** '(foot) to be numbed' (< OS ܛܢܒ **tnb**).[107]

7. In comparison with OA/OS, some words in NA lose vowelless consonants, often resulting in an open syllable and long vowel: (1) In medial position: **xāṣa** 'back' (OA חרצא); **kāsa** 'belly' (OA כרסא); **qāna** 'horn' (< OA קרנא); **kāpa** 'shoulder' (OA כתפא); **ʾēta** 'church' (OS ܥܕܬܐ); **xāṯa** 'new' (OA חדתא); ***ruwwa** (Z)/**rurwa** 'big' (OA רברבא); **bazarʾa** (Z)/**barzarʾa** (NT) 'offspring' (OA בר זרעא); **qteʾle/qtēle** 'he cut' (OA קטע) ;[108] (2) In final position **ʿōlām** (Z)/**ʿōla** (RivSh181) 'world' (H עולם); **gēhınnām** (Z)/**gēhı/anna** (NT, RivSh) 'hell' (H)[109]; **xā** 'one' (OA חד); **ṣīṣi** 'prayer shawl' (H ציצית): **šāme(ʾ)** 'he hears'; **qū** 'Get

---

[106]Cf. TA in Epstein 18-19: עלס/אלס < לעס 'to chew'; ליגרי > ריגלי 'feet'; and outside of our group: **qamla** 'louse' (Khan 577)= Z **qalma**.

[107]At times it is difficult to tell which one is the 'original' root and which has the metathesis, e.g., נ-ג'-ו **n-j-w** 'to snatch, tear away and escape' — I consider it to be from Ar √ نجو 'to escape, get away'; but cf. Garbell 286 **j-n-v** < K/T?; MacD. 54 **jānū** 'to seize, snatch' < Ar جنا pluck/OS ܓܢܒ steal?

[108]Cf. TA in Epstein 18: קדמא=קמא 'first'; אודנא=אונא 'ear'.

[109]Hebrew has two pronunciations of this word **gēhinnōm** and **gēhinnām**; the former is mostly Biblical, while the latter is more Rabbinical, probably due to Aramaic influence, and is especially current among the Near Eastern Jewish communities; cf. OS ܓܗܢܐ ; Ar جَهَنَّم ; see *Leshonenu* 62 (1999):266f.

up!' (OA קום/קו)[110]; **(y)tū** 'sat down' (OA יתב);[111] (3) Varia (only a selection): **zılle** 'he went' (< *אזיל לה); **ʾāzi** 'they go' (OA אזלין); **sī** 'Go!';[112] **mırre** 'he said' (< *אמיר לה); **mār** 'Say';[113] **xēna/xēta** 'another' (m./f.).[114] Omission of initial originally participial **m** is rare in our group, e.g., **(m) rōḥımle** 'he showed mercy' (RivSh172); **(m)gōbēṯa** 'chosen' (RivSh 196);

8. ASSIMILATION. Partial consonantal assimilation (due to devoicing or voicing, etc.): (a) **b › p**: **pısra** 'meat' (OA בסרא); **qaṣāpa** (NT קצאפא) /**qaṣāba** (Z) 'butcher'; ⁺**rapṯa** (D רפתא) 'big' (f.) (OA רבתא); **gupta** 'cheese' < OS ܓܒܬܐ / ܓܘܒܬܐ; **s-p-r** 'to hope' (OA סבר); **x-p-q** 'to hug' (already in TA/OS עפק/חבק); **k-p-s** (Am)/**k-b-s** (Z) 'to conquer'; **š-p-y** 'to resemble' (Ar **šbh**); (b) **p › b**: **šabūḏa** 'skewer' (OA שפודא); **bız[‹ ḏ]āna** (Z)/**bıṯāna** (NT2)/**pıṯāna** (NT3) 'plow' (OA פדנא); (c) **d /ḏ › t/ṯ**: **ʾēspaṭīre** (Z) 'Passover' (< איד-פטירי); OS ܟܬܝܬܐ > **kṯēṯa** 'hen'; **ʾasqad** 'so much' (< **ʾaḏ-qadr**); **hatxa** 'like this' (< < האדך הדכא); (d) varia: **mpāqa** 'going out' (OA נפק); **mpāla** ''falling' (OA נפל); **rıfqa** 'Rebecca' (H רבקה); **x/ġzāya** 'to see' (OA חזי); **š/žġāla** 'to work' (Ar شغل); **ġ/xlāqa** 'to close' (Ar غلق); **x/ġẓāda** 'harvest' (OA חצד); **ʾ-s-p** 'to borrow (food only)' < OA יזף/OS ܐܙܘܦ 'to borrow'?; for assimilated variants of suffixed and prefixed particles, see above V, §§2.7-3.2.

8.1. Total assimilations: **ʾaššat** 'this year' (< אד שאתא); ⁺**marıtta** 'bitter' (f.)(< **marırta**); It is common at verbal morphological boundaries: **txır-re** 'he remembered' (< **txir-le**); **taxrıt-te** 'you remember him', etc.

9. DISSIMILATION. **qırša** 'straw' < OA **qaššā** (vs. **qāša** 'priest' < OS **qaššā** < OS/OA **qaššīšā**); **nābēn ‹ mā bēn** 'between'; **g-x-k** 'to laugh' < ***g-x-x** (OA גחך) (see above VI, §2); but Kapeliuk 1997: 528 assumes influence by a noun such as **gıxka** 'laughter'); **l-k-x** 'to lick, eat secretly' < ***l-x-x** (OA לחך; but already OS **lkḥ/lḥk** 'lick'); **r-k-x** 'to be soft'< **r-x-x** or < **rukxa** [< ***ruxka** / ***rukkıxa**?] 'boneles chicken breast'l; see also above VI, §2.

10. Pharyngealization or emphatic pronunciation[115] (known in Arabic as تفخيم,

---

[110]See Epstein 89; cf. ibid: תיקום/תיקו 'It will stand'; מיקם/מיקא 'to stand'.

[111]Cf. TA in Epstein 18: אזא=אזל 'go'; שקא=שקל 'take'; אמא=אמר 'say'; תו=תוב 'again'.

[112]For the various forms of the verb אזל in TA, see Epstein 58-60, e.g., אָזֵי~אָזֵיל 'he goes'; זִיל~אִיזִיל 'Go!'.

[113]For the various forms of the verb אמר in TA, see Epstein 61-67, e.g., אֵימָא/אֵימָר 'Say!'; אִמִיר 'said' (p.p.); מֵימָא 'to say'.

[114]Cf. TA in Epstein 19: חיתי=חריתי(א).

[115]That is, the pressing of the blade of the tongue against the palate in the formation of certain consonants.

marked in JNAD by an elevated cross to the left of the word) is an important prosodic feature of NA in general[116]. In addition to the traditional emphatic consonants **ṭ ṣ ẓ**, it usually affects words or syllables[117] with **+b, +č, +d, +l, +m, +p, +r, +z**, e.g., Z **+čōʾa** 'smooth'; **+palla** 'coal'; **+māya** 'water'; **+marīra** bitter'; **+plīma** 'twisted' (cf. above V, §2.7). However, while certain words may be emphatic in most dialects (e.g., variants of Z **+tlāha** 'three' < OA תלתא), others may vary from dialect to dialect, e.g., NT טעל **+t-ʿ-l**, emphatic,'to play' vs. Z **t-ʿ-l** (plain); NT **ṭōla** 'drum' (< OA טבלא) vs. Z **dōla**[118]; Z **+d-m-s** 'to dip' vs. NT/D דמס **d-m-s**; Am **+ʾɪrxa** 'guest' vs. Z **ʾarxa**; Am **+gōra** 'man' vs. Z **gōra** (Hob97: 317; 333); Z **tāḥli** 'bitter' (K) vs. NT טהלי **ṭahli**; Z **nūra**, Gz **+nūra**, fire; Z **sōrāya** vs. Gz **ṣoráya**.'Christian'; and, outside of our group: Arbil **+māl** 'property'; **+talta-sar** 'thirteen'; **+t-r-y** 'be wet' (Khan 574; 583) vs. Z **māl**; **tɪltaʿsar**; **t-r-y**.

10.1. In case of serial words one or more may be emphatic but not the other(s), e.g., Z **+ʾɪsra** 'ten', but **ʾɪsri** 'twenty'; **+tmāne** 'eighty', but **tmanya** 'eight'; **+tlāha** 'three', **+tlāsi** 'thirty', but **tɪltaʾsar** 'thirteen'; **+māya** 'water', but **mɪyāna** 'soft, liquidy'.

10.2 There are a few cases of phonemic contrast between emphatic and non-emphatic words/roots, usually the emphatic being a loanword, e.g. (all Z): **+tōra** 'Torah' (H) vs. **tōra** 'ox'; **+ōda** 'room' (Ar < T) vs. **ʾōda** 'slave'; **+rīx** 'dung' (K) vs. **rīxa** 'smell (OA); **+k-r-y** 'to rent' (Ar) vs. **k-r-y** 'be short' (OS); **+g-z-r** 'to decree' (H) vs. **g-z-r** 'to circumcise' (OA); **+qōri** 'teapot' (IrAr < P) vs.'**qōri** 'they bury' (OA קברי) ; in some cases both words are loanwords: **+čanta** 'suitcase' (IrAr < T) vs. **čanta** 'shoulder bag' (K< T); **+z-n-j-r** 'to sizzle' vs. **z-n-j-r** 'to chain'; **+ġīra** 'disappeared' vs. **ġīra** 'zeal'; **+karam** (Ar) 'kindness' vs. **karam** 'Karam' (p.n., K< Ar); **+mɪrad** 'wish; Murad' (Ar) vs. **mɪrad** 'Murad' (K < Ar); in some cases both are native: **+mɪrre** 'became bitter' vs. **mɪrre** 'he said'; **+qīra** 'pitch' vs. **qīra** 'cold' (OA); **+m-l-y** 'to fill' vs. **m-l-y** 'to be enough'; **+r-p-y** 'to be set against' vs. **r-p-y** 'to be loose'.

10.3. De-emphatization. Compared to the more common emphatization, there are only a few cases of de-emphatization: **t-x-n** 'to grind' and **txuna** 'flour' < OA טחן; **sɪxwa** 'clear sky' <OA צחוא; **tɪḥāla** 'spleen' < OA טחלא/Ar طحال; **dōqa** 'baking pan' < OA טפקא; **dōla** (Z; but **ṭōla**, NT) 'drum' < OA **ṭavlā**; **tarz** 'manner, form' (< Ar طرز); **haʿēs** (H העץ from the blessing בורא פרי העץ) 'fruit of the tree'. OS ܡܛܠ > preposition **ta** 'for' (Z), but NT **ṭla**, and Z **ṭāli** , **ṭālox** 'for me, for you, etc.', and **ṭamā** 'what for, why'; cf. also פצחה/פסח **fɪṣaḥ/fisaḥ** 'clear (tongue)'; קצתא/קסתא **qɪṣta/qɪsta** 'story'; צהיון/סחיון **ṣɪhyon/sɪḥyon** (H ציון)

---

[116]Cf. Hob85; Hob91, passim; Hob97:316-18; Mutz 19-20.

[117]Normally the entire word or even compound is affected; cf. Mutzafi 2000a: 301.

[118]Cf. Khan 559: **ṭʿl** 'play', but **tšy** 'conceal' (= Z **ṭšy**); **tpy** 'stick' (= Z **ṭpy**); and vice versa: **ṭxn** 'grind' (= Z **txn**).

'Zion' (SaLH; Amedi 63 'thirst' by mistake); **ṣ/sanduq** 'box' (Ar صندوق; but OS ܣܢܕܘܩܐ, and so in many Arabic dialects).[119]

11. Occasional interchange of **q/k/(x/g)**: the Present prefix **g-/k-/q**;[120] Z **k-s-m** 'to swear' < Ar قسم; **p-r-k** 'to break off partnership' < OA פרק; **pukta** 'belch' < OS ܦܘܩܬܐ; **p-k-ʾ** 'to belch' < OS ܦܘܩܐ 'yawn, hiccough'/OA פקע 'burst'?; ***qaqra** 'very talented or rich person' < OA ככרא; **gagna** 'vat' < OA כַּגְנָא 'pan' (?); **yaqsir** 'prisoner' but NT יכסיר = **yak/xsir** < K **yaxsir**; Z **qčīn** 'as the size of', but NT אקג'ין/אכג'ין; **qāza** 'beetle' < K **kez**; **ʾīko/ʾaqo** 'Jacob' (H יעקב); **qutta** 'short person' (P **kutāh**); and perhaps: **qūṭa** 'vagina' < K **quz**/P/Ar **kuss**; **qīyaᶜ** 'grime' < H כִּיחַ?[121]; **kazza** 'moss' < Ar **qazz** 'silk'.

12. Cases of **w/y** interchange: **hāw/ye** 'they will be'; **j-w/y-b** 'to answer' (Ar جوب); **r-j-y** 'to request' (NT) < Ar رجو; **yalunke** (Z) /ולונכי **walunke** (RivS 122-3) 'children'. Note also that Z **ʾamōya** 'paternal uncle', **xalōya** 'maternal uncle', **sapōya** 'snack' - all end with **-wa** instead in MacD.

13. Phonetic variations of hypocoristic forms of proper names seem to follow K patterns of consonnantal shift: **čīmo** 'Siman-Tov'; **ʾıččo** 'Isaac' (cf. K **mıčo** 'Mustafa'); **ḥamo** 'Rahamim' (cf. K. **mıḥo** 'Muhammad'); **ʾusaka/osīka** 'Joseph' (but K **ʾīsıf**); **ḥale** 'Rachel'.[122]

14. Varia: **tınna** 'smoke' < OA/OS **tınānā**; **kāšīya** '(tea) glass' < Ar **kās**? **ṭarpıšna** 'fallen leaves' < **ṭarpe** 'leaves' +**šna** 'change'?; **ḥušta** 'pretext'; pl. **ḥujyāṯa** < Ar حُجّة.

15. VOWELS. For a detailed vowel description of our group see Hob97:322-30. In the following only some general rules, which have more historical-lexical relevance, will be mentioned.

15.1. There are seven vowel qualities: **i ı e a o ü u**. The vowel **ı** sounds almost like schwa or as **e** in English **under**. The vowel **ü** is like **ı** plus rounding of the lips and both often interchange as reflected by variant spellings even in the same manuscript (v. above V/§3.4). The other vowels do not need further explanation. Final phonemically long vowels, normally unaccented, are realized in context as short or long (left unmarked in JNAD): **kálba** 'dog',

---

[119]Cf. Mutz 25; OA עקס/עקץ 'to sting', etc.

[120]See above V, §3.1. Already in OA קָא ~ כָּא (OS ܟܐ; SokBA 976).

[121]Cf. TA כיטא/קיטא 'summer'; כמצא/קמצא 'locusts', etc; Mutzafi 2000a:302 on the reflexes of ***q**; Mutz 205, 221, 222 **ḥqy** 'to talk' (Z **ḥky** < Ar حكي); **qnš** 'to sweep' (but Z **knš** < OA כנש); **qanušta** 'broom' (Z **kanušta**); **qušāba~xušāba** 'Sunday'; cf. in TA, Eshel 62f., 227ff., 251: בי כיפי/בי קופאי a locality (perhapsrelated at least by name to Tel-Kepe near Mosul?); כרדו/קרדו (similar change in OS) 'Cordyene = Gzira or Jazirat Ibn-'Umar = T Cizre.

[122]For more details see Sabar 1974c.

knísta 'synagogue'; **ḥámmaš** 'book'. Penult long vowels (**ā ē ī ō ū** in open syllables) are usually realized as long: **qaṭūṯa** 'cat' (accent on vowels marked as long is unmarked due to technical reasons), **šrāʾa** 'lamp', **sēpa** 'sword', **šamīna** 'fat', **ḥakōma** 'king'. Antepenult unaccented vowels in open syllables may be realized as short or long: **rō/omāna** 'high'; **ro/ōmā/anūṯa** 'height'; **gū/urāne** 'husbands' (< **gūre** 'men'); **ṣī/iwāye** 'loggers' (< **ṣīwa** 'wood'); **ʾē/enwāṯa** 'wells' (< **ʾēna** 'well'); **zā/axōnāya** 'one of Zakho'; **ba/ābıwāṯa** 'fathers' (< **bāba**, sg.); **qaṭūṯa** 'cat' (f.) < **qāṭa** (m.); **xawōra** river' (< OA חָבוֹרָא); **šamīna** 'fat' (< OS **šammīnā**).

15.2. Certain old vowel **a** > **e** before **ʾ** (< OA ע): **tōleʾṯa** 'worm' (OA תּוֹלַעְתָּא); NT תיאלא **teʾla** 'fox' (OA תַעְלָא); **reʾwa** 'zest, gusto' (OA רַעֲוָא 'wish'); **ʾarbeʾma** 'four hundred', but **šwaʾma** 'seven hundred'. Note also in verbal forms **ı** > **e**: **qāṭeʾ** 'he cuts' (vs. **šāqıl**), **šāmeʾ** (> **šāme**)'he hears', **šmeʾle** 'he heard' (vs. **šqılle**), but with (recent) Ar loan roots **ı** is retained before **ᶜ**: **ṭāmıᶜ** 'he desires', **qālıᶜ** 'he goes away', **qlıᶜle** 'he went away', etc.; exceptions with older borrowings: **nāfeʾ/nfeʾle** 'benefit' < Ar نفع.

15.3. Old and new vowels **ū** and **ī/ē** may interchange, or perhaps the new vowels continue old non-literary dialects: **xızūra** 'wild boar' (OA חזירא); **zarzūra** 'starling' (OA זרזורא); **šarqīᶜa** 'slap' (OS ܨܪܩܘܥܐ); **xašūka** 'dark' (OA חשיכא, but OS ܚܫܘܟܐ); **xarūpa** (Z)/**xarīpa** (NT) 'sharp' (OA/OS **ḥarīfā**); **raʾīḏa** 'tender' (OS ܪܟܝܟܐ); **ʾamūqa** 'dark (color), deep' (OA/OS/Ar **ʾamīq(a)**, but H עָמֹק); **tūra** 'twig' (K **tīre**); **tēra** 'saddle-bag' (K **tūr**); **bībi** 'pupil' (< K < Ar بُؤبُؤ, OA/OS **bāvā**, P **babak**); **bahwarī/ūṯa** 'trust'. Note also the shifting of short vowels: **dıpna** 'corner' (OS ܕܘܦܢܐ, OA דִּפְנָא); **našuqta** 'kiss' (OA נשיקתא/ נושקתא; OS ܢܘܫܩܬܐ).

15.4. Vowel **ā/a** > **ō/o** in Am/Arodh next to emphatic or labial consonants, e.g. **ṭūrōne** 'mountains' (Z **ṭūrāne**); ***rōba** 'much' (Z ***rāba**); **ṭōṯe** 'plate' (Z **ṭāse**); **mōṭo** 'why?' (Z **māṭo**); **⁺ᶜarōḏen** 'Aradhin', ***bōš** 'good' (Z **bāš**);[123] cf. also NT קורבונה/קרבונה **qürbōne/qurbāne** 'sacrifices'; אסחוק **ʾısḥoq** 'Isaac' (Z **ʾísḥaq**); פינחוס **pınḥos** 'Phineas' (Z **pínḥas**). For an opposite case, perhaps morphological, Z has **ō**, **yārōna** 'illicit lover', vs. יארארא **yārāna** in NT5 399 and RivSh 229).[124] Note also the following: **smōqa** (NT+) 'red' < OA (+OS/Mand) סומקא **summāqā**; **kōma** 'black' < OA/OS אוכאמא **ʾukkāmā**[125]; **pıddōma** (Z) 'stopper, cover' < OA פִּדְמָא, פדאמא (Ar فدام < P **padām** 'mask for the mouth').

15.5. Long vowels in open accented syllables become short when the syllable is closed and may change quality: **šamīna** (m.) (spelled שמינא) 'fat' > **šamınta** (f.) (usually spelled without י: שמנתא); **xlīma** (m.)'thick' > **xlımta** (f.); **kōma** (m.) (כומא) 'black' > **kumta** (f.) (כומתא); **šahāra** (m.) (שהארא) 'blind' > **šaharta** (f.) (שהרתא); **ʾīṯ** (אית) 'there is' > **ʾıtli** (אתלי) 'I have'; **lēṯ** 'there is not' > **latli** 'I have not' (cf. below VI. §6). Complimentarily,

---

[123]Cf. Hob97 324.

[124]Cf. MacD 122 **yārānā**.

[125]See SokBA 88, but also אִיכּוּמָא **ʾıkkūma**, which seems the source of the NA form.

short vowels in closed syllables become long when opened and accented: **nāmus** 'law, custom', pl. **nāmūse**; **ḥákim** 'healer', pl. **ḥakīme**; **bāžır** 'city', pl. **bāžēre**; **ḥēwan** 'animal', pl. **ḥēwāne**.

15.6. Arabic sg. nouns with original short or long vowel in the last syllable (usually becoming short and unaccented in NA) tend to lengthen the vowel when a pl. suffix is added: **ḥákim** : **ḥakīme** 'healers'; **fáqir** : **faqīre/-īn/-īm** 'poor people'; **falak** : **falāke** 'zodiac signs'; **ṭalab** : **ṭalābe** 'demands (from horse to gallop)'; **zaman** : **zamāne** 'periods'; **ḥúdud** : **ḥudūde** 'borders', **túxub** : **tuxūbe** 'regions'.[126]

15.7. Open non-accented short vowels are often attenuated (> ı), e.g., ***mırāqa/*marāqa** 'soup'; **bābıwāṯa/bābawāṯa** 'fathers'; **tıxurya/tuxurya** 'memory'; **beʾe(!)/bıʾe** (Z) 'eggs'; **šızāna** (Z)/**šīdāna** (Am)'mad' < **šēḏa** 'demon' (cf. above VI, §15.5).

15.8. Diphthongs. Old Aramaic diphtongs are usually monophthongized **bēṯa** 'house' (< OA בֵּיתָא); **mōṯa** 'death' (OS ܡܰܘܬܳܐ); similarly: **kōda** 'liver' (< כַּבְדָּא **kav/wdā**);[127] some exceptions: **ʾay** (OS ܗܰܝ) 'that' (f.) vs. **ʾē** 'this' (f.); **ʾaw** (OS ܗܰܘ) 'that' (m.) vs. **ʾō** 'this' (m.); and in a few loanwords: **ḥawja** 'need' (< Ar √ حوج); **gawda** 'upper body' (T); **fayda** 'benefit' (Ar); **qaysi** 'dried apricots' (K/T); and in geminated semivowels: **hayya** 'fast!'; **hawwa** 'good'. However, in Am and NT more diphthongs are retained: כוודנתא **kawdınta** 'mule' (OA; Z **kōzınta**); **nıw/vya** (NT נבייא/נווייא) 'prophet' (Z **nūya**) **ḥawš** 'yard' (Z **ḥōš**; Ar);**ʿayš** (NT עייש)'living' (Z **ʿīš**; Ar); **ʾaykar** (NT אייכר) 'then, that time' (Z **ʾēga**); **hawna** 'behold' (Z **hōna**); and even **tawleʾe** (Am/NT תוולאה) 'worms'.[128]

15.9. Arabic loaords in NT show traces of **ā** › **ē**:[129] רמאלין/רמילין **rammā/ēlīn** 'geomancers'; חאכם/חיכם **ḥā/ēkım** 'ruler'; אימן **ʾēmın** 'secure' (< Ar آمن); cf. Z**jērīye** (< جارية) 'maid'; **dunye** (< دنيا).

16. ACCENT. Normally the accent in our group (Z, Am, D, Arodh) is on the penult syllable (so assumed for NT and other related written texts), as occurs in NENA in general (excluding the Jewish dialects of Eastern Iraq and Iran, which place the accent usually on the final syllable). Since lexically we are mostly concerned with nouns (rather than conjugated verbal forms), the exceptions to the penult accent are as follows: (a) On the final syllable:

---

[126]On the syntax of number see below VII, §9.2.

[127]In contrast to ChNA; see above I, §5; It is interesting to note that while OS retains many diphtongs the contemporary Jewish Aramaic (=SokBA) does not, e.g., ܒܰܝܬܳܐ, ܚܰܝܠܳܐ vs. בֵּיתָא, חֵילָא; ܝܰܘܡܳܐ: ܝܰܘܢܳܐ vs. יוֹמָא, יוֹנָא, etc.; but also ܛܰܘܣܳܐ, טַוְוסָא 'peacock' (< Gr ταωζ).; ܫܰܘܩܳܐ, חַוְוקָא 'step of stair' (< Ak **xūqu** rung of a ladder? Cf. Z **ḥuqqa** 'rung of a ladder' !)

[128]Cf. Hob97: 325f.

[129]This phonetic shift, known as **imāla** in Arabic, is typical to **qeltu** dialects; see Sabar 1984: 202, n. 10.

H and Ar pl. endings **-īm, -īn, -ōṯ**: **ḥāxāmím** 'sages'; **ᶜawōnóṯ** 'iniquities'; **rammālín** 'geomancers' (but Ar **-āt** ending is shortened and unaccented: **jēríyat** 'maids' (Ar جـــاريات); varia: **gıruvír** 'round' (K) **ʾevaddón** 'hell' (H); **ṭamá** 'why?'; (< **ṭamáh a**); **ʾīlá**'God' (< **ʾiláh a**); certain construct forms and numbers: **palgús-báḥḥar**; **kōlán-māṯa** 'village alleys'; **xamšá ʾalpe** 'five thousands'; **šātá palgé** 'a year and a half'; **balé** 'yes, indeed' (vs. **bále** 'but'/**bále** 'his mind'); **zāqén** '(respected) old man' (H) but **záqen** family name; **ṣaddíq** 'righteous' but **ṣáddiq** personal name; **ḥáxam/ḥāxám** 'Sage, rabbi'; **baxávoḏ/baxavóḏ**/'respectfully' (H); **wazára** 'ministry' (f. sg., وزارة) vs. **wázara** 'ministers' (pl. Ar وزراء); **maᶜayyén** 'certainly' (Ar مُعيّن); a few Ar words retain the original accent, e.g., **maᶜlúm** 'obviously', but most are naturalized and receive a penult accent (with the final long vowel becoming short): e.g., **máḥṣul** 'profit'; **máᶜbud** 'idol'; **ẓáᶜif** 'weak'; **xášim** 'simpleton' (Ar غشيم); **ḥákim** 'healer' (Ar حكيم); **qánun/qānún** 'law' (Ar قانون) ; Am **májbur** 'forced' but Z **majbúr** (Hob97:331). (b) On the first syllable (words with 3 syllables): **ʾáxtōxun** 'you'; **wálōxun** 'Hey you!'; **ʾápāwa** 'he too'; **mbínōke** 'morning' (OA מִ-בְּ-נָגְהֵי); **láxaṯma** 'how much more so' (< H על אחת כמה וכמה); **mbúhdıla** (p.p.) 'confused'; **múqīma** (p.p.) 'raised'; **láwmān(e)** 'therefore, because of this' (Ar لوما) ; **bár-taxti** 'downwards'; **dúrtıdyom** 'next day' (c) Varia: **+bárux-xábba** 'welcome' (H); **+bárux-ʾátta** 'you too'; **šōʾí-ga(he)** 'although' (lit. seventy times); **hēdí-hēdi** 'slowly'; **ṭūré-ṭūre** 'via mountains'.[130]

130Note: Penult accent, being quite regular, usually is not marked in JNAD (with exeption for clarity), especially so for words known only from written texts (manuscripts and printed books) which do not indicate accent in any way. However, in all other cases, the accent, if known, is usually marked.

VII. Observations on Morphology

1. NOUNS. Most of the native Aramaic nouns appear with the reflex of the OA definite suffix **-a** (m.), **-ta** (f.), regardless of their being definite or not in NA: **xmāra** 'donkey' (also a/the donkey); **xmarta** 'she-ass' (a/the she-ass). A few exceptions: **lēle** 'night' (m.); **gāre** 'roof' (m.); **sūse** 'horse' (m.); **xuwwe** 'snake' (m.);[131] **mındi** 'thing'; **čēri** 'autumn'; **nēri(ya)** 'he-goat'; **kālo** 'bride'; **ʿēqu** 'trouble' (f.); **wardo** 'thigh-muscle'. Optional common means to make nouns definite or indefinite: **xa kalba** 'a dog'; **ʾaw kalba** 'the/that dog'. A few formally indefinite (but semantically definite) nouns remain, especially in adverbial expressions: **kud yōm** 'every day'; **ʾıdyo** 'today'; **palgıdyom** 'noon'; **bōma-xın** (< OA אחרינא) 'on another day"; **ʾıd̲lal** 'tonight'; **kud̲lal** 'every night'; **palgıd̲lal** 'midnight'; **lēlxın** 'last night'; **kuššat** 'every year'; **ʾaššat** 'this year'; **ʾaxgıb** 'this side, hither'; **tangıb** 'over there' **bē/byā-ʾal** 'this/that side'.

1.1. Loanwords may be naturalized and take the m./f. reflex suffixes: **xafīfa** (m.)/**xafıfta** (f.) 'light' (< Ar); **ḥadāda** (< Ar) 'blacksmith'; **ṣafāra** 'coppersmith' (< Ar); some remain unsuffixed: **ḥakim** 'healer' (< Ar); **faqir** 'poor' (Z < Ar); **ḥāxam** 'Sage' (< H); ⁺**rāʿ** 'evil' (< H); with some the suffix is optional: **taxt(a)** 'chair' (K/P); **sanduq(a)** 'box' (< Ar); **mískin** 'humble' (< Ar مسكين) is inv. in Z, but in NT: **mıskēna** m. (< OA/OS מִסְכֵּינָא), **mıskēta** f., **mıskēne**, pl.

2. Construct forms. Possessive-genitive relations between nouns are as follows: (a) Suffixing of **d** (OA -ד/די) is most common, e.g., **bēt̲ıd ḥakōma** (ביתד חכומא) 'house-of king, palace'; (b) prefixing of **d**: **bēt̲a dḥakōma** (ביתא דחכומא, rare in speech); (c) without **d** (some old construct, common especially in certain expressions, as well as some more recent neologisms): **bēt̲ ḥakōma**; **bır mōše** 'son of Moses'; **brat ʾamōyi** 'daughter of my uncle'; **bax-bāba** 'step-mother' ('wife of father'); **ʾen-yōma** 'eye of day, sun'; **kōz yatūme** 'a constellation, Orion?' (lit., a group of orphans); **nāš-gyana** 'relative'; **bır-nāše** (!) '(not a blood) relative'; **mar(e)-bēt̲a** 'house owner, landlord'; **dıdūt̲ dūša** 'bee' (fly of honey); **makīn-xyāt̲a** 'sewing machine'; **massīn qahwa** 'coffee pot'; and with demonstratives: **xōr dō** [<dʾo] **nāša** 'a friend of this person'; **nāš dē baxta** 'a relative of this woman'; (d) redundant **d**: **šımmıd dʾılāha** (NT שמד דאילאהא); **šımmıd dīde** (שימד דידה) 'His name' (rare in our group but common in others; cf., **lišānıd didan** 'our language', Khan 219).

2.1. Construct forms may neutralize sg./pl. endings: **nāš-gyāna** ='relative/relatives' (**naš**=**nāša**, sg./**nāše**, pl.); **ṣīwıd gōza** 'nut-tree(s)'; **raqqıt māya** 'frog(s)' (PolG).

2.2. Some nouns undergo changes in their construct stem followed by another noun or relative clause (preposition, or even verb), e.g., **xabra** 'word' > **xabır-bābox** 'word of your father' (but **xabre** 'his word'); **ʾıpra** 'dust' > **ʾıpır-**; **brōna** 'son' > **bır-(/brōn-)**; **baxta** 'wife' > **bax-**; **bēt̲a** 'house' has two forms, with some distinction: **bē-** 'family of', **bēt̲-** 'house of', thus: **bēs bē zāqen** (Z) 'the house of the Zaqen family' . Cf. Goldenberg 2000 80: **lyāp(ıd) lišāne** 'studying languages'; **ʾō mıṭır kušle** 'This rain that came

---

[131]See Mutzafi 2000b: 298, n. 6, on a possible reason for the-**e** ending.

down'; **šūl ʾuzlu** 'the work that they did'; **ʾan nāš ʿımme** 'the people who are with him'; PolG: **la šqāl ṭımʾıd xabra ula fhām maʿne dīde** 'without (really) getting the (full) meaning of the matter and understanding its (complete) sense/implication.'

2.4. Nouns are attached to pronominal possessive suffixes either directly or with **dīd/d-**: **bēṯi** or **bēṯa dīdi (/bēṯıd dīdi)** 'my house'; **bēṯēni** or **bēṯa dēni** 'our house'; some of these forms may be ambiguous: **bēṯa** = 'house' or 'her house'; **kalāṯa** = '(her) daughters-in-law'; **xmāre** = '(his) donkey(s).' Foreign words usually are attached only with **dīd**: **⁺trambēl dīdi** 'my car'; **ḥanukka dōhun** 'their Hanukkah candelabrum'.

2.5. A noun may be attached to another noun in construct **d-** form (instead of the regular apposition of noun and adjective), serving as qualifier: e.g., **ṣaddīq dmōše** 'The righteous Moses'; **rāšāʿ dparʿo** 'the wicked Pharaoh'; **ṭōpıd šırmāsa** 'huge buttocks' (lit. 'cannon of buttocks').

3. Common noun formations (including prefixed/suffixed morphemes). In addition to the basic root consonants, nouns and adjectives have native or loan reflexes of nominal morphemes. Here is a selection (usually m. forms):[132]

3.1. Several formations indicate profession or tendency to do something (agent nouns): **qaṭāla** 'killer, one who kills'; **ʾaxāla** 'glutton'; **šaqāla uyahāwa** 'trader' ('taker and giver'); **qarāya ukaṯāwa** 'literate' ('reader and writer'); **kapōra** 'infidel'; **naxōpa** 'shy'; **duglāna/mdaglāna** 'liar'; **malpāna** 'teacher'; **mṭapyanēṯa** 'female baker'; the **-āna** suffix may be added to loan words or roots as well, e.g., **yıkkāna** 'an only child' (< K **yak** 'one'); **⁺mkōbırāna** 'muezzin' (< כ-ו-ב-ר **k-w-b-r** 'to say **allāhu akbar**')

3.2. Gentilic: **hōḏāya** 'Jew'; **sōrāya** 'Christian'; **mušulmāna** 'Muslim'; **ʾēzıdnāya** 'Yezidi'; **zāxōnāya** 'one from Zakho'; **baġdannāya** 'Baghdadi'; **ʾıngleznāya** 'English'; **tırkāya** 'Turkish'; but also: **muṭurbāya** 'Gypsy musician' (< Ar مُطرب), **ḥambıšāya** 'giant', **qātırčāya** 'muleteer, trader'.

3.3. Nouns of action and verbal nouns (theoretically they can be derived from any verb, but only those attested are listed in the JNAD): **ʾixāla** 'eating'; **mšadōre** 'sending'; **mafhōme** 'explaining'; some indicate individualized or kind of 'action': **ʾixalta** 'one's way of eating';[133] **ʾizalta** 'way of going'; **qyamta** 'one's way of rising'; **dmaxta/dmaxīṯa** '(kind of) lying, carnal relations'; **npalta** '(kind of) falling';[134] **swaʾta** as in **xōl swaʾtox** 'Eat your fill'; **ryamta uytōta dīde** '(She) was looking at) his movements, the way he conducted himself' (lit., his rising and sitting (PolG); **šqaltıt ʾilāha** craziness '(God's taking [of one's brain])' (PolU 267).

---

132 For f. forms see below, VII, §4, Gender.

133 Cf. **ʾixalte ʾixaltıd ʾarya** 'his eating is like that of a lion; he eats a lot and well.

134 Cf. **npılle xa npalta, rēše mpušpıšle** 'He fell such a hard fall that his head was smashed.'

3.4. Abstract nouns ending with **-ūṯa(/-tūṯa)** (very common)/-**īṯa** (less common), including with loan stems: **⁺rabūṯa** 'greatness'; **hawūṯa** 'goodness'; **xmarūṯa** 'stupidity' (jack-ass behavior); **šwawūṯa** 'neighborhood, neighhborliness'; **nāšūṯa** 'humanness, good human relationship'; **xıtnūṯa** 'groomhood, matrimony'; **kalūṯa** 'bridehood'; **rāᶜūṯa** 'evilness' (H); **daᶜūṯa** 'plea' (< ***daᶜwūṯa** < Ar √ دعو); **šēx(āt)ūṯa** 'sheikdom'; **šahyānātūṯa** 'joyfulness of celebration' (PolG) < **šahyāna** '(royal) celebration'; **pāšrōžūṯa** 'end-of-days-ness' (NT); **ᶜıšq-u-havīnūṯa** 'desire-and-amour-ness'; **twarīṯa** 'defeat, brokenness'; **škalīṯa** 'beginning'.

3.4.1. Formation **qaṭṭalīṯa** seems to indicate excessiveness: **ṭapparīṯa** 'excessive heat; **parraṭīṯa** 'excruciating work'; **šarraqīṯa** 'excessive sun heat'; **⁺zarradīṯa** 'tantrum'; **sarraxīṯa** 'excessive aggression'; **kallawīṯa** 'dog-like aggression'; **čarrapīṯa** 'excessive sudden fear'.

3.4.2. Nouns indicating a single of a kind (اسم الوحدة, n. unit.): **xıṭṭīṯa** 'a wheat grain' < **xıṭṭe** 'wheat'; **⁺saᶜarta** 'barley grain' < **⁺saᶜāre** 'barley'; **ʾınūṯa** 'a grape' < **ʾınwe** 'grapes'; **ṭluxta** 'a lentil' < **ṭlōxe** 'lentils'; **bıṭımṯa** 'a terebinth nut' < **bıṭme** 'terebinth nuts'.[135]

3.5. Adjectives. Some typical formations: **sqīla** 'beautiful'; **ʾatīqa** 'old, ancient'; **raqīqa** 'thin'; **gamūʾa** 'deep'; **bahūra** 'clear'; **yarūqa** 'green' **smōqa** 'red'; **zrōqa** 'blue'; **xwāra** 'white'; **kōma** 'black'; **kurkmāna** 'yellow'; **komnāya** 'blackish'; **xwarnāya** 'whiteish'; **smoqnāya** 'reddish'; but some of these formations are also used for nouns: **xmīra** yeast; **qaṭīʾa** 'stick'; **xabūša** 'apple', **šabūqa** 'rod'; **šabūḏa** skewer, **zāxōnāya** 'resident of Zakho'.

3.6. Diminutive forms of some family members (mostly morphological, rather than semantic): **brōna** 'son' (OA ברא) ; **sāwōna** 'old man' (OA סבא); **sōtınta** 'old lady' (OA סבתא); **baxtunta** '(little) lady' (< **baxta** 'woman'); **bratunta** '(little) daughter, girl' (< **brāta**); **xalunta** (NT) 'sister' (< **xalta** 'maternal aunt' or **xāṯa** 'sister'); **xımyāna** 'father-in-law' (so already in OS, but OA חָמָא) .

3.6.1. Kurdish/Persian suffixes (some quite productive and attached to even H stems): (a) Diminutives (indicating variety of notions: affection, belittling, 'our ..', or just a doublet of the regular form): **-ko/-(ōš)ka** (m.)/**-(ōš)ke** (f.): **⁺rāᶜíko/-ke** '(little) bad person', n., vs. **rāᶜ**, adj. ; **gōra** man vs. **gōrınka** 'our guy/ fellow' (in FT); **ᶜānīka** '(little) poor guy'; **faqīr(ōš)ka/-(ōš)ke** '(little) poor person'; **ḥannōke** '(little) Hanna, Annie'; **qaḥbe/ qaḥbıke** 'prostitute'; (b) vocative **-o** (common especially in hypocoristic names or pejorative epithets, regardless of gender): **⁺ʾavro** 'Abraham, Abe'; **ḥanno** 'Hanna, Annie'; **čāro** 'Sara, Sarita'; **mᶜarṭo** 'farter'; **qaṭōṭo** 'quarrelsome' (< H קטטה?); **flankaso** (m.)/**flankase** (f.) 'So-and-so'; (c) abstract suffixes: **šalaqīna** 'excessive heat' < **š-l-q** 'to boil'+-**īna**.; **mılkīni** 'possession' < Ar ملك + -**īni**.; **xudāni** 'care, providence' < P

---

[135] Or using phrases such **xa rēša xasse** 'one head of lettuce'; **xa kakta tūma** one clove of garlic.

xuda 'God'; **xulāṣi** 'salvation' (Ar خلاص); **ʾazādi** 'freedom'; **sahnāyi** 'easiness'; **baqqıki** 'swimming frog-like'; (d) games: **kabʾāne** 'knucklebone game'; **tabalāne** 'marbles game'; **hēkāne** 'egg-cracking game'; **dajalāne** 'polemics, arguing contest'; **qōčāne** 'goring game'; (e) doer, agentive: **xıšūfkar** 'sorcerer'; **gunahkar** 'sinner'; (f) onomatopoetic sounds, such as of hunters chasing after their game, or speedily sailing on a river; see examples below VIII, end of §13.

3.7. Kurdish/Persian prefixes (with varying degrees of productivity, if any): **be-ṭabᶜat** 'ill-natured'; **be-ḥaya** 'shameless'; **be-ᶜaqlūṯa** 'foolishness' ('no smartness'); **ná-ṣax** 'not-well, sick'; **ná-xwaš** 'unpleasant, not-tasty'; **du-/sē-ṭabaqi** 'two/three-floor (structure).'

4. GENDER. Most nouns and adjectives belong clearly to either the masculine or feminine gender. Some nouns do not have a clear gender (see below). While most m. nouns remain unmarked, the f. are suffixed with **-ta/-ṯa**, usually as inherited from OA/OS or by analogy: **šabṯa** 'Sabbath, week'; **mḏīta** (NT < OA מדינתא) 'town'; **šāta** 'year'; **šāṯa** 'fever'; **kṯūta** 'amulet' (< OA כתיבתא); **parta** 'sawdust'; **qarṯa** 'cold weather'; **ʾarṯa** 'rival wife'; **kalṯa** 'daughter-in-law'; **⁺rāṯa** 'lung'. The suffix may be added to a loan stem: **nālnālta** 'aching, suffering' < K/P/T **nāl** 'lamentation'.

4.1. The f. form of several nouns, adjectives, participles is quite predictable and regular: **qaṭāla** (m.)/**qaṭalta** (f.) 'murderer'; **šahāra/šaharta** 'blind'; **xmāra** 'Jack-ass', **xmarta** 'she-ass'; **malūxa/maluxta** 'salty'; **yaqūra/yaqurta** 'heavy' (but **gamūʾa/gamoʾta** 'deep'; **xamūṣa/xamüṣta**); **xafīfa/xafıfta** light'; **kpīna/kpınta** (p.p.) 'hungry'; **sqīla/sqılta** 'beautiful' ('polished')'; **kırya/krīṯa** 'short' (p.p., R_3y); **mīra/mırta** 'said' (p.p. R_1ʾ); **qīma/qımta** (p.p., R_2y) 'standing'; **(y)tīwa/ (y)tūta** 'seated, sitting' (p.p., R_3w); **mšudra/mšōdarta** 'sent' (p.p., II); **muʾmıra/muʾmarta** 'built' (p.p., IV); **šulxāya/šulxēṯa** 'naked'; **⁺ᶜarabaya/⁺ᶜarabēṯa** 'Arab'; **kurdināya/kurdinēṯa** 'Kurd'; **komnāya/komnēṯa** 'blackish'; **duglāna/duglanta** 'liar'; **mıyāna/ mıyanta** 'watery, not too thick'; **yıkkāna** : **yıkkanta** 'only child, unique' (< K **yak** 'one'), but **mamṣāna** (NT) 'pedagogue'/ **mamṣanīṯa** 'wet nurse'.[136]

4.2. Some f. nouns, indicating people and animals,use a more modified m. stem with f. suffix: **kalba** 'dog', **kalıbṯa** 'bitch'; **tōra** 'bull', **tawırta** 'cow'; **xōra** (m.)/**xawırṯa/xūratṯa** (f.) 'friend'; **ʾarya/ʾaryōṯa** 'lion'; **qāṭa/qaṭūṯa** 'cat'; **sūse/susta** (NT) 'horse'; **xımyāna** 'father-in-law'; **xmāṯa** 'mother-in-law'; **brōna** 'son'; **brāta** 'daughter'; **mıskīna/mıskīta** (NT < OA מסכינתא) 'poor'; **ʾaxōna** 'brother', **xāṯa** 'sister'; **⁺ʾurwa/rurwa/⁺ruwwa** (m.) 'big', but f. **⁺rabṯa**; **ṣaddīq** (< H, m.) 'righteous person', but f. **ṣaddāqa**. A rare form of adjective is **bxāye** (NT בכאייה) 'alive' (inv.), which literally means 'in life'. (cf. H בחיים 'alive').

4.3. Some f. nouns seem to be syncopated, missing the final vowel **yíqruṯ** 'nightmare; heaviness'; **píṭxuṯ** 'width'; **yírxuṯ** 'length'; **šíxnuṯ** 'warmth'; and perhaps **palgús**

---

[136]See also below VII, §§4.3.2; 5.7; 5.8.

(**baḥḥar**) (Z) 'in the middle of (the sea').

4.3.1. Some f. nouns end with -o[137]: **kālo** 'bride' (vs. **kalṯa** 'daughter-in-law'); **wardo** 'thigh-muscle' (vs. **warīḏa** 'sinew, root, vein'); **xıppo** 'bridal veil' (cf. H. חֻפָּה) ; **šalqo** 'small pox, boils'; **balqo** (K?) 'brier'; **jar'o** (K?) 'stomach'; **mēdo** 'Sabbath table' (JAB < Ar مائده ?).

4.3.2. Many f. Arabic/Kurdish loan nouns and adjectives end witn -e: **xıdme** 'service'; **xasse** 'lettuce'; **ʿāde** 'custom'; **pışṭuwwe** 'collar'; **pıškūre** 'ceiling'; **bıllūre** 'flute'; **paraṣuwwe** 'rib cage'; **pırtuwwe** 'shed hair'; **ʿarje** (m. **ʿarja**) 'lame'; **karre** 'deaf' (m. **karra**); **šange** (m. **šanga**) 'sweet, playful'; **qutte** 'short woman' (m. **qutta**) ; **čappe** 'left (hand)', and, due to analogy, **yamme** 'right (hand)' (< OA ימינא); also some native words ending with -**e** take f. qualifiers due to analogy: **xıṭṭe mıyanta/paqoʾta** 'liquidy/cracked wheat' (OA pl.); **gınūne sqılta** 'beautiful weddding chamber' (OA גנונא. m.); and perhaps **mabōṯe** (vn II of **b-y-ṯ**) **šaxınta** 'warm Sabbath dish'; **kēpāye bassımta** 'special Sabbath dish of stuffed sheep's stomach and intestines' (no other form known in Z (K? < P **gīpā**, same meaning).[138]

4.3.3. Kurdish (diminutive) suffixes **-(ōš)ke** (f.), may be attached almost freely to native and borrowed words (from Arabic and Hebrew): **qaḥbıke** '(little) prostitute' (< Ar); **rāʿıke** '(little) evil woman' (< H); **faqīrōške** 'a poor woman'; ⁺**šuršurke** 'profuse water/sweat drops' has a doublet ⁺**šuršurta** (PolU 103, 121); an interesting case of semantic distinction is **ʾarmılṯa** (OA) 'widow' vs. **ʾarmalke** 'husband doing housewife's work'; **faqīr(ōš)ke** 'little poor woman'

4.3.4. Some f. Arabic loanwords, mostly via Kurdish/Persian, retain the literary Arabic f. marker t, plus the Aramaic ending -**a**: **qıṣta** 'story' (< Ar **qiṣṣa(t)** < P **qıṣṣat**); **ṣaneʾta** 'skill' (Ar/P **ṣināʿat**); **xılēʾta** 'gift' (Ar/P **xılʿat**); but **daʿwa** '(invitation to a) wedding' (< Ar دعوة > K **dāwat**).

4.3.5. Some f. nouns are without any f. marker (mostly inherited from OA/OS: natural females; dual parts of the body, and others by analogy) in one dialect or more: **yımma** 'mother'; **ʾızza** 'she goat'; **nuqwa** 'female' (NT, but Z **nıqqūsa**); **ʾīḏa** 'hand'; **ʾaqla** 'foot'; **ʾēna** ' eye' (but **kāka** 'tooth', **xıḏya** 'breast', m.); **šırma** 'buttock' (OS); **tıḥāla** 'spleen'; **kōda** ''liver'; **qḏāla** 'neck'; **dıpna/dıpınṯa** 'corner'; **dūka/dukṯa** 'place'; **qınna** (Z)/**qınṯa** (NT) 'nest'; **ʾarʾa** 'earth'; **bāžır** 'city'; **ʾaṯra** 'place' (NT).

4.4. The gender of some nouns may be different from what we have in (literary) OA/OS (dictionaries), or, in case of loanwords, from the original language, and from dialect to dialect, probably due to analogy, with a synonym, or 'same' noun in a contact language, e.g., **zambīla**

[137] Perhaps with K influence; cf. above, VII, §3.6.1.

[138] See below n. 147.

'basket' (Z+Ar+OS : m., but OA f.[139]); **zuwwāde, zawāde** (=H צֵדָה, PolG: Jud 20:10) 'provisions for journey' is f. sg. in Z, like Ar زوّادة, but OA זְוָודֵי is m. pl.(SokBA 401); **yāma** 'sea' (NT: f./m.; OA:m.); **kōda** 'liver' (f. in Z and OS, but OA כַּבְדָּא, m.); **dıqna** 'beard' (NT/OA: m., but Z: f.); **dıpna** 'side, corner' (Z/NT: f.; OA: m.); **dıdwa** 'fly' (NT/OA: m.), but Z **dıdūsa** (f.); **dıbbōra** 'hornet' (Z: m.; NT: f.); **bāqa** 'gnat' (OA m., but has also בַּקְתָא f. 'she-gnat', while Z has only **bāqa** f., for males and females; an opposite case is **dıdwa** (m.), **dıdūṯa** (f.), 'fly'; but OA only דִּידְבָא, m. (for males and females); **brat naᶜama** 'ostrich' (Z., f., but OA בר נעמיתא, m.); **ʾıstūna** 'pillar' (NT: m./f.; Z: f.); **tallīsa** 'sack' (Z: f. < OS ܛܠܝܣܐ, m.); **ᶜōlām** 'world' (Z: f.< H: m.); **gālūṯ** 'exile' and **zaxūṯ** 'merit' (m./f. < H, usually f.); **nēs** 'miracle' (m./f. < H: m.)⁺**markab** 'ship' (NT: f.; Z, Ar: m.); **ᶜaskar** 'army' (f. < Ar: m.); **baḥḥar** 'sea' (Z/Ar:m.; NT: f.); **lašša** 'body, flesh' (NT: m.; Z: f.); **nūra** 'fire' is m. in Z, but f. in Gz (perhaps influenced by H. אש); **kurāxa** 'shroud' is generally m. but clearly f. in Socin 159 (Did its gender change since 1880?).[140]

4.5. The gender of some nouns, such as. ⁺**sıfra** 'table', or verbal nouns such as **mšadōre** 'sending', **maʾmōre** 'building', could not be ascertained by texts or informants (and is left either unmarked in JNAD, or, in case of doubt, with a question mark); **ʾarmalke** has a f. suffix **-ke**,[141] but it denotes 'husband doing house/wife's work'.[142]

5. NUMBER. Most nouns have a plural form (one or more; see below). Most of the m. nouns have just an **-e** ending replacing the **-a** ending of the sg.: **xmāra** (sg.): **xmāre** (pl.) 'donkeys'; **ḥakōma** : **ḥakōme** 'kings'; **nāša** : **nāše** 'people'; **gumla** : **gumle** 'camels'.[143] Most of the f. nouns have the endings **-āṯa/-yāṯa/-wāṯa** in pl.: **baxta** (sg.): **baxtāṯa** (pl.) 'women'; **xmarta** : **xmaryāṯa** 'she-asses'; **nunīṯa** : **nunyāṯa** 'fish'; **qarīṯa** : **qaryāṯa** 'beams'; **xātun** : **xātunyāṯa** 'noble women' (T); **naṣūṯa** : **naṣwāṯa** 'wars'; **qaṭūṯa** : **qaṭwāṯa** 'cats'; **kālo** : **kalawāṯa** 'brides'; **xāṯa** : **xaṯwāṯa** 'sisters'.[144]

---

[139]See SokBA 397: זבילה גדולה; זבילא בתריתא last basket

[140]Including dialects outside our group, e.g., **ṣapya** m. 'cloth strainer' = **ṣapyo** f. in Koy Sanjaq (Mutz 228).

[141]See above, VII, §3.6.1; below VII, §5.8.

[142]On the syntax of gender see below VII, §9.1.

[143]Note that such forms, when in construct, neutralize the sg./pl. difference, e.g., **ṭeʾnıd/ṭeʾen** = "load(s) of"; see above VII, §2.1.

[144]Note that while many nouns have the same ending as in OA/OS (e.g., **kēpa**: **kēpe** כיפי 'stones'; **beʾta**: **beʾe** ביעי 'eggs'), others do not, e.g., the NA pl. forms of **ʾıškaṯta** (f.) 'testicle', **ʾāxa** (m.) 'brother', **bısma** 'resin, spice', **bırka** 'knee', **brōna** 'son' (OA ברא), **dıdūṯa** 'fly' (OA דִּידְבָא) are, respectively, **ʾıškāṯa**, **ʾaxawāṯa**, **bısme**, **bırkāke**, **bnōne**, **dıdwe**, but in OA are, respectavely, **ʾēškē**, **ʾaḥē**, **busmānē**, **birkē**, **bnayyā**, **dedvāṯā** (דִּידְבָתָא).

5.1. Some m. nouns have f. endings in the pl.: **yōma** : **yōmāṯa** 'days'; **xıḏya** : **xıḏyawāṯa** 'breasts'; **bāba** : **babawāṯa** 'fathers'; **ʾaxōna** : **ʾaxawāṯa** 'brothers'; **xıtna** : **xıtnawāṯa** 'grooms'; **gāre** (!): **garıwāṯa** 'roofs'; **sūse/susta** : **sūsawāṯa** 'horses'; **lēle** : **lēlıwāṯa** 'nights'; **mare** : **marıwāṯa** 'owners'.

5.2. Some f. nouns have the m. pl. ending: **tōleʾṯa** : **tōleʾe** 'worms'; **beʾta** : **beʾe** 'eggs'; **ṭlımṯa** : **ṭlımme** 'flat breads'; **mısta** : **mızze** 'hairs'; **qundarta** : **qundare** 'shoes' (K/T < Gr).

5.3. Some irregular pl. stems reflect specific OA/OS phonetic features: **gōra** : **gūre** (< גּוּבְרֵי) 'men'; **kalba** : **kalwe** (< כַּלְבֵי) 'dogs'; **ʾırba** : **ʾırwe** (< עִרְבֵי) 'sheep'; **brāta** : **bnāṯa** 'girls'; **brōna** : **bnōne** 'boys'; **šāta** : **šınne** 'years'; **mḏīta** : **mḏınyāṯa** 'cities' (NT); **⁺māya** 'water' (pl. only; OA מַיָּא) (see also below §5.12).

5.4. Some nouns reduplicate the last consonant of the sg. in the pl. and precede it with **ā**, especially when the sg. form has, or originally had, a geminated consonant, and others by analogy: **lıbba** : **lıbbābe** 'hearts'; **ṭılla**: **ṭıllāle** 'shades'; **sıkṯa** (< סִכְּתָא): **sıkkāke** 'pegs'; **kāwa** (< כַּוָּא): **kawāwe** 'air-holes'; **pımma** : **pımmāme** 'mouths'; **swāne** : **swanāne** 'roof-edges'; **pısra** : **pısrāre** 'meats'; **qırwa** : **qırwāwe** 'abouts'; **qāna** : **qanāne** 'horns'; **lᶜōya** (< לְגוֹ): **lᶜawāwe** 'indoors'; **ṣadra** : **ṣadrāre**' 'chests' (Ar); **baḥḥar** : **baḥrāre** 'seas' (Ar).

5.5. Some nouns have **-āne** ending in pl. (originally < Ak): **gūda** : **gūdāne** 'walls'; **ṭūra** : **ṭūrāne** 'mountains'; **šūra** : **šūrāne** 'city walls'; **šūqa** : **šūqāne** 'markets'; **čamma** : **čammāne** 'lakes'. This suffix is also used for mostly Kurdish game names: **hēkāne** 'egg-cracking game' < K **hēk** 'egg', **kabʾāne** 'knuckle-bone game', etc. (see above §3.6.1. (d)), but some have just regular pl.: **⁺karte** 'card game'; **ḥalūse** 'pebble game'.

5.6. Some nouns end with **-āye/-āhe/-āʾe** in the pl. (regardless of gender and origin): **xaṭa** : **xaṭāye/-he/-ʾe** 'sins' (Ar); **bala** : **balāye** 'troubles' (Ar); **darga** : **dargāhe/-ye** 'doors' (K); **tarʾa**: :**tarʾāye** 'gates'; **šımma** : **šımmāye/-he** 'names'; **dımma** : **dımmāhe** 'bloods.'

5.7. Adjectival phrases of the type:**rēše/-a šaxīna** 'his/her head hot'= 'hot headed' have the pl. **rēšu šaxīna** 'their head hot'; **lıbbu bassīma** 'their heart pleasant'= 'happy'; **pāṯu kumta** 'their face black'= 'embarrassed'; **ʾēnu kıpta** 'their eye lowered' ='humble'.

5.8. Most sg. nouns ending with the K suffixes **-ka** (m.)/**-ke** (f.) have the pl. suffix **-at** (< Ar **-āt**): **ᶜānīka**:**ᶜānīkat** 'beggars'; **taxtonka**:**taxtonkat** 'stools'; **jıddıke**:**jıddıkat** 'midwives'; **maymunke** : **maymunkat** 'monkeys'; but **mbınōke**: **mbınokwāṯa** 'mornings'.[145]

5.8.1. Suffix **-at** is also used with Arabic sg. f. nouns ending with **-a/-e**: **kafīya** :

[145]The stem is < **bınhe** 'tomorrow' < OA בְּנַגְהֵי 'at lights', + the K diminutive suffix **-ke**.

kafīyat 'scarfs'; **jērīye: jērīyat** 'maids' (but also **jērīye!**); **ġazāla : ġazāle/ġazālat** 'gazelles'; **maṭlabe: maṭlabat** (but also **maṭlabyāṯa**) 'requests'; but **+saᶜᶜa : +saᶜᶜe** 'hours'; occasionally with other native and borrowed words as well: **raᶜōla : raᵓōlat** (D)/**raᶜōle** (NT) 'brooks' (< OS); **mabōṯe** [< **b-y-ṯ**, IV, v.n. 'cook over night']: **mabōṯat** 'Sabbath dishes'; **tānj : tānjat** 'crowns' (< Ar).

5.8.2. Also Kurdish sg. nouns ending with **-e** may have the **-at** ending in pl.: **pıškūre: pıškūrat** 'ceilings'; **pıṣṭuwwe: pıṣṭuwwat** 'collars'; **bıllūre: bıllūrat** '(plain reed) flutes', but **+zurne: zurnāye** (AmU2) '(shrill wooden) flutes'.

5.8.3. The same suffix is used with sg. nouns ending with T-**či**: **qundárči : qundarčíyat** 'shoemakers'; **čāyíči : čāyičíyat** 'owners of tea shop'; but **daftarči : daftarčiye** 'clerks'.

5.8.4. The same suffix is used with sg. nouns ending with **-o**: **sāko : sākōyat** 'coats'; **qulo-qulo : qulo-qulōyat** 'bagel-shaped pastry'; **alo-ᶜalo : ᶜalo-ᶜalōyat** 'turkeys'; but **kālo: kalawāṯa** 'brides'.

5.9. As in other Semitic languages, some nouns have only or mostly a pl. form (pl. tantum): **xāye** 'life, lives'; **šımme** 'sky, heavens'; **+māya/māye** 'water(s)'.

5.9.1. However, the following category of body excreta, being in pl., seems to be typical of this group: **ᵓıxre** 'excrement(s)'; **jōre** 'urine(s)'; **rōqe** 'spit(s)' (but OA, ChNA **-ā**, sg.); **xmōṭe** 'nasal mucus'; **nāve** 'inner liquids, diarrhea'.

5.9.2. Some adverbs appear in pl. or pseudo-pl. form only: **qamāye** 'firstly, olden days'; **xarāye** 'lastly, afterwards'; **šıtqe** 'last year' (OA אשתקד); **talṯe** 'two years ago'; **rōᵓe** (< OA רבעי) 'three years ago'.

5.9.3. Cereals and some vegetables, fruits, and dishes, usually are in the pl.: **ṭlōxe** 'lentils'; **māše** 'cow peas'; **šušme** 'sesame'; **+saᶜāre** 'barley'; **ṭōle** 'coriander seeds'; **ṣayīḥe** 'cracked wheat'; **+xırnūfe** 'fresh carob fruit'; but **xıṭṭe** 'wheat -only when cooked?)' is f. sg. (see above VII, §4.3.2), and **gırsa** 'cracked wheat', **+rızza** 'rice' are m.; **xasse** 'lettuce' seems to be pl., because for 'one' one says **xa rēša xasse** 'one head of lettuce',[146] but its qualifiers are f., e.g., **xasse bassımta** 'delicious (f.) lettuce'; **+kīrāte** leeks (no sg. in use; but OA כָּרָתָא, sg.; כָּרָתֵי, pl.); **kēpāye** 'a Sabbath dish' perhaps originally was pl.,[147] but later seems to be f. sg.: **kēpāye šaxınta** 'warm k.'.

5.9.4. Varia: Some nouns seem to have very low distribution in sg., and are mostly known in their pl. form, e.g.,**(ᵓe)škāṯa** 'testicles'; sg. שכתתא **škaṯṯa** ;others are known only

[146] Cf. OA חַסָּא; OS ܚܣܐ; pl. ܚܣܐ; Ar خس; the NA form seems to be related to the OS pl. form.

[147] Cf. Garbell 315 **kipayta**; pl. **kipae**; Mutz. 197 **j/čipāta**; pl. **j/čipāᵓe**; the sg. is unknown in Z.

in plural for no apparent reason, e.g., šumʾāṯa 'rumors, reports';[148] paṭīre 'unleavened bread' in Z only in Pl. and in ʾēz-paṭīre 'Passover', but in NT also sg. paṭīra.[149] Note also cases like: bır-nāše 'kin by marriage', lit., 'son of people'; there is no singular *bır-nāša.

5.10. Loan nouns from Hebrew and Arabic may retain their original pl. form, or have a NA pl. ending, or both: ṣaddīqīm 'righteous ones'; ḥāxāmīm 'sages'; sg. talmid ḥāxām 'a learned Jew' (PolU 288) has pl. talmīḏe ḥāxāmim (< H תלמידי חכמים, NT); malʾāxīm/n/ne, malʾāxe, 'angels'; ṣārōṯ 'afflictions'; nıšāme/nıšāmōṯ 'souls'; mıṣwōṯ/mıṣwāye 'precepts' (H); mazzālōṯ/mazzāle 'fortunes'; רובי רבאבות rubbe rıvāvōṯ.(RivSh 195) 'huge number'; sōfēre (סופירה) 'scribes';[150] falāke/ʾaflāk 'wheels of fortune' (Ar); māʿbūdīn/maʿbūdat/ maʿbūde 'idols'; note that an original Ar broken pl. may become sg. in NA: háyam 'time, period' < Ar ايام 'days' (has no attested pl.); tıjjar (< Ar تجّار , pl.), pl. tıjjāre 'merchants'; rısūm(e)/-mat 'rules, laws'; maqābır(e) 'graveyards; tasābīḥ(e) 'hymns'; in šarṭe ušurūṭe 'all necessary conditions' the Ar. pl. is used as a compound with the NA pl.; H ṣārōṯ 'afflictions' is at times treated as sg. (preceded by xa 'a') in women's speech. In some case K/P pl. forms are used alone or with NA ending as well: ẓābıṭān 'officers' (sg. < Ar ضابط); šēxyāne 'tribal chieftains' (sg. < Ar شيخ); rēspiye/rēspiyāne 'elders' (sg.< K respi 'white bearded'). The compound malkílmot (< Ar 'angel of death') has the pl. malkılmōte 'aggressive persons, bullies'.

5.11. Some irregular pl. forms (native and loaned): yāla : yalunke (Z) 'children'; zwaʾta : zudyāṯa 'loaves'; mısta : mızze 'hairs'; ṣaboʾta : ṣubʾāṯa 'fingers';; qaḥba /-e: qaḥbıkat 'prostitutes'; ʿılle :ʿıllıtyāṯa 'grief, malignant growth'; ḥušta : ḥujyāṯa 'pretexts'; mındi 'thing' has pl. mındiye in NT, but ʾawāye (a suppletion) in Z; gēba : gēbe 'things', has also the contracted form gıb (.e.g., kullu gıb 'all things'); the exact morphological relation of some pl. forms with the sg. is not certain, e.g., ʾēš : ʾēš-u-nāle '(all kind of) ailments'; dard : dard-u-balāye 'diseases and misfortunes'; dāra : dāre-dāre 'trees'.[151]

5.12. The pl. and/or sg. form of some nouns is unknown or could not be ascertained; especially uncommon nouns ending with -e can be sg. or pl., e.g., ⁺taqfe which is known only from the idiom xamūṣa x-⁺taqfe 'as sour as __', meaning, gender and number unknown; ṭīme 'worth, value' (< Gr timé) is usually considered pl., and the sg., טימא ṭīma, is rare; the pl. form of bır-nāše 'a non-blood relative', would be *bnōnıd nāše, but it is not attested (or used ?); šaqlāve 'wave(s) reaching the shore'; the pl. form of čēri 'autumn' (< תשרי '(month of) Tishre') is assumed to be čēriyat (in analogy to nēri 'billy goat': nēriyat

---

[148]Perhaps pl. of šmoʾta (cf. ṣaboʾta : ṣubʾāṯa 'fingers); but šmoʾta has its own pl.: šmoʾyāṯa.

[149]Cf. Khan 576.

[150]Cf. Sabar 1999.

[151]See also above VII, §5.3.

?)[152]; **gıvāne, gavanāne** shore(s) of (sea, river) (< OA/OS גיף/ ܓܒܐ side, shore?).

5.13. Plurality is often quite shifty and unstable. Various speakers or writers of even the same dialect give (at times hesitantly) different plural forms for the same noun.[153] Some of these forms are inherited from OA/OS, e.g., **yōma:yōme/yōmāṯa** 'days' (cf. H -ימים/ימות) ; **nehra :nehrawāṯa/nehre** 'rivers' (cf. H נהרים/נהרות). Others seem to be due to analogy, e.g., **dımma** 'blood' was given two pl. forms by the same speaker:(a) **dımmāye**, probably in analogy to **šımma** : **šımmāye** 'names'; (b) **dımmāṯa**, in analogy with **yımma** : **yımmāṯa** 'mothers'.; **tarʾa** : **tarʾāye** 'gates'in analogy to **darga** : **dargāhe/-ye** 'doors' (K); **xıtna** : **xıtne/xıtnawāṯa** 'bridegrooms', the second form seems to be an analogy with **kalawāṯa** 'brides'[154]; **jērīye** : **jērīyat/jērīye** 'maids', the second in analogy with **ʾōde** 'slaves'. The following are a few examples of nouns which have more than one pl. form attested in written or oral texts: **bēṯa** : **bāte/batāne/beṯawāṯa** 'houses'; **dūka** : **dūkāne/dūkawāṯa** 'places'; **dıpna** : **dıpnāṯa/ dıpnāne** 'sides, corners'; **karta** : **kartāṯa/karāṯa** 'loads' (OS); and including loanwords: **bala** : **balāye/balıtyaṯa/balwityāṯa** 'misfortune' (Ar); **bıhēma** : **bıhēmat/ bıhēmōṯ/bıhēme** 'animals' (H); **sāko** : **sākōye/sākōyat** 'coats'; in some cases the different pl. forms are dialectal: **xuwwe** : **xuwwāsa** (Z)/**xuwwāwe** (D) 'snakes'; **bızʾa** : **bızʾe** (Z, NT)/ בִּיזְאָאֵי **bızʾāʾe** (PolG:D); **mīṯa** : **mīse** (Z, NT)/**mīṯāne** (NT) 'dead ones'; ⁺**māya** (pl. Z)/**māye** (pl. Am, NT, D, and Z, but only for rhyming purpose); **sıkṯa** : **sıkyāṯa** (NT)/**sıkkāke** (Z) 'pegs'; **lıbba** : **lıbbābe/lıbbawāṯa** 'hearts'; **xōra** : **xūrāṯa/xūre/xūrāne** 'friends'; **xēma** : **xēmāsa** (Z)/**xēmāme** (Am) 'tents' (< Ar); **ġulāma** : **ġulāme/ġulamwāṯa** 'servants' (< Ar); **ʾāġa** : **ʾāġāwat** (RivSh 277)/**ʾāġāyat, ʾāġālarat**[155] (PolU 444)/**ʾāġāye** (AmU2 5b)/**ʾāġawātat** 'aghas' (K/T); **dehwa** : **dehwe** (Z, RivSh), **dehwat** (PolG:D) 'kinds of gold'. At times the different pl. forms indicate different meanings: ⁺**ruwwa** :⁺**ruwwāne** 'great men, leaders', vs. ⁺**ruwwe** 'big, great'; **gōra** : **gūrāne** 'husbands, strong men', vs. **gūre** 'men'; **tūṯa** : **tūṯe** 'mulberries (fruit)', vs. **tūṯawāṯa** 'mulberry trees'. A rare pl. is used only idiomatically, e.g., **šınṯa** : **šınyāṯa** 'sleeps', used only in: **d-m-x šōʾa šınyāṯa** 'to sleep seven sleeps, sleep a very deep sleep' (SaAC 22).

5.13.1. On the other hand, a plural form may belong to more than one sg. noun, e.g., **ṭabāqe** is the pl. form of **ṭabaq** 'basket' and **ṭabāqa** 'storey'.

6. VERBS. Active (**qāṭıl**) and passive (**qṭıl-, qṭīla**) participles are at the basis of

---

[152]However Mutzafi 2000b 299 has **čıryawā(ṯa)**.

[153]E.g., in PolU 294, the pl. of ⁺**pōlis** 'a police' is given as ⁺**pōlīse** and ⁺**pōlīsat** on the same page and by the same informant. Therefore, a special effort is made to indicate the source of most text-attested plural forms.

[154]But already so in OA: חַתְנֵי, חַתְנְוָותָא, SokBA 491.

[155]The suffix **-at** is added to the T. -pl. **-lar**.

the verbal system, which includes also the imperative (**qṭol**) and the infinitive (gerund, verbal noun) (**qṭāla**). The active participle (a.p.) forms usually serve the present-future tenses, and the past participle (p.p.) forms usually serve the past tenses, e.g., **šāqıl** 'he takes'; **šaqlın** 'I take', etc.; **šqılle** 'he took'; **šqılla** 'she took'; **šqōl** 'take!'.[156] The examples of the basic forms given above are from the ground conjugation (I< OA פְּעַל/פְּעֵל). For the derived forms (II-IV), see below, User's Guide. The conjugation of a root may occasionally differ from one dialect to another, **ḥ-k-y** 'to speak' and **x-l-ṣ** 'to rescue' are in conjugation IV (< אפעל) in Z, but mostly in II (< פַּעֵּל) in NT and Am; **ṭ-l-q** 'to divorce' is in II in Z (**mṭalōqe**), but in NT in both I (**ṭlāqa**) or II. **d-b-l** 'to wrestle' is in II (**mdabōle**) in Z, but in I (**dbāla**) in NT; **t-y-m** 'to annihilate' is I in Z (**tyāma**), but in IV (**matōme**) in Am. A root may appear in two different conjugations in the same dialect (text) without any obvious difference in meaning: **r-p-y** II/IV 'to set off, let loose' (RivSh 155, 216; NT5 384). Note that many verbs are 'transitive' (vt) and 'intransitive' (vi) as well[157], e.g., **ṣlıxle** 'he/it split' (vi/vt); **xlıṣle** 'he/it finished'; **pṯıxle** 'he/it opened'; **ġlıqle** 'he/it closed'; **xlıqle** 'He created or he/it was created, came into being'; ⁺**mlēle** 'he/it filled'; **turre** 'he/it broke'; ⁺**mrıčle** 'he crushed or was crushed'; **mhujjıjle** 'he wandered or caused one to wander'; and most of quadriradicals: **mpušpıšle** 'it wore out (vi)/ he wore out (vt)'; **mbuhdılle** 'ridiculed or became ridiculed'; **mgundırre** 'rolled' (vt/vi); some tri-radical roots are secondary roots from old **t**-reflexive-passive conjugations (which otherwise disappeared in NA): **t-ʾ-r** (1) 'to wake up' < OA אתעיר; **t-x-r** (1) 'to remember' < דכר/אדכיר; **t-n-x** II 'to sigh' (AvidH 29) < OA אתאנח.[158]

6.1. The infinitive (verbal noun, gerund) is used for certain aspects (at times preceded by preposition **b(ıd)**): (a) **wēlu bixāla** 'they are eating' (continuous); (b) **pıšlu bırqāḏa** 'they began dancing' (ingressive); **škōl mṣalōye** 'Start praying'; **škılle bīxāla** 'He began eating'; **škıllu (bıt) msafōre** 'They began traveling' (PolG);[159] (c) at times, with negation, it is equivalent of p.p.: **yāle gzīre ula gzāra** 'circumcized and uncircumcized children' (RivSh 264); **dıqne yrıqta ula yrāqa** 'His beard has barely sprouted' (PolG);. **šımša la šrāfa** before the sun is set (PolU 423); **hēš ʾāna ṣax la-myāsa** 'while I am (still) alive not-dead' (PolU 57); (d) for the passive voice with the verb **ʾ-ṯ-y** (Z **ʾ-s-y**) 'to come'; cf. these Bible translations:[160] **sēle (l)xšāwa** 'it was considered' (=H נֶחְשַׁב); תֵּילֵי לִיכְרַהַא **ṯēle lıkrāha** 'was detested' (=H נִבְאַשׁ, PolG); **ṣurre dēni sēlu kšāfa** 'Our secrets have been revealed' (PolG); **ʾāsētun mẓarōbe** 'you will be routed' (=H תִּנָּגְפוּ); **sēla masōye** 'she was brought' (=H הוּבָאת); **qıṭla** is often used instead **qṭāla**: **sēlu lqıṭla kuṭṭlāhun** 'all

[156]Note, however, how a good story-teller can switch from one tense to another to express the historical past tense: **nıšāme qızla, lıbbe gımkēzır, wēle mparpōṭe, nāve umēlāke qızlu** 'His soul burned, his heart is roasting, he was squirming, his bowels and guts burned' = 'He had a great pity' (PolU 373).

[157] Mostly due to the loss of the OA reflexive-passive **t**-conjugations; see below.

[158] Cf. also in a loan root: **t-f-q** 'to meet' < Ar اتّفق.

[159]Same development as in English: 'She is walking' has developed from 'She is a-walkinging' < 'She is on walking' ('walking' being a gerund, not a participle); v. Goldenberg forthcoming.

[160]Similar use in K/P; see Kapeliuk 1999:12-15.

three of them were killed' (Zaken 392); **bāset lqiṭla** 'You will be killed' (PolG); **sēlu qiṭla bid sēpa** 'they were killed by sword' (Sa83c 36, Z); (e) for emphasis (much like the Biblical Hebrew שָׁמוֹעַ שָׁמַעְתִּי "I verily heard'): **dunye ḥmilla ḥmāla** 'the weather is very opressive' (lit. 'the world has stood a standing', i.e., there is no breeze).[161]

6.2. The passive voice may be expressed by other means as well: (a) Impersonal verbal forms, e.g., **qṭīla** 'they killed her/she was killed'; **qṭīli** 'they killed them/they were killed'; **krīdi** 'they were expelled' (=H גֹּרְשׁוּ, AvidH 46, but AlfH 55 **sēlu krāda**); **xēli munxil** 'my strength was exhausted'; (b) p.p. (mostly in NT): **xīl** 'it was eaten'; **qwīr** 'he was buried'; **mīr** 'it was said'; **mḥōke** 'it was told'; משה קט לא וילה ולא כליק אלא מתלא וילה **mōše qaṭ la wēle ula xlīq, ʾilla maṯala wēle** 'Moses didn't exist and was not created at all, but rather was a parable' (NTU4 161a); **la snīq** 'it isn't necessary'; **muxw-axni** 'we were shown'; **mulp-axni** 'we were taught' (NT5 411); **nhīb-axni...mupq-ax** 'we were plundered...taken out (of our homes)' (Sa83c 36, Am); או יומא דבליא יונה **ʾaw yōma dblīʾ yōna** 'the day that Jonah was swallowed' (NT6 134); למן כליקיתן **lman xlīqētin** 'by whom were you created' (NTU4 158b); **wal mōqiḏ** 'was burnt (already)'; אכתיף אל באבה **iktīp ʾil bābe** '(Isaac) was bound by his father' (NT3); **wal mqōteʾ** 'was dissected (already)' (BaBin 154). NT has also forms of R_3**y** verbs without the agentive **-le, -la,** etc.: **mṭe waʿdox** 'your time has arrived' (=Z **mṭē-le**); **yṯe** 'he has come'; **xze** 'he saw' (!) ; **iyṯin** (איתן) 'I have come' (NT5 365, n. 167).

6.2.1. NT and Am infix the 1st and 2nd object pronoun (but Z paraphrases): **mulp-ax-lu** 'they taught us' (= taught-us-they) (but Z **qam malpī-lan**); **xlīq-an-ne** 'He created me (f.)' (= Z **qam xāliq-li**); **mufhim-in-na** 'she made me understand' (= Z **qam mafhimā-li**); **muḥib-it-ti** 'I loved you' (= Z **qam maḥīb-in-nax**); **muʾūr-ax-le** 'He helped us cross' (=H הֶעֱבִירָנוּ, AvidH 42, but AlfH **qam maʾur-ran**); **mšudr-in-ne** 'he sent me' (מְשׁוּדְרְנֵי, Rivsh 146); **musim-in-nu** 'they hated me' (Sa83c 16, Am); **marʾūṯa dwiq-in-na** 'Pain seized me' (Sa83c 22, Am); **xizy-at-ti** 'I saw you (f. sg.)' (=H וָאֶרְאֵךְ, AvidH 27, but Z **qam xāzin-nax**, קָם כָזֶנַךְ, AlfH 39); קרתי **qr-it-ti** 'You called me' (=Z **qam qārit-ti**).

6.2.2. Passive participles may serve in future perfect and other tenses as well: **hīl ʿaṣirta gibe ʾaxlax** [=**hāwax xīle**]...**bēsa hāwe knīša, hāwax xīpe kullu gūre ubaxtāsa** 'By the Eve (of Yom Kippur Fast) we must eat [have eaten]..., the house be swept, (we) all men and women be bathed (already)' (SaAC 4); **ʾalpa bšimma wēlu nuble** (p.p.pl.) **yalunke go ʿarabāye, murūye** (p.p.pl.) **dōhun** Many like her had been taken (as) children among the Arabs (and) were raised by them' (SaAC 17); **miryam ...ʿarabāye-lu mumṣe** (p.p.pl.) **dīda** 'Miriam...Arabs have nursed her' (ibid.).

6.2.3. All dialects have verbal forms with the 3rd person object pronouns, as follows: **qṭille** 'he killed him' (meaning also just 'he killed'); **qṭillan** 'we killed (him)'; **qṭillu** 'they killed (him)', etc.; **qṭīlā-le** 'he killed her' **qṭīlī-lox** 'you (m.sg.) killed them', etc.

---

[161]Cf. dialectal Arabic (*JSS* 40, 1995: 60, 61): **yisūq sōq** 'It (a plant) grows a growing' = very fast; **šālōhum šēl** 'They snapped them up'.

Note also uses like these: **zıllu, darga twīrın** (p.p. m.sg. + nunation), **twīrın darga, sulṭan qṭīlın, baxte qṭīla** (f.), **umpıqlu** 'They went, broke the door, broke the door, killed the sultan, killed his wife, and left.' (PolU 79).

6.2.4 A verb may take two objects (rare and only with a.p. and imperative): **yāwıl-lē-li** He will give it to me; **hállū-le-li** 'Give it to me'.

6.2.5. An imperative form may take one or more intensifying particles:**de ke me halli** 'Give me!' (PolU 31).

6.3. Weak Verbs: Some OA R_1א (ʾ) verbs (פ"א) are reflected as R_1**y** verbs (פ"י): **y-r-x** (OA ארך) 'to be long'; **y-s-r** (OA אסר) 'to tie' (Z **ysīra** but NT **sīra**); **y-l-p** (OA אלף) (NT)/**l-y-p** (Z) 'to learn'. Others retain the ʾ in some forms (when followed by a vowel), while in others (when vowelless), it is changed to **y** or omitted altogether: **ʾāxıl** 'he eats', but **xılle** (Z, NT)/**yxılle** (+NT) 'he ate'; **xōl** 'Eat!"; **ʾixāla** '(Z, NT)/**yxāla** (+NT) 'eating'; **ʾizāla/yzāla** 'going'; **ʾiṯāya/yṯāya** 'coming'; **ʾaṯya** 'she comes', but (**y**)**ṯēle** 'he came'; **ʾamrax** 'we say', **ʾimāra** 'saying', but **mırran** 'we said'. Note also in causative forms: **māxıl** 'he feeds' (< ***maʾxil**), **maxōle** 'feeding'; but **mayrıx** 'he prolongs'; **mayrōxe** 'prolonging'; **mēṯe** 'he brings' (< ***mayṯe**); **mēṯōye** 'bringing' (+Z **masōye**). See also below §6.6. Some irregular forms: **ʾāzi** 'they go' (< ***ʾazli**); **si** (m.)/**se** (f.)/**sāwun** (Z)/**suwwun** (NT) (pl., c.) 'Go!'; **yṯa** 'Come!' (sg., c.).; **mār** 'Say'.

6.4. Reflexes of OA R_1**y** verbs (פ"י) retain the **y** in most verbs: **yāme** 'he swears'; **ymēle** 'he swore'; **ymāya** 'swearing. However, in some common verbs **y** is often omitted when vowelless: **yātu** 'he sits', but **tīwa** (Z)/**ıytīwa** (NT איתיוא; OA יתיבא) 'seated, sitting' ; (**ıy**)**tūle** 'he sat'; **tu** 'Sit'; **yāʾe** 'he knows' (OA ידע), but (**ıy**)**ḏeʾle** 'he knew'; reflexives of the causative: **muymēle** (NT)/**mōmēle** (Z) 'he made him swear'; **muyḏeʾle** 'he made known'; but **matwi** 'they seat, put'; **muttūle** 'he seated (him)'; **mattu** 'Put!'; **mattōwe** 'seating'; some irregular forms: **yāwıl** 'he gives' (OA -יהב+ל); **yāwi** 'they give' (OA יהבין) ; **hulle** 'he gave' (OA יהיב לה); **hīwa** 'given' (OA יהיבא); **hāl** 'Give' (OA הב+ל); **yhāwa/hwāya** 'giving' (but **yhōta/yholta** 'gift'); **mābıl/nābıl** 'he carries away' (< מַוְבֵל; cf. H מוֹבִיל) ; cf. 6.3.

6.4.1. Some R_1**y** verbs are secondary developments (mostly due to metathesis) from OA roots (some other than פ"י): **y-s-q** 'to go up' < OA סלק (נסק*); **y-ʾ-l** 'to enter' < OA עלל (due to metathesis: עֲיֵל > **yāʾıl**) ; **y-r-m** (occasionally, NT)< **r-y-m** (NT, Z) 'to rise'; **y-ḏ-l** 'to give birth' (OA ילד); **y-q-ḏ** 'to burn' (NT, OA) appears in Z as **q-y-z**; **y-w-š** 'to dry' (NT, OA יבש) appears in Z as **w-y-š**. Reflexes of the causative: **māsıq** 'he brings up'; **māqıḏ** (Z **māqız**) 'he burns' (vt); +**mārım** 'he raises'; **māwıš** 'to dry (vt)', but **mayʾıl** 'he brings in'; v. also below 6.10.2; VII, 1.

6.5. The root **w-ṣ-y** (< Ar, II) is conjugated as **mwōṣēle**. etc., 'he enjoined' in NT, but Z **mōṣēle**; **w-j-b** (< Ar, IV) = **mūjıble** 'he obliged (vt)'.

6.6. OA verbs with R_1ע (ʿ) have coalesced with R_1א (ʾ) verbs, but they usually retain the ʾ, while original R_1א verbs usually omit it when vowelless (see above §6.3): **ʾzılla** 'she spun' (OA עזל; Ar غزل); **ʾmırre** 'was built' (OA/Ar عمر); **ʾzāla** 'spinning'; **ʾmāra** 'being built'; **maʾmır** 'he builds'.

6.7. Geminated OA, Ar, and H roots, $R_1R_2R_2$, are reflected as R_2**y** in conjugations I (**qṭāla**, פעל) and IV (**maqṭōle**, אפעל): **kyāpa** <OA כפף 'to bend (vi)'; **makōpe** 'to bend (vt)'; **xyāpa** <OA חפף 'to take a bath'; **ryāʾa** <OA רעע 'to grind'; **fyāra** < Ar فرّ 'to fly, flee'; **mafōre** 'set flying'; **maḥōbe** < Ar حبّ 'to love'; **maḥōle** <H חלל 'to desecrate, break laws of Sabbath'. However, in conjugation II (פַּעֵּל), the doubling is usually retained: **mxaṯṯōṯe** 'to renew' < OA **xāṯa** 'new'; **mjassōse** 'to spy'; **mčakkōke** 'to arm' < **čakka** 'weapon' (K); **mḥallōle** 'to make permissible, kosher' < **ḥalāla** 'kosher' < Ar.

6.8. OA roots with R_2**w** (ע"ו) have totally coalesced with R_2**y** (ע"י): **qyāma** (OA קום) 'to get up'; **maqōme** < ***maqyōme** (IV) 'to raise'. However, **w** may be retained in Ar loan roots: **mjawōbe/mjayōbe** (II) 'to answer'. Note also that **w** that is a reflex of OA ב רפה (fricative, **v**) is either retained or elided **kwāša** 'going down' (OA כבש); **kwıšle** (כְּוִישְׁלֵי, AvidH 25; אכוישלה **ıkwıšle**, NT)/**kušle** (Z) 'he went down'; **mak(w)ōše** 'to bring down'; **gwāra** 'to marry'; **gwırre/gurre** 'he married'; **mag(w)ōre** 'to marry off'; **qwāra** 'to bury'; **qurre** 'he buried' **swāya** 'to get old' (OA סיב, metathesis), **swēle** (Z) 'he became old'. The loan root **k-y-f** (Ar) appears only in II (פַּעֵּל): **mkayōfe** 'to have fun (vi); to entertain (vt)'. Irregular or obscure roots: **mēnōxe** (Z)/**mʾēnōxe** (NT) 'to look, gaze' < OA אניח 'to rest (one's eyes on??)'[162]; **č-y-m** 'to close, lock' < OA אטם/טמם ? **č-y-q** 'to tear' < Ar شقّ ? **ṣ-y-ḥ** 'to have free time'; **maṣōḥe** 'to visit, call on someone' < Ar صيح 'call' ?

6.9. OA roots with R_3 ב רפה (**v**) are reflected as R_1R_2**w**: **qrāwa** (OA קרב) 'to come near'; **qāru/qarwa** 'he/she comes near'; **qrūle** 'he came near'; **maqrōwe** 'to bring near'; **xšāwa** 'to think'; **gnāwa** 'to steal'; **kṯāwa** 'to write'; **kṯu** 'Write!' (sg. c.); **kṯuwun** (NT)/**ksūn** (Z) 'Write!' (pl.).

6.10. Reflexes of OA verbs with R_3**y** (ל"י), including **y** <ʾ (ל"א; see below §6.10.1), retain **y** only when followed by vowel: **xzāya** 'to see'; **štāya** 'to drink'; **šatya** 'she drinks'; **maštōye** 'watering'; **mšanōye** 'changing (residence)'; **hwāya** 'to be'; **qrāya** 'reading'; **maqrōye** 'to teach'; **mṭūya** 'roasted' (p.p.); **šıtya** (p.p.) 'drunk'; **ṣıpya** (Z)/**ṣpīya** (Arodh) 'pure, purified'. Otherwise, **y** is elided or monophthongized: **šāte** 'he/they drink(s)' (but Gz73 58: pl. **šāti, dāri, qāri** 'they drink, put, read'); **štēle** 'he drank'; **štīṯa** 'drunk' (p.p.f.); **muštēṯa** 'watered'; **mṭōwēṯa** 'roasted'; **xzi** (Z:m.; Am:c.)/**xze** (f.) 'See!' **y** >**w** in some forms: **mıṭūwe** '(low) level' (< **m-ṭ-y** 'reach'); **hwāwun** 'Be!' (pl.); **xzāwun** (Z, pl.)/**xzuwwun** (Am)'See!', but **(ı)xzūn** (NT2), **qrūn** 'Read!' (NT5 404); **tlūle** 'Hang him!' (NT5 403). Some irregular forms: **la-mṣēle** 'he was not able'; **la-mṣe** 'he cannot'; vowelless **h** in **h-w-y** is elided when it means 'to be', but retained to indicate 'to give birth': **wēle** 'he was'; **hwēle** 'he was born'; note also: **pāwe** 'he/they will be' (< **b+hāwe**) vs.

---

[162]For a different explanation (deriving it fron **ʾēna** 'eye'), see MeAl 180, n. 27.

bhāwe 'he/they will be born'; **kāwe** 'he is/they are' vs. **ghāwe** 'he is/they are born [small/big, etc.]'; **štāwe/štāye** <**šud** + **hāwe** 'Let it be!'

6.10.1. In speech forms of R_3ʾ <OA R_3ע, the vowelless glotal stop may become silent and coalesce with R_3**y** (OA ל״י/ ל״א): **šāmeʾ** (normally spelled שאמא < OA שמע) 'he hears' is often realized as **šāme**; **šmeʾle** 'he heard' as **šmēle**; this realization is often reflected in the spelling of less learned scribes, e.g.: לבי גמארי **lıbbi gmāre** 'my heart aches' (< OA מרע) (BaBin141); זְדֵילוּ **zdēlu** 'they feared' (OA אתזיע)(RivSh 130); גנאפי **gnāfe** 'is useful' (Ar نفع) (BaBin 143). Note also **yāʾe** 'he/they know(s)' (Z < OA ידע), but NT pl. **yāʾi/ -e** (יאאי/ יאאיה) .

6.10.2. A root may develop two or more variant stems; a good example is **s-j-d** (Z < Ar سجد) 'to worship, bow', which has also: **s-d/t-j** (PolG:D), **s-j-j**, **s-y-j** (NT); cf. above, VII, §6.4.1.

6.11. Reflexes of the quadriradical verb conjugation (=III, variant of II) are as follows: **mtafsır** 'he explains/Explain!' (< **táfsir** 'commentary' < Ar تفسير); **mtufsırre** 'he explained'; **mtafsōre** 'to explain'; **mburbızle** 'scattered' (OA בזבז); **mkurkımle** 'yellowed'. Some irregulars with R_2vowel: **mhēmın** 'he believes'; **mhīmınne** 'he believed'; **mšēḏın** 'he gets mad'; **mšīḏınne** 'he became mad'; **mkōšōre** 'to wash meat according to kosher rules'; **mkōbōre** 'to recite (the Muslim prayer) **allāhu ʾakbar**'; a very irregular verb is **h-n-n-l** 'to say this and that'< **hınna** 'that thing': **hnılle** 'He did what you call it'; **bhınnıli** 'they will say this and that'.

6.12. New verbal roots may be derived from existing native and loanwords (nouns, adjectives, etc.), usually in the II (< **paᶜel**) conjugation: **mdamdōme** 'to bleed' < **dımma** 'blood'; **mxaṯṯōṯe** 'to renew' < **xāṯa** 'new' (OA חדתא); **mtafsōre** 'to interpret' < **tafsir** 'interpretation' (Ar); **mkarrōre** 'to become deaf' < **karra** 'deaf'; **mtarbōže** 'to sneeze' < **tēr bıži** 'bless you' (lit., 'Long live!'); **mdarmōne** 'to medicate' < **dırmāna** 'medicine'.

7. Adverbs are, besides some inherited old ones, mostly nouns modified by prepositions, demonstratives, plural forms, adjectives, suffixed elements (e.g. K -**(k)i**), loanwords, etc., as follows (selection): **tımmal** 'yesterday'; **ʾıdyo** 'today', **ʾıḏlal** 'tonight'; **ʾaššat** 'this year'; **šıtqe** 'last year' (OA אשתקד); **qamāye** 'firstly, in olden days'; **x(a)rāye** 'lastly, afterwards'; **talṯe** 'two years ago'; **rōʾe** (< OA רבעי) 'three years ago'; **bın(ıʾ)he** 'tomorrow' (OA בנגהי 'at lights, at dawn'); **bōma-xın** 'the day after tomorrow/before yesterday'; ⁺**rāba** 'much, many'; **lqīṭa** (p.p.) 'diligently'; **ᶜōgıb** 'inside'; **wargıb** 'outside'; **ʾaxgıb** 'this side, hither'; **tangıb** 'that side, thither'; **lʾēl** 'above'; **ltēx** 'below'; **lxırxaṣ** 'on the wrong side (of clothes), inside out'; **lqıšṭaṣ** 'on the right/correct side'; **ᶜanqaṣti** 'on purpose' (Ar-K); **mērkānī**'in man-style (clothes); **pāšpāški** 'backwards'; **baqqıki** '(swimming) frog-like'; **yammıki** 'to the right'; **čappıki** 'to the left'; **žnıgva** 'suddenly' (K); **žnu** 'anew, only now'; **-ši** (suffixed) 'too' (**ʾāna-ši bāzın** 'I too will go'); **hēdí-hēdi** 'slowly, calmly'; **haʾ-ha** 'right now!'; **bḥamdox** '(You) take it easy, do patiently' (lit., 'at your praise', Ar);

blazzi 'quickly, in a hurry'; **byārūṯa** 'in friendly manner, in jest' (< K/P يار 'friend'); **bxurṭūṯa** 'by force, reluctantly'; **bitwār qzāle** '(He came) unfortunately (lit., at the breaking of his neck) (PolU 424); **bxāye** (NT בכאייה) which literally means 'in life' but its common sense is 'alive'; **ʾap-/ʾup-** 'too'; an assertive **la** seems to indicate 'certainly, after all, Isn't it' (cf. H הֲלֹא): **la ḥakōmit kullu ḥēwānē-le ʾarya**. After all the lion is the king of all animals' (Avin78 94); **la faqīr hādax-īle** Certainly the poor is (=behaves) like that (PolU 433).[163]

8. Prepositions include many old ones and a couple of new ones: **ʾil** 'to, on' (OA אל/על); **b-/ʾibb-** 'at'; **barqul** 'across, against'; **go/gāw-** 'inside of'; **qam** 'before (spatial)'; **mqabil** 'before' (temporal); **baṯir** 'after, behind'; **ʾimm-** 'with'; **(l)kis(l-)** 'chez, at'; **m-/min** 'from' (Z, NT)+ 'with' (Am/D); **ṭla** (NT)/**ta** (Z) 'for' [decl.: **ṭlaṯ-** (NT)/**ṭāṯ-** (Am)/**ṭāl-** (Z)]; **ʾix/muxwāṯ** 'like, as'; **riš** 'over, on top' (OA ראש 'head'); **xōr** 'like' (< **xōra** < חברא 'friend', inv.; cf. **sqilta xōr dē brāta lēs** 'Pretty like this girl — there isn't' = 'There is nobody as pretty as this girl'.

9. Syntax is beyond the scope of a dictionary. Here are some useful highlights:

9.1. Gender agreement exists between m. sg., f. sg., and m. pl. noun and their qualifiers: **brōna zōra** 'little son'; **brāta zurta** 'little daughter'; **bnōne zōre** little sons'; note, however, that there is no f. pl. form, and m. pl. qualifier is used instead with f. pl nouns as well: **bnāṯa zōre** 'little daughters'; **baxtāṯa sqīle** 'beautiful women'; however, foreign qualifiers normally remain (at least partly) invariable: **brāta ẓáʿif** 'weak daughter' (Ar); **baxta rāʿ/ṣar-ʿáyin** 'bad/stingy woman' (H); **yalta na-ṣax/be-ʿāqil** 'sick/stupid girl' (K); and even when the noun itself is a loanword: **šidde** (Ar, f.) **ʿaẓīm** (Ar, m.) 'great hardship'; cf.above VII, §5.10.

9.2. Native adjectives agree in gender and number, except that m. pl. serves f. pl. as well: **bnōne/bnāṯa sqīle** 'beautiful boys/girls'; I found only one exception in NT: **imqablanyāṯa** (אמקבלניאתא הודיאתא) 'Jewish midwives',[164] perhaps a calque. However, foreign adjectives usually remain invariable in gender and number[165]: **nāše ⁺rāʿ** 'bad people' (H); **yalunke baš** 'good children' (T); **bnāṯa ẓaʿif** 'weak girls' (Ar); **baxtāṯa ⁺stawir** 'barren women' (K). However when used as nouns they take Ar pl. (all from NT): **rāstīn** 'righteous men' (K); **naxwašīn** 'patients'; **maḥrūmīn** 'indigent people' (Ar); **šākirīn** 'grateful people' (Ar); **naṣāxīne** 'sick people' (Ar+NA pl **-e**); **pappūkin** 'poor ones' (=H מִסְכֵּנִים, PolG).

9.3. Only a couple of notes on some typical sentences: (a) Topical/Fronting: many sentences begin with the psychological subject, rather than the grammatical one: אילאהא פשלה לביה מיונה **ʾilāha pišle libbe myōna** 'God - His heart became angry at Jonah' (BT6 132); רשעים

163Cf. the various uses of **la** in Khan 111, §8.12.

164Cf. Goldenberg 2000 74.

165See above VII, §4.5.

קטילי ומגורגשי גו כולאנא **rašāʿīm qṭīli umgurgıši go kōlāna** 'The wicked ones - (Jews) killed them and dragged them in the street' (NT5 403); הם אתירה מצה דיהון לא האויה בשאכר יאן בדושא מכלילא **uham ʾaṯīre maṣṣa dēhun la hāwe bšākar yān bdūša maxlēla** 'and the rich, too - their matzah - they should not sweeten it with sugar or honey.' (NT5 408); **yalunke - mād ʾamrıttu la gōzi bxabrox** 'Children -whatever you tell them -they don't obey your words' (Z); **pılıštāye - baxtıt šımšon iẓbiṭālu** 'The Philistines -the wife of Samson - they captured her' (RivSh 216); **qınyāne dōhun mšulxi, mubli, mušte ⁺māya** 'Their animals - (were) undressed, led, and watered' (= They removed the saddles off their animals, and led them to water to drink) (PolU 115);[166] (B) Postponing the subject to the end, especially in rhymed texts: כוון תאוורו מנד שמיה ומנדילה דפתארוה מלאיל ה' **xawan tāwırru mınnıd šımme umandēle daftāruh mılʾēl ʾilāha** 'May he-defeat-them from-Heaven and-cast-(away) their-book (of life) from-above - God' = 'May God defeat them etc.' (NT5 394); כימן דשמאלה איא כברא שולטאנא **kīman dıšmeʾle ʾayya xabra šulṭāna** ...'When he heard this word - the king...' = When the king heard about this.. (ibid.); **mbuhdıllu kullu usēlu lqıṭla ʾan hōzāye** 'They were humiliated all of them and were killed, those Jews' (Z); **ba xāyu wēlu ta baxtāsu ʾafandiyāne** 'Indeed their lives are for their wives, the effendis' (=The effendis like their wives very much) (PolU 420); **latli pıšta nıšāma** 'There is not to me left a soul' (=I have no soul left, became very week); (c) Calque translations (NA lexicalification) of common Kurdish everyday phrases: **šımmox mayle** 'name-your what-it-is' (=What is your name); cf K **naveta čīya**; **ʾo bır manīle** 'this(one) son-of who-he-is' (=Whose son is this one?) = K **ʾava kure kīya** (see also below on calque translations).[167] Cf. also the use of relative-possessive pronoun as object pronoun: **bıqṭāla dīde** 'killing him' (also: 'his killing'); **bınšāqa dīda baxta** kissing the woman; cf. OA ולא שבעת עד דכבשתן לדידי 'you will not be satisfied until you have subdued me (SokBA 328).

---

[166]Cf. above the example at the end of VII, §8.

[167]Cf. the unique syntax of the Passive, above, VII, §6.2.1.

VIII. Observations on Semantics and Language Registers

1. Doublets. The vocabulary includes many native and loan doublets (the following all from Z), often with some semantic differentiations: **kalsa** (OA) 'daughter-in-law' vs. **kālo** (< OA) 'bride'; **warīza** (< OA) 'root, vein, sinew' vs. **wardo** (< OA, f.) 'thigh-muscle' (=H גִּיד הַנָּשֶׁה); **qarʾa** (< OA, m.) 'zucchini' vs. **qareʾsa** (f.) 'pumpkin'; **qōqa** (< OS, m.) 'cooking clay pot' vs. **quqta** (f.) 'clay jar for preserving meat'; **sāqa** (< Ar) 'sock, leg warmer' vs. **šāqa** (OA) 'leg'; **⁺šarwal** (Ar) 'native baggy trousers' vs. **šırwāla** (OA) 'underpants'; **kabʾa** (K< Ar كعب) 'anklebone' vs. **kaᶜbīye** (Ar) 'heel'; **mıᶜāra** '(H) 'Cave of Machpelah' vs. **⁺mığāra** '(any) cave'; **karapíssa** (OA) 'parsley for Passover Seder' vs. **⁺kírafıs** '(regular) parsley'; **xābūr** 'Khabur River' (Ar) vs. **xawōra** (OA חבורא) 'any river'; **ġazāla** 'gazelle' vs. **ġazāle** 'Gazelle' (f.p.n.); **šmoʾta/šmeʾta/ šumᶜāṯa** (pl. only) - all three mean 'rumors'; **š-ṭ-x** 'hang clothes to dry, spread out' (OA שטח) vs. **š-ṭ-ḥ** (OA שטח?) 'lie down, stretch oneself on the ground or bed'; **x-l-p** II (OA חלף) 'to exchange' vs. **x-l-f** (Ar) 'to deviate, disobey'; **q-ṭ-p** (OA) 'to pick up at one go' vs. **q-ṭ-f** (Ar) 'to pick (fruits, flowers)'; **g-w-l** (< OA גְּבַל) 'to smear, mix, soil' vs. **g-m-b-l** (OA גְּבַל) 'to mix and roll (wheat-meat balls)' vs. **j-b-l** (Ar cognate) 'to mix water and soil for plastering walls); however, **b-r-x-š /x-r-b-š** both mean 'to look feverishly for something"; cf. also above VI/§10.2 for emphatic variants.

1.1. Dialectal doublets (with phonological-morphological variations), as expected, exist within our group for the same meaning: **māṯe** (NT)/ **tarteʾma** (Z) 'two hundred'; **dıdwa** (NT, m.)/**dıdūsa** (Z, f.); **yōmās dīna** (Z)/**yōmāṯa ddīne** (NT יומאתא דדיניה) 'weekdays'; **⁺dōrtıd yōm** (Z)/**dʾartıd yōma** (NT< OA) 'the next day'; **ṭōla** (NT< OA טבלא) /**dōla** (Z) 'drum'; **lūna** (NT< OA לבנא)/ **lubna** (Z< Ar) 'brick'; **qufla** (Z, Ar)/**qulfa** (NT) 'lock'; **sūse** (Z)/**sūsa** (סֻוסָא, PolG:D); **zēṯa** (NT, D< OA)/**zaytūna** (Z< Ar) 'olive'; **f-n-d-š** (Z)/ **š-n-d-f** (D) 'destroy', and many more.[168]

1.2. Examples of dialectal semantic variations of even the same word: **māsa** in Z is only 'village', but **māṯa** in NT and D means also 'city'; **nehra** is 'river' in NT and Am, but 'laundry' in Z; **hırge** is 'rags, torn clothes' in Z, but '(regular) clothes' in NT and Am; **kallaš** 'dead body' in Z, but '(living) body' in NT and Am; **f-r-ḥ** 'be startled, scared' in Z, but 'rejoice' in NT (and Ar); **m-s-y** is 'to wash clothes (only)' in Z, but is 'to wash body and clothes' in NT; **š-p-x** is 'to overflow (vi)' in Z, but 'to spill (vt), pour' in Am; **r-m-y** 'to lay (only hen: eggs)' in Z; but 'to overlay' in D; **mın** is 'from' in Z, but 'from' and 'with' in Am (see also below VIII, §3)

1.3. A meaning may be reflected by a different root/word in each dialect, e.g.: 'place' is **dūka** in Z, but **ʾaṯra** in NT (and unknown in Z!); 'to go out' is **n-p-q** in Z, but **p-l-ṭ** in NT/Am; 'to touch' is **n-ḥ-q** in Z, but **n-q-š** in NT (which in Z is 'to embroider'); 'fox' is **rūvīka** (< K) in Z, but **teʾla/teʾlona** (OA תעלא) in NT; 'tiger, leopard' is **⁺pılıng** (< K) in Z, but **nümra** in NT; 'dunghill' is **kāvılta** (< K) in Z, but **sulta** in Am; 'east' and 'west'

---

[168]See above, VII, §§ 6.4.1, 6.10.2.

are mušrıq and muġrub (< Ar)in Z, but mızraḥ and maᶜarav (< H) in D; 'very' is ⁺rāba (< OA) in Z, but qawi in NT/Am/D (< Ar).

2. Hendiadys and similar combinations, with 'and' or without, are quite common in native and loan expressions: nıxle-brıxle 'he disencumbered himself (of certain responsibilities)' (lit. 'rested-kneeled'); šulxāya-purʾāya 'bare (due to poverty)'; ṣāx-salīm 'alive and well'; ḥāl-u-qıṣta '(details of this) story' (Ar); mana-salwe 'delicacies' (lit., 'manna-quails'); mıkkōnīye-mᶜaddale 'good housewife'; ʾēš-u-nāle '(all kinds of) ailments'. Theoretically, any noun can be used with its m-'doublet' (=the real noun but with its first consonant replaced with m-) to indicate 'all kinds of, and the like', with some belittling, e.g., julle-mulle 'clothes, rags'; pılda-mılda 'hair residue, and the like'; pīrakat-mīrakat 'old women and the like' (PolU 58);[169] nšāqa umanšōqe 'kissing and the like" (PolU 202); šarṭe ušurūṭe 'all kinds of necessary conditions'. In curses: ⁺rāᶜ ⁺mıṣurrāᶜ 'real evil' ('evil-leper' < H)); qṣīfa mqurṣıfa / ġbīṭa mġubṭa / qṭīʾa mquṭqıṭa 'Have a short-life, Get killed!' ([Be] 'minced'). Due to borrowing, there are expressions with redundancy: xāč-u-ṣalib 'the cross' (T 'cross'+Ar 'cross'); yāmıd baḥer qulzam 'the Red Sea' (OA+Ar; AvidH 53); gıntıd gan-ᶜēdın 'the Garden of Eden' (OA+H; NT3); dunyıd ᶜōlam 'the entire world' (SaAC 7).

2.1. Two identical words repeated one after another indicate distributive and other nuances, such as constancy, persistence, emphasis, variety, etc.: xá-(b)xa 'one by one'; tre-tre 'two by two'; ʾarbí-ʾarbi, ṭlāsí-ṭlāsi drāʾe 'about forty, thirty, cubits each' (PolU 422); ʾımmēhun-ʾımmēhun (NT2) 'constantly with them'; qamēhun-qamēhun 'constantly before them' (NT5 405;); baṯru-baṯru 'persistently/closely after them' (RivSh 169; cf. ibid. 181: qam-qāme; bas-basre) kullu-kullu 'all of them, none excluded' (RivSh 227); kud yōm kud yōm 'each and every day' (RivSh 189); jōqe-jōqe 'many groups'/ʾorde-ʾorde 'many camps, hordes' (RivSh 270); xarje-xarje 'all kinds of taxes' (RivSh 267); sınjāqe-sınjāqe 'many banners' (NT5 405); šıklé-šıkle 'all kinds of shapes and colors' (Z); šaqqé-šaqqe '(He cut her into) many pieces' (PolG); būᶜé-būᶜe boils (all over the skin); bēsa bbēsa '(entered) one house after another' (SaAC 9). Note also verb examples: gmenxa bıd do yāla, hama wal gmabrıq, gmabrıq, gmabrıq 'She looks at this child, behold, he shines, he shines, he shines' (= extremely beautiful) (PolU 79).

3. Examples of semantic changes from OA/OS, or, in the case of loanwords, from the original language. While the meaning of many words remains totally, or almost,[170] unchanged, there are others which undergo major semantic shift, or extend range of meaning (at least when

---

[169]Cf. K/P/T [> Ladino] m-, which replaces first consonant of a real word to indicate 'and its kind, etc., whatever'.

[170]E.g., in both OS and Z the meaning 'to vomit' is expressed by the verb 'to return' (vt), but in each it is a different root: OS: ܬܠܐ, Z: madʾōre. Also, as expected, the dictionaries of even the same language and period do not always agree on certain form or meaning, e.g., Zkwāra f. 'receptacle for grain' seems to be related to M. Jastrow 617 כְּוֶורֶת/כְּוַורְתָּא 'receptacle of grain', but SokBA 565 has only כַּוְּרָא 'bee-hive' (same in OS and Ar).

compared with the literary written sources): **xayēṯa, xēṯa** (BT3, D; BaBin 32), lying-in woman (= H יוֹלֶדֶת, BT3, D), but OA (+OS) חַיְּיתָא 'midwife';[171] **loʾta** 'chewing gum', but OA/OS **lūʿā** 'jaw'; **xabūša** 'apple (only) ', but OA/OS 'name of a fruit, quince, apple, peach'[172]; **sparıgla** 'quince', but OA/OS 'plum, quince, apple'; **ʿınjāṣe** 'prunes', but Ar 'pear, plum' (cf. H אגסים/עוגסים 'pears'); **kapōra** 'a giant; merciless person, infidel (rare)' < OS 'infidel (only)'; **kulka** 'inferior sticky residue of wool' < K/P/OA כּוּלְכָּא 'soft wool from goat's hair'[173]; **qınna** is 'nest' as in OA/OS but also edible 'meat' part of walnuts[174], etc.;[175] √ קמח = 'to dress hides with flour' in OA (TA); in OS = 'to make flour'; in Z (**q-m-x**) = 'to be sprinkled with flour, to taste flour-like'; √ עקש = 'to be hard , stale,' in TA, 'to be erect (penis) in OS, 'to be thick (soup, liquid); be rigid, too serious (person)' in Z; **x-t-m** 'to overfill' in Z, but 'to seal' in OA (חתם); **x-w-y** only in **ḥısse xwēle/xūya** 'He has a hoarse voice; lost his voice' but in OA חבי = 'hide';[176]; **ṭ-w-ʾ** 'to fall asleep' (OA טבע 'to sink'; but OS also 'to fall asleep'[177]; **s-m-x** 'to become pregnant' (Z), but 'to lean, uphold' in OA (+NT, and other dialects); **ḥ-m-l** 'to stand', but in Ar 'to bear, carry, be pregnant'; √ ברי **b-r-y** in OA/OS = to create, but in NA = 'to happen' (for 'to create', Ar خلق is used); **g-w-y** 'to beg food, alms' < OA גבי 'to collect (money, taxes, dues); **g-w-r** 'to marry' < OA גבר 'prevail, excel'[178] **h-l-k** 'to be soiled, get dirty', but in Ar 'to destroy'; **x-r-j** 'to sell well', but in Ar 'to exit'; **š-k-l** 'to begin', but in Ar 'to form'; **ḥamd** 'patience, calm' (cf. **si bḥamdox** 'Go leisurely/calmly'), but in Ar 'praise';[179] **qunbara** in NT means 'cave, tunnel' but 'bomb' in Z and Ar; cf. also **laġam** < Ar 'bomb', but 'cave' in Z; **ʿaṣamōṯ** 'obstinate, rigid person', but in H 'bones'; **šāmaʿti** 'obedient wife', but in H 'I heard'; **ṭōṭāfōṯ** 'waste, down the drain', but in H 'frontlet, phylacteries'; **k-w-n** II 'to look intently, examine' < H 'to pray with intention, concentration' (see also above, VIII, §1.2).

4. Examples of verbs that drastically change their meaning according to the necessitated preposition: **dʿēla ʾılle/ṭāle** 'she cursed him/prayed for him'; **māxē-le/-ʾılle/-ʾıbbe** 'he hits him/ betrays him/insults him; **flıtle mınna/ʾılla** 'he slipped away from her/had

---

[171]It is interesting to note that a NA pl. **xayāṯa** translates H חָיוֹת, in Exod. 1:19.

[172]See M. Jastrow 417; SokBA399 and sources given there.

[173]Cf. MacD 133 **kilkā** < AzT 'wool of the cotton-plant; silk-remnant'.

[174]This meaning is listed in Brockelmann 674, but as NA, i.e.: "neosyr. nucleus.'

[175]Even when the meaning seems to be identical, yet its uses may be limited, e.g., both **brīxa** and **mburxa** = blessed in NA and OA, but in NA **brīxa** is used only in the sense of Ar مبروك 'Use it well!', while **mburxa** = 'blessed' in the general sense : **mburxa šımme** 'Blessed be His name!'

[176]Cf., however, OA חסי נחבי/OS ܚܣܐ ܩܠܐ to lower one's voice, SokBA 425.

[177]Cf. Arnold (forthcoming) §2.4.2 **aġreḳ** 'to fall asleep' < Ar غرق 'sink'.

[178]Probably more directly from **gōra** 'man, husband' < OA גברא 'man'.

[179]Cf. H √ שבח 'praise', 'calm'; v. Ps. 89:10 בְּשׂוֹא גַלָּיו אַתָּה תְשַׁבְּחֵם.

intercourse with her'; **mᶜāmır ᵓılle/ᵓıbbe** 'he bosses him around/shows concern for him'.

5. Reborrowings. Some new loanwords in NA from Kurdish and other languages seem to have been originally native NA/OS words, or already naturalized loanwords in OA/OS, before being reborrowed in NA: **ᵓāman**'vessel' < K **mān** < OA **mānā** (מאנא); **ᵓınjāne** 'urn' < A **ᵓijjāna** < OA/OS **ᵓaggānā** < Ak **ᵓagannu**; ⁺**tašt(e)** 'large basin'< K/P > OA טשטקא; **gēr**: 'threshing' < K **gēre**<OS ; **xılōlāyi** 'cavity' < K < OS/OA חלולא; **kulka** 'inferior wood residue' (K/P < OA); **barxa** 'lamb' < K < OA/OS בַּרְחָא/בראחא 'he-goat'; **čamma** 'lake, meadow' <K< OA אגמא < Ak **agammu** 'marsh'; **nēčir-vān** 'hunter' < K; cf. OA נחשירכן **naḥšir ka**… < P; **ḥayzaran** 'bamboo' < K < OA חיזרא; **nıkkıla** 'beak'< K < OA **maqqōrā** ? ?)]; **gındōr**: 'melon' < K < NA/OA **g-n-d-r** 'to roll'? **ḥíllıq** 'mixture of dates and nuts paste eaten on Passover night' < JAB < rare OA **ḥ/halīqā**;[180] **kıllōra** 'bagel-shaped bread-cake' < K < OA קילורית < Gr; **kıškıri** 'fine burghul' < K (?) < OA כושקרא < P **xuškār**; **sımmēdīye** 'semolina dish' < Ar/P < OS/OA סמידא < Ak **samīdu**; **jornat** 'water troughs' < K < Ar (PolG)/**gorne** OA (Z/BT); **hındās** (pl. **hındāze**) 'measure' (NT, D); מטרייה **maṭ(ṭ)arīye** (?) 'coat' (NT2) < Ar **mamṭar** 'coat' < OA מנטר 'protection cover'; **tıxub** K/P 'border'/**tuxum** 'kind, type' < OA **tıḥūmā**; ⁺**panni** 'shady' < K **peni** < OS **pānyā** 'evening'? See also below, VII §16.

6. Archaisms or learned (including Hebrew) words are more common in literary texts (NT, BT, SaLH, etc.) or in learned people's speech: **māṯēn** 'two hundred' (NT מאתין); יומד מאלד אידא **yōmıd m(ᵓ)ālıd ᵓēḏa** 'the Eve of Holiday' (NT5 407 < OA מעלי 'entrance'; unknown in Z) vs. the common **ᵓırōta** 'Eve (of Sabbath, Holiday)' (< OA ערובתא); **n-ᵓ-h** 'to light, to dawn' (NT; unknown in Z, except in **bınhe** < בנגהי 'at lights, at dawn' > 'tomorrow'); **b-y-ṯ** I 'to spend the night' (NT < OA), but in Z only **mabōse** (IV) 'to cook overnight'; **mṣadōᵓe** 'to violate, to rape' (BT< Ar صدع 'cause pain'); **karapıssa** 'parsley' (Z < OA) only in the Passover Haggadah, but ⁺**kırafıs** < Ar in everyday use; **malka** 'king' (Z < OA) only in SaLH, but otherwise **ḥakōma** (< Ar حكم); **ṭ-l-l** 'to find shelter' (OA) (BaBin 37; Ruth 2:12; unknown otherwise); **bāsār ᵓādām** (!) 'flesh and blood, a human' (PolU 260 H בשר ודם); **bārūx maḥayyīm-mēsīm** 'Blessed be the reviver of the dead' (PolU 227 < ברוך מחיה המתים (H), said after being saved from a disaster); **maḥīla** 'sorry, forgive me' (H מחילה); **ᵓahavá-šālōm** 'amicable relations' (< H אהבה ושלום 'love and peace').

6.1. Archaic words are also common in proverbs, especially the rhyming word, e.g. **dıxra** 'treasure' (< Ar ذخر) appears only in **ᵓaw gmāẓıᶜ buxra, gmāẓıᶜ dıxra** 'Whoever loses a firstborn, loses a treasure' (SaAC 18); the informant after quoting it, added: **la kīᵓan dıxra mayle, xšu xa xızēna** 'I don't know what **dıxra** is; (I) think (it is) a treasure'; **dōla** 'bucket' appears only in the following proverb: **zılle xōla basır dōla** 'The rope followed the bucket' (one loss follows the other), but the Z informants confuse it with **dōla** 'drum' which has coalesced with it, and explain it differently: 'A Wife has to follow her husband'; the pl. form **nūne** (OS/OA **nūnē**) replaces the common form **nunyāṯa** only in this saying

[180]See Avishur 1993a:44-45; 1993b:14-15.

ʾaw gdāwiq nūne, ktarya ʿūne 'He who catches fish, his buttocks get wet' (Segal #47);[181] **ṭarpa la gnāpil mʾīlāna la b⁺ʾimir ʾilāha** 'a leaf does not fall from the tree without God's order' (OA אילנא 'tree' is rare in Z; **ṣīwa** is the regular word).

7. Euphemisms. Spoken JNA includes some very crude and obscene curses and expressions , even for plain mundane terms such as **ʾēr qīra dabuqāna** 'sticky as a penis of tar'. said about a pest; **kīʾin kma mizze ʾīs bširma** 'I know how many hairs are on her anus [= vagina]' = I know her very well'; **kutru mxa ʾēra-lu umin xa širma** 'siblings (who look very much alike)' (lit., 'both are from the same penis and from the same anus [= vagina]' (PolU 68); However, there are, as an antidote, a few euphemistic expressions, especially in literary texts and among the Hakhamim: **xōr-⁺sudra** 'underpants' (lit., a companion of undershirt); **zille/tūle riš ⁺māya** 'he went to have/had a bowel movement' (lit., went/sat onto water); **kiflūṯa** 'bowel movement' (lit., necessity, BT; cf. H צורך גדול) **ḥawējibe** 'genitals' (lit., covered things, BT); **barva** 'vagina' (lit. front door); **gō-ʾaqla** vagina (lit., in-between her legs); **pištva** 'anus' (lit., back door); **du-ṭāyi** 'buttocks' (lit., two sectioned); **ḥzirre/dmixle/kisla** 'he had intercourse with her' (lit. was present/slept with her); **pišlu gōra-baxta** 'They had consumed their marriage' (lit., became husband-wife); **mṣadōʾe** 'to rape' (lit., 'to cause pain', Ar); **⁺barradāyi** 'prostitute' (lit., one open to all, Ar-K); **⁺murpēle pōxa** 'he farted' (lit., he released wind); **širma gyāwa ʾilli, bāla la gyāwāle ʾilli** '(My wife) avoids me' (PolU 45) (lit., She gives me her buttocks; her face [=front] - she doesn't give me) ; **ʾ-z-l rēš** 'to mate' (lit., go over); **ʿ-l-q** 'to become pregnant (people)' (< 'to be kindled, touched'); **d-w-q bara** 'become pregnant (animals)' (< 'catch seed/fruit'); **ṣōre(x) qāṭān/gāḏōl** 'urination/bowel movement' (lit., small/big necessity, H); **ʾōṯ mīla** 'circumcised penis' (lit., sign of circumcision, H); **gilda ugarma** '(She was) gang-raped' (lit., [They left her] skin and bone (PolU 11); **ṯlāha ʾaqle** '(to have) an erection' (lit., three legs) (PolU 2-); the verb **h-n-l** II 'do that thing, have intercourse' < **hinna** 'that thing'; **la min kāsā ula min xāṣa** 'Both parents were not able to have any children' (lit., [neither] from the [mother's] belly nor from the [father's] back [= loins]); **nyāxa** or **ʾizāla qam raḥmit ʾilāha** 'He passed away' (lit., rest or go before God's mercy).

8. Pejorative words especially regarding rituals of Gentiles: **mnaʿōle** 'horseshoeing' or **⁺mpartōme** 'grafting' for 'Gentile marriage' (vs. **gwāra/mqadōše/mbarōxe** 'Jewish marriage'); **mʾabōye** 'to impregnate' (lit. 'inflate') for out of wedlock or Gentile pregnancy vs. **masmōxe** for regular pregnancy; **mtapōle** 'Muslim praying/prostrating' < H **tiflā** 'folly' or H **tifillā/hitpallel** 'pray' (?) vs. **mṣalōye** 'Jewish prayer'; **xiṣwa** (Ar) 'Gentile or misguided act of charity' (lit. 'castration') vs. **miṣwa** (H); **ġēẓa** 'Gentile Holiday' (Ar غيض 'rage') vs. **ʾēḏa** '(Jewish) Holiday'; **mōqēš(ka)** 'Gentile Holiday' (Heb מוקש 'trap'); **ʾīšo mšīḥa** 'Jesus Christ' and **⁺mat-miryam** 'Lady Mary' are said about an only child who is too spoiled or 'worshipped' by his parents.

9. Blessings and curses, like in any traditional society, are very common and part of

---

[181]In some cases an archaic word may be a borrowing from the ChNA, e.g., **ʾēwa smoqa bispāre, šqōl xaṭōra uysa lgāre** 'Red cloud in the morning, take a pounder and beat the roof,' in which **bispāre** (< OA צפרא) 'in the morning,' is not used in Z.

everyday speech of men and women, although there are some more typical to each grou Women's curses can be as vicious as men's, but obscene curses and swear-words were mo common in men's talk. Inspite of a plethora of blessings, they don't include replicas of mode general European expressions such as 'thank you', 'sorry', 'excuse me', but have more elaborat formulas said in similar situations, e.g., when one wants to thank someone, one will say one c the following, depending if the addressed person is young or old, rich or poor, man or womar etc. : **ʾilāha nāṭırrox/nāṭır yalunke dīdox** 'May God keep you/your children'; **ʾilāh ma'mır bēṯox** 'May God sustain your house'; **zēdi xāyox** or **sōʾıttu xāyox** 'May you liv long' (lit. "be satiated of your life"); **raqḏax bdaᶜwox** 'May we dance at your wedding' **xōra pāṯox** 'May you be proud' (lit., May your face be white). Some greetings are connecte with special occasions, e.g., **blıbba bassīma** '(Use it) with a joyous heart'; **ʾēnox bahūr** '(May the good news) brighten your eyes'. There is an equivalent of "I am sorry, excuse me" **mfāḥılli,** lit., 'forgive me!', but it is used only in solemn and religious circumstances, a when addressing God. It is interesting to note that the major word for blessings and curses is th same: **daᶜwāṯa** , which may be translated 'prayers, pleas'; and so is the verb **d-ᶜ-y** (Ar) except when followed by a differentiating preposition: **dᶜēla ʾılle** 'she cursed him', vs. **dᶜēl ṭāle** 'she blessed him'. However the synonym **ṣuᶜrāṯa** means only 'curses', and the ver **mṣaᶜōre** (OA צער; cf. Ar صغّر 'belittle'). Curses are often negative formulas of the blessings, e.g., **la sōʾıttu xāyox** 'May you not live long'; **kēma pāṯox** 'May you be humiliated' (lit. your face become black); **hājım bēṯox** 'May your house be destroyed'; however, paradoxically some curses are used as positive formulas, e.g., **xāru bēṯe** It/He is wonderful (lit., May his house be destroyed; cf. Ar. **yixrib bētu**)[182] A person may curse oneself as well, to express sorrow, helplessness, e.g., **qıṭma brēši** 'Woe to me' (lit., Ashes on my head). A commor obscene curse is **qūṭıt yımme** 'The vagina of his mother' (a calque of Arabic), and others much worse, which, however, are softened by paraphrases such as **hatxa (ʾuzli) myımme** '(I did) thus to his mother'. In the daily JNA speech of the Hakhamim Hebrew blessings o curses are common, e.g., **ᶜeser makkōṯ mıṣrāyim** (עשר מכות מצרים) 'the Ten Plagues of Egypt' said after hearing a fart, and **leḥayim ṭōvīm** (לחיים טובים) 'for good life!' after a sneeze. However some Hebrew curses are common only in women's speech, e.g., **(yım)maḥ šamō wazıxrō** (ימח שמו וזכרו) 'May your (lit., his) name and memory be erased!', and women who use it very often are known as **wazíxro**.

9.1. Interestingly, Hebrew blessings and other formulas are used in folktales even when the characters and the milieu are altogether Muslim-Kurdish, e.g.: - **šālom ᶜalēxem, bābo!** - **way ᶜalēxem šālōm, bārux-xábba, go ʾēni, hā ḥasan čalabi** 'Peace upon you, Father!' -'Upon you, too, most welcome, O Hasan Chalabi!' (PolU 33); **ḥızzāq bārūx** 'Bravo' (PolU 105); **ʾilāha umōše rabbēnu hāwe wakil dīdox** 'May God and our Master Moses be your agents' (= I swear that I am not lying) (PolU 157); **zılwāli lṣōre(x) qāṭān** 'I went to urinate' (PolU 219); **muṣlıḥ wıt, ṣaddīq wıt, yāre ṣāmāyim wıt** 'You are a benefactor, a righteous, a God-fearing (person)' (said by one Gentile to another) (PolU 245).

---

[182]Cf En. He is terrific = very good, and similar negative = positive expressions in other languages.

10. Cryptic language, mostly Hebrew, used in the presence of Gentiles or children: **šīn-qōf-rōš** (!) (=H שקר) 'I am intentionally bluffing, I don't mean to act on what I am saying'; **l-y-x** 'to go away, leave quietly (so the children will not notice, or before any problem sets in)' (< H הלך/ילך); **šuttāfe** '(let us be) partners (in this deal)' (H שותפים); **ḥāṣi šılli ḥāṣi šıllox** 'half (of the profits) are mine, and half are yours' (H חצי שלי, חצי שלך); **šattí-ʿērev** 'cross' (H שתי ערב 'warp and woof') (normally **xāč-u-ṣalib**).

10.1. Taboo words. A frightening disease, such as cancer, is usually not mentioned by name and referred to as **ʾaw dla gmēṯe baḥṯe** 'that which is not mentioned'; 'ashes' are often referred to as **brēš dıžmıne** '(May be) on the head of the enemies'; demons are called **ʾan bıšṭom mınnan** 'those who are better than us', or **šēna mʾaxgıb** '(May) peace (be) on our side'; angel of death is **ʾaw bxa ʾēna** 'he who is with one eye'; the dead are **ʾan dlēwu ʾaxxa** 'those who are not here'. In translations from Hebrew whenever the text includes a curse of the Jews by a Gentile, the translator paraphrases it, e.g. דבר פרעה למחות את שמם ולהאביד את זכרם 'Pharaoh said to erase their name (=Children of Israel) and obliterate their memory' is translated as ...**šımmıd gyāne** ... **tuxurye** '...his own name (=Pharoah's)...and his memory' (AvidH 51), or 'Israel' is substituted by 'enemies of Israel'; note also the interpolation of the narrator in the following curse: **la sōʾıttu, ʾaw dlēwe ʾaxxa, xāyox** 'May you - he who is not here (among the audience)- not live your life fully'. Any word that the speaker doesn't feel comfortable saying in public, he or she will use the word **hınna** 'that thing' and assume the context will provide the meaning. Gentle women follow any word that may have any sexual connotation, such as 'stick, enter, penetrate' by **be-maʿna** 'without (sexual) intention' (ironically, the result is the opposite); cf. also above VIII, §8.

11. Metaphors and unique idioms: **šamāmōke/qaqwāna/qaramta** 'good looking girl' (lit., musk-melon/partridge/pancake); **ʾēn-yoma go pāsa, šımšıd sehra go ṣuṣyāsa** 'Sun (radiates) on her face, moon - on her braids (said of a pretty woman); a wife/woman of good character is: **ʾıšša kašēra; xa yalta raḥat; ʾēna kīpe; xa beʾta dla pımma** 'a decent/lawful woman', 'a calm girl', 'her eyes lowered=humble, shy'; '(quiet like) a mouthless egg = not too talkative' (PolU 407); **mamṣanīs gurge** 'mighty mother' (lit., one who nurses wolves); **ʿarnūwa** 'ugly/angry face' (originally 'rabbit'); **qareʾṯıd-⁺māya** 'turtle' (lit., water-pumpkin); **kalbıd⁺māya** 'avid swimmer' ('sea dog'); **ʾēn-yōma** 'sun (disc)' (lit., day's eye); **ʾēn-xmāṭa** 'Chinese' (lit., [one with slanted eyes like] the eye of the needle); **ʾēn ʾilāha ʾılle** 'He is fortunate (lit., God's eyes are upon him!); **ʾēr-qīra** 'pest' (lit., [He is like a] penis [made] of tar); **kūr-dugle** 'frequent liar' (lit., kiln of lies); **qaṭra mjōbāna** 'echo; impudent' (lit., 'responding rock'); **qūna [!] qaḥbe** 'free-for-all place' (lit., prostitute's arse); **qınnıd dıbbōre** 'large family' (lit., nest of hornets); **ʾıprıd qam kanushyāṯa** 'null and void' (lit., (like) the dust before brooms (NT5 406); **ʾıyāla smīxa** 'embryo' (lit., 'pregnant', expectant, child, NT); **brāta brat-bēṯa** 'virgin' (lit., daughter-of-the house daughter); **sehrıd ṭlāha sehre** 'the third month' (lit., moon of three moons, NT); **qanāne štílu-le** 'he was astonished' (lit., horns sprouted on his (head); **xwarūṯa** 'snow', 'dairy food' (lit., whiteness); **p-y-š ʾōqad xıt** 'be very happy' (lit., be twice as big); **ʿ-l-q** 'to become pregnant' (< 'to be kindled, touched'; also a euphemism?); some of these metaphors are even less transparent, e.g., **bqanya rēšan kēse grāʾa** 'we are very strong/smart' (lit., our head can be shaved by a reed) (PolU 4); **la ʾāwa šqılle xāṣa māwa, la ʾāwa** 'neither prevailed over the other (in a duel)'

(lit., neither he overtook the back [which presumbly is more vulnerable, or get behind?] from him, neither he); **kullu wēlu xe fıṣṣıd ʾasıqse** 'All of them are under his control' (= under the jewel of his ring); **kṭawīla mın mušruq umın muġrub** It is worth a great deal (lit., from east and west) (PolU 102); **bšīr ušakır** 'with milk and sugar' (K)/**bšeʾze ušākar** 'with almonds and sugar' = (raise a child) with luxury and pampering; **gıgıl ʾabrēsım** 'very much in love' (lit. silk skein, because in FT a couple much in love put it around their neck while making love) (PolU 110); **la mxa lıbba, mın ʾımma uʾısri uʾıšta lıbbābe qam ʾıbāle** 'She loved him not from one heart, (but rather) from one hundred twenty and six hearts' (PolU 405).

12. Traditional oral literature, folktales, formulas. Certain phrases are especially typical to folk narratives, such as the following beginnings and ends: **ʾıṯwa laṯwa, bıšṭof mın ʾilāha laṯwa** 'There was, there wasn't, better than God there was none'; opening phrase in folktales, similar to 'Once upon a time'; **kud šmiʾāle xāye ukud la šmiʿāle xāye** "whoever has heard the story - may he live! And whoever hasn't heard it - may he live (as well)', said at the end of a story (cf. Socin 166; PolG); sometimes an additional humorous formula is mentioned by the narrator: **muṯēli mın tāma ṯlāha xabūše, xa ta maḥkyān ḥıkkōṯa, xa ṯāli uxa ta yōna'** I have brought from there three apples, one for the story-teller, one for me, and one for Jonah (the narrator's name) (PolU 76)'; **upıšla xızyūsa ušahyāna ʾıllu uʾıllıd kullu (bani) yisrāʾēl uta kullu bani ʾādam** 'They had joy and a great celebration and so may all Jews and peoples' (an alternative formula for a story with a happy end of; cf. PolU 377); **xa yōma myōmaṯa** 'one day...; ever; never' (with negative particle) (MeAl 176); **gıbıt xa yōma, gıbıt trē yōme** '(they searched for her,) be it for (lit., you want) one day, be it for two days (be it...)' (Socin 165); **bamrıt ʾıdyo lēwe mīsa; ʾıdyo ʾısri uʾıšta šınne wēle mīsa** 'You could say, He did not die today; he has died twenty six years ago (he looked so 'dead')' (PolU 22); **hatxa wēle ḥāle kullu yōmās ʾilāha** 'His situation remained like this all his life' (lit., all days of God); **mın yōmıd muttūle dunye uhīl xarwa dunye** 'never ever' (lit., from the day He set the world and till the day the world is ruined); **ḥakōma dīwıt bassīma** 'Long live the King' (MeAl 178); **baxad ʾilā(ha) ubaxatox** 'I beg you, for God's sake' (MeAl 179) (lit., mercy of God and yours); **ʾuḏlu daʿwa šōʾá yōme ušōʾá lēlawāṯa** 'They made a wedding for seven days and seven nights' (MeAl 193); **har nāša hānēle ʾāxıl ušāte umēnıx bḥusn-u-jamal dē brāta** 'May a person be always happy to eat and drink and look at this girl's grace and beauty' (MeAl 188; cf. PolU 4); praising someone may also be done indirectly, by praising God instead: **qurbān xalāqa** '(May I be) a sacrifice of her/the Creator' (=She is most beautiful) (SaNR); **ʾanya - har hāwe mpuṣna šımme, har hāwe mburxa, mqudša šımme, ʾaw ʾilāha-le, lēs ⁺ġēre, lēwın xızya yāla xōr danya kutru** 'These (boys) - May God's name be always praised, may His name always be blessed, sanctified, He is the God, none else but Him - I have never seen a child (as smart) as these two.' (= extremely smart) (PolU 151). Note the sequential verbs in the following formula: **zılle yōma, ṯēle yōma** 'days went by' (lit., a day went, a day came) (Avin78 94); **⁺rımle tūle** 'whatever he did' (lit., he got up, he sat down) (ibid.); **mād ʾuḏle la ʾuḏle** 'no matter what he did'; **mušmeʾla muštıqla** 'she heard [but pretended not to hear] and kept quiet' (MeAl 188); **bēṯa zılle ṯēle, zılle ṯēle** 'the house shook (during an earthquake)'; **yōma gnēle, lēwe gınya, gnēle, lēwe gınya** 'The sun was just about to set' (lit., the day declined, is not declined, etc.) (PolU 423); **qīme tīwe mızġas** '(They) were raised (lit., got up, sat down) together, got along very well' (PolG). To make the listener more involved in

the story, the narrator often uses present-future verbal forms (often including the fictitious pronoun 'you'), 'historical present', instead of the expected past tense: **masyālox ṭlāha man zudyāsa** 'she brings-you (=me) three of those loaves of '; **šāqıllox** ***ʾısra zudyāsa** 'He takes-you ten loaves' (PolU 427). For this purpose 'invented' questions, answered by the narrator himself, are used as well: **ḥıkkōsa ma waʿda xliṣāli** 'At what time did I finish the story?' (PolU 428). In addition, non-sensical or sounds are used to describe movements, sounds, emotions, etc., e.g.,[183] **ḥım-ḥah** indicates the start of galloping (PolU 47); **day day day day day** sounds and movments of horse speedily galloping; **gır gır gır** sounds of speeding donkey or wagon (PolU 429); **tık tık tık** sound of energetic steps; **ṭır ṭır ṭır** sounds of farting; **zrıng zrıng zring** sound of key turning in a lock; **pırrr** bird's take off or landing; **tırnīni, tırnāna/ḥıng-u-dıng/šarp-u-ṭarp** sounds and energetic movements of dancers; ***xırrēna umıššēna, šraqqēna uṭraqqēna,** ***bādēna uxarpēna** - all indicate energitic movements and sounds of hunters chasing after their game, or loggers floating speedily over the river; ***mırč-u-mırč-u-mırč** sounds of kissing; ***mırra-*mır** '(a divan session) with all due pomposity'; **nıxxx** (< **n-y-x** 'to rest'?) sound and movment of animal dropping down to rest or to mate; **wul-wul-wul** sound of angry birds; **hayhū, hayhū** indicates shock, sadness, yearning; **wāḥ/waḥḥ** indicates puzzling situation; **xulım-xulım** commotion, tumult (as reaction to an abnormal birth); **ṭrappenta** 'thump'; **ʾē, ʾe** indicates slight change of the subject or shift to another scene by the narrator. A consonant or syllable may be dragged to indicate emphasis or duration: **sssar-rast** 'rrright ahead'; **bxēlēēē uqımle** 'He cried for a lo-o-ng time and then got up' (PolU 430); **hīīīīl** 'unti-i-i-i-l'.

13. Women's Speech. Certain words, idioms, curses and blessings were used almost exclusively by women folks, e.g., calling months by the Holiday or fast in which it occurs, e.g., **yarxıd ʾēḏīlāne** 'the month of Arbor Holiday' (= the Hebrew month of Shevat); **yarxıd ṣōma ʿazīza** 'the month of the Venerable Fast (Yom Kippur)' (= Tishri); **yarxıd ṣalīḥōṯ** 'the month of singing hymns' (= Elul); **ʾeḏ-praṭīle** Holiday of Hard Labor = Passover (because women worked very hard preparing for it), pun with **ʾeḏ-paṭīre** Holiday of Unleavened Bread; many blessings or curses which include the H words ***kappāra** or **qorbān** 'sacrifice, expiation': **pēšan** ***kappārox** 'May I become your expiation!' (a blessing said by mothers to their sons); **pēšat** ***kappāri** 'May you become my expiation!' (a curse exchanged by quarreling women); **yımmaḥ šamo wazıxro** 'May your ('his') name and memory be obliterated!' (H ימח שמו וזכרו); this curse is usually accompanied, for extra emphasis, by a motion of one's palm facing the cursed person; the last word **wazıxro** has acquired an independent meaning: 'accursed woman' or 'a woman who curses a lot'; **ʾīze yarıxta** 'lecher' ('his hand long', likes to touch women). The taboo words mentioned in 10.1 above are much more frequent in women's speech.

14. Baby Talk. Very small children, and adults talking to babies and children, used a special vocabulary limited to a child's needs and body parts (and usually not used by adults when talking to each other), e.g., **ṭūṭıla** 'child's penis'; **ʿūna** 'buttocks'; **čıčča** 'breast'; **tatte**

---

[183]Only a selection is included in the dictionary. Cf. Polotsky 1961:18 on the numerous onomatopoetic reduplications in NS (= ChNA; mostly loans from K) dialects and their syntactical use as adverbs and predicatives.

'hands'; **pappe** 'feet'; **mamma** 'bread' **ʿamm** 'eat'; **ʾaḥḥ** 'sweet, drink'; **žažža** 'meat' **qaqqe** 'nuts'; **naʿʿe** 'raisins'; **jōje** 'pee'; **ʿāʿe** 'kaka'; **kıxx** 'dirty, don't touch'.[184]

15. Calque translations from Kurdish and Arabic are not unusual in the spoken registers and from Hebrew in the literary Midrashic and Bible translational registers, e.g., **rıš** 'on top, over' (prep., lit. 'head'; cf. K **sar** 'head; on'); **rıš rēši** 'welcome; willingly' (lit. over my head; cf. K. **sar sarēmın**; Ar **ʿala rāsi**) ; **banjāne smōqe** 'tomatoes'; (lit. 'red b.'); **banjāne kōme** 'eggplants' (lit. 'black b.'; cf. K. **bajāne sōr/raš**); **pāṯe kımla/xurra** 'became embarrassed/proud' (lit., his face became black/white; similar in IrAr, K, and others); **gyāwıl šırme** 'homosexual' (cf. K **qūn-dahe** 'anus-giver'); **turra qḏāle** 'he suffered a great loss' (lit. 'his neck broke'; cf. K **⁺stu škasti, gardan xalāyi**); **xılle ʾıxre** 'he made a big mistake saying this ; I vehemently disagree!' (lit. 'he ate shit'; cf. K/P **gu xwār**) **mēka ʾıtlēni** 'How do we know?" (=H מנין לנו, NT); **gṣaʿda mʾıḏox** 'you can afford it' (=H עולה בידך) (NTU4 161b).[185]

16. Etymology. An effort was made to find the language of origin (for native or loan words) and the etymology of most words. While in many cases the origin of a word is quite obvious, there are many cases that the language of origin and the etymology are ambiguous or remain unknown. The available dictionaries of Aramaic, Syriac, and of contact languages: (Literary) Arabic, Iraqi Arabic, Syrian Arabic, Anatolian Arabic, Kurdish (Kurmanji and Sorani), Persian and Turkish, often fail to record words which belong to the colloquial register, or are recorded differently from how they are known/pronounced in our JNA group.[186] In some cases the pronunciation and/or the meaning are different from that of the original contact language, suggesting an intermediary language, e.g., Arabic words borrowed via K/P/T, and even OA/OS words may be re-borrowed through K[187] or JAB.[188]

16.1. OA/OS words are not always recognizable due to regular or irregular phonetic changes, e. g., the origin of **rōḏāna** (Z **rozāna**; MacD 290 **rōḏānā**) 'earthquake' is not given anywhere (e.g., MacD); at first it seems to be related to **h-r-ḏ** 'to shake' < OA חרד; or **r-y-ḏ** 'to move' < OA רעד(?), a more likely origin would be OS **nawḏānā** (ܢܘܕܢܐ) 'earthquake',[189] but a rare spelling, רְאוֹדָנָא **rʾōdāna** (=H חַלְחָלָה, AvidH, twice; cf. now Mutzafi 2000b: 298 **⁺rawdāna** etymologized ***rāʿōḏānā**!), suggests OA רעד as its origin (however, Garbell 328 **⁺rotana**, Mutz 224 **⁺rotāna**, may be from OA רתת). For **x-r-ʾ** < ר-ח-ע, see above IV, §1.

---

[184]For a full list see Sabar 1974b.

[185]For examples of very literal Bible translation, see Sabar 1983a: 28-31.

[186]Cf. the observation in Sokoloff forthcoming, p. 7, §4.1.2 on many spelling variants in the manuscripts mostly homogenized in standard printed editions, and "[m]any Jewish Babylonian Aramaic words occurring even in the printed editions are absent from the lexica." n. 34 ad loc.

[187]Cf. Chyet 1995, 1997.

[188]See also above, IV, §§1-2; VII, §4.3.1; VIII, §6.

[189]Suggested by Simon Hopkins in a private communication.

16.2. Similarly, **zwa'ta** 'a loaf of bread enriched with sesame and egg-yolk'; pl. זודיאתא **zudyāṯa** (=H עֻגּוֹת, BT1, D; PolG); it may be derived from OA זְוָודְתָא, זבדתא/Mand זאואדתא/Ar زوّادة provisions for journey (> + OA 'shrouds', euph.); or < OS ܙܘܐܬܐ (!) 'a cake of fine flour' ? (Cf. other NA variants: MacD 90 **zattā, zwātā** 'a cake for children'; Garbell 342: **zatila** 'cake of bread made with oil'; Mutz 241 **zatila** 'a kind of big pita bread'/242 **zwāta** 'thin and dry bread').

16.3. Words whose etymology was discoverd by chance, e.g., **'ılpa** 'eyelash', pl. **'ılpāpe**, could not be found in any dictionary, and seemed unrelated to any apparent word for 'eyelid' in the various native and contact languages; then by mere chance I came across **ṭılpā** in MacD 112 <OS **talīpā** ܛܠܝܦܐ.[190] Similarly, **dōqa** 'arched thin iron used for baking thin bread': the search for the origin of this very common tool in all relevant dictionaries was quite frustrating;[191] eventually, while perusing Sokoloff's forthcoming dictionary, I came acrooss the word /טַבְקָא טַפְקָא 'baking/frying pan' < OA/OS < P > Ar طابَق (SokBA 492), which is no doubt the 'mother' of our **dōqa**.[192]

16.4. The following roots and nouns have irregular sibilant shifts: The root **č-h-y** 'to be tired' has been assumed to be from OS **g-h-y/k-h-y** (?) (Segal), or OA/OS **š-h-y** 'tarry, pause' (MacD); however, Sokoloff has שהי #2 specifically meaning 'to be tired, lethargic'.[193] Similarly, **m-s-y** 'to wash (NT: body/clothes; Z: only clothes)' seems to be a loan root from Ak **mesū** 'to wash', rather than OA/OS **m-š-y** (משי) 'to wash, soak, rub' (SokBA 712; right meaning, wrong sound), or **m-s-y** (מסי) 'melt, flow, drip' (SokPA 320)/'to condense' (SokBA 690; right sound, wrong meaning); so **q-ṯ-r** 'to tie' (cf. H. ק-ש-ר) is not listed in OA/OS dictionaries (!), and instead they have קטר **q-ṭ-r** 'to tie'; and vice versa with the word for rock: NA has **qaṭra**, but OA/OS קתרא; **kāšīya** 'drinking glass; goblet', but OA/OS/Mand כָּסָא/Ar كاس.

16.5. The etymology or origin of a root or a word may remain ambiguous despite - or

---

[190]Perhaps the initial **t** was re-analyzed as the possesive **d-** similar to En 'a norange' > 'an orange'; 'a napron' > 'an apron'

[191]As far as I know, no other scholar has found its origin; cf., e.g., Mutz 200; no origin given; Maclean ܛܦܩܐ **ṭapqa** wooden bowl (no origin given! not listed in Khan, Garbell).

[192](SokBA 1064); for the phonetic change **af** > **ō**, cf. **nafšā** > NA **nōša**, etc. (above, VI, §2.6.); cf. also OA variant טבהקי. The emphatic **ṭ** seems to be reduced to plain **d**, somewhat unusual; cf. however **ṭ** > **ḍ/d** : **ṭ/ḍabīla** 'ritual bath' (< H טבילה), **ṭ/ḍabanja** 'revolver' (T/K), **dōla** (Z; **ṭōla**, NT) 'drum' < OA **ṭavlā**.

[193]See SokBA 1064: שהי ליה ושתיק ליה [= **šhē-leh uštiq-leh**] 'he was tired and quiet'; note the Gaonic comment to this in Hebrew: ריש לקיש יגע ביותר באותה שעה ומיגיעתו לא יכל לדבר ולפיכך שתק שיגיעה כזאת נקראת בלשוננו שיחיא [=שיהיא] '....such fatige is called in our language (= Aramaic) **šihya**.

because of - several possible explanations, e.g., the root **ṭ-p-r** 'to burn'; it may be related to Ak **ṭipāru** 'torch' (v. above IV, §1); or to **ṭıpra** 'claw'; cf. MacD: **ṭ/tāpir** 'put the claws into; attack; interfere; stick to, be kindled'; cf. **ʿ-l-q**; **mṭāpir** 'incite, stick' (but no source is given); PolG assumes: ܐܬܛܦܪ/ܐܬܛܦܪ (v. Brockelmann 560: 'iratus, indignatus'); Arabic طفر 'leap' (also:'drive away, ruin, etc.') seems less likely because Arabic **f** is usually retained in Jewish Zakho, and indeed PolG has **ṭ-f-r** 'to be weary (of one's life)' (but AnAr has **ṭ-p-r** 'fall asleep'!). One is tempted to also assume OA טפל **ṭ-f-l** 'attach, cling to', same etymology as the synonym **ʿ-l-q** (< Ar) 'attach, kindle'. However if the major meaning 'to kindle, burn' is related to the meaning 'to put the claws into' > 'to attack' (both unknown in Z), hence 'to catch fire, be attacked by fire, burn', and metaphorically 'be incited', then all may indeed be derived from **ṭupra** 'nail, claw'. Similarly, **bībi** 'the pupil of the eye' is an example of a word that has very similar sounds in a few languages; cf. OA/H בבבה **bābā**; Ar **buʾbuʾ**; P **babak** (cf. other NA variants in MacD 24, 30 **bibiltā**; **bābāgī** (pl.), **bībīyī**). So **mērge/a** 'oasis' could be < OS **margā**/K **mırk**/P **marġ** (Ar/**marj**)? So **kāka** 'tooth' < OA/OS/Mand כַּכָּא 'molar tooth', or P ککا **kakā** 'the teeth' (Steingass 1039; cf. **kākıllo** < K 'toothy'). So **ʿabra** 'raft, barge' sounds very 'Arabic', but I could not find it in any Ar dictionary; instead it appears in a K dictionary (Jaba-Justi 140) as **ḥabra** 'barque'; but cf. H עֲבָרָה 'raft' (2 Sam 19:19); OS ܥܒܪܐ 'crossing'; and perhaps even a metathesis of OA /OS ערבא, ארבא 'boat'. The common word for 'child' is **yāla** assumed to be from OA ילדא, but in NT it is איאלא **ʾıyāla**, showing perhaps a derivation from Ar **ʿiyāl** 'children, family'. **masta** 'yoghurt' seems to be from K/P ماست; but cf. OA/Mand מַסּוּתָא/OS ܡܣܘܬܐ/ ܡܣܘܬܐ 'curdled milk' < √ מסי 'to condense'. **ṭ-ʿ-l** (NT), **t-ʾ-l** (Z, PolG) 'to play (games); to mock', e.g., **mtōʿılle brēši** 'He made a mockery of me' (< H הִתְעַלֵּל?; Garbell 292 **⁺t-y-l** 'play'; but Krotkoff 129-30 < **taʿla** 'fox'). **mēnōxe** (Z)/**mʾēnōxe** (NT) 'to look' seems to be blending of **ʾēna** 'eye' and the causative of **n-y-x** 'to rest' (vt), i.e., 'resting the eye on something' > 'look'.[194]

16.6. The etymology of some words, including some common everyday ones, remains unknown, e.g., **pıškūre** (Z) 'ceiling'/**bıškūre** (PolG)/**škūrī** (MacD; no source is given and I could not find it in any other dictionary; perhaps from ***bēṯ-škūre** ?); similarly, **marimōye** 'mourning session, sitting shiva'; **gōʾa** 'saffron, stalk of lettuce'; **šwa** 'for no reason' (e.g., **ʾawa šwa zılle** He went for nothing (having no special reason) < H לשוא/שָׁוְא ?); **zāya** 'recurrent time; case, matter, it', and less common such as **ṭufur** 'precious, valuable'; **ṭapōla** 'blow on the head with both hands', **tarlāl** 'dandy',**tafṣıkyāṯa** 'sycamore fruits'; **⁺sa(ʿ)karra(ḥ)/ sakkáraḥ** 'anguish' (as in **ṣaʿkarrıd lıbbu turra/tūla** 'They calmed down, their anguish subsided'); **sarnīʾa** (NT)/**sırn/moʾta** 'grape skin'. See also above IV, §§1-2; VIII, §6.

[194]Cf. MeAl 180, n. 27.

A USER'S GUIDE TO THE DICTIONARY

(1) All the lexical items (nouns, prepositions, adverbs, etc., except verbs for which see below), whether attested in written or printed texts or from the spoken registers, are listed in Hebrew alphabetical order (see above VI, §1), usually according to the prevailing spelling conventions attested in the 'classical' manuscripts of Nerwa Texts (see above V, §1). Note I: Since vowel letters are used profusely and not consistently, not all variations are listed as lemma with reference. Therefore, it is advised to look for e.g., **pü/ımma** 'mouth' first under פמא rather than the occasional variants פימא/פומא;[195] Note II: Since the letter ג̇ represents **č** (ג̇)/j (ג̄)(**ž**), and כ = **k** (כּ, כ)/**x** (כ̄) etc. (see V above), one has to look in the other(s) if he doesn't find it in the first. The Hebrew spellings are followed with their (partly assumed - in case of old written texts -) phonetic transcription and English translation. Verbs are listed according to their root; see below §§14-16.

(2) Following the Hebrew spelling of each entry, the OA/OS[196] probable cognate, or simply comparable form,[197] is given. For loanwords, the original language (Arabic, Kurdish, Persian, Turkish, etc.) is given[198] whenever it could be found in the dictionaries. If not found, but assumed to be in one of the above languages, the language is marked by an *, e.g., ג̇לל **jalal** is marked by *K < Ar شلال.

(3) Since in unvocalized texts some letters are used for more than one consonant, one has to check an unknown word in other possible places, e.g., words beginning with כ should be checked in כ/**k**, and, if not found there, then in כ/**x**; (so with ת/**t**, ת/**ṯ**; פ/**p**, פ/**f**; ד/**d**, ד/**ḏ**; ג̇/**j**, ג̇/**č**; ב/**b**, ב/**v**). We preferred this separation, since some of the consonants represented by the same letter are historically not related, e.g., כ represents variants of OA/OS phoneme **/k/** as well as **/ḥ/**.

(4) Significant spelling/vocalized variations (suggesting a different/possible/dialectal pronunciation, etc.), are listed as well with cross-reference to the main entry, e.g., בזרא

---

[195]See above V, §5.4 for other such examples.

[196]When the OA/OS form/meaning are almost identical (with each other and with NA), usually only one cognate word is quoted, if any, e.g., בוכרותא (OA/OS בּוּכְרוּתָא) **buxrūṯa** first birth; כלבא (OA/OS) **kalba** dog; כוזא (OA/OS/Mand/Ar/K/P) **kūza** jug, jar; however, when form/meaning are significantly different from the cognates, they are quoted, e.g., כאוא (Mand כאוא; OA/OS כַּוְּותָא) **kāwa** little window; בסמא (OA בּוּסְמָא/OS ܒܣܡܐ spice) **bısma** resin; בסתאנא (Ar بُستان/OA/OS בּוּסְתָּנָא < P **bostān**) **bıstāna** garden, orchard; גומלא **gumla** 'camel' (OA/OS גַּמְלָא; Mand גומלא).

[197]At times a form may be given simply for contrast, e.g., פסחא (OA פִּסְחָא; OS ܦܨܚܐ) m. **pısḥa** Passover; the OS form, with **ṣ** instead of **s**, is given to show that the JNA form is derived from OA, rather than OS.

[198]The actual form usually is not given, except when it is somewhat different.

[**bazarʾa**] v. ברזראא [**barzarʾa**] ('offspring, seed'); רסק [**rɪsq**] v. רזק [**rɪzq**] ('livelihood'); מַרְטַבֵּי v. מרתבה ***martabe** ('high rank'); גופתא [**gupta**] v. גובתא [**gubta**] ('cheese'); טרוסא v. תרוצא ***trōsa** 'truth'; both spellings (as well as other variations) suggest emphatic pronunciation of the entire word or shifting parts of it, marked in JNAD by superlinear cross (*) to the left of the transcription.

(5) Secondary or additional spellings/pronunciations are marked by regular + sign to the left of the abbreviated source, e.g., +NT = 'NT has, in addition to the first spelling, also this one'. Alternate spellings with prosthetic aleph, such as אטלאהא **ɪṭlāhā** for the regular טלאהא **ṭlāha** ('three'), usually are ignored. However, whenever the prosthetic aleph has been lexicalized, e.g., אשתא **ʾɪšta** 'six', אכרה **ʾɪxre** 'excrement', it appears under א.

(6) The very regular Z variants with **z** < **d̲**., **s** < **t̲**, usually written with ז, ס, respectively, in texts originating from Z, are not reflected in our H spelling, but noted in parentheses in the phonetic transcription, e.g., אידא **ʾīd̲a** (Z **ʾīza**)'hand'; ביתא **bēt̲a** (Z **bēsa**) 'house'. However, the Z variants of words with the common f. sg. and pl. endings **-t̲a** are not given even in the phonetic transliteration, e.g., רבתא **rabt̲a** 'large'; רבותא **rabūt̲a** 'greatness', כלואתא **kalawāt̲a** 'brides'.

(7) In case of two or more homographs, they are followed by numbers 1, 2, etc., e.g., טלא 1 **ṭla** 'for'; טלא 2 **ṭɪlla** 'shade'.

(8) Irregular plurals, such as **šɪnne** 'years', pl. of שאתא **šāta** are usually listed with cross-reference to the singular.

(9) The plural form of many nouns and adjectives, when attested or otherwise known, is given, excluding, usually, those which are quite predictable; see above VII, §5.

(10) The gender of nouns, adjectives, etc. (m./f./c./inv.) is listed only when attested in a written or oral text or has become otherwise known to me. The f. adjective is listed together with the masculine form, usually with no additional reference, e.g., סקילא, סקלתא **sqīla, sqɪlta** 'beautiful'. The common plural (סקילה **sqīle**) is not listed.

(11) Predictable f. forms, such as adjectives or p.p. forms (see above VII, §4.1), usually are not given a separate entry but rather given with the m. form with no further reference. However, if the f. form has an independent lexical life, e.g., **mṭapyanēt̲a** 'female oven-baker' (lit. 'one who sticks (the dough on the oven-wall)', because only women baked like that in our community.

(12) The context citation samples after certain entries - if taken from written texts, are usually quoted in their original Hebrew spelling, followed by a phonetic transliteration, but those from the spoken registers - are given in phonetic transcription only. Usually citations from written sources (manuscripts, prints) are given first, followed by citations from oral sources.

(13) Entries or sub-entries and their meanings which are known to me from the spoken register of Z are usually left unmarked. However, all other entries are marked by their written or published source, e.g., NT= Nerwa Texts; BT=Bible Translations, etc. (see abbreviations, below). Words which are attested in NT as well as other written and oral sources are matrked by NT+. Words which are attested only once or twice the exact written source (and a context quotation, if not too long) is given, e.g., כוואז **kawwāz** 'potter' (NTU4 157a); **ʾašāra** 'signal' or **ʾōqāna** 'distress' (PolG); מאלא/ה* (OA/OS מַעְלָא; -מַעֲלֵי entrance, eve of) **māla/e** attested only once in יומד מאלד אידא **yōmıd m(ʾ)ālıd ʾēḏa** Eve of Holiday (NT5 407). However, a written source is given also in case of many common words (usually marked by "cf.", followed by the source), especially if a new context or source further supports the meaning or pronunciation or other features of the word.

(14) For words whose meaning, etymology or other features are obscure a reference is made to some old as well as recent academic literature, that may shed some additional light on it. Also all nuances of meaning, usually based on attested context, are quoted or at least indicated.

(15) VERBAL FORMS are generally listed according to their (triradical or quadriradical)roots, e.g., context טלבלה **ṭlıble** will be in the entry ט-ל-ב **ṭ-l-b**; מפולטלו **mpōlıṭlu** in פ-ל-ט **p-l-ṭ**.; מכושבננן **mxušbınnan** < כ-ש-ב-ן **x-š-b-n** 'to calculate'.[199] However, weak verbal forms whose roots are not easily identified, are usually listed with a cross-reference to their root, e.g., מרו v. א-מ-ר 1; תו v. י-ת-ו; -כיא v. י-ד-א; מארז v. ר-י-ז; האל v. י-ה-ו-ל. The basic irregular forms, especially if attested in oral or written texts, are also given in the major entry in square brackets (v. e.g., א-ז-ל, ה-ו-י) .

(16) The basic VERBAL FORMS are indicated by Arabic numerals as follows:

1 = passive participle (p.p.) forms (used in past tenses).

2 = active participle (a.p.) forms (used mostly in present-future tenses).

3 = imperative forms.

4 = infinitive forms.

(17) The VERBAL STEMS are indicated by Latin numerals as follows:

I = the ground stem (verbal noun **qṭāla**), parallel to OA פְּעַל, usually left unmarked in JNAD.

II = parallel to OA פַּעֵּל (**mqaṭōle**) .

---

[199]The reason for listing the verbs differently from nouns, etc., is because the relation of most verbal forms to their roots is much more transparent than that of nouns. The verb has only three or so patterns while the nouns come in many formations and include many loanwords from non-Semitic languages, whose root would be difficult to abstract.

II2 = same as II, but with roots whose R_2=R_3 (**mjassōse** <**j-s-s** 'to spy').

III = same as II, but with quadriradicals (**mtafsōre** < **t-f-s-r** 'to interpret').

IV = the usually causative stem, parallel to OA אַפְעֵל (**maqṭōle**).

(18) Passive participles and other verbal forms which have independent lexical value are usually listed under the m. form, e.g., סקילא, סקלתא **sqīla** (p.p.m.), **sqılta** (f.) adj. 'beautiful' (< **s-q-l** etymologically 'be polished, adorned'); מכובלא, מכובלתא **mxubla, mxōbalta** 'leper, grimy' (< **x-b-l** 'be a leper, have damaged flesh' < OA חבל).

(19) The necessitated preposition of verbs, especially when lexically meaningful, is given, e.g., **dᶜēle ṭāla** 'he prayed for her'; **dᶜēle ʾılla** 'he cursed her'.

SIGNS USED

< (derived, borrowed) from (language, previous form)

> (changed) to, resulting in, incorporated into

/ or (variant word, vowel, alternative form/meaning)

~ alternates with

√ indicates (abstract) root, often alternatively with division (i.e., √קטל = ק-ט-ל)

+ plus (morpheme plus morpheme)

- between letters indicates NA verbal roots (e.g., ק-ט-ל **q-ṭ-l** to kill); connects construct utterances of two words or more, bound particles (**l-, ʾımmıd-, bır-, d-/-d,** etc.); left out part of a word, e.g., **zāxōnāya** (m.), **-nēṯa** (f.), 'resident of Zakho'

— stands for the whole left out word when repeated in a quotation, etc.

* (1) restored form; (2) Arabic or Kurdish word/form known to me from childhood, but not found in the dictionaries; (3) a Hebrew source (in the Bibliography).

() includes info on language, source, etc

[] includes necessary attested verbal forms (of irregular verbs); external comparative info (other NA dialects, sources, or Semitic or non-Semitic languages, when relevant).

{} includes redundant words in English translation (to reflect literal NA phrase or idiom)

LIST OF GRAMMATICAL AND LANGUAGE ABBREVIATIONS

adj. = adjective

adv. = adverb

af. = אַפְעֵל

Ak = Akkadian (see Black, CAD)

Am = the JNA dialect of **ʿAmidya**

AnAr = Anatolian Arabic (see Vocke, S. - Waldner, W.)

a.p. = active participle

Ar = Arabic (usually literary)

arch. = archaic

Arm = Armenian

Arodh = the JNA dialect of **ʿArōḏın**

Az = the JNA dialects of Azerbaijan

AzT = Azeri Turkish

BA = Biblical Aramaic

BT = JNA Bible translations

c = common (gender)

ChNA = Christian Neo-Aramaic (general term; also words that are used occasionally in JNA, as in proverbs and folk songs)

coll. = collective form

constr. = construct form

cryptic = part of the cryptic language used by the Jews (when they didn't want the Gentiles or children to understand what they were saying)

D = the JNA dialect of Dihok (as attested in Bible translations; see Sabar, BT1-BT5; PolG)

decl. = declined forms (selection attested in the texts)

dim. = diminutive (caritative, indicates variety of notions, affection or belittling, etc.)

E = (general) European

En = English

euph. = euphemism

f. = feminine

Fr = French

FT = Folktales style

Gr = Greek

Gz = the Jewish Dialect of Gzira (Turkish Cizre, near Zakho; see Nakano)

H = Hebrew

hypo. = hypocoristic forms (indicate variety of notions: diminutive, affection, belittling, etc.)

interj. = interjection, exclamation

inv. = (partly or totally) invariable foreign adjective

IrAr = Iraqi Arabic (see Woodhead, D.R. - Beene, W.)

IsrH = Israeli Hebrew (loanwords; usually excluded)

It = Italian

JAB = the Judeo-Arabic dialect of Baghdad (see Avishur, Ben-Jacob, Mansour; Rajwan — Yona-Swery).

JNA = Jewish Neo-Aramaic (general term)

K = Kurdish (usually the Kurmanji dialect)

L = Latin

lit. = literally

m. = masculine

Mand = (old) Mandaic

n. = noun, note

N = the spoken JNA dialect of Nerwa

NA = Neo-Aramaic (general term)

n. abst. = noun with abstraction suffix: **-(t)ūṯa, -(t)īṯa**

n. act. = noun of (kind of) action (**qṭalta, ʾixalta, ytōta**)

n. ag. = agent noun (**qaṭāla, maqṭılāna, mqaṭlāna, mtafsırāna**)

n. unit. = nomen unitatis

NT = Nerwa Texts, or the literary dialect of Nerwa (17th century; see Sabar); see below, Bibliography NT1-NT6.

NTU = yet unpublished Nerwa Texts, mostly hymns, freely translated from Hebrew; see Bibliography: NTU1-NTU4

OA/OS = old classical literary (Jewish) Aramaic or (Christian) Syriac lexemes as listed in dictionaries (Aruch, M. Jastrow, Levy, Sokoloff; Brockelman, Paine Smith) a convenient general term vs. Neo-Aramaic

onomat. = (native) onomatopoetic

P = Persian (of varying periods, general term)

pa. = פַּעֵל conjugation

pejor. = pejorative

pl. = plural

p.n. = proper name

p.p. = passive participle

pron. = pronoun

R = Russian

sarc. = sarcastic

SyAr = Syrian Arabic (see Barthélemy)

T = Turkish (modern and Ottoman)

TA = (Babylonian) Talmudic Aramaic

Targ = Targumic (Onqelos, Jonathan)

vi = intransitive verb

v.n. = verbal noun (infinitive)

voc. = vocative (form)

vt = transitive verb

Z = the JNA dialect of Zakho

Bibliography

Note: An asterisk in this list (*) indicates a publication in Hebrew

*AlfH = Alfiye, Sh., 1986 (5746) *הגדה של פסח בשפה כורדית זאכוית* [Passover Haggadah in Jewish Neo-Aramaic of Zakho], Jerusalem.

*AlfM = Alfiye, Sh., 1987 (5747), מדרש משה, מדרשים ואגדות חז"ל בתוספת פטירת משה בשפה הכורדית [Legends on Moses in Neo-Aramaic of Zakho], Jerusalem.

Am = JNA Dialect of ʿ**Amidya** (BT1, BT2; Avidani; Hob85, Hob89; see also above II/3, and below, ZU)

Amedi, Y. = יצחק עמדי, "ממנהגי יהדות כורדיסתאן," *ילקוט מנהגים*, ערך אברהם בן יעקב, ירושלים, תשכז, עמ' 73-43

AmU1 = ʿ**Amidya** texts in the Ben-Zvi Institute ms. no. 18 ("שירים ותפסירים")

AmU2 = ʿ**Amidya** texts in the Hebrew University National Library ms. no. 8°2950

Arnold., W., 1989-1991, *Das Neuwestaramäische*, 5 vols (Semitica Viva)., Wiesbaden.

____, forthcoming, "Western Neo-Aramaic", chapter in *Aramaic Handbook*, ed. David Sperling.

Arodh = the JNA Dialect of ʿ**Arodhin** (BT2; plus oral communication)

**Aruch Completum (ערוך השלם)*, ed. A. Kohut, Vienna, 1878-1892.

*AvidH = Avidani, A., 1959 (5719), *סדר הגדה של פסח עברי-כורדי* [Passover Haggadah in Jewish Neo-Aramaic of ʿ**Amidya**], Jerusalem.

*Avin74 = Avinery, I., 1974, "ספור בניב הארמי של יהודי זאכו" [A Story in the JNA dialect of Zakho], *Sefer Hanokh Yalon*, pp. 8-16 (included in Avinery 1988 as well).

Avin78 = Avinery, I., 1978, "A Folktale in the Neo-Aramaic Dialect of the Jews of Zakho," *JAOS* 98:92-96 (included in Avinery 1988 as well).

*Avin88 = Avinery, I., 1988, *The Aramaic Dialect of the Jews of Zakho*, Jerusalem.

Avinery, I., 1976, "The Israeli Contribution to the Study of Neo-Syriac," *Afroasiatic Linguistics* 2/10, pp. 39-47.

*Avishur, Y.,1989, "מלים קשות בתרגום רס"ג," *מסורות* ג-ד (תשמ"ט), עמ' 146-131.

*___,1993a, "יסודות מן הלהג הערבי בעיראק בלשונו הערבית-יהודית של רב סעדיה גאון," *חקרי עבר וערב, מוגשים לפרופ' יהושע בלאו במלאת לו שבעים שנה*, ערך חגי בן-שמאי, ת"א-ירושלים, עמ' 35-52.

*___, 1993b, "יסודות ארמיים קדומים בערבית היהודית של עיראק," *מסורות* ז, עמ' 1-24

*___, [2001], *עברית שבערבית היהודית, המרכיב העברי והארמי בערבית היהודית של קהילות יהודי עיראק, סוריה ומצרים*, תל-אביב-יפו, תשס"א

Azerbaijani-English Dictionary, 1996, compiled under the guidance of O.I. Musayev, Baku.

*Bar-Adon, P., 1930/31, "מהארמית המדוברת אצל היהודים הכורדיים," [=several JNA proverbs], *Tsion (Yedi'ot)* I/1, pp. 12-13.

*BaBin = Barukh, Sh. - Binyamin, Y., 1973, *ספר טעמי המצוות* [JNA translations/paraphrases of Hebrew hymns and *Azharot* mostly in Z].

Barthélemy, A., 1935, *Dictionnaire Arabe-Français, Dialectes de Syrie. Alep, Damas, Liban, Jérusalem*, Paris.

*Ben-Jacob (בן-יעקב), A., 1981(2nd ed.), *Kurdistan Jewish Communities* , Jerusalem.

*___, 1985, *עברית וארמית בלשון יהודי בבל* [Hebrew and Aramaic loanwords in the Judeo-Arabic of the Jews of Baghdad].

Black, J., et al., 2000, *A Concise Dictionary of Akkadian*, Wiesbaden.

Blanc, H., 1964, *Communal Dialects in Baghdad*, Cambridge, Mass.

Blau, Joyce, 1965, *Kurdish-French-English Dictionary*, Bruxelles.

*Br48 = Brauer, E., 1948, *The Jews of Kurdistan, An Ethnological Study*, Jerusalem.

Br93 = Brauer, E., 1993, *The Jews of Kurdistan*, completed and edited by R. Patai, Detroit.

Brock. = Brockelmann, C., 1928, *Lexicon Syriacum*, Halle.

BT = Bible Translations in JNA (Z, D, Am, Arodh); see also PolG

BT1 = Sabar 1983a

BT2 = Sabar 1988a

BT3 = Sabar 1990a

BT4 = Sabar 1993

BT5 = Sabar 1994

CAD = The Chicago Assyrian Dictionary, Chicago, 1956-

Chyet, M.L., 1995, "Neo-Aramaic and Kurdish, An Interdisciplinary Consideration of Their Influence on Each Other," *Israel Oriental Studies* 15, pp. 219-252.

____, 1997, "A Preliminary List of Aramaic Loanwords in Kurdish," in *Humanism, Culture, and Language in the Near East, Studies in Honor of Georg Krorkoff, ed. A.Afsaruddin and A.H.M. Zahniser*, Winona Lake, pp. 283-300.

Clarity, B.E., et al. ed., 1964, *A Dictionary of Iraqi Arabic:English-Arabic*, Washington, D.C.

Cohen, D., 1971, "Neo-Aramaic," *Encyclopaedia Judaica vol 12: cols. 948-951.*

D = JNA dilact of Dihok, mostly as attested in BT1-BT5; see also PolG.

Denizeau, C., 1960, *Dictionnaire des parlers arabes de Syrie, Liban et Palestine; supplément au Dictionnaire arabe-français de A. Barthélemy*, Paris.

Dozy, R., 1927, *Supplément aux Dictionnaires Arabes* (2nd ed.), 2 vols., Leiden - Paris.

Drower, E. S. — Macuch, R., 1963, *A Mandaic Dictionary*, Oxford.

Duval, R., 1883, *Les dialectes néo-araméens de Salamas*, Paris [includes Jewish texts].

*Epstein, J.N., 1960, *A Grammar of Babylonian Aramaic*, Jerusalem-Tel- Aviv.

*Eshel, B.-Z., 1979, *Jewish Settlements in Babylonia During Talmudic Times, Talmudic Onomasticon, Including geographical locations, historical notes, and indices of place-names*, Jerusalem.

Fassberg, S. E., 2000, "A Contribution of Western Neo-Aramaic to Aramaic Lexicology: rḥṭ/rwṭ and rḥᶜ" *JSS* 45/2:277-291.

Fox, S. E., 1994, "The Relationships of the Eastern Neo-Aramaic Dialects," *JAOS* 114:154-62.

Fraenkel, S., 1886, *Die Aramäischen Fremdwörter im Arabischen*, Leiden.

*Friedman, Sh., 1992, "Studies in Talmudic Lexicography: אזדא," in *Language Studies* V-VI, ed. M. Bar-Asher, Jerusalem, 327-345 (English summary, p. xxxv f.).

Garbell, I., 1965, *The Jewish Neo-Aramaic Dialect of Persian Azerbaijan*, The Hague.

Garbell, I., 1965a, "The Impact of Kurdish and Turkish on the Jewish Neo-Aramaic Dialect of Persian Azerbaijan and the Adjoining Regions," JAOS 85:159-177.

*Gavish, H., 1999, *Changes in the Jewish Community of Zakho...in Folkloristic-Historic Contexts*, Ph.D. Thesis, University of Haifa.

Gewrani, A.S., 1985, *Ferhenga Kurdi Nujen Kurdi Erebi* [Kurdish Arabic Dictionary], Amman.

Greenfield, J. C., 1991, "The Verbs for Washing in Aramaic," *Semitic Studies in Honor of Wolf Leslau*, ed. A. S. Kaye, vol. I, pp. 588-594.

___, 1995, "Aramaic and the Jews," *Studia Aramaica* (JSS Supplement 4), Oxford, pp. 1-18.

*Goldenberg, G., 1988, Review article of Sabar 1984a, *Pe'amim* 36:141-156.

Goldenberg, G — Zaken, M., 1990, 'The Book of Ruth in Neo-Aramaic," *Studies in Neo-Aramaic*, ed. W. Heinrichs, Atlanta, pp. 151-157.

Goldenberg, G., 2000, "Early Neo-Aramaic and Present-Day Dialectal Diversity," JSS 45/1, pp. 69-89.

Goldenberg, G., forthcoming, "Semitic Linguistics and the General Study of Language (Gerund)," *Israel Oriental Study* 20 (in press).

Gz73 = Nakano 1973

Hava, J.G., 1964, *Al-Faraid, Arabic English Dictionary,*, Beirut.

Hob85 = Hoberman, R.D., 1985, "The Phonology of Pharyngeals and Pharyngealization in Pre-Modern Aramaic," *JAOS* 105:221-231.

Hob89 = Hoberman, R.D., 1989, *The Syntax and Semantics of Verb Morphology in Modern Aramaic, A Jewish Dialect of Iraqi Kurdistan* [= **ᶜAmidya**], New Haven.

Hob90 = Hoberman, R.D., 1990, "Reconstructing Pre-Modern Aramaic Morphology: The Independent Pronouns," *Studies in Neo-Aramaic* , ed. W. Heinrichs, Atlanta, pp. 79-88.

*Hob91 = Hoberman, R.D., 1991, "Neo-Aramaic and the Comparative Reconstructing Method," *Masororot* 5-6: 51-76.

Hob93 = Hoberman, R.D., 1993, "Chaldean Aramaic of Zakho", in R. Contini, F. Pennacchietti and M. Tosco (eds.), *Semitica: Serta Phililigica Constantino Tsereteli dicata,* Turin, 115-126

Hoberman, R.D., 1996, “Modern Aramaic” [= Christian Neo-Aramaic, Orthography], *The World’s Writing Systems*, ed. P. T. Daniels and W. Bright, New York, 504-510.

Hob97 = Hoberman, R.D., 1997, "Modern Aramaic Phonology," *Phonologies of Asia and Africa*, ed. A.S. Kaye, 313-335.

Hoberman, R.D., forthcoming, "Modern Aramaic **šımma** 'Name' and Semitic 'Triradicality'"

Hopkins, S., 1991, Review of *Studies in Neo-Aramaic*, ed. W. Heinrichs, Atlanta, in *JAOS* 111:789-790.

*___, 1993, "יהודי כורדיסתאן בארץ ישראל ולשונם," [The Jews of Kurdistan in Eretz -Yisrael and their Language], *Pe'amim* 56: 50-74.

___, 1999, "The Neo-Aramaic Dialects of Iran," *Irano-Judaica IV*, ed. Sh. Shaked - A. Netzer, pp. 311-27.

Hony, H.C., 1957, *A Turkish-English Dictionary*, Oxford.

*Israeli, Y., 1998, The Jewish Neo-Aramaic Language of Saqqiz (Southern Kurdistan), Ph.D. Dissertation, Jerusalem.

Jaba, A. - Justi, F., 1879, *Dictionnaire Kurde-Français*, St. Pétersbourg.

Jastrow, M., 1950, *A Dictionary of the Targumim, the Talmud Babli and Yerushalmi, and the Midrashic Literature*, New York.

Jastrow, O., 1989, "Notes on Jewish Maslawi," *Jerusalem Studies in Arabic and Islam* 12: 282-293.

___, 1990a, "Personal and Demonstrative Pronouns in Central Neo-Aramaic: A Comparative and Diachronic Discussion Based on Turoyo and the Eastern Neo-Aramaic Dialect of Hertevin," *Studies in Neo-Aramaic*, ed. W. Heinrichs, Atlanta, pp. 89-103.

___, 1990b, *Der Arabische Dialect der Juden von Aqra and Arbil*, Wiesbaden.

___, 1997, "The Neo-Aramaic Languages," *The Semitic Languages*, ed. R. Hetzron, London, pp. 334-377.

Kaufman, S.A., 1974, *The Akkadian Influences on Aramaic*, Chicago.

*Kapeliuk, O., 1997, "Spirantization of **t** and **d** in Neo-Aramaic", in. M. Bar-Asher, ed., *Massorot: Studies in Language Traditions and Jewish Languages* 9-11, Jerusalem,.pp. 527-544.

___, 1999, "Regularity and Deviation in Peripheral Neo-Semitic," *Tradition and Innovation, Norm and Deviation, in Arabic and Semitic Linguistics*, ed. L. Edzard -M. Nekroumi, Wiesbaden, pp. 11-21.

Khan, G., 1999. *A Grammar of Neo-Aramaic, The Dialect of the Jews of Arbel*, Leiden.

Krotkoff, G., 1985, "Studies in Neo-Aramaic Lexicology," *Biblical and Related Studies presented to Samuel Iwry*, Winona Lake, pp. 123-13.

Lane, E. W.,1863-93, *Arabic-English lexicon*, Lahore. Reprint 1978., London.

Levy, J., 1881, *Chaldäisches Wörterbuch über die Targumim*, etc., Leipzig, 2 vols.

MacD = Maclean, A.J., 1901, *Dictionary of the Dialects of Vernacular Syriac*, Oxford.

MacG = Maclean, A.J., 1895, Grammar of the Dialects of Vernacular Syriac, Cambridge.

MacKenzie, D. N., 1961, *Kurdish Dialect Studies*, vols. I-II, London.

Macuch, R., 1965, *Handbook of Classical and Modern Mandaic*, Berlin.

___, 1993, *Neumandäische Texte im Dialect von Ahwaz* unter Mitwirkung von Guido Dankwarth, Wiesbaden.

*Mansour, J., 1983, *The Judeo Arabic Dialect of Baghdad: Dictionary* (part one), Haifa.

MeAl = Meehan, Ch. — Alon, J., 1979, "The Boy whose Tunic Stuck to Him: A Folktale in the Jewish Neo-Aramaic Dialect of Zakho," *Israel Oriental Studies* 9:174-203.

Mengozzi, A., 2000., A Story in a Truthful Language, Neo-Syriac Poems by Israel of Alqosh and Joseph of Telkepe, North Iraq, 17th Century, Ph.D. Dissertaion, Leiden.

Mokri, M., 1975, *A Kurdish-Arabic Dictionary*, Beirut.

Morag, Sh., "קוי תיחום ויחסי מבנה," *לשוננו* נא (תשמ"ו), pp. 42-59.

*Mutz = Mutzafi, H., 2000a, The Jewish Neo-Aramaic Dialect of Koy Sanjaq (Iraqi Kurdistan), Phonology, Morphology, Text, and Glossary, Ph. D. Thesis, Tel-Aviv University.

Mutzafi, H., 2000b, "The Neo-Aramaic Dialect of Maha Khtaya D-Baz, Phonology, Morphology and Texts," JSS 65/2, pp. 293-322.

Nakano, A., 1969, "Preliminary Reports on the Zaxo Dialect of Neo-Aramaic: Phonology," *Journal of Asian and African Studies*, Tokyo, vol. 2: 126-142.

___, 1970, "Text of Gzira Dialect of Neo-Aramaic," Institute for the Study of Languages and Cultures of Asia and Africa, Tokyo, vol 3: 166-203.

___, 1973, *Conversational Texts in Eastern Neo-Aramaic (Gzira Dialect)*, Tokyo.

Noeldeke, Th., 1868. *Grammatik der neusyrischen Sprache am Urmia-See und in Kurdistan*, Leipzig.

NT1 = Sabar 1976a

NT2 = Sabar 1984a

NT3 = Sabar 1991a

NT4 = Sabar 1983b

NT5 = Sabar 1965

NT6 = Sabar 1981b

NTU1 = Hebrew University National Library ms. no. 8°496 ("שומרון קול תתן")

NTU2 = a page from a Nerwa ms. owned by late Hakham A. Avidani ("שוכני בתי חומר")

NTU3 = Columbia University ms. no. X893 J7382 ("לכה דודי לקראת כלה")

NTU4 = A Nerwa ms. copied in 1680, owned by Moshe Yona of Maoz Zion, Israel.

Oraham, A.J., 1943, *Dictionary of the Stabilized and Enriched Assyrian Language*, Chicago.

Payne Smith, R.+J., 1903, *Compendious Syriac Dictionary*, Oxford (offprints 1957, etc.).

Pol = Polotsky, H.J., 1967, "Eastern Neo-Aramaic: Zakho," *An Aramaic Handbook* II/1, ed. F. Rosenthal, pp. 73-77; glossary II/2, pp. 104-111.

PolG = Polotsky, Glossary cards (many of them just for attested grammatical forms) for mostly unpublished Zakho-Dihok texts; they include folktales (Z), and some translations from the Bible (Pentateuch, Judges, Samuel I-II, Kings I-II, Esther, Canticles, Ruth, and a Haggadah, probably, to judge from the spelling and vocalization, all from manuscript written by Hakham Mizrahi-Dihoki); however, loanwords from Palestinian Arabic, such as **nāmūsīye** 'bed', **s-k-r** 'to lock', and Israeli Hebrew, such as **s-d-r** 'to arrange', **s-m-ḥ** 'to be glad', which were incorporated *after* the emigration to Israel, usually are excluded from JNAD.

PolGr = Polotsky, Grammar of Jewish Neo-Aramaic of Zakho (unpublished notes).

PolU = Polotsky, Unpublished texts (numbers indicate page number of typewritten pages, mostly recordings made, copied and typed by Y. Sabar for Polotsky in the 1960's of folktales told by Yona Gabbay and some by Ishaq Shekh, both from Zakho; some very short texts are in the neighboring Christian dialects; see ChNA, above).

PolUL = Polotsky, unpublished folktales told by Simha Levi.

PolUR = Polotsky, unpublished folktales in the Dihok dialect (by Hakham Avraham Elyahu Mizrahi Dihoki, with many loanwords from Palestinian Arabic, not included in JNAD), named "Sippurim (Rivlin)", indicated by §.

*Rajwan, R., - Yona-Swery, G., 1995, *Dictionary of Iraqi Judeo-Arabic [Baghdad] Dialect*, Jerusalem.

*RivPr = Rivlin, Y.Y., 1945-1946, "פתגמים בלשון תרגום," [=Neo-Aramaic Proverbs] *Reshumot* n.s., I, pp. 207-15; II, pp. 209-214 (some quoted by proverb number marked by #).

*RivSh = Rivlin, Y.Y., 1959, *שירת יהודי התרגום* [Neo-Aramaic Biblical epics in various dialects: Zakho, Nerwa, Urmi, etc.; some with mixed dialects and many misspellings/ misprints; only Zakho and Nerwa texts were used for JNAD].

Ruth = Goldenberg — Zaken

Sa83c = Sabar 1983c

SaAC = Sabar, Y., "Agonies of Child Bearing in Kurdistan," as told by my mother Miriam Sabar.

*Sabar, Y., 1965, "Tafsirim (Commentaries) of the Bible and Hymns in the Neo-Aramaic of the Jews of Kurdistan [Nerwa]," *Sefunot* 10: 337-412.

*___, 1974a, " The Hebrew Elements in the Neo-Aramaic Dialect of the Jews of Zakho in Kurdistan," *Lešonenu* 38: 206-219

___, 1974b, "Nursery Rhymes and Baby Words in the Jewish Neo-Aramaic Dialect of Zakho (Iraq)," *JAOS* 94: 329-336.

___, 1974c, "First Names, Nicknames and Family Names Among the Jews of Kurdistan," *Jewish Quarterly Review* 65: 43-51.

*___, 1975a, "The Hebrew Elements in the Neo-Aramaic Dialect of the Jews of Azerbaijan," *Lešonenu* 39: 272-294.

___, 1975b, "The Impact of Israeli Hebrew on the Neo-Aramaic Dialect of the Kurdish Jews of Zakho: A Case of Language Shift," *Hebrew Union College Annual* 46: 489-508.

___, 1976a, Pešaṭ Wayhi Bešallaḥ, *A Neo-Aramaic Midrash on Beshallah (Exodus), Introduction, Phonetic Transcription, Translation, Notes and Glossary*, Wiesbaden.

___, 1976b, "Lel-Huza: Story and History in a Cycle of Lamentations for the Ninth of Ab in the Jewish Neo-Aramaic Dialect of Zakho, Iraqi Kurdistan," *JSS* 22: 138-162.

___, 1978, “Multilingual Proverbs (Neo-Aramaic, Kurdish, Arabic) in the Neo- Aramaic Dialect of the Jews of Zakho,” *International Journal of Middle East Studies* 9:215-235.

___, 1978, “From Tel-Kepe (A Pile of Stones) in Iraqi Kurdistan to Providence, Rhode Island: The Story of a Chaldean Immigrant to the U.S.A in 1927,” *JAOS* 98:410-415.

*___, 1981a, “Qistit Hanna: A Neo-Aramaic Rhymed Legend on the Martyrs Hanna and Her Seven Sons,” *Pe’amim* 7:83-99.

*___, 1981b, “A Midrashic Commentary on the Book of Jonah in the Neo-Aramaic of the Jews of Kurdistan,” *Jewish Thought in Islamic Lands*, ed. M. Zohory, Jerusalem, pp. 131-143.

*___, 1981c, ”מילון מונחים” (glossary of jewelry and material culture) in *יהודי כורדיסתאן: אורח חיים, מסורת ואמנות*, Jerusalem:Israel Museum, catalogue no. 216, pp. 266-69; an English edition: *The Jews of Kurdistan, Daily Life, Customs, Arts and Crafts*, Israel Museum, Jerusalem, 2000.

___, 1982 “The Quadriradical Verb in Eastern Neo-Aramaic Dialects,” *JSS* 27:149-76.

*___, 1983a, *The Book of Genesis in Neo-Aramaic in the Dialect of the Jewish Community of Zakho, Including Selected Texts in Other Neo-Aramaic Dialects, and Glossary*, Jerusalem: The Hebrew University, Language Traditions Project.

*___, 1983b, “A Midrashic Commentary on Isaiah 10:32 - 12:6 in the Neo-Aramaic of the Kurdish Jews,” *Studies in Aggadah and Jewish Folklore* VII, ed. I. Ben-Ani, J. Dan, Jerusalem, pp. 317-336.

*___, 1983c, “Two Midrashic Commentaries to Jeremiah 8:13 - 9:23 in the Neo-Aramaic Dialects of Zakho and Amidya,” *Aramaeans, Aramaic and the Aramaic Literary Tradition*, ed. M. Sokoloff, Ramat-Gan, pp. 11-41.

*___, 1984a, *Homilies in the Neo-Aramaic of the Jews of Kurdistan for the Biblical Portions of* Wayḥi *(Genesis),* Beshallaḥ *and* Yitro *(Exodus)*, edited and translated into Hebrew with comparative Midrashic notes and glossary, Jerusalem: Israel Academy of Sciences and Humanities, Jewish Language Series.

___, 1984b, “The Arabic Elements in the Jewish Neo-Aramaic Texts of Nerwa and ‘Amadiya, Iraqi Kurdistan,” *JAOS* 104: 201-211.

*___, 1988a, *The Book of Exodus in Neo-Aramaic, in The Dialect of the Jewish Community of Zakho, including selected texts in other Neo-Aramaic dialects and a glossary*, Jerusalem:The Hebrew University, Language Traditions Project.

*___, 1988b, “The Neo-Aramaic Dialects and the Other Languages Spoken by the Jews of Kurdistan,” *Studies in Jewish Languages*, ed. M. Bar-Asher, Jerusalem, pp. 87-111.

___, 1989, "Substratal and Adstratal Elements in Jewish Neo-Aramaic," *Studia Linguistica et Orientalia Memoriae Haim Blanc Dedicata*, ed. P. Wexler et al, Wiesbaden, pp. 264-76.

*___, 1990a *The Book of Leviticus in Neo-Aramaic in the Dialect of the Jewish Community of Zakho, Including selected Texts in Other Neo-Aramaic Dialects and a Glossary.* Jerusalem: The Hebrew University, Language Traditions Project, 1990.

___, 1990b, "General European Loanwords in the Jewish Neo-Aramaic Dialect of Zakho, Iraqi Kurdistan," *Studies in Neo-Aramaic*, ed. W. Heinrichs, Atlanta, pp. 53-66.

___, 1991a, *Targum de-Targum, An Old Neo-Aramaic Version of the Targum of Song of Songs (Introduction, Eclectic Text, English Translation, and Glossary)*, Wiesbaden, 1991.

___, 1991b, A Review-Article of: I. Avinery1988, *JAOS* 111: 653-656.

___, 1991c, "The Hebrew Bible Vocabulary as Reflected through Traditional Oral Neo-Aramaic Translations," *Semitic Studies in honor of W. Leslau*, ed. A.S. Kaye, Vol. II, Wiesbaden, pp. 1385-1401.

*___, 1993, *The Book of Numbers in Neo-Aramaic in the Dialect of the Jewish Community of Zakho, Including selected Texts in Other Neo-Aramaic Dialects and a Glossary*, Jerusalem: The Hebrew University, Language Traditions Project.

___, 1994, *The Book of Deuteronomy in Neo-Aramaic , in the Dialect of the Jewish Community of Zakho, Including selected Texts in Other Neo-Aramaic Dialects and a Glossary*, Jerusalem: The Hebrew University, Language Traditions Project.

___, 1995, "The Christian Neo-Aramaic Dialects of Zakho and Dihok: Two Text Samples," *JAOS* 115: 33-51.

___, 1996, "Christian Neo-Aramaic Love Songs in a Jewish Manuscript," *Israel Oriental Studies* 16 *(Studies in Modern Semitic Languages*): 85-91.

___, 1999a, "The Hebrew Elements in Written Jewish Neo-Aramaic Texts (in Manuscripts and Printed Texts)," *Vena Hebraica in Judaeorum Linguis, Proceedings of the 2nd International Conference on the Hebrew and Aramaic Elements in Jewish Languages (Milan, October 23-26, 1995)*, ed. Sh. Morag et al., Milano, pp. 387-397.

___,1999b, "Parallel Patterns of Development in Jewish Neo-Aramaic and Modern Israeli Hebrew," *Leshonenu* 62 (5759/1999): 333-344.

___, (forthcoming a) "Zakho", *Encyclopaedia of Islam*, new edition

___, (forthcoming b), "The Story of the Two Brothers Ali and Amar in the the Jewish Neo-Aramaic Dialect of Zakho (as recordeb by A. Socin in 1870)," Otto Jastrow Festschrift.

SaLH = Sabar 1976b

SaNR = Sabar 1974b

Sara, S. I., 1974, *A description of modern Chaldean*, The Hague.

Segal, J.B., 1955, "Neo-Aramaic Proverbs of the Jews of Zakho,", *Journal of Near Eastern Studies* 14: 251-70 (quoted by proverb number).

ShiKC = Shilo, V., 1986, *הבישול הכורדי* *(Kurdistani Cooking)*, Jerusalem.

Shilo, V., 1995, *מילון עברי-ארמי-אשורי בלהג יהודי זאכו* [Hebrew Neo-Aramaic:Zakho], Jerusalem.

Socin, A., 1882, "Der Dialekt der Juden von Zacho," in *Die Neu-Aramaeischen Dialecte von Urmia bis Mosul, Tübingen*, pp. 159-66.

SokBA = Sokoloff, M., forthcoming, A Dictionary of Jewish Babylonian Aramaic of the Talmudic and Gaonic Periods.

SokPA = Sokoloff, M., 1990, *A Dictionary of Jewish Palestinian Aramaic of the Byzantine Period*, Ramat-Gan.

Steingass, F., 1963, *A Comprehensive Persian-English Dictionary*, London.

Stowasser, K. — Ani, M., 1964, *A Dictionary of Syrian Arabic:English-Arabic*, Washington D.C.

Vocke, S. — Waldner, W., 1982, *Der Wortschatz des anatolischen Arabisch*, Erlangen.

Wahby, T. — Edmonds, C.J., 1966, *A Kurdish-English Dictionary*, Oxford.

Wehr, H., 1966, *A Dictionary of Modern Written Arabic*, Ithaca.

Woodhead, D.R. — Beene, W., 1967, *A Dictionary of Iraqi Arabic, Arabic -English*, Washington.

*Yona, M., 1989, האובדים בארץ אשור, יהודי כורדיסטאן וזאכו, Jerusalem.

*___, 1999. מילון ארמי-כורדי-עברי [=Kurdish Aramaic-Hebrew Dictionary, i.e., Jewish Neo-Aramaic of Zakho], Jerusalem.

Zaken, M., 1997, "'גורלם של ממציאים', סיפור עם בארמית חדשה של יהודי זאכו" [folktale in JNA of Z], *Massorot* 9-10-11, pp. 383-394.

ZU = Zakho unpublished, Hebrew University National Library ms. no. 8°494 (some of the texts, mostly translations of Hebrew hymns, seem to have originated in Amidya).

Dictionary

א (ʾ)

א (H; OA/OS אָלֶף)f. **ʾāle/af** the first letter of the Hebrew alphabet; **xa** one. cf. אלף-בית.

א-, אה-, ה- (OA ה-) **-a(h)** (NT), **-a** (Z), her, hers (suffixed pron.)

אא (<הא) **ʾā** hah, so?! (indicates wondering) (MeAl 191).

אבאהי, אאבהי, אאב'אהי (K < P آبادي) inv. **ʾāvāhi** settled, populated (place) (NT+).

אאבה (K) f. **ʾāve** stream, current (PolU 375).

עאגורא, אאגורא (K < Ar < P/OS < Ak **ʾagurru**) f. **+ʾājurra, +ʾā-** kiln-fired brick; pl. עָאגֻרֵי **+ʿājurre** (BaBin138).

אאג'א (K/P) m. **ʾāġa** master, agha; **ʾāġāti** My agha, Sir; — **mtangēba** 'our guy' (=the story's hero; lit., my gentleman from that side) (PolU 17); pl. אַגַ'וַת **ʾāġāwat** (RivSh 277); **ʾāġāyat, ʾāġālárat** (PolU 444); **ʾāġāye** (AmU2 5b); **ʾāġawātat**.

אאדי (OA הדי) c. **ʾādi** this, that one (NT); cf. אידי, אד [Khan 561 **ʾadi**].

אאדמי (Ar) m. **ʾādami** human being (NT); cf. אדם, נאשא.

אאהו, אאהון, אהון, אָהוּא (OA הַהוּא, הָהוּ that one; אִיהוּ he; OS ܗܘ; Mand האהו) **ʾāhu(n)** he, that one (m.); cf. אאוא, או 1 (NT, BT1:D, Am; BT4, D; AvidH 20).

אאהופ (< ?) inv. **+ʾāhūp** stark naked; often following שולכאיא **šulxāya** naked, with nothing at all (cf. PolU 144).

אאהי, אאהין, אהין, אָהִי, אאיי (OA הָהִיא, הָהִי, אִיהִי) **ʾāhi(n), ʾāyi** she, that one (f.); cf. אי 1 אאיא, (NT, BT1:D, Am; BT4, D; AvidH 24).

אאהת 1, אאהד, אָהֶת (OA אַתְּ, אַנְתְּ) **ʾāhıt/d** you (m.sg.); may be used as object pronoun: אָנָא אָהֶת לַגְ גְשׁוֹקֶינָא **ʾāna ʾāhıt lag gšōqēna** I'll not forsake you; cf. לוך-, יתן- (NT+) [Khan 81 **ʾat/ʾāti**].

אאהת 2 (OS ܐܢܬܝ) **ʾāhat** you (f. sg.); cf. אתן-לך-, (NT+) [Khan 81 **ʾat**].

אאוא (< אאהו) **ʾāwa** he, that one, it (m.) (NT+).

אאור (K) m. **ʾāwar** farina dish made with fried fat; cf. ארכאבכה.

אאזא, אזיי, אזאיי, אזאדי (K/P) inv. **ʾāza, ʾazāyi, ʾazādi** set-free, liberated (slave) (NT+).

אאזכתא (K **āsik** آسك) f. **ʾāzıkta** gazelle; pl. אאזכיאתא **ʾāzıkyāta** (NT); cf. ג'זאלא.

אאז'ארה (K vintage) pl. **ʾāžāre** green vegetables used for soup (ShiKC 93).

אאי (OA) interj. **+ʾāy** Woe! Auch! **hēš lē(we) mīra ʾāy rēši** It (= cooked meat, etc.) is still rare, not cooked enough (lit., has not said : Auch, my head!); cf. אאך.

אאיא 1 (< אי 1) **ʾāya** she, that one, it (f.); ולא אאיא ובס **ula ʾāya ubass** And not only that (but also ...); cf. אאדי (NT+).

אאיא 2 (Ar) f. **ʾāya** any one of the Ten Commandments (v. עשר אאית); נטארד איאתוך **naṭārıd ʾayātox** keepers of Your Commandments (= Israel) (NT5 392).

אאיי, אאי (< אאהי ?) **ʾāyi** (mentioned) above (?) (NT1).

אאך, אך, אוך (P/K) interj. **+ʾāx, +ʾōx** Auch! Alas! **ʾāx ʾāx** What a pity (said after reminiscing of painful memories); **ʾāx-ʾōx** pain, suffering (RivSh 116); cf. א-כ-א-כ.

אאכא (OA אחא) m. **ʾāxa** brother; cf. אכונא; pl. אכואתא **ʾaxawāta** (NT).

אאכורא (AnAr/K < P; cf. OA אָהֻוֶרְיָרָא stable master) f. **+ʾāxōra** stable, manger.

אאכרי (Ar-K) adv. **ʾāxıri** finally (PolG).

אאלא (K آلی side, border) f. **ʾāla** side, direction; **ʾāl šarqi** eastward (=H מִזְרָחָה, BT); **zılle bēʾal** (< **b+ʾe-**) He went this way; **bēʾal, byāʾal** this way, that way; all kinds of things, etc. (SaAC 1); **mın ʾıdyo ulēʾal** from today on; **ʾāl lıʾal** to the other side (Socin 163); also used as accusative marker in BT (=H אֶת): **šqōl ʾāl brōnox** Take your son; pl. אלאלה **ʾalāle** (cf. PolG) (NT+) [Khan 573 **lāʾa**!].

אאלאכא (<אאלא) **ʾālāka** side of face (PolU 229).

אלג'י v. אאלג'י

אאלנאיה (< אאלא?/P **ʾalān**, Iranian people near the Caspian Sea?) pl. **ʾālanāye** outsiders (?) enemies (?); usually in hendiadys with כפורה **kapore** infidels: **kapōre uʾālanāye lag ʿāfe ldan hōzāye** Infidels and enemies don't show mercy unto those Jews (SaLH 152); **kapore u'ālanāye hāwe bḥāli** May infidels and enemies be in my condition (said by a suffering woman when asked how she was doing).

אאמן, אמאן (OA/OS/Mand מָאנָא, מָאן < √אני; cf. Ak **unūtu** vessel) m. **'āman** (Z), **'amān**? (NT5 410) vessel, dish; pl. אמאנה **'amāne** (NT+)[MacD 152 **mānā, āmānā, āmān**].

אאן v. יאן

אאנא, אנא (OA אֲנָא; OS ܐܢܐ) **'āna** I (c.); may be used as object pronoun: בַּלֵי אַהִית אֲנַא לַאת גִימַחֲבֵיתִין **bale 'āhıt 'āna lat gımaḥübētın** But you don't love me (RivSh 223) (NT+).

אאני, אאנה (OA הָנְהֵי, הָנֵי) **'āni, 'āne** (+NT), they (c.); cf. אהנון.

אאסא, עאסא (OA/OS אָסָא < Ak **āsu**) m. **'/ʿāsa** (Z) aromatic myrtle (used for benediction בורא עצי בשמים) [Garbell 298: **asse**].

אאסמאג'ון (P) m. **'āsmajun** sky-blue cloth. NT3.

אאסנא, אאסרא (K?) m. **'āsın/ra** valley, territory (PolU 295).

אאפה (Ar) f. **'āfe** misfortune, mishap; pl. אאפתיאתא **'āfıtyāṯa** (NT+).

אאפורא (K?) **'āfōra** odd whatever (PolU 80).

אאפרא (K) m. **'āfırra** fodder; pl. אאפרה, אאפרת, **'āfırre, 'afırrat**.

אאקא (OA עקא) f. **'āqa** trouble; cf. איקו; pl. אאקתיאתא, אאקה, **'āqıtyāṯa, 'āqe** (NT5 398).

אאקו (< יעקב) **'āqo** Jack (hypo. of Jacob); cf. איכו.

אארא (OA אגרא) m. **'a'ra, 'āra** reward, payment (NT)[cf. Mengozzi 189 **'ārā, 'aġrā**]

אאשא (OA עשא) m. **'āša** moth; cf. אכלא.

אאשיבכה (K) f. **'āšīvke** waterfall, cascade; pl. **'āšīvkat**.

אאבאהי v. אבאהי

אב בית דין (H) m. **'āv bēṯ dīn** supreme judge in a Jewish court (NT).

אבד 1, -אב v.-ב 1

אבד 2, אבדאן (K<Ar) adv. **'abad, 'abadán** ever, never; אבתה אבתאן **'abaté-'abatán** never-ever (=H לְעוֹלָם וָעֶד, BT, AlfH 93); אבדאן ואצלאן **'abdán wa'ṣlán** never, in no way! (SaLH 150); totally: - **tīmīle** he totally annihilated them (PolU 33).

אבדון (H) m. **'evaddón** (!) hell: **zıllu b'evaddón** They went to hell, were lost (and I don't care; don't bother me).

אַבָדִי (< אבד 2) inv. **'abādi** eternal; **'-w-ḏ** – to eternalize (=H לְנַצֵּחַ, AvidH 71).

אבדנותא (< אבד 2) **'abadanūṯa** eternity (=H נֶצַח, AlfH 93).

אבוקאט (AnAr < T < It avvocato) m. **'abuqáṭ** 'advocate' (sarc.), smooth talker.

אבות (H) pl. **'āvōṯ** the Forefathers; **bzaxus d'āvōs** (Z) By the virtue of the Forefathers (said when invoking God's help) (NT+).

אבזארא (OA אַבְזָרָא < P **abzār** instrument) m. **'avzāra** comb in a loom [MacD 1< OS].

אבזונא (Ar إبزيم/K < P **awzīn** > OA אב/פזינא) m. **'avzūna** buckle, ring.

ב-א-י 1 v. ב-א-י

א-ב-י 2, ע-ב-י II (OA ע-ב-י) **'-b-y, ʿ-b-y** (NT4; Arodh; AmU2 5b), to swell (vi/vt), inflate, impregnate (pejor.); die (pejor.); cf. מְאַבְיינַא.

אביאנא (OA עוביאנא) m. **'ıbyāna** swelling.

אבינו (H) **'āvīnu** our forefather (following the name of Abraham, Isaac, Jacob) (NT+).

אַבִינִי, אַוִינִי (K ئەڤين 'love') **'av/wīni** grace (=H חֵן, PolG).

אֲבֵלוּת (H) f. **'ıvēlūṯ** mourning period (=H אוֹן, BT5, D).

אבנוס (OS, Ar) m. **'abanōs** ebony.

אבן שתייה (H) f. **'ēven šaṯīya** the foundation stone in the Temple on which the world was founded. NT2.

אבני אפוד (H) pl. **'avné 'ēfóḏ** the precious stones on the breast garment of the high priest. NT2.

אבראזא (K) m. **'avrāza** steep slope, hard climb. Pol 105; pl. **'avrāziyat** (PolU 430).

אברד v. ברונא

אברהם, אברו, אבי (H) **+'avrāham, +'avro, +'avvi** Abraham, Abe, Aby (hypo.).

אבריסם (Ar < P > OA אַבְרֵישׁוֹם) m. **'abrēsım** silk (NT+).

אבתא (< ב-א-י) f. **'ıbbıta** (?) wish, will: אני באבתיה אילו צלואתא דיני **'ınni b'ıbbıteh-īlu ṣlawāṯa dēni** Because our prayers are {in} His wish (NT2 97; NT5 390; NTU4 148a).

אבתה אבתאן v. אבד 2

אבתי (< אבד 2) inv. **'abatí** eternal, good for long time (Zaken 391).

אגר 1 (K/P/T) conj. **ʾagar** if, even if.
אגר 2 (< K 'fire'?) m. **agar** anguish: **mayle – lıbbu** What is anguishing them? (PolG).
אגאא, אגׄאה (OA תשעא) **⁺ʾıčʾa** nine (c.); דאגאא **dʾıčʾa** the ninth (NT+).
אגאי (OA תשעין) **⁺ʾıčʾi** ninety (NT+).
אגאמא, אגאא אמאייה (OA תשע מאה) **⁺ʾıččaʾma** (NT), **⁺ʾıčʾa ʾımmāye** (Z), nine hundred.
אגאסר (OA תשע עשר, תְּשַׁסַר) **ʾıččaʾsar** nineteen (NT+).
א-ג-ב (< ע-ג׳-ב) **ʾ-j-b** to wish, to want [1:**ʾjıblēle** he wanted/it pleased him; 2: **ʾājıble** he wishes/it pleases him) (NT+).
אגבונא (< א-ג׳-ב) m. **ʾıjbōna** desire, wish.
אגו (< יצחק) **ʾıččo** Isaac (hypo.).
אגרסי (IrAr?) inv. **ʾačrasi** a type of fine dates.
א-כ-ב v. א-ג׳-ב
אכדאדה v. אג׳דאדה
אאג׳את v. אַגַ׳וַת
אד (OA אִידֵי, הדי) **ʾad** this (c.), the; בד [< +ב אד] **bad** in this (NT).
א-ד-ב II (Ar) vt **ʾ-d-b** to educate, teach good manners (including by punishment) (PolG).
אדב (Ar) m. **ʾadab** good manners, education; reproach (=H מוּסָר, BT) (NT+).
אדב-כאנא (IrAr/T) f. **ʾadab-xāna** (public) restroom (euph.); pl. **ʾadab-xānat**.
אכדאדה v. אדג׳אדה
אדוא, אִידְוַא (OA/OS עַדבא, עדווא) m. **ʾıdwa** (Z **ʾızwa**) lot, fate (=H גּוֹרָל, BT3, D) (NT+).
אדודא (<?) m. **ʾadōda** pestle.
אדוני 1 (H) **ʾadōnāy** (Z **⁺ʾazōnāy**) God (mainly in Hebrew rituals).
אדוני 2 (H) **ʾadōni** Master, Rabbi; טפאיד אדונים **ṭappāyıd ʾadōnīm** the Rabbis' Hill (Cemetery) (Am, Br48 169).
א-ד-י II(Ar) vt **ʾ-d-y** to hurt, damage (NT+).
אדיא (< אד) **ʾadya** this (c.); בדיא **badya** in this. NT; BT1, Am **ʾadya**; AvidH 17: לֵילֵי אַדְיָא **lēle** (m.) **ʾadya** this night; ibid. 46: מַצָּה אַדְיָא **maṣṣa** (f.) **ʾadya** this matzah (NT+).
אדיו (< אד+יומא) adv. **ʾıdyo** (Z) today; **(m) – tmanya** a week ago/a week from today (NT+).
אָדִייֵ (Ar) f. **ʾadīye** harm, affliction (=H צוּקָה, AvidH 67).
אדלל (< אד+לילה) adv. **ʾıdlal** (Z **ʾızlal**) tonight.
אדמא (<?) **ʾıdma** (Z **ʾızma**) brother-in-law; cf. אידמתא [MacD 9:< OS ܝܒܡܐ **yabmā**].

אדן (Ar) **ʾıdın** (Z **ʾızın**) permission (PolG).
אדר (H) m. **ʾādar** (Z **⁺ʾāzar**) the Hebrew month of Adar (March); **bēbūn** – anemone(s).
אהאלי (Ar) pl. **ʾahāli** population, people.
אהבה שלום (H) **ʾahavá-šālōm** love and piece; **pıšla (!) — gawōhun** to have amicable relationship (PolU 351).
אהד, עהד (K < Ar عـهـد) m. **ʾahıd** (Z), **ʿahıd** (NT3) oath, promise; **drēle ʾahıd ʾıl gyāne** He put himself under an oath; **ʿahde ʿarabi** irreversible ('Arab') oath (PolG).
א-ה-ד II (< אהד) **ʾ-h-d** to promise (PolUR 2).
אאהוא, אהון v. אאהון
אאהין v. אהין
אהיה אוד אהיה (H) **ʾehye ʾōd ʾehye** I am what I am (BT2).
אהנון, אַהֲנוּן (OA אִינְהוּ/הנון/אינון) **ʾahnun** they (c.)(NT; AvidH 36; BT4, D; Sa83c, Am); cf. אאני; אאהון אאהין.
אהת v. אאהת
או 1, אוו, אַיו (< אאהו) **ʾaw** the, that (m.); בו **baw** in the; לְיו, לוד **law(d)** to that which; cf. אאוא אוכין, (NT+).
או 2, אוד (< או 1) **ʾō (d)** the, this (m.)(=H אֲשֶׁר, BT, inv.); cf. אוהא.
או 3 (K) voc. O; also suffixed: **ʾō, gāvānō** O Cattleman (PolU 6); cf. אודא 3, אי.
אואדא 1 (< א-ו-ד) m. **ʾawāda** (Z **ʾawāza**) maker; אואדת עגאבה **ʾawādıt ʿajābe** Maker of wonders (God) (NT+).
אואדא 2 (< א-ו-ד) v.n. **ʾwāda** (Z **ʾwāza**) doing, making (NT+).
(א)וא(הא) (< אאוא) **(ʾa)wā(ha)** that one there; **wā yāla** (MeAl 179) that boy yonder;v. אוהא.
אוואיה (Ar اوانی 'vessels' ?) pl. **ʾawāye** (material) things; **zunnu ⁺rāba ʾawāye** They bought many things [Khan 562 **ʾawaʾe**].
אוארא 1 (<א-ו-ר) m. **ʾawāra** passerby; **ʾawāre napāqe** visitors (MeAl 190, n.72).
אוארא 2 (<א-ו-ר) **ʾwāra** to pass, enter; entering, crossing (NT+).
אוג׳ג, אוגׄך (T 'fire-place, hearth') m. **ʾōjaġ/x** (extended) family, clan; pl. **ʾōjāġe**.
אוג׳לן (T) m. **⁺ʾoġlan** jack (in deck of cards).
א-ו-ד (OA עבד) **ʾ-w-d** (Z **ʾ-w-z**) to make, do, perform; לא אויד לאלי **la ʾwīd lāli** (The

sin) was not committed by me (NT3); **ʾilāha la ʾāwız** May God not do it (= let it happen, said about a misfortune; SaAC 3); **⁺rāba ʾuzle brēšan** He caused us a lot of pain (cf. PolG); **la gōzi ʾımmıd xauxıt** They don't get along; **ʾuzla xāʾ ʾılle** She (verbally) attacked him so much, that [1:ʾwid-/ʾuz-; 2: גאאוד **gʾāwid** (NT), **gēwız** (Z), **gō(zı)t; mōz-** (‹ma+ʾōz-; PolU 210); 3:ʾōz]; IV to employ, make work: **xmāsi gmaʾuzābi ⁺rāba šūla** My mother-in-law makes me do a lot of work; **lmaʾōze** to fix (= H לתיקון, PolG).

אודא 1 (OA עבדא) m. **ʾōda** slave; pl. **⁺ʾōde** (NT+).

אודא 2 (IrAr < T) f. **⁺ʾōda** room; pl. **⁺ʾōde**

אודא 3 (< או+דאיה 3) voc. **ʾō-dā** OMother, Ma!

אודותא (OA עבדותא) **ʾōdūṯa** slavery (NT+).

אודם (H) **ʾōdem** ruby (BT2).

אוהא, דוהא (< או 2) m. **ʾ/dōha** this (one here); **ʾōha bištof-īle** This one is better; **hulli ta dōha** I gave to this one; cf. אואהא.

אווא (<?) inv. **ʾuwwa** painful, it hurts (baby talk).

אוטו(ף) (< או+טוף) adv. **ʾōto(f/v)** thus, like this, this manner (MeAl 192); cf. מאטו בשטוף.

א-ו-י II (< איוא) vt **ʾ-w-y** to cloud.

אוי v. אי...אוי

אַוִינִי v. אַבִינִי

אוך v. אאך

אוכי (K) interj. **ʾuxay** Hurrah! Very good! (NT1); אוכי אוכי (NTU4 183a)[cf. Garbell 323 **⁺oxxay** 'exclamation of relief'; MacD **ʾuxay**].

אוכין, אוכינא (< או+כינא) m. **ʾawxın, ʾāwxēna** the other one (NT+).

אול, אוול (Ar) adv., adj. **ʾawwal** first(ly) (NT+).

אוולי (K < Ar) f. **ʾawwali** beginning.

אוולא (Ar) inv. **ʾawla** able, skillful (cf. PolU 391).

אוליתא v. אליתא

אומבאשי (T **onbaşı**) **umbāši** Turkish officer, colonel (PolU 364).

אומות העולם (H) pl. **ʾummōṯ haʿōlām** world's nations, Gentiles (NT+).

אומיתא v. אמתא

און v. יאן

און-גליות (OS-H) **ʾāwen-gālīyōṯ** the Gospels (sarc.); cf. אנגיל.

אונס (K < Ar) p.n.m. **ʾūnıs** Jonas (PolU 231).

אוסו, אוסיכא, אוסכא (< יוסף) **ʾūso, ʾōsīka, ʾūsaka** Joe, Joey (hypo. of Joseph).

אווסלא (<?) m. **ʾawısla** wine-press (NT4; RivSh 278:אַוִסְלָא, אַבְסְלַא) [MacD 6 **ʾāwislā** 'reservoir'].

אוסתאדא v. אסתאדא

אוצמלי (T) inv. **⁺ʾosmalli** Ottoman (PolUR 48).

אוף, -אוף v. -אפ

אוקד(א), אתקד(א) (< או, אד+קדרא) adv. **ʾōqad(da), ʾaṯqad(da)** (Z **ʾas-**; RivSh 137, 235: אוֹקַת **ʾōqat**, אַתְקַד; Hob89 182 **ʾaqqat**) so much, that many; hardly: **ʾōqad mōnıxli, xa xuwwe wēle bıxyāša xazri** I hardly looked, and there I saw a snake crawling near me; **ʾōqad ʾībi** I cannot continue any more; **tré-ga ʾōqat xét/ʾıl ʾōqad** twice as much (PolG); **p-y-š ʾōqad xıt** become very happy.

אוקאנא (< א-י-ק) **ʾōqāna** strait, distress (PolG; PolU 139).

א-ו-ר (OA עבר) vi **ʾ-w-r** enter, pass, cross; **ʾurra go ʾēne** He became very angry; **čuxa la ʾurre qam ʾēne** None seemed fit to him; didn't like anyone (to marry); **ʾurra ʿanne** She forgave him (cf. PolU 340); **ʾurta wēla bšınne** She had been quite old (NT+).

אורגֿא (<?) f. **ʾurja** fried meat kebab; pl. **ʾurje**.

אורוא v. רורוא

אורופא (T/IrAr < It) f. **⁺ʾuruppa** Europe.

אורזא (K < Sanskrit **vrsa**) m. male (NT+).

אורזותא (< אורזא) f. **ʾurzūṯa** masculinity; foreskin (=H עָרְלָה, BT2, D; penis (=H שָׁפְכָה, BT5).

אורים ותומים (H) pl. **ʾūrīm utummīm** Urim and Thummim (oracles)(NT, BT).

אורכא (OA אורחא) f. **ʾurxa** road, way; **-d ʾızāla ula dʿāra** (Have) a one-way trip! (curse); **māt sēla bʾurxe** whatever life brought his way; pl. אורכאתא **ʾurxāṯa**; v. -מ כ-י, ד-ו-ק (NT+).

אורתכא (OS ܐܘܪܬܟܐ) f. **ʾurtxa** packing needle.

אותי (IrAr/AnAr < T) f. **ʾūti** flat iron; **mxēle**

b'ūti He ironed.
אותיל (IrAr/AnAr < Fr) m.'utēl hotel.
אזא, איזא (OA עזא) f. 'ızza she-goat; pl. אזה 'ızze (NT+).
אזאדי v. אאזא
אזאלא 1 (<א-ז-ל 1) m. 'azāla walker, traveler; 'azāle u'asāye travelers.
אזאלא 2 (< א-ז-ל 2) 'zāla spinning, to spin.
אזבני (K) 'azbani Sir, 'I am your slave' (PolU 116).
א-ז-ל 1 (OA אזי/אזל) '-z-l to go; שמה זלה בכולא עולם šımme zılle bkulla ʿōlām His name became famous all over the world; 'īze la gēzi qāṭılla He cannot bring himself to kill her (MeAl 179); 'aqlās xa mınnu la zıllu None of them moved (PolG); לשא גיזיל וכיסי lašša gēzıl ukēse Her body shivers (ZU 72a); trē-ga zılle sēle bxabra He repeated it twice (SaAC 18) [1:zıl-; 2:gē(zı)l; bā(zı)l;'ā(zı)l; qū dāx Get up, let us go; 'āzi; 3:sī (m.), sē (f.); sūn (NT, RivSh 122)/sāwun (Z, Zaken 390) (pl.c.); 4:'izāla/yzāla] (NT+).
א-ז-ל 2 (OA אזל/עזל; cf. Ar غزل) '-z-l to spin (a yarn) [1:'zıl-; 2:'āzla; 3:'zōl; 4:'zāla].
אזלא (< א-ז-ל 2) m. 'ızla yarn; 'ızlıd qōta spider's web; pl. 'ızlāle.
אזלתא (< א-ז-ל 2) f. 'azalta spinner (of yarn).
אִזְמַרֶיגֿ (Ar < Gr) 'ızmarej sapphire, emerald (=H סַפִּיר, BT2, D).
אזן v. אדן
אֶזְנַוָותַא (<?) pl. 'eznawāṯa torments, prayers (=H נַפְתּוּלִים BT1, D).
אז'דהר (K/P) m. 'aždahar dragon, monster; vicious person; pl. 'aždahāre.
אח (<?) 'aḥḥ inv. delicious, sweet, goody-goody (baby talk); cf. אח.
אחמקין (Ar) pl. 'aḥmaqīn fools (PolU 41).
אחסאן (Ar) m. 'ıḥsān favor, kindness; pl. אחסאנה 'ıḥsāne (NT5 385).
אי 1 (< אאהי) c. (NT)/f. (Z) 'ay that, the; bay šāta in that year; hīl day šāta till that year; 'ay xa šāta It has been a year; 'ay 'āhıt, 'ay 'āya This is now up to you and her; cf. או 1.
אי 2 (< איהא) c. (NT)/f. (Z) 'ē this, the.
אי 3 (K) 'ay O (vocative) (BT4); cf. אי'.

אי 4, הי (OA הֵן, אֵין; OS اِی) 'ē, hē yes; 'ē-'e yes indeed, well then (said as a summation before moving to a new subject) [Khan 562 'e]
אי...אוי (onomat.): la 'uzli la 'ay la 'oy I din't say a thing, I kept very quiet (PolU 119).
איא, אייא, אִיַא, אַיַן (< אדיא) c. 'a/ıyya(n) this; לדייא ריזא ldayya rēza as follows, in this order (NT; BT1, Am; AvidH 16; RivSh 245, 265); cf. אנא [Khan 'iyya].
איא(הא) (< אאיא 1) 'ayā(ha) f. that one there; cf. איהא.
איאלא, יאלא (< עיאל/OA ילדא) '(ı)yāla (NT), y'āla (Hob89 182), yāla (Z), child; איאלא סמיכא 'ıyāla smīxa fetus (NT3); ילתא yalta f. girl (=H עַלְמָה, BT2); pl. אייאלה '(ı)yāle (Sa83c 38, Am [cf. Mengozzi 181 (')yālē]); yalunke (Z), walonke (RivSh 122f.), yāle (RivSh 264) [Mutz 240 assumes an unattested form of OA עול, influenced by Ar عيال ? cf. OA/OS אילא/עילא 'foal' ?].
איאלותא, יאלותא, יְלוּתַא (< איאלא) f. ('ı)yālūṯa childhood, youth (AmU2 10a; ZU 72a; =H נְעוּרִים, BT1, D).
איאקא (< א-י-ק) m. 'yāqa tightness (of spirit) (=H קֹצֶר רוּחַ, BT2).
איב- (<-ב איח) 'īb- there is in -; 'ībe It (m.) contains/weighs; 'ības 'ıllōhun We can defeat them; 'ību 'ısri nāše There are about twenty people.
איבארייה (K) f. 'ēvārīye (early) evening.
איגא (< אי 2+K gāh 'recurrent time') adv. 'ēga so then, now then; cf. נקלא, אייכר.
איגר (< אייכר) adv. 'ēgar then.
אידא 1 (OS) f. 'īḏa (Z 'īza) hand; לאידת l'īḏıt by, by means of (NT); zılle līze he shook his hand/they reached agreement (Socin 159); pl. אידאתא 'īḏāṯa; 'īzāse la zıllu He did not have the heart (to do it) (NT+).
אידא 2 (OA אידא, עידא) m. 'ēḏa (Z 'ēza) holiday; 'ēzīlāne/'ēz tım'e Arbor Holiday; *'ēzyāra Shavuoth (lit. Holiday of Visiting [the shrines]); 'ēzmağılla Purim; 'ēsukka Succoth; 'ēspaṭīre Passover (also 'ēz-mōše Moses' Holiday; PolU 432); cf.

פסחא; - א-ו-ד ʾ-w-d̲ - celebrate; pl. אידואתא **ʾēd̲awāt̲a** (NT+).

אידאנא, עידאנא (<אידא 2) **ʾēd̲āna, ʿīdāna** (Z) holiday gift (usually a tray of food) (AvidH 6, 8) [cf. MacD 233].

אידי (<אאדי?) f. **ʾēd̲i** such one, one like that (NT2).

אידמתא (<אדמא) **ʾīd̲amt̲a** (Z **ʾīzamsa**) sister-in-law; pl. אידמיאתא **ʾīd̲amyāt̲a** (Ruth 1:15).

איהא, דיהא (v. אי 2) f. **ʾ/dēha** this one (here); v. אוהא; cf. איא(הא).

איו- (< ה-ו-י) **ʾīw-** copula for 1st and 2nd person (v. איל- 1): אאנא פלאן איון **ʾāna flān ʾīwın** I am (m.) so-and-so; **ʾīwan** I am, f.; **ʾīwax(ni)** we are; **ʾīwıt/ʾīwat** you (sg., m./f.) are; **ʾīwētun** you (pl. c.) are (NT, but Z: **wētun**, etc.; cf. RivSh 202: /אִיוַכְנִי וַכְנִי).

איון (Ar/P) **ʾīwan** ante-chambre, portico; holy chamber (=H דְּבִיר, AlfH 69); cf. ליון [cf. Khan 569 **haywan** veranda, porch, K]

איוא (OA עיבא) m. **ʾēwa** cloud; cf. אינאנא; pl. איואוה **ʾēwāwe** (cf. Polg) (NT+).

איונתא (OA ענא) f. **ʾīwanta** ewe; pl. איואנה **ʾīwāne** (NT+) [MacD 81 ܥܘܢܐ **wānā**; Mutzafi 301 ⁺**wāna** ‹ *ʿ**wāna**].

איזאלא (< א-ז-ל) v.n. **ʾizāla** going, to go (NT+).

איזבל (H) **ʾizēvel** Jezebel, wicked woman (pejor. in men's talk).

איזידנאיא (K) **ʾēzidnāya** Yezidi, member of the non-Muslim Kurdish sect; cf. דצנאיא.

איזלתא (< א-ז-ל) n. act. **ʾizalta** a go, a walk (RivP 209), one's kind of walk.

איזר (Ar إزار < OS ܐܙܪܐ; OA איזרא coarse inexpensive garment) m. ⁺**ʾīzar** woman's shawl, wrapper (=H צָעִיף, BT1, D).

א-י-ז-ר III(< איזר) ⁺ʾ-**ī-z-r** to veil oneself [4: ⁺**mʾīzōre**].

איכא (OA היכא/איכא/OS ܐܝܟܐ) **ʾēka** where; איכילה **ʾēkēle** (NT), **kēle/ʾēka-le** (Z), Where is he? ליכא **lēka** Where to? How far? מיכא, מֵיכַּאֶן **mēka , mēkaʾen** (+POLG), From where?; מיכא אתליני **mēka ʾıtlēni** How do we know? (cf. H מנַיִן לנו).

איכאלא (< א-כ-ל) v.n. **ʾixāla, יכאלא yxāla** (+NT), eating, to eat; ביכאלוך **bixālox** at your eating, while you eat; דלא יכאלא ודלא שתאיא **dla yxāla udla štāya** without eating or drinking; food; pl. **ʾixāle**; **rāba – uštāye** many foods and drinks (PolG).

איכו (< יעקב) **ʾīko** Jack (hypo.); cf. אאקו.

איכ-טבקי (K) inv. **ʾēk-ṭabaqi** one-floor structure, first floor (BT1).

איכית, איכיתא (< אי+כיתא 1) **ʾayxıt, ʾayxēta** the other one (f.).

איכלתא (< א-כ-ל) n. act. **ʾixalta** (kind of) eating (RivP 209).

איכן v. אנכן

אייכר, איכר (< אי 1+Ar **karra**) **ʾaykar** that time, then, therefore; cf. איגא, נקלא (NT).

איל (OA עֵיל/OS ܠܥܠ upward, above) **ʾēl** up; אלאיל **ʾılʾēl** high up, above; מלאיל **mılʾēl** from above, from the top (NT+).

איל- (OA אית+ל-) **ʾīl-** copula for 3rd p. (cf. איו-): **ʾīla** she is; אילה **ʾīle** he is; אילו **ʾīlu** they are; also: (י)לא, (י)לה- **-(ī)la, -(ī)le,** etc.: איכילה **ʾēkēle** (NT/Am)/ **ʾēkā-le** (Z) Where is he; דילה **dīle** who/which is, etc.; may be fronted: **la kıs mōṣel** It (f.) is near Mosul (Hob89 184); **lax bixāla ṣaʿar** We are grieving (ibid.).

אילאהא (OA/OS אֱלָהָא; Mand אלאהא) m. **ʾi/īlāha, ʾilā(ha)** (Z) God; אילאהא דעלמין/ אלעלמין **ʾilāha dʿalmīn/alʿalmīn** (NT) God of the universe; cf. אסתאד-עולם (NT+).

אילאהותא (OA) n. abst. **ʾilāhūt̲a** Divinity (NT).

אילאנא (OA) m. **ʾilāna** tree; אילאנא דתמרא **ʾilāna dt̲amra** fruit tree (NT3); אילאנא דכרשי **ʾilāna dxarše** barren tree (NT3, BT1, D+Am; but Z only in **ʾēz-īlāne** Arbor Holiday; and **ṭarpa la gnāpıl mʾīlāna la bʾımır ʾilāha** a leaf does not fall from the tree without God's order; cf. ציוא

אימא (OA) **ʾēma** Which (c.)? בימא **bēma** In which? At what? cf. אימי (NT+).

אימאן v. אימן 3

אימאן-סז (T) inv. **ʾimān-sız** faithless; cf. דין-סז.

אימארא (< א-מ-ר) v.n.. **ʾimāra** saying, to say; בימארא ויוא **bīmāra wēwa** He was saying; לימארא **limāra** to say, saying (NT, BT).

אים-וואגב (K-Ar) **ʾēm-u-wājıb** fodder-and

necessary staff for horses (PolU 12).

אימי (OA) ʾēmi Who? Cf. מן 3; כו אימי **ku ʾēmi** whoever, anyone; בימי פאתא **bēmi pāṯa** How does one dare (lit. with which face)?

אימם (Ar) m. **ʾīmam** Imam (PolU 21, 256).

א-י-מ-ן v. ה-י-מ-ן

אימן 1, אימל (OA אֵימַת) **ʾīman, ʾīmal** (Sa83c 16, Am), When? כו אימן ד- **ku ʾīman d-** whenever, each time that (NT+).

אימן 2 (Ar) inv. **ʾēmın** confident, trusting (NT+).

אימן 3 (Ar) m. **ʾīman** faith; **wēle +mılya hīl dīne uʾīmāne** He is totally loaded (with money, etc.).

אימנאהי (Ar-P) f. security, peaceful time.

אימנתא (Ar) f. **ʾīmánta** faith, trust (PolG); ביקין דאימנתא **byaqīn dʾīmánta** in absolute faith, wholeheartedly. NT.

א-י-ן, י-א-ן IV(< ע-י-ן 1) **ʾ-y-n, y-ʾ-n** (Hob89 220) to help [2:**māʾın** (Z), **mayʾın**](NT+).

אינא (OA עינא) f. **ʾēna** eye; spring, well; אינא רעה/סריתא **ʾēna rāʿa/sriṯa** the evil eye; אין-יומא, איניומא **ʾēn-yōma** sun (disc) (RivSh 176, 197); **ʾēn-yoma go pāsa, šımšıd sēhra go ṣuṣyāsa** sun (radiates) on her face, moon - on her braids (said of a pretty woman); cf. ביבי; **ʾēn ʾilāha ʾılle** He is lucky! ('eyes of God upon him'); **ʾēn ʾilāha hōya ʾıllox** May God protect you (PoU 305); **ʾēn xmāṯa** the eye of the needle; (one with) slanted, 'Chinese', eyes; **ʾēn-lıbba** center of the heart (PolG); **ʾēne kıpta** humble ('his eye lowered'); **ʾēne kpınta** greedy ('his eye hungry'); cf. כפינא; **ʾēn-lıbba** center of the heart (Pol 105); **bʾēna** by sight, not by weight; **ʾēna bʾēna** eye to eye, face to face (NT5 383); **ʾēne la kṭaʾna** He is envious (lit. his eye doesn't bear); **ʾēnu wēla xa ldaw xıt** They are jealous of each other; pl. אינה **ʾēne**; **ʾēnox ʾılle** Watch him, take care of him; **go/rıš ʾēni** Most welcome (lit. on/in my eyes); **+rāba muxwēle ʾēna** He caused her much suffering (lit. much he showed her eyes); **čımındi la kēse qamʾēne** nothing is valuable to him; **ʾēna xurru** She suffered a lot (from hard work; lit. her eyes became white); **ʾēne pıšlu lʾēn ʾurxa** His eyes were fixed on the road (anxiously waiting for someone); pl. **ʾēnāṯa, ʾēnawāṯa** springs, wells; **lʾēnāṯe** compared to him (NT+).

אינאנא (OA עֲנָנָא/OS ܥܢܢܐ) m. **ʾinānа** cloud; פרדא דאינאנא **parda dʾināna** screen of cloud (NT5 404) cf. ג'מאם, איוא. NT.

איניתא (Ar>P عنايت / نيّت) f. **ʾīnıta** intention, wish, interest; **ʾīnıtox mayla** What is on your mind ? **ʾīnıtta** [!] **xrūta** evil intention (PolG) (NT+).

א-י-נ-כ v. נ-י-כ

איסנא v. אלווסנא

איסר (H/OA אִיסָרָא punishment, charm; lit. binding) m. **+ʾīsar** knot, bond; charm (?); used only in greeting to 'old maids' or barren women: **ʾilāha šāre +ʾīsar dīdax** May God untie your knot (i.e., be lucky and get married or become pregnant); שְׁרֵילוֹך אִיסָרָא דִידִי **šrēlox ʾisāra dīdi** You have untied my bond (=H פִּתַּחְתָּ לְמוֹסֵרָי, AlfH 83).

איפאדא (Ar) f. **ʾifāda** testimony, deposition (PolU 155).

א-י-ק (OA ע-י-ק) **ʾ-y-q** to be tight, narrow; אקליה בגיאנה/ אקלא אלה **ʾıqle bıgyāne/ʾıqla ʾılle** He became distressed; **behne ʾıqle** He became impatient; IV to make tight, narrow (NT+).

איקא, אקתא (OA עיקא) adj. **ʾīqa,ʾıqta**, narrow, tight; פשליה קוי איקא מגיאנה **pišle qawi ʾīqa mıgyāne** He became very distressed; איקת גינאתא **ʾīqıt gyanāṯa** (those of) distressed souls (NT5 391); **behne ʾīqa** (he is) impatient (NT+).

עיקו, איקו, איקותא (OA עיקותא*; cf. OA עַיְקָא weariness) f. **ʾiqūṯa** (Z), **ʾ/ʿēqo** (NT1; BT1, D; Hob97 324), trouble, affliction; pl. איקוייה **ʾīqūye** (Sa83c 24, Am), אֶקוֹבֵי (AvidH 61) **ʾēqōve** (?).

אייר (H) **+ʾıyyar** the Hebrew month of Iyyar (=May).

אירא (Ar) **ʾēra** penis; **ʾēr qīra dabuqāna** pest, nag (lit., a sticky penis of tar); pl. **ʾērawāṯa, ʾēre** foul curses.

איראני (K-Ar) adj. **ʾirāni** Iranian (border) (PolU 379).

איש, אישא (K) m. **ʾēš(a)** ailment, plague; **ʾēš**

ʿālıq go bēse May a plague touch his house; **ʾēš uʾalam** (any kind of) ailment (PolU 137); pl. only with hendiadys: **ʾēš-u-nāle, ʾēš-u-žāne; ʾilāha mābıllu ʾēš-u-nāle dīdox lṯūre xrīwe** May God carry away your ailments to bad mountains (NT+).

אישו (משיחא) (OS) **ʾīšo (mšīḥa)** Jesus (Christ); very spoiled child (sarc. said about an only child whose parents 'worship' him).

אישלא (Ar) **ʾʾīšalla** God willing (Socin 163) ; **ʾīšalla raqzax bdaʿwox** May we dance at your wedding; cf. שאלן.

אישלכה v. הילכה

אית, איתן (OA) **ʾīṯ, ʾīṯın** (Z **ʾīs, ʾīsın**) there is/are; אִיתֵינַא וְאִיתֶין **ʾīṯēna uʾīṯın** certainly there is (=H יֵשׁ וָיֵשׁ, 2Kings 10:15, PolG); **ʾıtla, ʾıtle** she has, he has, etc.; **ʾıtlox ʾılli** I owe you (5 dinars); I am obliged to you (to do so and so);**ʾıṯwa** there was/were; **ʾıswābu ʾımma nāše** There were about 100 persons; **ʾıswābe ʿıllōx** He could win the match against you; **ʾıṯwāle** he had, etc.; cf. לית, -איל, -איב (NT+).

איתא (OS ܥܕܬܐ **ʿedtā**) f. **ʾēta** church; pagan temple (BT1); minaret (PolG); pl. **ʾētāṯa**.

איתאיא (< א-ת-י) m. **ʾiṯāya** coming, to come; פשלה ביתאיא בתריהון **pıšle biṯāya batrēhun** It (m.) was following them (NT+).

איתן v. אית

אך (OA/OS איך; היך) **ʾıx** (Z **x-/ġ-**) as, like; cf. אכגן, אכואת, דך, מוך, (NT+).

אכא (OA/Mand הָכָא, האכא; OS ܗܪܟܐ) **ʾaxxa** here; **ʾaw did lēwe ʾaxxa** excluding you (lit. he who is not here; said after quoting a curse); לכא **laxxa**, לך **lax** (NT), (to) here; מכא **maxxa** from here, hence; **bʾaxxa btamāha** by (doing) this and that (PolU 145); **maxxa laxxa** one way or another, be it be it that (Pol 213) (NT+).

אכאברה, עכאברה (Ar) pl. **ʾ⁺/ʿakābıre** magnates, distinguished people (cf. PolU 149).

א-כ-א-כ III (< אאך) **ʾ-x-ʾ-x** to be in pain, make sounds of pain; גייאני בד חצרא ומאכאוכי פישלא **gyāni bıd ḥaṣra umʾaxʾōxe pıšla** My soul was sighing and suffering (RivSh).

אכאכתא (< א-כ-א-כ) **ʾaxʾaxta** sound of pain, sighing (PolG).

אכלא, אכלתא (< א-כ-ל)adj. **ʾaxāla, ʾaxalta**, glutton, one who eats a lot.

אכגב (< אכא+גיבא) adv. **ʾaxgıb** this side, this way.

אכגן, אֶכְגִ'ין (< אך?) **ʾıxjın, ʾıkčın** (NT; PolG **kčın**?), אקגן/אקג'ין **ʾıqčın** (+NT), קג'ין **qčın** (Z), מַכְג'ִין **maxčın** (RivP #39; PolUR 54), the size of.

אכדאדה (OA אהדדי; OS ܚܕ̈ܕܐ) adv. **ʾıxḏāḏe** (Z **ʾıx/ġzāze**, אכדה **ʾıxḏe** (+NT), together; **la sēlu lıġzāze** They did not get along or reach mutual agreement; מכדה/מאכדה **mıxḏe** (Z **mıġzaz, mızġaz, mıġzāze**) from/with one another; אמד אכדה **ʾımmıd ʾıxḏe** with one another, together [Khan 567 **dixle**].

אכואת, כואת, כות (OS ܐܟܘܬ/OA -כוואת/-כְּוָות) **(ʾı)xwāṯ, xuṯ**, מכוות **mıxwaṯ** (Z **ʾıxwās, mıxwās, xus**), as, like; cf. אך (NT+).

אכונא (OS ܐܚܘܢܐ little brother; OA אֲחָא) m. **ʾaxōna** brother; pl. אכואתא **ʾaxawāṯa** (OA אחי; OS ܐܚܐ); cf. אאכא.

אכותא (OS ܐܚܘܬܐ) f. **ʾaxūṯa** brotherhood.

אכז-ועטא (Ar) **ʾaxz-u-ʿaṭa** (Z) exchange give and take, political negotiations (PolU 91).

אכיד (Ar) adj./adv. **ʾakīd** sure, surely.

אכיר (Ar) m. **ʾaxīr**, אָכֶיר **ʾāxır** (BT4, D), end (of days); באכיר/לאכיר **b/lʾaxīr** at the end of days, eventually; הל אכיר **hal ʿaxīr** forever; cf. אאכרי (NT+).

אכירתא (< אכיר) f. **ʾaxīrıta**, end, edge.

א-כ-ל (OA) **ʾ-x-l** to eat; כיל אלד כלוה **xīl ʾıllıd kalwe** was eaten by dogs (NT2 283); **kēxıllu pār nāše** He doesn't pay back debts (lit. He eats people's money); **la kıxli xa ldaw xıt** They don't go together, don't fit with each other; **ʾalpa līre kēxıl ʾılle** It is worth thousand pounds more than the other one (cf. PolU 267); **xılle ʾıxre** He lied, bragged (lit. ate shit); — **ṣaṯra** received a blow on the face (PolU 229); **wal kıxlaxle laxmēni** We are living well; **kıxli ġamme** They take care of it (PolU 187) [1:-כל **xıl-**; 2: כיכל **kēxıl**, באכל **bāxıl**; 3: כול **xōl**; 4: איכאלא/יכאלא **ʾixāla/yxāla** (+NT); ביכאלא **bixāla**]; IV to feed [1:-מוכל **mōxıl**; 2/3: מאכל **māxıl**; 4:מכולה **maxōle**].

אכלא (OA/OS) m. **ʾıxla** moth.

אַכַּנְגִ'י (K farmer < T pioneer) **ʾakanji** settler;

p-y-š ʾakanji settle (=H להשתקע, AlfH 37).

אכנוכון v. אכתון

אכני, אכניני, אכנן (OA אֲנַחְנָא, אֲנַן; OS ܚܢܢ) ʾaxni, ʾaxnēni, ʾaxnan we (c.). v. כני-, כ- (NT+) [Khan 562 ʾatxan we; ʾatxun you]

א-כ-פ, א-ג'-ב II(K آخفتن) ʾ-x-f (NT), ʾ-ġ-v (Z), to speak, be on speaking terms with; la gmaġvi xawxıt They don't speak with each other (due to anger) [1: mōġıv-; 2/3: מאאכף mʾāxıf (NT), māġıv ; 4: maġōve].

א-כ-ר II (OA אחר/Ar اخر) ʾ-x-r to be late; to delay (vt) [1: מוכר-.מאוכר- mōxır-/mʾōxır-]; cf. ת-א-כ-ר.

אכראמותא (Ar) f. ʾıkrāmūṯa generosity (RivSh 190); cf. כראמתא.

אכרה (OA חריא; OS ܚܪܝܐ) pl. ʾıxre excrement; ʾıxre lqōre to hell with him (lit., shit on his grave); v. א-כ-ל [Khan 585 xre].

אכתון, אכתוכון, אכנוכון (OA/OS אנתון/אתון) ʾaxtun, ʾáxt/nōxun you (pl.c.); cf. אכני (NT+).

אכתייאר (Ar) ʾıxtıyār choice, wish (NT).

אכתייר (K < AnAr) inv. ʾíxtyar, ʾxítyar old (person) (PolU 10).

אכת-ל-קחב (Ar) ʾıxt-ıl-qaḥb prostitute's brother (common curse) (PolU 107)

אכתר (Ar) ʾakṯar much, excess: ומנד אכתר מחובה דמוחיבילוך umınnıd ʾakṯar mıḥubbe dmuḥibīlox and out of much love that You loved them (NT5 387, 396).

אל, איל- (OA אל, על) ʾıl, ʾıll- to; on; by means of; accusative marker [cf. Khan 573]; cf. אאלא, ל-; ʾıtlox ʾılli I owe you, I am obliged to you (to) (PolU 21).

אלא (OA) ʾılla except, unless, but, only, on the contrary, but rather; behold, suddenly (NT+).

אלאיא, אליתא (OA עליא) adj. ʾılāya, ʾılēṯa, high; טבאקה אלאיה ṭabāqe ʾılāye the higher layers (firmaments) of Heavens (NT+).

אלאיל v. איל

אלאי קומנדר (T) ⁺ʾalāy ⁺qomandar the Chief of Staff (PolU 40).

אלג'י, אאלג'י (T) m. ʾı/a/ālči king's emissary, tax-collector, ambasador, police officer (PolU 295); pl. ʾalčiyat (PolU 38).

אלה (Ar) ⁺ʾallā(h) Allah, God; ⁺ʾalla karīm uʾalla raḥīm God is merciful (said about possible difficult times ahead; cf. PolU 340); ʿal ⁺ʾalla God will show a way (PolU 29); v. יא (NT+).

אלו (< אליהו) p.n.m. ʾılo Elie(hypo. of Elijah).

אלווסנא, עלווסנא (OA אילווא [<עלוא*] aloe+ אסנא bush) m. ʾılwasna (NT, BT2), ʿılwasna (Z) thornbush, bramble; also: אסנא (+NT, BT5, Z)/ אִיסְנַא/אֶסְנָה(BT2, D; AlfM 27) ʾısna, סנה (+NT < H) sıne.

אלול (H) ʾíllul the Hebrew month of Ellul.

אליה (H) p.n.m. ʾelīya Elias.

אליהו (H) p.n.m. ʾılyāhu(n) Elijah; אליהו הנביא (RivSh 272 אֵלִיהוּ הַנָּבִיּ) ʾılyāhu-nnāvi the prophet Elijah; often used in blessings: ʾılyāhu-nnāvi xāzır qāmox May the prophet Elijah protect you (lit. be around you); v. שומר ישראל.

אלים (Ar) inv. ʾalīm painful (NT).

אלינא v. לאינא

אלישבע (H) p.n.f. ʾelišēvaʿ Elisheba, often shortened to שבע (q.v.).

אליתא, אֲלִיתַא, אוליתא (OA אֲלִיתָא) f. ʾülīṯa, ʾılīṯa (BT3,D), sheep's tail, fat; pl. ʾülyāṯa (OA אַלְיָיתָא).

אלכנס (Ar الخنّاس Satan) inv. ʾalxanas evil person: la kīʾıt ma ʾalxanas-īle You don't know how evil he is!

אלכסנדרוס, אלסכנדוס (H < Gr) ʾaleksandıros, ʾaleskandos Alexander (the Great)(NT3).

א-ל-מ (OS 'to keep anger'?) ʾ-l-m to be able to utter, usually with negation: gjār la ʾlımle He didn't utter a word at all (due to fear).

אלם (Ar) m. ʾalam pain (NT+).

אלמזיני (Ar?) almazīni kind of fabric (PolU 214).

אלמץ, אלמס (Ar) m. ⁺ʾálmaṣ diamond (NT3: אאלמס/אאלמאס; BT2, D: אַלְמַאץ).

אלעזר (H) p.n.m. ⁺ʾılʿāzar Elazar.

א-ל-פ 1 v. ל-י-פ

א-ל-פ 2 II (Ar) ʾ-l-f to be blessed, used only in greetings; mʾalfıt May you be blessed (=have a thousand blessings?); cf. מאולפא.

אלפא 1 (OA) m. ʾalpa thousand; v. כארא; pl. אלפה ʾalpe; xamšá ʾalpe five thousand;

אלפאיה, אַלְפָאהֵי **ʾalpāye, -he** (AvidH 68), thousands (of), many (NT+).

אלפא 2 (OS ܐܶܠܦܳܐ) m. **ʾılpa** eyelid; **ʾēni uʾılpi ʾāhıt wıt** You are all I have (PolU 305); pl. אלפאפה **ʾılpāpe** (Sa83c 34, Z); **drēle rıš ʾılpāpıd ʿēne** He liked it very much (lit., put it on his eyelids); **l – šımme** 'to the sky's eyelashes' = '(fly) way up to the sky' (PolU 226) [MacD 112: **ṭilpā** < OS; cf. Mutzafi 317 **tulpa**; pl. **tulpāpe**].

אלף-בית (H) **ʾālef-bē(ṯ)** the Hebrew alphabet; initial Hebrew studies.

אלפונא (< OA א-ל-פ) **ʾılpōna** a learned habit; cf. ל-י-פ.

א-ל-ק II/IV (?) (Ar) **ʾ-l-q** to shine: ושופריה לאלפא רנגיה גמאלק **ušufre lʾalpa range gmaʾlıq** (?) His beauty shines a thousand shades of color (AmU2 5a); cf. ע-ל-ק.

אלתיך v. תכית

אמ-, אמד (OA עם) **ʾımm-** (with suffixed pron.), **ʾımmıd** with; cf. מן; אמוך אמוך **ʾımmōx-ʾımmōx** constantly with you (NT2) (NT+).

אמא, אימא (OA מְאָה/OS ܡܐܐ/Mand מא) **ʾımma** hundred; pl. אמואתא **ʾımmawāṯa** (NT; cf. OS ܡܐܘܳܬܐ)), **ʾımmāye/-he** (Z), but **tarteʾma, ⁺tıllasma** two hundred, three hundred, etc. (cf. OA תלת מאה, ארבע מאה, etc.); cf. מאתה.

אַמָא (Ar) **ʾamma** however (RivSh 173).

אמאניה, אמאנתא (K < Ar) f.**ʾamāne, ʾamānıta,** trust, deposition in trust; **ʾamānıti ʾıllōxun** I entrust with you; pl. **ʾamānıtyāṯa** (NT+).

אמויא (K **amo** < Ar **ʿammu**?) m. **ʾamōya** paternal uncle; **bır-/brat-** cousin; cf. 2, אמתא מאמו; pl. **ʾamowāṯa** [Mutz. 187: **ʾamōna** <OS ܚܡܳܢܐ!].

אמונה (H) f. **ʾımūna** faith, trust; **lēbe ču ʾımūna** you can't trust him (lit., there is no trust in him) (RivSh 255: אֶמוּנָה **ʾamūna**).

אמין (Ar) inv. **ʾámin** trustworthy, reliable; pl. **ʾamīne** (PolGr); cf. אימן, כאפר.

אמינתותא (< אמין) f. **ʾamīnatūṯa** trustworthiness. (BaBin 144)

אמירא, מירא (Ar, K) m. **ʾamīra** (NT), **mīra** (Z), emir, prince, lord.

א-מ-נ (Ar) **ʾ-m-n** to trust (PolG); II to reassure, make someone trust you (Segal #95); cf. ה-י-מ-נ.

אמן 1 (H) **ʾāmēn** amen (response in prayer).

אמן 2, אמאן (K/Ar امان) **⁺ʾama/ān** mercy!; cf. דכיל; **halli ⁺ʾaman** Be patient, Give me a break! Give me some time (cf. PolU 144); **lēs ču – faltın** There is no chance for me to escape (PolG).

א-מ-צ̇ II (Ar) **⁺ʾ-m-ẓ** to sign (one's name).

אמצא, אומצא (Ar) f.**ʾümẓa** signature.

א-מ-ר 1 (OA) **ʾ-m-r** to say [1: **mır-**; 2: **gē(mı)r** (Z), **kēmır** (NT); **bāmır**; 3:**mār, māl** (NT1; RivSh 174); 4: **ʾimāra, bimāra, limāra** (=H לֵאמֹר, BT); v. מאר, מרי-מרוך, במרי מימורי,.

א-מ-ר 2 II (Ar) **⁺ʾ-m-r** to command, issue an order (PolU 224); cf. ע-מ-ר, אמר.

א-מ-ר 3 (Ar/OA/OS **ʿmr**) **ʾ-m-r** to be built, sustained; **dunye ʾmırra** the weather improved (following rain and storm); IV to build, sustain; **ʾilāha maʾmır bēsox/bēsox ʾmīra/bēs ʾilā ʾmīra** Thank you, Thank God (PolU 426; PolG).

אמר, אִמֵיר, עמר (Ar) m. **⁺ʾımır** (BT5, D), **ʿımır** (NT5 395), order, command; cf. א- 2 מ-ר (NT+).

אמרא (OA עמרא) m. wool; cf. אמרתא (NT+).

אמריכא (IrAr < E) f. **ʾamrīka** America (PolU 214).

אמרתא (< אמרא) **ʾamırṯa** fleece; pl. **ʾamıryāṯa**.

אמת (H) **ʾemeṯ** (Z **ʾemēs**) truth, mostly in swearing: **beméz-⁺attōra** (I swear) by the truth of the Torah (that what I said is right)!

אמתא 1, אִמְתָא, אומיתא (OA אוּמְתָא) f. **ʾümmıta** nation; pl אמתיאתא, אֻומִיתְיַיאתָא (BT3, D), **ʾümmıtyāṯa** (OA pl. אוּמֵי).

אמתא 2, אמתו (< אמויא) f. **ʾamta, ʾamto** (voc.), paternal aunt; pl. **ʾamtāṯa**.

אן 1(OA הני) **ʾan** those (c.), the; לן/לנד **lan/land** to those; cf. אאני, אנה, אניא (NT+).

אן 2 (OA/Ar) **ʾın** if; ואן לא **uʾın la** and if not, otherwise; cf. אנכן (NT+).

אן 3 (< יאן) **ʾān** or (NT+).

אנא, אנה, אני (< אניא, אן1) **ʾa/ınna/e/i** these,

those (c.); בני **banni** in those; לני **lanni** for those (NT; BT1, Am); cf. אייא [Khan 561 **ˀanne, ˀinna**].

אנא-, (א)ן- (< אאנא) **-āna, -an** I (f. subject pron. with a.p.): הויאנא **hōyāna** I (f.) shall be; בסמן **basman** I (f.) shall heal; מצליאן **mṣalyan** I (f.) shall pray; cf. ינא- (NT+).

אנא(הא) (< אן 1) **ˀanā(ha)** those (c.) over there; **mın danāha** from those over there; cf. אוא(הא).

אנגליזי, ענגליזי (K/IrAr) **ˀ/ᶜınglēzi** English (language); **ˀ/ᶜıngliznāya** (m.),**-nēṯa** (f.) English (person) (SaAC 17, 19; cf. JAB, Blanc 147).

אנגֿאנה (Ar. **ˀijjāna** <OA/OS **ˀaggānā**) f. **ˀınjāne** urn, basin, washing tub.

אנגֿאצה, ענגֿאצה (K < Ar 'pears'; cf. H-OA עוגסים/אגסין) pl. **ˀ/ᶜınjāṣe** dried prunes

אנגֿיל, ענגֿיל (K < Ar) m.**ˀ/ᶜınjil** the Gospels, the New Testament.

אנגֿק (T) adv. **ˀınjaq** barely, hardly; **ˀāwa bxamša ˀınjaq dāˀır** He will hardly be back by five (cf. PolG **ˀınjax** perhaps, hardly).

אנגֿר (K) adv. **ˀınjar** this time, then, now (NT).

אנה v. אנא

אנ(ה)ו (Ar) **ˀınn(ah)u** that is to say (MeAl 190; PolG); cf. אני.

אנואר (Ar) pl./f. **ˀanwār** fire, light; usually in אסתונד אנואר **ˀıstūnıd ˀanwār** the pillar of fire (in Exodus) (NT) (=Z **stūnıd nūra**); אַנְוָאר שְׁכִינַא גנַהְרָוַא **ˀanwār šaxīna gnahrāwa** the light of the Shekhina was illuminating (RivSh168).

אנותא (OA עִינְבְּתָא; pl. עִינְבֵי) f. **ˀınūṯa** a grape; pl. אנויה **ˀınwe**; v. סרניאא (NT+).

אני 1 (Ar) **ˀınni** because; אני אמתא מקודשתא ויתון אכתון **ˀınni ˀımmıta mqōdašta wētun ˀaxtun** because you are a holy nation (NT+).

אני 2 v. אנא

אניא (v. אן1) **ˀanya** these (c.); בניא **banya** in these; מניא **manya** from these. (NT+).

אניה (Ar) **ˀınne** that is (NT5 409); cf. אנהו.

א-נ-כ v. נ-י-כ

אנכן, אן כאן, איכן, אסכן, כַאן (Ar) **ˀınkan, ˀīkan, ˀıskan, kān** (PolG), if; cf. הכן, אן 2 (NT+).

א-נ-כ-ר, ע-נ-כ-ר III (Ar) **ˀ-n-k-r** (NT), **ᶜ-n-k-r** (Z), to refuse, to be obstinate (NT+).

אנסאן, ענסאן (Ar) m. **ˀınsān** (NT), **ᶜınsān** (Z), a human being (NT+).

אַנְקַרָא (OA אנגריא < Gr) **ˀanqara** forced labor (RivSh 139).

אנתקאם (Ar) **ˀıntıqām** vengence, revenge (NT).

אסאס, אסס (Ar) m.**ˀısas** foundation; pl. אסאסה **ˀısāse** (NT+).

אסבח (Ar) inv. **ˀasbaḥ** the best hymn (NT3).

אסחק, אסחוק (Ar < H יצחק) **ˀısḥaq, ˀısḥoq** (NT), Isaac; cf. אגֿו

אסטנגא (K) **ˀasṯanga** narrow passage.

אסכנדרייא (Ar) **ˀıskandarīya** Zoan (BT4), Alexandria.

(א)סטמבול (T) **(ı)sṭambul** Istanbul (PolU 223).

אנכן v. אסכן

אסכר, עסכר (Ar, P) f./m./coll. **ˀaskar** (NT)/**ᶜaskar** (Z), soldier, army; pl. **ˀ/ᶜaskarāye, ᶜ/ˀaskarāṯa, ᶜaskāre; ᶜ/ˀaskarnāye** (RivSh 169 עסכר רבסא **ᶜaskar rabsa** (f.); ibid. 278 כולא עסכר **kulla** (f.) **ᶜaskar**; ibid. 281 עסכר דוהון כולו **ᶜaskar dōhun kullu** (coll.) (NT+).

אסלאם, אסלם (Ar) **ˀıslām** (NT),**ˀíslam** (PolU 123), Islam; cf. מושלמנותא.

אסמר (K < Ar) inv. **ˀasmar** brown; **ˀasmar-širīn** 'sweet-brown' shade (considered ideal for woman's skin).

אסנא v. אלווסנא

אסנת (H) p.n.f. **ˀasnad/t** Asenath.

א-ס-ס II2 (< אסאס) **ˀ-s-s** to found; to be founded.

א-ס-פ II (< OA יזף, OS ܐܘܙܦ to borrow money/objects?) **ˀ-s-p** to borrow food (only); **mˀōsıpli xapča qamxa** I borrowed some flour (from neighbors); v. אספא.

אספא (< א-ס-פ) m. **ˀıspa** borrowed-food (from neighbors to return its equal later): **šqılli xapča qamxa bˀıspa** (=**mˀōsıpli xapča qamxa**) I borrowed some flour.

אספניכ (IrAr/T < E) **ˀasfanīk** phenic acid.

א-ס-ק v. י-ס-ק

אסקד(א) v. אוקד(א)

אִיסְקֻופְתָא v. סקופתא

אסקתא (OA עזקתא) f. **ˀasıqṯa** ring, seal;

ʾasıqtıd xyāṯa thimble; pl. ʾasqāṯa, ʾasıqyāṯa (cf. PolGr 55).

אסר, איסר (OA עסר) f. ʾıssır (?) ten ; אסר צ̇רבתיאתא ʾıssır ẓarbıtyāṯa the ten plagues of Egypt (NT5 386) [MacD ʿiser, but AvidH 8 אִסַּר ʾıssar].

אסרא, אצרא (OA עשׂרה) m./c. ʾısra (?)(NT), ʾıṣra (Z), ten; דאסרא dʾısra the tenth (c.); מִן אִיסְרַא כַא mın ʾısra xa tenth (=1/10)(BT3, D); xa uʾıṣra ten times (bigger); pl. אסרואתא ʾısrawāṯa (NT), ʾıṣrāye (BT2, Z).

אסראתא (< OA אסרתא 'band(?)' ?) pl. ʾısrāṯa bracelets (=H צָמִיד, BT4, D); cf. י-ס-ר.

אסרי (OA עשׂרין) ʾısri twenty (NT+).

אסתאדא, אוסתאדא (Ar) m. ʾustāḏa (Z ʾıstāza) master, teacher; ʾıstāz ʿōlām Master of the Universe, God (BT); ʾıstāy ⁺murdax Master (=Rabbi) Murdakh (a title used with the first name of local Rabbis); cf. הוסטא; pl. ʾıstaḏ(a)wāṯa (cf. PolG); v. אסתתא.

אסתונא, סתונא, סִיתֻונַא/אִסְתֻונַא (OA/OS ʾesṭūnā < Gr, m.) ʾestūna (NT, m./f.; PolG:D), stūna (Z, f.), column, pillar; stūn bēsa the house pillar, important figure (PolG); pl. stūne.

אסתיור v. סטויר

אסתכפר אללה (Ar) ⁺ʾıstaxfar ⁺ʾalla God forbid! This is a blasphemy! (PolU 156).

אסתר (H) ⁺ʾıster Esther; אסתר שולטנתא ʾıster šulṭanta Queen Esther (NT5 394); cf. אתה.

אסתתא (< אסתאדא) ʾıstatta mistress, lady-in -charge, female mentor; pl. ʾıstattat (?).

אעז (Ar) ʾaʿaz dearer, most dear (NT3); cf. עזיזא.

אף, -אפ, אוף (OA/OS/Mand אַף) ʾap-, ʾup too, also: אפאהת ʾapāhıt you (m.sg.) too (BaBin 133); אופאהת ʾupāhat you (f.) too (NTU1 43a); ʾapāna I too; ʾapēha she too, this one (f.) too, etc.

אַפִילוּ (H) ʾafıllu (not) even (one) (BT2, D; AlfH 29; MeAl 181).

אפלאך v. פלכ

אפלאטון (Ar < Gr 'Plato') ʾaflāṭōn super-Genius, the devil; ʾaflāṭōn lēbe ʾılle (Even) the devil cannot worst him.

אפנדי (T/IrAr < Gr authentes) ʾaffandi an official, effendi; ʾaffandi bala maʿaš an unemployed official (humorously said about a person dressed well but without an income); pl. afandyāne (PolU 420; PolU 36).

אפסארא, הפסארא (OA/OS אַפְסָרָא < P) m. ʾ/hafsāra bridle; pl. hafsārē (Pol 107).

אפרא (OA/OS עַפְרָא) m. ʾıpra dust, mortar; pl. ʾıprāre (NT+).

אפרז (Ar افراز 'discharge') ʾıfraz allotment (deed of land), partition (PolU 289).

אפרים (H) ⁺(ʾı)frāyim Ephraim; cf. פהו, פרו.

אצעב (Ar) inv. ʾaṣʿab more difficult (NT); cf. צעבא.

אצרא v. אסרא

אקאלא (Ar عقال?) ʾaqāla rope-ring (AmU2 10b); cf. עגאלא;

אקבא (OA עקבא) f. ʾaqba heel; pl. ʾaqbawāṯa (RivSh 120) [MacD ʿıqba/ʿıqwa].

אקבל (Ar) m. ʾıqbal (bad) luck, fate; ʾıqbal dīda kōma-le She is unlucky (lit., her luck is black) (SaAC 17; cf. PolG ʾuqbal luck).

אקגן, אכגן v. אקגן

אקדם, אקדאם (Ar) inv. ʾaqdam first in importance (NT2).

אקוברא (OA עקברא, עַכְבְּרָא; OS ܥܘܩܒܪܐ) m. ʾaqubra mouse; pl. ʾaqubre.

אקל (Ar) inv. ʾaqal less (than) (NT5 410).

אקלא (OA עקלא 'bend'?) f. ʾaqla foot; ʾaqli ʾımmıd ʾaqlox I will go wherever you go, I'll follow you (PolU 83); magnate, pillar of community (PolU 364); pl. אקלאתא ʾaqlāṯa; אקלה ʾaqle (NT+) [Krotkoff 130].

אקלתא (< אקלא) f. ʾaqılta little foot (MeAl178); pl. ʾaqlāṯa (PolG).

א-ק-ר (OA עקר) ʾ-q-r to uproot; be uprooted.

אקרא (< OA עִיקָּרָא?) m. ʾıqra root, bottom, end; ʾıqır dunye the end of the world (far away place); mın rēša hil ʾıqra from start to finish; pl. אקרארה ʾıqrāre (PolU 426) (NT+).

אקרוא, אַקְרוּבַא (OA עַקְרַבָּא m./f.; OS ܥܩܪܒܐ, f.) f. ʾaqırwa (Z; PolG), ʾaqruba (RivSh 257), scorpion.

אראא, ארא, ארא, אראה (OA ארעא) f. ʾarʾa, ʾara land, ground; אַרֶד ʾared land of (RivSh 122); pl. אראאתא ʾarʾāṯa.

אראורא (OS ܐܪܐܘܪܐ) m. **ʾarʾūra** manna (BT); sweet secretion collected from tree leaves.

אראקא 1. ארקתא (< א-ר-ק) .**ʾarāqa, ʾaraqta** runner, one who escapes

אראקא 2 (< א-ר-ק) v.n. **ʾrāqa** running, escape, pursuit (NT+).

א-ר-א-ר III (< אראורא) **ʾ-r-ʾ-r** to spoil (a child), to pamper too much.

ארבא 1, ארבאא (OA/OS ארבע, ארבעה) **ʾarba** (f./c.), **ʾarbıʾa** (m., +NT) four; /דארבא דארבאא **dʾarba/dʾarbıʾa** (NT5 411) the fourth.

ארבא 2 (OA ארבא, ערבא; SoBA 146; OS ܐܪܒܐ) **ʾırba** sheep; ארבד ואלא **ʾırbıd wāla** wild sheep (NT); pl. **ʾırwe** (Z; PolG), but AvidH 26, 34, 50 אִרְבֵּי; RivSh 231 אִירְבֵּי = **ʾırbe** [cf. Mengozzi 292 **ʿerbē/ʿerwe**; Khan 562 **ʾırba, ʾırbe**].

ארבאלא (OA/OS ערבלא/ארבלא < Ak **arballu**; Ar غربال) f. **ʾırbāla** coarse sieve; cf. מכלתא.

ארבאמא, ארבא אמאיה, אַרְבָּא אִמָּא (OA ארבע מאה) **ʾarbeʾma** (Z), **ʾarbá -ʾımmāye** (BT), **ʾarba ʾımma** (AvidSh 24), four hundred.

ארבאסר (OA ארבעה עשׂר, אַרְבָּסַר; OS ܐܪܒܥܣܪ, m.; Mand ארבאסאר) **ʾarbaʾsar** fourteen, c.

ארבושב (OA ארבעה בשב(א)) **ʾarbōšıb** (Z), **ʾarbūšıb** (BT1, Am).

ארבי, ארבאי (OA ארבעין) **ʾarbi, ʾarbıʾi** (+NT; NT5 384, 386, 410), forty.

ארגאלא (Ar اجل?) m. **ʾırjāla** lifetime, the end of one's life.; cf. עומר 1 (NT+).

ארג׳ו (Ar 'I beg') n. **ʾarju** request; בארג׳ו מנוך **bʾarju mınnox** I beg you.

ארג׳ואן, ארג׳וון (Ar; cf. OA/OS אַרְגְּוָנָא) m. **⁺ʾarjawan** purple, crimson (garment).

א-ר-ו (OA ערב) **ʾ-r-w** to be mixed; ארולו באכדיה **ʾrūlu bʾıxde** they gripped one another (in wrestling); IV to mix (vt), to cross-breed (BT3) (NT+).

ארואנא (< ארבא 2?) m. **ʾırwāna** sacrifice, charity meal; בארואנוך **bʾırwānox** kindly, with your charity; **ʾaxlax bʾırwānox** May we eat at your charity meal (as in Bar-Mitzva, wedding, etc.) (NT+).

ארוה v. ארבא 2

ארויל (OA ארביל) **ʾárwil** the town of Arbil; **ʾarwilnāya** a resident of Arbil [Khan 2 **arb/wīl** < Akk. **arba-il** < Hurrian **u/arbilum**].

ארוילנאיא, ארוילניתא (< ארביל) **ʾarwilnāya, -nēta** (f.), resident of of Arbil; pl. **-nāye** [Khan 561 **ʾarbelna/ʾarbinna** (m.); **ʾarbelta** (f).; pl. **ʾarbinne**].

ארון (H) **ʾarōn** the Biblical Ark; v. היכל.

ארור (H) **⁺ʾārūr** a cursed one; common in **ʾārūr bır ʾārūr** a cursed son of a cursed one! (cf. PolU 234).

ארותא (OA ערובתא) f. **ʾırōta** eve of Sabbath or Holiday; cf. מאלא; יומ(ד) ארותא **yōm(ıd) ʾırōta** Friday; pl. **ʾırutyāta** (PolGr 56) (NT+) [RivSh 199 אַרוֹתַא **ʾarōta**].

א-ר-ו-ס v. ה-ר-ו-ס

ארזא (OA) m. **ʾarza** cedar (NT).

ארזאלא (OA ערסלא/ אַרְזָלָא/OS ܐܪܙܠܐ/Ar عرزال hummock in a fruit garden) **ʾarzāla** hut (NT6 136) [cf. MacD 244].

ארזאני (K/P) f. **ʾarzāni** abundance (of crops); period of cheap prices (NT+).

ארזאק, ארזק v. רזק

ארזן (K/P) inv. **ʾarzan** cheap, abundant.

א-ר-ז-נ III(< ארזן) **ʾ-r-z-n** to become cheap.

א-ר-י (OA ערי) **ʾ-r-y** to be of sufficient volume; to hold (cf. PolG); **la ʾrēlu kıslēni** We didn't have enough room for them; IV to make sufficient room, make do with less; to solder (PolG); to curdle [MacD 243; Mutz.:191: 'freeze, curdle].

אריא, אריה (OA) m. **ʾarya** lion; pl. ארייה אריואתא, **ʾarye, ʾaryawāta** (NT+).

אריותא (OS) f. **ʾaryōta** lioness (=H לָבִיא, BT) [but PolG **ʾurīta / ʾıryōta**].

א-ר-כ (< ארכאבכה?) **ʾ-r-x** to become thick and starchy (soup).

ארכא, ארכתא (OA ארחא) m. **ʾarxa** (Z), **ʾırxa** (Hob89 186), **ʾarıxta** (f.) (PolU 185), guest; pl.**ʾarxe**.

ארכאבכה (K آر+خاف raw flour) f. **ʾarxāvke** a thick cold flour dish mixed with sugar.

ארכה (OA רחיא) f. **ʾırxe** mill; **mare ʾırxe** miller; pl. **ʾırxāta** [Krotkoff 128; Khan 563 **ʾırxel**].

ארכותא (< ארכא) **ʾarxūta** accomodation, stay as guest (PolGr 73).

ארכן (OA ערכן/OS ܐܪܟܘܢ < Gr arkon?) **ʾark/xan** (?) ruler (?); pl. ארכאן **ʾarkān** ministers, officers (NT2).

ארמאלכה (< א-ר-מ-ל/K **har+māl** always (at) home?) **ʾarmālke** husband doing house or wife's work.

ארמותא, ערמותא (OA רמונא) f. ʾ'/ᶜ**armōta** pomegranate; pl. ᶜ**armōne**. cf. רימונייה (NT+) [Hoberman 1985 226; Mutz. 192].

א-ר-מ-ל III (OA/OS/Mand) ʾ**-r-m-l** to become a widower.

ארמלותא (OA/OS/Mand) f. **ʾarmılūṯa** widowhood.

ארמלתא (OA/OS/Mand) f. **ʾarmılṯa** widow; pl. **ʾarmılyāṯa** (cf. PolGr 55).

ארמן (Ar) **ʾarman** Armenia, Armenians; Aram (BT1); ארמנאיא **ʾarmanāya** Armenian; Aramean (NT; BT; AvidH 25; PolG).

ארמרנג̇ (K ارماغ < P آماج) **ʾarmaranj** (?) target (AmU2 10a).

ארנווא, ערנווא (OA/OS ארנבא) **ʾarnuwwa**, ᶜ**arnūwa** (Z), hare (BT3, D); sour puss (Z, pejor. in women's talk).

ארץ ישראל (H) **ʾereṣ yiṣrāʾēl** Land of Israel; cf. ירושלים (NT+).

ארץ תקח ולא תתן (H) **ʾéreṣ tíqqaḥ wálo títten** hell, very bad place (lit., land that takes and doesn't give).

א-ר-ק (OA ערק/ ארק) ʾ**-r-q** to run, flee; **ʾrīqāle** He ran away, left in a hurry (lit., he ran it); **wēlu ʾrīqe dīda** They had run away (PolG) IV to cause to flee (RivSh 166), run with, elope.

ארקא (< א-ר-ק) m. **ʾırqa** run, running (MeAl 184; PolG); **si bʾırqa** Run, hurry!

ארקתא (< א-ר-ק) f. **ʾraqta** escape (=H מְנוּסָה, NT5 394).

ארתא (OA ערתא) f. **ʾarṯa** rival wife (in poligamy); pl. ארתאתא **ʾarāṯa**.

אשארא (Ar) **ʾašāra** signal; pl. **ʾašārat** (PolG).

אשה כשרה (H) f. **ʾíšša kašēra** (Jewishly) proper wife (PolU 400); cf. אשת איש, אשת חיל.

אשה רעה (H) **ʾíšša rāᶜa** bad, evil wife.

אשוא v. שואא

אשואסר v. שוואסר

אשכאל v. שכל

אשכאתא, שכאתא (OA/OS/Mand אִשְׁכֵּי) pl. **(ʾe)škāṯa** (+Z **reškāsa**, folk-etymology 'on the belly'?) testicles (=H מְבוּשִׁים, BT5); sg. שכתתא **škatta** (OA/OS/Mand אִשְׁכְּתָא) [cf. Mutz 229 **šıčyalta**].

אשכבה v. השכבה

אשכרא, אשכראיי (P/K) adv. **ʾaškara**, **ʾaškarāyi** publicly, openly; **pıšle ʾaškara** became known, revealed (AvidH 46).

אשמדאי (H) **ʾašmaḏay** (Z **ʾašmazay**) Asmodeos (the king of the devils): **ʾašmazay lēbe ʾılle** (Even) Asmodeos cannot worst him.

אשר, עאשר (H) ʾ/ᶜ**āšır** Asher (common name).

אשת 1 (< אד+שאתא) adv. **ʾaššat** this year[Khan 562 **ʾayšat** 'this year'].

אשת 2 (OS) **ʾıššıt** six (f.); סאעא אשֶׁת **sāᶜa ʾıššıt** the sixth hour (NT5 408).

אשתא (OS) **ʾıšta** six (c.); אוד אשתא **ʾōd ʾıšta** the sixth (c.) (NT+).

אֶשֶׁת איש (H) **ʾēšeṯ ʾīš** married woman (BT3, D).

אשתאסר (OS; OA שֵׁית עֲשַׂר, שִׁיתַּסַר) **ʾıštaʾsar** sixteen (NT+).

אשתג̇ל (Ar) **ʾıštıġāl** business (NT).

אשת חיל (H) **ʾēšeṯ/t ḥāyıl** good woman (Ruth 3:11; PolGr 228)

אשתי (OS) **ʾıšti** sixty (NT+).

אשתמא, אשתא אמאיה (OS) **ʾıššıtma, ʾıšta ʾımmāye** (BT), six hundred (NT+).

אתא (OA הַשְׁתָּא < הא שעתא?) **ʾatta** now; any moment (from now) (PolU 31); מתא **matta** from now, from this moment; cf. חַסְדַּ֫ [v.Mutz. 187 **ʾatta**; Khan 562 **ʾatta(neha)**].

אתה, אתוכה (< אסתר) hypo. **ʾıtte, ʾıttōke** Esther.

אתונא (OA/OS/Mand < Ak **atūnu**) m. **ʾatūna** furnace, oven, kiln(NT+).

א-ת-י, י-ת-י (OA) ʾ**/y-ṯ-y** (Z ʾ**/y-s-y**) to come; auxiliary for passive: **sēle (l)qıṭla** He was killed (cf. Zaken, 392; Sa83c 36, Z); **la kēse mınnu** They cannot afford it; **ma kēse mınni** What can I do? I am helpless (PolU 129); **ʾo ʾixāla la kēse ʾılle** This food doesn't agree with him (he is allergic to it); **bēṯa ṯēle uzılle** The house shook (lit. came and went) (RivSh 227); **lašša gēzıl ukēse** Her body shivers (ZU 72a); **sēla** lucky strike! (lit., It has come!) (PolU 426) [1: **(ʾıy)ṯē-**; **ʾıṯya** (m.), **yṯiṯa** (f.); 2: **ʾāṯe, bāṯe, kēṯe/gēṯe**

(NT5 382, 408); 3: (ʾıy)ta (sg.c.), (ʾıy)tāwun (pl. c.) (Zaken 390; Sa83c 16, Z; PolG: אִיתָוִון)); (ī)sálōxun (PolG); tuwun (Hob89 184); 4: ʾitāya, bitāya]; IV to bring; **la gmēse xa pāra** It is not worth a penny; **ʾilāha qam mesēla** lucky strike! (lit., God has brought it) (PolU 428) [1: **motē**-; 2: **mēte**-; 3: **mē(ti)** (m.), **mē(ti/-e)** (m./f.); **mētun** (pl. c.); 4: **me/atōye**; PolG] (NT+).

אתיקא, אתקתא (OA עתיקא) adj. **ʾatīqa**, **ʾatıqta**, old, ancient; cf. א-ת-ק (NT+).

אתיקותא (OA) f. **ʾatīqūta** antiquity, old state.

אתירא (OA עתירא) m. **ʾatīra** rich, wealthy (NT) [cf. Mengozzi 191 **ʾatīrā**].

אתירותא (OA עֲתִירוּתָא) **ʾatīrūta** wealth (NT; Sa83c 40, Am).

אתכאל (Ar) **ʾıttıkál** trust in God (NT); cf. ת-כ-ל.

א-ת-ל (Ar عتل to carry?) **ʾ-t-l** to take, to buy (crypt.):**ʾtulle, ʿıvrāya, mbalaš-īle** Buy it, fellow-Jew, it is a real bargain!

אתן-, ת- (< אאהת 2) **-ātın, -at**, you, f. sg. subject pron. with a.p.: אודאתן **ʾōd-ātın/-at** You will do (NT+).

א-ת-ק (OA עתק) **ʾ-t-q** to become old (things); IV to make old, use long time; v. מואתקא.

אתקד v. אוקד

אתרא (OA/OS/Mand) f. **ʾatra** place, estate; אתרא מקודשתא **ʾatra mqōdašta** the Holy Place, the Temple in Jerusalem (NT); cf. דוכא.

אתראנא, אֶתְרָנִיתָא (<?) **ʾıtrāna** (m.), **ʾıtranīta** (f.)(BT4, D), ladle; **šqōl bkōčıksa uhāl bʾıtrāna** Take (borrow) with a spoon, and give (back) with a ladle (= be generous); pl. אִתְרַאנֶי **ʾıtrāne** (BT4, D) [Khan 582 **trāna**].

אתרוג (H)m. **⁺ʾítroġ** citron (used in Succoth).

ב, בּ (b)

ב (H) **bēṯ** (Z **bēs/be**) the second letter of the Hebrew alphabet; **tre** two.

-ב 1, -ב, -אב, אבד (OA) **b-, -b, ʾıbb-, ʾıbbıd** in, at, with; **dūka bdūka** (he searched) one place after another (PolU 376) [NT:/ביכון אביכון **(ʾıb)bēxun**; Z **ʾıbbōxun**; מבשליבו **mbašlību** they cook in them NT5 409].

-ב 2 (< -ב 1?) **bı** attached to the infinitive to indicate the continuous aspect: בספארא ועדא אילה **bıspāra waʿda ʾīle** He is awaiting the time; פשלו במסבוחה **pıšlu bımsabōḥe** They began singing hymns; often omitted in Z with infinitive of II-IV: **škıllu mbaqōre dīde** They began asking him (questions); **pıšla mbakbōke** She began whining; **wēle maʾmōre** He is building (NT+).

-ב 3 v. בד

-ב, -בא (K?) **ba** proclitic particle to indicate mild puzzlement, wonder, complaint: **ba-kēle** So where is he (=H וְאַיּוֹ, BT2, Exod 2:20); **ba-qay la zıllox** Why, then, you didn't go? בא דיתכור **ba-dı-txōr** Please (try to) remember (BaBin 113); במאטוף **ba-māṭof** Why then (BaBin 105; cf. PolG) [cf. Khan 564 **ba-** 'jussive particle' **ba-šatele** 'Let him drink it!'].

-באב (< Ar/OA 'gate'?) **bāb-** only in the idiom **bču bābıd dunye** not for the world, in no way (MeAl 178; Zaken 389; PolG).

באבא (OS/K; cf. OA פאפא) **bāba** father; באבו **bābo** Dad!; My God! (voc.; cf. RivSh 133/240/252 יא באבו/ואי באבו **ya bābo/wāy bābo**); **bābi (wēlox)** 'my friend' (PolU 443); **⁺bāba darweš** Father Derwish, Your Holiness (PolU 107); בבא **babba** daddy!; באבא-ימא **bāba-yımma** parents; pl. ב(א)בואתא **ba/ābawāṯa** ; cf. אבות (NT+).

באבאכי (K/P) inv./adv. **⁺bābāki** angrily, humiliated (?) (PolU 233).

באבה-פלאכה (< באבא+פלכ?) **bābe-falāke** high society (PolG); but v. באלא.

באדינא (K/onomat?) **⁺bādēna** speeding sounds and movments of floating on river (PolU 8).

באג' v. בוקג' ובאג'

באורה (Ar **baʿr**) pl. **baʾōre** dung, dried cattle's droppings (used as fuel).

באז (K/P 'arm'?) f. **⁺bāz** energy, agility (PolU 74).

באזא 1 (Ar) m. **bāza** hawk (NT+).

באזא 2 (IrAr) m. **bāza** cotton flannel; **fistan bāza** a dress made of cotton flannel.

באזבנד(א) (IrAr < P) m. **⁺bāzband(a)** amulet worn on the upper arm; **⁺bāzbān-dsulṭāne** emblem of kings (worn on arm) (PolU 369).

באזר (K/P) m. **⁺bāzar** trade, business; **ʾ-w-ḏ ⁺bāzar** to bargain, negotiate the price; cf. ב-י-ז-ר, באגר.

באזרגן (P) **⁺bazırgan** trader; pl. **bāzırgāne**.

באזרגנותא (< באזרגן) f.**⁺bāzırganūṯa** trading.

באז'ור (< ב-ג'-נ?) sg./pl. **bāžūr** fantasy, delirium, troubling thought(s) (cf. PolG).

באז'ר (K < באזר) f. **bāžır** city, town (Z); pl. בַּאגְ̇רֵי **bāžēre**.(RivSh 277; cf. PolG); cf. מאתא, מדיתא [MacD 29].

באטני (Ar) inv. **bāṭınī** ghost(s), the invisible (PolU 37).

א-ב-י, ב-א-י (OA בעי; or אבי??) **b-ʾ-y** (NT, Am, RivSh 163; Hob 89 215)), **ʾ-b-y** (Z), to want; דלא באיי **dla bʾāyi** against my wish; **gıbe** it's necessary; **gıbe ʾāzax** We should go; **gıbıt...gıbıt** Be it...be it; either...or (BaBin 88; Socin 165)[1:**bʾē-/ʾbē-**; 2: **gbıʾe** (NT גבאה) /**gıbe** (Z); 3: **bʾi/ʾbi**;4: **bʾāya/ʾbāya**].

באייד אילאהא (< ב-א-י) **baʾāyıd ʾilāha** God seeker, pious (NT6 133).

באיה פלאכה (< באלא+פלכ?) **bāye falāke** 'winds-fortune-wheels, only in **latlu hāyi m-** He is not aware of anything going on (PolU 358).

באיה סמורה (K < P بادي سمومي scorching wind) pl. **bāye samūre** winds of deadly pestilence (=H קֶטֶב מְרִירִי, BT5).

באלא (OA/Ar) **bāla** attention, face; **d-r-y/y-h-w-l bāla ʾıl** to pay attention to, take care of (cf. Avishur 1993b 17); **la yāwıt bālox ʾılle** Don't mind him; **zılla mbāli** I forgot it; **sēla lbāli** I remember (it now); **latle hāyi mbāle-falāke** He is totally out of it (= very sick) (PolU); **láswālu bāla mın gyānu** They were not aware of what they were doing (PolG); direction: **bēsa** ...**bāle bāl čōl** the house's front was facing an open area (PolG).

באמא (< ?) f.⁺**bāma** fat and short woman; (looks like a) marten.

באמיא (Ar/K) f. ⁺**bāmya** okra, gumbo.

באנהה, בנהיה (OA נַגְהָא/OS نوگها/Mand ניהגא break of day) **bɪʾinhe** (NT), **binhe/bine** (Z), morrow, tomorrow; בדלד באנהה **ba<u>d</u>lɪd bɪʾinhe** (NT)/בְּדֵיל בִּינוֹכֵי **ba<u>d</u>ɪl binōke** (BT1, D) dawn, the last shift of the night; cf. בנוכה, נ-א-ה, נאהתא.

באסוכא (< באסכא) m. **bāsōka** heavy smoker (of traditional pipes).

באסכא, בַּסְכָּא (K < P بازو) **bāska** (NT; cf. Mutz 194), **baska** (BT2/5, D; PolG), (upper) arm; pipe-stem (of long traditional one); cf. זנדא [Khan 565 **bāsk** 'upper arm'].

באפושיית (K **bavšīn** blowing [hot] air?) pl. **bāfūšīyat** nonsensical, exaggerated, sarcastic talk (cf. PolU 205).

באקא (OA/OS בָּקָּא, באקא, m., בָּקְתָּא, f. < Ak **baqqu**) f. **bāqa** gnat; pl. **bāqe** (NT+).

באקי, מבאקי (Ar) (**ma**)**bāqi** remainder (NT+).

באקלה (Ar/K/P; cf. OA בקלא, בקילא, pl. בקילי; SokBA 212); type of beans, Vicia Zaba;) pl. **bāqɪlle** fava beans (which caused favisim, allergic anemia, to many who ate it).

באר (K بار/بر fruit/charge?) **bār** in the idiom: **hīl ʾaxla bār dīda** until she (a she-ass) is not useful anymore, too old (PolU 431).

באראנה (K) **bārāne** strong rain (PolU 378).

בארוד (Ar) ⁺**bārud** gunpowder.

בארילי (P **bar**+OA עלי?) adv. **bárēli** upwards, up; **mɪn bɪr ʾɪsri ubárēli** (beginning) from twenty years old and up; cf. ברתכתי (cf. PolG).

בארכאנא (P) ⁺**bārxāna** loads, goods (of traveling merchants) (PolU 115).

באש (K < T) inv. ⁺**bāš** good; cf. הווא.

באשותא (< באש) f. **bāšū<u>t</u>a** goodness (AlfH 95).

באשי v. חכם

באתא 1 (< בראתא) **bāta** girl (babytalk); cf. בונא.

באתא 2, ביאתא (OA בֵּיעֲתָא, בֵּיתָא) f. **beʾta** egg; **beʾta dɪlme** very soft boiled egg; **beʾta šlɪqta** hard boiled egg; **beʾta dla pɪmma** very quiet (and pleasing!) woman (SaAC 15); pl. ביאיה (NT5 410) **beʾe** (OA בֵּיעֵי); **beʾe qɪlye** fried eggs, omelet.

באתה, באתי v. ביתא

באבא v. בבא

בבא עווא (Ar بُعبُع?) m. **babba ʿuwwa** Father Monster, bugaboo, bogeyman.

בבג׳א (Ar < It **papagallo**) **babġa** parrot; jabberer (cf. PolG).

בבואתא v. באבא

בברושכא (K?) **bavrōška** youngster (PolU 2).

בג (T) m. **bag** lord; pl. **baggat, bagalarat**.

בגירא, בגרתא (< OA/OS בגר to be weak, lean?) oilless (dish only), not oily enough to be delicious [MacD 25 **bagīrā** < OS lean, thin].

בג׳א (T **pīč**) m. ⁺**bɪčʾa** bastard; mischief; f. ⁺**bɪčeʾ<u>t</u>a**; pl ⁺**bɪčʾe** [MacD 30 **bīčā**].

ב-ג׳-ב-ג׳ 1 III, , ב-י-ג׳ (<?) **b-j-b-j, b-y-j** to crawl (baby, insect); cf. בג׳וג׳א.

ב-ג׳-ב-ג׳ 2 III (<?) vi ⁺**b-č-b-č** to simmer, boil gently.

בג׳וג׳א (<?) m. **bajōja** cockroach, insect.

בג׳ירכה, בַּרְגִ׳ילְכֵּי (K?) f. **bɪčirke** (Z), **barčilke** (BT4, D), pancake, cheese omelet. (=H צַפִּיחִית 'wafers', BT2); pl. **bɪčirkat**.

בג׳ם (JAB < T?) **bɪčɪm** face, 'ugly face' (used mostly in insults).

ב-ג׳-נ (Ar?) **b-j-n** to talk and curse deliriously; cf. באז׳ורא.

בג׳דאד, בג׳דד (Ar-P) **baġdad** Baghdad; Babylon (NT, BT).

בג׳דנאיא, בג׳דדאיא, בג׳ג׳דנאיא(< בג׳דד) **baġdad(n)āya** (NT), **baġdannāya** (Z), Baghdadi; Babylonian (NT, BT).

בד, בת, -ב (OA -בעי ד) **bɪd, bɪt** (NT), **b-** (Z), indicates future tense with a.p.: בד כאטיה **bɪd xā<u>t</u>e** They will sin; **ʾīman bdāʾɪr** When will he return? **ma bāxɪl** What will he eat? with negated future sentence it is replaced with the present particle: **la gdāʾɪr** He will not return. In NT also with p.p.: בד מרואלה **bɪd mɪrwāle** He should have said (NT2).

בדאנא, בתאנא, פתאנא (OA פדנא) m. **bɪ<u>d</u>āna** (Z **bɪzāna**), **bɪ<u>t</u>āna** (NT2), plow, plowshare; **ʾ-w-<u>d</u> pɪ<u>t</u>āna** to plow (NT3) [Krotkoff 125; Ar فدّان].

בדאנותא (< בדאנא) **bɪ<u>d</u>anū<u>t</u>a** agriculture; v. ב-ד-נ.

ב-ד-ד II2 (Ar) vi/vt **b-d-d** to scatter, separate;

nāše wēlu mbuddıde ʾanya yōmāsa (Even related) people are scattered (all over the world) these days.

בדואייא (Ar) **badwāya** Bedouin (Sa83c 18).

ב-ד-ל II (Ar) **b-d-l** to exchange, to substitute (BT3, D).

בדל 1 (Ar) m. **badal** a fee paid for exemption from military service; אִמְבַּדַל **ımbadal** recompense (=H חֵלֶף, BT4, D).

בדל 2, בדיל (< OS?) **badıl**-(Z **bazıl**-) **mbınōke** morning shift, dawn (NT5 394; PolG; cf. MacD 25); v. באנהה.

בדלא (Ar) f. **badla** suit, set of clothes; pl. **badle, badlat** (PolG)

בדם (T < Ar بعد ما) **badam** if so, why then; v. יח . NT2 [MacD 25]

ב-ד-נ (< בדאנא) **b-d-n** (Z **b-z-n**) to plow (cf. PolG).

בדן (K < Ar) m. **badan** a traditional short coat (cf. RivSh 257; PolG)

בדנכאת (< בדן?) pl. **bıdankat** ailments (=H מַדְוֵי-, PolG).

ב-ד-ק (OA/H) **b-d-q** (Z ⁺**b-z-q**) to examine (if an animal is kosher for slaughtering).

ב-ד-ר, ב-ז-ר (?) (OA/OS/Mand בדר; OA בזר?) vt **b-d-r** (NT3), **b-z-r** (Z; cf. PolG), to scatter (NT3); sprinkle spices, salt, etc. (Z); cf. ביזירה, ב-ר-ב-ז.

בדרא (OA בי אדרא, בית אדרי, בידרי) f. **bıdra** threshing floor; a heap; **bıdır-⁺māya** toilet (euph.); pl. בדראתא **bıdrāta** (NT+). [Krotkoff 130].

בדר אל זמאן (Ar) **badr-ıl-zamān** The Full Moon of (Her) Time, an epithet of Queen Esther (NT5 397).

בהבהי (K?) inv. **bahbahi** pink.

ב-ה-ד-ל III (Ar) vt/vi **b-h-d-l** to ridicule, humiliate; be at a loss, confused.

בהדליתא (OA) **bahdalīta** humiliation, confusion. (Pol 105)

בהורא, בהורתא (OA בְּהוֹרָא, בְּהִירָא/OS ܒܗܪܐ dim, pale) adj. **bahūra, bahurta**, shining, bright; enlighted (heart); **bahūra zahūra** very bright; **ʾēnōxun bahūre** May your eyes shine (said after hearing announcement about marriage, etc.) [cf. Khan 564 **bahira** 'bright'].

בהורותא (< בהורא) **bahūrūta** brightness; glory (=H הוֹד, BT4, D).

בהוורותא, בהווריתא (K) **bahwarī/ūta** trust; **bahwarīse la kısya ʾıllan** He doesn't trust us.

ב-ה-י (Ar) **b-h-y** to rejoice (NTU4 163b; PolG), shine with joy (about good news).

בהייא (< ב-ה-י) adj. **bahīya** cheerful, full of light (place) (AmU2 5b).

בהיתא, בהתתא (< נ-ה-ת) adj. **bhīta, bhıtta** astonished, confused person (NT+).

בהלול (Ar/P) inv. **bahlul** jester (name of a wise-fool character in FT).

בהלולכא (OA בלל?) m. **bahlulka** growth in the eye (=H תְּבַלּוּל, BT3).

בהלולכאנא (< בהלולכא) m. **bahlulkāna** (one with) wen, cyst, tumor (=H יַבֶּלֶת, BT3).

בהמה, בְּהֵמָא (H) f. **bıhēma** animal (BT5, D); pl. בֶּהֶמָאת **bıhēmat** (BT4, D), בְּהֵמוֹת **bıhēmōt** (RivPr #93), בהימה **bıhēme** (NT6 135-6).

בהנא, בינא, בהן (K) m. **behna, bıhen** respite, breath, moment; abdomen (=H חֹמֶשׁ, PolG); **behna ʾıqa** impatience; **behna rwīxa** patience; **mayrıx/marwıx behnox** Be patient! **behne dʾırre** He recovered, felt better; **xa bēna** just a minute (Socin 162); suddenly (FT).

ב-ה-ר (OA) vi **b-h-r** to light, to clear; (**dunye**) **bhırra** the weather cleared; **ḥmōl hıl bahra** Wait till dawn; **bahra ʾıllax** Bless you, Bravo (Avin78 94); **ʾēne bhırru** He was delighted; IV to clarify (meaning) (NT), to light (vt); **ʾilaha mabhırra ʾıllōxun** May God shine upon you (=Have a good news); **ʾilaha mabhırra ʾıllox, mubhırālox ʾılli** Thank you, you helped me a lot (PolU 132); to appear (God) (=H הוֹפִיעַ, BT5, D) (NT+).

בהר (K/P) m. **bahar** the spring season.

בהרא 1, ביהרא (OA) m. **behra** (day)light (NT+).

בהרא 2 v. בירא

בהרתא (< ב-ה-ר) **bharta** daybreak (PolGr 33).

ב-ה-ת (OA/OS/Ar) vi **b-h-t** to be astonished, frightened; v. בהיתא (NT+).

בהתי (Ar-P) inv. **bahti** panic-stricken (NT2); פשלא בהתי וחרתא **pıšla bahti uḥırta** She became astonished and at a loss (=H תמיהה ושוממה, NT5 397).

בוג'ום (< Ar بَغـوم groaning/T knot?) **buğum** unfriendly, keeps to oneself (SaAC 6).

בודאקא (OS) **budāqa** blast furnace (=H כּוּר, BT5).
בוהראיי (K-OA/Ar) m. **bohrāyi** light; pl. **bohrāyiyat** (=H מְאֹרֹת, BT1).
בוטאלי, בֻּוטְלָאנִי (K-Ar) **buṭāli** (Z), **buṭlāni** (D), rest, no work (=H שַׁבָּתוֹן); pl. **buṭāliyat**. (=H שַׁבָּתוֹת, BT2, BT3).
בוטלא, טוטלא (OS ܒܘܛܠܐ anus?) m. **būṭıla, ṭūṭıla** penis (babytalk); cf. זנגלא, אירא.
בויא (<?) f. **bōya** (snack) seed of melons, and pumpkin; pl. **bōye**; cf. בושאדא [cf. Garbell 300 **bota, boe**; Mutz194 **bāwya** 'almond'].
בויך (T) m. **bōyax** shoe polish, dye.
בוימא (T?) f. **bōyama** a kind of head scarf.
בוימבאך (T/IrAr) **boyambáx** (modern style) tie.
בוכארי (Ar < ב-כ-ר) ***buxāri** incense (=H קְטֹרֶת, BT); herb; pl. ***buxāriyat** (NT+).
בוכס(א) (IrAr < En) **bux(a)**, box, punch (Z; BT2, Arodh) [Khan 565 **boks**].
בוכר (Ar) **bukır** virgin (NT3); cf. כמתא.
בוכרא 1, בוכ(ו)רתא (OA בּוּכְרָא, בּוּכְרְתָא) **buxra, buxı/urta** first-born (NT+).
בוכרא 2 (Ar/IrAr) f. **bukra** spool of thread.
בוכרותא (OA/OS בּוּכְרוּתָא) **buxrūta** birthright, first birth.
בוכתאן (K < Ar بهتان) **buxtān** libel, false charge (NT2); pl. בוכתאנה **buxtāne** (NT5 384) [cf. Mutz 197].
בוכתאנכר (K) **buxtānkar** libelous (NT5 401).
בוכתנצר, בוכתת נצר, בוכתד נצר, נבוכדנצר (Ar-H) **buxta(d/t)naṣṣar** (NT3), **navuxasnēṣar** (Z), Nebuchadnezzar.
בולא (<?) m. **bōla** hair (on head only); cf. מזתא (NT+) [MacD 27 **būla** wisp of hair < **šbūlā** ear of corn].
בולקא (OA בלעא?) m. **bulqa** mouthful, gulp.
בולק-בולק (onomat.) **bulq-bulq** sound of boiling; **mande bulqe** it boils (PolU 375).
בומא (Ar/OS) f. **būma** night hawk, owl (= H תַּחְמָס, BT3).
בומכין, בומא כן, בומכד, בומכת (< ב+יומא+כינא/כיתא) adv. **bōmaxín/d/t** the day after tomorrow, or before yesterday (usually preceded by **bınhe/tımmal**) tomorrow/yesterday (NT+).
בונא (< ברונא) **bōna** boy (babytalk); cf. באתא.
בונוד (P-Ar) **bunūd** conspiracy, banding: דוקלו בונוד אמיה **duqlu bunūd ʾımme** They conspired against him (NT2); cf. בנד, בנודה.
בועה-בועה (OA בּוּעֲתָא abcess; pl. בּוּעֵיי, בּוּיֵי) pl. **būʿé-būʿe** boils (all over) (=H אֲבַעְבּוּעוֹת, BT2).
בוקארא* (OS) **buqāra** advice, question; pl. בּוּקָרֵי **buqāre** (RivSh 274); cf. בקרתא.
בוקגא (K/T **bohçe**/P بغچه) m. **buqča** bundle, cloth used for keeping or carrying clothes (RivSh 148); **buqčıd kālo** bride's bundle, trousseau; pl. **buqče**.
בוקג'-ובאג' (K/P; cf. OA/OS/Mand בָּגָא, באגא < P) pl. **buqč-u-bāġ**luxurious garden (PolU 302); pl. **-ġat** (Pol 9).
בוקד/בוקל נפירא (Ar) f. **bōqıd/bōqıl ⁺nafīra** trumpet; pl. **bōqıd/bōqıl ⁺nafīrat/⁺nafīre** (BT4, BaBin 32; PolG).
בֻּוקְתָא (OA/OS בוקא jar) f. **buqta** bottle, liquid measure (= H הִין, BT3, D); cf. בקבקייה.
בור (K) **bōr** (river-)crossing (=H עֵבֶר, BT5; PolU 363); pl. בּוֹרַאת **bōrat** (=H מַעְבְּרוֹת, PolG).
בורא מאורי האש (H) ⁺**bōrē** ⁺**mōrē hāʾēš** (Blessed be) the Creator of Fire Lights (said on the exit of Sabbath; and followed by: **kıtte mın gōyīm la pāyıš, uʾawd pāyıš, rēše wāyıš** May none of the Gentiles survive, and if one does, may his head wither; cf. Amedi 49).
בורא עולם (H) **bōrē ʿōlām** Creator of the world (ZU 72b; PolU 160).
בורבוראנא (< K/onomat.?) adj ⁺**borbōrāna** loud, reverberating (voice); cf. ברברתא.
בורג'א (Ar) m. ⁺**burja** fortress (RivSh143).
בורהאן (Ar/P) m. ⁺**burhān**. miracle, divine sign; pl. בורהאנה⁺**burhāne** (NT, BT).
בורי (IrAr < T) m. ⁺**bōri** pipe, tube; pl. ⁺**bōriyat**.
בורכתא, ברכתא (OA בִּרְכְּתָא) f. **büraxta** (NT), **baraxta** (Z), blessing (NT), the Jewish wedding ceremony in which the seven benedictions are recited; לילד ברכתא **lēlıd** – wedding night (NTU3 1b); pl. ב(ו)רכאתא **bürxāta** (NT2) (OA בִּרְכָּאתָא.
בוש, בושאהי, בושאיי (K) **bōš, bōšāhi/yi,** strong (fire) (Zaken 388)), torrential (water), huge crowd (SaNR; =H הָמוֹן, PolG) (NT+).
בושאדא, בושיאדא (< בויא+שאדא?) **bōšeʾda** (Z

bōše'za) dry almond; v. שאדא.; pl. **bōše'de**.

בושאלא (OS) **bušāla** cooked food, pottage. (NT).

ב-ז-א (OA/OS בזע; Mand בזא) vi/vt **b-z-'** to break, to crack (NT), to pierce (BT2, Arodh); **lıbbi bze'le** My heart is broken; **qam bāze'le lıbbi** He broke my heart. (NT+).

בזא (OA בזיא) **bızza** wretched, humiliated man (NT2); בזא ומסכין **bızza umıskīn** humiliated and destitute man (NT5 392; NTU4 163a).

בזאא (OA/OS בִּיזָא, בִּיזְעָא) m. **bız'a** crack; pl. **bız'e**, בִּיזְאָאֵי **bız'ā'e** (=H חֹרִים, PolG:D) (NT+).

בזב (K) **bızav** hyperactivity; **'-w-z bızav** to be hyperactive, in constant motion.

בזבאנא (< K?) f. ***bızbāna** cigarette butt.

בזוטא, בִּיזֻּודְּכַּא (K) m.***bızzōta**, ***bızzodka** firebrand, torch (BT1, D; PolG); pl. ***bızzōte**, ***bızzotkat** (RivSh 216).

ב-ז-י II (OA בזא/OS/Mand בסא) vt/vi **b-z-y** to humiliate, be humiliated (RivSh 259); cf. בזא; to plunder: מִיבַזְיַיאנֵי **mıbazyāne** (=H שֹׁסִים, PolG).

בזיאתותא, בִּיזְיָיתֻותָא (< ב-ז-י; cf. ביזיון) f. **bızyātūta** humiliation (BaBin 121; = H בִּזָּיוֹן, PolG).

בזמא (AzT) **bızma** cuff (of shirt, dress); bracelet made of chain of coins [MacD **buzmā** plaid, fold].

בזמארא (K < Ar **mismār**) m. **bızmāra** metal nail (cf. PolG); pl. **bızmāre**.

ב-ז-מ-ר III (< בזמארא) **b-z-m-r** to nail; to have a 'rusty' and hard section (melons).

בזף (K بزاو 'haste') **bızaf** agony, struggle; — **mōsa** death agony, hard work (SaAC 10).

ב-ז-ר 1 v. ב-ד-ר

ב-ז-ר 2 (IrAr) ***b-z-r** to sire (pejor.); cf. ב-ד-ר.

ב-ז-ר-א III (< ברזרא) vi **b-z-r-'** (woman:) to retain seed (=H נִזְרְעָה, BT4, D).

בז'וז'ינכה (K) f. **bıžužinke** large needle.

בז'נו-באל (K بژن < P بشن 'stature' + K/P بال 'tallness') **bažn-u-bāl** stature and body, good looks (PolU 10).

בז'נות v. ז'נו

בז'רב v. בשרב

בח (K/Ar?) **baḥ** all gone (baby talk).

בחייך הטובים (H) **baḥayyēxa haṭṭōvīm** By your (good) life (an oath) (NT2); cf. כאייה.

ב-ח-ל-ק III (IrAr) **b-ḥ-l-q** to stare with eyes wide open; cf. ב-ל-ק.

בחס (T/P < Ar بحث) **baḥs** (bad) report, talk: **nāše mosēlu baḥsan** People talked badly about us; **mpıqle baḥs lxa *palavan** Rumors spread about an acrobat (PolG); **'aw dla gmēse baḥse** cancer ('that which is not mentioned', taboo idiom); cf. פגגא שיר.

בחר (Ar) ***baḥ(ḥ)ar** sea, ocean (cf. PolG); the Nile (=H יְאוֹר, BT2); pl. בחריה **baḥre** (NT; BT3), בחארי **baḥ(ḥ)āre** (BaBin 138; PolU 305), ***baḥrāre** (Z); cf. יאמא.

בחרי(תא) (Ar) **baḥri, -rēta** (in FT: horse) able to cross oceans fast (PolU 129, 162).

בחר מלכא (OA מלחא) ***baḥḥar mılxa** the Dead ('Salt') Sea (BT4).

בחר קרם, בחרד קלזם (Ar < Gr klysma) f. **baḥrıd qılzam** (NT), ***baḥḥar *qırram** (Z), the Reed (Red) Sea (AvidH 53 יָאמִיד בַּחֵיר קְלְזַם)

בחריכה (Ar-K) f. **baḥrīke** lake, river; pl. בַּחְרִיכַּאת **baḥrīkat** (=H יְאוֹרִים, BT2, D).

בַּטַּא (IrAr) f. **baṭṭa** scar in the eye (BT3, D).

בטאטא (Ar < It) f. **baṭāṭa** potato.

בטאנא (Ar)f. **baṭāna** lining of clothes.

בטאנייה (Ar) f. **baṭānīye** blanket;pl.**baṭānīyat**.

בטי, בטיכא (< בטא) **bıṭṭi**, **bıṭṭīka** one with a scar in the eye.

בטילא, בטלתא (OA/OS בַּטִּילָא) adj. **baṭīla**, **baṭılta** unemployed, idle (often in hendiadys with עטילא **ʿaṭīla**); **xılmıd lēle baṭīla** (May your) night dream be of no consequence (said when one tells of a bad dream).

בטילתותא (< בטילא) f. **baṭīlatūta** idleness (Segal #88).

בטל (IrAr < En) m. **bıṭṭıl** bottle; pl. **bıṭle** [Khan 565 **boṭil**]

ב-ט-ל (OA/Ar) vi **b-ṭ-l** to stop (working, etc.); II/IV to annul (vows) (BT4), cancel, interrupt (RivSh 232); cease (PolG) (NT+).

בַּטְלַאנִין (OA בַּטְלָנָא/Ar بطلان) pl. **baṭlānīn** shirkers (=H נִרְפִּים, BT2, D).

בטמא (OA בוטמא; OS ܒܛܡܬܐ) f. **bıṭma** terebinth nut (tree = H אֵלָה, PolG); n. unit. **bıṭımta**; pl. **bıṭme**.

ב-ט-ר (Ar) **b-ṭ-r** to become haughty, arrogant;

to kick (=H וַיִּבְעַט, BT5).

בטראנא, בטרנתא (Ar) adj. **baṭrāna, baṭranta,** haughty, arrogant.

-בי 1 v. ביתא

-בי 2 (K/P) **be-** without, devoid of (privative).

ביאל v. אאלא

בי-אדב (K) inv **bē-adab** uncouth, (one) without manners.

ביאטא (<?) m. **bıyāṭa** ax (RivSh 115).

ביא-אל v. אאלא

בי-אלאייה (< ביתא+אלאיא) pl. **bē-ʾılāye** the upper floor residents (SaLH 161); cf. -בי. כתאייה

בַּיַּאר (K < Ar باثر) inv. **bayar** desolate; **pēša** —will become desolate (=H תֵּשָׁם, PolG).

ביאתא v. באתא

ביב (K?) **bēb** together with; **ʾāwa ubēb ʾaxōne sēlu** He came together with his brother; **kāšīya bēb saḥnāye** (tea) glass together with (its) saucer (cf. BT3; BT5; BaBin 108; PolG).

ב-י-ב II (< ביבי?) **b-y-b** to look around, search with one's eyes.

בי-באבא (< ביתא+באבא) **bē-bāba** (bride's) parents' house (cf. PolGr 59)

ביבאנכס v. פלאנא

ביבונא (Ar/K/P) m. **bēbūna** wild flower, camomile; **bēbūn ⁺ʾāzar** anemone; **bēbūn nīsan** cyclamen ('flower of Adar/Nisan').

ביבי (K < OA בּוּבִיתָא, בבביתא/Ar بؤبؤ/P بَبَك?) **bībi** the pupil of the eye (NT4; BT5); — **dyōma** sun (PolU 376); cf. אינא; pl. **bībīye** (but v. NT5 389 ביבי דאינוה בד פלטי **bībi dʾēnuh bıd palṭi**) [MacD 24, 30 **bibilta**, pl. **bābāgi, bībīyī**; Mutz 195 **bibılka**].

בי-בכת (P) inv. **be-baxxat** dishonest; v. בכת.

בי-בכתותא (< בי-בכת) **be-baxtūṯa** dishonesty; **drēle ʾılla bē-baxtūṯa** He falsely accused her (SaLH 150).

ביגוינא (OA בית גבינא) **begwīna** eyebrow (BT3); pl. **begwīne** (Hob97 325).

ביגוינאנא (< ביגוינא) adj. one with no (or thick?) eyebrows (=H גִּבֵּן, NT3).

ביגר (< ברינגר?) **bē/īgar** (?) yoke, burden? ביגר דידוך גטאנך בד דונייה – **dīdox gṭaʾnax bıd dunye** We carry your yoke in this world (NTU4 150b).

ב-ג̇-ב-ג̇ v. ב-י-ג̇

-ביד לב (< ב+אי+ד+לבא) **bēd lıbb-** intending: **tūle bēd lıbbe yātu unāyıx** He sat, intending to sit and rest (PolG).

בידאדיית (K) pl. **bedādīyat** annoying caprices; **mare-bedādīyat** capricious, troublesome; הַי דאד ובֵידַאד **hay dād ubedād** Alas, what a suffering! (Babin 160).

בי-דולת (P) inv. **be-dōlat** unfortunate, unlucky.

בי-היבי (K) inv. **be-hīvi** hopeless (Ruth 1:18).

בֵּיוַעִיד (P-Ar) **be-waʿıd** suddenly (BT4, D).

ב-י-ז (OA בזז) vt/vi **b-y-z** to spill (NT+).

ביזא (< OA בית אידא?) f. **bēza** sleeve (Z); pl. **bēzāsa** (Z).

ביזוי (H) **bızzūy** usually: **p-y-š** — to be humiliated, disgraced (woman, old person).

בִּיזַּיוֹן (H; cf. OA בִּיזְיוֹנָא) **bızzāyón** humiliation; with **p-y-š** to become humiliated (BT1, D); cf. בזיאתותא.

ביזירה (< ב-ז-ר/Ar بزر/OA בְּ(י)זְרָא seed?) pl. **bızīre/bızre** (?) spices, seeds (NT5 408).

ב-י-ז-ר III (< באזר) **⁺b-ē-z-r** bargain (cf. PolG) [1:**⁺mbīzır-**; 2/3: **⁺mbēzır**; 4: **⁺mbēzōre**].

בי-חאל (P-Ar) inv. **be-ḥāl** very sick; very poor: **faqir...beḥāl waxni** We were poor and destitute ((PolU); v. חאל.

ביחד (P-Ar) inv. **be-ḥád** without limit (NT3).

בי-חזאנה (OA-H) **bē-ḥazzāne** Cantors' House (name of shrine and synagogue in Amidya).

בי-חיא (P-Ar) inv. **be-ḥaya** shameless.

בי-חכומא (< ביתא+חכומא) **bē-ıakōma** king's house (PolGr 59).

בי-טבעת (K-Ar) inv. **be-ṭabʿat** ill-natured.

בייא v. ביתא

בייטרכאנא (T/IrAr) f. **bayṭarxāna** veterinarian hospital; **bayṭarxanči** veterinarian.

בֵּי-כָּאבִי (K) adv. **be-kavi** (hurting someone) unintentionally (Z); suddenly (BT4, D).

ביכודן (K) inv. **be-xudān** (one with) no protection or care (BaBin 162); v. כודאני.

בי-כס (K) inv. **be-kas** one without immediate relatives [cf. Khan 565 **bekas** 'orphan'].

בי-כירת (K) inv. **be-xīrat** lazy; v. כירתא.

בי-כמרא (OA בית חמרא) **bē-⁺xamra** wine-cellar.

בי-כתאייה (< כתאייא) pl. **bē-xtāye** lower (first) floor residents (SaLH 161); cf. -בי אלאייה.

נ-ב-ל v. ב-י-ל
ביני v. בילי
בילא (< בילי/ביני) adj. **bēla** medium (not good or evil): פראת הויה ובילה **parā'ıt hawwe ubēle** (God) rewards the good and medium people (NTU4 181a, 183b).
בילומא (K without blame?/Ar بلومة with blame?) **belōma** terrible, unfortunate: **yā rabbi** – My God, how terrible (the situation is)! (PolG; SaAC 12)
בי-מענא (K-Ar) **be-maᶜna** no (sexual) inuendo (said after mentioning a word that might have sexual connotation).
בי-מעריפתא (K-Ar) inv. **be-maᶜrīfıta** lacking good manners, crude.
בֵי מִירַאד (K-Ar) **be-mırād** disappointment; **qısmi – lēwe ınpīqa** My lot has not resulted in disappointment, I am lucky (PolG).
בי-מרוות, בֵימִירְוַוד (P-Ar) inv. **be-mırwat/d** cruel, lacking ideal manly manners.
ב-י-ן II (Ar) **b-y-n** to seem,to appear; **gımbēna** It seems (NT+).
בי-נאמוס (P) inv. **be-nāmus** ill-mannered.
בי-נאמוסותא (P) f. **be-nāmūsūt̲a** ill manners (PolU 182).
בי-נגמא (P-Ar) inv.**be-najma, bınjama** uncouth; usually hendiadys with בי-עצל.
בינאת(א) (OA) adv./prep. **bēnāta** (!) meanwhile, between it (PolG).
בין השמשות (H) **bēn-haššımāšōt̲** twilight (NT2).
ביני, בילי, בֵין, בֵית (OA בֵינֵי, -בֵינָת/OS ܒܝܢܬ ,ܒܝܢܝ:) prep. **bēni, bēli** (NT2), **bēn** (BT3, D), **bēt** (BT4, D) among, between; ביני ובינוך **bēni ubēnox** between me and you; cf. -לאל.; ביני אינד **bēni 'ēnıd** on the forehead of (NT3); cf. גובאינא.
בין כך ובין כך, בין כך לכך (H) adv. **bēn kax lıxax, bēn kax uven kax** in the meantime (NT2).
בי-נסל (P-Ar) inv. **be-nısıl** childless (BT1).
ביס אל מציר (Ar) **bīs-al-maṣīr** bad luck, bitter end (NT2).
בִיסְמַא (OA) **bısma** frankincense (=H לְבוֹנָה, NT3, D).
ביסת ויכ (K) **bist -u-yak** twenty-one (popular card game).
ב-י-ע II (Ar) **b-y-ᶜ** to sell (NT5 408); cf. -ז-ב-ן.

בי-עאקל (P-Ar) inv. **be-ᶜāqıl** (< **ᶜaql**) mindless, simpleton; pl. בֵיעָאקִילֵי **beᶜāqıle** (AvidH 61).
ביע ושרה (Ar) **bayᶜ ušıre** trade, buying and selling (NT5 408); cf. ש-ק-ל.
בי-עצל (K-Ar اصل) inv. **be-ᶜáṣıl** ill-mannered, of no (good) origin; **be-ᶜáṣıl ubınjáma** (< **ube-najma**) very ill-mannered ('no [noble] origin and no star') (cf. PolG).
בי-עקלותא, בֵיעַקְלוּתַא (< בי-עאקל) **be-ᶜāqılūt̲a** mindlessness. BaBin 132, NT+
בי-ערז (K-Ar عرض) inv. **be-ᶜarz** dishonored; **'-w-z be-ᶜarz** to dishonor (Pol 105); cf. ערז.
בי-פיידא, ביפאידא (P-Ar) inv. **be-fayda** (Z), **be-fāyıda** (NT2), useless, of no benefit.
בי-פעול (P-Ar) inv. **be-fıᶜol** sexually ill-mannered.
בי-פעלותא (< בי-פעול) **be-fıᶜlūt̲a** disapproved sexual behavior.
ב-י-צ II (OA) vt/vi **b-y-ṣ** to glitter; **'amāne dīda wēlu mabōṣe** Her dishes are glittering (being so clean).
בִיקַא (Ar?) **bīqa** bottle, jar (=H הִין, BT3, D); cf. בקבקייה, בוקתא.
בי-קדר (K-Ar) inv. **be-qadır** disrespected (Segal #109).
ביקור חולים (H) **bıqqūr ḥōlīm** (the religious obligation of) visiting the sick (NT2).
בירא, בהרא (OA/OS/Mand) m. **bēra** (NT), **behra** (Z), water well; בירד אריואתא **bērıd 'aryawāt̲a** lions' den; pl. ביראתא **bērāt̲a** (NT), **behrawāt̲a** (cf. PolGr 54)[Khan 565 **bira**].
בֵירָאקָא (T) **berāqa** flag, troop, ensign (BaBin 107, 119)[cf. MacD 30; Khan 565 **berāq**].
בירובה (K) f. **bīrōve** psoriasis (=H בַּהֶרֶת, גָּרָב, BT3); pl. **bīrōvat**.
בירובנתא, בירובכאנא (< בירובה) **bīrōvanta** (D), **bīrovkāna** (Z), (one suffering from) scurvy (=H יַלֶּפֶת, BT3).
בירית̲א (<?) f. **bērīt̲a** dancing circle (cf. PolG); **d-w-q bērīt̲a** to make a dancing circle; pl. **bēriyāt̲a** (PolU 18).
ביראמשי, בירמאשה (OS) **bēramāše** (at) evening, sunset (NT2), yesternight (BT1, Z).

בירנגי (T 'first') inv. **be/ırınji** excellent, 'numero uno' (PolU 115).

ביש (K) m. **bēš** quota, share (PolU 59).

ביש בלכ (T) **bēš bıllık** Turkish gold coin used in necklaces.

בי-שודה (< שודה) **be-šōḏe** (Z **be-šōze**) 'house of joy' = the first visit of the bride to her parents' house after the wedding (cf. PolU 375; Bt93 145)

בי-שרם (K/P) inv. **be-šarm** shameless.

בישתא (OA) only in מלאכד בישתא **malʾāxıd bišta** angels of evil (NT3).

ב-י-ת (OA/OS/MAnd) **b-y-ṯ** to spend the night (=H לִין, BT1, D; PolG); VI **mabōṯe** (Z **mabōse**) to cook overnight; cf. מבותה; to keep overnight (=H הֵלִין, BT3, D; מים שלנו, NT5 409).

ביתא, בייא (OA) m. **bēṯa** (Z **bēsa**), **bayya** (PolU 207: ChNA), house; **bēs(ıd) bē zāqen** the house of the Zaqen family; **bēs bābi** My dear friend (lit. house of my father)(PolU 421); **bēs ʿilāha ʾmīra** Thank God (PolU 422); pl. באתיה **bāte**; **batāne** (MeAl 190), **bēṯwāṯa** (AlfH 49; PolG) (OA pl. בָּתֵּי, באתי) ; v. בי-באבא, בי-חכומא (NT+).

בית אילאהא (< ביתא) **bēṯ-ʾilāha** house of God, synagogue (PolU 390).

בית דין (H) **bēṯ dīn** Jewish court (NT+).

בי ישראל, ביתד ישראל (H) **bē(ṯıd) yısrāʾēl** the House of Israel (NT).

ביתד מדרש (H; cf. OA בי מדראשא) **bēṯıd mıdraš** Jewish school; pl. מדראשיה **mıdrāše** (NT+).

בי מקדש, ביתד מקדש (H) **bē(ṯıd) mıqdaš** (NT3; Z **bēsammíqdaš**) the Temple (in Jerusalem).

ביתונכא (< ביתא) m. **bēṯunka** (Z **bēsunka**) little house; toy-house; pl. **bēṯunkat**.

ביתכה (K?) f. **bētıke** trousers' hem to hold the string-belt.

בכאיא, בכיתא (< ב-כ-י; cf. OA בָּכְיָא) adj. **baxāya**, **baxēṯa** crybaby, weeper.

בכאיה v. כאיה

בכבאבא v. בכתא

ב-כ-ב-כ III (Ar) **b-k-b-k** to whine, moan, pretend weeping (child).

בכו (K) **bakko** an evil character, a spoiler (from the famous Kurdish epic Mam-u-Zin).

בכור (H) ⁺**bıxōr** firstborn (as a religious term; cf. בוכרא)(NT2).

בכורים (H) **bıkkūrím** first-fruits (BT3).

ב-כ-י (OA) **b-x-y** to weep.

בכיא (OS ܒܟܝܐ) m. **bıxya** weeping, cry; pl. בכיה **bıxye**; באואדא עזאיה ובכיה **beʾwāḏa ʿazāye ubıxye** lamenting and crying (NT+).

בכיתא (< ב-כ-י; OA בְּכִיתָא) f. **bxēṯa** cry (NT5 397).

בְּכִיִיתָא (<?) pl. **bıxyāṯa** aftergrowth, remains (=H סָפִיחַ, BT3, D).

ב-כ-ר II (Ar) ⁺**b-x-r** to burn incense, to perfume (=H קִטֵּר, BT; cf. PolG); cf. בוכארי.

ב-כ-ש (OA/OS בחש) vt **b-x-š** to mix, stir.

בכד, בכת (IrAr/P) m. **bax(x)at/d** mercy (cf. PolG); **baxxat ʾilāha ubaxxatox** for the mercy of God and yours (MeAl 191-2, n. 79); cf. בי-בכת.; **má ile ʾóha báxxat ilá** What is this (thing) for God's sake? (Gz).

בכתא (OS 'spinster') f. **baxta** woman, wife; בכבאבא **baxbāba** stepmother (Babin 84); בך-חכומא **bax-ḥakōma** queen; **la-baxta** bachelor, without a wife (PolU 351a); pl. **baxtāṯa** (NT+) [Krotkoff 131-32, 134].

בכתונתא (< בכתא) **baxtunta** (little/fellow) lady; pl. **baxtunyāṯa** (PolGr 56).

ב-ל-ע, ב-ל-א(OA בלע, בלי) **b-l-ʾ**, **b-l-ʿ** (RivSh 141) to swallow; או יומא דבליא יונה **ʾaw yōma dblīʾ yōna** on the day that Jonah was swallowed (NT6 134) (NT+).

בלא 1 (Ar) f. **bala** misfortune, trouble; pl. **balıtyāṯa, balāye, balwıtyāṯa** (Sa83c 34); v. דרד (NT+).

בלא 2 (Ar) **bala** without; **bala** ⁺**nēzır** with no (religious) obligation; **bala (mal)qós šabbás** without (suffering) the punishment (of breaking) the Sabbath (rules)(said by women after mentioning some work forbidden on Sabbath).

בלא 3, בלתא (K/T **bellu** known) **bılla (ta)** only in **ta -ıd ʾilāha** for God's sake, doing a favor pro bono (PolU 295, 308, 437).

בלבול (H) **bılbūl** confusion (NT2).

בלבולכא (Ar بُلْبُلَة jug with spout) m. **balbulka** spout; pl. **balbulkat**. [cf. MacD **banbūlā**].

ב-ל-ב-ל III (OA to mix, disturb) **b-l-b-l** to search, look for: **mbalbıl go jēbox** look in your pocket; to feel by fingers (BT1); to confound (BT1).

בלבל (Ar) **bılbıl** nightingale; **kīʾēla mux bılbıl** He knows (to chant) it very well.

בלבליסכה, באבליסכה (K) f. **balbaliske** (Z), **bābaliske** (NT5 388), storm.

בלג'ם (Ar < Gr) m. **balġam** phlegm.

בלד (Ar) f. **balad** city, country; cf. -(ת)בר אלבלד; pl. **balāde, baládat** (PolG, SaAC 17) (foreign) countries, abroad.

בלדייא (Ar) f. **baladīya** city government.

בלדירכאת v. ברנדירכה

בלי, בלה (K < Ar) adv. **bale** yes indeed; **la zıllox ʾıl šūqa? bale** Didn't you go to the market? Yes (I did); however, moreover (NT+).

בלואתא (OS ܒܠܘܥܬܐ sink, sewer; OA בלועא throat) f. **baloʾta** throat; **lak kāwıš bbaloʾti** I don't like him very much (lit., He doesn't go down in my throat) (NT+).

בלובכתא (K?) f. **bıllōvıkt̲a** a measure of grain, about one עולבא, for grinding in the mill (cf. PolU 395).

בלוז (IrAr < Fr) f. **blūz** woman's blouse.

בלוטא (OA/OS בַּלּוּטָא) m. **balūṭa** acorn; **dārıt** — acorn tree.

בלולא (OA?) m. **balōla** rolled (carpet, etc.).

בלועא (Ar; OA בָּלוֹעָא throat, chasm) f. **ballōʿa** drain, sewer; cf. בלואתא.

בלור (Ar/P < Gr) **bıllur** crystal, beryl.

בלורה (K) f. **bıllūre** flute; **bıllūre bo gāyi bēža** Play a flute for a cow (said when one fails to convince an ignorant); **ʾ-m-r/m-x-y bıd** — to play flute; pl. **bıllūrat** (BT2; PolG).

בלחש (H) adv. **balaḥaš** by whispering (a Jewish prayer) (NT2).

ב-ל-ח-ת III (Ar بحث) **b-l-ḥ-t̲** (Z **b-l-ḥ-s**) to search out, poke about.

בלטיתא (OA בולטיתא) f. **bıltīt̲a** worm in wood.

בלי 1 v. בלה

בלי 2 (IrAr) **billi** ace (in cards).

ב-ל-י (OA) vi **b-l-y** to wear out (=H בָּלָה, BT5, D); לשוך בד באלה גו קורא **laššox bıd bāle go qōra** Your flesh will be consumed in the grave (NTU4 163b); II vt to wear out (NTU4 150b).

בלכ (K 'alert'?) **bılık** (horse) shared alternately by two riders (PolU 250).

בלכין, בלכון, בַּלְכֵּית, בלכיד, בלכי (AnAr/IrAr/P/T/K < Ar بل يكون?) adv. **balki(d/t)** (RivSh 137), **balku/in(+Z)**, perhaps, lest (NT+).

בלם (IrAr) **balam** small row boat (PolU 215); food tray (shaped like boat ?) (PolU 193).

בלסאן, בלסם (Ar < Gr) m. **balsan** (NT), **balsam** (Z), balsam.

בלסתירכה (K?) f. **balastīrke** sparrow (Z); בְּרַאסְתִּירְכֵּי **barastīrke** stork? (=H חֲסִידָה, BT3, D); pl. **balastīrkat**.

בלעא (Ar) **bılʿa** gulp (?), used only in: **bılʿe mpıqle** He has a back-breaking task; **bılʿi qam māpıqle** He made me work very hard.

בלעם (H) **bılʿam** Balaam, a malicious scheming person.

בלצא (Ar) f. **balṣa** bribe; pl. **balṣe**.

ב-ל-ק (Ar) **b-l-q** to gloat (with eyes wide open); cf. ב-ח-ל-ק; **ʾēne blīqe** big ugly eyes.

בלקו (K?) **balqo** a kind of thistle leave eaten pickled or in soups [cf. H בַּרְקָן?].

בלקיר בלגהנם (Ar) **bılqīr bıljahannam** (to go) to hell of hells (PolU 365); cf. קירא גיהנם.

בלש, בלאש, מבלש (Ar) adv. **(b)balaš, mbalaš** for free, at no cost; צנם בלאש **ṣanam balaš** vain idol (NT5 397); **mbalaš ʿalaš** absolutely free (cf. PolU 410).

במבא (K/Ar < E) f. ***bımba** bomb.

במבאלא (K?) f. **bımbāla** balloon (made of sheep's bladder).

במבלושכה (K?) f. ***bambalōške** soap-bubble; swollen skin; bloated fruit.

במה (H) **bāma** pagan altar (NT2).

במרי (< א-מ-ר) **bamri** one might say (Pol 105).

בנא (Ar بنّاء; OA בַּנָּאָה; OS ܒܢܝܐ) m. **banna** mason, bricklayer.

בן אדם, בן אאדם, בני אאדם (H) m. **ben-ʾād̲am, bani-ʾādam** (Pol 105) a human being (NT+).

בנאס- (K) **bnās-** fault of-: **bnāsox-īla** It is your fault, you are to blame.

בנאתא v. בראתא

בנבוב (K?) inv. **bınbūv** hollow.

בנג'אנא (K < Ar) f. **banjāna kumta** eggplant; — **smuqta** tomato; pl. **banjāne kome/smoqe**.

בנד (P) adj. **band** bound, stuck; captive, enslaved.(NT2).

בנדא (K) f. **banda** a kind of Kurdish epic song.

בנדאקא (Ar < Gr pontika) f. **bındāqa** hazel-nut; **naxīr-bındāqa** beautiful nose shaped like a hazel-nut (SaNR 332).

בנדואר (K بنده وار retarded) inv. **bandawār** neglected (kids), left with no care (PolG).

בנדובא (K) m. **bındūva** vagina.

בנדיזה (K) f. **bındīze** cushion-ring put on head when carrying loads.

בנהיה v. באנהה

בנודה (K? cf.בנד, בונוד) pl. **bınnūde** strips used to tie a baby to a cradle, diapers.

בנו, בניו (< בנימין) **bino, bınyo** Benjy (hypo).

בנוכה מבנוכה (< באנהה) f. **(m)bınōke** morning; pl. **mbınokwāṯa**.

בנונה v. ברונא

ב-נ-י 1 (OA) **b-n-y** to build; דאבנה לשלמה **dʾıbne lšalōmo** Which was built by Solomon (NT3); IV to make someone build; או בניאנא דמובנילו אבד ישראל **ʾaw bınyāna dmubnēlu ʾıbbıd yısrāʾēl** that building which they (Egyptians) made Israel build (for them).

ב-נ-י 2 (OA בין) **b-n-y** to select, pick out (dirt, tiny stones, bad seeds, from rice before cooking); **wēla mbanōye dīde ⁺rızza** She is clearing the rice.

בן אדם v. בני אדם

בניאנא (OA/OS/Mand) m. **bınyāna** building, structure.

בני בשר (Ar) **bani-bašar** human, any single person (PolU 86, 151).

בניכה (K) f. **bınīke** socket (BT2, Am).

בנימין, בניאמי (H) **bınyāmin, bınyāme** Benjamin.

בני ישראל (H) **bane-⁺yisrāʾel** Children of Israel (NT).

בניית (P بنیاد 'basis') m. **bınyat** one's genealogy, origin (PolU 94).

בנכ (Ar < E) m. **⁺bank** bank; cf. בנקנוט.

בן עולם הבא (H) m. **ben-ʿōlām-habba** one who deserves the World to Come (NT+).

בן פורת יוסף (H) m. **ben-porāṯ-yosēf** (May you be like) Joseph a fruitful bough (Gen. 49:22) (said to a child by an adult after being helped or shown an act of kindness).

בנקנוט (Ar < En) m. **banqanōṭ** banknote, money bill (in contrast to coins); pl. **banqanōṭe**.

בס, בסא (K/T/P/IrAr; cf. OA בַּס (הא) < P bas indeed) adv. **bas(sa)** only, just (that), that is enough; ולא אאיא ובס **ula ʾāya ubas** and not only that (but also...); בַּס סַנְחֵרִיב שׁוּקְלֵי **bass sanḥēriv šuqle** He left (alive) only S. (RivSh 278); **bassi** I am full; **bassox**? Did you have enough (to eat)? (NT+)

בסו v. בתיה

ב-ס/צ-ט II (Ar) **b-ṣ-ṭ** to spread, exhibit (Socin 161).

בס/צטא (Ar) **basṭa** spread, exhibit (fabrics).

בסטרמא (T) m. **⁺bastırma** heavily salted and peppered sausage.

בסימא, בסמתא (OA/OS/Mand בַּסִּימָא sweet, pleasant) adj. **bassīma, bassımta** alive, well (NT); delicious, pleasing (Z); **blıbba bassīma** (Use it) in good health! **hāwıt ṣāx ubassīma** Stay well! Long live (Zaken 390); **gyānox/ṣaḥḥıtox (ʾalpaga) bassımta** Bravo! lit., May your self/health be (thousand times) well! (PolG).

בסימותא (< בסימא) f. **bassīmūṯa** well-being, pleasantness; **bassīmūsox** Stay well!

בסירה (OA) pl. **bassīre** sour grapes.

בסכא 1 v. באסכא

בסכא 2 (K) m. **bıska** curl; pl. **bıske** (cf. PolG).

בסכו (K) inv. **bısko** curly (girl)

ב-ס-מ (OA/OS/Mand be pleasing, cheerful, intoxicated) **b-s-m** to be pleased; (the world:) to be sustained (NT); to recover from illness (NT); (the weather:) to improve (Z); to be delicious (Z); **basma gyānox** Be well, Bravo!; IV/II to heal (vt), to please, to make delicious; to sing well (Z): **qam mabsımla ⁺rāba** He sang very pleasingly; to exaggerate, make it more appealing (PolG).

בסמא (OA בּוּסְמָא/OS ܒܣܡܐ spice) m. **bısma** resin (used as dry powder to heal wounds); pl. **bısme** (=H בְּשָׂמִים, PolG) (OA pl. בּוּסְמָנֵי).

בסמתא (< ב-ס-מ) f. **bsamta** well-being (BaBin 140); healing, good news (Sa83c 18, Z).

בסקא (OA בזקא) m. **bısqa** pebble, little stone; pl. **bısqe**.

בסתא (K) n./inv. **bısta** certain(ty):- **dīde zılla** He lost his confidence; confident (SaAC 11), has a sure hand; **māxıtte hādax** – You hit him with a sure hand (PolG); cf. בסתהי.

בסתאנא (Ar بُستان/OA/OS בּוּסְתָּנָא < P **bostān**) m. **bıstāna** garden, orchard; pl. **-e**.

בסתה (K/P) f. **baste** dry area in a river, river bank; **xılle kēpıd baste** He starved.

בסתהותא (< בסתא) **bıstahūṯa** confidence (PolG).

בסתהי (< בסתא) **bıstahí** confidently (BaBin 140); confidence (NTU4 182a; PolG).

ב-ע-ב-ע III (Ar بحبح) **b-ᶜ-b-ᶜ** to be prosperous.

בעבעתא (< בעה) f. **baᶜbaᶜta** bleating (cf. En **baa** 'bleat')

ב-ע-ב-צ III (IrAr) **b-ᶜ-b-ṣ** to poke lewdly with finger; to poke about (in drawers).

ב-ע-ג̇ (Ar to dent) vt/vi **b-ᶜ-j** to lay heavily on someone; be out of breath due to a heavy load (NTU4 165a) [MacD **p/b-ᶜ-j** to nearly die].

בעה (< ב-ע-י) m. **baᶜe** sheep (babytalk).

בעויר, בעוירכא, בעוירכה (Ar) inv. **baᶜwir, baᶜwirka** (m.), **baᶜwirke** (f.), half or almost blind, cross-eyed; cf. עוירא.

ב-ע-י (OA פעי) **b-ᶜ-y** to bleat (RivSh 183).

בעל הבית (H) m. **baᶜal-abbáyit̲** (Z -s) the owner of the house (BT2, Z); the master; the host (PolU).

בעל זכות (H) **baᶜal záxut̲** meritorious (NT+).

ב-צ-ב-צ III (OA/Ar) **b-ṣ-b-ṣ** to glimmer (PolUL 407).

בפשא (K?) m. **bafša** rectangular piece of wood to stir fried meat.

ב-צ-ט v. ב-ס-ט

בצלא (OA) m. **bıṣla** onion; **bıṣle yarūqe** scallions.

בצלאל, בצלו (H) p.n.m. **baṣálʾel, baṣlo** (Hypo.) Bezalel; talented craftsman, inspired person.

בקא (K) f. **baqqa** frog; **⁺garrıd baqqe** family with many noisy children ('pond of frogs').

בקאלא (Ar) **baqāla** green grocer (PolU 287).

ב-ק-ב-ק III (Ar) **b-q-b-q** (stomach:) to be swollen from drinking too much (water or soup); to popple (=H פעפע, AlfM 15).

בקבקייה (Ar; cf. BH בַּקְבֻּק) f. **baqbaqīye** small jug (cf. PolU 16); pl. **baqbaqīyat**; cf. ב-ק-ב-ק ; cf. בוקתא [Khan 564 **barbaqi** K; probably all onomatopoeic of water-pouring sound].

בקה (K?) **⁺bıqe** peek-a-boo (babytalk).

בקכי (< בקא) adv. **baqqıki** (swimming) frog-style.

בקל (Ar) m. **baqıl** beet leaves (Hob89 182).

בקלאוא (T/Ar) f. **baqlāwa** sweet Turkish pastry.

בקמארא (K) f. **⁺baqmāra** crocodile; turtle (?) =H צָב, BT3).

בקצמא (Ar/OA פכסם < Gr) **baqṣımma** hard buiscuit, zwieback.

ב-ק-ר II (OA) **b-q-r** to ask, inquire, consult with (NT+).

בקרתא, בִּיקֻורְתָא (OA) f. **baqarta** (Z, NT), **bıqurta** (+PolG), question, request (for advice); **qıṭla dla – lag barya** Execution without investigation is not possible (PolU 155); cf. בוקארא; pl. **baqaryāt̲a**; בקורייתא **bı/uquryāt̲a** (Babin 105; PolG) [Mutz 196 **baqurta**; pl. **baqurye**].

בקשא (K) m. **baqša** pebble; pl. **baqše** children game with five stones (trying to jump them from inside the palm to the back of hand).

בקשיש (Ar/P) m. **baqšiš** bribe; pl. **baqšīše**.

בר 1 v. ברונא

בר 2 (K) prep. **bar** only in **bar ḥukum/ mutuᶜ d-** under the rule of (PolU 341,350).

ברא 1 (K) **bırra** f. crowd, group, flock (of birds); pl. **bırre**.

ברא 2 (K/P) m. **bara** seed, fruit, mostly in: **d-w-q** – to become pregnant (animal) (PolU 63).

בראדה (Ar) f. **⁺barrāde** water cooler

בראזא (K) m. **bırāza** pig.; pl. **⁺bırāze**.

בראיה אכרתי (K-Ar?) **brāye ʾıxrati** '(swear by) adopted (?) brotherhood' (PolU 362).

ברא-בוכאת/בז'כת (K) pl. **bara-būkat/ bēžakat** relatives of bride and groom who throw seeds and candies on the newlyweds' head for a blessing (PolU 168).

ברא-טנגה v. טנגא

בראייכותא, בְּרָאכֻּתָא (K) f. **barā(yı)kūt̲a** priority (NT); prep. towards (=H לִקְרַאת, BT1 D; RivSh 264 לְבַרְכוּסַא; +PolG בְּרֵיהִיכֻותִית).

ברכה v. בראכא

בר(ת)-אלבלד v. בר-אלבלד

בראנא (K) m. **⁺barāna** ram, male sheep; pl. בָּרָאנֵי כִּיבִי **barāne küvi** (=H אֵלִים, AvidH 50).

בלסתירכה v. בראסתירכי

ברא-פאשבא (K) adv. **bara-pāš/žva** backwards (PolG).

בראתא (OA בְּרַתָּא, OS ܒܪܬܐ) f. **brāta** daughter; בראתא בוכר **brāta bukır** (NT3)/**brāta brat-bēsa** (Z) virgin; cf. ברתותא; v. באתא; pl. בנאתא **bnāt̲a** (NT+).

ברבא (K) **barva** front (euph.), vagina (PolU 71); v. פש(ת)בא.

ברבאטה (< ב-ר-ב-ט?) pl. **bırbāṭe** sparks (?), only in **bırbāṭe dnūra fırru m'ēne** He became very angry (lit., sparks of fire flew from his eyes)(cf. PolG; PolU 104).

ברבאנכה (K) f. **ba/ırbānke** patio, semi-open hall (cf. PolG); pl. **ba/ırbānkat**.

ב-ר-ב-ז III (OA/OS בזבז) vt/vi to scatter, to waste; cf. ב-ד-ר (NT+).

ב-ר-ב-ט III (Ar) **b-r-b-ṭ** to dabble, move like a fish; struggle (=H הִתְרוֹצֵץ, BT1).

בר-בנא (K) **bar-bınna** lowland (BT5; PolU).

ב-ר-ב-ע III (Ar بُعبُع 'bogey' ?) vt/vi to suddenly alarm someone or be alarmed (cf. PolG).

ב-ר-ב-ק (Ar بربخ drain, gutter?) **b-r-b-q** vi/vt to splash or be splashed .

ברבר (K) prep. **barbar** towards, very close to (a certain time), about (cf. PolG); cf. ברמבר.

ברברכאנא (P/IrAr?) **⁺barbarxāna** necessary goods for home (?) (PolU 362).

ברברתא (K) f. **bırbırta** uproar, talking sounds; cf. בורבוראנא.

בר בתרא v. בתר

ברגוזא, ברגוס (K?) m. **bargūza, bargus** woolen vest (and pants); coarse wool.

ברגיל (AnAr < K/P) m. **bargil** beast of burden, old horse; decrepit, bony, lean (person).

ברגילכי v. בגירכה

בַּרְגִילֶכְּתַא (K?) f. **barjīlıkta** crop (in bird's gullet) (=H מֻרְאָה, BT3).

ברג'י (Ar) m. **⁺bırği** a screw; pl. **⁺bırğiye** (PolU 350).

ב-ר-ד (Ar) **⁺b-r-d** to file, to rasp (cf. Zaken 388; PolG); cf. מברד.

ברדא, ברברדא (OA בַּרְדָא) f. **barda** (NT), **barabarda** (Z), hail (stones); v. כיפא1.

ברדאיי, בַּרַדַּהִי (K) **⁺barradāhi** prostitute (euph.) (BT1); open, non-walled area (=H חֲצֵרִים, BT3, D), non-walled city (BaBin 27).

בַּרְדֻונְגֵי (K bardūv) **bardūnge** backbone (in sheep's tail) (=H עָצֶה, BT3, D).

בַּרְדִיפִּין (K-OA) **bardıpın** corner, edge (of) (BT, D); cf. דפנא.

ברנדירכה v. ברדינכי

ברדקאנייה, בַּרְקַאנִיֶה (K) f. **bardıqānīye** (Z), **barqānīye** (RivSh 247; PolG), slingshot; cf. ברקוסכה.

ב-ר-ה-נ III (Ar) **⁺b-r-h-n** to demonstrate (by miracles, wonders).

ברוך הבא (H) **⁺bārux-xábba** Welcome! (used even by Gentiles: PolU 7; said to a woman as well, PolU 288); ברוך אתה **bārux-'átta** Blessed be you, too! (response).

ברוך הוא וברוך שמו (H) **⁺bārūx-(h)ū(n) ubārūx šamō** Blessed be He and blessed be His name!

בָּרֻוךְ הַשֵּׁם, ברוך השם (H) **bārūx-haššēm** Blessed be his name, Thank God (NT2; PolG; PolU 321).

ברוך מחייה המתים (H) **bārūx maḥayyim-mēsīm** Blessed be the reviver of the dead (said after being saved from a disaster) (cf. PolU 227).

ברונא (OA ברא, בר) m. **brōna** son, boy; const. אברד **ıbrıd** (NT), **bır** (Z): **bır-'amōya** cousin; **bır-bāba** bachelor; **bır-ḥakōma** prince, king's son; but **brōne, brona** his/her son, etc.; pl. **bnōne, brōne** (RivSh 264) (OA בְּנֵי, בנין; OS ܒܢܝܐ).

ברונ(נ)כא (< ברונא) m. **brōnı(n)ka** (little) son, boy (cf. PolU 320).

ברוסכא (K) m. **bırūska** sudden pain, birth contraction; ghastly image, lightning (PolU 352); pl. **bırūskat**.

ברוור (K) **barwar** shortcut route (PolU 436).

ב-ר-ז (Ar?) **b-r-z** to be dry; **wıšle brızle** (food) became dry, lost its freshness.

בָּרָאזִיו, ברזיב(K?) **barazīv, -zīw** (AvidH 50), flint (=H חַלָּמִישׁ. BT5; AlfH 59).

בר-זיקא (K-Ar) **bar-zīqa** front of collar.

בר-זיר v. זיר-ובר-זיר

בר-זראא, בזראא (OA בר זרעא, בַּזְרָא seed) m. **bar-zar'a** (NT), **bazar'a** (Z), offspring(s).

בר-חליא m.(OA-Ar حلي tender thistle?) **bır-ḥalya** fresh anise.

ברטיל (Ar) m. **barṭil** bribe, gift (NT, BT); ransom (BT4); bride-price (Z); pl. ברטילה ברטילאת, **barṭīle, barṭīlat**.

ב-ר-י (OA/OS create) **b-r-y** to happen; **brēla naṣūsa** a war broke out (PolU 309); **ma brēle ʿıllox** What happened to you? **lag barya** It is impossible; **lag bāre mınnan** We cannot afford it; **lēwa brīsa ula gbarya** Nothing (amazing) like this has ever happened or will ever happen (Ft; PolG); to be born, to result (RivPr 212); IV to cause to happen; **apēha ʾilāha qam mabrēla brēšan** This too God wanted to happen to us (said after misfortune); to create (BT1, Am) (NT+).

ברי (K) m. **bıri** (main) weight, heaviness, focus, force.

בריייא (Ar) f. **barīya** wilderness, desert.; pl. **barīyat** (NT+).

בריה (H) f.⁺**bırya** creature, human being; **ču ⁺bırya lēba fatla gzāza ʾılle** No creature can trick him (twist a string around him); pl. בְּרְיֵי **bırye** (=H בריות, AvidH 67).

בריכא, ברכתא (OA/OS/Mand blessed, God, people, things) adj. **brīxa, brıxta** blessed, but used only when having something new, much like Ar مبروك, Use it well!: **jullox brīxe** Use your (new) clothes well! V. מבורכא.

ברינגר (< K برگران?) **báringár** (heavy) burden; **p-y-š** – to become a burden (PolG); cf. ביגר.

ברינדר (K) **b(ı)rīndar** wounded, ailing; **ʾ-w-d̲** – to wound (PolG); pl. **b(ı)rındāre**; cf. ברינה.

ברין, ברינה (K) f. **b(ı)rīne** (Z), **bırīn** (NT), wound, injury; pl. ברינה **bırīne** (NT; cf. PolG), **bırīnat** (Z).

ברירא, ברירתא (OA clear) adj. **barīra, barıtta** (food) dry,lacking fat or oil, crisp.

ברית מילה (H) ⁺**barīt̲ mīla** Covenant of Circumcision; cf. ששה (NT+).

ב-ר-כ 1 (OA) **b-r-x** to kneel, to rest; אבי גניכי וגברכי כולו ישראל **ʾıbbe gnēxi ugbarxi kullu yisrāʾēl** On it (the Sabbath) all Jews rest and relax (NT); **nıxle-brıxle mınne** He does not worry about it any more; II to bless; to wed, to marry (RivSh 211; MeAl 187); cf. בורכתא, מבורכא.

ב-ר-כ 2 II(Ar) ⁺**b-r-k** to dedicate a house; greet with a gift (for a new house); bring 'blessed' candy after visiting a shrine; cf. תברכ.

ברכא 1 (K برخ < OA/OS בָּרָחָא, בראחא) m. **barxa** (young) lamb; cf. ברכתא 2; pl. **barxe** (NT+).

ברכא 2 (OA/OS/Mand בּוּרְכָּא) f. **bırka** knee; pl. ברכאכה **bırkāke** (cf. PolG) (OA pl **-kē**) ; (NT+).

בר-כאל v. כּאל-ובר-כאל

ברכה 1 (Ar) f. ⁺**bırke** pool [PolG ⁺**bırka**]

ברכה 2 , בראכא, בְּרָכָא (H) f. ⁺**bırāxa** blessing; food (over which blessing is recited); ברכת כוהנים **bırkat̲ kōhanīm** Benediction of Priests; pl. ברכות, בְּרָכוֹת ⁺**bırāxōt̲** (AvidH 6, 71).

ברכיות (< ברכה 2) pl. ⁺**baraxiyót** presents (fruits, cakes) exchanged at the circumcision (Gz 28).

ברכה לבטלה (H) **bırāxa lıvaṭṭāla** a blessing in vain (NT2).

בראייכותא v. ברכותא

ב-ר-כ-נ III (< ברכא 2/Ar?) vi ⁺**b-r-k-n** to squat, to sit with legs crossed.

ב-ר-כ-ש, כ-ר-ב-ש III (< ב-כ-ש) **b-r-x-š, x-r-b-š** search, poke about.

ברכתא 1 v. בורכתא

ברכתא 2 (< ברכא 1) f. **barıxt̲a** young ewe (BT3).

ברכתא 3 (K) f. **barrıkt̲a** a type of kilim-rug used to lie on; **pšōṭ ʾaqlox qčīn barrıksox** Stretch your feet according to the size of your rug (be frugal).

ברכתא 4 (K **berik**) f. **barrıkt̲a** bullet (Zaken 389; PolG).

ברכת הלבנה (H) **bırk(at̲)-allıvāna** the Hebrew prayer over a new moon.

ברכת המזון (H; OA ברכת מְזוּנָא) **bırkat̲-hammazon** (NT5 411), **bırkal[!]-ammāzo(n)** (Z; cf. PolU 306), the Hebrew grace over food.

ב-ר-מ (Ar) vt/vi ⁺**b-r-m** to twist.

ברמבר (K) **barambar** equal to (in merit, power) (NT); opposite of (BT2, Arodh); in front of (AvidH 66) [Khan 564 **barambār** 'beside, opposite']

ברמוט (IrAr) m. **bırmuṭ** snuff; cf. תתון.

ברמילא (Ar) f. **barmīla** barrel, vat (cf. PolG).

ברמל (K) m. **barmal** kilim-type rug; pl. **barmāle** hangings (=H קְלָעִים, BT4).

ברמנן (OA-H) ⁺**barmınnān** How awful, terrible! (PolU 14); What a mess! **qımle xa pōxa** , – What a horrible wind it was! (SaAC 7).

בר-מצראעא (K-Ar) f. **bar-mıṣrāʿa** top (child's toy).

בר-מקאבל (K-Ar) **bar-maqābıl** in front of (for all to see) (BT2, Arodh).

בר-מקלוב (K-Ar) **bar-maqlūb** inside out, the wrong side, turned over.

בר-מתוע (k-Ar مُطيع) inv. **bar mıto^c** servant (PolU 97)

בר-נאשה, ברת-נאשה (OA בר אנש; OS ܒܪ ܢܫܐ person, human being) m. **bır-/brat-nāše** kin by a recent marriage, not a blood relative (to whom one feels more obliged) (SaAC 20); cf. ברונא, בראתא.

בַּרַנְדִירָא (K) m. **barandīra** young male sheep (BT2, D).

ברנדירכה, בַּרִינְדִירְכָּא, בַּרְדִירְכֵּי (K) f. **bar(ın)dīrke** young female sheep; pl. ברנדירכת, בַּלְדִירְכַּאת **barındīrkat, baldīrkat** (BT1/3/4, D).

ברנייא (Ar) **⁺barnīya** jug of oil (m.)(NT2); disk-shaped wheat dumpling stuffed with fat meat (f.)(Z); pl. **⁺barnīyat**.

בר-פילכה (K) **bar-pēlke** stumbling stone, obstacle; **drēle xa – – qāmi** He misled me.

בר-פשתה (K) **bar-pıšte** backpack, back pad.

ב-ר-ק (OA) vi to shine (NT); IV to polish, to shine (vi/vt) (Z).

ברקא (OA/OS בַּרְקָא, Mand בירקא) m. **bırqa** lightning; pl. **bırqe** (NT+).

בַּרְקַאמְתַּא (K-OA) **barqamta** frontlet (BT2, D).

ברקוכה (K-Ar برقوك reflexion) f. **barraqōke** shining shell (?); pl. **–kat** (SaAC 16).

ברקול (Kbar + OA -לקובל) **barqul** in front of, against, versus, erqual to (NT+).

ברקוסכה (K) f. **barqōske** slingshot; cf. ברדקאנייה.

ברקייא (Ar) f. **bırqīya** telegram; pl. **bırqīyat**.

ברקתא (K) f. **barıqta** lead bullet.

בראתא v. ברת

ברת-אלעיל (Ar) adv. **⁺barrat-ıl^cēl** outside of the family quarters (PolU 292)

בר(ת דיד)-אלבלד (Ar) adv. **⁺barr(at-did/)ılbalad** abroad; open country (Pol 105; PolG).

ברתונתא (< בראתא) f. **bratunta** baby girl (SaAC 21), young lady (MeAl 190); pl. **bratunyāta** (PolGr 56).

ברתותא (< בראתא) f. **bratūta** virginity (=H בְּתוּלִים, BT3); v. נ-פ-ל.

ברתכתי (K-OA) **bar-taxti** downwards, down the river; cf. באריליי (NT+).

ברת-נעאמא (OA בַּר נַעֲמִיתָא; Ar نَعامة) f. **brat-na^cāma** ostrich (=H בַּת הַיַּעֲנָה, BT3).

בש, ביש (P; cf. OA בי good, better < P **bih**) **bıš** more (than); v. בשרב, בשטו (NT+).

בשא (Ar بَشّ cheerful?) inv. **bašša** hyperactive (often with **be-muhlat** restless).

בשו-בשו (K) **bıšo-bıšo** wash, bath (babytalk).

בשטו, בשטוף, בשטום, בֶּשְׁטוֹם (< בש+טוף) **bıšto(f/m)** better; **ʾan bıštof mınnan** ghosts, spirits (lit. those who are better than us) (cf. PolU 95; PolG/RivPr 211) [Mutz 195 **bıštam** < OA טב) (NT+).

בשכורה v. פשכורה

ב-ש-ל (OA) **b-š-l** to be cooked well; II to cook.

בשר ודם (H) **bāsār ʾādām** (!) a flesh and blood, a human, a weakling (PolU 260).

בשרב, בז'רב, בֶּשְׁרַב (< בש+ראבא) adv. **bıš/ž-⁺rab** (much) more (AlfH 65).

בששים ולא בששה (H) **bašıíšim wálo bašíšša** (Pay) sixty rather than six; It is better to buy things of good quality even if more expensive.

בד v. בת

בדאנא v. בתאנא

בתיה, בתיא, בתו (H) **batya, batto** [Z **basya, basso**) Bithia (RivSH 155).

בתנה v. תנה

בת-ציון (H) **bāṣīyon** Bath-Zion; cf. ג'ייא.

בת-קול (H; cf. OA b, ekt) **bat-qōl** (BaBin 128; Z**basqōl**; cf. PolU 290) Divine voice (NT+).

בתקורא (OA בי/בית קברא) **bıtqōra** cemetery (NT2).

בתר (OA) prep. **batır** (Z **basır**) after, behind; בתר האדך **batır hādax** afterwards; -בר בתרא/בתרא/לבתרא בְּ תְ רַ א בְּרַא אֶל **bar-batra/lbatra** (NT), **ʾıl bara-batra** (=H אַחֲרַנִּית, PolG; Z), backwards, in reverse.

ב, ב̇ (v)

באלק (K?) inv. **vālıq** old (maid) (PolU 344).

בארה (K) **vāre** away, further (PolU 60, 428).

בג̇יעא, בג̇עתא (< ב-ג̇-ע) adj. **vjīᶜa, vjıᶜta** weird person

ב-ג̇-ע (< Ar/K وجع pain?) **v-j-ᶜ** to become weird.

בג̇עוס, וג̇עוס (< ב-ג̇-ע) **v/wajaᶜōs** weird (woman).

ב-ד-י (K?) **v-d-y** to jitter, swerve (cf. PolG).

בזרין (T/IrAr? < En) **vazarin** vaseline, petroleum jelly.

ב-ז'-נ-ק III (K) **v-ž-n-q** to be startled (horse).

ב-ר-ב-ר, ב-י-ב-ר III (K) **v-ē/r-v-r** to spin the hand in the air, hurl far away, to spin (eyes), be temporarily blinded: **ʾēne mvīvırru** his eyes were almost blinded [2: **mvēvır**].

בירא v. גירא 3

ב-ל-ק-נ III (< K?) **v-l-q-n** to be spotted (sheep); v. מבולקנא.

ב-נ-ב-נ III (K?) **v-n-v-n** to hum, utter sounds (=H הָגָה, AlfH 78).

בר (onomat) **vırrrr** bird's take off (Polu 32), flying, ejection; cf. פר.

ברברוכה (K) f. **vırvırrōke** swivel; whirligig; diligent (woman).

ברג̇ (onomat.) ⁺**vırč** sound of sudden escape (PolU 202).

ג, גּ (g)

ג (H) **gīmal** the third letter of the Hebrew alphabet; **ṯlāha** three; v. 'ג.

-ג, -כ, (-ק) (OA קָא [< קָאֵם], כָּא, -כָּ; OS ـقـ, SokBA 549) **g-, k-, (q-)**, a prefix with the a.p. to indicate the general present: גדאאר **gdā'ır** he returns; כימר **kēmır** (NT)/**gēmır** (Z) he says; כיתה **kēṯe**/גיתה **gēṯe** (both NT, but Z **kēse**) he comes; כיאה **kī'e** he knows; גשאמא **kšāme'**; (ג)קארו **(q)qāru** he approaches (MeAl 179, n. 23); it may be suffixed to the negation particle: לך, לג **lag, lak**; and with redundant spelling; לג גקטאי **lag gqaṭ'i (=la qqaṭ'i)** they don't cut (NT3); in negated future it replaces ב-/בד **b-/bıd**: בדאאר **bdā'ır** he returns; לג דאאר **lag dā'ır** he does/will not return.

גא v. גאהא

גאבאנא (K) m. **gāvāna** herdsman of cattle, 'cowboy' (PolU 6).

גאבאדר (K) **gāvadar** streetwalker, prostitute (RivPr 210).

גאבה (K) f. **gāve** footstep; pl. גבאתא **gavāṯa** (BaBin 1; PolG); cf. פינגבי.

גאדא (OA/OS גַּדָּא) m. **gāda** luck; **gāde xwāra/kōma** He is lucky/unlucky (lit. , his luck is white/black; cf. OA ביש גדא unlucky).

גאהא 1, גַּהָא, גא (K/P) f. **gāha** (NT), **gaha** (BT1, D), **ga** (Z), recurrent time; **xá-ga** once, sometimes; **gā-xıt/n** again, once more; **ču-ga** never; pl. גאהה **gāhe** (NT), **ga** (Z); **trē-ga** twice; **ṯlāhá-ga** thrice, etc.; **-trē-ga l'ōqad** twice as much (cf. PolG); **šō'í-ga d-** inspite of, even if.

גאהא 2 (K) f. **gāha** place; mostly in pl. in the invocation **la 'āse banya gahāsa** May he not come in these places, said after mentioning a deceased person's name, due to a superstition that the dead come sometimes after the living.

גאוד v. גו

גאזינו (IrAr<E) f. **gāzīno** modern cafe, 'casino'.

גאזנדא, גאשנא (K) f. **gāzında** (Z), **gāš/žına** (NT2), complaint; **'-w-z gāzında mın** to complain about (cf. PolG).

ג-א-י (OA) vt **g-'-y** to be haughty; **⁺rāba ggā'e bıgyāne** (cf. PolG, but RivSh 277 גַּאנֵי מוּגְּאֵילֵי) **gāne mug'ēle**, IV) He shows off a lot (NT+).

גאיא, גאיתא (OA) adj. **ge'ya, g'īṯa**, haughty; often as hendiadys **ge'ya sıṭya** conceited, cocky (NT+).

גאיותא, גיאיותא (< גאיא) **ge'yūṯa** haughty (NT+).

גאלא (K?) m. **gāla** a certain kind of rug, kilim-style (cf.ברמל), but heavier; pl. **gāle**.

גאמישא (K/P) m. **gāmēša** buffalo; large and asymetrically built person (pejor.) (NT+).

גאנא v. גיאנא

גאצא (OA/OS גַּצָּא > Ar جص < Ak < **gaṣṣu**) m. **gāṣa** gypsum, lime.

גאראנה (K) f. **⁺gārāne** herd of livestock (PolU 6)

גארה (OA אִיגָּרָא < **igāru** wall) m. **gāre** roof; pl. **garıwāṯa** [Krotkoff 128].

גארס (K) m. **gārıs** millet; **xapča gārıs laswābe zāwınwa, mād wēle faqir** He couldn't buy even some millet, being so poor.

גאזנדא v. גאשנא

גד v. גאת

גב- v. גיבא

גבאי (H) m. **gabbay** synagogue treasurer (also common family name); גַּבֵּיתֵי צְדָאקָא **gabbēṯı(d) ṣadāqa** female treasurer (Br48 191, Am).

גבאנה, -גיבאנית, -גבננית (< OA גיף/כיף נהרא riverside, shore, SokBA 578); pl. (?) **gıvāne, gavanāne** shore(s) of (sea, river) (MeAl 19; PolG).

גבארא, גברתא (OA גִּיבָּרָא/OS ܓܢܒܪܐ) **⁺gı/abāra** (cf. PolG),**⁺gıbarta**, mighty (person), hero (NT+).

ג-ב-ג-ב III (<ג-י-ב /IrAr to swell?) vi **g-b-g-b** to foam up (a bit), boil over (soup); cf. גבו.

גבה v. ב-א-י

גבו (<ג-ב-ג-ב). f. **gıbbo** foam [cf. PolG; MacD].

גבורה (H) f. **gıvūra** Omnipotence (God)(NT2).

ג-ב-י IV (OS) **g-b-y** to select, chose (NT+).

גביר (H) m. **gávir** lord, dignitary; pl. **gavērīm** (!) (PolU 39).

גביתא v. גבאי
גברותא, גבורותא (<גבארא) ⁺gıbarūṯa, (+NT) gıbbōrūṯa (?), might, heroism (NT+).
גבת, גבה v. ב-א-י v.
גגלא (OS ܓܓܠܐ <OA גלגלא; Mand גירגלא; circle, wheel) m. gıgla skein of yarn; spindle; -d ʾabrēsım silk skein (used by lovers making love)(PolU 110); pl. gıgle.
גגנא (< OA כַּגְנָא m. frying pan?) f. gagna vat, cask; pl. gagnāṯa.
יגגאר v. גגאר
גד, גַּאת (OA כד) gad/t as, when (=H כִּי, BT1, Am, D).
גדולי רומי (H) gıḏolē rōmi the magnates of Rome (NT2).
גדאדא (OA/OS/Mand גְּדָדָא) m. gḏāḏa (Z gzāza) thread, yarn, string; pl. גִּידַאדֵי gḏāḏe (=H פְּתִילִים, BT2, D).
גדיא, גִּידְיָיא (OA/OS/Mand גַּדְיָא) m. gıḏ/dya kid, baby goat (NT4; BT1, D; BaBin 109); cf. גיסכא.
גדי, גדיכא, גדיכה (K < OS kid) voc. gıdi, gıdīka (m.), -ke (f.), youngster, (my young) fellow (PolU 126; PolUR 38).
גדילים (H) pl. gıḏīlīm (Z gızīlīm) the tassels on the prayer shawl; גַּדְלֵי gadle (BrH 309).
גדישא (OA) m. gadīša stacked grain (=H גָּדִישׁ, BT2).
ג-ד-ל (OA/OS/Mand) vi g-ḏ-l (Z g-z-l) to plait, to twine.
גהא 1 (K geh link?) gaha thumb, big toe
גהא 2 v. גאהא
גהפרא (K) m. gahparra nape (=H עֹרֶף, BT).
גו, כו, גאוד (OA גאו, גו) prep. go, ko (+NT, with unvoiced consonants), gāwıd, inside, in, among; כו פלגא ko palga in the middle; ʾīs mahkēsa go palga Can one argue about this?! (PolU 83); כו כלמא ko xılma in a dream [decl. גאויהון gawēhun (NT), gāwu (Z)]; pl. gawāwe insides, entrails (=H קְרָבַיִם, BT2).
גואא (<?) m. gōʾa saffron (Cf. PolG); stalk of lettuce.
גואיא 1 (<ג-ו-י) v.n. gwāya begging alms; cf. גווייתא (NT+).
גואיא 2, גויתא (<ג-ו-י) adj. gawāya, gawēṯa beggar (cf. PolG).
גווארא (<ג-ו-ר) v.n. gwāra marriage (NT+).
גובא (OA גובא, גּוּבָא pit) m. gūba loom (usually in a pit).
גובאינא (<גו+ב+אינא?) m. gobʾēna forehead (NT+).
גובתא v. גופתא
גוג ומגוג (H) gōġ-u-māġōġ Gog and Magog (NT; RivSh 276); quarrel (Z): pıšla – go bēsu There was much quarrel and strife in their house.
ג-ו-ר-ג-ר v. ג-ר-ג-ר 2
גוּג (K<T koč) m. gūj toil, hardship (NT+).
גוג'ין, גוזין (T güzin) inv. gūj/zin desirable, good (BT1, Am); pl. גּוּזִינֵי gūzīne (AvidH 6).
גודא 1 (OA/OS/Mand גּוּדָא) m. gūda wall; pl. גודאנה gūdāne (cf. PolG) (NT+).
גודא 2 (OA/OS/Mand < Ak gūdu > P كوزه earthen bottle?) m. gūḏa (Z gūza; cf. PolG) leather bottle, churn; pl. gūḏe; cf. גּוֹדא jōda.
גוודא (T gövde) f. gawda (trunk of) body; mare - corpulent (cf. Pol 106; PolG).
גודגודתא (K/OA) f. gudguda tumult.
גוהדר (K) inv. guhdar good listener (PolU 244).
גוזא (OS ܓܘܙܐ; pl. ܓܘܙܐ; OA אַמְגּוֹזָא; Mand אנגוזא) gōza walnut; gōza mšaqrıqāna noisy nut, said about lively child; pl. gōze.
גוזכא (K/P گوزك) m. gōzaka ankle (cf. AlfM 28; PolG); pl. gōzakat.
גוז'גוז'תא (<ג-ז'-ג-ז') f. gužgužta buzz (of fly).
ג-ו-י (OA/OS/Mand גבי collect) vt g-w-y to collect alms, be a beggar; cf. גואיא, גויתא.
גוי (H) gōy Gentile; f. בכתא גויה baxta gōya Gentile wife (BaBin 71); pl. כוריה גוים xūre gōyīm Gentile friends (NT5 408).
גויא (<K/P 'so to speak/'golf ball'?) gōya a kind of words or ball game (?) (PolU 204).
גויזכתא, גְוִזְכְּתָא (K?) f. gwīzıkta, gūzıkṯa (PolG), stalk, ear of corn (=H גִּבְעוֹל, BT2); pl. gwīzıkyāṯa [MacD 46 peppercorn].
גוירא, גורתא (<ג-ו-ר) adj./pp. gwīra, gurta/gwırta, married (person).
גווייתא (<ג-ו-י) f. gwayīṯa alms begging (PolU 80).
ג-ו-ל (OA/OS/Mand גבל knead, prepare fodder, be created) vi/vt g-w-l to mix up; אגולה עקל דידה ıgwılle ʿaqıl dīde He mixed his mind up (NT2); to soil, be soiled; gwılle bmūne he suffered a lot, was destroyed (lit., soiled with mire); gulta bdımma udeʾsa

(Be)soiled (f.) with blood and sweat (curse) (PolG); cf. ג-מ-ב-ל, ג'-ב-ל (cf. Avishur 1993b 18).

גולאגא (K?) m. **gulāga** sideburn; pl. **gulāge**.

גולבהר (K) m. **gulbahar** spring flower.

גולברוש (K) m. **gulbarrož** sunflower.

גולג'יג'כא (K) m. **gulčičaka** (wild) flower.

גולול, גְלוֹל (K fondu) **gulol** rice-and-milk dish (eaten on Shavuot Holiday) (Amedi 62).

גּוּלִייֶה (K?) pl. **gulīye** ears of corn(?) (=H מְלִילוֹת, BT5, D).

גּוּלִילְתָּא (<OA גלל) f. **gulılta** loaf, round bread; pl. גּוּלִלַייאתַא **gulılyāta** (=H חַלָּה, חַלּוֹת BT3, D; עֻגּוֹת, AvidH 46); cf. דורכתא.

גוליפכא (K) m. **gulifka** fringe (in carpets).

גולכא (K) m. **gōlıka** young bull (NT4; Sa83c 26, Am); pl. **gōlıkat**; גולכתא f. **gōlıkta** heifer, young cow; pl. **gōlıkyāta** [Khan 569 golka, f. heifer].

גולם (H) m. **gōlem** lifeless (RivSh 112).

גולפא (OS<**gappā**) m. **gulpa** wing (NT2).

גּוּלְתַא (OA) f. **gulta** (PolG) ball, cylinder, capital of column (=H שְׂבָכָה, PolG); pl. גוליאתא **gulyāta** hooks (=H וָוִים, BT2); sockets (=H אֲדָנִים, BT4, D).

גומא (T **küme**) **gūma** heap, pile (NT5 397).

גומאאנא, גומאנתא (OS ܓܘܡܐ pit) adj. **gumʾāna, gumʾanta**, deep; cf. גמואא.

גומאנותא (<גומאאנא) f. **gumʾanūta** depth (NT+).

גומבולאנא, גומבולנתא (<ג-מ-ב-ל) adj. **⁺gumbōlāna, ⁺gumbōlanta**, round, circular.

גומבולתא (<ג-מ-ב-ל) f. **gumbülta** ball, any round -shaped thing; pl. **gumbülyāta**.

גומג'א (<ג-מ-ג) m. **⁺gumča** fistful, handful; pl. **⁺gumče**.

גומטלא (<?) m. **gumṭıla** clod, lump; pl. **gumṭıle**.

גומלא (OA/OS גַּמְלָא; Mand גומלא) m. **gumla** camel; pl. **gumle** (NT+).

גומלונכא (<גומלא) m. **gumlonka** (little/certain) camel (PolU 132).

גומרכ (IrAr<T) **gumrık** customs duty or tax.

גונדכניתא, גונדכנאיא (< גונדכה) adj. **gundıknāya, -nēta** villager.

גונדכה (K) f. **gundıke** village; pl. **gundıkat**.

גונה v. גנאהא

גונהכר (K/P) **gunahkar** sinner, guilty (BT).

גונייא (K/IrAr< Hindi) f. **gūnīya** gunny sack, burlap bag; pl. **gūnīyat, -ye** (PolG); cf. כסתא, תליתא.

גוסא < גותא* (<?) f. **gussa** (Z) ball of yarn or threads; pl. **gussat** (PolU 325) [cf. Mutzafi 304 **gutta, gutta**;MacD 49 **güttā** < OS **gullā**].

גוסנא (<?) **gōsına/gusna** ? celebration: גג'ילא בכלולא וגוסנא **žgīla bxılōla u-** busy in feast and celebration (AmU2 6a).

גועדכא (K **guʿıtk**) m. **gōʿıdka** young camel (PolU 292-3); also a common family name.

גופאלא, גופלתא (K) **⁺gōpāla** (m.; cf. PolG), **⁺gōpalta** (f.; BT2, Am), walking cane.

גופתא, גובתא (OS **gvittā**) f. **gup/bta** cheese; **pıšlu skīna ugupta** They hated each other (cf. PolG) (NT+).

גוצא (< OA dwarf?) m. lump of dough; pl. **gūṣe**.

ג-ו-ר (< גורא; OA גבר prevail, excel) **g-w-r** to marry; IV to marry off; לא גורי ומגורי מאכדאדה **la gōri umágūri mʾıxdāde** They should not intermarry; **ʾīman magūrıtta brātox** When will you marry off your daughter? (NT+).

גורא (OA/OS/Mand גַּבְרָא man, husband) m. **gōra** man, husband; **gōra-baxta** married couple, (lit., husband-wife), sexual relation (euph.) (Avin78, 93; RivSh 267); cf. גורותא, גורנכא; pl. **gūre** (< OA גּוּבְרֵי) men, **gūrāne** husbands, strong men (NT+).

גורגא (K/P) m. **gurga** wolf; pl. **-e**; cf. דיוא.

גורגומתא (< ג-ר-ג-ם) f. **gurgumta** thunder; cf. הרהמתא; pl. **gurgumyāta**; גּוּרְגוּמֵי **gurgume** (RivSh 180).

גורגור, גירגור, גרגור (<AnAr **burġul**?) m. **gürgur** bulgur; grits (SaAC 11; =H גֶּרֶשׂ, BT3, D).

גורגורי (<גורגור?) inv. **gurguri** color of burghul (?) (PolU 4)[K **gurgur** crackling of fire?].

גורגורתא (OA) f. **⁺gurgurta** throat (Pol 106); **-ıt qzāla** under the chin (PolG); cf. קולקולתא.

גורג'י, גורג'יה (IrAr<T) **gurji, gurjīya** 'Georgian', common male/female names.

גורד ומרד (K?) **gurd-u-mırd** somewhat strong ('un peu forte') (PolG).

גורותא 1 (< גורא/OA גַּבְרוּתָא) f. **gōrūta** manliness, manhood (cf. PolUR 64).

גורותא 2, גורוה v. גרותא
גורזא (<P 'club, pestle') **gurza** neck, trunk - **id qzāle mux xa qurma** His neck (was) like a log (PolU 113, 347); log, club (PolU 348).
גורי (K) **gōri** sacrifice; response to **dāye** Mom is **dāye gōri(yox)** Mom (be) your sacrifice.
גורייא (K) **gurrıya** flame: **mux xa gurrīyid nūra bıšʿāla go libbe** (the insult was) like a flame of fire burning in his heart (PolG).
גּוֹרָל (H) **gōrāl** fate, lot (BT3, d; BT4, D); pl. **˚garalōs (!)** (PolU 291).
גורמא (OA גומרא) **gurma** burning coal (NT3) [Khan 569 **gurme** 'hot coals'].
גורנה (OA) f. **˚gōrne**, גּוֹרְנִית מַאשְׁתּוֹיֵי **gōrnıt maštōye**, water trough (=H שֹׁקֶת, BT1, D); pl. גּוֹרְנַאת **gōrnat** (=H רְהָטִים, BT2, D) (NT+).
גורנכא (<גורא) m. **gōrınka** (little) man, fellow (Pol 106).
גורפאלא (<?) m. **gurpāla** funeral meal (rice dish); **ʾaxlax gurpālox** May we eat your funeral meal (a curse).
גו-רצץ (K; v. רצץ) **gú-rısaṣ** alloy (Zaken 388).
גותא v. גוסא
גזאלא (OA) m. **gazāla** robber (AvidH 70; Sa83c 24, Am).
גזארא 1 (<ג-ז-ר 2) v.n. **gzāra** circumcision; cf. ששה; **yāle gzīre ula-gzāra** circumcized and uncircumcized children (RivSh 264).
גזארא 2 (<ג-ז-ר 2) m. **gazāra** circumcizer.
ג-ז-ג-ז III (K **gizgizin** 'fever, tremor') **g-z-g-z** to have fever with chills
גזגזתא, גסגסתא (<ג-ז-ג-ז) f. **gız/sgız/sta** unrest (PolU 90); **mare -** 'movers and shakers', people prone to revolt (PolU 418).
גזגזיתא (ג-ז-ג-ז) **gazgazīṯa** fever with chills; consumption (=H שַׁחֶפֶת, BT3, D).
גזילה (H) f. **gazēla** robbery, excessive charge.
גזירא 1 (<ג-ז-ר 2) **gzīra** circumcized (p.p.) (NT+).
גזירא 2 (OA partition) f. **gzīra** island; the town of Jazira (T Cizre).
גזירנאיא, גזירניתא (<גזירא 2) **gzīrnāya** (m.), **gzīrnēṯa** (f.), resident of Jazira.
גזירא 3, גזירה (H) f. **˚gazēra** (evil) decree; pl. גזירות **˚gazērōṯ** (MeAl 190) (NT+).

ג-ז-ל (H/OA/Mand גזל; OS ܓܙܠ) **g-z-l** to rob; cf. גזאלא.
גזל, גיזל (H) **gēzıl** loot, excessive price.
גזר (K) inv. **gızır** dry, oil-less, crispy (dish).
ג-ז-ר 1 (H-OA) **˚g-z-r** to decree; cf. גזירא 3 (NT+).
ג-ז-ר 2 (OA shear, cut, be circumcized, decree) **g-z-r** to circumcize (only) (NT+).
גזרא (<OA?) m. **gızra** a pile, a heap (of chopped wood, etc.); ציוד גזרא **ṣīwıd -** firewood (AmU2 2b); used for sacrifice (NTU4); pl. **gızrāre**.
ג-ז'-ג-ז' III (<K?) **g-ž-g-ž** to buzz; cf. גוז'גוז'תא.
גז'נז'ה (K) pl. **gıžnıžže** tiny filigree balls or cradles and bubbles on top layer of sour cream or yoghurt; cf. קרושתא.
גט (H) **gēṭ** divorce writ; גט גרושין זמן temporary divorce writ (NT2).
גיאנא, גַאנַא (K/P) f. **gyāna** (Z, NT), **gāna** (RivSh 119, etc.), self, soul; מני ומגיאני **mınni umıgyāni** of my own initiative (NT1); **la xzēle bıgyāne** He did not feel up to it (lit., see in himself); **wın š-gyāni** I am still healthy, look young (PolU 444); **wēla muġ gyāna** It remained the same (=unaffected); **la qam mapqınna gyāni ʾıbbe** I didn't show interest in him, pretended not to see him; **ʾ-w-z -** to pretend, claim to be (PolG); **qṣīfıd (la) gyāna** May your life (not) be short; **bdaqīqıt gyāna** at that very moment, right away (PolU 151); pl. **gyānāṯa** individuals (=H נֶפֶשׁ, BT).
גיאנזור (P) **gyānzawer** living creature (NT2).
ג-י-ב (OA גבב?) vi **g-y-b** to boil over, to foam up (sea, soup); cf. גבו, ג-ב-ג-ב [cf. Mutzafi 2001 203].
גיבא (OS ܓܒܐ ܓܒ back, side; OA גַּבָּא back. side, top, body) m. **gēba** side, direction; **ʾıl barīya gēba** towards the desert; **mılʾēl-/mıltēx-gēba** upwards/downwards; **lʿogıb** inwards; **lwargıb** outwards; **ʾaxgıb** hither; **tangıb** thither; **šēna mʿaxgıb** Peace (be) hither (said after mentioning demons); **mın-/m-gēb** instead of (cf. PolG); **kullu gēbe/gıb** (SaAC 22) all kinds of things (NT+); cf. גבאנה [Khan 568 **geb** near, in the home of].
ג-י-ג' 1 (K/P/T) **g-y-j** to feel dizzy; have headache, head-spin; IV to cause headache.

ג-י-ג̇ 2 (<K **kotin**) ⁺**g-y-č** to eat fruits, such as melons, from the rind or meat off the bone; chew bread in a hurry.

גיגבאנה, גיגבנתא (<ג-י-ג̇ 1) f. **gējıbāne, gējıbanta** jabbering woman; headach-causing woman (PolU 444).

גיג̇ותא, גייש'ותא (<ג-י-ג̇ 1?) f. **gēj/žūṯa** hardship (BaBin 105).

ג-י-ד (OS/OA גדד 'cut off, level') **g-y-d** to eat the entire (delicious) dish, 'clean' the plate.

גיהנם, גֵיהֶנָא, גיהאנא(H-OA גֵיהִנָּם; OS ܓܗܢܐ; Mand גוהנאם) **gēhınnām, gēhínna** (RivSh 111, 185), **gēhanna** (+NT) hell; **si bgēhınnē-gēhınnām** Go to hell of hells! Cf. גֹהנם.

גיזארא (OS/P) **gizāra** carrot; pl. **gizāre**.

ג-י-ש'-נ, ג-י-ז'-נ III (< ג-י-ג̇ 1 ?) **g-ī-ž-n** to feel dizzy, to faint (BaBin 108) [1: **mgīzınne**].

גיכא (<OA גיחא cavity?) m. **gīxa** line or circle drawn on ground in games such as hop-scotch; pl. **gīxe** (=H עוּגה, AlfM 19).

גימל (H) f. **gīmal** (the Hebrew letter) Gimel.

גֵיסֶין (K) **gēsın, gēsın ja^cōḏa**, (the iron edge of) plough (=H מַחֲרֵשָׁה, PolG); pl. גֵיסִינֵיה **gēsıne** (=H מַחֲרֵשׁוֹת, PolG) [Khan 568 **gāsin** plough].

גיסכא (K) m. **gīsıka** kid, baby-goat; cf. גדיא; pl. **gīsıkat** (NT+).

ג-י-ר II (H) vt/vi ⁺**g-y-r** convert to Judaism (NT+).

גירא 1 (OA) m. **gēra** arrow, bread roller; **gēra uqašṭa** arrow and bow (PolG); pl. **gēre, gērawāṯa** (NT+).

גירא 2 (K) m. **gēra** threshing (=H דַּיִשׁ, BT3); **ʾ-w-z gēra** to thresh (BT5).

גירא 3 (K) **gēra** f. commotion, tumult; often in hendiadys: **gēra-u-vēra** (raining) cats and dogs; **gēra-u-gozambo** pandemonium.

גִירַאשֵׁי (<ג-ר-ש) **gırāše** distilled (grape) juice (=H מִשְׁרַת [עֲנָבִים], BT4, D).

גירו (K?) inv. **gīro** confused; **gīro-parganda** wonderer (=H נָע וָנָד, RivSh 116)[MacD 50].

גכוכא, גכוכתא 1 (OS ܓܚܘܟܐ; OA גַחְכָנָא; Mand מגאהכאנא) **gaxōka, gaxukta** one who laughs a lot, jester.

2 *גכוכתא (< ג-ח-כ) f. **gıxukta** laughter; dimple; pl. **gıxukyāṯa** [cf. MacD 50].

ג-כ-כ, ג-כ-ג, כ-כ-כ (OA גחך; cf. OA עחך* > אחך) **g-x-k/g, k-x-k** (NTU4 183a), to laugh, (-**ʾıl/^cıb**) make fun (of), dally (with)(MeAl 191); VI to make someone laugh, amuse [Khan 553 **gḥk**].

גכּכא (<ג-כ-כ) m. **gıxka** laughter, jest; **bgıxka** jokingly, in jest [Khan 569 **giḥka**].

גלא (OA/OS/Mand גִילָא straw, chaff) m. **gılla** grass; pl. גלאלה **gıllāle** (NT+).

גלאיא (<ג-ל-י) m. **galāya** revealer; גלאייד סוריה וכאפאיית **galāyıd ⁺surre uxafāyat** Revealer of secrets and mysteries (=God)(NT2); גְלַאיִית טִישְׁיֵיה **galāyıt ṭıšye** revealer of hidden things (=Joseph=H צָפְנַת פַּעְנֵחַ, BT1, D).

גלאלא (?) (OA גללא) m. **glāla** (?) bolt of fabric; pl. **glāle** (PolU 422); cf. תובא **ṯōba**.

ג-ל-ג̇ (OA גלש?) **g-l-j** to skip obligatory reading, read too fast.

גלגול נשמות (H) **gılgūl nıšāmōṯ** reincarnation.

גלגל (H) **galgal** zodiac sphere; pl. גלגלים **galgallīm** celestial spheres (NT2).

גלדא (OA/OS) m. **gılda** leather, skin (NT+).

גלדנאיא (<גלדא) adj. **gıldanāya** covered with skin or leather (PolU 336).

גלואזא (K) f. **galwāza** necklace; string of summer vegetables and fruits hanging to dry.

גלוב (IrAr<En globe) ⁺**gılōb** light bulb.

גלוי וידוע (H) **gālūy uyāzūwa^c** One that every thing is revealed and known to Him (epithet of God) (PolU 273).

גלוי עריות (H) **gıllūy ^carāyōṯ** incest (NT+).

גלות (H) m./f. **gālūṯ** exile; cf. גלֹוה (NT+).

ג-ל-י (OA/OS/Mand) vt/vi **g-l-y** to reveal, uncover; be uncovered; **d-r-y lgılye** reveal (PolG) (NT+).

גלי 1 (K) **gali** winding valley, gully (cf. PolG).

גלי 2 (K) **gali** all: **gali nāše** (You) all people! (SaLH 148; PolG)

גליזא (K) m. **galīza** saliva.

ג-ל-פ (OA) **g-l-p** to hull, blanch (almonds, sesame seeds); **wēle xīla šušme glīpe** He behaves recklessly, arrogantly (like a horse fed hulled sesame); to bruise one's skin.

ג-ל-פ-ס III (K?) **g-l-p-s** to be or make grimy.

ג-מ-א (OS ܛܡܥ dive; OA גמע, גמי swallow) **g-m-ʾ** to become deep; IV to make deep, deepen; cf. גמואא.

ג-מ-ב-ל III (OA גרבל, גַּבֵּל roll. knead) vt/vi

g-m-b-l to shape into balls (specially wheat and meat balls); **gulle mgumbılle** He became totally mixed up; cf. גומבולאנא גומבולתא,; ג-ו-ל, ג׳-ב-ל.

ג-מ-ג׳ (OA גמש) ⁺**g-m-č** to scoop with one's hand; take a handful [= MacD **g-m-š**].

גמואא, גמואתא (< ג-מ-א) adj. **gamūʾa, gamoʾta** deep.

גמורא, גמורתא (< ג-מ-ר) adj. **gamūra, gamurta** pungent, too sour.

גְמִיבָאנַאת (T-K) **gamīvānat** sailors (PolG).

גמייא (T) f. **gamīya** ship; cf. ספינא, גמייא פאפור,.

גמילות חסדים (H) **gamīlūṯ ḥasaḏīm** charity acts (NT+).

ג-מ-צ (<OA dig?) **g-m-ṣ** to smile coyly; **gmīṣāle** smiled (Pol 106; Zaken 390; PolG).

ג-מ-ר (<OA to finish?) **g-m-r** to tan leather; **bābe qam gāmırra lašše** His father beat him to pulp (to educate him); cf. גמורא.

גמשא, גמשו (<גאמישא?) **gamša** (m.), **gamšo** (c.), corpulent, bulky looking person.

גאנא-גרג׳א (K) **gana-garča** castor oil plant.

גונה, גנאהא (K/P) **günāha, gunah** sin (=H אָשָׁם/עָוֹן, BT); מגנאהד **mgünāhıd** in punishment for (NT+).

גנאוא 1 (<ג-נ-ו) v.n. **gnāwa** stealing, theft (NT+).

גנאוא 2, גנותא (OA/OS/Mand גַּנָּבָא) **ganāwa, ganōta**, thief, one who steals, kleptomaniac.

גנאוותא (OA גַּנָּבוּתָא; cf. גנאוא 2) f. **ganāwūṯa** stealing, larceny.

גנאיא (<ג-נ-י) v.n. **gnāya** waning; בגנאיית יומא **bıgnāyıt yōma** at sunset; **yōmā barbar gnāya** at about sunset (PolG) (NT+).

גנדורא (K) f. **gındōra** melon; pl. **gındōre**.

ג-נ-ד-ר III (OA/OS/JAB **gndr**) vi/vt **g-n-d-r** to roll down (Avishur 1993b 15-16).

גנדרה (K **gandan** 'earn'/OA גנדר 'embellish'?) f. **gandare** prostitute (?) (PolU 323).

ג-נ-ו (OA/OS/Mand גנב) **g-n-w** to steal; **ggānūla gyāne** He sneaks in (NT+).

גנוא (<ג-נ-ו) **gınwa** stealth; בגנוא **bgınwa** stealthily, secretly (NT2).

גנונה (OA גְּנוּנָא/OS ܓܢܘܢܐ < Ak **ganūnu**) f. **gınūne** bridal chamber (NT+).

ג-נ-ז (OA/H) **g-n-z** to hide (texts) (NT2).

ג-נ-י (OA/OS/Mand lie down, sleep) **g-n-y** to set (sun), to end (day); waste away (sick person); **yōma ggāne, qaẓa-bala dīde lag gāne** The day is gone, but its troubles linger on; IV to spend the evening (=H הֶעֱרִיב, PolG) (NT+).

גניזה (H) f. **ganīza** chamber in synagogue for burial of discarded sacred material.

גנם גיג׳כה (K) f. **ganım gējke** jabbering woman.

גַּנְעֵדֶן, גן עדן (H) **gan-ᶜēḏın** (Z **ga/ınᶜēzın**) Garden of Eden (RivSH 189; PolU 204); כבושה דגן עדן **xabūše dganᶜēḏın** apples of Eden (NT3); **ṭımʾıd ganᶜēzın (ʾılōhīm)** (like) the Divine taste of Paradise, very delicious, luxurious (PolU 229); גנתד גן עדן**gıntıd gan ᶜēḏın** the garden of Gan-Eden (NT3), גן עדן דעולם הבא **gan ᶜēḏın dᶜōlam habba** The Garden of Eden of the world to come (NT5 405).

גנתא 1 (OA גִּינְתָא vegetable garden; OS ܓܢܬܐ) f. **gınṯa** garden; pl. גניאתא **gınyāṯa** (NT3; RivSh 114; AmU2 4b; PolG); cf. חדיקא.

גנתא 2 (<גגנא?) f. **ganta** large clay bowl.

*גסא (OA) **gıssa** (?) loin; pl. גִיסַאסֵי **gisāse** loins (=H כְּסָלִים, BT3, D).

גסגסתא v. גזגזתא

גס רוח (H) inv. **gaz-⁺rūwaᶜ**(!) difficult person.

גסתי (P) **gasti** draught, hunger (NT+).

ג-פ-ג׳-ל III (<פ-ג׳-ל?) vi/vt ⁺**g-f-č-l** to be or make grimy, messy.

ג-פ-ג-פ III (<?) **g-f-g-f** blow harshly (wind).

ג-פ-ר v. כ-פ-ר

גפריד v. כברית

גר (צדק) (H) **gēr (ṣēdēq)** (righteous) proselite (NT+).

ג-ר-א (OA/OS גרע; Mand גאר be inferior, shave the head, reduce) vi/vt **g-r-ʾ** to shave (NT+).

גרא 1, -גר (K) f. **garra, -gar**, recurrent time; **ʾápe gárra** This time too; **xá-gar** once, **ʾımmá-gar** hundred times (PolG); **gár-xēta** once more; turn **ʾaššat gárrax-īle** This year it is your turn (PolG); pl. גרה **garre**; cf. 1 גאהא. NT+

גרא 2 (K) f. ⁺**garra** deep section of sea or river.

גרא 3, גִּירַא (K) m. **gıra** hillock; mountain summit (=H הֹר הָהָר, BT4, D); pl. **gırāre, gıre** (PolG); cf. גרונכא, גרא-זורכא.

גראאא, גראאה (OA גרעא) m. **garāʾa** shaver,

barber; cf. חלאקא.

גרא-גרא v. גרגרא

גראוא (<?) m. **gırāwa** coarse whitish cotton material [cf. MacD 55].

גרא-זורכא (K) m. **gıra-zūrka** hillock; cf. גרא זורא 2,

ג-ר-א-ל, ג-ר-ע-ל, ג-ר-ו-ל (<OA געל) **g-r-ʾ/ʿ/w-l** to roll in ashes (in mourning), be smeared in blood; מְגוּרְוְלְתָּא smeared (=H מִתְבּוֹסֶסֶת, AvidH 27) (NT+) [Mutz. 190 **ʾrgl**].

גראג' (IrAr<En) ⁺**garrāj** inter-city bus station.

גראנא, גרנתא (<גריתא 1) adj. **gırrāna, gırranta** hot-tempered, one with many tantrums.

גראני (K) **gırāni** high cost of living, dearth.

גראשא (< ג-ר-ש) **garāša** one who pulls, draws; **garāšıd ⁺māya** waterdrawer; _ **sēpa** swordman (NT5 386).

גראתא, גריאתא, גריתא (<ג-ר-א) f. **gareʾta, garēta** (RivSh 280), straight razor (=H מוֹרָה, PolG); pl. **gareʾyāta, garʾāta** (PolU 326).

גרג (T) adv. **garag** probably, it seems.

גרגדן (K/P) m. **gargadan** rhinoceros; corpulent and strong person.

גרגופא (<?) m. **gargūpa** very old person, out of shape, delapidated.

גרגור v. גורגור

ג-ר-ג-ט III (OS ܓܪܓܛ 'scribble'?) **g-r-g-ṭ** to tickle (cf. PolG).

ג-ר-ג-מ III (<?) **g-r-g-m** to thunder; cf. גורגומתא.

ג-ר-ג-ר 1 III (< גרא 3) **g-r-g-r** to roll downhill (cf. PolU 33).

ג-ר-ג-ר 2, ג-ו-ג-ר III (OA) ⁺**g-r/o-g-r** to rumble (stomach), to stir (the heart of one in love) [1:**mgurgır-/mgōgır**] (Pol 108, 152).

גר-גר-גר (onomat) **gır-gır-gır** sounds of speeding horses, etc. (PolU 12); cf. די-די-די.

גרגרא, גרא-גרא (K) m. **garagara, gıra-gıra** vizier, magnate, leader (PolU 12, 157) [cf. MacD 56: 'noble, elder'< **gōra**<K]

גרגרתא (K) **gırgırta** the sound of rolling heavy objects, running, galloping.

ג-ר-ג-ש III (<ג-ר-ש) **g-r-g-š** to drag, pull behind (NT+).

גִּרְגַּלָּה v. כפגאלא

ג-ר-ד (O/OS scrape) **g-r-ḏ** (Z **g-r-z**) to scratch, to scrape.

גרדנא (K) m. **gardana** heavy gold or silver necklace (cf. PolG); **gardanox ʾāza** you are free (of other obligations) (PolU 109).

גרהאני (K) **gırhāni** guarantee, surety (NT2, NT5 381).

גרובר (K) inv. **gıruvír** round-shaped.

גרודאנא, גרודנתא (<ג-ר-ד) **garūḏāna, garūḏanta** scratchy, uneven (surface).

ג-ר-ו-ל v. ג-ר-א-ל

ג-ר-ו-נ III (O/OS גַּרְבָא leprosy) **g-r-w-n** to become a leper (cf. PolU 123), be extremely grimy.

גרונכא (<גרא) m. **gırōnka** hillock (PolU 250).

גרוסא, גרוסתא (<ג-ר-ס) adj. **garūsa, garusta** large, big, full (seed) (NT+).

גרוסתא (<ג-ר-ס) f. **garusta** handmill (cf. PolG); pl. **garısyāṯa** (Pol 80).

גרותא, גורותא (OA/OS גּוּרְבָּא, pl. גורבי < P گـوراب short socks) f. **gı/urūṯa** sock; pl. **gı/urwe** [Khan 569 **gorita**, pl. **gorye**, K].

ג-ר-ז-ב III (K?) **g-r-z-v** to roll (in dust, ash) (BaBin 114; =H נתפלש, AlfM 19); cf. ג-ר-כ-ל.

גרידאיי (K) inv. **gıredāyi** followers, animals that stick with the herd (in contrast to strugglers)(=H מְקֻשָּׁרוֹת, BT1).

גריתא 1 (K) f. **gırrīta** tantrum, seizure, anger (PolU 104); **d-w-q** - to have a tuntrum.

גריתא 2 v. גראתא

ג-ר-כ-ל, כ-ר-ג-ל III (< K **xergele** untidy) **g-r-x-l, x-r-g-l** to be or make dirty, roll in soil; cf. ג-ר-א-ל, ג-ר-ז-ב, ג-ר-כ-ל, ג-ר-מ-כ.

גרמא (O/OS גַּרְמָא; Mand גירמא) m. **garma** bone; **garmıd xāṣa** backbone; **garme xafīfe/yaqūure** He is pleasant/unpleasant (lit., his bones light/ heavy) (NT+).

גרמאנא, גרמאנתא (<גרמא) adj. **garmāna , garmanta** bony, one with big bones (NT+).

ג-ר-מ-כ III (K) **g-r-m-x** to be or make dirty, grimy; cf. ג-ר-כ-ל.

ג-ר-נ (<גראני) **g-r-n** to be expensive, go up in price; IV to raise the price (BaBin 47).

גרן (K/P > OA/Mand גְּרָאן expensive) inv. **gıran** expensive; cf. גראני.

ג-ר-ס (OA/OS/Mand גרס break into pieces) **g-r-s** to grind coarse with a handmill; cf. ת-כ-נ; in ritual slaughter to cut the throat less than necessary; cf. ד-ר-ס.

than necessary; cf. ד-ר-ס.

גרסא (OA גירסא ground flour) m. **gırsa** large-sized cracked wheat [Khan 569 **girse** groats].

ג-ר-פ (OA/OS/Mand גרף rake, scrape clean) **g-r-p** (water:) to sweep away.

ג-ר-ש (OA/OS גרש, pa. divorce; but M. Jastrow 273: *גַּרֵשׁII to hoist up; SokPA 137 גרש to pull, lead, extend; cf. OS ܓܪܫ drag, draw) vi/vt **g-r-š** to pull, draw (cf. גראשא); to last, continue; to distill; pull away, steal; to mate (=H הִרְבִּיעַ, BT3, D; euph.); attract (heart) (NT3); forgive ('draw back') an insult (v. נאכאמי); **grıšle ʾılli** He attacked me (verbally); **grıšle lišānu** He tried to elicit information from them ('pulled their tongue') (Pol 106).

גשרא, גִישֶׁיר (OA/OS גישרא < Ak **gišru**) m. **⁺gıšra , gıšır** - constr.(RivPr #85), bridge (of); **⁺gıšra ⁺ruwwa/⁺gıšır nīmo** the Big Bridge/Nimo's Bridge (a well-known old stone-bridge in Zakho); pl. **⁺gıšrāre** (cf. PolG).

גשתי (<K گهشتي 'reached, riped, mature') inv. **gašti** reachable, found (PolU 207: ChNA).

ג, ג̇ (j)

גאגא (T) m. **jāġa** spoke, spike; pl. **jāġe**.

גאג'יכ (K/T) m. **jājik** soft herbal cheese.

גאדא, גהדא, גַעְדֵי (T/Ar) f. **jādda, jahda** (NT4), **jaᶜde** (BT1, D; PolG), paved road, highway; pl. **jāddat,** געדייאת **jaᶜdīyat** (BaBin 11; PolG).

גאודא (<Ar جزء to split?) m. **jaʾōda** (Z **jaᶜōza**) axe, hatchet, cleaver; pl. גְאוֹדֵי **jaᶜōde** (=H אֵתִים, PolG) [cf. Krotkoff **juʾutta**; Mutz. 205 **jahota** (+**jawtta, goʾoda**)<OA גדע?].

גאכית (IrAr/T <Fr) f. **jākēt** jacket; pl. **jākētat**.

גאלדא (Ar) f. **jālda** stroke with leather whip.

גאמ(א) (Ar) **jāma** glass pane.

גאמי (T **čam** pine, fir) **jāmi** gopher wood (=H גֹפֶר, BT1); bulrush (=H גֹמֶא, BT2).

גאן (K/P) **jān** self; only in: **qarār hāwe mpīla l — dīdi** I solemnly promise (lit., May a decision fall on my self)(cf. PolU 102).

גאסוס(א) (Ar) m. **jāsūs(a)** spy; pl. **jāsūse** (NT+).

גאפאן, גאפון (AnAr **+čāpūn** linen < En Japan?) m. **+jāpun, čāpān** coarse linen (used for traditional underwear).

גאר (K) f. **jār** recurrent time; אול גאר **ʾawwal jār** first time (NT2); cf. גגאר.

גארא (P) f. **jāra** escape, refuge, good advice (against evil decree); trick (RivSh 220).

גאר-ובאר (K) **jār-u-bār** at times, from time to time [Khan 571 **jarubar** 'sometimes'].

גבאתה (Kجقات<Ar جماعة) f. **jıbāte** group, congregation (=H מַקְהֵלָה, AlfH 91).

ג'-ב-ל (Ar) **j-b-l** to mix mortar; cf. ג-ו-ל.

גבלא (Ar) f. **jabla** mixed mortar; mess.

ג'-ב-ר (Ar) vi/vt **+j-b-r** be hard (of heart); to force or be forced, feel reluctant, obliged; to be healed (fractured bones); II to overcome, prevail; make strong or hard, give patience (God:man); IV to force (Heb89 184) (NT+).

גבראי (Ar) **jabrāyi** coercion (PolG).

גגארא (IrAr/T<E) f. **+jıgāra** cigarette; pl. **+jıgāre**; **š-t-y** - to smoke (cigarettes).

גגדא (<OA שגד/רונא hip-disease?) m. **jıgda** swelling and pain in the thigh (with fever).

גגר (P liver, heart; sorrow, compassion) **jagar** beloved, dear child (NT+).

ג'-ג-ר (Ar جكر be vexed) **+j-g-r** to be angry, enraged (cf. PolG); IV to make angry.

גגרא, גכרא (<ג'-ג-ר) m. **+jıgra, jıkra** (NT5 395), wrath, vexation (NT+).

ג'-ג'-ל v. ש-ג'-ל

גד (Ar 'seriousness') m. **jıd** effectiveness, ability to cure (PolU 69).

ג'-ד-ד II2 (Ar) **j-d-d** to renew (NTU4 156b).

ג'רידאנה v. גדידאנה

גדכה (K<Ar جدّة old lady) f. **jıddıke** midwife; pl. **jıddıkat**.

ג'-ד-ל, ד-ג'-ל II (Ar) **j-d-l, d-j-l**, to contest, argue, dispute (cf. PolG).

גהאזה (Ar) pl. **jıhāze** bridal outfit, paraphernalia.

גהאזי (Ar) m. **jıhāzi** a small gold coin used in necklaces and other jewelry; pl. **jıhāziyat**.

גהדא v. גאדא, גידא

גהדאסי (K) **jahdāsi** rye, oats (Segal #15).

גהה (Ar) f. **jıhe** separate side, aside (NT+).

גחיל, גהל (K<Ar) **jıhıl, jıḥıl** (Z, Babin 136; PolG) uncouth, inexperienced youth; pl. גהילין **jıhılīn** (?) fools (NT2).

גהילותא (<גהל) **jıhēlūta** foolishness, ignorance, inexperience. NT+

גַחַנֵּים, גהנם (Ar/K) **jah/ḥannem** hell (AlfH 75); cf. גיהנם.

גואב (Ar) m. **jıwāb** (written) response (NT+).

גואהר (Ar) m. **+jawāhır** gemstone; pl. **+jawāhıre/+jawāhırat** NT+

גואמיר(א) (K) m. **jwāmēr(a)** noble, generous person; pl. גְוָאמֵירֵי **jwāmēre** (AvidH 49).

גואן (K) inv. **jwān** young (PolG).

גְיוּוַנְגַאי, גואנגא (K) m. **jwānaga(yi)** young bull (=H בֶּן בָּקָר, BT; PolG); pl. **jwāngāye**.

גואנה (K) f. **jwāne** young and pretty woman (SaNR); **jwāna jīre** very young woman (who gets pregnant fast) (SaAC 20); cf. גונקא.

גואנייה (K) f. **jwānīye** young horse (RivPr).

ג'-ו-ב, ג'-י-ב II (Ar) **j-w/y-b** to answer [1:**mjōw/yıb-**; 2:**mjāw/yıb**; אמגובנה **ımjōbanne** He answered me (f.) (NT3);

but Hob89 185, AvidH 63-64, 67: מוֹגְבְּלִי **mōjıble**; מַגְבָּנָא **majbāna** (=H עוֹנֶה)]; v. קטרא; גואב (NT+).

גוברִיכ (<K **jibrōk** mole?) m. **jūbírrīk** cockroach; restless person; **jūbırrīke** f. restleess woman.

ג-ו-ג (OA זוז move/T **juš** commotion?) vi **j-w-j** to crawl, to teem; stir, budge, become loose (=H נָזַח, BT2, D); set out (=H נָסַע, BT2, Arodh); IV מְגוֹגַאנָא **majōjāna** shaker (=H מַחֲרִיד, BT3, D) מַגוּגְלִי **majujli** (whoever) removes me (RivSh 128) (NT+).

גוגא (K<T) m. **jūja** dwarf, midget (PolU 95); **jūja-jınna** little devil, Tom Thumb; pl. **jūje**.

גוגה (<גורה) pl. **jōje** urine, peepee (babytalk).

גוגו (<גוגה) **jōjo** one who wets his pants.

גוגייא v. ז'וז'ייא

גודא 1 (IrAr < Ar abundant rain) **jōda** skin bottle (BT1; PolG); cf. גודא 2.

גודא 2, גודאא (K/P; cf. OA דְזוּד separate < P) adv. **jud(ʾ)a** separately, alone.

גוהארא, גֻוהַלָא (K/P > OA/OS/Mand גְוָאלְקָא) **juhāl/ra** sack, large sturdy bag (BT1, D); pl. גֻוהַלֵי **juhāle** (cf. PolG) [Krotkoff 124].

גוזא v. גזא

גוזי (Ar جوزه narghile?) f. **jōzi** coffee kettle.

ג-ו-י v. ג-ו-י

גוין(א) (K?) f. **jwīn(a)** group, team (Pol 107); pl. **jwīne** (cf. PolG) (NT+).

גולא (Ar) **julla** garment (SaAC 22); pl. **julle**; cf. ג-ל-ל. NT+

גומלתא, גמלתא (Ar) **jümlıta** totality, sum (NT2).

גונכא (K) adj. **jōnaka** dark-colored (BT1).

גונקא (K) m. **jwqanqa** lad; cf. גואנה.; pl. **jwanqe**.

גונקונכא (<גונקא) dim. **jwanqonka** youth, lad (Pol 107); pl. **jwanqonkat** (Hob97 325).

גונקותא (<גונקא) n. abst. **jwanqūṯa** youth.

ג-ו-ק II(Ar) **j-w-q** to form a group (NT3).

גוקא, גפקא, גואקא (Ar) f. **jōqa, jafqa, joʾqa** (?) (AmU2 10a), sect, group. pl. **jōqe**, שוקי-שוקי **ž/šōqe-ž/šōqe**? (RivSh 172) (NT+) [Khan 570 **jafqa**].

ג-ו-ר II (Ar) **j-w-r** to oppress (NT3).

גור(א) (Ar) **jōr(a)** burden, yoke (NT).

גורדא (Ar) m. **jurda** mole, field-rat; pl. **jurde**.

גורה (Arm **jur** water) pl. **jōre** urine; cf. ג-י-ר, גוגה [cf. Garbell 313; MacD 50 **jyūrī**; Khan 571 **jore**].

גוֹרְנַאת (Ar) pl. **jornat** water trough (= H רְהָטִים, PolG); cf. גורנה.

גורעתא (K<Ar جرأة) ⁺**jurʿıta** audacity, courage; **mare-jurʿıta** courageous, audacious.

גותיארא (K) m. **jotyāra** ploughman; pl. **jotyāre**.

גותכא (K<P جفت) **jōtıka** pair, duo; pl. **-kat**.

גזא, גוזא, גוּזַא (Ar) f. **jı/uza** punishment, fine; recompense (good or bad)(NT2; RivSh 121); pl. גזאיי **jı/azāye** (BaBin 123); **bıd jazāye** with much suffering (cf. PolG).; cf. ג-ז-י.

גזאיותא (<גזא) f. **jızāyūṯa** suffering, sorrow.

גזדאן (IrAr<P/T) f. ⁺**jızdān** wallet.

גזוכה, גזונכה (K?<Ar جزء 'section [of Koran]'?) f. **jızūnke, čızūke**, booklet (of religious or magic nature) (PolU 251).

ג-ז-י II (Ar) vi/vt **j-z-y** to punish, torture; to suffer, to pine (for a beloved one) (NT+).

גזיא (Ar جزة) f. **jızya** fleece; גזיית אמרא **jızyıt ʾamra** a fleece of wool (BaBin 129).

גזירא (Ar) f. **jızīra** island (NT3); cf. גזירא 2; pl. גזיריית **jızīrīyat** (BT1).

גזירכה (Ar-K) f. **jızērīke** isle (PolU 109).

גזמא (Ar/K/T) f. ⁺**jazma** boot; pl. ⁺**jazme**.

גזינה (K?) f. **jızīne** (shoulder) bag (PolU 72); cf. כורגניאתא.

ג-ח-ד II (Ar جهد) **j-ḥ-d** to quarrel, argue, resist, fight back (Pol 136; PolG).

גחדתא, גְחַתָא, גְחַת, גחדותא (<ג-ח-ד) f. **jaḥadta, jaḥat(ta), jaḥdūṯa** (+PolG) quarrel (=H רִיב, מְרִיבָה, BT4/BT5, D); pl. **jaḥadyāṯa** (PolGr 33).

גחיר v. ז'חר

גחל v. גהל

גחנם v. גהנם

גחשא (Ar) m. **jaḥša** young donkey; jackass (=H עַיִר, PolG) (NT+).

ג-י-ב v. ג-ו-ב

גיבא (Ar) m. **jēba** pocket; pl. **jēbābe** (cf. PolG).

(-מ) גיד, גִית, מגיד (<גודאא) **(m)jīd/t** apart from, besides of (מִן מִיגִיד דִידוֹך **mın** [!] **mıjīd dīdox** =H מִבַּלְעָדֶיךָ, AvidH 67).

גידא, גהדא (K<Ar جَهْد diligence) adv. **jēda**,

jeḥda (also **jēd-gyāna, har jēda**), right away (cf. PolG).
ג-י-ז (Ar) vi **j-y-z** to be possible (NT+).
גיל, גילה (Ar) **jīl** (m.), **jīle** (f.), generation, period; קמלא כדא גילה כיתא **qımla xda jīle xēta** another generation has risen (NT5 385).
גימכה, גימכת (K) pl. **jēmıke** (NT3), **jēmıkat** (+Z), twins (NT+).
גימע (IrAr<Ar جامع) f. **jēmaᶜ** mosque.
גינדרכה (K **jindar** diviner) **jindarke** trickery (Sa83c 26) [MacD 54<AzT].
גיניכה 1 (K<Ar) f. **jēnīke** garden; pl. **jēnīkat**.
גיניכה 2 (K) f. **jēnīke** temple (right or left side of the head, including the ear).
ג-י-ר (< גורה) **j-y-r** to urinate (cf. PolG); IV help (a child) urinate (Hob89 218).
גירה (K diligent, lively) f. **jīre**; v. גואנה.
גירייה, גירי (K<Ar) f. ⁺**jērīye**, ⁺**jēri** (BT2, Am), female slave, concubine (=H פִּילֶגֶשׁ/שִׁפְחָה/ אָמָה, BT); pl. גירייה **jērīye** (NT; especially with ʾōde slaves'; PolGr 57), ⁺**jērīyat** (Z; PolG).
גירן, גירנתא (K<Ar) n./inv. **jīran, jīránta**, neighbor; cf. שואוא; pl. **jīrāne**.
גיש, גאייש (Ar) **jayš** army (NT3); cf. אסכר.
גית v. גיד
גגרא v. גכרא
גלד ,גלאד, גַלַּת (Ar) m. **jállad/t** (RivSh 271) hangman, executioner; pl. גלאדין **jallādīn** (NT), **jalllāde** (Z; PolG).
גלאלתא (Ar) f. **jalālıta** honor, glory (NT+).
גלב (Ar) **jalab** herd (cf. PolG); logs dispatched over the river; pl. **jalābe** (NT+).
ג-ל-ג-ח III (Ar جلخ/جرح) **j-l-j-ḥ** to have a superficial wound (cf. PolG).
ג-ל-ד 1 II (Ar) vi **j-l-d** to freeze.
ג-ל-ד 2 II (Ar) vt **j-l-d** to bind a book (usually with a leather cover).
גלודא (<ג-ל-ד 2) m. **jıllōda** leather bound book.
גלוה (Ar) f. **jalwe** exile (NT3). cf. גלות.
ג-ל-ט (Ar shave) **j-l-ṭ** to wipe clean (a plate of a delicious dish).
ג-ל-י (Ar) **j-l-y** to polish, rinse (dishes); II to reveal Oneself (God to man)(NT, BT).
ג-ל-כ (Ar) vt **j-l-x** to slightly wound, to scrape.
גלכא (Ar) m. **jılxa** wound (=H פֶּצַע, BT1).
ג-ל-ל II2 (Ar) **j-l-l** to cover, to clothe (for glorification)(NT3); cf. גולא.
גלל (Ar شلال) **jalal** brook (= H נַחַל, AlfM 13), waterfall; cf. רעולא, כזלא; pl. **jalāle**.
ג-ל-ק (Ar?) **j-l-q** to flirt, tease, have an affair.
גמאעא (Ar) f. **jımāᶜa** (Jewish) congregation, comminity (=H הַקָּהָל, PolG); pl. גמעיתייתא **jımaᶜıtyāṯa** (BaBin 106) (NT+).
גמאעוכה (<גמאעא) f. **jımāᶜōke** gang, group (BaBin 143; Sa83c 24, Z)); pl. **jımāᶜōkat**.
גמבא (Ar جنب) m. **jamba** one side of double saddlebag (PolU 132).
ג-מ-ד (Ar) vi **j-m-d** to freeze, become cold (hot food); IV to freeze (vt), to confiscate.
גמדאני (K **čemedān**) f. **jımıdāni** checkered kefiya used by Kurdish men as circular headgear; pl. **jımıdānīyat**.
ג-מ-ט (Ar?/OA שמט?) **j-m-ṭ** to become slippery, loose (PolU 346); IV to remove the foliage and branches of a tree (PolU 347).
גַמִילֵי (Ar) f. **jamīle** favor (=H חֶסֶד, BT1, D).
גמיע (Ar) **jamīᶜ** all (NT3).
ג-מ-ל (Ar) **j-m-l** to include; to decorate (?)(NT3).
גומלא, גמלא (Ar) **jı/ümla** wholesale.
ג-מ-ס (OA כמש/Ar تشمس?) vi **j-m-s** to wither, wilt (flower, plant); to lose vivacity (a person); to wait too long; be silent (out of fear) (cf. PolU 409); cf. ג-ר-מ-ס **č-r-m-s**.
ג-מ-ע (Ar) **j-m-ᶜ** to assemble (vi); II to gather (vt) (NT+).
גנא, גניתא (Ar) **jınna** (m.), **jınnīṯa** (f.), jinni, ghost, demon; smart, mischievous, 'devil'.
גְנַאוִר (K/T<P جانوَر) **janāwır** wild boar (=H עַכְבָּר BT3, D).
גנאזה (Ar) f. **jınāze** funeral, hearse (NT).
גנגארא (K/P ژنگار) m. **jıngāra** rust; **d-w-q jıngāra** to become rusty.
גנגאראנא, גנגארנתא (<גנגארא) adj. **jıngārāna, -anta**, rusty.
גנגארי (<גנגארא) inv. **jıngāri** rusty color (PolU 4).
ג-נ-ג-ר III (<גנגארא) **j-n-g-r** to rust.
גנגיר (<Ar/K?) m. **jınjir** hammock; **-īre**.
גנגר (<K جنجره<P جندره) m. **janjar** threshing sledge [cf. MacD 55 **jerjer**<OS ܓܪܓܪܐ; Khan

571 **janjar** 'threshing machine', K].

גנדאיא, גנדיתא (K galant<Ar soldier) adj. **jındāya, jındēṯa**, of good quality (people, things), kind, good-looking (cf. PolG).

גנדארא (P) **jandāra** soldier, bodyguard (NT2).

גנדרמא (IrAr<Fr) m. **jandırma** gendarme; pl. **jandı/ürme**.(RivSh 125; PolG).

גַנֶיג (<זנכ) **janıg** blight (=H שִׁדָּפוֹן, BT5, D).

גנן (Ar جنان heart) **jınan** patience; **latli gjār jınan dīde** I don't have any patience for him.

גנס (K<Ar<L) **jıns** (human) kind, usually in hendiadys **ʿıns-u-jıns** (any) living creature; **kma jıns ʿınsān xlıqlox go dunye** (O God,) how many sorts of people have You created in the world? (PolU 294).

גנסייא (Ar) f. **jınsīa** identity card; pl **jınsīyat**.

גנפאץ (IrAr) **jınfāṣ** sackcloth, canvas.

גסד (Ar) m. **jasad** body: **la mṣēla doqāle jasad gyāna** She couldn't hold her body (PolG).

ג-ס-ס II2 (Ar) **j-s-s** to spy; cf. גאסוסא (NT+).

ג-ס-ר II(Ar) ⁺**j-s-r** to have the audacity.

גַעְדֵי v. גאדא

ג-ע-ל (Ar) **j-ʿ-l** to make, turn into; אילאהא גאעליה כלמוך שלום **ʿilāha jāʿılle xılmox šālōm** May God turn your dream into a peacful result (cf. PolU 324).

גראדה, דראגה, דרנגה (Ar) f. ⁺**jırāde** (Z), **darāje** (NT), **darınje** (PolG; PolU 15), ladder (Z), stair(s), rank(s) (NT); pl. גְרַדְיָיתָא **jıradyāṯa** (=H מַעֲלוֹת, PolG), דַרְנְגַאת **daranjat** (PolG).

גראדוכה (<גראדה) ⁺**jırādōke** step(s); pl. ⁺**jırādōkat**.

גראו (K?) **jarʿo** stomach (=H קֵבָה/קֳבָה, BT4/5).

גרארא (Ar جرّار potter?) ⁺**jırāra** maker of ground sesame sauce; very grimy person.

ג-ר-ב, ג-ר-פ, ש-ר-ב (Ar) ⁺**j-r-b**, (+NT) **ž-r-p/b**, to try, to test; to prefer (NT2) (NT+).

ג-ר-ב-א III (Ar) **j-r-b-ʾ** to have scabby skin (=H גָּרָב, BT3).

גרבה (Ar) pl. (?) **jarbe** only in **mapōqe mın jarbe** to test someone by conversing with him (like an interview) (cf. PolG).

גרבהי (K-Ar) **jarbahī** attempt, trial (PolG).

גרבואה (Ar) pl. **jırbōʾe** scabs (H אֲבַעְבֻּעֹת, PolG).

גרבונא (<ג-ר-ב) m. ⁺**jırbōna** trial, test (=H מַסָּה, BT5); pl. ⁺**jırbōne** (BaBin 151).

גרבתא, גרביתא, גרביי (<ג-ר-ב) f. ⁺**jarbıta** (NT2), **jarbīye** (NTU4 151a), trial, test; pl. גרבתיאתא ⁺**jarbıtyāṯa**.

גרגור (Ar?) m. ⁺**jarjur** a kind of necklace.

גרוטא, גרוטתא (<ג-ר-ט) adj. ⁺**jarūṭa**, ⁺**jaruṭṭa** slippery.

ג-ר-ז (Ar) **j-r-z** to be dissected, mostly with **nāve** 'guts': be tortured (emotionally); IV **qam jārızlu nāvi** He caused me a lot of pain.

ג-ר-ט (K) **j-r-ṭ** to slip; IV cause to slip (NT+).

ג-ר-י 1 (Ar) ⁺**j-r-y** to flow, to ooz; IV to fulfill: ⁺**maram dīda qam** ⁺**majıryāle** She fulfilled her wish (PolG) NT+

ג-ר-י 2 (Ar جـــور) **j-r-y** to live as neighbors (NT4).

גרידאנה, גדידאנה, גדידה (K) **jar/dīdāne, jıdīde** (PolU 286), equesterian race or game by Kurdish knights; **m-x-y** - to race (FT).

ג-ר-מ II (Ar) ⁺**j-r-m** to impose a fine, punish.

גרס (Ar) m. ⁺**jaras** (modern) doorbell; cf. זנגלא.

ג-ר-ב v. ג-ר-פ

ג-ר-ק II (Ar?) ⁺**j-r-q** to respond with impudence; give impolite answer.

ג', ג̇ (č)

גאבא-דר (K) inv. **čāva-dar** errant wife whose eyes are always on the door, anxious to go outside.

גאגונא (K/P چوگان) m. **čāgōna** staff, club.

גאגכתא (<K?) f. **čāčıkta** the meat of shoulder blade (=H זְרוֹעַ, BT4; PolG); pl. **čāčıkyāṯa**.

גאדרא (P) f. **čādıra** tent; pl. **čādırrat** (PolG).

גאויש (T/Ar) m. **čāwıš** personal attendant, courtier (=H סָרִיס, BT1); pl. גַאוִישֵׁי **čāwīše** taskmasters (=H שׁוֹטְרִים, BT2, D), שאווּשֵׁה **šāwūše** eunuchs (=H סריסים, NT5 394).

גאונא, גאונתא (<ג'-א-נ) adj. **⁺ca'ūna, ⁺ca'unta** greasy.

גאיי (IrAr/K/T/P) m. **čāy(i)** tea.

גאייגי (T) **čāyıči** tea man, owner of tea house; pl. **čāyıčīyat**; v. קנדג'.

גאייכאנא (T) f. **čāyixāna** tea house.

גאלה (P) f. **čāle** pit, canal; גאלד ארייה **čālıd 'arye** lion's pit (NT2); pl. גלאתא **čalāṯa** (BaBin 152; PolG), **čalawāṯa**.

ג'-א-נ (<K?) **⁺č-'-n** to be greasy; cf. גאונא.

גאפא (K) m. **⁺čāpa** overhand stroke of water.

גאקויה (K/AnAr<T) f. **čāqōye** penknife; — **'ıngīīzi** English (=Swiss?) penknife (PolU 15); pl. **čāqōyat**.

גארא (K) f. **čāra** shawl, tunic (NT2), ephod (BT2).

גאר-גאב (K) **čār-čāv** four-eyed (a monstrous mule), very vigile (?) (PolU 113).

גאר-גוקול (K) **čār-čuqul** cross (PolG).

גארדא-צאלי (K) inv. **čārda-ṣāli** most youthful (lit. 'fourteen-years old') (PolU 244).

גארוכה (<שרה) f. **čārōke** Sarah, Sarita (hypo.).

גארכ (IrAr/K<P چهاریك) m. **čārık** quarter.

גארנכאר, גארכנאר (P) **čārnıkār, čārkınār** all around, all the four corners (PolG; RivSh 181/274 אַרְבַּא כְּנָארֵי/גאר כִּנֶרֶת); cf. ג'-ר-כ-נ (NT+).

גארפאיא (IrAr) m. **⁺čārpāya** (quadruped) modern wooden bench, bed (PolG).

גאשני (P) **čāšıni** taste, sample, resemblance (NT2; NTU4 153b) [MacD 141].

גגא (K) m. **čıčča** breast, tit (babytalk).

גגמא (JAB<P<T **česme**) f. **čačma** lavatory.

גהוא, גוֹהְוָא/גוּהְוָא (<ג'-ה-י) m. **čehwa** (cf. PolG), **ču/ohwa** (AvidH 29/30), exertion (NT+).

ג'-ה-י (OA שהי be tired; SokBA 1064: 2# שהי) vi **č-h-y** to be tired, exert oneself; IV make weary (Segal #85 < OS**ghy/khy**?) (NT+).

גהיא, גהיתא (< ג'-ה-י) p.p. **čehya, čhīṯa** tired (NT+).

גו (OA שום/K **ču/**) **ču** no (one); v. גוכא 1 גמנדי,., גוגא (NT+). [cf. Western NA **ču**].

גואא/גואאנא, גואתא/גואנתא (<ג'-י-א) adj. **⁺čō'a/ ⁺čō'āna, ⁺čo'ta/⁺čō'anta** smooth (surface).

גואותא (<גואא) f. **⁺čō'ūṯa** smoothness (cf. PolG).

גוגא (<גו+אהא 1) adv. **čuga** never, not even once.

גוגא (K 'chick'?) adv. **čūča** a little bit, some [Khan 566 **čúča** 'somehow', K].

גוגה (K) f. **čūče** bird (babytalk); cf. גוגכתא.

ג'-ו-ג'-י III (< ג'-ו-י) **⁺č-o-č-y** to whine, complain.

גוגכתא (K) f. **čūčıkṯa** (any small) bird, sparrow; pl. **čūčıkyāṯa** (cf. PolG); cf. גוגה.

ג'-ו-י (<?) **č-w-y** to complain, scold (NT2); cf. ג'-ו-ג'-י.

גוית (IrAr<T) m. **čıwit** indigo, washing-blue.

גוך (IrAr) **čōx** heavy broadcloth (PolU 425).

גוכא 1, גו כא (<גו+כא) **čuxa** none, nobody.

גוכא 2 (K) f. **čōka** the back of the knee; pl. גוֹכַאכֵי **čōkāke** jointed legs(=H כְּרָעַיִם, BT3, D).

גוכלא, גוקלא (K) m. **čukıla, čuqıla** (PolG), tree branch, hook, leg of aleph; pl. **čukılāle** (MeAl 178), **čuqqolāle** (PolU 327); cf. גאר-גוקול.

גוכר (<גו+כארא) **čukar** never (RivSh 200); cf. גוגא.

גול (IrAr<T) m. **čōl** wilderness, countryside [also **čōl-u-čōlistān/čawal**; Pol 106]; **čōl-bır** open area (after mountains)(PolU 430).

גונא (< ציון) m. **čūna** Zion (hypo.); cf. גייא.

גוקלא v. גוכלא

ג'-ו-ר (K?) **⁺č-w-r** to wink, to blink (cf. PolG).

גז (K/onomat.) **⁺čızzzz** sound of sizzling (cf. PolUL 390).

ג'-ז-ג'-ז III (K) **⁺č-z-č-z** to frizzle, sizzle.

גזוכה v. גזונכה
גזי-וזי (K crude violin) ⁺čızi-wızi obscure, unknown language, 'Barbarian'.
גטל (<T?) čaṭal silver or gold talisman locket.
גחו (<רחל) f. čaḥo Rachel (hypo.).
גי ...גי (K) čī...čī (n)either...(n)or, (PolG); **či naṣya, či la naṣya** whether she fights or not (SaAC 1).
ג-י-א (OA שעע) ⁺č-y-ʾ to be smooth; IV to smooth, beautify (cf. PolG); cf. גואא.
גיגלכא (P چچله lingula) m. čičılka clitoris.
גיגנא (<גגא) m. čičına nipple, nipple-like.
גיגרכא (K چیـــر crackle) m. ⁺čičırka pest, nagger; cf. גיר-נכווש, ציצרכא.
גייא (<בת-ציון) f. čīya Bath-Zion (hypo.).
ג-י-כ (<OA סכך/סִכָּא pin?) vt č-y-k to stick in, insert, squeeze in; **ʾaw dčāyık rēše go tanūra qqāyız bıd nūra** He who sticks his head in the oven gets burned by fire.
גיל v. שילא
גילכא (K) m. čīlıka dry twig, kindling; **kutēle bčīlıka** dumpling on a stick (popular snack among children); pl. **čīlıke** (cf. PolG)
ג-י-מ (< OA אמץ/עמץ to close the eyes?) vt/vi ⁺č-y-m to close (usually eyes); cf. ג-מ-ג-מ, ג-ע-מ-צ, [cf. MacD 12 ʾ-č-m/č-y-m].
גימו (<סימן טוב) čīmo hypo. of סימנטוב Simantof.
גין (P/K/T<R) čīn (military) epaulet (RivSh 274 [cf. MacD 275].
גין-ומאגין (K/P) **čīn-u-māčīn** China; end of the world, a far away, legendary, place.
גינכו (T<It) f. **čīnko** zink, enamel ware.
גיק (K) m. **čīq** screen of reeds (for privacy).
ג-י-ק (Ar شق) vt/vi **č-y-q** to tear; **julle čıqlu** His clothes became torn; to have intercourse (vulgar, in curses) [=Khan 552 **čqy** stab?].
גיקכי (<גיק?) adv. **čīqıki** diagonally.
גירוכה (K) f. ⁺**čīrōke** folktale; pl. **čīrōkat**.
גירי (OA תשרי) m. **čēri** fall, autumn (beginning with month of Tishri).
גיריו (IrAr<En) **čīryo** Cheerio (used as a toast).
גירכיני (< ג-ר-כ-נ?) adv. **čirkīnī** secretly, calmly, quietly (PolG).
גיר-נכווש (K) inv.⁺**čīr-naxwaš** pest, nagger (lit., no-good sound); cf. גיגרכא.
גיר-צארכה (K) f. **čēr-ṣārke** idle talking woman.
גיר-צארותא (K) f. **čēr-ṣārūṯa** idle talk.
גיתי (IrAr/T<Hindi) m. **čīti** light painted/printed cotton cloth, chintz.
ג-כ-ג-כ III (K/onomat) **č-k-č-k** (?) to cast out (=H גרש, NTU4 164b) [MacD 175 **mkačkič** tear to pieces/**mčakčik** to creak?].
גכגכתא (<ג-כ-ג-כ) f. **čakčakta** (?) outcast (NTU4 150a].
גכה (K) pl. **čakke** weapons; jewelry (NT+).
גכוג (T) m. **čakkuč** hammer.
גכווגי (<Ar شكوة accusation?) slanderer, talebearer (=H רָכִיל, BT3).
גכווגותא (<גכווגי) f. **čakwačūṯa** slander, ill-will (BaBin 144; Sa83C 26, Z); cf. גינדרכה.
גכון, גכין v. גנכי
ג-כ-כ II2 (<גכה) vt **č-k-k** to put on weapons (cf. PolG).
גכמגא (IrAr<T) f. **čakmača** drawer.
גכלוכא (K) m. **čıklōka** chick, young bird; pl. **čıklōke** (cf. PolG), **čıklōkat**
גכלית (IrAr<En) m. **čıklēt** wrapped candy (such as toffee); cf. שכרוכא; pl. **čıklētat**.
גלא (K) **čılla** forty, only in **čıllıd sıswa** (Z) mid-winter, the worse 'forty' days of winter.
גלאנא, גלנתא (K?) adj. **čıllāna, čıllanta** glutton, one too eager to eat (as a guest).
גלאקא (<JAB 'kick') **čıllāqa** slap.
גלא-סבכ (K **čalak** diligent+**sivik** quick<P سبك) inv. **čala-sıvık** quick, diligent (PolU 251).
ג-ל-ב II (IrAr) vt **č-l-b** to cling, to stick to.
גלבי (T) inv. **čalabi** noble, elegant, gentleman.
גלכ (K?) **čılk** menstrual blood.
גלנג (K) inv. **čalang** diligent, agile (PolU 74).
גמא (K<OA אגמא?) m. **čamma** meadow, lake, reed grass (=H אָחוּ, BT1); pl. **čammān/me** (=H אֲגַמִּים, BT2; PolG)[v. MacD 130, 134; but Mutz 198 **čom** 'forest'<K **čam** 'pine'].
גמאד (OA -כמה ד?) **čımmād/t** as much/many as (cf. Pol 106; PolG).
ג-מ-ב-ל III(<גמבלא) **č-m-b-l** to hook, to ring.
גמבלא (K) m. **čımbıla** handle (of a kettle, jar) (SaAC 11); pl. **čımbılāle** (cf. PolG).
ג-מ-ג (OA כמש?) vi ⁺**č-m-č** to shrivel; ⁺**čmīče** (p.p.pl.) shriveled (=H צְנוּמוֹת, BT1).
גמגא 1 (K/T) m. **čamča** ladle; pl. **čamče**.

גמגא 2 (< ג-מ-ג) ⁺**čımča** hard mucus (in the eye); pl. ⁺**čımče**.
ג-מ-ג-מ III (<ג-י-מ) ⁺**č-m-č-m** to have bleary eyes (due to smoke); cf. ג-ע-מ-צ.
ג-מ-י (OS ܥܡܐ be dark?) iv ⁺**c-m-y** to be extinguished; IV to extinguish (vt), turn off; annihilate, get rid of (enemy) (PolU91)
גמינתו (T<It) m. **čımīnto** cement.
ג-מ-כ (OA צמק?) vi **č-m-k** to shrink in size.
גמנדי (<גו+מנדי) **čımındi** nothing; **čımındí-čımındi** minimum, the least.
גן (K) **čan** some, a: **xa čan muqdar** (I'll come with you) a certain distance (PolU 427).
גנאגא (<K **čannān** a few?) **čanāča** a bit, small section (PolG).
ג-נ-ג II (<גנגא) **č-n-g** to scoop (=H קָמַץ, BT3; צָבַט, PolG< Ruth 2:14).
גנגא (K) m. **čanga** wing; handful (RivSh 276; =H חֹפֶן); cf. כי-גנגא; pl. **čangāge** (cf. PolG).
גנגאלא (K/T) m. **čıngāla** hook, talon, fork (=H מַזְלֵג, PolG; latch; pl. **čıngāle**.
גנגולא (K?) **čıngōla** rag (SaAC 16); cf. גנגרתא.
ג-נ-ג-ל III (<גנגאלא) **č-n-g-l** to hook, fasten together.
גנגלתא (<גנגאלא?) f. **čangılta** arm (bend) (PolU 20); pl. **čangılyā**t**a** (cf. PolG).
גנגרתא (K) f. ⁺**čıngırta** rag; pl. ⁺**čıngırre** (cf. PolG).
ג-נ-ג-ל III (<נ-ג-ל?) vi/vt **č-n-č-l** to tear to pieces: תולאתא אכלאליני ומגנגלא בכאכא פסריני **tōle'ṯa ʾaxlalēni umčančıla bkāka pısrēni** (In the grave) a worm will eat us and tear our flesh with her teeth (NTU4 165b).
גנטא (IrAr<T) f. **canṭa** (modern) suitcase; pl. **canṭe, canṭat** (cf. PolG); cf. גנתא.
גניכא, גניכה (K?) n./adj. ⁺**čınnīka, -ke** miser.
גנכי, גכין, גכון (K/T/P چونكه) **čınki, čıki/un** because (cf. PolG).
גנתא (K<T) f. **čanta** shoulder bag; pl. **čanyāṯa** (PolU 174).
געגורכא, געגורכה (<גרגועא?) n./adj. ⁺**caʿačurka, -ke** tramp, messy looking, light-headed.
ג-ע-מ-צ III (OA עצם/עמץ 'close eyes'/Ar عمص 'have bleary eyes'?) ⁺**č-ʿ-m-ṣ** to have bleary or narrow eyes; cf. ג-מ-ג-מ.
גפאיא, גפיתא (<גפה) adj. **čappāya, čappēṯa** left-handed.
גפגולכא, גפגולכה (T-K) n./adj.⁺**čappačulka, -ke** slovenly, untidy person, ragamuffin.
ג-פ-ג-פ 1 III (<גאפא) ⁺**č-p-č-p** to clap, beat the water (beginning swimmer).
ג-פ-ג-פ 2 (OA טפטף?) **č-p-č-p** to drip, drizzle; cf. גפכתא.
גפגפיסכה (K) f. **čapčapīske** butterfly; pl. **čapčapīskat**.
גפה (K) f. **čappe** left (hand); bad luck (RivSh 186); **čappıki** adv. to the left (PolU 227); cf. גפאיא [Khan 566 **ʾilit čopa** 'left hand'].
ג-פ-כ II (<גפכתא) **č-p-k** to drizzle; cf. ג-פ-ג-פ.
גפכתא (<OA טיפתא?) f. **čıppıkṯa** a drop; pl. **čıppıkyāṯa**.
ג-פ-ל (Ar جفل) **č-f-l** to be startled, take fright (BaBin 158; =H וַיִּלָּפֵת, Ruth 3:8; PolG).
גפלתא (<ג-פ-ל) n.act. **čfalta** fright (PolUR 35).
גפקא v. גוקא
גפר (K) m. **čappar** palisade, hiding place, shield (=H סִתְרָה/מָגֵן, BT5); **d-w-q — ʾıllu** to ambush them; **p-y-š — ʾıl-** protect (PolG).
ג-ק-ג-ק III (onomat) **č-q-č-q** to make noise [=MacD 177]; to rob (=H גָּזַל, BT5, D).
גקגקוכה (onomat) f. **čaqčaqōke** noisemaker.
גקמק (T) m. **čaqmaq** (modern) lighter; cf. קדותא; diligent, 'ever ready' housewife; pl. **čaqmāqe**.
גרא (K/P) **čara** pasture (=H מִרְעֶה, BT1).
גרא-הורכה, גרורה(K) f. **čırta-hūrke, čırūre** (PolUL 407, but PolG 'child talk'!), candle flame, light-spot; pl. **čıra-hūrkat**.
גראכא, גרכתא (<ג-ר-כ) n. ag. **čarāxa, -axta** loiterer, one who spends much time away from home (pejor.).
גרגאפכה (K) f. **čarčāfke** veil, shawl (=H צָעִיף, BT1); pl. **čarčāfkat**.
גרגועא (K) f. ⁺**čırčōʿa** disgusting concoction; cf. געגורכא [Mutz.193:ʿ**ırča**<OS ܥܪܐ 'filth'].
ג-ר-ג-ע III (<גרגועא) vt/vi ⁺**č-r-č-ʿ** to become/ make a messy concoction, mishandle [cf. Mutz.198, 223 **črčʿ, rčʿ**].
גרגק (K/P/T?) **čarčaq** the shoulder blade of

cattle (also used as toy for children).
גֵּרְוָאן (K) **čerwān** pasture (AvidH 26); cf. גּרא.
גּרוכּ (T) inv. **čıruk** inferior, ignoble.
גּר(ו)כגותא (<גּרוכּ) f. **čırükčūṯa** small trade, the business of גּר(ו)כגי **čırükči** small trader.
גּרופא, גּרופתא (<ג-ר-פּ) adj. **čarōpa, čarüpta** timid (cf. Pol 106; PolG).
גּרורה v. גּרא-הורכת
ג-ר-כ (<גּרכא) vi **č-r-x** to walk around (searching for something), loiter; cf. גּראכא; IV to sharpen (BABin 118), to whet (on grinding wheel); move (dog: tongue) (=H חָרַץ, BT2).
גּרכ(א) (P) m. **čarx(a)** wheel; **čarx-u-falak** the zodiac wheel; **g-r-š čarxe** be an intriguer (NT+).
גּרכי (T) m. **čarxi** Turkish coin; pl. **čarxīye**.
ג-ר-כ-נ, ג-ר-נ-כ III (< גּארכנאר) **č-r-k-n, č-r-n-k** to crouch (cf. Pol 108; PolG).
ג-ר-כ-ס (T?) **č-r-x-s** to insult, humiliate (Avin78 93).
גּרמכתא (K/P) f. **čarmıkṯa** foreskin (=H עָרְלָה, BT); **mare-čarmıkṯa** uncircumcized (=H עָרֵל, BT1).
ג-ר-מ-ס III (OA כמש/Ar تشمس?) vi **č-r-m-s** to wither, wilt (flower, plant), to lose vivacity (a person); to wait too long; cf. ג-מ-ס **j-m-s**.
ג-ר-נ-כ v. ג-ר-כ-נ
ג-ר-ס II (IrAr **č-r-z**) **č-r-s** to eat roasted seeds and small nuts to pass the time [cf. Khan **čaraze** sweets, K].
גּרס (K/IrAr چرز<T) **čaras** dry fruits and nuts used as snack.
ג-ר-פּ II (<?) **č-r-p** to startle or be startled (Avin78 94; =H נִבְעַת, PolG); cf. גּרופא.
גּרפיתא (<ג-ר-פּ) f. **čarrapīṯa** sudden fear (=H מֹרֶךְ, BT3; cf. PolG).
גּרק (onomat/K?) **čraq** sound of sudden and difficult door opening.(PolU 15).

ג, ג' (ġ, غ)

ג, ג' (H) **ġimal**, fricative variant of ג Gimel.
ג'- v. כ-
ג'אפל (Ar) **ġāfıl** unaware, ignorant (NT3); pl. ג'אפלין **ġāfılīn** fools (NT3).
ג'ארא (K<Ar) f. ⁺**ġāra** raid (PolU 47).
ג'בארא (Ar) f. ⁺**ġabāra** straw dust (Ruth 3:2).
ג'-ב-ט 1 (Ar خبط) **ġ-b-ṭ** to die untimely; common in curses: **ġabṭıt/ġbīṭa** May you die untimely; II to urge, hasten (=H הָאִיץ, BT1).
ג'-ב-ט 2 v. כ-ב-ט
ג'ביטא, ג'בטתא (< ג'-ב-ט)p.p., adj. **ġbīṭa, ġbıṭṭa** (May you be) untimely dead, accursed.
ג'בין (Ar) inv. **ġabīn** fraudulent (NT3).
ג'בינה, מג'בינה, מְכַבִּינֵי (Ar) interj. **(m)ġabīne, mxabīne** What a loss, deprivation! (RivSh 192); cf. חיף (NT+).
ג'-ב-ן I/II (Ar) **ġ-b-n** to deprive (NT2).
ג'בריתא (Ar) f. **ġabbarīṯa** excessively dusty and humid storm.
ג'-ד-א v. כ-ד-א
ג'דאיא (Ar) **ġadāya** lunch, breakfast (Pol 107; PolG; RivSh 108); - **mīri** late 'royal' breakfast (PolU 429).
ג'-ד-י II(Ar) **ġ-d-y** to lunch, to breakfast (cf. Pol 108; PolG).
ג'-ד-מ v. כ-ד-מ
ג'-ד-ר 1 (Ar) **ġ-d-r** to deceive in business, to betray.
ג'-ד-ר 2 v. כ-ד-ר
ג'-ו-ג'-י III (<?) **ġ-ō-ġ-y** to coo, bubble (baby sounds before being able to talk).
ג'וואצא (Ar) **ġawwāṣa** diver; v ג'-ו-צ.
ג'ולאמא, ג'ולמתא (Ar) ⁺**ġulāma,** ⁺**ġulamta** servant (boy, girl); slave (BT2, Arodh); pl. ג'ולאמה ⁺**ġulāme** (NT2; NTU4 151b), ⁺**ġulamwāṯa** (m., =H נְעָרִים, BT1; RivSh 236), **ġulamāṯa** (PolG); **ġulamyāṯa** (f.).
ג'ולמותא (< ג'ולאמא) f. **ġulamūṯa** (but PolG **ġulumwasūsa**) apprenticeship.
ג'מאם v. ג'ומם
ג'-ו-צ (Ar) **ġ-w-ṣ** to dive, to dip.
ג'זאלא, כזאלא (K<Ar) f. **ġ/xazāla** gazelle; **ḥalāla x-pısır** - as kosher as the gazelle meat (=very kosher);- **(b)barīya mṭaše gyānax** Hide and Seek; pl. **ġ/xazāle/-lat** (PolU 3).
ג'זאלה, כזאלה (K/Ar) p.n. f. **ġ/xazāle** Gazelle.
ג'-ז-ד-ג v. כ-ד-ז-ג
ג'זו (Ar) **ġazu** tribal raid (PolU 290).
ג'-ז-י v. כ-ז-י
ג'-ז-ן v. כ-ז-ן
ג'-ז-ר v. כ̇-ד-ר
ג'יבה (Ar) p.p. pl. **ġībe** only in **ʿašāyıd ġībe** the charity dinner in the memory of the deceased ('absent') ones.
ג'יר (Ar) ⁺**ġēr** without, except; בג'יר הואן **bġēr hawān** untimely (NT2); **pıšle** ⁺**ġēr nāša** He became a different person; **ʾo** ⁺**ġēr mındī-le** This is a different thing; **kıtte** ⁺**ġērox la kīʾe** No one, except you, knows (about this); **la kšaqla** ⁺**ġēri** She will not marry anyone else besides me (PolG);⁺**ġēr?** eh? ok? (SaAC 13).
ג'-י-ר 1 II (Ar غير) vi/vt ⁺**g-y-r** to change, to be different (cf. PolG). NT+
ג'-י-ר 2 (Ar غور) ⁺**ġ-y-r** to disappear (BaBin 132; PolG), to sink; IV to conceal, to annihilate (NT+).
ג'ירא 1, ג'ירתא (< ג'-י-ר 2) p.p. ⁺**ġīra,** ⁺**ġırta** lost.
ג'ירא 2, ג'ירתא (K<Ar) f. **ġīra, ġīrıta** zeal; cf. כירתא; מרה ג'ירא **máre-ġīra** zealot(s) (NT+).
ג'לאקא (< ג'-ל-ק) v.n. **ġlāqa** closing; **ġlāqıd tarʾe** Locking of Doors (on the first day of Adar; a custom associated with Purim (BrE 344; Amedi 57).
ג'-ל-ב, כ-ל-ב (Ar) **ġ-l-b, x-l-b** (RivSh 263) to win, overcome; שטן ג'אלב אלה **sāṭān ġālıb ʾılle** Satan overcomes him (NT+).
ג'לבאוי (Ar) m. **ġalabāwi** wrangler (RivPr 214).
ג'-ל-ט, כ-ל-ט (Ar) **ġ-l-ṭ, x-l-ṭ** (+NT), to err; IV to mislead; to correct an error made by someone reading aloud the Biblical text in synagogue.
ג'לט (Ar) inv. **ġalaṭ** mistaken (cf. PolG).
ג'לטא (Ar) m. **ġılṭa** error, mistake; pl. **ġılṭe**.

ג'לטאי (Ar-K) adv. **ġalaṭāyī** by error (PolG).

ג'-ל-ק, כ-ל-ק (Ar) vi/vt **ġ-l-q, x-l-q** (+NT), to close, to lock.

ג'ם, ג'מתא (Ar) m. **ġam, ġammıta,** concern, care, worry; ליוו בג'מי **lēwu bġammi** They are not concerned about me; **manī-le bġammox** Who (or nobody) cares about you! **ġammıd ʾilāha uġammıti** God and I will take care (of it) (PolU 69); pl. **ġamme** (cf. PolG).

ג'מאם, ג'ומאם (Ar) m. **ġa/umam** (the Pillar of) louds (NT), cloud (BT2, Arod, BT3, D); cf. איוא, אינאנא.

ג'-מ-ג'-מ III (Ar) **ġ-m-ġ-m** to mumble, stutter.

ג'-מ-מ IV (Ar) **ġ-m-m** to go numb (heart) (=H פָּג, BT1, D).

ג'-מ-ר (Ar) vi **ġ-m-r** to faint; לבא ג'מרה **lıbba ġmırre** She fainted (lit. her heart flooded)(NT2).

ג'מתא v. ג'ם

ג'-נ-י (Ar to be rich) **ġ-n-y** to be (suddenly) lucky (BaBin 136; PolG); **ġnēle/yımme ġnēla** Lucky him! IV to make someone lucky.

ג'פארא (< ג'-פ-ר) v.n. **ġfāra** atonement (NT+).

ג'-פ-ל (Ar) **ġ-f-l** to neglect (a duty) (NT+).

ג'פליה, ג'פלא (Ar) f. **ġafle/a** suddenness; **rıš ġafla** suddenly; cf. ז'ג'פלתי.

ג'-פ-ר, כ-פ-ר (Ar) **⁺ġ/x-f-r** to atone (NT+).

ג'צב (Ar غصب) m. **ġaṣıb** aggression; בגצב **bġaṣıb** aggressive(ly) (NT2); **bġaṣbıd ʿanne** unwillingly, reluctantly.

ג'צ̇אדא (OA/OS חצָדָא, חצאדא) v.n. **ġẓāda** harvest; v. ג'-צ̇-ד

ג'צ̇ב, ג'צ̇אב, כזב (Ar غضب) m. **ġaẓab, ⁺xazab** (NT5 392), wrath, anger (NT+).

ג'-צ̇-ב, כ-צ̇-ב (Ar) **ġ/x-ẓ-b** to be angry (NT+).

ג'צ̇בותא (< ג'צ̇ב) f. **ġaẓabūṯa** anger (PolU 386).

ג'-צ̇-ד, כ-צ̇-ד (OA/OS חצד to harvest) **ġ/x-ẓ-d** to harvest (cf. PolG) [Mutz 238 **xṣl**]

ג'ראפא (Ar) f. **ġarrāfa** rower; oar; cf. ג'-ר-פ.

ג'ראקא (< ג'-ר-ק) v.n. **⁺ġrāqa** sinking (NT+).

ג'-ר-ב (Ar) **⁺ġ-r-b** to feel homesick, miss someone: **⁺rāba ⁺ġrıblan mınnox** We missed you a lot (when you were away).

ג'רבי (Ar) **ġarbi** west; cf. מערב.

ג'רבייה (< ג'ריב?) f. **ġarbīye** homesickness (PolU 392); cf. ג'ריבותא.

ג'-ר-ג'-ר III (< ג'-י-ר 2?) vi **⁺ġ-r-ġ-r** to become blurred (script), be hoarse (voice).

ג'-ר-ז (Ar خرز to string) vt **ġ-r-z** to swarm (=H שָׁרַץ, BT1).

ג'רז (Ar) m. **ġa/ırz** a swarm (=H שֶׁרֶץ, BT).

ג'ריב, ג'ריבנאיא, ג'ריבשא (K<Ar) m/inv. **ġarib(nāya), ġaribša** (NT2), stranger, one far away from home, nostalgic, homesick; strange: **barīya rabsa uġarib** big and strange/lifeless desert (PolG); cf. ג'רבייה.

ג'ריבותא (< ג'ריב) f. **ġarībūṯa** (being in) foreign country, nostalgia, homesickness (NT+).

ג'ריק (Ar) m. **ġarīq** sinking (NT2).

ג'רם (Ar<E) m. **⁺gıram** gram; pl. **⁺grāme**.

ג'-ר-מ IV (Ar) **⁺ġ-r-m** to repay (=H שִׁלֵּם, BT1).

ג'-ר-פ (Ar) **⁺ġ-r-f** to row; cf. ג'ראפא.

ג'רץ̇ (Ar aim) **ġarẓ** partiality (NT2), revenge (NT3); grudge (NT5 386); intention.

ג'-ר-ק, כ-ר-ק (Ar) vi/vt **⁺ġ/x-r-q** to drown; ג'רקנה סיפי בדמיהון **ġarqınne sēpi bdımmēhun** I shall sink my sword in their blood (NT+).

ג'-ש-מ (Ar) **ġ-š-m** to be ignorant or innocent (=H נוֹאַל, BT4, D); cf. כשים.

ד, דּ (d)

ד (H) **dālet̲** (Z **dāles**) the fourth letter of the Hebrew alphabet; **ʾarba** four.

-ד, ד-, ת- (OA/OS ד-) **d-, -d, -t** relative-possessive pronoun, including with prepositions: ביתד **bēt̲ıd** house of; שַׂאתִית **šatıt** year of (BT, D); טורת סיני **t̲ūrıt sīnay** Mount Sinai (NT5 383); אלד **ʾıllıd** upon; אפרד קם כנושיאתא **ʾıprıd qam kanušyāt̲a** (like) the dust before brooms; דילה **dīle** who is; דמירן **dmīrın** that was said; יונה דלא גנאהא **yōna dla gnāha** blameless dove (NT3); **jwanqıt xwāsox dalāla uʿazīza** pampered and precious young man like you (PolG) ; דהאדך **dhādax** For thus...; **h̲akōma dīwıt bassīma** Long live the king (MeAl 191); באילי דנובלואלו **bʾēle dnōbılwālu** He wanted to lead them (NT5 384); **qu dā(za)x** Get up, let us go! May connect an epithet and a name: צדיק דמשה **ṣaddīq dmōše** the righteous Moses; רשע דפרעה **rāšāʿ dparʿo** the wicked Pharaoh. May be used redundantly: שמד דאילאהא **šımmıd dʾilāha** God's name (NT3); שמד דידה **šımmıd dīde** His name (normally **šımme/šımma dīde**). May precede a quotation: מרו דאכני לתלן **mırru dʾaxni latlan** They said:'We don't have...'; v. also דיד, די.

דאבסתי (K) inv. **dābasti** fattened animal (NT+).

דאג'א (K/P) m. **dāğa** branding rod; **wēle xa dāğa š-lıbba** She is suffering ('her heart is branded/ burning'); cf. ד-ג'-י.

דאדא (K) f. **dāda** Aunt, Sister (+p.n.) (SaAC 7).

דאדה v. דאיה

דאדוכה (K) f. **dādōke** wet nurse; substitute mother; cf. דאיה; pl. **dādōkat**.

דַאהִינֵי v. דאיינה

דאהינתותא (<דאהיני) n. abst. **dāhīnatūt̲a** wet-nursing (SaAC 14).

דאווד אפנדי (K **dāwūdī** <IrAr?) **dāwūd affandi** chrysanthemum.

דאויסכא (< דוד) **dāwıska** (Z) David, Dave.

דאיה, דאדה (K; cf. OA דדי mother; דדי רבתי grandmother, SokBA 314) f. **dāye, dāde** Mother; וַאי בַאבו ואיי דַאיֵי **wāy bābo, wāy dāye** Woe, Father, Woe, Mother (RivSh 240); cf. אודא 3, דאדוכה, ימא.

דאיינה, דאיה, דַאהִינֵי (K) f. **dāy/hīne, dāye** (PolG), wet-nurse (=H מֵינֶקֶת, BT1, D), midwife (=H מְיַלֶּדֶת, BT2, D), caretaker (of a child) (=H אוֹמֶן, BT4); pl. דַאיינַאת **dāyīnat** (BT2, D); cf. דאדוכה, דאהינתותא, דאפירכה, ממצניתא.

דאים, דַאיֶים, דַאיימַאן (Ar) n./adv. **dāyım(an)** eternity, always, (BT4; PolG); cf. ד-י-ם (NT+).

דאיפא 1 (<ד-א-פ) **daʾīpa** fold away thin bread.

דאיפא 2, דאפתא (<ד-א-פ) p.p./adj. **dʾīpa, dʾıpta** folded; דאפתא ומודאפתא **dʿıpta umudʿapta** many folds (=H כְּפוּלָה וּמְכֻפֶּלֶת, AvidH 42).

דאיירא (Ar) f. **dāyera** office (PolU 281).

ד-א-כ (OA דעך) vi **d-ʾ-x** to be almost extinguished (fire, candle); become dispirited; IV to quench, extinguish (NT+).

דאכל (Ar) **dāxıl** inside, within (PolU 223).

ד-א-ל (OS ܕܓܠ) vi **d-ʾ-l** to (be able) to see (NT5 383); **pıšle sāwōna, lag dāʾıl** He has become an old man, he cannot see well.

דאלרה (K?/OA דרדרא thistle?) f. **dālare** a thistle, centaury leaves (eaten pickled or cooked).

דאמנה (K/P) f./pl. **⁺dāmane** coat-tail(s), flap(s) (=H שׁוּלַיִם, BT2; כְּנָפַיִם, Ruth 2:12); דַהְמַנַאת **dahmanat** shoulder-pieces (=H כְּתֵפוֹת, BT2, D).

דאן (K/P) m. **dān** portion of rice or other grains prepared for each cooking: **hēš lēwa drīsa dān** She has not put the grains portion (in the boiling pot) as yet.

דאנא (OA עדנא) f. **dāna**, time: **ku dānıt ʾāhıt yad̲lātın** each time you give birth (RivSh 117); **t̲lāha dāne ʾıxāla** three meals (MeAl 189; cf. PolG meal); Jewish school shift; **dān mbınōke** morning shift; **dan xāzaxle** when we see him (Hob89 184); **bé-dana** so now (ibid.).

דאעי (Ar) m. **dāʿi** prosecutor (NT); cf. מדעי.

ד-א-פ (OA/OS עטף wrap/ע/אפף fold?) vi/vt **d-ʾ-p** to fold, bend or be bent; cf. דאיפא (cf. PolG) [MacD 113: **ṭ-ʿ-p** < Ar **ḍ-ʿ-f**/OS **ʿ-ṭ-f**].

דאפא, דַאפַא, דפא (OA/OS דַפָּא < Ak **dappu** wooden board ?) m. **da'pa** (Z), **dāpa** (PolG), **dappa** (NT, BT2, Arodh), board, plank; school tablet (for beginners) (Z); pl. **da'pe, dāpe, dappe** (NT+).

דאפירכה (K) **dāpírke** midwife ('little old mother'); pl. **dāpírkat** (BT2, Arodh; PolG).

ד-א-ר (OA) **d-'-r** to return (vi); **d'ırru riž hıšše dōhun** regained their composure (Zaken 392); — **'ıbba** to repent (PolU 1); v. אורכא; IV to restore, take or bring back, repel; vomit (Z) (NT+).

דארא (K) m. **dāra** tree; **dār-bıṭma** terebinth-tree; **dār-balūṭa** oak-tree; **dār fēka** fruit-tree; **dār kıtwe** thorn-tree (PolG); **dār-qaṣbe** palm-tree; **dār-ṣanam** idol-tree (=H אֲשֵׁרָה, BT5); דַארֵית דַרְמַאנֵי בַסִּימֵי **dārıt dārmāne bassīme** aloes (=H אֲהָלִים, BT4, D); pl. **dāre-dāre** woods.

דארבסתה (K scafolding) **dārbaste** bier, board for washing and carrying the dead; common in curses: **rıš dārbasate xēpīlox** May you be bathed on the bier!

דארג'ין (K/P; cf. OA/OS דָרְצִין cinnamon < P) m. **+dārčin** cinnamon (China wood).

דארג'יתא (K) f. **dārčīta** a cut tree with branches used to hang hunted animals on it (PolU 14).

דארה רקסה (K-Ar) **dārē raqsē** magical entertaining tree that when touched at various spots starts dancing, singing, reading poetry, etc. (PolU 324).

דארובר (K outdoor and front?) **dār-u-bar** odds and ends, various needs: **qẓēla dār-u-bare dīda uzılla** She took care of her various needs and went away.

דארייא (*IrAr) f. **+dārīa** Western style woman's dress; vs. פסתאנא; pl. **-at** (SaAC 23).

דארתא (<ד-א-ר) f. **d'arta** a return, come-back; דארתת/דירת יומא **d'artıt/dērıt yōma** (NT), דֵּיר יוֹם (BT3, D) **dēr yōm**, the following day; ד(א)רתד שאתא **d(')artıt šāta** (same season) the year after (NT5 396); cf. דורת(ד)-יום.

ד-א-ש v. ד-י-ש

ד-א-ת (OS ܕܐܬ) vi **d-'-ṯ** (Z **d-'-s**) to sweat.

דאתא, דיאתא (OA דיעתא) f. **de'ṯa** sweat.

דבא, דיבא (OA דּוּבָּא; OS ܕܒܐ) f. **dıbba** bear; **dıbbıd go māše** a bear in lentils (field), ridiculous; pl. **dıbbe, dıbbāṯa** (PolG)

דבאבא (Ar) f. **dıbbāba** (military) tank.

דבאשא (< ד-ב-ש) **dabāša** honey; v. דבורא.

ד-ב-ב II2 (Ar) **d-b-b** to teem (=H דָּגָה, BT1, D); cf. דביבא.

ד-ב-ג' (Ar) vi **d-b-ġ** to be stained.

דבוליבה (K) pl. **dav-u-lēve** mouth and lips, lower parts of the face; **davulēvi tlīxlu bdımma** My lower face is bleeding.

דבוקאנא (OA דְבוֹקָא glue/OS ܕܒܘܩܐ viscous) **dabuqāna** a nag (lit., sticky); **qīra u —** sticky situation (lit., tar and glue)(PolU 136); v. אירא; cf. טפוסא.

דבור (H) **dıbbūr** any one of the Ten Commandments (NT); cf. אאיא 2.

דבורא (OA דבורי f. bee, SokPA 138) f. (NT)/m. (Z) **dıbbōra** wasp; **qınnıd dıbbōre** hornet-nest; תרתיה דבוריה **tarte dıbbōre** two (f.) bees (NT5 384); a family with many (unruly) children; דַבוּרֵית דְבַאשַא **dabbūrıt dabāša** honey bees (RivSh 212); **dūšıt dıbbōre** honey of bees (PolG).

דבושא, דבושתא (<ד-ב-ש) adj. **dabūša, dabušta** sticky (liquid, food).

ד-ב-ח v. ד̇-ב-ח

דביבא (Ar) m. **dabība** insect; cf. ד-ב-ב (NT+).

דביר v. דברא

ד-ב-ל I(Z)/II(NT) (Ar/OA?) **d-b-l** to wrestle (<to be enmeshed together?) (cf. PolG); cf. דבלא, ד-ב-ל-ב [cf. Khan 552 **dbl** cast down].

דבלא (<OA cake of pressed figs? MacD honey cake?) m. patched cloth or small blanket to cover food; **dıbıl mabōse** pot warmer of the Sabbath meal; **dıbıl lēša** dough-cover; pl. **dıblābe/dıblāle**.

ד-ב-ל-ב III (<דבלא) vi **d-b-l-b** to patch, sew roughly together [MacD to be double-faced; be much patched].

דבנג'א, טבנג'א (T/K) f. **+d/ṭabanja** pistol; cf. ורור.

ד-ב-ר (Ar دبّر economize, manage; OA/OS/Mand דבר conduct oneself, live) vi **d-b-r** to be sustained, make a living; II to sustain, to support (=H כַּלְכֵּל, Ruth 4:5; cf.PolG) (NT+).

דברא, דביר (< OA/OS/Mand דַבְרָא field; Ar تدبير economy, housekeeping?) m. **dabra, dabır** (+NT), food, sustenance, provision (=H מָזוֹן, AlfH 67).

דברג'י (<דברא) m. **dabrači** provider (PolG).

דברי תורה, ד"ת (H) **dıvrē-tōra** words of Torah, Jewish studies (NT).

ד-ב-ש (OA/Ar دبس?) **d-b-š** to be or become sticky; cf. דובשא, דבושא, דבאשא.

דגדן (P?) m. **dıgdan** laver's stand (=H כַּן, BT2), big pot with hot water in which smaller dishes are soaked [MacD tripod over fire for holding saucepans<P **dīkdān**].

ד-ג-ל II (OA) **d-g-l** to lie.

ד-ג-מ-ג III (<K دگنك 'big baton'<T دكنك?) **d-g-m-g** to be cumbersome, stocky; **mdugmıga** cumbersome (=H מְסֻרְבָּל, PolG).

ד-ג-ל v. ג-ד-ל

דג'לאנה (K<ג-ד-ל) **dajalāne** polemics, dispute; ʾ**-m-r** —to argue, discuss (PolU 21).

דגמן v. דז'מן

ד-ג'-י II (Ar?) **d-ġ-y** to brand, to apply burning-red metal for medical use; cf. דאג'א.

דדוא, דדותא (OA דֵּידְבָא) **dıdwa** (NT, m.), **dıdūṯa** (Z, f.), a fly; **dıdūṯ dūša** bee; cf. דבורא; pl. **dıdwe** (OA pl. דֵּידְבָתָא).

דה v. די

דהבא (Ar دابّة) m. **dahba** animal; uncouth, dumb; pl. **dahbe** (=H עָרוֹב, BT2)(NT+) [cf. Mutz 198 **daʿba**].

דהדורה (<ד-ה-ד-ר) pl. ⁺**dahdūre** plans, conditions; **mare** —one who sets conditions (slightly pejor.).

ד-ה-ד-ר (<IrAr roll?) ⁺**d-h-d-r** to plan, make conditions.

דהוא (OA/OS/Mand דהבא) m. **dehwa** gold; pl. דֶהְוֵי **dehwe** gold coins (RivSh162); **dēwe** (PolU 431); דֶהְוָואת **dehwat** (PolG).

דהוכ (K? ChNA ʾıttok) **dıhok** Dihok, town in Iraqi Kurdistan with Neo-Aramaic speaking Jewish (and Christian) community.

דהוכנאיא, דהוכניתא (<דהוכ) **dıhoknāya, -nēṯa,** resident of Dihok.

ד-ה-ו-ר III (Ar to crumble) ⁺**d-h-ō-r** (**mdohōre**) to spend money recklessly.

דהינא, דהנתא (OA/OS דַּהִינָא) adj. **dahīna, dahınta** oily; **mzōrafta udahınta** plump (PolG)

דהמנאת v. דאמנה

ד-ה-נ 1 (OA/OS) **d-h-n** to be oily; II to oil.

ד-ה-נ 2 v. ד-י-נ

דהנא 1 (OA/OS דּוּהְנָא, SokBA 314; דַּהֲנָא, M. Jastrow 281, fat) m. **dehna** boiled/melted meat fat; **dehna ṣıpya** fat oil; **dehna umıšxa** meat fat and milk fat (Babin 63) (NT+).

דהנא 2 v. דינא 1

דהפארא (P-T) **dahpāra** Turkish coin (PolU 9)

ד-ה-ש v. ת-ה-ש

דואה (OS ܕܘܓܐ sour skim milk<P **dōġ** 'whey' > OA דּוּגֵי drops of melting fat?) pl. **doʾe** yoghurt drink; cf. דוג'בא.

דואמה (Ar) f. **dawwāme** spinning top (NT6 134); cf. בר-מצראעא.

דואקא 1 (<ד-ו-ק) v.n. **dwāqa** holding, keeping; דואקד שבתא **dwāqıd šabṯa** keeping the Sabbath; דואקד סהרא/שמשא **dwāqıd sēhra/šımša** moon/sun eclipse.

דואקא 2 (<ד-ו-ק) m. **dawāqa** occupier, conqueror; דואקת-סיפא **dawāqıt sēpa** swordsmen (NT+).

דוארא (T **davar** 'sheep') m. **dawāra** (riding) animal; pl. **dāwāre** (Socin 164) [cf. MacD 63 'mule' < T طوار]

דווארא (Ar) f. **dawwāra** rotary, hand on watch, the rotating mule of huge grinding stone.

דובא (OA דּוּבָא/OS ܕܘܒܐ flow) m. **dōba** clear honey; cf. דושא.

דובית (<?) **dubēt** a kind of silky cloth.

דוגא (OS 'dumb') **dōga** common family name.

דו-גוני (K) **du-gūni** dual layer bag (PolU 236).

דוגלא (OA) m. **dugla** a lie; **bdugla/e** falsely, jestingly (cf. PolG); נוייה דדוגלא **nūye ddugla** false prophets (NT3) (NT+).

דוגלאנא, דוגלנתא (< דוגלא; OA/OS/Mand דַּגָּלָא) adj. **duglāna, duglanta** liar (Segal #126); ⁺**trōsāna yān** —truthful or liar (PolG)

דוג'בא, דוג'אבכה (K/P) **dōġava, dōġāvke** meat and milk dish; non-kosher food.

דוג'רי (T) adv. **dōġıri** honestly, straight (cf. PolU 361)

דויד ,דוד (H) **dāwiḏ** (Z **dāwıs**) David; cf. דאויסכא.

דודייא (Ar/K?) f. **dōdīya** rocking-cradle; **dōdīyıd pōxa** swinging ('wind') cradle.

דודכתא (K/T) f. **dudıkṯa** flute, lullaby (?) (RivSh 149-150).

דוהא v. אוהא

דוזינא (Ar/K<En) f. **dōzīna** dozen, set; cf. דרזן.

דו-טאיי (K) inv. **du-ṭāyi** double-stringed; buttocks (=H שָׁתוֹת, PolG).

דו-טבקי (K) inv. **du-ṭabaqi** two-layered.

דווייה (Ar) f. **dawayye** inkwell; pl. **dawayyat**.

דוכא, דוכתא (OA/OS/Mand דּוּכְתָא; Targ דוכא) f. **dūka, dukṯa** place; **dūka bdūka** each and every place; **šūla/xabra lál dūke** inappropriate thing (PolG); pl. דוכאנה, דוכואתא **dūkāne, dukawāṯa** (NT5 407) (NT+) (OA pl. דּוּכָּאתָא, דּוּכְתֵי, דּוּכְוָתָא) [Khan 567 **dukka: dukke, dukkāne**.].

דוכטור, טוכטור, תוכטור (AnAr<E)⁺**d/tuxtor** medical doctor (vs. **ḥakim** traditional healer) — **bāši** chief doctor (PolU 299) [Khan 567 **dixtor**].

דוכטורותא, טוכטורותא (<דוכטור) f. ⁺**d/tuxtōrūṯa** medicine, healing (PolU 280).

ד-ו-ל (<דולא 2) **d-w-l** to drum, beat the drum.

דולא 1 (OA דּוֹלָא, דַּוְולָא/OS ܕܘܠܐ bucket) **dōla** (NT) bucket; **zılle xōla basır dōla** The rope followed the bucket (both fell in the well, i.e. double loss)(Z); cf. דולכתא 1.

דולא 2 (K) m. **dōla** drum; cf. טולא.

דולא 3 (Ar) **dawla** only in — **rēš ʾilāha** thank God (for this fortune) (PolU 176).

דולאלה (Ar) **dulāle** luxury (NT3); cf. דלאלותא.

דולא-ריש (Ar) **dawla-rēš** thanks to, with the help of (lit., luck upon, sarcastic):**dawla rēšox la muḥṣıllan čımındi** 'Thanks' to you we didn't make any profit.

דולב (K/P) m. **dōlab** wheel; cupboard; pl. **dōlabe**.

דולב-הווא (Ar) m. **dōlab-hawa** air-wheel, 'aeroplane' (in FT only; cf. PolU 226).

דולכתא 1, דּוֹלִיכְּתָא (<דולא 1) f. **dōlıkṯa** (little) bucket (BT2, D; PolG); pl. **dōlıkyāṯa** (BT4).

דולכתא 2 (K tail) f. **dūlıkṯa** extended sleeve; foreskin; pl. **dūlıkyāṯa**; cf. דלגא.

דולמא (T) f. ⁺**dōlama** vegetables stuffed with rice and meat (a festive dish).

דולמנדותא (<דולתמנד) f. **dōlamandūṯa** wealth (BaBin 150).

דולשמא (<K **dulet** 'two parts') m, **dulšama** box or cradle with two compartments for twins (PolU 318).

דולתא (Ar/P) f. **dawılta** wealth; good fortune (NT5 394); cf. דולא 3; government (NT+).

דולת)מנ(ד (P) inv. **dōla(t)mán(d)** wealthy (cf. PolG) (NT+).

דומאה v. דמאתא

דומאיכ, דֻּומַאהֵיךְ (K) n./adv. **dūmāy/hık** edge, end; at the end; remains of; **bdūmāyık yōmāṯa** in days to come (BT); דֻּומַהִיכֵּית **dūmāhīket** ends of (=H אַפְסֵי [אָרֶץ], BT5, D).

דומכא, דומא (K **dunk**) m. **dūmıka, dūma** (PolG), tail; **pıšle dūmıka dēni** We are stuck with him; pl. **dūmıkat**.

דונדרמא (IrAr<T) ⁺**dōndırma** ice-cream.

דוני (K<Ar) inv. inferior (character), unreliable (person) (SaLH 150).

דונייה (K<Ar) f. **dunye** world; **mpılle ž** — He began a journey (PolU 15); — **hatxa zılla uhatxa sēla** This is how the world turns; — **ta čuxa la kpēša** Nobody will live forever; —**ıd ʿōlām** the entire world (SaAC 7); cf. עולם, עאלם.

ד-ו-ס (Ar) **d-w-s** to press down (to make more room in a bag) (cf. PolG)

דוס (Ar 'trampling') m. **dōs** trail (PolU 57); **dōs sar-re** trail to a main rout (PolU 258).

דוסיתא (< ד-ו-ס) f. **dwasīṯa** pressure (PolG).

דוסת (K/P) inv. friend, buddy; pl. **dōste**.

ד-ו-ק (OA/OS/Mand דבק) **d-w-q** to hold, to arrest; to delay; to blame; to grasp (PolU 151); אדוקלה כייד **ıdwıqle kayd** He held a grudge; דויקלה כילא **dwıqle xēla** He gained strength; דאוק עזתא **dāwıq ʿızzıta** He honors; דאוק סהיל **dāwıq sahıl** He belittles; דוקי שבתא **dōqi šabṯa** They keep the Sabbath; דוקי דיארי **dōqi diyyāri** They prepare a gift; דוקיתון נובא אלה **dōqētun nōba ʾılle** You guard him in shifts; **dwıqle ʾurxıd** He set for, took the road to (MeAl 182); **duqle ʾadab** He learned his lesson, was disciplined (=H נוֹסַד, BT3); **d-w-q ʿāqıl** to grasp, to realize (PolU 229); **la dōqıt ʾılle** Don't be angry at him (cf. PolG); **duqle ʾīzi** He lent me some money, he helped me; **duqle kımın** He lay in wait; IV to hand over to the enemy (SaLH 148); **lıbban duqle** We ate to our fill, became stronger (PolU 427; PolG); IV to cause the arrest of someone by police, etc.: **gıbat maduqátti** Do you want me arrested?(PolG); cf. דואקא, דוקיתא.

דוקא (OA/OS טַבְקָא/טָפְקָא baking/frying pan < P **tābag** > Ar طابَق; SokBA 492) m. **dōqa** arched thin iron sheet used for baking thin bread; used also as a cooking pot by Jews eating at Gentiles home since normally it was used only for backing bread; pl. **dōqe**. [cf. Mutz 200; no origin given].

דוקיתא (< ד-ו-ק) **dwaqıṯa** holding; **dwaqıṯut ʾıḏa** help (=H עֲזוּר וְעָזוּב, PolG).

דור (H/Ar) m. **⁺dōr** generation; דור המבול **dōr hamabbūl** the biblical flood generation; **⁺dōr-⁺dōr** each and every generation; pl. דורה **dōre** (NT; RivSh 236), דורות **⁺dōrōs** (Z) [Khan 567 **dawr** 'generation, time, K<Ar]

ד-ו-ר 1 (< OA/Ar go around; make enclosure?) **d-w-r** to darn (woolen socks, etc.).

ד-ו-ר 2 II (Ar) **⁺d-w-r** to give up one's fiancé for another suitor (PolU 129) [⁺**mdu(w)r-**].

דור(א) (Ar) m. **⁺dōr(a)** waiting turn (cf. PolG, PolU 381).

דורבין (K/P/T) f. **dōrbin** binoculars.

דורבינג'י (K/P) m. **dōrbīnči** one on look-out.

דֻּורְדֵּי (K/Ar/OA דורדא<P) pl. **durde** seeds (of grapes) (=H חַרְצַנִּים, BT4, D).

דורדור (K/T) adv. **dūradūr** (looking) far and around; being at a loss (Pol 106; PolG).

דורדוכנא (< דֻּורְדֵּי?) m. **⁺durduxna** sediments, dregs; cf. ד-ר-ד-כ.

דורה, דֻּורַא (Ar دُرّة/OA דּוּרָא) f./m. **durre/a** pearl (BT2, D); pl. דורה **durre** (NT3).

דו-רו (K) inv. **dū-ru** two-faced, of dual character.

דורוסת, דרוסת (K; cf. OA דְּרוּסְתְּ truth < P **drust** right) inv. **dürust** honest; straight; correct (cf. PolG)

דורייא (Ar) f. **dawrīya** patrol police.

דורייאנכי v. דרגא

דּוֹרִכְּתָא (K **dorik**) f. **dōrıkṯa** loaf, round bread; pl. דּוֹרִכְּיַיאתָא **dōrıkyāṯa** (=H חַלּוֹת, BT3, D) [but MacD: a kind poem].

דורמנדור (K) adv. **dōramandōr** around (BT2).

דורת(ד)-יומ(י) (Ar) adv. **dōrt(ıd)-yōm(e)** the following day(s) (PolU 186); v. תינד-יום.

דּוֹרְתֵּיתְּשַׁאת **dōrtıtšat** the following year (BT3, D; PolG); cf. דארתא.

דושא (OA דּוּבְשָׁא, דבשא, OS ܕܘܫܐ) m. **dūša** honey; cf. דובא, ד-ב-ש.

דושב, דושאבכה (K/P) **dōšav** (m.), **dōšāvke** (f.), grape/honey syrup.

דו-שטיכה (K) f. **du-šaṯṯıke** a kind of fish (PolU 263); cf. שקלא 2, שקלא, עפריכה, דמבכ.

דּוֹשִׁיכְּתָא (<דושכ) f. **dōšıkṯa** earth-bench (=H מַצָּבָה, BT1, D); altar (NTU4 152a); pl. **dōšıkyāṯa** earth-beds(cf. PolG; PolU 14).

דושכ (K/P) m. **dōšak** mattress; pl. **dōšāke**.

דושלמא (T) **dušlama** hard-boiled sugar

דזגא (K) f. **dazga** a set (of dishes; cf. PolG); workshop; birthstool (=H אָבְנַיִם, BT2); guarding shifts (BT4).

דסגורכה, דזגורכה (K) f. **daz/sgōrke** glove; pl. **dazgōrkat**.

דזו, דזה (K) **dızo** (m.), **dıze** (f.), (little) thief (PolU 218).

דִּיזְ'וַואר, דז'וור (K) inv. **dıžwar** pungent.

דז'מן, דגמן, דושמין (K<P) **dıžmın, dušmın** enemy; pl. **dıžmıne**; **ʾawd brēš dıžmıne** ashes (lit., that which is on the head of enemies, a taboo for **qıṭma**, ashes used by mourners) (NT+).

ד-ז'-מ-נ II (<דז'מן) **d-ž-m-n** to be hostile (=H צָרַר, אָיַב BT3).

דז'מנאיותא, דז'מנתותא (<דז'מן) f. **dıžmınātūṯa, -nāyūṯa** (RivSh 120, NT5 396) hostility, enmity.

דחלה (AnAr/K) f. **daḥle** forest, woods.

דחליכא (K) m. **daḥlīka** forester (family name).

די, דה (K) **dı, day, de(h)**, so, now, well then; די מרי **dı marri** Tell me (then); דיקו **dı-qu** Get up (RivSh 191); **dı-tū** Sit (=H שְׁבִי, Ruth 3:18); דֵי שְׁפּוֹךְ **de špōx** Pour (AvidH 59); די דיסקך **dı dyasqax** Let us go up; די אתה אאהת כיאת **dı ʾatta ʾāhıt kīʾıt** Now, you know (that...); די האי די /די היידה **dı hay-dı** instantly, relent-lessly (NT2; NTU4 183a); דֵימַיְידִיאוּלַאן **de-máydıʾūlan** Let us know (=H הוֹדִיעֻנוּ, PolG); **dı šud ʾāzi** Let them go; **de ma ʾōzax** So what shall we do (implying anxiety)?

דיין v. דייאנא

דיאני (Ar/K?) **dıyāni** obedience (?)(NT5 393).

דיארי (K<Ar house gift) f. **dıy(y)āri** gift; pl. דיארייה **dıyyārīye** (NT3); דיאריית, דיארתיאתא, **dıyyārīyat, dıyyārıtyāṯa** (NT2) (NT+).

דיד (OA -דיד < -דיל; cf. -ד) **dīd** possessive/relative/objective pronoun: **bēsa did ḥakōma** king's house; **ʾaw nāša did ʾāmır** The person who says...; **bıqṭāla dīde** killing him (also: his killing); **bınšāqa dīda baxta** kissing the woman; because, when (=H כִּי, BT); [decl. **dīdi,** my, etc. (sg. prons.); **dēni** ours, **dēxun, dēhun** (NT), **dōxun, dōhun** (Z), yours, theirs]; cf. -ד.

די-די-די (onomat) **day-day-day** sounds describing speed of racing animals (cf. Socin 163; PolU 12); cf. גר-גר-גר; די.

דיהא v. איהא

דיוא 1 (OA/Mand דֵּיבָא/OS ܕܐܒܐ) m. **dēwa** wolf (NT); cf. גורגא.

דיוא 2 v. דהוא

דיואן, דיון (Ar) m. **dīwan** divan, council (NT+).

ד-י-כ (Ar **d-k-k**) **d-y-k** to pound, beat hard, dance very energetically (by stamping the floor); cf. דכא.

דיכלא (Ar-K) m. **dīkıla** rooster; cf. כתיתא; pl. **dīkıle** (cf. PolG).

דיכלא פורא (K) m. **dıkıla pōra** hoopoe (=H דוּכִיפַת, BT3).

-דיל v. -ד

ד-י-מ (Ar) **d-y-m** to last, live long; IV to prolong life: **ʾilāha mādımlox** May God prolong your life (= thank you) (cf. NT5 411; PolG); cf. דאים.

דין 1 (H) m. **dīn** judgment (Jewish) law; דין שמים **dīn šāmāyim** Heavenly judgment; דין תורה **dın tora** biblical law (RivPr #90); אודלה דין אביהון **ʾudḻe dīn ʾıbbēhun** He sentenced them harshly; pl. דינים **dīnīm,** דינין **dīnīn** (NT3); v. דינא 2, אב בית דין, מדת-הדין.

דין 2 (Ar) **dīn** religion; **dīn hōzāye** Judaism; **dīn mušılmāne** Islam; **dīn sōrāye** Christianity; **dawāqıt dīn** religious (PolG); **wēle ⁺mılya hīl dīne uʾīmāne pāre** He is 'loaded' with money; **⁺wulla dīne la gbınne** By God, I hate his guts; **dīnu wēle kısli** They liked me very much; **gıbınna, mgō dīnox mēsıtta** I want her, you must find her no matter what (PolU 214),

דיין, דין 3, דייאנא (H-OA/OS/Mand דיאנא, דַּיָּנָא, דַּיָּן) m. **dayyān, dayyāna** (BaBin 82) judge (in Jewish court); pl. דיינים, דינים, דייני, **dayyānīm, dayyāne** (NT+).

ד-י-נ, ד-ה-נ II (Ar) **d-y/h-n** to give or take a loan (=H לָוָה/הִלְוָה, BT5; PolG).

דינא 1, דהנא (K<Ar) m. **dēna, dehna** debt, loan; **šqılle bdēna** He bought by credit.

דינא 2 (OA/Mand יומא דְּדִינָא weekday, SokBA 530) **dīna** workday, weekday, only in the idiom: יום דינא **yōm dīna** weekday, secular day (not a Sabbath or holiday); pl. יומאתא דדיניה **yōmāṯa ddīne** (NT), **yōmās dīna** (Z); פלגיה מיומאתד דינילה... ופלגיה מיומד.. אידילה **palge myōmāṯıd dīnēle...upalge myōmıd ʾēḏēle** (the Eve of Passover -) half of it is (considered) Holiday ... and half of it is a work day (NT5 407; cf. NTU4 162a).

דינדארא, דינדרתא (K) **dēndāra, dēndarta** debtor; creditor (=H נוֹשֶׁה, BT2); obliged (NT5 410).

דינו, דינה (K) **dīno** (m.), **-e** (f.), crazy, madly enamoured (PolU 208).

דין-סז (T) inv. **dīn-sız** infidel; cf. אימאן-סז.

דינר (Ar < L; cf. OA/OS דינארא, דִּינָרָא < L) m. **⁺dīnar** dinar; pl. **⁺dīnāre.**

ד-י-ק (OA/OS/Mand דיק/דקק) **d-y-q** to grind (grains or meat by pounding); **qam dāyıqla lašše** He beat him hard ('pounded his flesh'); **gdāyıq prızla qarīra** He pounds cold iron, his efforts are useless; to knock on (door) (PolG), pulsate (heart, blood in veins) (Pol 106; SaAC 7).

דיקתא v. צִיקתא

דירא (OS/Ar) m. **dēra** monastery, convent; **šuqle dēre, mpılle basır ʾēre** He left his monastic life to follow his penis (=became a hedonist); pl. **dērāṯa.**

דירת יומא v. דארתא

ד-י-ש, ד-א-ש (OA/OS/Mand דוש) **d-y-š, d-ʾ-š** (Hob89 215), to tread upon, step over, run over; **lag dēšınne bēse** I'll never step in his house (being very angry at him) (NT+).

דך, דאך, דכד (<ד+אך) **dıx, dax** (RivSh 118), **dıxxıd** how, just as (NT).

דכא 1 (Ar) m. **dakka** punch, hard blow; cf. -ד י-כ.

דכא 2 (K<Ar) **dıkka** bench; **bḥanukka sıswa tūle 1-** On Hanukkah winter sits on a bench.

דכאלא (Ar) inv. **daxāla** protégé (PolU 248).

דכאנא (Ar دُكّان shop; OA דוכאנא, דּוּכָּנָא platform < Ak **dakkānnu(m)** doorway?) f. **dık(k)āna** shop, stall (cf. PolG); cf. דכא 2; pl. **dıkkāne**.

דכאנדר (K) m. **dıkkāndar** shopkeeper; pl. **dıkkāndāre** (cf. PolG).

דכאנוכה (<דכאנא) dim. **dıkkānōke** little shop (PolU 311).

דכיל (Ar) inv. **daxil** (one) suffering (SaLH 153); **ʾamān (u)daxīl** I beseech you (PolG).

דַּכִילַא (Ar) **daxīla** reserve (=H פִּקָּדוֹן, BT1, D).

ד-כ-ל (Ar) **d-x-l** to enter (PolU 392).

דכלא 1 (Ar) m. **daxla** crops, grains.

דכלא 2 (Ar) f. **daxla** entrance to the wedding chamber to have intercourse (PolU 183).

דכניתא (<דכאנא) f. **da/ıkanīṯa** earth-bench; pagan pillar (=H מַצֵּבָה, BT); terrace; pl. **-yāṯa; -yās-ṣanāme** (=H מַצֵּבוֹת, BT5; PolG).

דכרא (<Ar ذخر treasure?) m. **dıxra** treasure, known only in **ʾaw gmāẓıᶜ buxra, gmāẓıᶜ dıxra** Whoever loses a firstborn, loses a treasure (SaAC 18).

דלא (OS/OA דוללא) m. **dılla** woof (=H עֵרֶב, BT3).

דלאלא 1 (Ar) m. **dal(l)āl(a)** herald, hawker (cf. PolG); pl. **dal(l)āle** (NT+).

דלאלא 2, דללתא (K<Ar) adj. **dalāla, dalalta** pampered, gentle (=H רַךְ, BT5); of fine quality (cf. PolU 306); **dalāl-lıbba** very dear (PolU 43).

דלאלותא (<דלאלא 2) f. **dalālūṯa** pampering, gentleness (=H רֹךְ, BT5).

ד-ל-ד-ל v. ד-נ-ד-ל

דלה (Ar/OA?) **dılle** poverty; **rwēle bqılle-dılle** He grew up in abject poverty; cf. דלילא (NT+).

דלול (K/Ar دليل?) m. **dılul** (leading?) horse (PolU 53, 56).

דלופה (OA/OS דִּילְפָּא) pl. **dalōpe** rain drops leaking through the roof; cf. ד-ל-פ.

דל-וצואץ (K-Ar) inv. **dıl waṣwāṣ** hesitant, of doubting mind/heart.

דליל (Ar) inv. **dalil** mentor (NT2).

דלילא (< דלה) m. **dalīla** poor (=H אביון, NT5 404).

דליתא (OA) **dal(l)īṯa** vine (cf. PolG); pl. דליאתא **dalyāṯa** (NT3; PolGr 55) (NT+).

דלכוש (K/P) inv. **dıl-xwaš** happy-hearted.

דלכושותא (<דלכוש) f. **dılxwašūṯa** happiness.

ד-ל-כ-ש III (<דלכוש) vt/vi **d-l-x-š** to console or be consoled (=H נִחֵם, הִתְנַחֵם, BT).

ד-ל-ל II2 (Ar) **d-l-l** pamper; cf. דלאלא 2 (NT+).

דלמה (K) inv. **dılme** soft boiled (egg).

ד-ל-פ II (OA/OS) **d-l-p** to leak; cf. דלופא.

דלק (< דלקא?) **dalaq** strait-jacket (?) only in **napāqıd mdalaq** efficient, smart (lit., extricates oneself of...)(cf. PolG).

דלקא (Ar/K/P) **dalqa** mourning cloth, sack (NT+).

דמא 1 (OA/OS דְּמָא) m. **dımma** blood; **dımme qırre** He was unable to act (SaLH 148); pl. **dımmāhe** (PolG)/**dımmāye/ dımmāṯa** (BT3);v. ד-מ-ד-מ 2 (NT+).

דמא 2 (K) f. **damma** time, moment; **dammōxun bassımata** Have a pleasant time! **ʾay-damma** right then (NT5 394); (**ʾay**) **dammıd** when, the moment that; **ku-dammıd** whenever.

ד-מ-א II (OA/OS דמע) **d-m-ʾ** to shed tears (eyes) (BaBin 129; PolG).

דמאתא (OA/OS דִּמְעֲתָא) f. **dımeʾṯa** tear; pl. **dımʾe** (cf. PolG), **dümʾe** (דומאה, NTU4 152b, 181b) (OA/OS דמעי) [Khan 567 **dimᶜa**, pl. **dimᶜe**].

דמבוס (IrAr) m. **dambus** safety pin.

דמביכא (K) m. **dambīka** fist (=H אֶגְרוֹף, BT2, Arodh).

דמבכ (<?) m. **dımbak** carp (cf. PolU 263).; pl. **dımbāke/-at**.

ד-מ-ד-מ 1 III (OA/Mand דמדם/Ar دمدم

grumble; onomat.) ⁺d-m-d-m to grumble.
ד-מ-ד-מ 2 III (<דמא 1) vt/vi **d-m-d-m** to bleed (PolU 39, 92) ; v. מדומדמא.
דמדמא (K/P دمدمي capricious?) inv. **dımdıma** huge, big (house, etc.)[cf. Macd 67 'fool']
ד-מ-י II (OA) **d-m-y** to resemble; imagine (NT).
דמיר (IrAr) m. **damir** brocaded coat.
ד-מ-כ (OA/OS) **d-m-x** to lie down (cf. Avishur 1993b 18); to have carnal relations (=H שָׁגַל, BT5); IV to put to sleep, to rest (vt).
דמכיתא, דמכתא (<ד-מ-כ) n. act. **dmaxīṯa, dmaxta** carnal relation (BT4).
דמן (Ar ضمان) **dáman** protection tax, bail (PolU 434).
ד-מ-ס, ד-מ-צ (Ar) vi **d-m-s/ṣ** to sink, have concave lines (BT3, D); to dive (Z); vt to sink (?): גמעתררה וגדאמסלה **gmāᶜṯırre ugdāmısle** (God) makes him stumble and sinks him (NTU4 183a).
דנגא 1 (K?) m. **dınga** massive strong wall.
דנגא 2, דנגושכא (K?) m. **danga, dangoška** big wooden mallet; **rēš danga** bulky, unshapely head (of person, animal).
ד-נ-ד-כ III (K) **d-n-d-k** to pick (a vineyard) bare (=H עוֹלֵל, BT3).
דנדכרכה (<דנדכתא?) pl. **dandıkāke** provisions (Zaken 391)
דנדכתא (K) f. **dındıkṯa** a grain, kernel; a tiny bit; pl. **dındıkyāṯa** (NT+) [Khan **danka** 'grain'].
ד-נ-ד-ל, ד-ל-ד-ל III (OS/IrAr) vi/vt **d-n-d-l** (Z), **d-l-d-l** (NT6 133) dangle, hang down.
דנתא (OA דנא) f. **danta** barrel, big jar (NT).
דזגורכה v. דסגורכה
דסכרא (Arتذكره) f. **daskara** document, writ (of a liberated slave (NT+).
דסנאיא v. דצנאיא
דסתא (K; cf. OA/OS דִּסתאנא porttion of food sent to guests at a meal < P ?) f. **dasta** a set, dozen, pack, suit (of clothes (RivSh 119); pl. דסתאתא **dastāṯa,** דִּסְתֶּי **daste** portions of food given to guests (=H יְדוֹת, BT1, D).
דסת בדסת (K) **dast bdast** from hand to hand, non-stop (baking of matza) (NT5 410).
דסתא-ברא (K) m. **dásta-brá** loyal friend (Socin 160; PolU 139)
דסתה (Ar/P) f. **dıste** copper pot (=H דוּד, PolG); pl. **dıstāṯa, dıstat** (PolU 79).
דסתה-ראסת (K) **daste-rāst** prime ('right-hand') (minister) (PolU 278).
דסתור (Ar/P) ⁺**dastur** permission, licence (NT+).
דסתיכה (K?) **dastīke** pumpkin (?), used only in **bōyıd** — (roasted) seeds of pumpkin.
דסתכתא (K) f. **dastıkṯa** handle, haft (=H נִצָּב (הַלַּהַב), PolG).
דסת-נמיז' (K) **dast-nımēž** hands ablution before Islamic prayer (PolU 92).
דעוא (Ar call, invitation) f. **daᶜwa** wedding, celebration (AvidH 65); **muttūlu** — They prepared a wedding (PolG); regarding: **daᶜwıd mōs bābi** regarding my father's death (PolU 434; cf. PolG); pl. **daᶜwıtyāṯa**.
דעו-דוזה (Ar/K?) pl. **daᶜu-dōze** complains, demands; **mare daᶜu-dōze** complaining or demanding person.
דעווה (Ar) f. **daᶜwe** plea; pl. דַּעְוַאיֵי **daᶜwāye** (RivSh 229)(NT+).
דעוייה (Ar) f. **daᶜwīye** concern, affair (=H מַעֲשֶׂה, PolG); concerning (prep.).
דעותא (<ד-ע-י) f. **daᶜūṯa** plea (from God); curse (=H אָלָה, BT5) or blessing; pl. **daᶜwāṯa**; דעואתיני קבולו **daᶜwāṯēni qbūllu** (God,) accept our prayers (NTU4 156a).
דעותא-שיר (K) **daᶜwata-šīr** 'wedding-sabres?', groom's best men (who accompany him to the pre-wedding bath on the river (PolU 227).
דעותנאיה (<דעוא) pl. **daᶜwıtnāye** wedding guests (PolU 168
ד-ע-י (Ar) **d-ᶜ-y** to pray, to plead (from God): **dᶜēle ṯāla** He prayed for her; to curse: **dᶜēle ʾılla** He cursed her; IV to demand, to sue; to pray (NT5 385; NTU4 152b) (NT+).
דעת (H) f. **daᶜaṯ** (Z **daᶜas**) knowledge; **nāše mare ḥoxma u-** wise and knowledgeable people; **latla** — She isn't too smart; **ʾıtlu ḥoxma, ᶜıtlu** — They have wisdom and knowledge, they are intelligent (PolU 294).
דפא v. דאפא
ד-פ-י II (<Ar waggle?) **d-f-y** become loose,

old (teeth) (PolU 431).
דפכתא (K<Ar) f. **daffıkta** hand-drum; pl. **daffıkyāta** (=H כִּנּוֹרוֹת PolG).
דפנא, דפנתא (OA/OS/Mand דּוּפְנָא, דַּפְנָא side, wall, rib) f. **dıpna, dıpınta** side, direction; **ʾıl dıpın** next to, by; **dıpın baḥḥar** seaside, shore; pl. **dıpnāta** (cf. PolG), **dıpnāne** (OA pl. דפנאתא, דּוּפְנֵי).
ד-פ-ע II (Ar) **d-f-ʿ** to pay; **dfıʿle mgēbi** He paid for me.
ד-פ-ת II v. ד-ב-ת (**d-b-t**), ת-ב-ת (**t-b-t**)
דפתר, דפטר (Ar<Gr) m. **ᐩdaftar** ledger, notebook, book (=H סֵפֶר, BT5, D); pl. **ᐩdaftāre** (NT+).
דפתרג׳י (Ar-T) m. **ᐩdaftarči** clerk, bookkeeper; pl. דפתרג׳ייה **daftarčīye** (NT5 396), דַּפְטַרְגִ׳יַיאת **-yat** (PolG).
דסנאיא, דצנאיא (K?) **ᐩdasnāya** Yezidi (Am); Chaldean (RivSh 174); cf. איזידנאיא.
דקא 1 (OA) f. **daqqa** moment; **el daqqe dpalgıd yōm** exactly at noon (Socin 162); pl. **daqqe**.
דקא 2 (OA) m. **dı/aqqa** ground rice; **lak tōrınne daqqe** I will not hurt his feelings (PolU 440); **hēš dıqqa lēwe twīra** She is still inexperienced, unhurt (PolU 131).
דקא 3, דקה (Ar) f. **daqqa/e** tattoo (BT3, D).
דקא 4 (<דקא 2) m.
דקאשא (<ד-ק-ש) **daqāša** goring (ox)(BT2).
ד-ק-ד-ק III (H-OA) **d-q-d-q** to be meticulous: מדקדק בעמאלוך **mdaqdıq bʿamālox** Be meticulous with your deeds (NTU4 163a).
דקדוקין (H-OA) **dıqdūqīn** minutiae (NT3); **dúqduq ʿınyūs** hard life (<H דקדוקי עניות, PolG).
דקוקא, דאקוקא (OS) m. **daqōqa** stone pestle.
דקיקא 1, דקקתא (OA/OS, SokPA 154) adj. **daqīqa, daqıqta** thin, tiny; **daqīqa-daqīqa** very thinly; **pare daqīqe** small change, coins; **yalunke daqīqe** small children (PolG) (cf. OA דַּקָּא pupil, child SokBA 348) (NT+).
דקיקא 2 (Ar) f. **daqīqa** minute; pl. **daqīqe**.
דקנא (OA/OS/Mand) m./f. (NT/Z; PolG) **dıqna** beard; pl. **dıqn(aw)āta**, but PolGr 52: **dıqnāne** [Khan 567 **dqinta**, sg.].
דקנאנא, דקנו (OA/OS דַּקְנָנָא) **dıqnāna, dıqno** (pej.) bearded man, 'beardo'.

ד-ק-ס (Ar?) vi **d-q-s** to become small, shrink (old person); II to keep small, prevent (child) from growing.
ד-ק-ר, ד-ר-ק (OA דקר?) **d-q-r** to hurt (NTU4 153b), **d-r-q** to gore (BT2, Am); cf. ד-ק-ש.
ד-ק-ש (<?) **d-q-š** to gore(=H נָגַח BT2); cf. ד-ר-ק.
דר (P) **dar** upon, only in עאלם דר עאלם **ʿālam dar ʿālam** multitudes, great many (NT2).
דראאה (OA/OS דְּרָעָא, דראעא, Mand דרא) m. **drāʿa** arm (NT3); cf. זנדא; local yard or meter (Z); cubit (=H אַמָּה, BT); pl. **drāʾe** (PolG), דְּרָיֵא **drāye** (RivSh 169).
דראג׳ה v. ג׳ראדה
דראעא (Ar) f. **darrāʿa** (child's) apron.
דראשא (OA דַּרְשָׁנָא) **ᐩdarāša** darshan, commentator on Judaism (in Synagogue).
דראתא v. דרתא
ד-ר-ב (Ar ضرب) **d-r-b** to injure (=H נָגַף, BT2, Arodh).
דרבא 1 (T<Ar ضربه, f.) m. **darba** a blow, a hit; an opportunity; pl. **darbe**; cf. דרביי, צ׳רביה.
דרבא 2 (K) adv. **darva** outside; external.
דַּרְבִיֵי (Ar) f./pl. **darbīye** blow(s) (AvidH 37).
דרגא (K) m. **darga** door; דַּרְגִּית דּוּרְיַיאנְכֵּי **dargıt dūryānke** crossroad, the (town's) gate for distant traveling (=H פֶּתַח עֵינַיִם, BT1, D); pl. **dargāh/ye** (cf. PolG).
דרגבן (K) m. **dargavan** gate keeper; pl. **dargavāne** (=H שֹׁעֲרִים, PolG); **-at** (PolU 231) (cf. OA דרבאנא doorkeeper <P).
דרד (K) m. **dard** ailment; **ču dard ʾēnax la xazya** Stay well!; **kmālēli bdardi uḥāli** I have enough problems of my own; pl. דרדה ובלאייה (NT5 382), דַּרְדּוּ בַּלַאיֵי (BT1, D; BT5; BaBin 59) **dard(e)-u-balāye**.
דרדומאג׳ה (<K?) pl. **dardumāğe** the lower parts of the face, jaws; cf. דבוליבה.
ד-ר-ד-י III (<דרד) **d-r-d-y** to languish for, be love sick.
ד-ר-ד-כ, ד-ר-ד-ש III (< דורדכנא) vi/vt **d-r-d-x/š** (water or any liquid) to make or become turbid, muddy, mixed with dregs (cf. PolG).
דרדשאנא, דרדשנתא (<ד-ר-ד-ש) adj.

dırdıšāna, -anta, muddy, turbid (PolU 276).

דר(ה)ימתא (Ar درهم to produce) f. **dar(h)īmıta** produce, crops (=H תְּבוּאָה, BT, PolG)[cf. MacD 70].

דרהם (Ar<Gr) m. **dırhım** dirham (Iraqi coin); pl. **dırhıme**.

דרואזא (P) m. **darwāza** gate (RivSh 145).

דרואנכתא (K) f. **darwānıkta** curtain (=H פָּרֹכֶת, BT2, Am).

דרוישכא, דרויש(א) (K/P) m. **darwēš(a)/ka** dervish, singer-beggar; also proper name; pl. **darwēšīn** (PolU 317)/**-šat** (PolU 369).

דרום (H) m. ⁺**dārom** south (NT5 383; BT; PolU 321) (cf. OA דרומא)

דרוסת v. דורוסת

ד-ר-ז (K) vt/vi **d-r-z** to crack, slightly open (Avin 78 94).

דרזא (K) m. **dırza** crack, small opening.

דרזי באשי (Ar-T) m. **darzi bāši** master tailor (PolU 233).

דרזן (IrAr<En) **darzan** dozen, set.

דרחל (P-Ar) **darḥal** immediately, right away (AvidH 46; RivSh 125; PolG).

דרחק (P-Ar) **darḥaq** with regard to (NT).

ד-ר-י 1 (OA/OS דרי < דרע, OS, carry, bear, sustain) **d-r-y** to put, to place; **drēle ʾēne** He paid attention; he coveted; - **behra** He shed light; - **bıqdāli** He imposed upon me (NT); blamed me (Z); - **ṭīma** He quoted a price; - **mınta ʾıllēni** He did us a favor (so that we have to reciprocate); - **šımma** He named; - **targum** He translated; - **bāle** He paid attention; - **šalōmōs** He gave regards; - **mıṭra** It rained; **drēla uma drēla** It rained like hell; - **rāyi/tagbir** He advised; - **hawāre** He screamed; **qam dārelan go pımmıd nāše** People gossiped about us because of him (lit., He put us in the people's mouth); - **qam pāt- (gyān-)** to have an excuse (PolG); **ʾımmi** He quarreled with me; **ʾilāha drēle go lıbbe** God inspired him (to do the right thing); **ʾımmıt nērīya rıš ṭūra la dāret** Don't engage with a billy-goat on top of the mountain (PolG) (NT+).

ד-ר-י 2 (OA) **d-r-y** to winnow (=H זָרָה, Ruth 3:2; NT5 388, 408).

דרי, דריבא (K) **da(r)ri, darīva** escape, opening, opportunity (cf. PolG); cf. כיסי.

דריזאנה, דְּרַזִינְכה (K **derazink**) **darīzāne, dırazinke** threshold (PolG); cf. סקופתא.

דרימתא v. דר(ה)ימתא

דרמאנא (K/P) m. **dırmāna** medicine; care, cure; spice; **dırmāne qıṭla-le** The only way to get rid of him is by murder (cf. RivSh 161); **hulle —e** He punished him as he deserved (Pol 170); pl. **dırmāne** (NT+).

ד-ר-מ-נ III (<דרמאנא) **d-r-m-n** medicate (PolG).

דרנגי (K) adv. **drangi** late; **drangid lēle** late at night (MeAl 187; PolG); **pıšla drangi** It is getting late.

דרנגה v. ג'ראדה

ד-ר-ס (H-OA) **d-r-s** in ritual slaughter: to improperly press on the knife; v. ג-ר-מ.

דרסאד, דרסאת, דרסד, דרסית (P درساعت) adv. **darsa(ʾ)ad/t, darset** right then, at that very moment (NT2).

דרפא (Ar ظرف vessel; envelope; waterskin) ⁺**darfa** tanned and inflated sheepskin (used as swimming aid, or many of which are tied to logs to make a large barge; PolU 8).

ד-ר-ק v. ד-ק-ר

ד-ר-ק-ל, ת-ר-ק-ל III (OA תקל) **d-r-q-l** (Z), **t-r-q-l** (PolG), to stumble.

דרקלתא, תַּרְקָלְתָּא (OA תקלתא) **darqalta** (Z), **turqulta** (AvidH 53), obstacle, snare (=H מוֹקֵשׁ, BT2); pl. דרקליאתא **darqılyāṯa**.

דרש, דרוש (H) m. **daraš, daruš** sermon, homily.

ד-ר-ש (H/OA) **d-r-š** to give a (Jewish) sermon, to preach (BaBin 128; Hob89 215).

דרתא (OA) f. **darta** courtyard; pl. דראתא **darāṯa** (NT5 406).

דשדאשא (IrAr) **dısdāša** ankle-length robe.

דשו (AnAr<K) **daššo** laver (for washing hands in Jewish rituals)(cf. PolG).

ד-ש-נ II (Ar) vt **d-š-n** to wear new clothes, shoes, or use a new house, etc., for the first time; **mdašōne** dedication (=H חֲנֻכָּה, BT4).

דשתא (P > OA/OS דִּישְׁתָּא, דַּשְׁתָּא) f. field; pl. דשתאתא **daštāṯa** (NT+).

ד, ד̇ (̇d̲, ẓ [+d/ḍ?])

ד-ב-ח, ד-ב-ח-, צ̇-ב-ח (Ar ذبح; cf. OA דבח; + זבח < H. SokBA 373) vt **d̲/d-b-ḥ** (NT; Hob89 215 **d-b-ḥ**); **ẓ-b-ḥ** (Z; cf. PolG), to slaughter, to sacrifice (NT+) [Khan 552 **dbḥ**].

דביחא, צ̇ביחא, צ̇ביחתא (Ar) f. **d̲/d/ẓabīḥa, ẓabīḥıta** slaughter, sacrifice; pl. **ẓabīḥıtyāt̲a** (BT2; PolG) (NT+).

ד-ב-ט v. צ̇-ב-ט

ד-ב-ת, ד-פ-ת I/II(Ar ثبت?) **d/d̲-p/b-t** (PolG **d̲-b-t** to prepare, be ready, H נָכוֹן; Hob89 215 **d-p-t** to heal, mend) to be well founded (BT4, D); to set (in place) (RivSh 197), to arrange (BT2, Arodh); to establish (BT5, D) [cf. MacD 60 **d̲ābit** be established].

דִילִים v. צ̇ולום

ד-י-ע v. צ̇-י-ע

ד-ל-מ v. צ̇-ל-מ

דמתא v. זמתא

ד-ר-ב v. צ̇-ר-ב

דַּרְבָּא v. צ̇רבא

ה (h)

ה (H) **he** the fifth letter of the Hebrew alphabet; **xamša** five; **ʾilāha** God (NT).

ה- 1, יה- (OA) **-e** (Z). **-e(h)** (NT), his.

ה- 2 v. א-

הא, הה (OA/OS/Mand הָא this, that; lo, here is!) **ha(h)** behold, here (=H הֵא, BT1); Beware (PolU 96); Yes? What? eh? I am here (said when one's name is called from some distance); Oh! הא אאהת והא אאנא **ha ʾāhıt uha ʾāna** Between you and me, let us see who will prevail! (NT2); **ha ʾatta mmāyıs, ha xapča xıt** He may die at any moment; הא הא **haʾha(ʾ)**, הֵיהַא **hayha** (RivSh 277), right away, this instant; at any moment (Socin 163; PolG); cf. הייא [cf. Khan 569 **ha-** presentative particle].

הַא (H -הֲ/ Ar هل?) **ha** interrogative particle (=H -הֲ, BT1, D); cf. הלא.

האגא (K (h)aga) **hāga** attention; usually as hendiadys with האיי [cf. Garbell 309 **haga**; Mutz.: 187:ʾ**āgā**; Khan 569 **hāga**].

האגא (AzT) m. **hāča** axle, forked bar for plowing [cf. MacD].

האדך (OA הדא הך) **hādax** thus, so; **lhādax, mhādax, ṭla ḥadax** therefore, hence, because of this (NT); **baṯır hādax** afterwards; cf. הדכא (NT+).

האדמה (H) **hāḏāma** (Z **hāzāma**) the blessing as well as the fruit of the ground on which one has to recite בורא פרי האדמה; cf. העץ.

האהא v. הא

האוון (K/P) **hāwan** mortar (to grind nuts); pl. **hāwāne** (PolG).

האוונטא (IrAr) **hāwanṯa** cheating, bluff.

האוור(תא) (K) **hāwar(ta)** call for help; **hay hāwār** Help! (socin 164); **mu hāwar-īle** What is the rush? pl. **hāwāre** (cf. PolG); **drēlu hāwāre** They screamed for help.

האיה-לאיה, האיה-האיה (K?) **h/lāye-h/lāye** lulling sounds chanted while putting child to sleep (SaNR).

האיי (< K هاير) **hāyi** apprehension; האי לג האוילי מצו כברא **hāyi lag hāwēli mču xabra** I am not aware of anything (NTU4 184b); **latli hāyi mınnox** I am not aware of any conflict with you, leave me alone; **latli - mın hıšši** I am totally confused (PolU 273); often with האגא; (Pol 107; PolG; BaBin 163; Segal #90).

האל, הל, היל, חיל (OS) prep. **hā/al, hī/il, ḥīl** (BT 2, Am), till, (from) to; **hāl ʾābad** forever.

האנא (K) **hāna** help, military aid, assistance (NT2; NTU4 165a).

הַאר וִיהַאר (K?) adv. **hār-wi-hār** (?) here and there (=H אָנֶה וָאָנָה, PolG:1 Kg 2:42).

הארון (Ar<H אהרן) p.n. ⁺**hārun** Aaron; **dawıltıd hārūn qārūn** great wealth (PolU 1).

-הארית (K **hārī** zeal) **hārīt-** support (due to zeal): **qımle hārītī** He stood by me (while fighting or arguing with others) **qımlu hārītıt ḥakōma** They stood by the King's side (cf. PolG).

האת-ובאת (K) **hāt-u-bāt** 'going and returning', a difficult journey with a slim chance of coming back alive.

ה-ב-ב II2 (Ar) vi **h-b-b** to blow, hover (=H רִחֵף, BT1; cf. PolG)); cf. ר-פ-ר-פ.

הבדלה (H) **havdāla** Sabbath's exit ritual; ʾ**-w-ḏ havdāla** to perform this ritual.

הבינותא (K (h)ewīn) love, amour; often as hendiadys with עשק: ʿ**ıšq u-** deep love.

הבכה (Ar حُبْكَة twist?) f. **habke** weaving comb.

הבלנגא (K) m. **havlınga** brother-in-law.

הבפשכת (P) inv. **habpaškıt** equal (in rank, virtues)(NT2).

הברייא (IrAr) f. **habrīya** thin scarf.

ה-ב-ר-כ III (K) **h-v-r-k** to provoke (=H הִתְגָּרָה, BT5).

הברכתותא (< ה-ב-ר-כ) **havrekatūṯa** arguing, provocation.

הגדה (H) f. **haggāḏa** (Z **haggāza**) Haggada, the narrative of Passover.

הגעלה, עג'אלא (H) f. ʿ**agāla** (!) the ritual of making the dishes kosher for Passover use.

הגארא (< ה-ג-ר) v.n. **hjāra** desertion (NT3).

ה-ג-ג, ה-י-ג II2 (Ar) vi/vt **h-j-j, h-y-j** (NT6 133) to wander, migrate; to stir (vi); open (a wound) (PolG) to make one wander (=H הִתְעָה, BT1, D) (NT+).

ה-ג-י II (Ar) **h-j-y** to spell, pronounce, study

Hebrew alphabet with the diacritical points.

הג'יג (Ar) **hajīj** burning hot (NT2).

ה-ג'-מ 1 (Ar) vi/vt **h-j-m** to destroy or be destroyed; attack (physically or verbally); IV to destroy.

ה-ג'-מ 2 v. ח-ג'-מ

ה-ג'-ר (Ar) **h-j-r** to desert (husband:wife); II to emigrate.

הדודא (Ar?) **hadūda** horse, charger; הרגמתד הדודיה ועסכארה **hargamtıd hadūde uʿaskāre** the uproar of charging horses and armies (Sa83c 18); cf. מהינה, סוסה [cf. MacD 72].

הדאיתא (< ה-ד-י) f. **hadāyıta** equanimity; **la kese lču hadāyıta** They don't reach any compromise, can't live peacefully together.

ה-ד-י (Ar هدء) **h-d-y** to calm down (vi), stop crying (baby); IV to calm down (vt).

הדייה (Ar) f. **hadīye** gift (PolG); pl. **hadiyat**.

הדכא, התכא (<האדך; cf. OA האכי, הָכֵין; OS ܗܟܢܐ thus;) adv. **had/txa** so, like this; also euphemistic substitute of vulgar curses: **gēmır hatxa mın yımmox** He said vulgar things about my mother (cf. SaLH 148) (NT+).

ה-ד-ר II (Ar) **h-s-r** to risk, waste (PolU 130).

הו (K) interj. **hūū** Oh, Ho! (SaAC 19); v. הי.

הוא 1, הוה (Ar) **hawa** air, space (NT2).

הוא 2, הוה, הויתא (<?) adj. **haw(w)a, hawēta** good, fine; all right, yes (cf. PolG) (NT+).

הואיא (< ה-ו-י) **hwāya** birth.

הואן (Ar اوان) **hawān** term, liftime (NT2).

הוגא (< ?) m. **hōga** mouth vapor (NT+) [cf. MacD 73 **hōgā** steam; **mhāwig** air the fire].

הוגן, הוגם (Ar حوجب?) **hōjan/m** on the condition that, as long as (NT2).

הודא v. יהודא

הודאיא, הודיתא (OA יְהוּדָאָה/OS ܝܗܘܕܝܐ) **hudāya, hudēta** (Z **hōzāya. hōzēsa**; PolG: **huzāya**) Jew, Jewess; pl. הודַאיֵי **hūdāye** (=H הָעִבְרִים, BT2, D); הודאיאתא (NT2) **hūdāyāta** (=H הָעִבְרִיּוֹת, BT2, Am); cf. עבראיא.

הודאיותא (< הודאיא) f. **hōdāyūta** Jewish Neo-Aramaic; Jewishness, Judaism.

הוונאת (Ar) pl. **hawanāt** troubles, ignominies.

הווס (Ar) m. **hawas** frenzy, craze (PolU 112).

הוותא (< הוא 2) f. **hawūta** favor, act of kindness (=H חֶסֶד, BT); pl. הויאתא **hawūyāta** (NT+).

ה-ו-י (OA) **h-w-y** to be; לא האויה **la hāwe** Let it not be (that...), It is forbidden to; **štāw/ye** (< **šud hāwe**) Let it be so; **la hāwe zīle ši** (I hope) they haven't gone already; to be born; to give birth; **hwēlu/e-la tre bnone** She gave birth to two boys (cf. PolG); **ʾīman bhāwēla** When will she give birth? **ʾīman hwēlox/wıt hūya** When were you (m.sg.) born? **la hōyanwa ula baryanwa** (I wish) I (f.) had not been born at all [1:**wēli, wēlox** I was, you were, etc.; ויוא **wēwa** (NT) he was/they were; 2:**hāwe, pāwe** (‹**bhāwe**), כהאוה **khāwe**(NT)/**kāwe** (Z); **hōya**, אגהויא **ıghōya** (NT3)/**kōya** (Z); איוך **īwax** (NT)/**wax** (Z); וין/ון **wın** I (m.) am/**wan** I (f.) am; וונוא **wınwa** I (m.) used to be; 3: **hwi** (m.), **hwe** (f.) **hwā/ōwun** (PolU 152)]; 4:**hwāya**]; IV aid at birth (Hob89 218), deliver (PolG) [2: **máhuya**; **qam mahūyánna** I delivered her].

הוירנאיא (K) **hawernāya** Haweri Kurd.

הויתא 1 (< ה-ו-י) n. act. **hwēta** birth (PolGr 33).

הויתא 2 v. הוא 2

ה-ו-ל v. י-ה-ו-ל

הולא (< הא+וילא) **hawlā** There she is; **hawlē** There he is (PolU 427); **hawlū (ha)** There they are (PolU 350).

הונא (< OA -הונ interj. here it is for...! < Ar هُنَا? SokBA 373) **hōna** (Z), **hawna** (BT2, Arodh), Behold (=H הִנֵּה, BT; הונוך **hōnox** =H הִנְּכָה, PolG); cf. הָלַאן [cf. MacD 74].

הוסטא (K) m. **hosta** skilled person, master; pl. **hostāye** (PolU 320).

ה-ו-ר II (K) **h-w-r** call for help (MeAl 192; PolG) [2:**mhāwır, mhōra**; 4: **mhawōre**].

הוש (K) **hušš** hush!

הי 1 (OA הן, אין) **he** yes; היבלי; הי בליה **hē-bale** (Yes,) however (NT5 382; NTU4 148a); **hē ⁺wālla/wınne** Yes, indeed ('by God'); cf. הה.

הי 2 (K) **hay** O (you); **hay-hē/hō/hū/lā/lō/⁺wāy** interjections to express various mood nuances, such as yearning, puzzlement.

הי 3 (K) **hī** interj. used to express mild anger: 'This is ancient; it was long time ago!'

היא, הייא (OA הַיָּיא, חַיי quickly; Ar هَيَّا) adv. **hayya** fast, quickly; early; **hayyá-hayya** very diligently; cf. הה (NT+) [cf. Khan 569

háyya quickly, K].
היבה, היבתא (Ar) f. **haybe, haybıta** awe (NT).
היבי, היוי (K) f. **hīvi,** (+NT) **hīwi,** hope, plea; אתלי היבי מנה **ʾıtli hīvi mınne** I pray to Him; **gōzın hīvi (mın ʾilāha u) mınnox** I beg (God and) you; cf. בי-היבי; **hīvid ʾilāha** God will have mercy (SaAc 1); **ḥmōl hīvīti** Wait for me (cf. PolG); pl. **hīvīye** (MeAl 177).
היבלי v. הי 1
היבן (K) m. **hēvın** rennet.
ה-י-ג̇ v. ה-ג̇-ג̇
היג̇ (T) **hīč** no, none, nothing (whatsoever).
היג̇ס-האג̇ס (IrAr) **hīčıs-hāčıs** like this-like that (imitation of Arabic speech) (PolU 71).
הידי (K<Ar; v. ה-ד-י) adv. **hēdi, hēdí-hēdi,** calmly, slowly (BaBin 164).
הידיכאנה (K) adv **hēdikāne** Well then (SaAC 8).
הי-האי/ת (K) interj **hay-hāy/t** indicates surprise and amazement (PolU 18, 381).
היהתא (< K **hay**) **hayhıta** cheering sounds, clamor (PolU 26); cf. הי 3, הי 2.
היי (K you have) inv. **hayī** rich; **ʾāni rāba hayī wēlu** They were very wealthy; **hayī-nayī** rich and poor; the haves and the have -nots, everybody; one in-charge (PolU 77).
היכאנה (K) pl./f.? **hēkāne** an egg-game played by Jewish children during Passover.
היכל 1 (H; cf. OA/OS/Mand היכלא) m. **hēxal** (+Z **ʾēxal,** SaLH 151) sanctuary; inner room in the synagogue where the Torah scrolls and Elijah's chair were kept.
היכל 2 (Ar) m. **hēkal** form; as hendiadys: **mēnıx bšıkle uhēkāle** Look at his shape! kind of amulet-jewelry.
היל (IrAr) m. **hēl** cardamum.
הילינה (K<P آلانه) **hēlīne** nest; cf. קנא.
הילכה, הישלכה, אישלכה (K/T) f. **h/ʾē(š)lake** vest.
היים (Ar ايام days) m. **hayam** time, period; **hayam zılle ta hayam** As time passed, many years later (FT; PolU 2).
ה-י-מ-נ, א-י-מ-נ III, א-מ-נ II (OA) **h-y-m-n** (Z, Hob89 218), **ʾ-y-m-n** (Gz), **ʾ-m-n** (+NT), to believe, to trust [1:**mhō/īmın-** (cf. RivSh 147; PolG); **mʾōmın-**; **mʾīmın-**(Gz); 2/3:**mhēmın, mʾēmın** (Gz), **mʾāmın** (Segal #95) (NT+).

הֵימַנְתָּא (OA) f. **hēmanta** act of faith (BaBin 117; NT4).
הינגה, הַנְגִּי (K) adv. **hinge** (Z), **hangi** (RivSh 219) then, at that time.
הינ(נ)א (K) interj. **hayna(nna)** Is that so?! Yes, that is so! (PolU 212, 321).
ה-י-ר II/IV (< OA יהר be overbearing/OS ܗܪ annoy?) **h-y-r** to dare, to strive; מוהירא **múhīra**/ מהוירא **mhuyra** careful, cautious (NT2); לא מְהִירְין **la mahīrın** (RivSh 278)/**lag mehrın** (Z) I don't dare [Z, PolG:1: **mōhır-**; 2:**māhır** (m.), **mehra** (f.), etc.] [Mengozzi 256 **mhāyer** hurry<Ar هرع demolish<Ar هور].
היש, הישתאן (K; v. השתא) adv. **hēš(tan)** still, yet (NT4; **hēštan dīde** While he still (=H עוֹדֶנּוּ, BT1; cf. PolG) [cf. Khan 569 **heštan, -āne**].
הישכו (K) adv. **hēšku** at least (BaBin 143).
הישלכה v. הילכה
הכא v. אכא
הכן, הכא, היכן(K<Ar هل كان) **ha/ikan** (BT2), **haka** (PolG), if; cf. אנכן.
הלא (Ar) adv. **hala** surely, Is it not? (=H הֲלוֹא, BT1); cf. הָלַאן, הר? [cf. Khan 569 **hal** only; for shure].
הלא-הלא (< Ar الله/K clamor/P Bravo!) **⁺hallā-⁺hallā** external signs of great wealth (PolU 249); how fortunate! Cf. מאשלא.
הלאכ (Ar ruin) m., adv. **halāk** terribly (poor, sick, etc.), total loss (PolU 277, 431).
הלאל (Ar) m. **hilāl** crescent shaped amulet.
הלאלה (Ar) f. **halāle** 'Moonshine' (SaLH 139).
הָלַאן (< הלא+ן/Ar/T حالا at once) **hālan** lo (=H הֲרֵי, AvidH 19); cf. הונא [=MacD 76 **hālā** already; immediately?].
הלאתה (K) f. **halāte** precipice.
הלבד (K<Ar البتّة) adv. **halbad** certainly.
ה-ל-ה-ל 1 III (Ar) vi **h-l-h-l** to wear thin (clothes), become worn out.
ה-ל-ה-ל 2 v. ה-ל-ל
הלהלוכת (K) pl. **halhalōkat** cornel berries.
הלהלתא (K/onomat) f. **⁺halhalta** sounds of commotion (PolU 47, 116).
הלולא, חלולא, כלולא (OA/Mand הִילּוּלָא/OS ܚܠܘܠܐ wedding feast) **h/ḥ/xılūla** wedding

feast (AvidH 6; Br47 99, 118; Br93 414) [cf. Mutz 237 **xlūla** wedding].

הליסא, הריסא (Ar هريسة) f. **hal/rīsa** mushy porridge; soaked bread.; cf. ה-ל-ס.

ה-ל-כ (Ar) vi/vt **h-l-k** to destroy, cast dirt at (NT); become dirty, soiled (Z; PolG); IV to make dirty; to corrupt (=H שִׁחֵת, BT1).

הלכה (H) **hālāxa** Jewish law; cf. פתויה; pl. הלכות **hālāxōs** (PolU 390); – **šaḥīṭa** rules of ritual slaughtering (PolU 391) (NT+).

ה-ל-ל II, ה-ל-ה-ל III (OA/H) **h-l-l** (AvidH 48), **h-l-h-l** (AlfH 57) to recite the Hallel, to cheer (NT5 411) [cf. Blanc 158].

ה-ל-ס (Ar) vt **h-l-s** to come off the bone. (over-cooked meat).

הם 1, הַמִינִיךְ ,המיניך (K/P > OA/Mand האם, הם also) **ham(īnık)** (AvidH 24) also, same; yet (NT+) [cf. Blanc 158 **hammēn(a)**. **hámzēd(i)**; Khan 569 **ham** also].

הם 2 (Ar) m. **ham(m)** concern, worry; **ma ham dwīqāle lıbbox** What has been ailing you (PolG); pl. **hamme** (NT+).

המא, המאנ(כי) (K) adv. **háma(nki)** simply, just.(MeAl 184, n. 45; RivSh 158; PolG).

המדן (P) **hammádan** Hamadan (Iranian town), 'a far away place', 'the end of the world': **ṣōte dīda gēzi qam** - her screams reached the end of the world (SaAC 13).

המהויר, הָמָאוַר (K/P همـــوار) **ham(h)awēr** upright (=H יָשָׁר, AvidH 52); pl. הַמְהַוֵירַאת **hamhawērat** upright men (=H יְשָׁרִים, BT4. D).

המין, המינכא (OA/OS המיינא < P **himyān**) m. **hımyan(ka)** ornamental belt for women.

המפאיי(ד) (P) **hampāy(ad)** of equal rank or merit (NT2).

הנא (K **hīn**) **hınna** 'that thing', 'What do you call it?' [cf. MacD 78] cf. מישומא, ה-נ-ל.

הנאה (H) **hanā'a** pleasure (BaBin 67).

הנאויה, נאבה (K/P) pl. **hınāwe** (NT2; AvidH 70), **nāve** (Z), bowels, innards; **nāve zıllu** He has diarrhea; **nāve mkīzırru ṭāla** He has been pining for her (his guts burned for her).

הנארא (K) m. **hınāra** pomegranate tree; cf. ארמותא.

הינגה v. הנגי

הנג'אר (P) **hınjār** mason's rule, plumb-line (NT2).

הנד (Ar) f. **hınd** India; **hınd-u-ʾyaman** India and Yemen, far-away places, the end of the world; cf. המדן, ג'ין ומאג'ין.

הנדאבה (K) **hındāve** near the feet (RivSh 257).

הנדאס, הִינְדַאס (Ar/P هنداز measure > OA הַנְדָזָא measure) **hındās** measure (=H מִדָּה, PolG); pl. הנדאזיה **hındāze** measures, plans (NT2; NT6 136; BT4, D); cf. ה-נ-ד-ס.

הנדוכא, הנדאיא (< הנד; cf. OA הִינְדְוָאָה; OS/Mand הינדואייא) m. **hındōka, hındāya** (f. **hındōke, hındēṯa**) Hindu, Indian.

ה-נ-ד-ז, ה-נ-ד-ס III (OA הנדז to overlap, coincide < P **handāz** to plan, allot) **h-n-d-s/z** to dress up, spruce up (PolUR 50); מְהַנְדוֹזֵי (v.n.); **mıhandōze** measure (=H מְשׂוּרָה, BT3, D).

ה-נ-י (Ar; OA/OS/Mand) **h-n-y** to be pleased; **la ghānēle** It doesn't please him, he is reluctant (to spend money, etc.); **la ghānēli ʾıbbe** I want to spare him from trouble (PolU 305); **hnēlēli** It pleased me; cf. ת-ה-נ-י.

הנייה, הנייא (Ar; cf. OA הנייתא benefit; OS ܗܢܝܘܬܐ) f. **hanīye** pleasure; **hanīye ʾıllu** Lucky they are (said with envy); **hanīya hōyālox** Enjoy it, Bon appetite.

ה-נ-ל II (irreg.) (< הנא) **h-nn-l** to say this and that; to do this and that, have intercourse (PolU 112); **hnılle** He did what you call it (Ruth 3:9); **kullu bšamʾi, kullu bhınnıli** All of them will hear (about it) and gossip (SaAC 6, 8); **wēlu bıbxāya uhınnōle** They were crying and the like (PolU 306)

הנר, הינר, חנר (K/P) **hınnar** (NT), **ḥınnar** (Z), tactics, skill (NT); **mare -ḥınnare, ḥınnar-kare** skillful, trickster woman.

העץ (H) **hāʿēs** (!) tree fruits and the blessing בורא פרי העץ; **xōl hāʿēs-hāzāma** Eat fruits of tree and ground (and say the blessings).

הפטרה (H) f. **hafṭāra** the Prophetic portion read on Sabbath; pl. **hafṭārōṯ**.

הפסארא v. אפסארא

הקב"ה ,הב"ה (H) **h/ḥaqqādōš-bārūx-(h)ū** the Holy One Blessed Be He (NT+).

הר (P) adv. **har** always; since, in any case (cf. PolG), after all; **har jēda** right away (NT+). [cf. Khan 569 **har, hor** 'only, still; intensifying particle].

הרא 1 (P) m. **hırra** layer (of bricks) (NT2).

הרא 2 (< הר ?) **harra** (?) always/in vain? (NTU4 182b) [MacD 79 **harā** space between furrows< AzT; **herwā** in vain<K].

ה-ר-ב 1 II (H הרבה לספר?) **h-r-b** to talk, argue about the price too much (Jewish cryptic): **ʿıvrāya la mharbıt** Hebrew (Fellow), don't argue too much (=don't spoil the bargain with the Gentile).

הרגא (Ar/P خرقه patched garment?) f. **hırga** (good) garment (NT; BT2, Arodh); **go māta šımmox, bıd ʾurxa hırgox** In the village - your (good) name, on the road - your (good) clothes (RivPr 211); pl. **hırge** ragged garments (Z) [cf. MacD 107 **xirqā**].

ה-ר-ג-ל III (< הרגא) vi/vt **h-r-g-l** to wear out (clothes), to tear; cf. ה-ר-ד-ל.

הרגמתא v. הרהמתא

הרגׄה (K) f. **hırče** bearish woman, brute.

ה-ר-ד (OA ח-ר-ד?) vi/vt **h-r-d** (Z **h-r-z**); to shake (= H נִעַשׁ, PolG); cf. רודאנא (NT+).

ה-ר-ד-ל III (<?) vt/vi **h-r-d-l** to wear out, to tear to pieces, destroy things (by mischief).

הרה (K yes) **harē** only in **lā harē** to no avail, no response (cf. PolU 423).

הרהור (H; cf. OA הַרְהוֹרָא) m. ⁺**hırhūr** unchaste thought; אודיוא הרהור **ʾodīwa hırhūr** They were ill-thinking (NT2); הרהורית עברות **hırhūrıt ʿavērōt** thoughts of transgressions; cf. ה-ר-ה-ר.

ה-ר-ה-ם III (<?) **h-r-h-m** to thunder, roar; cf. ג-ר-ג-ם.

הרהמתא, הרגמתא, הַרְהַמּוּתָא, הרמהרמתא (< ה-ר-ה-ם) f. **harhamta**, **hargamta** (+NT), **harhamūta** (RivSh 205), **hırímhrímta** (PolG), thunder, lion's roar;].

ה-ר-ה-ר III (H/OA/OS) ⁺**h-r-h-r** to have unchaste thoughts; מְהַרְהוֹרֵית לִיבַּא **mharhōrıt lıbba** improper thinking of the heart (=H שְׁרִירוּת לֵב, BT5, D); have libidinous thoughts (Pol 108).

ה-ר-ו-ס, א-ר-ו-ס (< Ar هوس 'infatuate'?) **h/ʾ-r-w-s** to flirt (PolU 182).

הרזילא (OA ערסלא, ארזלא) **harzēla** elevated bed (Br47 61).

הרושא, הרושתא (< ה-ר-ש 2) adj. **harūša, harušta** muddy, unclear; ⁺**māya harūše** muddy water.

הריסא v. הליסא

הרמהרמתא v. הרהמתא

הרמיכה (K **hirmi**<P **armūd**) pl. **hermike** pears (Hob89 182); cf. כרגׄינה.

ה-ר-ש 1 II/IV (OA שרי?) **h-r-š** to begin (NT; Hob89 218); מהרשא שאתא אבד בורכאתא **mharša šāta ʾıbbıd burxāta** May the year begin with its blessings (NTU4 148a).

ה-ר-ש 2 (K 'spoil'/IrAr 'scratch'?) **h-r-š** to be unclear (liquid), have trachoma (SaAC 14)

הרשא (< ה-ר-ש 2) m. **hırša (dʾēne)** trachoma, eye infection (SaAC 14).

הש, הוש (K **aš**) **hıš, hüš** hush!

השיאר, השר (K/P) inv. **hıšyar** (NT), **hıššar** (Z, PolG), alert, careful, conscious, awake.

השיארותא (< השיאר) f. **hıšyārūta** (NT; Z **hıššarūsa**) caution, alertness (NT+).

השיה (P) pl. **hısse** senses, wits; נבלתו השיה You (God) take away his senses; - **zıllu mrēše** He lost his wits, became senile; - **sēlu brēše** He regained his composure (cf. PolG) (NT+).

השכבה, אשכבה (H) f. **h/ʾaškāva** prayer in memory of the deceased; **ʾ-w-d** - to recite it.

השם ישמרך (H) **haššēm yıšmarēxa** May God protect you, thanks (said by old Hakhamim to youngsters after being helped by them).

הֶשְׁתָא (OA הא שעתא? v. היש) adv. **hešta** now (AvidH 18).

התיכה (Ar) f. **hatīke** disgrace; cf. התכותא (NT+).

ה-ת-כ (Ar) vi/vt **h-t-k** to disgrace or be disgraced (=H חֵרֵף, PolG)

התכא v. הדכא

התכותא, הִיתְכֻותָא (ה-ת-כ) f. **hıtkūta** disgrace (=H חֶרְפָּה, PolG); cf. התיכה.

התרה (H) f. ⁺**hattāra** release from vows; **zıllan ʾuzlan** ⁺**hattara** We went (to synagogue) and had a release from vows (by the Hakham; cf. Amedi 51).

ו (w)

ו (H) **wāw** the sixth letter in the Hebrew alphabet; **ʾišta** six.

-ו, -וו (OA) **u-** and; may begin an apodosis: כימן דדארו...ומרולי **kīman dıdʾırru...umırrūle** When they returned ...{and} they said to him (NT1); often omitted in pairs: **yımma bāba** father (and) mother, parents; **gōra baxta** husband (and) wife; **tōra ʾarya** ox (and) lion (RivSh 153, 282) (NT+).

-ו v. -והון

וא v. אואהא

ואגֿב (Ar) m. **wājıb** (It is) obligatory, obligation; **n-p-q (m)** - to fulfill an obligation (cf. PolG); **q-y-m b-dīde** to look after him (NT+).

ואגֿבותא (< ואגֿב) f. **wājıbūta** obligation (=H חובה, AvidH 70).

ואה, ואח, וח (K?) interj. **wā/ah/ḥ** indicates very puzzling situation, bewilderment (PolU 15, 66, 263).

ואי, ווי, וי (OA/OS/Mand ואי ,ויי ,וָוי) **⁺wāy** woe (NT+); **wayli, wılli** woe unto me (SaLH); **qaṭlaxlōxun - wāy, ula qaṭlaxlōxun - wāy** (If) we kill you - woe (to us), and (if) we don't kill you - woe (to us) (PolU 295); pl. ואיי **wāye** (RivSh 240).

ואלא 1 (K) **wāla** wilderness, desert (NT3).

ואלא 2, ולא, ולהי, וונה (K<Ar) **⁺walla, ⁺wallahi, wü/ınne** by God; behold, suddenly, then ('empty word'): **bixāla wēle, ⁺walla gʾāwır xa nāša** He was eating, why, behold, a man comes in (MeAl 184; Zaken 389; PolG).

ואלי (Ar/T) m. **wāli** Turkish governor, vali.

וַאנַא דִיך (< T venedik) **wāna dīk** (superior gold of) Venice (=H מוּפָז, PolG:1Kg 10:18).

ואר 1 v. וריא

ואר 2 (K) m. **wār** camp, dwelling (PolU 17).

וארא (H) **waʾēra** only in **bšabsıd waʾēra sıswa kpāyıš gēra uvēra** On the Sabbath of **wāʾērā** (Exod 6:2) the winter becomes total chaos.

ובילא (AR?) **wabīla** (?) issue, problem (?): גנאפץ אידה מנד ובילה/כולו שואליה **gnāpıṣ ʾīde mınnıd wabīle/kullu shoʾāle** He washes off ('dusts off') his hands from the issue /all the issues (of third world) (AmU2 6a)

וג'(א) (K<Ar وجه) **waj(ja)** concern, care, need, thing (=H חֵשֶׁק, חֵפֶץ, PolG); **ʾāhıt ma wajjox** What do you care; **lē(we) wajjox** It is not your business! **la wájwali** I didn't care (Hob89 226); **ču mındıt waj lēbu** They are good for nothing (BaBin 137; MeAl 189, n. 70; AvidH 42).

ו-ג'-ב IV (Ar) **w-j-b** to condemn; impose, oblige.

וג'דאן (Ar) **wıj/ždān** conscience.

ו-ג'-ה II (Ar) **w-j-h** to meet face to face (= H נִתְרָאֶה פָּנִים, PolG: 2Kg 14:8)

וג'ארה (< Ar وغل to intrude, harry?) pl. **⁺waġāre** travels, only in **waġārox šālōm (hāwe)** May your travels be peacful, Have a safe trip! (cf. PolU 103).

ודוי (H) **wıddūy** confession; **ʾ-w-ḏ wıddūy** to confess (=H הִתְוַדָּה, BT3).

ודיפא v. וצ׳יפא

ו-ד/ז-ן II (Ar اذن) **w-ḏ/z-n** to call to Muslim prayer; **malla mōzınne** The mulla called for prayer; **mōzōn malla** mulla's call (PolG).

והון-, -יהון, -ו, -וה (OA הון-) **-ōhun** (Z), **-ēhun** (NT), **-u** (Z), **-u(h)** (+NT), of them, their (attached possessive pron., e.g.: **lıbbu(h)/ lıbbē/ōhun** their heart).

והמה (Ar) f. **wahme** confusion (polU 97).

וול-וול-וול (onomat.) **wul-wul-wul** sounds of angry birds (Pol 262).

וונה v. ואלא 2

וז(א)רא (Ar) **wazāra** ministery; **wázara** ministers (PolU 201)

וזא (Ar وزّ gander; cf. OA אֲוַוזָּא) **wazza** only in **ṭēra wazza** an exotic legendary bird (FT).

וזין (Ar) **wazın** (proper) weight (NT5 410).

וזיר(א) (Ar/OS) m. **wazīr(a)** vizier; **wazīra yammāya/čappāya** vizier sitting to the right/left of the king (MeAl 191); pl. **wazīre** (NT+).

וזכרו (H) f. **⁺wazıxro** accursed one; also: a woman who uses the curse ימח שמו וזכרו too often.; **wazıxro ʾılle** A curse upon him!

וזנא (Ar) f. **wazna** unit of weight/measure;

talent (=H כִּכָּר, NT5 396; PolU 434); pl. **wazne**.

וח v. ואח

ו-ח-ד II (Ar) **w-ḥ-d** to assert God's unity (NT3).

וחידא (Ar) m. **waḥīda** an only child (NT); cf. יכאנא; single, living alone (NT5 408).

וחידותא (Ar) f. **waḥīdūṯa** oneness of God (NT; RivSh 184).

וחל (Ar) m. **waḥıl** mud, slime (NT+).

וחשא (Ar) m. **waḥša** wild beast; uncouth (NT+).

וטן, מוטן (Ar) m. **waṭan, mawṭan** birthplace; pl. מוטאנה **mawṭāne**.

וטרא v. ותרא

וי (K) **wi, ⁺way** Ah!, Really?! (mild surprise).

-וי, -ויל v. ה-ו-י

ויקהל-פקודי (H) only in **bšabsıd wayyáqhel-paqūze, ⁺māya šxınnu go gūze** On this Sabbath (end of Exod.), water becomes warm in jars.

ויקרא (H) only in **bšabsıd wayyíqra, sıswa gʾāqır mın ʾıqra** On this Sabbath (Lev. 1:1), the winter is totally gone.

וירן, ויראני (K) inv. **wēran, wērāni** (NT3) ruined, desolate (place); awful(person).

וֵירֵיס (Ar وارث) **wērıs** inheritor; **bla wērıs** childless (=H עֲרִירִי, BT3, D).

ו-י-ש, י-ו-ש (OA/OS יבש) **w-y-š** (Z), **y-w-š** (NT) to dry, starve (vi); IV to dry, starve (vt)(SaAC 19); to keep someone waiting outdoors for too long [2:**māwš** (Z), מייוש **maywıš** (NT4; Hob89 220)]; cf. יושא ,יוישא.

וישא v. יוישא, יושא

וישותא v. יוישותא

-וך (OA ךָ-) **-ox** your (m. sg.) (NT+).

-וכון, -יכון (OA (י)כון-) **-ōxun** (Z), **-ēxun** (NT), your (c. pl., with sg. and pl. nouns).

וכי, וכו (K) adv. **waki/u** since, now that: **waki dsēle, šud pāyıš xapča ʾaxxa** Since he has come, let him stay here a bit; **la waku ʾamrētın** So that you won't say (PolU 31).

וכידי (< וכי) adv. **wakidi** otherwise (SaAC 22).

וכיל (Ar) m. **wakil** agent; pl. **wakīle**.

וכילותא, וכילתותא (< וכיל) f. **wakīl(at)ūṯa** agency; deposit (=H פִּקָּדוֹן, BT3, D).

ו-כ-ל II (Ar) **w-k-l** to appoint as agent [1:**m(w)ōkıl-**; 2:**m(w)ākıl** (PolG)] (NT+).

וכת (K<Ar وقت) m. **waxt** time; cf. וקת.

וכתא (< וכת) adv. **waxta** soon, in a short while (in future); about to: **waxta māyıs** He may die any moment (MeAl 177, n. 8; PolG).

ול, -ול (< ה-ו-י-ל?) **wal(-)** a particle used to add some emphasis to verb: **wal zıllu** They (surely) had gone; **wal gēzıl kudyom** He (indeed) goes every day; **uʾatta hōna ḥakōma wal gēzıl ʾıl qamōxun**=H וְעַתָּה הִנֵּה הַמֶּלֶךְ מִתְהַלֵּךְ לִפְנֵיכֶם (PolG: 1S 12:2); **hatxa wal mırre ʾıstaz ʿōlam** Thus has said the Master of the Universe (RivSh 238, 250; BaBin 148; Sa83c 16, 28); cf. ולוך.

ולא 1 (Ar/OA) **wála, ula** nor: **la xāzıtti wála xāzınnox** You'll not see me and nor I'll see you; **la ʿıns wála/ula jıns** Neither humans nor jinnis (could be found there) (PolG).

ולא 2, ולהי v. ואלא 2

ולא 3 (Ar وإلا) **wílla** or; **brōna-le – brāta-la** Is it a boy or a girl? (PolG),

ולד, ולאד (+NT) (Ar) **walad** child; **wa/ıld-ıl-ḥalāl** honest person (cf. PolU 242); cf. חלאלזאדא; pl. **walāde** (NT+).

ולדת ולדא (Ar) **wıldıt wıld-e** (provide for) several of his generations to come (Zaken 389; PolG).

ולוך (cf. IrAr **walak**) interj. (**hā**) **walox** (hey) you (m. sg., an informal address), say, look, **wálax** (f. sg), **wálōxun** (pl.c.) (BaBin 137; Pol 111; RivSh 236) [MacD 81].

ולחאצל (Ar) **walḥāṣıl** in short, to the point.

ולת, ולאת (Ar/P) f. **walat** region, province, unwalled city; pl. ולאתה **walāte** (NT5 396; Sa83c 18, Am) (NT+).

ונה v. ואלא

ו-נ-ס II (Ar) **w-n-s** to socially enjoy [1:**m(w)ōnıs-**; **emmūnıs** (PolG)].

וסך (Ar) **wasax** filth (NT).

ו-ע-ד II (Ar) **w-ʿ-d** to promise [1: -מוועד **mwōʿıd-**, מוועדה/אמוועדה/מויעדה **mwüʿde** (p.p.pl.) destined, promised](NT3).

ועד (Ar) **waʿıd** appointed term (NT).

ועדא (Ar/OS) m./f. ? **waʿda** time, term (PolG: **kulle waʿda** , m.; **pıšla waʿıd...**, f.); כימד ועדא **xēmıd waʿda** the Meeting Tent (=H אֹהֶל מוֹעֵד, NT3); cf. מחצר; - **hāwe mpīla**

ʾɪlli, or waʿdaubɪt (K), I swear, I promise (PolU 49, 224).

ועדותא (Ar وعد) f. **waʿdūṯa** promise; **waʿdūsa hōya mpɪlta ʾɪlli** I solemnly promise (FT).

ו-פ-ק II (Ar) **w-f-q** to agree (Avin74 9).

ו-צ-ו-צ III (IrAr) **w-ṣ-w-ṣ** to chirp in faint voice (dying bird).

ו-צ-י II (Ar) **w-ṣ-y** to command, to enjoin [1: אמווצכלה **ɪmwōṣaxle** He commanded us (NT); 1/2/3: **mōṣ-**(Z); מוּצְיֵי **mūṣye**, p.p.pl., PolG)] (NT+).

וצייה (Ar) f. **waṣīye** ordinance, will, instruction; pl. וציית/וצייד (NT2)/ וַצְיַּיאַת (BT3, D; PolG) **waṣīyat/d**; cf. מצוה.

וצלא (Ar) m. **waṣla** (connecting) piece; cut of meat; rib (=H צֶלַע, BT1); pl. **waṣlāle** (cf. PolG), **waṣle** (Pol 111).

וצ̇וצ̇תא (onomat) **waẓwaẓta** whimper (PolU 79).

וצ̇יפא, וְדִיפַא (Ar) f. **waẓīfa** official post (=H כֵּן, BT1, D [Gen 41:13]); pl. **waẓīfat**.

וקחותא (Ar وقح) f. **waqḥūṯa** insolence (NT2).

וקייא (Ar< Gr/L uncia > OA אוּקִיָא small weight) f. **waqīya** Turkish oka (about 240 gram or 1/12 of מניא; v. חוקא 1).

וקת (Ar) m. **waqt** time; בוקתד **bwaqtɪd** when; cf. וכת (NT+).

ורייא v. ור

ואראקא (Ar) f. **⁺warāqa** paper, note; cf. כאג'ז; **sɪppās ⁺warāqa** thin lips (mark of beauty) (SaNR) (NT+).

ורארה (< P وراغ flame?) pl. **warāre** signs of life (still shown by a very ill child, SaAC 8); condition, behavior (PolU 77) [MacD 82 **werwārī qiṭyī nā** He is very weak]

ורגב v. וריא

ורדא (OA/Ar < P) m. **warda** rose,flower; pl. **warde**; **-ɪt šɪmme** sky flowers (= stars?) (PolG); **⁺māyɪd** - rose water (NT+).

ורדה (Ar) p.n.f. **warde** Rose.

ורדו (< ורידא) **wardo** thigh muscle (=H גִּיד הַנָּשֶׁה, BT1).

ורור (K/IrAr<En?) m. **⁺warwar** revolver, pistol; pl. **⁺warwāre**.

ורזא, ורצ̇א (AzT) m. **⁺warza** vineyard [cf. MacD 82].

וריא (OA ברא) adv. **warya** outside; מלוריא **mɪlwarya** (NT3), **mɪn warya** (Z), from the outside; אל ור מ- **ʾɪl war m-** outside of (NT3); ואר ארץ ישראל **wār**... outside of Israel (BaBin 52); ורג(י)ב **wargɪ/eb** outward; the outside of a garment, etc. (cf. PolG; v. גיבא. (NT+).

ורידא (OS ܘܪܝܕܐ artery, nerve; OA ורדא lung ? < Ak **urʾudu** trachiae; H וָרִיד large blood vessel) m. **warīda** (Z **warīza**) root (of tree); blood vein; sinew; scion: **ʾɪnkan la hāwe mɪn -ɪt ḥakōme** If he is not a scion of kings; pl. **warīḏe** (PolG). cf. ורדו.

ו-ר-ע (Ar be pious, modest) **w-r-ʿ** be ashamed: **ʾēnu lag wárʿa** They have no shame (PolG).

ורצ̇א v. ורזא

ותרא, וטרא (Ar وتر) m. **⁺watra** tendon; string.

ושתי (H) **wašti** Vashti, stupid woman.

ז (z)

ז (H) **zāyın** the seventh letter of the Hebrew alphabet; **šōʾa** seven.

זאאה (OA/OS/Mand זָגָא cock < P زاق young of anything) m. **zāʾa** baby chick (Z); youngling (of doves, deer, lion) (NT; RivSh 212).

זאגא (OS) **zāga** bell's tongue.

זאד, צ̇אד (Ar/K)⁺**zād** grains, provisions.

זאורא, זורא (OA זעורא) adj. **zʾōra** (NT; RivSh 131; AvidH 60), **zōra** (Z), f. זאורתא **zʾurta, zurta**, young, small, little; cf. זאירא.

זאורותא, זורותא (< זאורא) f. **z(ʾ)ōrūṯa** youth, childhood; cf. זירותא.

זאיא (K?) f. **zāya** recurrent time; **zāyá-zāya** sometimes; **zāyıd treʾ** second time; אֵיזַא **ʾē-zā(ya)** this time (RivSh 214); case, matter, issue; **fhīmāle zāya** He got it, understood the issue (PolG); **qurra šēsa zāya** Come-on, really (mild complaint); [Garbell 341 **zaa** time].

זאירא, זארתא (OA זעירא) adj. **zʾīra, zʾırta** puny.

זאכו (< OS/OA בית-זכו place of victory?) **zāxo** Zakho (town in Iraqi Kurdistan) [Sabar forthcoming a].

זאכונאיא, זאכוניתא (< זאכו) **zāxōnāya, zāxōneṯa** resident of Zakho.

זאלטא, זלאטא (IrAr < It) f. **zālaṭa, zalāṭa** salad.

ז-א-פ (OA זעף?) vt **z-ʾ-p** to push away (=H נָדַּח, הָדַף, דָחַף, PolG:BT) (NT+).

ז-א-ר (OA זער) vi **z-ʾ-r** to diminish; IV to make smaller (BaBin 47).

זארתיאתא v. זיארא

זאת (T < Ar ذات) **zāt** self; **ʾāwa bzāte** He himself (and no one else; cf. PolG).

זבא (Ar) m. **zıbba** penis, genitals, pubic hair.

זבאלג̆י (Ar-T) m. **zabbālči** garbageman (cf. PolU 299).

זבאנא, צ̇באנא (< IrAr) f. ⁺**zıbāna** cigarette butt.

זבארא 1, זברתא (< ז-ב-ר) **zavāra, zavarta** loiterer, wanderer.

זבארא 2 (K) f. **zıbbāra** semi-voluntary communal work to help the local agha.

זבאשא (K/AnAr < Ar جـــــــبس) f. **zabāša** watermelon (cf. PolG); pl. **zabāše**.

זְבַגַא (Ar/P زبرجـد) **zabāja** jacinth (=H לֶשֶׁם, BT2, D); cf. סבג̇י.

זבו (< זבא) c. **zıbbo** one with large pubic hair or genitals.

זבון 1 (P) inv. **zabun** weak, helpless (NT+).

זבון 2 (IrAr) m. **zbūn** a belted and heavy robe.

זבון 3 (Ar; cf. OA זָבוֹנָא) **zabun** customer.

זבורא (< ז-ב-ר) **zıvvōra** roundish child.

זביבייה (AnAr? < Ar زبيب raisins) f. **zbēbīye** sweet raisin soup.

זבייא v. זויא

ז-ב-ל II (< זבלא/Ar/OA/OS, pa. to manure, dung) **z-b-l** to turn into a dump; not to take proper care of a place.

זבלא (Ar زبل; OA זיבלא) m. **zıbla** garbage, refuse; pl. **zıblāle**.

זבלסורכת (K?) pl. **zavlasurkat** youngsters (PolU 155).

ז-ב-נ II (OA) **z-b-n** to sell; cf. ז-ו-נ (NT+).

ז-ב-ר, ז-ו-ר (K) **z-v-r** (Z; PolG), **z-w-r** (Hob89 225), to turn (vi), walk around; **lēle zvırre rēšu** They didn't sleep well (MeAl 182); IV to turn (vt); take (a child) for a walk.

זברתא (< ז-ב-ר) f. **zvarta** turn, cycle.

ז-ב-ת v. ת-ב-ת

ז-ג̇-ל (Ar) **z-ġ-l** seduce, tempt (cf. PolG); II to forge, contaminate (PolG) (NT+).

ז-ד-א (OA אזדעזע tremble) **z-d-ʾ** to fear; IV to frighten (NT+).

זדאתא, זדיאתא (< ז-ד-א) f. **zdeʾṯa** awe, fear (NT+).

ז-ד-ג̆ (Ar سـجـد) **z-d-j** to bow down (BT1, D); cf. ז-י-ג̆.

זדואא, זדואתא (< ז-ד-א) adj. **zadōʾa, zadoʾta** fearful (Z); frightening, awe-inspiring (NT2; זַדּוֹאָה = H נוֹרָא, BT1, D); cf. מזדאאנא.

זדואתא (< ז-ד-א) f. **zdoʾṯa** fear; **mın -e** out of his fear; **-ṯıt ʾilāha** fear of God (cf. PolG) [Khan 586 **zdula**].

זהורא, זהורתא (< ז-ה-ר) adj. **zahūra, zahurta** glittering.

ז-ה-מ II (OA be foul smelling; OS be greasy, smell like bad fat) **z-h-m** to become impure (by eating meat or dairy food before the necessary time proscribed in Jewish law); cf. זוהמא [cf. MacD 166: to defile or put butter or milk into lenten food].

ז-ה-ר (OA) **z-h-r** to shine (=H זָרַח, BT5, D).

זואא (OA/OS זוּגָא < Gr) m. **zōʾa** pair, couple; בזואא **bzōʾa** (each) two together; **ʾōzıttu ʾaqlox ʾīzox zōʾa** May you die (lit, make your feet and hands a pair = stretched together) (NT+).

זואדה v. זוואדה

זואנא, זונתא (< ז-ו-נ; cf. OA/OS זָבוֹנָא) **zawāna, zawanta** buyer.

זואתא (OA זְוָודְתָא, זבדתא/Mand זאואדתא/Ar زوّادة provisions for journey (> OA shrouds, euph.); + OS ܙܘܐܕܐ a cake of fine flour?) f. **zwaʾta** a loaf of bread enriched with sesame and egg-yolk; pl. זודיאתא **zudyāta** (=H עֻגוֹת, BT1, D; PolG); cf. זוואדה (NT+) [cf. MacD 90 **zattā, zwātā** a cake for children; Garbell: **zatila** cake of bread made with oil; Mutz 241 **zatila** a kind of big pita bread/242 **zwāta** thin and dry bread].

זוגורדי (K < T) **zugurdi** destitute, vagabond, single person, footman (=H רַגְלִי, BT2).

זודאנא, זודנתא (ז-י-ד) adj. **zōdāna, zōdanta** exceeding, additional, superior (cf. Polg); בזודאנא **bzōdāna** exceedingly (NT+).

זודיאתא v. זואתא

זודנותא, זודניתא (< זודאנא) f. **zōdanūta, zōdanīta** (+NT), excess, majority (=H רֹב, PolG:Gen 16:10).

זוהמא, זומא (OA/Mand זוהמא, m./f.; OS ܙܘܗܡܐ stink, filth) m. **zohma, zōma** impurity: **lak xāšıx ʾaxlıt pısra; zohmox hēš lē(we) zīla** It is (ritually) inappropriate for you to eat meat; your impurity (time) is not over yet; v. ז-ה-מ.

זוהר (H) ⁺**zōhar** (the Kabbalistic book of) Zohar; **bzōhar** (I swear) by Zohar (that I am telling the truth; a very grave oath).

זוואדה, זַוַואדֵי (OA זְוָודֵי, זואדי, m.pl.; Ar زوّادة, f.) f. **zuwwāde, zawāde** (Zaken 387; =H צֵדָה, PolG: Jud 20:10), provisions (for journey); cf. זואתא, זאד.

זוזא (OA/OS/Mand זוזא < Ak **zūzu**) **zūza** coin; kind of tax; **la zūza, la ḥāṣa, la ṭāpo** (PolU 1) not any kind of tax; pl. זוזיה **zūze** (NT2).

זוזלק (T?) **zōzalaq** poplar (=H לִבְנֶה, BT1).

זוזן, זוזאנא (K) **zōzān(a)** pasture area; mountain (RivPr #22); (biblical) Bashan (בָּשָׁן, BT; cf. PolG: 2 Kg 10:33:D); cf. כויסתאני.

זוייא, זבייא (K < P زمين land) f. **zawīya** (NT2), **zavīya** (Z, PolG:D) field; **zawīyıt daxla/dašta** field of crop (=H חֶלְקַת הַשָּׂדֶה, BT1; 2 S 23:11; Ruth 2:3; קָמָה, BT2).

זולאזייה (K **tōlāzī**) pl. **zōlāzīye** wife abuse, infidelity; ⁺**rāba zōlāzīye mtōʿılle ʾıbba** He caused her much pain by his philanderings.

זולאל, זלל (Ar ماء زُلال) **zulāl** (NT3), ⁺**māyıd zalal** (Z), pure, sweet water; cf. זלולה.

זֻולמַאט (P/K < Ar ظلمة) ⁺**zulmāt** total darkness (=H עֲלָטָה, BT1, D); ⁺**zulmāta-raš** pitch dark.

זומא 1 (K) m. **zōma** (tribal) summer camp; group of villages which participate in common sheep shearing (PolU 438).

זומא 2 v. זוהמא

זומרת (Ar/P) **zumrıt** emerald (NT3).

ז-ו-נ (< ז-ב-נ) **z-w-n** to buy; **gzāwınna gyāne mın ʾaxōne** He kowtows to his brother [1: **zun-/zwın-**; 3: **zōn** (Z)/אִיזְוֹון **ızwōn** (PolG:D)] (NT+).

זונא (OA/Mand זיבנא/OS ܙܒܢܐ, SokPA 171; זימנא SokBA 384) **zūna, zōna** (Gz73 90), long time, only in **mın zūna** since a long time; **mın zūna lēwax xızye dōxun** We haven't seen you for a long time (cf. PolG).

זונה, זוֹנָא (H) f. **zōna** prostitute (BT1); cf. קחבא.

זוניתא (< ז-ו-נ) f. **zwanīta** purchase.

זוונתא (ז-ו-נ) n.act. **zwanta** sale (PolG).

זופא, צופא (IrAr **ṣōpa** < T **soba**) ⁺**zōpa** stove, heater.

ז-ו-ק II (Ar) **z-w-q** to nicely arrange (PolG:D).

זוקאק (Ar) **zuqāq** lane, river-bed (NT2).

זור, זורותא (Ar) **zōr** (NT2), **zōrūta** (NT5 392) force; very (RivSh 280); ⁺**bızzōr** by force, reluctantly (Z).

זוורא 1 v. זאורא

זורא 2 (K **zurg**) m. **zūra** hill; pl. זוראנה **zūrāne** (BaBin 10); cf. גרא-זורכא, גרא.

זורותא v. זאורותא, זור.

זורזורתא, זרזרתא, זורינתא, זוראנה (K) f. **zurzurta, zarzarta, zūrzénta, zūrāne** (pl.?), weeping-begging sound(s) (= H שַׁוְעָה, AlfH 91; cf. PolU 2, 392); cf. ז-ר-ז-ר.

זורינכא, זורינכה (< זאורא) adj. **zōrinka, -ke** tīny.

זורכא (< זורא 2) m. **zūraka** hillock.

זורכרת, זורכרה (K) pl. **⁺zōrkırat/-kırre** agressive youngsters, impudent fools (PolU 41, 157); cf. אחמקין.

זורנה v. זרנה

זוורתא (Ar زير porous jar?) f. **zawırta** small jar used as water cooler (=H צִנְצֶנֶת, BT2) pl. **zōrāṯa** (RivSh 257).

זחלקיתא (< Ar glide?) f. **zaḥlaqīṯa** shine: כשכלא זחלקיתד שמשא באיניהון אך ליליה **xšıkla zaḥlaqīṯıd šımša bʾēnēhun ʾıx lēle** Sunshine darkened in their eyes as night (=H מאור, NTU4 152b).

ז-ח-מ II (Ar) **z-ḥ-m** to harm, oppress (=H עִנָּה, BT2); be slightly injured, damaged: **rēše mzōḥımle** His head was slightly injured.

זחמה (Ar) f. **zaḥme** hardship, suffering; **zaḥmē-la ṭālox** It is difficult for you (to be in this condition); pl. **zaḥmıtyāṯa** (NT+).

ז-ח-פ (Ar) vi **z-ḥ-f** to be abundant, increase.

זחף (Ar) adv. **zaḥf** many; **zaḥf nāše/nāše zaḥf** many people; **b/mzaḥf** aplenty (PolU 21).

זיאנא (OA זְיָנָא, זיאנא, m. loss < P **zyān**) f. **zyāna** harm, damage (NT5 386); pl. זיאניה **zyāne** curses (NTU4 148a) (NT+).

זיארא, זירתא (Ar) **⁺zyāra, ⁺zyarta** a visit to a shrine; **ʾēḏ-⁺zyāra** Shavuoth Holiday (during which many visited shrines); **⁺z(y)ārıtyāṯa** (pl.)(visitis to) Jewish cemetery; **⁺bızyār bābi** (I swear) by my father's tomb.

ז-י-ג̆ (Ar زج) **z-y-j** to bow down (=H קָד, BT1, BT2; AvidH 70); cf. ז-ד-ג̆.

ז-י-ד (Ar) **z-y-d** to increase (vi), exceed, multiply; **zēdi xāyıt ḥakōma** Long live the King (Zaken 394); IV to increase (vt); **ʾilāha māzıdla, mın ṭīme mampılla, ʾarzāni ʾemnāhi, marʾa mōṯa kemnāhi** May God increase it, reduce its price, cheap prices and security, (rather than) pain, death (and) shortage (said after meal) (Amedi 72); cf. זיודא (NT+).

זידהי (Ar-K) f. **zēdahi** abundance; offspring (MeAl 177; PolU 1); bloating (=H שַׁחֶפֶת, BT5).

זיואנא, זיונתא (K) adj. **zīwāna, zīwanta** freckled; n. tare seed.

זיזייא (OA זִיזָא) **zīzīya** edge, projection (Avin88 228).

זיודא (< ז-י-ד) m. **zıyyōda** lefovers, remains.

זיזכ (K?) inv. **zīzık** fragile; **gyāna zīzık** gentle person, too delicate.

זימון v. זמון

ז-י-נ II (Ar) **z-y-n** to adorn (NT2).

זין, זִין (K/P) m. **zīn** horse riding equipment (Socin 162; =H מֶרְכָּבָה/רֶכֶב, PolG: 2Kg 5:21; 9:21).

זין וממה (K) **zīn-u-máme** Zin and Mame, better known as Mam i Zin (the lovers names in a Kurdish tragic love story by Ahmed Khani).

זִיפִית (Ar) **zifıt** tar (=H זֶפֶת, BT2, D); cf. קירא.

זִיַּפִיתָא (Ar ضيافة) f. **⁺zıyāfıta** hospitality, banquet (BaBin 162) [cf. MacD 86].

זיקא (Ar) m. **zīqa** shirt-front opening; **psıxla zīqa udʾēla** She opened her shirt and prayed (PolG); cf. בר-זיקא.

ז-י-ר (Ar) **⁺z-y-r** to visit (a shrine); cf. זיארא; to examine attentively (one's body)(Pol 111; PolG); IV to take children to shrines; to take candies to shrines, leaving them there overnight to be blessed and bring them back for children, sick people, etc. (NT+).

זיר-וברזיר (K **zīn** 'saddling'?) adv. **zīr-u-barzīr** tied securely? (PolU 87); cf. כאל-וברכאל.

זירווא (K) **zērūwa** leech.

זירותא (< זאירא) f. **zīrūṯa** babyhood, childhood (Pol 111); מִן זִירוּתִי **mın zīrūṯi** since my birth (=H מֵעוֹדִי, BT1, D); cf. זאורותא.

זירזמין (P) **zīrzamīn** underground (cave, water); pl. זירזמינה **zīrzamīne** (NT2) [Khan 586 **zerzamin** 'basement'].

זירכ (K/P) inv. **zīrak** diligent (person) (cf. PolG); **-e** diligent woman.

זירנגר (K) m. **zērıngır** goldsmith (cf. PolG).

זירתא v. זיארא

זיתא (OA זֵיתָא, זֵיתָא) f. **zēṯa** (Z **zēsa**, but rare) olive; **dehn zēṯa** olive oil; **ṣīwıt - olive** tree (= H עֲצֵי שָׁמֶן, PolG:D); pl. זיתה, זֵיתֵי **zēṯe** (NT, BT).

זיתונא (Ar) f. **zaytūna** olive (Z); pl. **zaytūne** [Khan 586 **zetunta**].

זכאי (H) **zakkāy** not guilty, innocent (cf. PolU 290) (NT+).
זכו (K) **zıko** short person with large belly.
זכו-פשת (K) adv. **zık-u-pıšt** (eating) hastily.
זכות (H) m./f. **zaxuṯ** (Z **zaxus**) merit; זכותוך טרוסתא **zaxūṯox** ⁺**trusta** Your true merit (NT6 137)(=H צְדָקָה, BT1, D); pl. זכויות זַאכִיות, זכיות, **zaxī/ūyoṯ** (=H חֲסָדִים, BT1, D).
ז-כ-י (< זכאי; H-OA זכי) **z-k-y** to be fortunate, to deserve (NT5 409); **did našāme zakyāwa** so that his soul will be meritorious (PolG); **did zākēna uʾāzēna lgınᶜēzın** so that I be fortunate and go to Paradise (PolU 288); II to let someone possess a merit (God:people): אילאהא מזאכיליכון **ʾilāha mzākēlexun** May you be meritorious (NT5 411;) declare innocent; cf. זכאי.
זכירא (Ar ذخيره) f. **zaxīra** treasure, storage (cf. PolU 317).
ז-כ-ת II (K **zixt** spur) **z-x-t** to goad, prick.
זכתכא (K) m. **zıxtıka** clown, assistant to פאלבן.
ז"ל (H) **zixrōnō livrāxā** of blessed memory.
זלאמא (Ar< OA צלמא?) m. **zalāma** person, man; pl. **zalāme** persons carrying no belongings, just by themselves (PolU 443).
זלא (T **sille** < P **sīlī**) f. **zalla** slap; pl. **zalle** (PolG); [cf. Garbell **zilli**; MacD 226 **silā**].
זלגא (K **zilik**) m. **zıllıga** twig; pl. **zıllıge** (cf. PolG: **zıllíg(g)a**)
זלובייא (Ar زلابية) f. **zlōbīya** pancake; pl. **zlōbīye** [cf. Mutz 241 **zlobta**].
זלולה (< זולאל?) ⁺**zlōle** only in ⁺**māyıd** ⁺**zlōle** soup with no substance (=pure water?).
זלומא v. צ̇לומא
זליכא, זליכאיי (P) **zılīxā(ye)** Zuleikha (Potiphar's wife; NT2, BT1).
זלל v. זולאל
ז-ל-מ v. צ̇-ל-מ
זלעום, צ̇לעום (Ar) m. ⁺**zalᶜum** gullet, larynx.
זלפנתא (*OA?) f. **zılpanta** chip of wood or fruit; pl. **zılpanyaṯa** marginal peelings (Avin88 228)[=MacD **zilpē** dry fruits?].
ז-ל-ק (< זלקא) **z-l-q** (chicken, birds) to defecate.
זלקא (K) m. **zılqa** bird droppings; pl. **zılqe**.
זמארא, זמרתא(OA) **zamāra, zamarta** singer; **sanduq zamāra** phonograph (singing box).
זמבילא (K/Ar < OA זַבִּילָא, f./OS ܙܒܠܐ ، ܙܢܒܝܠܐ, m<Ak**zabbilu, zanbilu**) m. **zambīla** basket made of woven reeds; pl. **zambīle**.
זמבלג (Ar/SA [Denizeau زمبلك/زمبرك) m. **zambalag** spring (of watch, etc.).
ז-מ-ב-ר, צ̇-מ-ב-ר III (Ar زنبر) ⁺**z-n-b-r** to sulk, be insulted ('stung by wasp'); cf. נ-א-ס [MacD 167 **mzanpir** be sulky, swell, swagger].
זמון, זימון (H) **zímmun** the additional Hebrew grace over food when three or more eat together (AlfH 65).
זמורתא (OA) f. **zımmurta** song, chant; pl. זמירייתא, זְימֻורְיַיתָא, **zımmı/uryāṯa** (BaBin 105; PolG).
ז-מ-ז-מ III (OA זמזם; OS ܙܡܙܡ) **z-m-z-m** to hum, to sing (מְזַמְזוֹמֵי =H זִמְרָה, AlfH 93).
זמזם (K/Ar) **zımzım** only in ⁺**mayıd zımzım** pure delicious water (FT).
זמן, זמאן (Ar) **zaman** time; מזמן דידה **mzaman dīde** all his life; pl. זמאנה **zamāne**; **ʾay kma zamāne** It has been long periods (NT+).
זמעא (Ar) **zamᶜa** shudder (NT2; NT5 389).
זמפארא (T) only in **kağaḏ**⁺**zımpāra** sandpaper.
זמתא (T < Ar ذمة) f. **zımmıta** conscience; **bzımmıti** I swear, I gurrantee
זניתא, זנאיא (< ז-נ-י) **zanāya, zanēṯa** adulterer (NT+).
זנביניייה (< ?) **zanbinīye** (?) evil messengers? מרפה איבן זנביניייה אכואתד כלויה סריכה **marpe ʾıbban — ʾıxwāṯıd kalwe srīxe** (Satan) looses against us his - (who are) like rabid dogs (NTU4 164).
זנבתא (Ar ذنب tail) f. **zınnabta** sting (of bee).
זנג v. זנכ
זנגין (K/IrAr < T) inv. **zangīn** rich, wealthy.
זנגלא (K) m. **zıngıla** hand bell; child's penis (euph.); pl. **zıngıle** bells of Torah scrolls.
ז-נ-ג-ר III (K echo) **z-n-g-r** to grate.
זנג̇ביל (Ar/P > OA/OS זנגבילא) **zınjıbil** ginger (tree) (NT+).
זנג̇ירא (Ar/P/K) m. **zınjīra** chain, ring; pl. **-e** (cf. PolG) [Khan **zinzira**].
ז-נ-ג̇-ר 1 III (< זנג̇ירא) **z-n-j-r** to chain.
ז-נ-ג̇-ר 2, צ̇-נ-ג̇-ר III (< ?) ⁺**z-n-j-r** to sizzle.
זנדא, זדנכתא (K < Ar) f. **zanda, zandıkṯa** elbow, arm; pl. **zand(ıky)āṯa** (cf. PolGr 53).

זנדאנא (P > OA/OS זֵנְדָּנְקָנָא jailer) m. **zındāna** jail, solitary cell (NT, BT); cf. חבס.

זנה (Ar) f. **zıne** adultery, prostitution (NT+).

ז-נ-ה-ר III (Ar/P) **z-n-h-r** to look/be amazed (cf. Pol 109; PolG).

זנות (H) f. **zınut** adultery, prostitution (BaBin 69).

ז-נ-ז-ק III (Ar زنزق) **z-n-z-q** to swing.

ז-נ-ט-ר (Ar زنتر) **z-n-ṭ-r** to grumble (NT2).

ז-נ-י (OA/OS/Mand/Ar) **z-n-y** to commit adultery, to prostitute; IV to make (one's daughter) a harlot (=H הַזְנָה, BT3) (NT+).

זנג, זנכ (K/P rust) **zank/g** blight (=H שִׁדָּפוֹן, BT5); **mıxye zang** scorched (by wind) (=H שְׁדוּפוֹת, BT1).

זנך (Ar) **zınx** rancid smell, especially of fish.

זנקא (OS < P زنخ) m. **zanqa** chin (cf. PolG).

זעטוטה, זעזוטה (OA/IrAr) pl. **zaᶜṭūṭe. zaᶜzūṭe** mischievous kids, children.

זעפראן (Ar) ⁺**zaᶜfaran** saffron; cf. גואא (NT+).

זעתר, זַעְטַאר (Ar) ⁺**zaᶜtar** thyme; hyssop (=H אֵזוֹב, BT2; PolG).

זפא (< ?) m. ⁺**zappa** large and thick excrement [=MacD **zapī, zirpī** chubby, plump female?].

זפתי (Ar) adj. **zıfti** unliked: מכרוה ונוא וזפתי **makrūh wınwa uzıfti** I was detested and unliked (NTU4 184a).

זקארא, זקרתא (OS) **zaqāra, zaqarta** weaver.

ז-ק-י (OA זקר?) vi **z-q-y** to stick out; have an erection; לשיה גמעאביה...גמזאקיה **lašše gımᶜābe ...gımzāqe** His body swells and sticks out (AmU2 5b).

זקן (H) m. **zāqēn** (learned) old man (BaBin 141); also family name: **bē-zāqen** the Zaqen family; pl. זקנים, זקינים **zaqēnīm** (RivSh 179); cf. ריספי, סאוא.

ז-ק-נ-ב (IrAr) **z-q-n-b** to eat poison (said when angry at someone).

זקנבות (K/IrAr) **zaqnabūt** (Eat)poison! Go to hell [cf. Blanc 151].

זקנות (H) **zıqnūṯ** old-age (=H זֹקֶן/זִקְנָה, BT1); cf. סיבותא.

ז-ק-פ (OA) **z-q-p** to raise (eyes) (NT2).

ז-ק-ר (OS زمر; OA stand up straight < Ak **zaqāru** build up high) **z-q-r** to weave.

ז-ר-א (OA זרע) **z-r-ʾ** to sow, to seed; IV to be sown (=H נִזְרַע, BT4).

זרא, צ̇רא (P زر old person?) inv. ⁺**zarra** huge (cf. PolG); **pıšle xa - gōra** He has become a huge man [cf. MacD 89 **zarā** gigantic].

זראא (OA זרעא) m. **zarʾa** seed, descendants (=H זֶרַע, PolG:Haggadah); cf. בר-זראא.

זראבוכה (K?) f. **zırāvōke** alley, path (Avin88 229); beautiful and nimble woman.

זראייכה (K) f. **zarāyīke** cold sweat (cf. PolG).

זראקא (< ז-ר-ק 1) **zrāqa** sunshine, east (NT4); ד- מדיתא **zrāqıd mdīta** east of town (NT6 136).

זראתא (< ז-ר-א) f. (p.p.) **zreʾta** vegetation, seed grain; cf. זרואתא.

זרב (K/P < Ar ضرب) **zarb** force; miracle (NT); בזרב **bzarb** strong, aggressive, strict (NT2), reluctantly (Z); terrible; כדא בלא בש בזרב מכולו **xda bala bıš bzarb mkullu** A trouble worse than all others (NT5 389).

זרבא, צ̇רבא (Ar) f. **zarba** (NT), ⁺**zarba** (Z), blow, stroke; plague; pl. ⁺**zarbıtyāṯa**; cf. דרבא.

זרביגכה, צ̇רביג̆כה (K?) f. ⁺**zırvījke** melted cheese.

ז-ר-ג (Ar زرك press against) ⁺**z-r-g** to (lewdly) penetrate; to sire (vulgar); to pierce (by lance) (PolU 75), push oneself against (snake:woman) (PolU 373).

זרג̆כונכא (K زرج) **zırčkonka** 'farter, wind-blower', weakling (PolU 34)

זרדאבה, צ̇רדאבה (K/P 'bile') f. ⁺**zardāve** poison.

ז-ר-ד-פ/ב (< זרדאבה) ⁺**z-r-d-f/v** to eat poison (said when angry at someone) (cf. PolU 413); cf. ז-ק-נ-ב.

זרדב, צ̇רדף (K/P/Ar سرداب) ⁺**zardav/f** cellar.

זרדיתא, צ̇רדיתא (< Ar زرد strangle?) ⁺**zarradīṯa** tantrum; **duqla ʾılle ⁺zarradīṯa** He has a tantrum attack.

זרואתא (< ז-ר-א) f. **zroʾta** vegetation, seeds (cf. PolG); cf. זראתא (NT+).

זרוכה (K) f. **zarōke** child bride (PolU).

זרוקא, זרוקתא (< ז-ר-ק 2) adj. **zrōqa, zruqta** blue.

ז-ר-ז-א III (OA זעזע) vt/vi **z-r-z-ʾ** to shake; **šımme uʾarʾa mzurzeʾlu ṭāle** heaven and earth shivered for him (at his death)(PolG);

to move the audience by chanting well (NT+).

זרזורא (OA זרזירא) **zarzūra** starling (RivP 211).

ז-ר-ז-פ III (OA) **z-r-z-p** to leak or drip profusely.

ז-ר-ז-ר III (K) **z-r-z-r** to beg with crying emotional voice.

זרזרתא v. זורזורתא

זרי(-כונזרי) (T/K/P **zirih**) **zıri(-kunzıri)** coat of mail (=H תַּחְרָא, BT2), armour (FT) [RivSh 233, 241 זירי וכום זירי **ziri ukum ziri**; **kum** = helmet, K].

זריזא (OA) **zrīza** competent, eloquent (BaBin 126, 151).

זריזותא (OA) **zrīzūṯa** diligence (NT3).

זרייכת (K?) pl. **zarayíkat** drops of sweat (Pol 111).

זרינג זרינג (onomat.) ⁺**zrıng** ⁺**zrıng** sound of key turning in a lock (PolU 232).

זריף (T< Ar ظريف) **zarif** good-looking, elegant (RivSh 265); cf. ז-ר-פ.

זרך (K) **zarık** jaundice.

זרכי (K) **zarki** mildew (=H יֵרָקוֹן, BT5, D).

זרכאנא (K) **zırkāna** (one with) jaundice, scurvy, boil-scar (=H גָּרָב, יַלֶּפֶת, BT3).

צֿרנה, זורנה, זרנה (K/T) f. ⁺**zı/ürne** shrill flute (played together with drum in weddings); **nōʿıt** - =H כְּלֵי זֶמֶר, PolG); pl. זורנאייה **zurnāye** (AmU2 6a; PolU 18); - **nuqra** = H סִפּוֹת כֶּסֶף, PolG: 2Kg 12:14 [Mutz 242]

זרניך (K/P/Ar < Gr) ⁺**zırnix** arsenic.

זרע (H) **zēraʿ** seed, descendants (NT2).

ז-ר-פ II (ظرف) **z-r-f** to be good looking, plump (=H סֹכֶנֶת, PolG: 1Kg 1:4); cf. זריף, דהינא.

ז-ר-ק 1 (OA scatter) **z-r-q** to shine, scatter light (NT4; Hob89 224) (=H זָרַח, BT1, D); cf. זראקא [cf. Mutz 242].

ז-ר-ק 2 (Ar) **z-r-q** to turn blue (due to cold); **yrıqle-zrıqle** was neglected, left unattended; became very fearful (MeAl 188); cf. זרוקא.

זרקתא, צֿרקתא (K **zerket**) f. ⁺**zarraqta** wasp, hornet; pl. ⁺**zarraqyāṯa** [cf. MacD 90 **zereqṭa**; OA ערעיתא, אורעיתא; H צרעה].

ז' (ž)

ז'-, שׁ- (K ži/OA ריש). ž-/š- on, over, on acount of, due to; **qṭıllu xa-ʾawxıt žde (/šde/rıš de/) xaʾ** They killed each other because of this one; v. ז'ג'פלתי, ז'נגבא, ז'נו.

ז'אן, שׁאן (K) **žān** sharp pain (=H חִיל, BT2; AvidH 50, 61; RivSh117); pl. ז'אנה **žāne** suffering, pains (NT); birth pangs (Z).

ז'אר(ה) (K) **žār, -e** (f.) poor; usually with פקיר (cf. PolG; PolU 207).

ז'-ג'-ל v. שׁ-ג'-ל

בְשְׁכַפְלַתִי, אֶשְׁכַפְלַתִי, אל, רש כפלתי, ז'ג'פלתי, כפלתי (K-Ar) adv. **ž/ıš/rıš/ʾıl/bıš ġ/xaflati** suddenly (BT4; = H בַּלָּט, PolG); cf. ג'פלה.

ז'האתי (K) inv. **žıhāti** good, nice (PolU 117).

ז'וזייא, גֻוגִ'יַיא (K) f. **žūžīya, jūjīya** hedgehog (Z); bustard (=H רָחָם, BT3, D); sand lizard (=H חֹמֶט, BT3, D) [cf. Mutz 242 **žūžık**].

ז'חר, גַחִיר, שׁחיר, גהר (K) **žaḥ(ḥ)ar** (cf. PolG), **žaḥer, žahır** (Sa83c 32, Am), **žaḥḥarīye** (PolU 108), poison (=H רֹאשׁ, BT5); pl גחרוותא **žaḥrawāṯa** (BaBin 102, 118).

ז'חראנא, גהראנא (< ז'חר) adj. **žaḥḥrāna** (Z, PolG, BaBin 116), **žah-** (NT5 384), poisonous.

ז'י v. שׁי

ז'ירנז'יר, ז'ירא-ז'ירא(K **žīrīn**) inv. **žēra(n)-žēr(a)** idiot, unimportant person (NT+).

ז'נגבא, רש נגבא (K **žiniškive**) **ž-/rıž-nıgva** suddenly (BT4; PolG).

ז'נו (K) **ž-nu** at last; only now/then; **basır mıtla yımme, žnu gurre** After his mother died, only then he got married; also: **bıžnūt, mıžnīd** (Pol 106; MeAl 193; PolU 428) .

ז'נוכא (K) **žnūka** only then, only now (PolG).

ז'נו-פיבא (K) **žnu-pēva** once again, anew.

ח (ḥ)

ח (H) ḥēṯ (Z ḥēs) Heth, the eighth letter in the Hebrew alphabet; **tmanya** eight.

חאדק (Ar) inv. **ḥāḏıq** sharp, intelligent (NT3; Sa83c 34, Am).

חאדר v. חאצ̇ר

חאכם, חיכם (Ar) **ḥākım, ḥēkım** (+NT), ruler, judge; cf. ח-כ-מ (NT+).

חאל (Ar) m. **ḥāl** situation, state (of health, etc.); **bē-ḥāl** very sick; often as hendiadys: **ḥāl-u-qısta/ḥawāl dīdi ʾēha-la** This is my story or the events that occurred to me (MeAl 182); **hatxa mınnox umın ḥālox** Curse upon you (PolU 431); **hatxa** pl. חואלה **ḥawāle** (NT5 403) (NT+).

חאלן (Ar) adv. **ḥālan** right away (cf. PolU 243).

חאצא (Ar/P حصّه) **ḥāṣa** share (of crops given to a ruler as tax) (PolU 1); cf. זוזא.

חאצלבן v. חצלבן

חאצל מרד (K<Ar) **ḥāṣıl mırad** an ideal child, one who is a wish come true.

חאצ̇ר, חאדר (Ar) **ḥāẓır, ḥād/ḏır** (NT), right away, ready, at your service; pl. חאצ̇רין **ḥāẓırīn** the present audience; שוקלה כאייה אבד חאצ̇רין **šuqle xāye ʾıbbıd ḥāẓırīn** He has deceased ('left life to those present here').

חאשך v. חשא

חבאבא (SA [Denizeau] 'sage femme') f. **⁺ḥabbāba** sheikh's wife (honorific title) (PolUR 48).

ח-ב-ב v. ח-י-ב

חבדנה v. חבורה

חבה (Ar) f. **hıbbe** love, affection; cf. מחוביה (NT+).

חבובא, חבי, חבו (Ar) **ḥabbūba, ḥabe/o** (hypo.) Beloved (f. name).

חבורה (K/Ar?) f. **ḥabbōre** a woman who is 'too' smart; **ḥabbōre-ḥabbadane** 'super smart' woman.

חביבא, חבבתא (Ar) adj. **ḥabība, ḥabıbta** beloved; pl. חביבין **ḥabībīn** (NT), **ḥabībe**.

חביסא, חבסתא (< ח-ב-ס) p.p. **ḥbīsa, ḥbısta** jailed.

ח-ב-כ II (Ar) **ḥ-b-k** to join (=H חִבֵּר, PolG).

חבכ-לבכ (Ar) **ḥabbık-labbık** 'Open sesame!'.

חבכא (Ar-K) f. **ḥabbıka** pill; pl. **ḥabbıkat.**

חבלוטייה (Ar?) **hıblōṭīye** hyper-activity.

ח-ב-ס (Ar) **ḥ-b-s** to jail (NT+).

חבס (Ar) m. **ḥabıs** jail, prison (cf. PolG).

חבראיא (H-OA) m. **ḥavrāya** member of burial society; cf. שיך.

חברא קדישא (H-OA) **ḥevra qaddīša** burial society (PolU 204).

חבש (Ar) **ḥabaš** Abyssinia, Kush (BT1) (NT+).

חבשאייה (Ar) pl. **ḥabašāye** Abyssinians (NT3).

חגאמא (Ar) f. **ḥajāma** cupping, blood-letting.

ח-ג̇-ג̇ II2 (Ar) **ḥ-j-j** to plot against, seek a pretext to attack someone (=H לְהִתְגּוֹלֵל, BT21). cf. חושתא; מחגגאנא.

חגול(-) (< Ar?) **ḥajul-māya** water spirit/ghost (?) PolU

חגולכא (Ar-K) m. **ḥıjūlka** anklet; pl. **ḥıjūlkat.**

חגומה (Ar 'muzzled') f. **ḥajūme** a woman wrapped-up by head scarf.

חג̇י, חג̇ייא (k< Ar) **ḥajji** (m.), **ḥajjīya** (f.), (Mecca) pilgrim; **ḥajji-⁺bāba** Hadji-Monster(a fictitious name to frighten children with); **ḥajji-laglag** stork; v. כוסיתא.

חג̇יאתא v. חשתא

חג̇י חסן (Ar) **ḥajji ḥasan** kind of fabric (PolU 214).

ח-ג̇-מ, ה-ג̇-מ (Ar) vi **ḥ-j-m, h-j-m** (+NT), to calm down.

חד (Ar 'border') **ḥad(d-)** daring; **ḥaddıd manīle** Who dares (to); **latle ḥad** He doesn't dare (to)[cf Khan 570 **ḥadd** impetuosity].

חדאדא (Ar) m. **ḥadāda** iron smith.

חדיקא (Ar) f. **ḥadīqa** garden, park; pl. **ḥadīqat**; cf. ג̇יניכה, חודא.

ח-ד-פ (OA הדף?) **ḥ-d-f** to cast away (NT5 408); cf. ח-ר-ד-פ [=MacD 97 **x-z-p?**].

חדקותא, חדקא (Ar?) f. **ḥadaqūṯa, ḥadaqa** impudence.

ח-ד̇-ר v. ח-צ̇-ר

חו-חו (onomat) **ḥaw-ḥaw** barking (PolU

116).

חואלא/ה (Ar transaction) f. **ḥawāla** money-order, unpaid bill (PolU 248); **-a/-e** a step from a high roof to a lower one, earth bench (SaAC 15).

חואלה v. חאל

חוברא (Ar) f. **ḥubra** ink (NT+).

חוגנא (IrAr<Ar حقنه) f. **ḥugna** enema.

חוג׳יאתא v. חושתא

חוג̆א (< כואג̆א?) **ḥōča** Hocha common Jewish family name in Zakho

חווג̆א (K<Ar) **ḥawja** need, only in **la-ḥawja** It isn't necessary, no need (MeAl 190; PolG).

חודא (K<Ar حوض) f. **ḥōda** (home) garden.

חוזור, חצ̇ור (Ar) ⁺**ḥızur** prediction, possibility (Pol 107); **la ʾuzle ⁺ḥuzur did bāsetun ʾıdyo** He didn't realize that you would come today; cf. ח-ז-ר.

ח-ו-י (Ar/K) vi/vt **ḥ-w-y** find shelter; provide a place to live, to accomodate (cf. PolG).

חֲוֵיג̆יבֵּי (Ar covers) pl. **ḥawējıbe** genitals (=the covered ones, euph. for H מְבוּשִׁים, BT5, D).

חוכום, חוכם, חכם (Ar) m. **ḥukum, ḥıkım** rule, jurisdiction, power (NT+).

חוכמה, חכמה (H) f. **ḥoxma** wisdom (NT+).

חול (H) m. **ḥōl** secular; **ʾ-w-ḏ ḥōl** to desecrate (=H חִלֵּל, BT1); cf. ח-י-ל.

חוול-בלא (Ar) f. **ḥawwıl-bala** trouble; cf. 1 בלא.

חוסן, חסן (Ar) m. **ḥüsın**, often as hendiadys: **ḥusn-u-jamal** (FT), beauty, grace (=H חֵן, BT) (NT+).

חופה (H) f. **ḥuppa** bridal chamber; cf. גנונה, כפו; mantle for the Torah scroll.

חוצה לארץ, חוץ לארץ (H) **ḥūṣ(a) laʾareṣ** outside of Ancient Israel (NT).

חוצלבן v. חצלבאן

חוצראתא (< חצר?) pl. **ḥuṣrāṯa** graves, holes (= H חוֹרים, AmU2 5a).

חוק (H) **ḥōq** law, rule, decree; **ʾ-w-ḏ ḥōq** to rule, decree (NT).

חוקא 1 (IrAr)f. **ḥuqqa** Iraqi oka (about 3 kg); v. וקייא.

חוקא 2 (OA/OS חֲווּקָא step of stair < Ak **xūqu**?) m. **ḥuqqa** rung (of a ladder).

חור, חורייא (Ar) **ḥūr** (NT), **ḥōrīya** (Z), nymph, fairy woman; - **baḥıšte** paradise beautiful woman (PolU 18); pl. **ḥōrīyat.**

חורא 1 (Ar) f. **ḥōra** bark-tanned sheepskin used for bookbinding.

חורא 2 (< ח-י-ר?) **ḥōra** ? mystery (?) (NTU4 157b).

חורא ודורא (Ar) f. **ḥurra udurra** free and (precious like) a pearl (PolU 343)

חורזא (Ar حرز) m. **ḥurza** necklace amulet.

חורייא V. חור

חורייתא (Ar) f. **ḥorīyıta** freedim (PolU 19).

חורין (H) **ḥōrīn** free people, not-slaves (NT2).

חורמיה, חורם, חרם (Ar) f. ⁺**ḥurm(e), ḥırım** (PolU 153), lady, wife. NT+

חויש (Ar) m. **ḥōš** (Z), **ḥaw/vıš** (BT2, Arodh; Hob89 183), courtyard; pl. **ḥōše** (Z), חַוְשִׁיֵי **ḥawšīye** (AvidH 62).

חושמה (Ar<T) f. **ḥušme** glory, pomp (NT3).

חוֹשֶׁן (H) **ḥōšen** breastpiece (BT3, D); cf. טליסם; **qčīn ḥōšen/⁺ḥēṭ uqčın mıšpāṭ** a very large number (of armies) (PolU 355, 384).

חושתא (K/Ar حُجَّة **ḥujjat**) f. **ḥušta** pretext; **mampıl/dāwıq/⁺mārım ḥušta** He uses a pretext, plots against (NT2, BT1) **q-ṭ-ʾ** - to thwart a plot (NT5 383); pl. חוג̆יאתא **ḥujyāṯa** (=H עֲלִילוֹת, BT5), **ḥuštyāsa** (PolG) (NT+).

חות 1 (Ar) m. **ḥūt** crocodile; pl. **ḥūte** (=H תַּנִּינִים, BT1).

חות 2 (K **hewd** 'cage') **ḥōt** encircled, trapped; **ʾ-w-z** - to trap, encircle (PolU 4).

חזו חֲלִילָה v. חס ושלום

חִיזֻורְתָּא, חוזרתא, חזורתא (< ח-ז-ר) f. **ḥüzurta, ḥızurta** riddle (NTU4 161a; =H שְׁנִינָה, PolG); sigh (?) (AvidH 52); pl. **ḥüzuryāṯa**.

חזינה (Ar) f. **ḥazīne** mourning; **ṣōm ḥazīne** the Fast of the Ninth of Ab.

חזיקא, חזקתא (< ח-ז-ק) adj. **ḥzīqa. ḥzıqta** strong.

ח-ז-מ (Ar) **ḥ-z-m** to fasten (belt) (cf. PolG).

ח-ז-נ (Ar) **ḥ-z-n** to mourn, to grieve (NT+).

חזן 1, חזין (Ar) m. **ḥızın** mourning, grief (NT+).

חזן 2 (H; OA חזאנא sexton < Ak **xazānnu** mayor) m. **ḥazzan** cantor, person leading the prayer; **bē-ḥazzāne** the Cantors' House (an old synagogue and shrine in Amidya).'

ח-ז-ק (OA/OS/Ar/AnAr/H) **ḥ-z-q** to be strong; IV to fasten, make strong (cf. PolG).

חזק ברוך (H) **ḥı/azzāq bārūx** Bravo! Well said! (cf. PolU 105, 254).

חַזַקִי (K/Ar?) **ḥazaqi** piercing thorn (?) (RivSh 115).

ח-ז-ר (Ar) ***ḥ-z-r** to predict, estimate (NT); reckon with (Pol 107; PolG); cf. חוזור חזורתא,.

חזרת (Ar) **ḥazrat** kind of fabric (PolU 214).

חטא (H) **ḥēṭ** sin (NT2); v. חושן.

חטאטא (IrAr?) f. **ḥaṭāṭa** white linen scarf.

ח-ט-ח-ט III (K?) **ḥ-ṭ-ḥ-ṭ** to be amorously excited.

חי, חאייכא (H 'alive') **ḥāy(īka)** p.n.m. Hay.

חיא (Ar) **ḥaya** shame; **bē-šarm ubē-ḥaya** totally shameless (NT+).

חיאת (Ar 'life') inv. **ḥayāt** very enjoyable.

ח-י-ב IV (Ar حب) **ḥ-y-b** to love, be in love with [1: **mōḥıb-**; 2/3: **māḥıb**; 4: **maḥōbe**] (NT+).

חיב, חייב (H) inv. **ḥayyāv** guilty (NT+).

ח-י-ד (< Ar حيد) vi **ḥ-y-d** to settle down; used mostly with negative: **la kḥāyıd lču dūka** He can't settle down anywhere, he is restless; **lak ḥēdīwa lbēsa** They would not stay at home (Zaken 387; cf. PolG).

חִידָא (H) **ḥīda** riddle (RivSh 215).

חי העולמים (H) **ḥē-haᶜōlāmīm** the Eternal One (NT2).

חיון (Ar) m. **ḥēwan** (Z), **ḥaywan** (BT1, Am), animal; pl. **ḥēwāne**, **ḥaywāne** (BT2, Arodh); cf. בהמה (NT+).

חי (ו)קיים (H) **ḥāy (wa)qayyām** the Eternal One (Ruth 3:13; AvidH 53; NT5 405); cf. קיים.

חיזה (K libertine<P sodomy) f. **ḥīze** one who leads dissolute life (PolU 218).

חיזרן (K [< IrAr **hayzar**] < OA חִיזְרָא, היזרא type of thorn) m. **ḥayzaran** bamboo cane; **qōmıd ḥayzaran** willowy body [Khan 584 **xayzaran**].

חיי העה"ב (H) **ḥayyē haᶜōlām habbā** eternal life (NT2).

חיים, חיו (H) p.n.m **ḥayim, ḥayyo** Hayyim.

חייכ (K?) interj. **ḥayk** Damn! (PolU 148).

חיכם v. חאכם

חיל 1 (IrAr) adv. (push, pull) with vigor (Avin78 95; = H חָזָק, PolG; SaAC 12).

חיל 2 v. האל

ח-י-ל 1 (H-OA) **ḥ-y-l** to be desecrated; **šabsi ḥılla** My Sabbath became desecrated/violated; IV to violate, desecrate [1:**mōḥıl-**; 2:**māḥıl**; 4:**maḥōle**]; cf. חול.

ח-י-ל 2 (Ar حل) **ḥ-y-l** to be permitted: **ma ḥıllēli/ḥılli mın ᵓilāha** What right do I have to...(lit., is permitted to me by God) (PolG; PolU4).

ח-י-ל 3 IV (Ar) **ḥ-y-l** to cheat (BT1, D).

חילא-מלא (K strength of shoulders) **ḥēla mıla**: **b-**very vigorously, with energy (PolU 251).

חילאנא, חילנתא (< חילה) **ḥīlāna, ḥīlanta** deceptor.

חילה, חִילֵי, חילתא (Ar) f. **ḥīle** (Z), **ḥīlıta** (NT5 394), ruse (=H מִרְמָה, PolG); **ᵓ-w-ḏ ḥīle** to cheat; pl **ḥīlıtyāṯa** (NT+).

חילתא (< חיל 1?) f. **ḥē/īlıta** courage; **mare-ḥīlıta** (inv.) courageous, strong.

חין (Ar) **ḥīn** age; **bxa ḥīn** (children) of same age (RivSh 264).

חיף (K<Ar) interj. **ḥēf** (also: **ḥēf umġabīne**, **ḥēf uṣat ḥēf**) What a loss! (RivSh 229).

חייפה, חיפי (Ar) **ḥayfe** (NT3), **ḥēfi** (Z), vengeance, retribution (cf. PolG).

ח-י-ר (Ar) ***ḥ-y-r** to wonder, be perplexed; **ḥırri bḥāli/bıgyāni** I am at a loss, don't know what to do (cf. PolG); II/IV to confuse.

חירותא (< ח-י-ר) **ḥīrūṯa** confusion (PolG).

חירחיר(תא) (K) **ḥīrḥīr(ta)** loud laughter.

ח-י-ש (Ar حوش) **ḥ-y-š** to penetrate, push in.

חישא, חשתא (< ח-י-ש) p.p. **ḥīša, ḥīšta** pushed-in (PolG).

חית, חטא v. חושן

חכאיתא (Ar) f. **ḥıkāyıta** story, event, case; pl. חכאיתיאתא **ḥıkāyıtyāṯa** (NT5 395) (NT+).

חכומא 1 (< ח-כ-מ) m. **ḥakōma** king., noble person; cf. מחכמא; pl. **ḥakōme** (NT+).

חכומא 2 (Ar) f. **ḥıkūma** government, authority.

חכומתא (< חכומא 1) **ḥakumta** queen, noble lady; pl. **ḥakumyāṯa** (cf. PolG).

חכותא, חוכיתא (< ח-כ-י) f. **ḥıkkōṯa** (Z), **ḥukkiṯa** (Hob89 27) folktale, story; pl. **ḥıkkōyāṯa**.

ח-כ-י II (NT)/IV (Z; but Hob89 218, PolG: II/VI)(Ar) **ḥ-k-y** to speak.

חכים (Ar) inv. **ḥakim** healer; **sāra /sımḥa ḥakim** Sara/Simha the healer. pl. **ḥakīme**.

ח-כ-מ (Ar) **ḥ-k-m** to rule, be in charge; to sentence; cf. מחכמא, חכומא, חאכם; IV to appoint as a ruler (NT+).

חכם (H) m./f. **ḥāxām** (+Z **xāḥām**) sage, rabbi; **pıšla xa qarēsa, ḥāxām** She became a reader, a sage (PolU 310); pl. חכמים **ḥāxāmīm, -īn, ḥāxāmīne** (MeAl 179) (NT+).

חכם באשי (H-T) **ḥāxām bāši** Chief Rabbi; חכם באשותא **ḥāxām bāšūṯa** the position of the Chief Rabbi.

חלאוה (Ar) f. **ḥalāwe** halva; **wın xīla laxma u- ʾımme** We are good friends (lit., We have eaten bread and halva together) (PolU 25).

חלאוג׳י (Ar/T) **ḥalāwči** halva-maker/seller.

חלאל(א) (Ar) **ḥalāl(a)** lawful, kosher; **ḥalāla x-pısır ġazāla** As kosher as gazelle's meat (= very kosher); **baxta ḥalāl/ḥalalta** lawful wife; cf. אשה כשרה; **wald-ıl-ḥalāl** honest, good person (NT+).

חלאלותא (< חלאל) f. **ḥalālūṯa** legality, kosher rules.

חלאלזאדא (Ar-P) inv. **ḥalālzāda** honest, rigteous (PolU 309); cf. ולד-אלחלאל.

חלאנא (K **hīlān**) m. **ḥıllāna** flat large flintstone (used for pavement, as well as baking of double face bread).

חלאקא (Ar) m. **ḥalāqa** barber; cf. גראאה.

חלה, חלא (H) **ḥa/ılla** Hallah, a small portion of dough thrown into the fire before baking (BT4; NT5 410).

חלו (Ar) **ḥılw** jam (Gz73 75); cf. מרבא.

חלוכא (K) f. **ḥılūka** plum; pl. **ḥılūke**.

חלולא v. הלולא

חלול שבת (H) **ḥıllūl šabbāṯ** desecrating the Sabbath. NT+

חלוסה (K?) **ḥalūse** a game of pebbles and board.

ח-ל-ח-ל III (Ar/K) **ḥ-l-ḥ-l** to melt (vi/vt), to crush (soul)(BaBin 115), excite (by singing well).

חלחלתא (< ח-ל-ח-ל) f. **ḥalḥalta** excitement; rush, exhaustion (sounds) (PolU 396)

חליק (JAB < OA חליקא/ הליקה) m. **ḥıllıq** mixture of nuts and dates eaten on Passover night (=H חרוסת; cf. Gz73 58; v. Avishur 1993a:44-45; SokBA 463).

ח-ל-ל II (Ar) **ḥ-l-l** to permit, consider kosher (NT5 411).

חלקון, חלקום (Ar) **ḥalqum/n** Turkish delight.

חלקושכה (< חלקתא) f. **ḥalaqoške** link, loop, ring; pl. **ḥalaqoškat** (cf. PolG).

חלק לעוה"ב (H) **ḥēleq lıᶜōlām habbā** a share in the world to come. NT+

חלקיז (< האל+כס?) **ḥalqiz** (?) even, so much so, to the point that (NT2; NTU4 153b).

חלקתא (Ar) f. **ḥalaqta** link, loop (one made of goat's hair serves as amulet against headache); pl. **ḥalaqyāṯa**; cf. חלקושכה.

חמאלא (Ar) m **ḥammāla** porter [cf. Khan 570 ***ḥambāla**].

חמאלותא (< חמאלא) f. **ḥammālūṯa** porterage (cf. PolU 145)

חמאמה (Ar) f. **ḥamāme** dove (BT3, D); female name (Z); v. יונה, כותרכא.

ח-מ-ב-ש III (< ח-ב-ש-ש) **ḥ-m-b-š** to become fat, gigantic.

חמבשאיא, חמבשיתא (< Ar **ḥabašī** Abyysinian/ turkey?) **ḥambıšāya, -ēṯa** giant, tall and fat person (cf. PolG); cf. כפורא.

ח-מ-ד (Ar) **ḥ-m-d** to praise (NT4; NTU4 150b); cf. ח-ב-ס.

חמד- (Ar praise) **ḥamd-** composure; זליה מחמדיה **zılle mḥamde** He was in panic, left his senses (NT2); **bḥamdox** At your ease; Don't rush yourself (Z; =H לְאִטְּךָ, PolG) (NT+).

עַל חַמְדִילַא, חמדלא, לחמד ללאה (ושכר) (Ar) **ḥámdılla (ušıkır), lḥamd lıllāh** (NT2), **ᶜal ḥamdila** (PolG); **el ḥámd-illa šíker** (Socin 165); Thank God.

חמה (< Ar حُمَّى heat/OA חמא sickness, SokBA 467) **ḥımme** curse, poison, sickness (?), used as a pun on וימלא הָמָן חֵמָה , when recited in the synagogue on Purim, the congregation responds: **ḥımme ṭāle uta yımme** sickness to him and his mother!

חמו, חמינא (< רחמים) **ḥamo, ḥamīna** hypo. forms of Rahamim, male p.n.

חם-חה (K) **ḥım-ḥah** indicates a start of galloping (PolU 47).

ח-מ-ל (Ar carry) **ḥ-m-l** to stand; חאמל קם אינך **ḥāmıl qam ʾēnax** May he be appreciated by you; **dunye ḥmılla ḥmāla** The air is standing still (=oppressive heat); **bıkma ḥmıllu ʾıllox** How much did they cost you? (cf. PolU 228); **ḥmılle rıš lıbbi** I have a heartburn; **ḥmōl ḥivīti** Wait for me! **ḥmōl ʾılli** Give me a grace period (to pay a debt); IV to rest (vt), make one stand or stop. NT+

חמם (Ar) **ḥammam** bath; **ʾ-w-z gyāna – l/namiš** She had a thorough (?) bath (PolG; PolU 216; PolUR 35); pl. **ḥammāme**.

ח-מ-ס II (IrAr<Ar **ḥ-m-ṣ**) **ḥ-m-s** to sauté.

חמץ (H) **ḥāmēṣ** leavened bread; cf. כמירא.

חמרא-פודרא (IrAr) **ḥamra-podra** make-up, rouge-powder and lipstick.

חמר-וחש (Ar) m. **ḥamır-waḥš** wild ass (=H פֶּרֶא אָדָם, BT1).

חמש (H חֻמָּשׁ Pentateuch) m. **ḥámmaš, ḥím-** (Gz73 75), any (Jewish) book (=H סֵפֶר, BT2); pl. חֻמָּאשֵׁי **há/ímmāše** (cf. PolG).

חֵן (H) **ḥēn** grace (BT2, D); cf. חוסן;חן וחסד **ḥēn-u-ḥēse(d)** grace and kindness.

חנא (Ar; cf. OA/OS חִינָּא) f. **ḥınna** henna.

חנג-ודנג (K) **ḥıng-u-dıng** sounds and mouvments of energetic dancing (PolU 18).

ח-נ-ד-ל III (< Ar be a dwarf?) **ḥ-n-d-l** to pamper, be playful; often as hendiadys with ש-נ-ד-ל.

חנדל-חות (Ar/K?) **ḥındıl-ḥōt** seesaw.

חנה, חנוכה (H) **ḥanna, ḥannōke** Hanna, Annie.

חנוך (H) **ḥınnūx** dedication; אודלה חנוך **ʾudle ḥınnūx** He dedicated (the Temple) (NT3).

חנוכה (H) **ḥanu/ıkka** Hanukkah Holiday/ candelabrum; **ḥanukka bammāyim,barāxa mıššāmāyim** Rain on Hanukkah is a blessing from Heaven; also male p.n.

חנונא, חנונתא (Ar/H) adj. **ḥanūna, ḥanunta** tenderhearted.

חנופה, חנופכרותא (H) **ḥınūfa , ḥınūfkarūta** flattery, malice; א-ו-ד חִינֻופָא **ʾ-w-d ḥınūfa** to flatter, bring evil (=H הֶחֱנִיף, BT4, D).

חנופכר(ה) (H-K) **ḥınūfkar(e)** flatterer, malicious (woman).

ח-נ-נ II2 (H) **ḥ-n-n** to beg, plead (NT2; BT1, D; =H הִתְחַנֵּן, PolG).

חנפייה (IrAr) f. **ḥanafīye** faucet; pl. **ḥanafīyat** (Gz73 75).

חנק (K) **ḥanaq** frivolity (NT); pl. חנאקה **ḥanāqe**; **ʾ-w-d** - to mock (Sa83c 22, Am).

חנרה v. הנר

חס (Ar) **ḥıs(s)** voice, sound; חסוך **ḥıssox** Be careful; חסיכון ובאליכון **ḥıssēxu ubālēxun** Be very careful; לא חס ולא פיג'ין **la ḥıs ula pējın** total silence; cf. קאלא.

חסאדא, חסדתא (< ח-ס-ד) adj. **ḥasāda, ḥasadta** jealous, envious.

חסאסא/י (Ar/K) **ḥasāsa/i** guard, night watchman (PolU 25); **ḥasāso wara mın bıgra** Guard, come and catch me (=If you're a thief, don't stop to talk to the guard).

ח-ס-ב II (Ar) **ḥ-s-b** to reckon (NTU4 184b)

חסד 1, חסאד (Ar) **ḥasad** envy (NT2).

חסד 2 v. חן

ח-ס-ד (Ar) **ḥ-s-d** to envy; to put the evil eye on someone (SaAC 24).

חס ושלום (H) **ḥāz-u-šālōm**, חַזו, חס וחלילה חֲלִילָה **ḥāz-u ḥalīla**, God forbid! Far be it! (= H חָלִילָה, BT1, D); cf. חשא (NT+).

חסיד (H) **ḥāsīḏ** (Z **ḥāsīz**) pious man; pl. **ḥasīḏīm**.

חסנה (Ar) **ḥısne** Grace (f.p.n.).

חסקו (H יחזקאל) **ḥasqo** Ezekiel (Hypo).

ח-פ-פ II2 (Ar) **ḥ-f-f** to cure or depilate.

ח-ב-צ, ח-פ-צ̇ (Ar) **ḥ-f/v-ẓ**, to keep (for the future), to maintain religious duties. (NT, BaBin 60).

ח-פ-ק v. כ-פ-ק

חפתיארא (K **keftar** hyena?) m. **ḥaftyāra** monstrous animal.

חצי שלי חצי שלוך (H) **ḥāṣi šılli, ḥaṣi šıllox** half (of the earnings in this deal) are mine and half are yours (crypt.).

חצירא (Ar) m. **ḥaṣīra** straw mat (cf. PolG).

ח-צ-ל (Ar) **ḥ-ṣ-l** to be made, to result, happen; חצליה **ḥṣılle** He was born, created (NT2); **ḥaṣli ⁺mırādōx** May your wishes come true; IV to fulfill (wishes); to earn, make profit.

חוצלבן, חאצלבן, חצלבאן (Ar غُصن اللُّبان galbanum) **ḥaṣılban** (NT), **ḥuṣılban** (Z) frankincense (=H שְׁחֵלֶת, BT2) [cf. SokBA 461 ad חלבניתא: = עסל אללבני ,عسل اللّبني milkey honey].

ח-צ-ר 1 II(Ar حسر) **ḥ-ṣ-r** to sigh, long for (NT+).

ח-צ-ר 2 II (Ar) **ḥ-ṣ-r** to besiege. NT+

חצר (Ar) **ḥıṣ(ṣ)ar** fortress, fortified (town)(=H מִבְצָר, BT4); pl. **ḥıṣ(ṣ)āre**.

חצרא, חסרא (Ar حسرة) f. **ḥaṣra** sigh; pl. /חצ סראתא **ḥaṣ/srāṯa** (Sa83c 20, Am; NTU1 43b), חצריתייאתא **ḥaṣrıtyāṯa** (BaBin 101).

חץ̇ (Ar) m. **ḥaẓ(ẓ)** luck (SaAC 17); cf. אקבל.

חצור v. חוזור

ח-ד-ר, ח-צ̇-ר (Ar) **ḥ-ẓ/ḍ-r** to be present, to attend; חצ̇ריה לכסלא **ḥẓırre lkısla** He slept with her (euph.); II to speak well of (NT2); IV to prepare, summon, bring (cf. PolG) NT+

חק(א) (Ar) m. **ḥaq(qa)** true; price (Z) **ḥaqqe kmaʾīle** How much does it cost? **ʾ-x-l** - to be delinquent on paying debts (PolU 432); **bḥaqqa** truly, justly; בחקא לה **bḥaqqa-le** He is right; פלטלה מחקד **plıṯle mḥaqqıd** He complied, retributed; succeeded; **šqılli ḥaqqi** I took what is mine (RivSh 135); **rıẓya bḥaqqi** content, satisfied with my portion(=H בְּחֶלְקִי, PolG); **ḥaqq-u- mıstaḥaq dīde qıṯla-le** He definitely deserves to die (PolU 75) (NT+).

חקאנא חקנתא (< חקא) adj. **ḥaqqāna, ḥaqqanta** right, just (person); cf. נחקאנא.

חקבאזות (K/P **ḥuqqa bāz** player of cups) **ḥaqbāzūt** deception, sleight (NT6 133).

חק ומסתחק (Ar) **ḥaq-u-mıstaḥaq** deserved punishment (PolU 236).

חק ונחק (Ar-K) **ḥaqq-u-naḥaq** right and wrong (BaBin 160).

חקותא (< חקא) f. **ḥaqqūṯa** truth, justice; **b-** justly (PolG).

חקייה (Ar) adv. indeed, truly (I just remember).

חקיקא (Ar) f. **ḥaqīqa** truth (NT2).

ח-ק-נ (Arbe congested?) **ḥ-q-n** to become tarnished; כמלי וחקני **kımli uḥqınni** I became black and tarnished (BaBin 142).

ח-ק-ק II (Ar) **ḥ-q-q** to verify, investigate; כברי מחוקקי **xabre mḥuqıqqe** verified words (BaBin 9).

חראמא, חרמתא (Ar) adj. **ḥarāma, ḥaramta** forbidden, unkosher; menstruating (=H נִדָּה, BT3); **ḥarāma x-pısır ⁺barāza** As unkosher as pig's meat; cf. חלאלא.

חראמג̇י (Ar-T) **ḥarāmči** thief; pl. **-čīyat** (PolU 411); cf. גנאוא.

חראמותא, חרמותא (Ar) f. **ḥaramūṯa** forbidden gain, prohibition (=H אִסָּר, BT4).

חרב (Ar) f. **ḥarb** (international) war; cf. נצותא.

חַרְבָא (OA) **ḥarba** sword, knife (=H תְּלִי, BT1, D).

חרבייא (Ar) s.n.f. **ḥarbīya** Warrior.

ח-ר-ד-פ III (< ח-ד-פ) **ḥ-r-d-f** to throw down (a structure); to fall in, collapse (cf. PolG); (NT+) [MacD 161 **mherdip**].

חרדפתא (< ח-ר-ד-פ) f. **ḥardafta** ruin (NT5 407).

ח-ר-ד-ק III (<?) **ḥ-r-d-q** to flirt, to joke (cf. PolG) [MacD 161 **mherdiq** play boisterously].

ח-ר-ז (Ar. حذر/حرز) **ḥ-r-z** be careful, devoted; to caution (=H הִזְהִיר, PolG); IV to caution (NT, BT2; Hob89 218); cf. מחרוז.

ח-ר-ח-ר III (K) **⁺ḥ-r-ḥ-r** to cackle, laugh boisterously [MacD 161 to yell].

חרחרתא (< ח-ר-ח-ר) f **⁺ḥırhırta** boisterous laugh.

חריפא (Ar) m. **ḥarīfa** colleague (NT5 404).

חריכתא (Ar) f. **ḥarīkıta** burst of energy (PolU 134).

ח-ר-כ II (Ar) **ḥ-r-k** to start moving (vehicle).

חרכא (Ar) f. **ḥaraka** movement, action; **ḥaraka baraka** Action is a blessing.

ח-ר-מ (Ar) **ḥ-r-m** become unkosher, forbidden (married woman to her husband after having sex with another man; cf. PolG); **šınse ḥrımla** He was unable to fall asleep; IV/II to forbid, declare unkosher (NT5 409/410); ban (sexual relations); cf. חראמא (NT+).

חרם (H) m. **ḥērım** excommunication, ban; **drīle bḥērım ubšamıtta** Ban him! Ignore him altogether!

חרם 2 v. חורמיה

חרפ (onomat.) **ḥarpp** sound of dog's catching by mouth food thrown at him (PolU 118).

ח-ר-ש, ח-ש-ר (Ar حشر) **ḥ-r-š, ḥ-š-r** (+NT3), to crowd, squeeze many people together; cf. חשר; crush together (RivSh 278); (woman) to mate (with animal) (=H רָבַע, BT3, D).

חשא, חאשך, חשאך (Ar) **ḥáša(k)** Far be it! (=H חָלִילָה, BT1; PolG); **ḥášak ḥāẓırīn/ dōxun** All present/of you excluded (said after saying a dirty word, such as dog, ass).

חשויא (< ח-ש-י) m. **ḥıššōya** (meat) stuffing.

ח-ש-י (Ar) **ḥ-š-y** to be stuffed; IV to stuff, fill.

חשכ (K dry) inv. **ḥısk** hard (currency) (PolU 289).

חשמה (T/Ar) f. **ḥašme** honor, majesty (NT2).

חשמוני, חשמונאי (H) **ḥašmōnay** Hasmonean (NT3).

ח-ש-ר v. ח-ר-ש

חשר 1 (Ar) **ḥašır** tumult, crowds (PolU 3).

חשר 2 (< Ar) inv. **ḥıššar** crowded, dense; cf. ח-ר-ש.

חשתא (Ar حاجة) **ḥašta** (needed) object (NT5 387); pl. **חג׳יאתא ḥājyāṯa** accoutrements, tools; pots and dishes (NT2; NT5 409)[cf. Khan 570 **ḥašta** work, job; **ḥājıta** tool].

ח-ת-ח-ת III (< H חתחת?) **ḥ-t-ḥ-t** to stir fire.

חתי (K<Ar) **ḥıtti** even, even if; **חתי שמשא כשכלא ḥıtti šımša xšıkla** Even the sun has darkened. (BaBin 107; SaAC 12); cf. אפילו.

חתי אלברכה (Ar) adv. ***ḥıttı-lbarake** You are welcome, have my blessing! (PolU 134).

ט (ṭ)

ט (H) **ṭēṯ** the ninth letter of the Hebrew alphabet; **ʾıčʾa** nine.

טא v. טלא 1

טאאנא, טאאנתא (< ט-א-נ) n. ag. **ṭaʾāna, -anta,** carrier (NT+).

טאבה, טאבייה (K) f. **ṭāve, ṭāvīye** downpour, shower (Avin74 9).

טאבוקא (< ט-ב-ק) m. **ṭābōqa** lid of box (BaBin 119).

טאג׳יכא (K) m. **ṭājīka** greyhound, scavenger.

טאויס (Ar/P) m. ***ṭāwis**; pl. טַוִיצַאת **ṭāwīṣat** (=H תֻּכִּיִּים, PolG: 1Kg 10:22).

טאולא (IrAr < It tavola) f. **ṭāwla** backgammon (Z); table (PolG).

טאונתא (OS) f. **ṭʾunta** fruit (on tree), produce (BaBin 59) [cf. MacD 113].

טאחין (Ar) m. **ṭāḥīn** ground sesame sauce.

ט-א-י (OA/OS טעי to err, get lost) **ṭ-ʾ-y** to search, look for; – **bšamʾe ušrāʾe** search very hard (lit., with candles and lamps) (NT+).

טאיא 1 (K) m. **ṭāya** branch (of tree); pl. טאיה, טאיאנה **ṭāye, ṭāyāne** (+NT3); cf. טַאנַא.

טאיא 2 (< טאיא 1) **ṭāya** layer: **1/bṭāyıṭ ṣudra** (wearing) just a shirt (no other layers) (P0lG).

טאייע (Ar) inv. **ṭāyıᶜ** obedient (NT).

טאיפא (Ar) f. **ṭāyıfa** community (NT).

טאיפי (K) inv. **ṭāyfi** a select kind of grapes.

טאלאנה, טאלאני, תאלאנה (K/T) f. ***ṭālāne/i** pillage, plunder (cf. PolG) (NT+).

טאלב (Ar) **ṭālıb** seeker; טאלבין דחקא **ṭālıbīn dḥaqqa** seekers of truth (NT).

טאם-וטאם (K < Ar/OS) **ṭām-u-ṭam** of superior taste; all kinds of delicacies (PolU 317);

טאמסאר (K) inv. **ṭāmsār** tasteless, boring.

טאן (K?) m. **ṭān** hedge, fence (=H גָּדֵר, BT4; BaBin 35); cf. סיאאה.

ט-א-נ (OA/OS טען; Mand. טאן) **ṭ-ʾ-n** to carry; to suffer (NT3); **ʾaw ṭāʾen uṣābır, ıbgjābır** He who bears patiently, will overcome (RivPr 212); **kāsi/ʾēnī la kṭaʾna ʾe xaʾ** I (lit., my stomach/my eye) cannot bear this; to swell due to infection and fever; IV to load (NT+).

טאנא (< ט-א-נ) m. **ṭeʾna** load; message, charge; **parṭeʾna ṭāʾın ṭeʾna** (It is as ridiculous as) a flea carrying a (heavy) load; constr. **ṭeʾen** (PolG); pl. **-e, ṭeʾınyāṯa** (SaLH 149) (NT+).

טַאנַא (< טאיא, טאן?) **ṭāna** branch (=H זְמוֹרָה, BT4, D).

ט-א-ס (OA) vi **ṭ-ʾ-s** to fly (RivSh 273).

טאסה (K/T < Ar; cf. OA/OS טַסָּא) f. **ṭāse** cup, bowl; pl. **ṭaṣāṯa** (cf. PolU 264).

טאעא, טאעתא (Ar) f. **ṭāᶜa, ṭaᶜıta** obedience, fear of God; זלו בטאעיה דידה **zıllu bṭāᶜe dīde** They obeyed him.

טאעון (Ar) m. **ṭāᶜun** plague; **ṭāᶜun šāre go bēse** May a plague dwell in his house! (cf. PolU 365).

טַאפַּא (< גאפא?) m. **ṭāpa** blow, slap on head (RivSh 136) [cf. Oraham 194 **tuppa**].

טאפו (T) **ṭāpu** title-deed; property tax; **ʾ-w-z ṭāpu** to register a transaction of title-deed.

טאק-ו-טאק (onomat.) **ṭāq-u-ṭāq** sounds of gun shots (PolU 116).

טאקא (Ar) f. **ṭāqa** wall, vault (PolU 426).

טאקתא (Ar) f. **ṭāqıta** strength (cf. PolG); **latli ṭāqıte** I don't have the energy for him.

תאריך v. טאריך

תַארִיסְטַן, טארסתאן (K) **ṭārıstān** total darkness (=H עֲלָטָה, BT1; אֲפֵלָה, PolG:Ex10:22).

טאת- v. טלא 1

טבא (Ar) m. **ṭıbba** healer, medicant (PolU 278).

טַבַּאכַא (OA/Ar) m.**ṭab(b)āxa** cook (=H טַבָּח, PolG:1S 9:24) [Khan 583 **ṭabbāx**].

טבאלא (K?) m. **ṭavāla** heavy layer (of fat).

טבאקא (Ar) f. **ṭabāqa** layer, storey; fastened down lid (=H צָמִיד, BT4); pl. **-e** (PolG); **-ıd šimme** the heavenly expanses; cf. טאבוקא, טבק טבקתא, (NT+) [Khan 583 **ṭab(a)qa** shelf; plate].

ט-ב-ז v. ט-פ-ז

טבילה (H) f. **ṭabīla** ritual bath, mikveh (NT+) [Mutz 234 **ṭabilla**].

ט-ב-ל (H-OA) **ṭ-b-l** (+Z **ḏ-b-l**) to have a ritual bath; האוה מקודשיה וטביליה בטבילה **hāwe mqudše uṭbīle bṭabīla** They should be sanctified and immersed in the ritual bath;

to wash blood from meat (Z); **pısra lāzım mkōšıríle uṭablīle** Meat has to be cleaned (made kosher) and washed; cf. כ-ו-ש-ר. NT+

טבנגא v. דבנגא

טבע (Ar) m. **ṭabᶜ** inclination; pl. טבעה **ṭabᶜe** (= H יצרים, NTU 158b)

טבעתא (Ar) f. **ṭabᶜıta** temper; **máre-ṭabᶜıta** temperamental (person); cf. בי-טבעת; pl. **ṭabᶜıtyāṯa** (=H מדות, AlfM 17).

ט-ב-ק (Ar) **ṭ-b-q** to fit well, fasten (lid of can); collapse inside (roof), bend (horse's back); PolG, PolU 3); cf. טבאקא.

טבק, טְבַאק (Ar) m. **ṭabaq** shallow basket; cf. סאלא; טבאקא; pl. **ṭabāqe** (cf. PolG).

טבקתא (Ar) f. **ṭabaqta** tablecloth; little blanket to cover dough, bread, etc. (=H מִטְפַּחַת, Ruth 3:15; PolG: סמרטוט, מגבת).

טבת (H) **ṭēveṯ** (Z **ṭēves**) the Hebrew month of Teveth (December).

טג'ארא (IrAr) f. **ṭaġāra** unit of weight equal to 2000kg; a huge earten vessel (= OA תִיגָרָא < P > SyAr **tiġār** earthen dish or bowl?).

טג'מא v. טמג'א

טהלי, תחלי (K) f. **ṭahli** (NT), **taḥli** (Z), bitterness, suffering.

טהרא, טחרא (OA טִיהֲרָא; OS ܛܗܪܐ) **ṭahra** (NT), **ṭaḥra** (Z), noon (heat) (NT3), excessive heat (Z).

טהרה v. קדושה

ט-ו-א (OS ܛܘܐ ܒܫܢܬܐ sank in sleep) **ṭ-w-ʾ** to fall asleep; IV to put to sleep; **muṭuʾāli gyāni** I pretended to be asleep [4: **maṭwōʾe**; cf. PolG)].

טוב v. טוף

טובאנא, טובנתא (< טוף) adj. **ṭōvāna, -anta** full of seeds (melons), has large seeds (cucumber).

טוטוכה (K) f. **ṭuṭūke** (child's) flute.

ט-ו-ט-ח III (IrAr) **ṭ-w-ṭ-ḥ** to stagger (drunk); be very drunk (cf. Pol 109)[4:**mṭōṭōḥe**].

טוטלא (Ar طلطلة uvula?) m. **ṭuṭıla** (child's) penis; cf. בוטלא.

טוטפות (< H [discarded] phylacteries? but cf. שטפות) **ṭōṭāfōṯ** (Z -s) waste; 'down the drain': **kulle māl dōhun zılle b-** All their wealth was wasted.

טוטרמא (H תרדמה/T **tutulma** being seized, in love) f. **ṭōṭırma** deep sleep (=H תַּרְדֵּמָה, BT1).

ט-ו-י 1 I/II (OA/OS/Mand) vi/vt **ṭ-w-y** to roast; to feel compassion; טוילילה לבא אבה **ṭwēléle lıbba ʾıbbe** She felt sorry for him (NT2).

ט-ו-י 2, ט-ו-א (OA טובי ל-) **ṭ-w-y** (NT), **ṭ-w-ʾ** (Z), to be happy (=H אַשְׁרֵי, BT5); טוילה **ṭwēle** (NT; PolG), **tweʾle** (Z) טוֹלֵי **ṭōle** (RivSh 197) Happy is he; to be valuable, to cost; **kma kṭāwe** (NT)/**kṭawīle** (Z) How much does it cost? What is its value? לגטוילא **lag-ṭawīla** It isn't worthwhile (BaBin 135).

טויאא, טויאתא (ט-ו-א, p.p.) adj. **ṭwīʾa, ṭweʾta** asleep (NT+).

טוילא, טוילכאנא (< Ar/P) f. **ṭawīla , ṭawilxāna** (PolU 2), (horse) stable (=H מְבוֹא הַסּוּסִים, PolG: 2Kg 11:16); pl. **ṭawilxāne** (PolU 3).

טוין, טוון (OA טובא אן) **ṭūwın** (?) Would that (NT) [cf. MacD 110 **ṭūwā d-**].

טוכטור(ותא) v. דוכטור(ותא)

ט-ו-ל II (Ar) **ṭ-w-l** to prolong, to grant a grace period (NT2), to tarry (cf. PolG).

טול (Ar) **ṭūl** length; **ṭūl ᶜumre** all his life (NT+).

טולא (OA/OS/Mand טַבְלָא musical instrument < Ak **tāp/balu**) **ṭōla** drum (NT); cf. דולא.

טולאזא (K) m. **ṭōlāza** fool, stupid (PolU 92).

טולה (K) f. **ṭōle** fresh, youthful female (SaLH); often as hendiadys: **tarr-u-ṭōle** (cf. PolG).

טוּמְאָה (H) **ṭumʾa** ritual pollution (BT3, D).

טוּמוּרְתָּא (< ט-מ-ר) f. **ṭumurta** (hidden) treasure (=H מַטְמוֹן, BT1, D).

טומיא, טמיא (OA טַמְיָא) m. **ṭūmya** , **ṭımya** (Z) ritually polluted; cf. ט-מ-י, מטומיא (NT+).

טומיותא, טמיותא (< טומיא) f. **ṭūmyūṯa** ritual pollution (NT+).

טוף, טוב (K) m. **ṭōf/v** seed (of fruits), kind, species; cf. אוטו(ף), בשטו(ף), מאטו(ף); pl. **anya ṭōve** =H סוג אנשים אלה, PolG) [Khan 583 **ṭam**].

טופ (T) m. **ṭōp** catapult (NT), cannon (Z); **ṭōp šāre go bēsox** May a cannon be loose on your house (curse) (PolU 253); big, gigantic: **ṭōpıd šırmāsa** huge buttocks (PolU 261); pl. טופה **ṭōpe**.

טופאנא; טופאן (OA/OS טוֹפָנָא; Ar طوفان) m. **ṭōpāna** (NT), **ṭawafān** (Z), flood, the Flood (NT5 384).

טופור (< ט-פ-ר 2?) **ṭúfur** precious: **sqile...mux**

— beautiful...like a precious thing (PolG: יקרים, מובחרים).

טופזא (K/T) m. **ṭōpıza** big (stick); cf. ט-פ-ז.

טופלא v. טפלא

טופרא, טפרא (OA/Mand טוּפְרָא; OS ܛܘܦܪܐ) m. **ṭüpra** nail; pl. **ṭüprāṯa** (cf. PolG); v. ט- 1 פ-ר [Mutz 235/Khan 583 sg. **ṭp/urta**].

טוקא (Ar) m. **ṭōqa** necklace (NT), brooch (Z); pl. **ṭōqıt dehwa** = H תּוֹרֵי זָהָב, PolG.

טורא (OA/OS/Mand) m. **ṭūra** mountain; טור סיני **ṭūr sīnay** Mount Sinai; pl. טוראנה, טורה **ṭūrāne** (cf. PolG), **ṭūre**. NT+

טוראיא, טוריתא (< טורא) **ṭūrāya, ṭūrēṯa**, mountaineer (SaLH).

טורבן (Ar) **ṭurban** turban (PolU 388).

טורטומתא (< ט-ר-ט-מ) f. **ṭurṭumta** complaint; pl. טורטומיאתא, תַּרְטַמְיַיאתַא **ṭurṭumyāṯa**, ⁺**tartam-** (BT4).

טוריתא (P طغرى) f. **ṭurīṯa** falcon (=H אַיָּה, BT3; דַּיָּה, BT5).

ט-ח-נ (Ar) **ṭ-ḥ-n** ache (body) (PolG); cf. ת-כ-נ.

טחרא v. טהרא

טיאנה v. טאיא

טייארא (Ar) f. **ṭayyāra** kite; airplane.

טייארג'י (Ar-T) **ṭayyārči** pilot (cf. PolU 91).

טימה, טִימֵי (OA/OS טימי < Gr; SokPA 223).f./pl. **ṭīme** value, cost (= עֵרֶךְ, BT3); sg. (?) טִימַא **ṭīma** (= H מְחִיר, PolG:1Kg 10:28) [cf. Murz 234 **ṭima**].

טינא (OA/OS/Mand; Ar) m. **ṭīna** mud (NT+).

ט-י-ע (Ar) **ṭ-y-ʿ** to obey (?) (AmU2 10b).

ט-י-פ (OA/OS/Mand טוף) **ṭ-y-p** to overflow, to float (NT+).

ט-י-ק (Ar طوق collar?) vi **ṭ-y-q** to lock; פומיה גכאתם וכטייק **pumme gxātım uktāyıq** His mouth gets sealed and locked (AmU2 5a).

טירא (Ar) m. **ṭēra** bird, fowl; טירא-וזא v. וזא (NT+).

טירכא-שבה (K) **ṭerka-šave** (Z), טֵירֵית לֵילֵי **ṭērıt lēle** (BT3, D), bat ('bird of night').

טיר-כולי (K) **ṭēr-kuli** a type of hopping bird.

ט-י-ש (Ar) **ṭ-y-š** to be unsteady, feeble (BaBin 127; to faint (heart)(PolG).

טכטיר v. טלא 1

טלא 1, טְלָא, תא/ -ת, דַא (OA מטולתא) **ṭla** (NT, AvidH 20, 24), **ta(-)** (Z), **da** (+RivSh 149, 189, 266), for, to, on account of [decl. טלאתי **ṭlāṯi**/ טאתי **ṭāṯi** (NT; cf. טתיהון **ṭaṯēhun** Sa83c 16, Am), **ṭāli** (Z), for me; **ṭlaṯēni/ṭalēni** for us]; טלא האדך טלהאדך **ṭla-hādax** therefore; טלא כאטר, טלכאטר, טכטיר, **ṭ(1)axāṭır** so that, in order to, for the sake of; it may be omitted: **dʾırru bara basra ʾāse lbēsa** They returned to come home; טלמהה, טלא מאהה, טלמא, טמא(הא) תא, מא **ṭ(1)amá(ha)** Why? What for? (v. also Avid H 40: תַּמָא; AlfH 49: טַה מַה); cf. קי, קמא.

טלא 2, טְלָא (OA/Mand טוּלָּא; OS ܛܠܠܐ) f. **ṭılla** shade; pl. טלאלה **ṭıllāle** (NTU2 40a); cf. טלניתא (NT+).

טלא(הא) (OA תלתא) **ṭlā(ha)** three; cf. טלת; יומד טלאהא יומה **yōmıd ṭlāha yōme** the third day (NT); cf. טלאתי [Hoberman 1985 228].

טלאהושב (OA תלתא בשבא) **ṭlāhošıb** (Z), **ṭlāhūšıb** (BT1, Am), Tuesday [Khan 583 **ṭlahušab**].

טלאקה v. ט-ל-ק

טלאשא (K< OS ܬܠܫܐ; cf. OA טולשא medlar?) m. **ṭılāša** chunk of wood for fire [cf. MacD 112].

טלאתי (OA תלתין) **ṭlāṯi** (Z **ṭlāsi**) thirty [Mutz 234/Khan 583 **ṭlāhi**].

ט-ל-ב (Ar) **ṭ-1-b** to request, wish; גטלבי למותוה ולא געאלק באידוה **gṭalbi lmōṯuh ula gʿālıq bʾıḏuh** They wish to die but cannot do so; **ṭālıblox xāye** May he ask (God) life for you (said after mentioning a deceased) (SaAC); to negotiate marriage with bride's parents (Z); cf. טליבא, טליבתא.

טלב (Ar) **ṭalab** kicking the horse on the sides to urge it to go faster; pl. **ṭalābe**: **m-x-y** - to gallop, to go fast (horse rider) (cf. PolG).

טלבאיה (< ט-ל-ב) pl./sg. f. **ṭalabāye** persons (groom's relatives)negotiating marriage with bride's family (cf. PolG); the ceremony of such negotiations (PolU 292).

טלבתא, טלובתא (< ט-ל-ב) p.p.f. **tlübta** fiancée, betrothed; cf. טליבא. (RivSh214; PolG).

טלג'ם, טלג'אם (T) inv. **ṭalġam** pure (silver, gold) (NT).

טלהא (Ar?) **ṭalha** trap (?): **mpılle go ṭalha dīda** He fell in her trap, She tricked him.

טלוכה (OA טְלוֹפְחֵי, OS ܛܠܘܦܚܐ) **ṭlōxe** lentils; טלוכתא **ṭluxta** a lentil (RivP 214) [cf. Mutz 235].

טלטא (< ?) **ṭalta** huge/heavy piece.

טליבא (< ט-ל-ב) p.p. m. **ṯlība** fiancé, betrothed (cf. PolG); cf. טלבתא.

טליסם (Ar< Gr) m. **ṭıllēsım** pendant amulet; breastplate (=H חֹשֶׁן, BT2); cf. תסלים?

טלית (H) f. **ṭalliṯ** (Z **ṭallis**) prayer-shawl (f.); pl. **ṭallīṯe, ṭallīṯat**.

טלכאטר v. טלא 1

ט-ל-ל II (OA/OS) **ṭ-l-l** to find shelter (BaBin 37; =H לַחֲסוֹת, Ruth 2:12; cf. PolG).

טלמא, טלמהא v. טלא 1

טלמתא (OA/OS טוּלְמְתָא, טוּלְמָא; Ar طُلْمَة) f. **ṭlımṯa** thin flat bread (= H פַּת-לֶחֶם, כִּכַּר-לֶחֶם, PolG); pl. טלמה **ṭlımme** (OA טוּלְמֵי) (NT+).

טלניתא (OA טַלָּנִיתָא; OS ܛܠܳܢܺܝܬܳܐ) f. **ṭıllanīṯa** shade, shadow; pl. **ṭıllanyāṯa**; cf. טלא 2 (NT+).

ט-ל-ק I/II (OA/Ar) **ṭ-l-q** to divorce; גט טלאקה **geṭ ṭalāqe** divorce writ (=H סֵפֶר כְּרִיתוּת, BT). NT+

טלק (Ar) **ṭalaq** exemption (from tax)(PolU 1).

טלת, טלאת, טילת (OA תלת) f. **ṭıllaṯ** three (NT); בשאתד טלת **bšātıd ṭıllaṯ** on the third year (NT5 392); ארבאי וטלת ביאיה **ʾarbıʾi uṭıllaṯ beʾe** forty-three eggs (NT5 410); טלתנו, טלתניהון **ṭıllaṯnu/-ēhun** (NT=Z **kud ṯlāhun**) all three of them; v. טלאהא.

-טלת v. טלא 1

טלתמא (< טלת אמא) **ṭıllaṯma** (Z **ṭıllasma**) three hundred (NT+).

טמא v. טלא 1

טָמֵא (H) **ṭāme** (ritually) polluted (BT3, D); cf. טומיא.

ט-מ-א (OA/OS טעם; Mand טאם) **ṭ-m-ʾ** to taste; IV to feed (=H הִלְעִיט, BT1, D) (NT+).

טמאה, טומאה (OA/OS טַעֲמָא) **ṭümʾa** taste, dish, new seasonal fruit; color: **šōʾa ṭımʾe ʾabrēsım** silk in seven colors (PolU 310); **la šqāl ṭımʾıd xabra ula fhām maʿne dīde** without really getting it; טֻומְאֵי **ṭumʾe** = H מַטְעַמִּים, PolG; **ʾēḏ ṭümʾe** Arbor Holiday (= חג האילנות).

טמאטא (IrAr< It) f. **ṭamāṭa** tomato; cf. בנגאנא.

טמאניאסר v. תמאניאסר

טמאנה v. תמאנה

טמאשא (T/K) f. **ṭamāša** show, spectacle (NT+).

טַמְבָוָא (K?) **ṭambāva** deep water (=H מְצוּלָה, AvidH 40).

טמבור, תמבור (Ar < P > OA/OS טַנְבּוּרָא) m. **ᵗtambur** long-necked string instrument (PolU 351a); cf. טמבלכה.

טמבלכה (K< P دنبك bagpipe?) f. **ṭımbılke** tambourine, small long-neck drum; pl. **ṭımbılkat** [cf. Blanc 151 **dumbug/dembek** a sort of drum]

ט-מ-ג' II (< טמג'א) **ṭ-m-ġ** to seal, to stain.

טמג'א (IrAr< P) f. **ṭamġa** stamp, seal, stain; טַגְ'מֵי טַג'מֵי **ṭaġmé-ṭaġme** (a sheep with) speckles (all over) (=H טָלוּא, BT1, D).

טֻומֻורְתַא (OA טימורתא, טְמוּרתא) **ṭumurta** buried treasure (PolG).

ט-מ-י (OA/OS) **ṭ-m-y** to be (ritually) polluted; II to pollute (NT+).

טומיא v. טמיא

טומיותא v. טמיותא

ט-מ-נ 1 II/IV (?)(Ar) **ṭ-m-n** to reassure (?) (AmU2 4b).

ט-מ-נ v. ת-מ-נ (**ṯ-m-n**)

ט-מ-ע 1 II (Ar طعم) **ṭ-m-ʿ** to overlay. NT+

ט-מ-ע 2 (Ar) **ṭ-m-ʿ** to covet; IV to make one to covet, seduce into buying (PolU 320) (NT+).

טמע (Ar) m. **ṭamaʿ** greed; **ṭammaʿ** greedy (NT+).

טמעותא (Ar) f. **ṭam(m)āʿūṯa** avarice (cf. PolG; RivSh 220 טְמַעְאוּתַא!

טמעכר (Ar-K) **ṭamaʿkar** avaricious.

טמפטור (IrAr **tabbadūr**< It tappo duro, tight cork) **ṭampaṭur** cork, stopper of corkwood.

ט-מ-ר (OA/OS) **ṭ-m-r** to bury, to hide (cf. PolG).

ט-מ-ש (OA/OS) vi/vt **ṭ-m-š** to dip (NT5 409).

טנגא (K) m. **ṭanga** saddle strap (Socin 162); pl. **ṭang-u-bara-ṭange** (PolU 12).

ט-נ-ג-ז' III (< T?) **ṭ-n-g-ž** to feel dizzy (cf. PolG); **rēši mṭungıžle** I have a splitting headache (from too much noise).

טנטופכא (< ?) m. **ṭınṭōfka** frontlet, charm locket on child's forehead [cf. H טוטפות].

ט-נ-ט-פ III (OA/Ar?) **ṭ-n-ṭ-f** to drizzle, drip.

טסלך v. תצלך

טסמה v. תצמה

ט-ע-ל v. ת-ע-ל

טעמים (H) pl. **ṭaʿāmīm** Biblical cantillation notes; halakhic points (BaBin 8).

טענה (Ar stab, hurt) **ṭaʿne** calumny; **gmaḥke**

b- He speaks with intention to hurt.

טַעְשִׁירֵי (Ar?) pl. **ṭaᶜšīre** entrails (=H קְרָבַיִם, BT3, D).

טפא 1, טפתא (OA טִיפְּתָא, pl טִיפֵּי) f. **ṭıppa** (NT3), **ṭıpta** (NT2), a drop; עצלוך טפתא ספסתילא **ᶜaṣlox ṭıpta spıstēla** your origin is a stinking drop (NTU4 158b) [cf. Garbell 337 ⁺**ṭippa** f. drop; MacD 113 dot].

טפא 2 (IrAr< T/OS) **ṭappa** hill, only in **zılle lqara ṭappa** He went to hell (what do I care), lit., to black hill; **ṭappıd rēša** headtop; cf. טפאיא.

טפאיא, טַפֵּיתָא (OS) **ṭappāya** (NT), **ṭappēta** (BT4, D; PolG:2Kg 17:10, D) hill(top) (=H גִּבְעָה); Z only in **zılle b-** He went to 'hell'; cemetery; pl. טפאייה **ṭappāye** (NT; cf. RivSh 197 טַפַּיֵּא), טַפַּיְתָא **ṭappayāta** (BT4, D); טַפֵּאָיָסָא **ṭappeʾyāsa** (AvidH 50) [cf. MacD 113 the shoulder of a mountain].

טפה (< טפא 2/K **tepek** kick?) f. **ṭappe** ball; **qaṭīʾa-ṭappe** a stick (and) ball game similar to baseball; pl. **ṭáppat** (PolG) [Khan 583 **ṭoppa**; pl. **ṭoppāye** ball, K].

ט-פ-ז, ט-ב-ז II (< טופזא) **ṭ-p/b-z** to pommel, beat hard with club.

טפולא (< OA/OS?) **ṭapōla** blow with both hands on one's head (PolG); cf. רשומא.

טפוסא<טפותא*? (< ט-פ-י/OA טפוסא ?) **ṭıppūsa** (Z)< *ṭıppūṯa ? nuisance, a nag; cf. דבוקאנא.

ט-פ-ט-פ III (OA טפטף/Ar طبطب) **ṭ-p-ṭ-p** to pat, to tap (a fainted/sleeping person to awake her) (PolU 340), caress lightly.

ט-פ-י (OA/OS טפי to close) vi **ṭ-p-y** to stick; overtake (NT5, 390); **ṭpēle ʾıbbi** He begged/nagged me (cf. **la ṭapyat ʾıbbi** =H אַל תִּפְגְּעִי-בִי, Ruth 1:16; טַפְיַיאטֶין ⁺**ṭapyātın** =H תִּדְבָּקִין, PolG:Ruth 2:21); cf. טפוסא; II/IV to stick (vt); **mutpēle gyāne ʾıbbi** He 'glued' himself to me (cf. PolG); to bake (stick loaves on oven walls); cf. מטפייניתא; cause to cling (Pol 109); close (door or window, without locking it) (cf. PolG); to falsely accuse: **mṭupya ʾıbbi** They accused me (PolU 337).

טפיתא v. טפאיא

טפלא, טופלא (Ar; cf. OA טַפְלָא; OS ܛܦܠܐ) m. **ṭūfla** baby, toddler; pl. טופלה, טפלה **ṭūfle** (NT5 396) (=H טַף, BT).

טפלאפא (K/T?) **ṭaplāpa** wobbling, slow moving, waddling person, a Golem; **-ıd mōsāna** deadly Golem cf. ט-פ-ל-פ.

טפלי-טפלו (K/T?) **ṭapli-ṭaplo** one (usually a girl) whose movements are funny and awkward; humpty-dumpty; cf. תקלי-תקלו.

ט-פ-ל-פ III (< טפלאפא) **ṭ-p-l-p** to wobble, waddle.

טפצכתא (K?) **ṭafṣıkta** sycamore; pl. טַפְצְכְיָתָא **ṭafṣıkyāta** (=H שִׁקְמִים, PolG: 1Kg 10:27).

ט-פ-ר 1 (< ט-פ-ר/טופרא 2/*OA< Ak **ṭipāru** 'torch'?) vi **ṭ-p-r** to burn; common in curses: **nūra ṭāpır** (or **šāre**) **go bēsox** May fire blaze up in your house!); be enraged, burst with anger (cf. PolG); to wander: **ṭāpır bıd dunye** to aimlessly wander in the world (PolG); IV to set on fire, kindle (vt); incite (NT+) [cf. MacD: **ṭ/tāpir** put the claws into; attack; interfere; stick to; catch fire, be kindled; cf. **ᶜāliq**; **mṭāpir** incite, stick. PolG: الطفر/الطفر ?].

ט-פ-ר 2 (Ar طفر 'leap'?) **ṭ-f-r** be weary, loathe: **ṭfırre mın roḥāyıt gyāne** He was sick of his life (PolG); v. טופור.

טפרא v. טופרא

טפריתא (< ט-פ-ר) f. **ṭapparīta** excessive heat (SaAC 12); inflammation (=H דַּלֶּקֶת, BT5, D).

טפרתא (< ט-פ-ר) f. **ṭparta** fire, conflagration (=H בְּעֵרָה, BT2; BaBin 110).

ט-פ-ש II (K) **ṭ-p-š** to grope (=H מִשֵּׁשׁ, BT5, D; BaBin 164; PolG).

טפש (H) m. **ṭıppēš** fool, dumb; **ṭıppēš-ᶜımya-gannāvēš** super dumb; pl. **ṭıppešīn** (PolU 204).

טפתא v. טפא 1

ט-צ-ד-ק v. ת-צ-ד-ק

ט-ק-ט-ק III (K/Ar) **ṭ-q-ṭ-q** to knock (on door), pound (PolG); do odd jobs (PolU 80).

טקטקושכה (K) f. **ṭaqṭaqōške** cracker, explosive cap; pl. **ṭaqṭaqōškat**.

טק טק טק (onomat.) **ṭiq ṭiq ṭiq** loud laughter.

טקטקתא (< ט-ק-ט-ק) f. **ṭaqṭaqta** sound of horse steps, etc. (PolU 322).

טר טר טר (onomat.) **ṭır ṭır ṭır** sound of farting (PolU 71).

טראגה (*IrAr) pl. **ṭırāge** a type of cheap slippers (bottom made of care tires).

טראחא (< Ar طرح to fell?) m. **ṭarrāḥa** logger.

טראחותא (< טראחא) f. **ṭarrāḥūṯa** logging and transporting trees as rafts on the river (a common occupation among Jews of Zakho).

טראכומא (Ar< E) **ṭrāxōma** trachoma.

ט-ר-ב-ל III (K?) **ṭ-r-b-l** to be cumbersome.

טרו-טולה v. טולה

טרוונדה v. תרוונדה

טרוסא, טרוסותא v. תרוצא, תרוצותא

ט-ר-ח (Ar) **ṭ-r-ḥ** to miscarry, have a miscarriage (RivSh 143).

טרח (Ar) m. **ṭaraḥ** still body (PolU 22).

טרחא (AnAr/K) m. **ṭarḥa** tendril, branch; pl. **ṭarḥe** (=H כַּפּוֹת תְּמָרִים, BT3).

ט-ר-ט-מ III (OS) **ṭ-r-ṭ-m** to complain, grumble (NT+) [cf. H/OA רטן].

טרטמיתא (< ט-ר-ט-מ) **ṭarṭamīṯa** complain (PolG).

ט-ר-ט-ק III (IrAr) **ṭ-r-ṭ-q** to explode, crack.

טרטרא (IrAr?) m. **ṭarṭarra** huge, very heavy.

טרטרוכה (K?) f. **ṭɪrṭɪrrōke** farter; cf. מערטו.

ט-ר-י (OA to dash, throw; OS to strike, drive away) **ṭ-r-y** to drive (animal, car), set in motion; lead (people); fly, go fast (NT5 384); II to bear fruits: **la smɪxla ula mṭōrēla** She didn't get pregnant nor bring any children (PolG).

טריחא, טרחתא (< ט-ר-ח) p.p. **ṭrīḥa, ṭrɪḥta** miscarried embrio, tiny baby (SaAC 19).

טְרֵיפָה (H) **ṭarēfa** non-kosher meat (BT3, D).

טרייק, תריאק (Ar< Gr) **ṭɪryaq** opium, balsam (=H צֳרִי, BT; BaBin 142; RivSh 123).

טריקא (Ar) **ṭarīqa** way, custom (NT2).

ט-ר-כ v. ת-ר-כ

ט-ר-כ-נ III (P?) **ṭ-r-x-n** to feel stuffed, suffer from indigestion, heartburn.

טרמא (K) m. **ṭarma** corpse, lazy, slow-moving; pl. טרמה **ṭarme** (=H פְּגָרִים, AvidH 61; PolG).

טרמביל (IrAr< E) m. **ṭrambēl** automobile, car, bus; pl. **ṭrambēlat** [Krotkoff 127].

טרמפא (T< It) **ṭarampa** trumpet; pump (PolG: **ṭramp** musical instrument).

טרנגא v. תרנגא

ט-ר-ס v. ת-ר-צ

טרעוזייא v. תרעוזייא

ט-ר-פ (OA/OS to knock, bang) **ṭ-r-p** to applaud, clap the hands (in celebrations for musical rhythm (cf. PolG).

טרף, טַרַף (Ar) **ṭaraf** side, only in: **mɪn - dīdi** as far as I am concerned; **m- de xa'** regarding this, because of this (cf. PolG).

טרפא (OA) m. **ṭarpa** leaf, petal; pl.**ṭarpe**; v. סלקא. NT+

טרפנתא (onomat) **ṭrappenta** thump (PolU 13).

טרפשנא (< טרפא+ש-נ-י?) m. **ṭarpɪšna** shedded leaves and fallen branches (cf. PolG)

ט-ר-ק (OA/Mand/Ar) **ṭ-r-q** to slam (door), to forge (metal).

טרק (Onomat.) **ṭraq** breaking sound (PolU 79).

טרקינא (onomat) **ṭraqqēna** beat (PolU 5).

טרש (K) m. **ṭarš** cattle (=H בְּעִיר, BT2).

טרשי (K) m. **ṭɪrši** pickles, pickled vegetables.

טרשתא (OS) f. **ṭarrašta** thicket, bush; pl. טרשיאתא **ṭarrašyāṯa**. NT+

טשוא (OA) m. **ṭɪšwa** hiding; בטשוא **bṭɪšwa** secretly, stealthily (cf. PolG).

ט-ש-י (OA/OS/Mand) **ṭ-š-y** to be hidden (NT); II vt to hide.

טשת, תשת, טַשְׁטֵי, תשטה, טשתה, טשתה (K/P > OA/OS טשטקא, טַשְׁתְּקָא) f. **⁺tašt(e)** a large basin for laundry, bathing, etc. (NT5 409; =H מִזְרָק, BT3); pl. **⁺taštāṯa**.

י (y)

י (H) **yōḏ** (Z **yōs**), the tenth letter in the Hebrew alphabet; אצרא **ˀıṣra** ten (NT+).

-י (OA) **-i** my, (to) me (attached pron.) (NT+).

יא 1 (Ar) **yā** O, hey (vocative particle); יא ה' **yā ˀilāha** (NT5 382)/**yā rabbi** (PolG) O God; יַא מַלְאַך **yā malˀax** O angel (RivSh 277); **yā brāti** O my daughter (Ruth3:10); יא אלה **yā ˀalla** (NT2), **⁺yallá-⁺yalla** (Z), hardly, at best, one wishes (it were so); **⁺yallá-yalla maḥsılax ˀısri dīnāre** We will at best earn twenty dinars; **⁺yallıd-yalla** finally, thank God (we have been rescued) (PolU 203); cf. ילא, יא נציב (NT+).

יא 2 v. יאן

-יאא v. י-ד-א

-יאו v. י-ה-ו-ל

יאכא (T/IrAr) f. **yāxa** collar of a jacket, pleat.

י-א-ל (OA עלל < עיל) **y-ˀ-l** to enter; **yˀılle bıd ġazab** He became very angry (BaBin 133) [1: **yˀıl-**; 2: **yāˀıl**; 3: **yˀōl**; 4: **yˀāla/ˀyāla**]; IV to bring in; cf. מאלא, יאלתא.

יאלא, יאלותא v. איאלא, איאלותא

יאלדוז (K<T) m. **⁺yāldūz** gilt; **wēle mabrōqe mux ⁺yāldūz** It is shining like gilt.

יאלתא (<י-א-ל) n. act. **yıˀalta** entrance (Zaken 388).

יאמא (OA) m./f. **yāma** sea (NT; AvidH 40; but RivSh 164 יַמַּא = **yamma**?); cf. בחר; a lot, a great deal (Z).

יאמיצא (OS ܚܡܨܐ) m. **yāmīṣa** rhubarb (Arodh); cf. ריבאזא. [MacD 121].

יאן, יא, יאאן, און (T/K/P) **yān, ya** (PolG), **ˀān, ˀōn** (BT2, Arodh), or (NT+).

י-א-נ v. א-י-נ

יאנכו (<יאן+Ar يكون?) **yānku** as if, so to speak.

יא נציב (Ar) **yā nāṣīb** lottery (lit., O luck).

יאקות (Ar) **yāqūt** hyacinth, ruby, precious stone.

יארדא (IrAr/T<It/Sp<En) m. **yarda** yard (measure of length).

יארונא, יאראנא (K/P **yār** friend) m. **yārōna** (Z), **yārāna** (NT5 399; RivSh 229), illicit lover [MacD 122 **yārānā**]; pl. **yārō/āne**.

יארותא (K/P) f. **yārūṯa** friendly play; **byārūṯa** jokingly, friendly way (RivSh 225; PolG).

יאריכר (K) m. **yārīkar** joker, jester.

יארכתא (K) f. **yārıkṯa** beloved, love; pl. **yārıkyāṯa** (PolG); v. יארונא.

יבון, יבום (H) **yıbbūn** (NT), **yabbūm** (Z), levirate marriage; נפלא ביבון **npılla byıbbūn** She has to have a levirate marriage; **ˀuzle yabbūm** He had a levirate marriage (=H יִבֵּם, BT1).

י-ב-ל v. ב-י-ל

יבם, יְבַאם (H) **yavām** (widow's) husband's brother; brother's widow (=H יְבָמָה, BT5, D).

יבשתתא, יפשתתא (OA יבשתא dry [grape]?) f. **yıb/pšaṯṯa** raisin; pl. **yıb/pšāṯa** [Garbell 296 **apišta**, pl. **apišye** currant, raisin; MUTZ 240 **yabıšta**].

יגגאר, גגאר (K) adv. **yıgıār** (NT), **gjār(kin)** (Z, SaAC 19), (not) at all; **gjār la kīˀax ma brēle ˀılle** We don't know at all what happened to him; **gjārī** (=H כָּלִיל, PolG).

י-ד-א (OA/OS ידע; Mand ידא/עדא) **y-ḏ-ˀ** (Z **y-z-ˀ**) to know [2 (irreg.): **yāˀe** he will know (Z, NT)/they will know (Z); **kīˀe** he knows (Z, NT)/they know (Z); כיאי **kīˀi** they know (NT); 3: **zōˀ**; 4: **y(i)zāˀa , līzāˀa** (PolG)].

ידואא, ידואתא (OA ידועא) **yaḏōˀa** (m.), **yaḏōˀta** (f.), expert, knowledgeable; pl. יְדוֹאֵי **yaḏōˀe** (=H חָיוֹת, BT2, D; יוֹדְעֵי עִתִּים, PolG).

י-ד-ל (OA) **y-ḏ-l** (Z **y-z-l**) to give birth; II/IV to beget, to father; cf. י-ו-ה [Mutz 240 **ydl**].

ידלתא (OA) n.ag. **yaḏalta** child-bearing woman.

ידעוני (H) **yıddaˁōni** familiar spirit; pl. **yıddaˁōnim** (BT3).

יהודה, יְהוּדַא (H) **yıhūḏa** (Z **hūza**) Judea, Judah (RivSh 123); cf. הודאיא, הודא; ליל-הודא (NT+).

י-ה-ו-ל (OA יהב ל-) vt **y-h-w-l** to give; גשקלי וגיאוי **gšaqli ugyāwi** they argue, trade; **hulle ˀıbba ⁺rāba** he paid a lot (of money) for her (as dowry); — **xabra** he informed, gave an order (PolU 247);— **xāye to ḥāẓırīn** He passed away; **xāye hīwīle ṭali** He liked me very much (PolU 255) [irreg.1:

-הול **hul-**(Z)/-הְוִל **hwıl-** (RivSh 148, 176), היוא **hīwa** (p.p.m.), הוותא **hıwta** (f.)(NT); היונה **hīwı/anne** he gave me (m./f.)(NT); 2: **yāwıl** he gives, **yāwın** I (m.) give, **yawıt** you (m. sg.) give, **gyāwi** they give.; 3: **hāl**; **hállan** Give us! **hállū-le-li** Give it to me (PolU 20); 4: **y(i)hāwa/ hyāw/va** (NT5 387 להיאוא; AvidH 48 לְהָיְבָא); cf. יְהוֹתַא (NT+).

-יהון v. -והון

יהושוע (H) **(yıho)šūwa**ᶜ Joshua; cf. אישו.

יְהוֹתַא, יהולתא (OA יהבתא) n. act. **yhōta** , **y(ı)hōlta** (PolG), gift (=H מַתָּן, BT4, D).

יונאיה, יואנאיה (H < Gr; OA יוֹנָאֵי) **yawanāye** the Greeks (NT3); cf. יוֹנַאן.

יובל (H) **yōvēl, yōvel** jubilee (year) (BT3).

(י)וישא, (י)ושתא (י-ו-ש, p.p./OA/OS יְבִישָׁא) adj. **(y)wīša**, **(y)wīšta**, dry; stingy (Z); **rēše wīša** rigid, obstinate; **wīša-brīza** totally dry, lacking moisture or oil (NT+).

יוישותא, וישותא (< יוישא) f. **ywīšū<u>t</u>a** (NT), **wīšūsa** (Z), dryness, dry land (NT5 404); cf. יושותא.

יוכבד, יוֹכֶבֶת (H) **yōxēve<u>d</u>/<u>t</u>** (Z **yōxēves**) Jochebed (RivSh157; cf. צְלָפְחַת).

יומא (OA/OS) **yōma** day; sun (NT3, SaNR; NT5 387 יומא וסהרא **yōma usehra** sun and moon); cf. אין-יומא; שמשא; כוד יום **kud yom** every day; pl. **yōmā<u>t</u>a, yōme**; **wēla rıš yōmā<u>t</u>a** She is about to give birth any day; **xa/bču yōma myōmā<u>t</u>a** one day, ever, never (NT5 407; MeAl 176, 192); cf. דארתא, דינא, אדיו, בומכין.

יום דין הגדול (H) **yōm dīn hagga<u>d</u>ol** the Great Judgment Day (NT3).

יום כפור (H; OA יומא דכיפורי) **yōm-kıppur** the Day of Atonement; cf. צומא עזיזא.

יומייה (Ar) f. **yōmīye** day pay (PolU 32).

יוֹנַאן (Ar; cf. OS ܝܘܢܢ) **yōnān** Greece (=H כִּתִּים, BT4, D); cf. יואנאייה.

יונה (OA יוֹנָא/H יונה) f. **yōna** dove; Jonah (very common male name among Kurdistani Jews, after **yōna bır mattay** Prophet Jonah son of Amitai whose traditional shrine is at Nineveh, near Mosul); pl. יונה **yōne** doves (NT, BT; cf. OA יוֹנֵי); cf. כותרכא.

יוסף (H) **yōsef** Joseph; v. אוסו.

יוקדאנא (< י-ק-ד) m. **yuq<u>d</u>āna** conflagration, burn (NT); blister (=H כְּוִיָּה, BT2, Arodh); **yoq<u>d</u>ān lıbba** pity, sorrow (BaBin 100).

יוקרא (OA) **yuqra** honor, prestige (NT5 395).

ו-י-ש v. י-ו-ש

יושא, וישא (OS ܝܘܫܐ) **yōša** (NT3; BT1, Am; AvidH 44; RivSh 199), **wēša** (Z, PolG, f.), dry land; river bank: **ma'urınne mın wēša lwēša** I'll help him to cross the river (Polg)

יושותא (< יושא) f. **yōšū<u>t</u>a** dryness; cf. יוישותא.

יזאלא v. א-ז-ל

יח, יח בדם (< אח/K?) **yaḥ (badam)** Hurrah! (NT2)[cf. H הֶאָח]; v. בדם.

יחזקאל (H) **yaḥasqel** Ezekiel; cf. חסקו.

יחידו של עולם (H) **yıḥī<u>d</u>ō šel** ᶜ**ōlām** the Universal Only One (God) (NT2).

יכאנא, יכנתא (K) **yıkkāna, yıkkanta** [PolG: **yakāna, yākanta** (!)] an only child; the Only One, the Incomparable (God) (RivSh 187; BaBin 11 אילהא יכאנא).

-יכון v. -וכון

א-כ-ל v. י-כ-ל

יכסיר, יקסיר (< K **yaxsīr**) **yax/ksir** (?)(NT), **yaqsir** (Z), prisoner, captive (=H שָׁבוּי, BT1); humble, quiet (Z); pl. יִקְסִירִין **yıqsīrīn** fugitives (=H פְּלֵטִים, BT4, D); cf. יקסירותא [Khan 586 **yaxsīr**].

יכסירותא, יקסירותא (< יכסיר) f. **yax/ksīrū<u>t</u>a** (NT 5 397), **yaq-** (Z), captivity (=שְׁבִית, BT4).

יכר (K/P) **yakkar** (of) one piece (=H מִקְשָׁה אַחַת/כָּלִיל, BT2); rigid, obstinate.

ילא (Ar) ⁺**yalla** Quick! Get up! Let us go (with God's help)! v. יא.

ילה- v. אילה

ילודא (OA) m. **yalū<u>d</u>a** baby (NT3).

ילונכה v. אילא

יְלוּתַא v. איאלותא

ימא (OA אִימָּא) f. **yımma** mother; **yımmıd** ⁺**māya** a female ghost that dwells in the river (Z); **yımmıd bēsa** a female ghost that dwells in the house; pl. **yımmā<u>t</u>a** (BaBin 149) (NT+).

ימאייא 1 (< י-מ-י) **ymāya** swearing, oath (NT+).

ימאיא 2, ימיתא (< ימה) adj. **yammāya, yammē<u>t</u>a** right-handed; v. וזירא.

ימה (OA ימינא, but formed like גּפה, ראסתה) f. **yamme** right (hand); cf. ימכי, ימין (NT+).

יַם הַמֶּלַח (H) **yam-hammēlaḥ** the Salt ('Dead') Sea (BT4, D); cf. בחר מלכא.

ימח שמו וזכרו (H) (yım) maḥ šamō wazıxrō May your ('his') name and memory be erased (for ever)! (a common curse among women, usually accompanied by pointing an open palm at the face of the accursed); cf. מחשמו וזכרו.

י-מ-י (OA) **y-m-y** to swear, to promise [1: **ymē** (Z)/-אִימֵי **imē-** (PolG); 3: **ymī**/אִייְמִי **iymī**] IV to adjure [1: **mōmē-/muymē-**; מומותולי (NT) **mōmütüli** I have adjured you (pl.); 2: מומנוכון **mōmınnēxun** I adjure you (pl.); מומיתיני **mumyattēni** You (f. sg.) adjure us]; cf. מומאתא.

ימינא, ימין (Ar يمين; OA/OS יַמִּינָא) **yam(m)īn(a)** right (hand) (NT; RivSh 244); cf. ימה.

ימכי (< ימה) adv. **yammıki** to the right (PolU 227).

ים סוף (H) **yam sūf** the Reed ('Red') Sea (NT); cf. בחרד קלזם.

-ינא, -ן (OA) **-ēna, -ın**, I (m.) (suffixed to a.p.: **mjarb-ēna/-ın** I try); cf. -אנא (NT+).

-יני, -ן (OA) **-ēni, -an** our (e.g. **bēṯan/bēṯēni** our house) (NT+).

יסורא (< י-ס-ר) m. **yıssōra** tie, rope (BaBin 1541; PolG)

יסורין (H-OA) pl. **yıssūrīn** suffering, ailments (NT)

יסמינה (P-Ar) **yasmīne** mandrakes (=H דּוּדָאִים, BT1).

י-ס-ק, + א-ס-ק ? (OA נסק/סלק) **y-s-q** to go up, to ascend [1: -יסק/-איסק/-סק **(ıy)sıq-**; 3: איסוק/סוק **(ıy)sōq**; 4: (א)יסאקא **(ı)ysāqa**]; IV to bring up [1: מוסקנה **musqanne** He brought me (f.) up (NT); 2/3: **māsıq**; 4: **masōqe**] [cf. Mutz 241 ysq~ʾsq].

יסק (T) inv. **yássaq** forbidden (PolG).

י-ס-ר, + א-ס-ר? (OA/OS/Mand אסר) **y-s-r** to tie [1: סירא **sīra** (p.p., NT), **ysīra** (Z); -אִיסִיר **ıysīr-** RivSh 217]; cf. איסר; יסורא; אסראתא [Khan 551 ʾsr].

יעני, יענו, יעניך (Ar) **yaᶜni/yaᶜnu** (Z), **yaᶜnix** (NT2), that is (to say), meaning (that).

יעקב (H) **yaᶜaqof** Jacob (referring to Jacob the forefather, or a learned person so named); **yaᶜqub** (for a lay person); cf. אאקו.

יפאיא, יפיתא (< י-פ-י) **yapāya, yapēṯa** (NT5 410) baker (=H אוֹפֶה, BT1, D; PolG); cf. מטפייניתא.

י-פ-י (OA/OS אפי) **y-p-y** to bake (NT+).

יפרך (K<T) **yaprax** stuffed grape-leaves (favorite festive dish); cf. דולמא.

יבשתתא, יפשתתא v. יפשאתא

יצחק (H) **yıṣ/sḥaq** Isaac (the forefather); cf. אסחק, אגו.

יצר הרע (H) **yıṣrarāᶜ** (Z) the evil inclination (cf. NT5 382), the devil; — **ʾurre go qalwe** He lost his bearing, the devil entered his body, he is possessed (NT+).

יצרתא (OA/OS יִצְרָא passion) (harmonious) character, inclination (PolU 243) [cf. MacD 121 **yiṣrā** mind, fancy imagination]

י-ק-ד, ק-י-ד (OA/OS יקד) **y-q-ḏ** (NT, RivSh 192), **q-y-ḏ** (Z **q-y-z**; ZU 72b **y-q-z**), to burn (vi); יאקדלו לבוה **yaqıḏlu lıbbuh** They feel pity; IV to burn (vt)[1: **mōqıḏ**; 2/3: **māqıḏ**; 4: **maqōḏe**].

יקורא, יקורתא (OA/OS יַקִּירָא dear, heavy) adj. **yaqūra, yaqurta** heavy; (of speech, = H כְּבַד פֶּה, PolG:Ex 4:10); oppressive; stale (taste); impressive (NT5 383); onerous (work) (SaAC 3); grievous (AvidH 62); **garme yaqūre** unpleasant person (lit., his bones heavy) (NT+) [Khan 585 heavy, difficult, expensive].

יקורותא (< יקורא) f. **yaqurūṯa** heaviness (BT2); cf. יקרותא.

יקורתא (< יקורא) f. **yaqurta** the Torah scroll (lit., the heavy/venerated one); **bay yaqurta** (I swear) by the Torah scroll; the Great Sabbath (before Passover=H שבת הגדול; but Amedi 49: Sabbath **ve-Yitro** in which the Ten Commandments are recited).

יקין (Ar) **yaqīn** total faith; ביקין דלבא **byaqīn dlıbba** wholeheartedly (NT2).

י-ק-נ II (Ar) **y-q-n** to believe wholeheartedly, be convinced (NT2); גמיקנכבוך **gımyaqnax-box** We trust in thee (NTU4 157a).

יכסיר v. יקסיר

יכסירותא v. יקסירותא

י-ק-ר (OA/OS increase in value, honor; ferment) **y-q-r** to grow heavy; to become stale (taste): **gōze tımʾu yqırre** the walnuts' taste has become stale; VI to honor (מויקרה, NT2; מייקורה, NT5 400; מייקרכלוך, NTU4 164a); to make heavy; **gmayqırra gyāne** He keeps his distance, remains aloof.

יקרות (OA) f. **yıqrūṯ** nightmare, incubus (heaviness).

יקרותא (OA) f. yıqrūṯa heaviness (NT+).

ירא שמים (H) inv. ⁺yāre šāmāyi(m) God fearing person(s)(cf. PolU 149, 285).

ירוקא, ירוקתא (OA/OS/Mand יוֹרָקָא, green, yellow; OA יָרוֹקָא yellow/OS ـــفـ pale) yarūqa, yaruqta green (NT+).

ירושלים (H) yırušaláyim (Z rošláyim) Jerusalem; the Holy Land (cf. RivSh 178, 196, 274) (NT+).

יריחו (H) yarīḥo Jericho; lanky person (humorous-pejor., pun with יריכא).

יריכא, ירכתא (OA/OS/Mand אריכא) adj. yarīxa, yarıxta long; ᵓīze yarıxta touches women lewdly (lit., his hand long), lecher; lišāne yarīxa one with sharp tongue, with impudent response to older people (NT+).

יריכאנא, יריכנתא (< יריכא) adj. yarīxāna, -anta, lengthy (cf. PolG).

י-ר-כ (OA/OS/Mand ארך) y-r-x to be long, to last; yarxi xāyox May you live long; ᵓe masale yrıxla ubtıxla This case has become overwrought; IV to prolong, extend (NT5 382); la mayrıxıtta Don't talk too much (I have enough)! muyrıxle lišāne ᵓılli He was impudent to me (PolG) (NT+).

ירכא 1 (OA/OS יַרְחָא) m. yarxa month; cf. סהרא; yarxıd ᵓēzīlāne the month of the Arbor Holiday (=Shebat; February); yarxıd ṣōma ᶜazīza the month of the Venerable Fast (Yom Kipur) (=Tishre); yarxıd ⁺salīḥōṯ the month of penitential prayers (=Ellul).

ירכא 2 (OA) yarka thigh (NT3); cf. עטמא.

ירכות, ירכותא, ירכנותא (< י-ר-כ; cf. OA/OS אוּרְכָּא) f. yırxūṯ(a) (Z; PolG), yırxanūṯa (NT4), length.

י-ר-מ v. ר-י-מ

י-ר-ק (OA/OS be pale) y-r-q to become green; to wait or be unused for a long time: yrıqlan ltāma uᵓāwa la sēle We waited for him a long time, yet he did not show up; to grow, bloom: dıqne yrıqta ula yrāqa His beard has barely sprouted (PolG).

ירקא (OA/OS יַרְקָא) m. yırqa greenery.

ירקותא (< ירקא) yırqūṯa greenery, greenness.

י-ר-ת (OA/OS) y-r-ṯ (Z y-r-s) to inherit; IV to let someone inherit (NT+).

יַרְתְּתָא (< י-ר-ת) n. act. yraṯṯa inheritance (PolG: Jdg 21:17).

ישיבה (H) f. yašīva yeshiva, traditional Jewish school or academy; night memorial service; pl. (באתד) ישיבות bātıd yašīvōṯ; cf. מדרש.

ישעיה, שעיה, שעו (H) yešaᶜya Isaiah; šaᶜya, šıᶜo hypo. forms.

ישראל 1, יצראל (H) ⁺yısrāᵓel, ᵓıs-(SaLH 149), Israel, Jew, Jewish (m. f. pl.); an Israel (not a Cohen or Levi); - גמאעת jamāᶜıt - the Congregation of Israel; - -בי bē- the House of Israel (NT+) [cf. Mutz 240].

ישראל 2, ישרו (H<ישראל 1) ⁺yısrāᵓel , ⁺yısro (hypo.) Israel, common proper name.

ישׂשכר (H) ⁺ᵓisāxar Issachar.

ישתבח שמו ויתעלה (כסא) הדרו (H) yištabbaḥ šamō wıyitᶜallē (kisse) hadārō May His name be praised and (the throne of) his glory exalted (NT2).

י-ת-ו (OA/OS יתב) y-t-w to sit; - ž māya to have a bowel movement (SaAC 7)[1: (y)tū-, (y)tīwa, (y)tūta; 2: yātu, yatwa; 3: (y)tū(lox), tūn (pl.)4: ytāwa]; IV to place, to seat [1: muttū-; 2/3: mattu, matwa; 4: mattōwe).

יתאוא, יתווא (OA יתובא) m. yatō/āwa resident, dweller (NT, BT), attendant (of school) (NT3); yatāwıt rāste dīde the (viziers) sitting to his right (Zaken 392).

יתומא, יתומתא (OA) yatūma, yatumta orphan; kōz yatūme Orion (?) (lit., a group of orphans; OA יוּתָא ? SokBA 532) (NT+).

-יתון v. -תון

יתותא (< י-ת-ו) n. act. ytōta (kind of) sitting: ryamta u — dīde (She was watching all his) movments (lit., rising snd sitting) (PolG); (specific) bowel movement (SaAC 7).

י-ת-י v. א-ת-י

-יתן v. -ת 2

כ (k)

כ (H) **kaf kafūfa** the bent Kaf; ך **kaf pašūṭa** the straight Kaf; the eleventh letter of the Hebrew alphabet; **ʾısri** twenty.

-כ v. -ג

כאבאנייה (K **kebani**) f. **kābānīye** skilled cook, housewife, servant woman; pl. **kābānīyat**.

כאבלתא (K **kāvil**) f. dump, ruined place; cf. סולתא; pl. **kāvılyāṯa** (BaBin 101; PolG).

כאברא (K) m. **kāvırra** very young sheep; cf.כורא 2.

כאג'ד, כאג'ז (P/K) **kāġaz/d** paper, piece of paper, note; cf. ורקא [Khan 572 **kaxta**].

כאדא (K) f. **kāda** baked turnover stuffed with cheese (**kādıd gupta**) or fried fat (**kādıd sısqe**); pl. **kāde**.

כאוא, כהוא (Mand כאוא; OA/OS כַּוּותָא/כַּוְּתָא/BA כַּוָּה; Ar كَوَّة) f. **kāwa** (Z, NT3, Segal #142; PolG), **kahwa** (NT2), air-hole, little window; pl. כוואתא **kawāṯa** (NT3), כהויה **kahwe** (NT2), כְוַואוֵוי **kawāwe** (Z; Sa83c 38, Am; =H אֲרֻבּוֹת, PolG) (OA/OS pl. כַּוֵּוי).

כאוה v. ה-ו-י

כואלה (K?) pl. **kawāle** sheep variety (?).

כאכא (OA/OS/Mand כַּכָּא molar tooth/P کَکَا **kakā** the teeth) m. **kāka** (any) tooth; כאכא דפיל – **dpīl** ivory;-**ıd gurga** cowry shell(s) (lit., wolf's tooth; used as a charm for a child after having his first tooth); -**ıd sōta** kind of spice (= cardamum?) or seeds; כאכא דרילו **drēlu** – They gnashed (their) teeth, held a grudge (NT2); **pısrıd kāke** gums; cf. ככתא, כאכלו.

כאכלו (K < כאכא?) inv. **kākıllo** toothy, one whose teeth stick out.

כ(א)לא (ריספי) (K) m. **kāla, kalla (respī)** a mythical old man, Father Time (keeps the track of day and night by winding a ball of yarn) (PolU 325).

כאלו (v. כלתא) f. **kālo** bride; pimple in the eye; cf. מאתא 2; pl. כלואתא **kalawāṯa** (NT+) [Khan 571-2 **kālo+kalla**, H].

כאל-ובר-כאל (K?) adv. **kāl-u-bar-kāl** tied securely (?) (polU 87).

כאלותא (< כאלו) f. **kālōta** doll, 'little bride'.

כאלכה (P) pl. **kālıke** cheap traditional sandals used by the villagers

כאן v. אנכן

כאסא (OA כַּרְסָא) f. **kāsa** belly, womb; **gıbēla kās gyāne** He likes to eat; **kāse kīʾa** He is smart; **d-r-y go** - to keep (insults) inside, to take it in (SaAC 14); pl. **kasāṯa**; **ʾıtla xamša** - She was pregnant five times (NT+).

כאסאנא, כאסנתא (< כאסא) **kāsāna, kāsanta** big-bellied; **pıšle kāsāna** became big-bellied (=H כְּשָׂה, BT5).

כאסכתא (K < Ar) f. **kāsıkṯa** cup; pl. **kāsıkyāṯa**.

כאפא (OA כַּפָּא, כַּתְפָּא; OS ܟܬܦܐ) m. **kāpa** shoulder; כברוך גמנדילה בתר כאפיהון **xabrox gmandēle baṯır kapēhun** They ignore your words (they throw your words behind their shoulders); pl. כפאניה **kapāne** (cf. PolG) (NT+) [cf. Khan 572 **kpāna**, pl. **kpāne**].

כאפר (Ar) **kāfır** infidel; **ʾamin wıt yan** - Are you co-religionist (?) or infidel? (PolUL 381); pl. כאפרין **kāfırīn**; cf. כ-פ-ר (NT+).

כאר (K/P) **kār** possibility, ability, occupation; **la kısya lkār** It cannot be described, beyond any description (SaAC 12; PolU 383) **kār-u-bār** preparations (PolG) (NT+).

כארא (Ar كَـرَّة) f. **kāra** recurrent time; ומי כארא לבתרא **umay kāra lbaṯra** from then on; בכא כארא **bxa kāra** (not) at all; כר כיתא/כינא **kar xēta/xēna** once more, again; שואי/אלפא כארה **šōʾi/ʾalpa kāre** (Z **šōʾi-ga**) even though; **ʾalpaga ʾilāha maʾmır bēse** I am very grateful to him (PolU 436); cf. איכר; גוכר (NT+).

כרוון v. כארוואן

כארובאר (K) **kār-u-bār** preparation (PolG).

כארטה (T< E) pl. **kārṭe** playing cards.

כאריזה (K) pl. **kārēze** only in **sehrān** - community picnic (in canals area ?) [cf. Khan 572 **kārēz** 'running water, canal', K].

כאר-כאנא, כרא-כאנא (IrAr< P) f. **kār-/karra-xāna** factory; brothel.

כארתא (IrAr) f. **kārata** shoehorn.

כאש-וכנדאלת (K) pl. **kāš-u-kandālat** steep hills and deep valleys (PolU 17); cf. כנדאלא.

כאשייא (< OA/OS/Mand כָּסָא/Ar كاس?) f. **kāšīya** drinking glass; goblet (=H גָּבִיעַ, כּוֹס, BT1); **kāšīyıd qıdduš** kiddush (wine ritual) cup; cf. כאסכתא; pl. **kāšīye** (Socin 161; PolG).

כאתב(ג׳י) (Ar) m. **kātıb(či)** scribe, clerk (=H סוֹפֵר, PolG); pl. כַּאתִבֵּי **kātıbe** (RivSh 123).

כבאא (K < Ar كعب) m. **kab'a** anklebone; cf. כּעבייה; pl. **kab'e** (NT+).

כבאאנה (< כבאא) **kab'āne** a game of anklebones (cf. PolU 320).

כבאבא (A; cf. OA כְּבָבָא roasting, כבב to roast < Ak **kabābu**) f. **kabāba** one kebab, ground meat broiled on skewer; pl. **kabābe**.

כבאבג׳י (Ar-T) m. **kabābči** seller of kebab.

כבוד (H) f. **kāvōḏ** (Z **kāvōs**), **kawód** (Hob89 66), respect (to elders or Rabbis; cf. BaBin121); בכבוד **baxavōs** (Z) Please, With respect (said to one called to read the Torah); cf. AvidH 45-47; also a family name (Z); cf. עזתא, קדר; מלאך (NT+).

כבוד אב ואם (H) **kıbbūḏ 'āv wa'ēm** (the duty of) honoring one's father and mother (NT2).

כבז׳א (K) m. **kavvaža** residue of hair or wool.

כבז׳ון (K **kewij** 'sexual heat'?) **kavažōn** (prey bird) in an attack position (PolU 106).

כַּבֵיכְוַואנֵי (< K **kawī** haughtiness/**xawe** tax paid by farmers to the village master) pl. **k/xavexwāne** oppressors (=H נֹגְשִׂים, PolG: Ex 5:6; var. מַאלְכְּוַואנֵי landlords).

כביכול (H) **kāvyāxōl** (!) if one could say, so to speak (used to avoid anthropomorphism of God; cf. AlfM 29).

כבלאנא (K?) m. **kavlāna** sheath (of sword; =H תַּעַר, PolG) [cf. MacD 124 **kāblān** <?].

כבנד v. כמרבנד

כ-ב-ס, כ-פ-ס (Ar/OS) **k-b-s** (NT5 402; RivSh 263; Z; PolG), **k-p-s** (BT1, Am; AvidH 64), to conquer (NT; PolG); to be bewitched and unable to get pregnant (Z); cf. כבסה.

כבסה (< כ-ב-ס; cf. Ar كابوس) f. **kabse** evil spirit bewitching menstruating woman or brides into sterility [cf. MacD 137 < OS **kefsē** menses; **kefsānīṯa** menstruating woman].

כ-ב-ר v. כ-ו-ב-ר

כ-ב-ר-ד III (< כברית) vi/vt **k-b-r-d** to burn, to char; to be overcome with feeling (lit., to have one's guts burning) (=H נִכְמְרוּ רַחֲמָיו, BT1; BaBin 104; PolG).

כברישכה (K) f. **kıvrīške** hare, rabbit; cf. ארנווא; pl. **kıvrīškat** (PolU 3).

כברית, כבריד, גפריד (Ar; OA כיבריתא) **kıbrit/d, gıprid** (?) (NTU4 162a), sulfur, brimstone (=H גָּפְרִית, BT1).

כגֹה (K) f. **kačče** girl, young lady (PolU 207: ChNA).

כגופה (K?) pl. **˚kačōpe** little stones (PolG).

כגכוכה (K) **kıčkōke** village girl; pl. **kıčkōkat**.

כגלא/ה, כגלוכא/ה (K) m. **kaččala** (m.)/-**le** (f.), -**lōka**/ -**lōke** (dim.), one with bald pate, one suffering from scalp disease (cf. PolU 238).

כגלותא (< < כגלא) f. **kaččalūṯa** scalp disease (=H שְׂאֵת/קָרַחַת, BT3).

כדא (Ar) **kadda** toil; the earnings from hard work.

כדונא (K **kedūn**/OS كدنا/ OA כַּדָּא) f. **kaddūna** jar.

כדכודא 1, כתכודא (K/P) **kad/txuda** alderman, wealthy (cf. PolU 8); pl. **kadxudāyin** (PolU 59).

כדכודא 2 (< ?) **kadkōda** stocky, well-built person.

כ-ד-ר II (Ar) **k-d-r** to distress, perturb (=H עכר, NT5 402).

כה, כילא (< K that?) interj. **kē(la)** Let (us, him, etc.)! **kē(la) mšadrun** Send (already)! **kē mjarbaxlu** Let us try them (PolG).

כהוא v. כאוא

כהונה, כּוּהְוּנָא (H) **kıhunna, küh-** (BT4, D), priesthood; cf. כוהנותא.

כ-ה-ל (OA) **k-h-l** to be able, to feel like (used with negation only): **lıbbi lak kāhıl maġvannu** I cannot bring myself (lit., My heart is unable) to talk to them(cf. PolG).

כהרא (K) **kahra** baby-goat; cf. כאברא.

כו 1, כוד (< כול ד -) **ku(d)** each, every, when; since; כו איכד **ku 'ēkıd** wherever that; כו אימי **ku 'ēmi** whoever; כוד יומא ויומא **kud yōma uyōma** each and every day; **kud-yōm** every day; **kuḏ-lēl** (Z **kuzlel**); **kuš-šabsa** every week, every Saturday; **kuš-šat** every year [Khan 581 **kud šāt**]; מכוד **mkud** once they ..., since; כומד **kumıd** whenever; כומד איויתון בסימה **kumıd 'īwētun bassīme** (=Z **čımmād hāwētun ṣāx**) as long as you live; כומד כיתה בהרא גזאיד **kumıd kēṯe behra** gzāyıd Its light increases more and more (NT2); kuttlāhun xabūše all three apples (cf. PolG); kutru (m./f.), kutırtōhun (f.) both of them; v. כול.

כו 2 (K/Ar يكون?) kū always (Socin 163).

כו 3 v. גו

כואוה, כוואתא v. כאוא

כוואז (*Ar) kawwāz potter (NTU4 157a); cf. כוזא [cf. MacD126 kūzačī potter; Krotkoff 124 kawāza pitcher]

כואלה (K?) pl. kawāle sheep variety raised in the yard of the house.

כוארא (Ar/OA/OS כַּוָּרָא 'bee-hive', SokBA 565; but M. Jastrow 617 כְּוֶורֶת/כוורתא receptacle of grain) f. kwāra bin, receptacle for grain; pl. kwarāre.

כָּוָאשָׁא, כָּוֹושָׁא (< כ-ו-ש) kawāša (Z), kawōša (AvidH 60), one who descends (=H יוֹרֵד).

כובא (K) m. kōva funnel.

כובאבא (Ar) f. kubbāba ball of yarn, spool.

כובי, כיבי, כוביכא (K) inv. kūvi (Z), kīvi (AvidH 50), kūvīka (PolG), wild; unusual; v. כמצתא, בראנא.

כובן (K) kōvan yearning pain; mıtla bkōvan brāta She died out of sorrow for her daughter; pl. kōvāne (BaBin 156; PolG).

כ-ו-ב-ר III (Ar كبّر) k-ō-b-r to pray (Muslim), say ᵓallāhu ᵓakbar God is great (PolU 255)[1/2/3:mkōbır; 4:mkōbōre].

כוגׄכא (K) m. kučıka little dog (cf. PolU 318).

כוגׄכה (K) f. kōčke guests area around the fire place (RivSh 142); stove (=H כִּירַיִם, BT3).

כוגׄכתא (K) f. kōčıkta spoon; -ıd lıbba the deepest spot of the chest (PolU 110); pl. kōčıkyāta.

כוגׄרנאיא, כוגׄרניתא (K) kōčarnāya, -nēta, nomadic Kurds.

כוד v. כו 1

כודא 1 (OA/OS/Mand כַּבְדָּא, m.) f. kōda liver.

כודא 2 v. כוזא 1

כודך, כודכד (< כוד+אך) kudax(d) just as, like; kudax basmālox as you wish (PolG).

כוודנתא (OA כּוּדַנְיָא/כּוּדַנְתָּא/OS ܟܘܕܢܐ ܟܘܕܢܬܐ/ Mand כודאנא < Ak kūdanu) f. kawdınta (NT; but Z kōzınta) mule; pl. kōdıne (cf. PolG)(OA pl. כּוּדְנְוָותָא/כּוּדַנְיָיתָא; SokBA 555).

כוהן (H) kōhē/en (Jewish) priest; a kohen; כוהן גדול kōhēn gādōl the High Priest; pl. כוהנאיה kohanāye, kōhanīm; cf. כומר (NT+).

כוהנותא (< כוהן) f. kōhanūta priesthood; cf. כהונה.

כוזא 1, כודא (K/P کوز hump) kōza, kōda (?) (PolG) pile (=H גָּלָל, PolG); kōzıd mılxa pillar of salt (BT1); kōzıd sahdūta mound of testimony (=H גַּלְעֵד, BT1); kōz yatūme a constellation, perhaps Orion (lit., a bunch of orphans); pl. kozawāta (PolU 87), kōze (kōde = H צִבּוּרִים, PolG).

כוזא 2 (K/P garden; sheep fold) kōza yard, open area (=H מִגְרָשׁ/חָצֵר, BT3).

כוזא 3 (OA/OS/Mand/Ar/K/P; +OA כּוּזְתָא) kūza jug, jar; pl. כוזיאתא kuzyāta (?)(NT5 406f.); cf. גודא 2.

כוזי-דאנכה (K) f. kūzi-dānke hole in the ground for holding the bottom of jars.

כוזיתא (< כוזא 2?) f. kōzīta (?) unobtrusive area, corner (NT2).

כוזייא (< K hump, dent) f. kūzīya round slice (of cucumber) (PolU 15).

כוזם (Ar?) k/xūzım brine (?) (NT5 409).

כווזרה (K?) f. kawzare beautiful lass (PolG).

כ-ו-י (OA/OS) k-w-y to be cauterized, seared; IV to sear (vt).

כוינא (K) f./m. kwīna black tent made of goat hair; pl. kwīne (cf. PolG).

כְּוִיסְתָּאנֵי (< K kī/ūvi-stān) pl. kıwistāne pastures (=H בָּשָׁן, AvidH 67); cf. זוזן, כובי.

כוכא (OA כּוּכָא/Ar كوخ hut) m. kūxa cavern; pl. kūxe; cf. כוכתא (NT+).

ככוביה, כוכויה v. כותא

כ-ו-כ-ר III (<?) ⁺k-ō-k-r vi/vt to be or make sad [1/2/3: mkōkır; 4: mkōkōre] [cf. Garbell 287 k-fk – r be sad].

כוכתא, כוככתא (OS ܟܘܟܬܐ) f. kuxta, koxıkta (PolG), shed; pl. כוכיאתא kuxyāta (NT5 406); cf. כוכא [MacD 126 kūxtā].

כול-, כולו, כולנתו (OA/OS/Mand) kull-, kullu, kullıntu (+NT), all (of them); cf. כו 1 [but Khan 572 kulla all, everyone].

כולאבא (Ar/OA) m. kullāba hook; pl. כֻּלַּאבֵּי kullābe (=H וָוִים, BT2, D).

כולאנא, כּוֹלַנְכָּא (K) m. kōlāna (Z; NT5 403), kōlanka (BT4, D), alley, path (=H מִשְׁעוֹל, BT4); pl. kōlāne.

כולב (K greedy/Ar كُلبة dearth) **kulb** hunger: **mgo kulb-ile ʾısya** He is gluttonous, starving.

כול בלכול (Ar) **kul bıl-kul** each and every thing (PolU 242, 390)

כולינה (K) f. **kulīne** platform to store bedding.

כוליתא (OA/OS) f. **kulīṯa** kidney; **kulīṯıd ʾaqla** leg's calf; pl. כֻולְיָיאתָ֗א **kulyāṯa** (cf. PolG).

כולכא (K/P/OA כּוּלְכָא soft wool from goat's hair) m. **kulka** inferior sticky residue of wool [MacD 133 **kilkā** < AzT wool of the cotton-plant; silk-remnant].

כולכה, כולכתא (K **kulek**) f. **kullıkṯa, -ake**, ulcer (PolU 73, 235);pl. כֻולֶיכְיַיתָ֗א **kulıkyāṯa** hemorrohids (= H עֲפָלִים, PolG); cf. בואסיר.

כול נדרי v. נדרא

כומא, כומתא (OA אוּכָּמְתָּא ,אִיכּוּמָא/אוּכָּמָא; OS ܐܘܟܡܬܐ ;ܐܘܟܡܐ; Mand עכומא) adj. **kōma, kumta** black; **gāde kōma** poor guy (lit., his luck black); cf. כ-י-מ (NT+).

כומד v. כו 1

כומותא (< כומא) f. **komūṯa** blackness (NT+).

כומנאיא, כומניתא (< כומא) adj. **komnāya, -nēṯa**, blackish, sort of black.

כומר (H; cf. OA/OS כּוּמְרָא) m. ***kúmmar** Christian/pagan priest (cf. BT1); angry, sour person (Z); pl. כּוֹמַּארִים **kommārīm** (BT4, D); cf. כוהן.

כומפיאלא (IrAr < It kombiale) f. **kumpiyāla** bill of exchange.

כ-ו-נ II (< כוונה/OA/OS כון) **k-w-n** to intend; do by design; (=H צָדָה, BT2, Am/תֵּאָה, BT4, D); to stare, examine: **mkōwınne bāš bıd dē xamsa** He intently looked long at this lass (PolG).

כונג'ירכא (K?) m. **kunjīrka** (=H דַּרְדַּר, BT1).

כונדרה v. קונדרתא

כוונה, כוונא (+NT) (H) f. **kawwāna** intention, concentration (in prayer, or religious duty).

כונכה (K) f. **kunnıke** underground hiding place, tunnel (=H מַחְתֶּרֶת, BT2).

כוסא 1 (AnAr/SA < P/T) only in **qarʾa kōsa** slim and smooth zucchini [MacD 128 'young man, smooth faced].

כוסא 2 (< K swordsman?) m. **kōsa** a Kurdish title, precedes proper name (PolU 11, 125).

כוסיתא (OS hat; cf. OA כסיתא covering?) f. **kusīṯa** hat; pl. **kusyāṯa**; **kusyās-ḥāji-lōkat** mushrooms (lit., hats of hadjis) (cf. PolG) [Khan **ksila**, pl. **ksiye**].

כוספא (OA/OS < Ak **kuspu/kupsu**; Ar كُسبة residue of dates, etc) m. **kuspa** dregs of sesame.

כופאיה (IrAr **kūb** cup/K-T **kūp** jar) f. **kōpāye** cup, glass (PolUR 3).

כופונה (IrAr < En) pl. **kupōne** coupons (for food rations).

כֻּפְּרוּתָא (< כּ-פ-ר) f. **kuprūṯa** denial of God (=H חֶסֶד, BT3, D).

כורא 1 (OA) m. **kūra** kiln, forge; כֻורִית פְּרִזְלָא **kūrıt prızla** iron forge (=H כּוּר הַבַּרְזֶל, PolG); **kūr dugle** fabricator of lies.

כורא 2 (K) m. **kūra** young goat; cf. גיסכא, כאברא.

כורא 3, כורה (K) adj. **kōra, -e**, blind; cf. שהארא.

כוראכא (< כ-ר-כ) m. (but Socin 159: f.) **kurāxa** shroud; common in curses: **dārēlox go kurāxa** May you be placed in a shroud (Segal #28).

כור פהים, כּוֹרָא פְּהֶם (K-Ar) inv. **kōr(a)-fahım** witless (=H נָבָל, BT5, D; ZU 72b); cf. כור-פהמותא.

כורג'אלכה (K) **kōrčālke** ditch (PolU 17, 328); cf. ג'אלה.

כורדי (Ar/K) **kurdi** Kurdish; cf. כורמנג'י.

כורדינאיא, כורדיניתא (Ar كردي+OA -נאיא.; cf. OA כּוּרְתִּיךְ, adj. Kurdish) **kurdīnāya, -nēṯa**, a Kurd; cf. קורדאיא

כורדיסתאן (K) **kurdistān** Kurdistan, Ararat (=H אֲרָרָט, BT1).

כוריסכא (K) m. **kurīska** foal, young ass or horse (NT+).

כורכ (K/T) f. **kurk** fur coat; **kurk-u-ʿabayyye** fur cloak (MeAl 182, n. 39).

כורכה (K < Ar قُرقة) f. **kurke** brood-hen, mother-hen.

כורכמאנא, כורכמנתא (< OA/OS כּוּרְכְּמָא crocus, saffron) adj. **kurkmāna, kurkmanta**, yellow, pale; cf. כ-ר-כ-מ (NT+).

כורמר, כורמאר (K) m. ***kōrámar** viper, python, asp; pl. ***kōramāre** (cf. PolG) (NT+).

כורמיסכה (K?) f. **kōramiske** anger, resistance, reluctance (PolU 56).

כ(ו)רמנג'י (K) **kı/urmanji** Kurdish,

Kurdmanji.
כורמתיכא (< ?) f. **kurmatīxa** chicken's breast meat.
כורסי (Ar < OA כּוּרְסְיָא < Ak **kussū**) m. **kursi** chair, throne; **kursīka** little chair, stool; **kursıt babawāṯa** the Forefathers' Chair (put in the Sukkah for the Seven Guests; Amedi 54f.); pl. כורסייה **kursīye** (NT+).
כור-פהמותא (< כּוֹרָא פְּהֶם) f. **kōr-fahmūṯa** foolishness (BT1).
כורתכ (K/P<R) m. **kurtak** robe, overcoat (cf. PolG); — **ʿarabāna** 'wagon robe', a kind of robe (PolU 208: ChNA); pl. **kurtāke**.
כורתכא (K) **kurtıka** (one with) short (neck) (PolU 92).
כ-ו-ש (OA/OS/Mand כבש press down, capture, subdue) **k-w-š** to descend, go down; **la kušla bbaloʾte** He disliked her (lit., She didn't go down his throat) [1: **kwıš-/kuš-**; 2: **kāwıš/kōš-**; 3: **kōš**; 4: **kwāša**]; IV to bring down; **ṭēre gmakušlu mın šımme** He brings the fowls down from the sky (by singing so well) (PolU 344)[1: **mōkıš-**; 2-3: **makwıš/makuš**] (NT+).
כושא (K lap) **kōša** dress part that can be used as a basket to carry smal things (PolU 79).
כושאיא, כושית/כושיניתא (OS ܟܘܫܝܐ; OA כּוּשָׁאָה) **kūšāya** (m., NT2), **kūšīnēṯa/kūšīṯ** (BT4), Kushite, Negro.
כושאנא, כושנתא (< כ-ו-ש) **kōšāna, kōšanta**, low, descending; inferior, humiliated (NT2) (NT+).
כ-ו-ש-ר III (H) ***k-ō-š-r** to clean the meat according to Jewish law (SaAC 4) [1/2/3: **mkōšır**; 4: **mkōšōre**].
כושת v. כו 1
כושתא 1 (< כ-ו-ש) n. act. **kwašta** descent; pl. **kwašyāṯa** (PolGr 33).
כושתא 2 (< OA/OS כושא hand spindle?) f. **kušta** knitting needle; pl. **kušyāṯa** [cf. MacD 129].
כותאנא (K?) **kōtāna** sheepfold; pl. **kōtāne** (=H גִּדְרוֹת צֹאן, BT4) [cf. MacD 129].
כותוא v. כתוא
כותילה (K **kutilk** < Ar كُبّة) f./pl. **kutēle** dumpling(s); **kutēl-pısra** meat dumplings.
כותך, כותכי, כותכותא (K) **kōtak, kōtakki, kōtakūṯa** reluctance, hardship (=H פֶּרֶךְ, BT2); אודליה כותכותא לגיאנה **ʾudle kōtakūṯa lgyāne** He forced himself; בכותך **bkōtak** reluctantly (cf. PolG) (NT+).
כותלא v. כמאטא
כותלה (K?) f. **kotale** dam, water reservoir.
כותרכא, כותֵירא (K) f. **kōtırka** (Z), **kōtıra** (AvidH 41) dove, pigeon; cf. יונה.
כזא (Ar قز silk?) m. **kazza** moss; **yarūqa x-kazza** very green (as green as moss).
כזאלכ (Ar) adv.**kızālık** the same way (Pol 137)
כזב (< כ-ס-ב) **kazab** offspring (=H יוֹצֵא חֲלָצַיִם, פְּרִי בֶטֶן, PolG).
כזוותא, כוזותא, כִּיסְוִיתָא (< כ-ס-י?) f. **küzwıta** (NT2; NTU4 161b), **kıswıta** (BT1, D), suit, vestment, garment (=H כְּסוּת, BT2, Am; סות, BT1, D; צניף, NT5 394); pl. כזותיאתא **kızwıtyāṯa** (NT2); cf. כסותא.
כזייא (K) f. **kazzīya** tress; pl. **-at** (PolU 49).
כז'א (AnAr < K/P inferior silk) m. **kažža** fine goat-hair, cashmere; cf. כזא.
כח (H) m. **kuwwaḥ** (Z) power (NT2).
כחיל, כחילאן, כחילא (K/Ar) **kıḥel, kıḥēlān** (+NT), **kḥēla** (f.), high-bred (horse), mighty (horse, woman); pl. **kıḥēle** (PolG).
כחלי (Ar) inv. **kıḥli** azure-colored (NT3).
כי- 1 (K **ka**) **ke-** come on, please (an optional particle used with the imperative: **ke-hallīle kēpa** (Please) give me the stone! **keme [‹ ke-mēsi] hallūli sanad** Give me a document! (PolU 78).
כי- 2 v. איכא
כיא- v. י-ד-א
כיבי v. כּובי
כייד (Ar) **kayd** grudge; ד-ו-ק כייד **d-w-q kayd** to hold a grudge, to plot against (NT); מרה כייד **mare kayd** grudging person (NT5 402).
כיון (H) conj. **kēwān** since, because (NT2).
כ-י-ז-ר III (K **kizirīn** grill) **k-ī-z-r** to roast, burn the skin clean from hair or feathers; **nāve mkızırru ṭāla** He pined for her ('His innards burnt for her'); suffer (SaAC 14).
כיכ (IrAr < En) **kēk** (European style) cake.
כ-י-ל (OA/OS/Mand) **k-y-l** to measure.
כילא 1 (OA/OS כַּיְילָא) **kēla** dry measure (=H אֵיפָה, BT3, D); cf. כ-י-ל.
כילא 2, כילה, כילו v. איכא
כילא 3 v. כה
כילו (IrAr < E) **kēlo** kilogram; pl. **kēlōyat** (PolU 444).

כ-י-מ (OA אכם) **k-y-m** to become black; **lıbbe kımle mınna** He doesn't love her anymore; **pāse kımla** He has been proven to be a liar, was embarassed; **kımla ʾılle** He is having bad luck; IV to make black; **qam mākımla pāsan** He (a family member) has humiliated us (by his behavior) (NT+).

כימא v. פמא

כימאיי (K) f. **kēmāyi** impotence, anemia, weight loss; **kēmāyi duqla ʾılle** He has lost a lot of weight (due to illness).

כימן, כימד, כים (OA כאימת) **kī/ēman, kīm(ıd)** when (NT; RivSh 180, 227: כֵּימַן, כֵּימֶית).

כימנאהי (K) f. **kemnāhi** shortage (Amedi 72); v. ז-י-ד.

כימר v. א-מ-ר

כ-י-נ II (< כין) **k-y-n** envy (=H קִנֵּא, BT1; PolG).

כין, כינותא, כִּינֵי (K/P) **kīn, kīnūṯa** (NT4), **kīne** (=H קִנְאָה, BT4, D), grudge, envy, jealousy.

כינאנא (< כין) adj. **kīnāna, kīnanta**, jealous, envious (=H קַנָּא, BT2; RivSh 185).

כִּינַאר (< K side?) **kinar** plain (=H אֶרֶץ הַכִּכָּר, PolG:Gen 19:28=misreading for כיכאר?).

כ-י-ס 1 (OA כבס?) **k-y-s** to launder, wash off; **qam kēsālu ʾan julle hil mobruqlu** She washed those clothes until they glittered.

כ-י-ס 2 II (< כ-ס-י?) **k-y-s** to close [1: **mokıs**; 2: **makıs**; p.p.: **muksa**] (Hob89 218) [cf. MacD 176].

כיס (OA/Ar) **kīs** money bag, pocket; מכיסד גיאני **mkīsıd gyāni** from my own pocket, at my own expense; **šti mkīsi** Have a drink on me! (cf. PolU 2).

כיסי (K < Ar كيس) **kēsi** treacherous opportunity; **dammıd nāppıllu kēsi, bqaṭlīle** When they have the opportunity, they will kill him; **la xāze ču kēsi ʾıbbe** May (his enemies) never succeed to plot against him (Zaken 394).

כִּיסִיל v. כס

כ-י-פ 1 (OA כפי/כפף bend over) vi **k-y-p** to bend; kneel (=H כָּרַע, PolG); look down; **ʾēne kıpta/rēše kīpa** (he is) humble, modest; IV to bend (vt), compel; מכיפי רישוה **makīpi rēšuh** they surrender (lit., lower their head) (NT5 382); **ʾēne mukīpīle** He lowered his eyes (being humiliated) (RivSh 281).

כ-י-פ 2 II (Ar) **k-y-f** to enjoy oneself, to have fun; **nāše mkōyıflu ʾıllēni** People rejoiced in our misfortune; **mkīfa/mkōyafta** (p.p. m./f.; cf. PolG) joyful (AlfH 57); **mkēfun, pšōqun** Rejoice, be glad! (BaBin 6).

כיף (Ar) m. **kēf** joy (=H שִׂמְחָה, BT1); **nšēlan kēf zımmıryāṯa** We forgot the joy of songs; **kēfox** as you wish; **māṭo kēfox** How are you (m. sg.)? **kēfe sēle** He rejoiced; **kēfa ʾısya** She is rejoiced, happy; **kēf nāše sele ʾıllan** People rejoiced by our misfortune; **la tōrıtte kēfe** Don't spoil his joy; cf. כיפג'י.

כיפא 1 (OA/OS כֵּיפָא) m. **kēpa** stone; kernel; **kēpa qadōḥa/kēpıd ıqdāḥa** flint (used by smokers to light tobacco)(=H צוֹר, BT2, D); pl. **kēpe**; **ṯlaha - dīda qam mandēlu** He cast her three stones = implying divorce (in Kurdish-Muslim tradition?) (PolU 271); **kēpıd bará-barda** hailsrones.

כיפא 2, כפתא (< כ-י-פ 1) p.p. **kīpa, kıpta** bent, humble; כיפא ועניו **kīpa uʿānāw** humble and modest (BaBin 7).

כיפאייה (K? cf. P. گيپا **gīpā**) f./pl. **kēpāye** favorite Sabbath dish made of sheep stomach and intestines stuffed with spiced rice and meat [Garbell 315 **kipayta**, pl. **kipae**; Mutz. 197 **j/čipāta**; pl. **j/čipāʾe**]

כיפג'י (< כיף) inv. **kēfči** comedian, joyful, funny.

כיפכווש (K) inv. **kēfxwaš** cheerful, comedian.

כיפכוושותא (K) **kēfxwašūṯa** joy, amity (PolG).

כיראתה, כיראטה (OA כראתי , כְּרָתֵי) pl. ***kīrāte** leeks [cf. MacD 141 **kīrāṯā** herb, perh. a leek].

כישכ-וכבאן (K) **kēšk-u-kavan** arrow-and-bow (BaBin 143; PolU 107);pl. **-at** (PolU 381).

כִּירַהְיִת v. כריתותא

כ-י-ת (Ar كت) vi **k-y-t** to run dry, boil dry, subside (=H שָׁכְכוּ, BT1); **behne kıtle** He became breathless (cf. PolG); IV to boil dry, dry up (vt, cf. PolG); נהרואתא מוכיתילה **nehrawāṯa mukītīle** He dried up the rivers (NT5 386); drink last drop (RivSh 278).

כיתי- v. א-ת-י

כך (K **kixkix**) interj. **kıx** (It's) dirty, not good to eat! (baby talk); cf. קיע. [Bunis כיח

kix].

ככו, ככא (K) **kakko/a** (husband's) brother (mostly vocative used by daughters-in-law).

כוכוא, ככותא (OA/OS/Mand כּוֹכְבָא, m., SokBA 558; but M. Jastrow 619: also כּוֹכְבִיתָא, כּוֹכַבְתָּא) f. **kıxūṯa** (Z), **kuxwa** (PolG), star; pl. כוכביה, כוכויה, כְּוֹכְוֵוי, **kuxwe** (Z; NT5 409, PolG), **kuxve** (NT2).

ככל- v. א-כ-ל

כ-כ-כ- v. ג-כ-כ

כ-כ-ל (OA/OS כחל) **k-x-l** to use eye-paint (cf. BaBin 71; PolG).

ככלא (OA/OS כּוּחְלָא < Ak **guxlu**) m. **kıxla** antimony, kohl, mineral eye-paint (=H פּוּךְ, PolG); v. מככאלא.

ככתא (< כאכא) f. **kakta** clove (of garlic); pl. **kakyāṯa**.

כלא v. שאכר 1, כאלא

כִּלְאַיִם (H) **kilʿāyim** forbidden mixture of two kinds (BT3).

כלאשה v. כלש

כלבא (OA) m. **kalba** dog (also common in curses); **kalba bır kalba** real base person, the worst of his kind; **kalbıd ⁺māya** seal; an avid swimmer; **kalba blišān kalba la kfāhım** A dog doesn't understand the tongue of (another) dog (said about noisy places); pl. כלוה **kalwe** (cf. PolG, RivPr 211 כַּאלְוֵוי); **kalwıd bāba** sons of a dog (a curse; lit. dogs of a father) cf. כלויתא, כ-ל-ו, כלבתא (NT+) [Khan 571 **kalba**, pl. **kalbe**].

כלבדון (IrAr **kalabdūn**) m. **kalavdūn** (cloth with) silver threads (=H בּוּץ, AlfM 27).

כלבתא (OA) **kalıb/pṯa** bitch; pl. **kalıb/pyāṯa**.

כלבתן (Ar/OA/OS) **kalbatan** pincers, forceps.

כ-ל-ו (OA כלב) vi **k-l-w** to be aggressive or unruly (like a dog); IV to encourage aggressive behavior; cf. כלבא, כליוא.

כלוה v. כלבא

כלויתא (< כ-ל-ו) f. **kallawīṯa** (dog-like) aggression; cf. סרכיתא.

כלורא (K **q/kur/lora**/OA קילורית < Gr) f. **kıllōra** bagel-shaped bread-cake; pl. **kıllōre** (=H עֻגּוֹת, BT4, D); cf. קלו-קלו.

כלותא (< כאלו) f. **kalūṯa** bridehood (NTU4 148b); **naqša lōšattu bkalūsax** May you wear them in your bridehood.

כליגא (K/P) f. **kılēča** dry stuffed pastry.

כליוא, כלותא (< כ-ל-ו, p.p.) adj. **klīwa, klūta** aggressive, unruly.

כלייה (K/Ar?) pl. **kalīye** alleys, usually as hendiadys with כולאנה (Pol 107, PolG).

כלילא (OA wreath) m. **k(a)līla** chain for scarf; interwined (=H מְשֻׁלָּב, BT2).

כליליית (onomat.) pl. **kılīlīyat** ululating sounds of women during celebrations; **d-r-y kılīlīyat** to ululate.

כלינא (K) f. **kalē/īna** moaning, cry (cf. PolG).

כליפותא (< כ-ל-פ) f. **klīfūṯa** excrement (lit., necessity; euph.; =H צֵאָה, BT5).

כלכ (IrAr/K/P/T < OS < Ak **kalakku**) m. **kalak** type of raft (made of bound logs only); pl. **kalāke**; cf. עברא, כרכא.

כלך (K) **kallax** dead (body), very tired; cf. כלש; pl. **kallāxe** (PolU 14).

כלכאלא (K **kāl** < Ar كهل) m. **kālkāla** very old man.

כלכבאנ(ו) (K) **kalakvān(o)** raftsman; also common family name (Z); cf. כלכ.

כלכלתא (K) f. **kalkalta** excessive heat.

כלם (Ar) m. **kalam** cabbage.

כ-ל-מ-ג̇ III (IrAr) vt **k-l-m-č** to handcuff.

כלמג̇א (IrAr < T **kelepçe**) f. **kalamča** handcuff.

כ-ל-פ I/II (Ar) **k-l-f** to cost, to have to pay.

כלש (K) m. **kallaš** dead body (Z); living body (AmU1 79a); pl. כלאשה **kallāše** (PolG) (NT+).

כ-ל-ש (< כלשא) **k-l-š** to whitewash (=H שָׂד, BT5); cf. ש-י-א.

כלשא (OS) m. **kılša** whitewash (=H שִׂיד, BT5).

כלתא (OA/OS כַּלְּתָא) f. **kalṯa** daughter-in-law; pl. **kalāṯa** (cf. Ruth 1:6) (OA pl. כַּלָּאתָא); cf. כאלו [cf. Khan 571 **kalda**].

כמא 1, אכמא (OA כמא/כְּמָה) **kma(ʾ), ıkma** (+NT), How many? How...! אכמא לכמא **ıkma lkma/** כמא וכמא אלד כדא כמא **ʾillıd xḏa kma ukma** (=Z **láxasma**) How much more so! **bıkma(ʾ) zwīnīlox** At what price did you buy them?; כמילו **kmaylu** (NT)/**kmaʾīlu** (Z; PolG)) How many are they? v. ככמא (NT+).

כמא 2 v. פמא

כמאכא (T/P **kamxā** silk fabric?) **kamāxa** thigh (meat) (cf. PolG).

כמאלה (< מ-ל-י) adv. **kmāle** (It's) enough; **kmālewalēni** It would have been enough for

Gentiles); pl. כנשיאתא knıšyāṯa (MeAl 190; PolG); cf. מדרש (NT+).
כנשתא 2 v. כנושתא
כנתא 1 (< OS/OA כְּנָתָא/pl. כְּנָוָתָא?) f. kınnıta related group, same type of people.
כנתא 2 (OA כַּנְתָּא ileum) f. kanṯa stomach fat.
כס, כסל, -כסל(ל) (OA גיס 'side') kıs, kısıl, (l)kısl- to , with, chez; zıllu kısle They went to him/his home; כְּסֵיל בַּאבֵּי kısıl bābe (RivSh 127 = Z kıs bābe (NT+).
כסא (K) m. kassa close relative, dear one.
כסאתא v. כאסא
כ-ס-ב, כ-ז-ב II (Ar كسب) k-s/z-b to earn, achieve (cf. PolG); cf. כזב (NT+).
כ-ס-ד (Ar to dull) k-s-d to preserve meat by much salt.
כסד, כסאד, כאסד (Ar) inv. kasad unsaleable goods (NT+).
כסדאיה, כשדאיה (OA) kasdāye Chaldeans (NT, BT).
כסויא (OA כִּיסוּיָא; OS ܟܣܘܝܐ) m. kıssōya cover, covering (=H מְכַסֶּה, BT1).
כסותא (OA כְּסוּתָא/< כ-ס-י) f. ksūta/kıssōta (?) garment, covering (NT2); cf. כזוותא.
כ-ס-י II (OA/OS/Mand) k-s-y to cover (NT+).
כסידא (< כ-ס-ד) p.p. ksīda heavily salted (meat).
כסיכא, כסכתא (< כ-ס-כ) p.p. ksīxa, ksıxta fatigued.
כסיתא 1 (OA) f. ksēṯa cover (=H כַּפֹּרֶת, BT2).
כסיתא 2 v. כתיתא
כ-ס-כ (OA/OS כסח to prune) k-s-x to be exhausted, fatigued; to prune: כרמא דידוך לא כסכיתן karma dīdox la kasxētın Don't prune your vineyard (BaBin 49).
כסל v. כס
כסלו (H) kıslew the Hebrew month of Kislev.
כ-ס-מ (Ar قسم) k-s-m to swear; mostly as hendiadys: gyāme ukkāsım He emphatically swears.
כסמא (P) f. kasma dry pastry; pl. kasme.
כסנה (OS) kısne tiny corals used as jewelry (=H אַלְמֻגִּים, PolG); ṭōqid kısne coral necklace.
כסרא (Ar) f. kasra breakdown, distress (=H מָצוֹק, BT5, D).
כסרוון (P?) kasrawan silk scarf [MacD 136 large turban].

us (=H דַּיֵּנוּ, AlfH 49); לְכַמַאלֵי It is not enough (BaBin 165).
כמבאכא (K) inv. kımbāxa damned, worthless.
כ-מ-ב-כ III (K) k-m-b-x to be damned.
כמהה (OA) pl. kımhe truffles.
כמונא (OA/OS כַּמּוּנָא/Ar كَمّون < Ak kamūnu) f. kammūna cummin.
כמיאן (K?) m. kamiyān (return after sickness to) a prior healthy condition (PolU 370).
כמין, כמינכה (Ar; cf, OA/OS כמן hide, conceal) kımīn(ke) ambush; d-w-q — ʾıl- to ambush (RivSh 22; PolG) (NT+).
כמירא, כמרתא (< כ-מ-ר) p.p. kmīra, kmırta stale.
כ-מ-ל (Ar) vi k-m-l to be complete (NT), be well done, ready (PolU 9), to recover, regain weight loss (PolU 337); II vi/vt to fill (PolG); have all present (BaBin 123).
כמנג̇א (IrAr < P) f. kamanča violin, fiddle.
כמר- v. א-מ-ר
כ-מ-ר (OA [heat, shrink]? SokBA 586: כמר 3#) k-m-r to become stale, smelly (food); cf. כמירא.
כמר, כמרבנד, כבנד (P; cf. OA/OS קַמְרָא) m. kamar(band), kaband waistband, sash (=H אַבְנֵט/פּוּמָז, BT2).
כמרבסתא (P) kamarbásta purse-belt (PolG).
כנא (< K that not?) kánā at least (PolG).
כנדאלא (K) m. kındāla steep slope, deep valley; zılle bkındāla Went to hell, down the drain.
כנונא (OA/OS/Mand כָּנוּנָא portable brazier< Ak ki/anūnu) m. earthen stove, fire-stand.
כנושתא, כנשתא (OA מְכַנַּשְׁתָּא/כְּנִישְׁתָּא sweeping, gathering; OS ܡܟܢܫܬܐ broom) f. kanūšta broom; pl. כנושיאתא kanušyāṯa (NT5 406) (NT+).
כנכנא (K?) m. kankana lord, tycoon, a VIP.
כנענאיה (OS ܟܢܥܢܝܐ, OA כנענאָה) kanaʿanāye the Canaanites (BT).
כנף (H) kanaf corner of prayer shawl (BT4).
כ-נ-ש (OA/OS/Mand כנש) k-n-š to sweep (by broom); mırrūte kkānıš ʾarʾa He is in a very bad mood (lit., his face sweeps the floor); to pile (=H צָבַר, BT2, D).
כנשתא 1 (OA/Mand כְּנִישְׁתָּא/OS ܟܢܘܫܬܐ) f. k(ı)nıšta synagogue; knıšta juhīya very noisy place (lit., Jewish synagogue, said by

כסתא (OA כִּיסְתָא bag) f. **kısta** small/medium bag; **kıstıd pāre** money bag, purse (cf. PolG); **kıstıd ṣīṣi(t̲)** the prayer shawl bag; pl. **kısyāt̲a**.

כסתאיה (OS **krestāyē**) **kestāye** the old Christian neighborhood in Zakho.

כעבייא (Ar) f. **kaᶜbīya** heal; cf. אקבא, כבאא; pl. **kaᶜbīyat**.

כעכא (OA/OS כַּעְכָּא, כַּכָּא/Ar كعك < P **kāk**?) f. **kaᶜka** dry pastry; pl. **kaᶜke**.

כפא (Ar كفّ; cf. OA/OS כַּפָּא) f. **kaffa** palm, hand; pl. **kaffāfe** (cf. PolG); **rıš kaffāfıd malāxīne ᵓāzıt** May you travel on angels' palms (=Have a safe trip).

כפאנה v. כאפא

כפגאלא, גרגאלא (< K **kivžāl**) m. **kıfjāla** Bar-Adon), **gırjāla** (RivPr 212), crab [MacD 138 **kirjālā**].

כפור v. יום כפור

כפורא, כפורתא (OS) **kapōra, kapurta** faithless, cruel person (NTU4 148a); giant (cf. PolG).

כ-פ-י (Ar) **k-f-y** to protect (God:people); **ᵓilāha kāfēlox ᵓēna rāᶜa** May God protect you against the evil eye.

כפייא (Ar) f. **kafīya** plain scarf; **kafīyıd qāma** handkerchief (used as purse as well) (cf. PolU 112); pl. **kafīyat**.

כפיל (Ar) inv. **kafil** guarantor; pl. **kafīle** (PolGr 36) (NT+).

כפינא, כפנתא (< כ-פ-נ, p.p./OA/OS/Mand כַּפִּינָא) hungry; **kāsa kpınta ksōᵓa, ᵓena kpınta laksōᵓa** a hungry belly is satiated, (but) a hungry eye is not; v. אינא.

כ-פ-כ-פ III (< ?) **k-f-k-f** (ᵓıl) threaten and nag [MacD 177 hiss, breath hard].

כ-פ-ל (Ar) **k-f-l** to be surety (=H עָרַב, BT1).

כפלתא (K < Ar duty, expense) f. **kıflıta** large family or household; pl. **kıflıtyāt̲a**.

כ-פ-נ (OA/OS/Mand) **k-p-n** to be hungry; IV to keep someone hungry.

כפנא (OA/OS כַּפְנָא/Mand כופנא famine, hunger) m. **kıpna** hunger (NT+).

כפנכ (K/P; but cf. OA כפניתא saddle on a donkey's back, SokBA 596??) **kappanak** shepherd's mantle (sitting on shoulders, and sleeveless) (cf. PolU 428).

כ-פ-ס v. כ-ב-ס

כ-פ-ר (OA/OS/Mand) **k-p-r** to deny (God); be very angry (Z) (NT+).

כפרה (H) f. ***kappāra** expiation (sacrifice); **pēšan *kappārox** May I become your expiation (commonly said by mothers to sons); **pıšla *kappārox** It has become your expiation (said after something is broken or lost); **pēšāt *kappāri** 'May you (f.) become my expiation! (curse); ***kappārıt brōna wēla** She was very devoted to her son [cf. Khan 571 **kapparox ġadren** 'I would lay down my life for you'].

כפרות (כ-פ-ר) f. **kıprut̲** (religious) denial (PolU 380).

כפש (K < Ar كشف) adv/inv. **kıfš** obviously, clearly (cf. Segal #36); visible (PolU 37).

כפשוטו (H) **kıfšūṭō** as its literal meaning is (NT2).

כפתא (K/P beaten?) inv. **kıfta** totally exhausted (cf. PolG).

כר (K) inv. **karr** quiet, still (Zaken 387).

כרא, כרה (K) **karra** (m.), **karre** (f.) deaf (cf. PolG); cf. כ-ר-ר, כרכרא

כראבא, כרבתא (כ-ר-ב) ***karāba, *karabta** one prone to get angry, distressed.

כאר-כאנא v. כרא-כאנא

כראמתא, כראם (Ar) ***karāmıta, krām** (PolU 128), honor, respect, generosity; miracle; cf. אכראמותא (NT+).

כראפייה (Ar ?) f. **kırrāfīye** poison, malignancy (used mostly in curses).

כ-ר-ב (Ar) ***k-r-b** to be angry (**mın** at, NT5 385); IV to distress (NT+).

כרבא (Ar) m. **karba** anger (NT+).

כרביתא (< כ-ר-ב) f. **karbīta** (excessive) anger (BaBin 139; PolU 348).

כרג'ינא (K) m. **karčīna** pear; pl. **karčīne**.

כ-ר-ד (Ar) **k-r-d** to chase out (NT+).

כ-ר-ה (Ar كره detest; OA/OS כרה/כרח be sick) **k-r-h** to detest (NT, BT; PolG); disprove (NT5 384).

כרה (K < Ar) f. ***kıre** rent, labor fees; **duqle b*kıre** He rented, hired; cf. כ-ר-י 2 (NT+).

כרוון, כארואן (K/P) f. **kārwan** caravan (=H אֹרְחָה, BT1); **xa – ᵓırba** herd of sheep (PolG).

כרואנג'י (T) **karwančı** caravan leader (PolG).

כרוב (H) ***karuv** cherub; pl. **karūvim** (BT2).

כרובא, כרובתא (< כ-ר-ב) adj. **karōba, karubta** one who tends to be anguished, sad (BaBin

106), angry (=H רָגֵז, BT5).

כרונכא (K) m. **kırrōnka** child (PolU 161).

כרוסא (Ar) f. **kırrōs/ta** coach (PolU 232).

כ-ר-י 1 (OS) **k-r-y** to be short, low (NT+).

כ-ר-י 2 (Ar) ***k-r-y** to rent (room, store, from; cf. PolG); to hire; IV to rent out (to).

כריא 1, כריתא (< כ-ר-י 1) p.p. **kırya, krīta** short; **krīta xlīta** brevity is sweet.

כריא 2, כריתא (< כ-ר-י 2) ***kırya, krīta** rented (p.p.), hired laborer (=H שָׂכִיר, BT2).

כריבא, כרבתא (< כ-ר-ב) p.p. **krība, krıbta** distressed, angry, alienated (NT+).

כרים (Ar) inv. **karim** generous, noble (NT).

כריתותא (< כרת) f. **kıretūta** ugly deed, outrage, abomination (=H נְבָלָה/תּוֹעֵבָה, BT; cf. PolG).

כ-ר-ך (OA) **k-r-x** to be attached (NTU4 149a); be exhausted (PolU 119); II to shroud; cf. כוראכא.

כרכא (OA?) m. **karxa** raft (similar to כלך).

כרכובי (K) **kar-kūvi** wild donkey (=H יַחְמוּר, BT5).

כרכוכנאיה (K/Ar) pl. **karkuknāye** residents of Karkuk in Iraqi Kurdistan (=H לְטוּשִׁים, BT1).

כרכיתא v. כארא.

כ-ר-כ-ם III (OA) vt/vi **k-r-k-m** to become or make yellow, pale (Pol 108); cf. כורכמאנא.

כרכספאלא (< ?) m. **karxıspāla** junk, delapidated gadget, vessel; worn-out person (PolU 55).

כרכרא (< כרא) m. **karkarra** strange, light-headed, totally dunce.

כ-ר-ם II (Ar) ***k-r-m** to show respect (NT+).

כרם (Ar) m. ***karam** (divine) act of kindness; **ta - ʿilāha** for God's grace; cf. כראמתא (NT+).

כרמא (OM/OS) m. **karma** vineyard; pl. כרמאניה **karmāne** (cf. RivSh 208; PolG).

כרמיאנא (K) m. **kırmıyāna** wormy.

כרמכתא (K) **kırmıkta** worm (=H רִמָּה, AlfM 29); pl. **kırmıkyāta**.

כרנבנדא (p) m. **karanbanda** slave (NT2).

כרנגה (K; cf. OA כְּנְגַּר artichoke < P) pl. **karange** a kind of thistle whose roots are pickled or cooked in soups; cf. בלקו.

כרסתא (< ?) **karısta** raw material (Zaken 391) [Khan 572 'instrument, implement'].

כ-ר-פ II (IrAr 'to scoop') ***k-r-f** to eat (pejor.), stuff it in (cf. PolU 440).

כרפורכת (K?) pl. **karpurkat** belongings? small things? children ? (PolU 145).

כרפס (IrA/Ar < P) m. **kírafs** parsley [Khan 572 **karawuz**, K].

כרפסא (OA כַּרַפְסָא < P **karafs** > Ar كَـرَفس) m. **karapıssa** parsley (arch., used only with the Seder ritual; Gz73 58).

כ-ר-ר II (< כרא) **k-r-r** to become deaf; to deafen.

כרת, כִּירָהִית (K < Ar كـــراهة) inv. **kırıt** (Z), **kırāhıt**, ugly, detestable; abomination (=H תּוֹעֵבָה, BT1,D); cf. כריתותא.

כ-ר-ת II (< כרת) **k-r-t** to use ugly trickery (=H נִכֵּל, BT4, D).

כרתא (OS) f. **karta** load (on one's back)(cf. NTU4 162B); pl. **karāta** (cf. PolG).

כ-ר-ת-ן III(Ar < E quarantine). **k-r-t-n** to suffuse or be suffused with smoke or smell.

כשאפד צורה (Ar) **kašāfıd *surre** Revealer of secrets (=H צָפְנַת פַּעְנֵחַ, BT1).

כשא (K/Ar) interj. **kıšša** Shoo! Cf. כ-ש-כ-ש.

כשכא 1 (IrAr) f. **kašxa** show-off (dress).

כשכא 2 (K/P) f. **kaška** dried yoghurt or butter milk; pl. **kaške**.

כשכג׳י (IrAr) **kašxači** one who likes to dress well to show off.

כשכייה (< כשכא 2) f. **kaškīye** dish made of butter-milk and grits.

כשכרי (OA כּוּשְׁקָרָא/OS ܟܘܫܟܪܐ < P(> Ar) خُشكار inferior type of flour) m. **kıškıri** a fine type of bulgur, semolina.

כ-ש-כ-ש III (K/IrAr) **k-š-k-š** to shoo away (=H הֵשִׁיב, PolG: Gen15:11).

כשכש ברא (IrAr). **kıškıš *barra** Go out and away! (Said after mentioning an ailment).

כשר, כשירא, כשרה (H) **kašēr(a)** (m.)(BaBin 105; PolU 390), **kašēra** (f.), righteous, honest; cf. כ-ו-ש-ר, חלאלא.

כתאבה (Ar) **kıttābe** book-keepers (PolU 246).

כתאוא 1 (OA כְּתָבָא script, amulet) m. **ktāwa** letter; writing.

כתאוא 2 (< כ-ת-ו) m. **katāwa** scribe; כְּתָאוִית תּוֹרָה **katāwıt *tōra** scribe of Torah (scroll) (=H מְחוֹקֵק, BT4, D); **qarāya ukatāwa** educated person, one who reads and writes (RivSh 192).

כתאנא (OA/OS/Mand כִּיתָּנָא flax, linen) m. **kıtāna** cotton; cf. כתן.

כתא (כורה) (K) **kıtta (kōre)** Go away, blind

(cat) (said to a cat or when one coughs).

כתב (Ar) m. **kıtıb** booklet (PolU 139).

כתה (K) **kıtte** one (of two or of a group) (=H פֶּרֶט, BT3; שָׂרִיד., BT4); none, not even one; odd number; cf. כתומאט, כתכתא.

כ-ת-ו (OA/OS כתב) **k-t̲-w** (Z **k-s-w**) to write [3: כתוון **kt̲uwun** (NT5 403)= Z **ksūn**].

כתוא, כותוא (< מכתווא?) m. **kı/ütwa** thorn; pl. **kı/ütwe**.(cf. PolG) (NT+).

כתובה, כתובא (H; OA כתובְּתא) f. **kat̲ubba** (Z **kasubba**) marriage contract (cf. PolU 271).

כתובים (H) **kat̲ūvim** the Hagiographia (NT+).

כתויתא (< כ-ת-ו) f. **kt̲awīt̲a** (hand) writing (NT+).

כתומאט (K) **kıtt-u-māṭ** odds-and-ends; cf. כתה.

כתותא (< כ-ת-ו) f. **kt̲ūta** (written) amulet; pl. **kt̲ūyāt̲a** [cf. Khan 572 **kliwta**].

כתיתא (OS ܟܬܝܬܐ) f. **kt̲ēt̲a** (Z **ksēsa**) hen; pl. **kıt̲yāt̲a** (cf. PolGr 55: **kisyāsa**) [MacD 142; Garbell 315 **klela**; Mutz. 207; **klela** ~ **klelta**, pl. **kle'e**].

כתכודא v. כדכודא

כ-ת-כ-ת III (< כ-י-ת?) vt/vi **k-t-k-t** to suffer or cause suffering (BaBin 114; NTU4 148b); **mıtle mkutkıtle ṭāla** He 'died' missing her (PolU 310); oppress (=H עָשַׁק/הוֹנָה, BT5, D).

כתכתא (< כתה) **kıtkıta** several (=H אחדים, PolG).

כתמא (Ar?) f. **katma** flea; pl. **katme**.

כתן (Ar) m. **kıttan** linen, flax; cf. כתאנא; **kıttan xumre** head linen-scarf with beads; pl. **kıttāne** (SaAC 16).

כ-ת-פ (Ar كتف bind; cf. OA כתף carry on the shoulders) **k-t-f** to bind; אכתיף לבאבה **ıktīf lbābe** He was bound by his father (NT3).

כ-ת-ר IV (Ar) **k-t̲-r** to augment (NT3); כתרו אלה ג'מה **kt̲ırru 'ılle ġamme** His concerns increased (NT5 401).

כ, כ̇ (x)

-כ, -ג׳ (OS ܐܝܟ) prep. **x-, ģ-** as, like, such; cf. אך.

-כ-, ך- 1 (< אכני) **-ax(-)**: (1) us (NT: היוכלה **hīw-ax-le** gave-us-he = he gave us); (2) we (אמרך **ʾamrax** we say; יאודכלה **ʾōdaxle** we do it); cf. כני- (NT+).

ך- 2 (OA) **-ax** your (f.sg.)(e.g., **bētax** your house) (NT+).

כא (OA/OS חד/חדה; Mand האד/הדא) **xa, xaʾ** (pausal or emphatic) one (m./f., but v. כדא), a (indefinite article): כא ישראל **xa yisrāʾel** a Jew; כא בקרתא **xa baqarta** a question; some, about: כא שואא תוראתא **xa šōʾa tōrāṯa** some seven cows; **xa xá yarxa** about one month (PolG); same, identical (=H אֲחָדִים, BT1); **kulla xaʾ-īla** It is all the same (MeAl 191); כא בכא **xa bxa** (+PolG **pxápxá**) one by one; אל כא תרי **ʾil xa tre/xa utreʾ** twofold, double; **xa ušōʾa** sevenfold (=H שִׁבְעָתַיִם, BT1); **xa (u)ʾalpa** thousandfold (NT6 136); **xa min xamša** one-fifth (=H חֲמִישִׁית, BT1); **xa-xin/-xēna/-xēta** another one; **la kēse lxauxit** They don't get along; כא מנדי **xa mindi** something (=H מְאוּמָה, BT4); **šuqlan min day xaʾ** Leave us alone from that thing, Forget about it! **ʾē-xa** such a thing (PolG); **bxa yōma wax ʾisye ubxa yōma bā(za)x** In one day we have come to this world and in one day we'll go away; **bxa-ʾēna** one eyed, one with one eye; **bxa-ʾīza** one handed.

כאב, כאף (K) inv. **xāv/f** raw, uncooked, unripe.

כאג̆ו צליב (K/P/T-Ar) m. **xāč-u-ṣalib** (the Christian) cross; cf. שתי-ערב.

כאטורא (OS ܚܛܘܪܐ) m. **xāṭōra** pounder (a board with handle); tadpole; cf. כ-ט-ר 1.

כאטר (Ar) m. **xāṭir** sake, wish; לא תורית כאטרא **la tōrit xāṭira** Don't hurt her feeling; **ṭlblu xāṭir min** They said goodbye to (cf. Hob89 183; PolG; PolU 105); v. טלא 1 סבכאטר, (NT+) [cf. Khan 585].

כאייה (OA חַיֵּי) pl. **xāye** life; בכאייד רישוך **bxāyid rēšox** (NT)/**bxudrēšox** (Z, PolG) (I swear) by the life of your head; **hulle xāye ṯālox/ʾillox** he passed away (lit., gave life to you); **yarxi xāyox** May your life be long, thank you (PolG); -בכאייה **bxāye** alive (inv.; cf. צאך); מיתיה ובכאייה **mīṯe ubxāye** dead and alive (people; cf. H הוא בחיים He is alive) (NT5 411, but AvidH 67 בֵּיכָאיֵי **bexāye**?).

כאיין (Ar) inv. **xāyin** traitor (PolG); cf. כ-י-נ.

כאלא (OA/OS חַלָּא, חאלא) m. **xāla** vinegar.

כאלו (< כלויא) **xālo** (maternal) uncle! (voc.).

כאלף (Ar) **xālif** in defiance of, in contrast to (NT; PolU 272).

כאלץ (Ar) inv. **xāliṣ** pure, free of guilt; pl. כאלצין **xāliṣīn** sincere people (NT).

כאלק v. כלאקא

כאמִש (OA/OS חֲמֵשׁ; Mand האמיש) f. **xāmiš/xammiš** (?) five: בסאעד כאמִש **bsāʿid xāmiš** at the fifth hour (NT5 407); cf. כמשמא.

כאן (T/P) m. **xān** market place; inn.

כאנא (OA חענא) m. **xāna** lap, knees, the lower part of dress, used also for carrying things: **qam ⁺malyāle xāna gōze** She filled her lap with walnuts (cf. RivSh 225; PolG).

כאנג̆י (< כאן) **xānči** innkeeper.

כאנמה (K/P) f. **xānime** lady, honorable woman.

כאסמין (OA חס מן) **xās-min** (Be it) far from (you)! Cf. חשכ (NT+).

כאסרת (Ar) pl. **xāsirat** flanks, loins (=H כְּסָלִים, BT3).

כאף v. כאב

כאצא (OS ܚܨܐ/OA חַרְצָא/Mand האלצא loin) m. **xāṣa** back; spine (PolG); support; **la ʾāwa šqille - māwa, la ʾāwa** neither prevailed over the other (in a duel) (PolU 61); **hullu** – departed (PolU 131); **mare xāṣa** powerful, with strong backing (PolU 293); cf. כרכאצא, סמרתא; v. ת-ו-ר (NT+).

כאתא 1 (OA אֲחָתָא, אחאתא; OS ܚܬܐ) f. **xāṯa** sister; cf. כלונתא; pl. **xaṯwāṯa** (OA/OS אַחְוָותָא) (NT+).

כאתא 2, כתתא (OA חַדְתָּא, m/OS ܚܕܬܐ; חַדְתַּי, f.) adj. **xāṯa** (Z **xāsa**), **xaṯṯa** new; v. כ-ת-ת, כתותא.

כאתון, כַאתוּ (T) f. **xātun, xātu** (RivSh 156) lady, princess, queen (NT5 402); pl. כאתונ(י)אתא **xātun(y)āṯa** (NT+).

כאתנותא (< כאתון) f. **xātinūṯa** queenliness (NT5

394).

כבאזא (Ar خبّاز; cf. OA כַּבָּזָא, כבאזא/OS ܟܒܙܐ baker, SokBA 521) m. **xabāza** baker; cf. מטפיניתא (NT+).

כבאזה (Ar) f. **xıbbāze** mallow plant (cf. PolU 341)

כבושא (OA חבושא apple, SokBA 399, but M. Jastrow 417 name of a fruit, quince; OS apple, peach) m. **xabūša** apple; **-ıt pāṯa** cheek-bone (PolG); v. גן עדן (NT+) [Mutz 236 sg. **xabušta**].

כ-ב-ט, ג'-ב-ט II (OA/OS חבט strike, throw down/Ar خبط) **x-b-ṭ** (NT), **ġ-b-ṭ** (BaBin 164), to beseech (by striking oneself; =H פָּצַר, הֵאִיץ, PolG), take pains (NT5 394), writhe in agony (NT); to mix or dip in oil (=H הֻרְבֶּכֶת, BT3, D); cf. ג'-ב-ט 1.

כביכוואני v. כביכוואני

כ-ב-ל II (OA חבל be sick, damaged/OS twist, be in pain/Ar خبل be confused, mentally damaged) **x-b-l** to be a leper, very grimy.

כבלותא, כבלווה (< כ-ב-ל) f. **xıblūṯa, xıblūwe** leprosy, hemorrhoid (= H עֳפָלִים, PolG) (NT+).

כ-ב-ק v. כ-פ-ק

כ-ב-ר II (Ar) **⁺x-b-r** to inform (by phone, telegram, etc.).

כברא (Ar) m. **xabra** spoken word, advice; rumor: **xabra bdugle la gnāpıq** No rumor goes out that is (entirely) false (Segal #119); **ʾuzle bxabre** He did as he said (Pol 111), followed the advice of (NT1 50); **mpıqlu bxabre** They confirmed his word, said the same thing (PolU 45); **xabrox go ʾēni** I'll gladly do what you say (Hob89 183); **xabrox-īle** You are right; **mırre xabre** He promised; pl. **xabre, xabrāne** (D) (NT+).

כגא 1 (< כא+גא) adv. **xaga** once, one time; **bxaga** at one go.

כגא 2 (OA חִיגָּא/OS ܚܓܐ celebration, חִינְגָא dance) **xıgga** dancing circle; celebration (=H חַג, AvidH 65).

כגׂכגׂוכא, כגׂכגׂוכה (K?) adj. **xıjxıjjōka, -ke** midget, shorty.

כ-ג̄-י (< OA חטט?)**⁺x-č-y** to damage one's eyes; II to pick one's teeth, nose, ear.

כ-ג̄-כ-ג̄ III (< כ-ג̄-י?) **⁺x-č-x-č** to scribble.

כגׂכׂוגׂה (< כ-ג̄-כ-ג̄) pl. **xıčxōče** scribblings, nonsense writing.

כ-ג̄-ל IV (Ar) **x-j-l** to embarrass, confuse (NT).

כ-ד-א, ג'-ד-א (Ar?) vt/vi **x/ġ-ḏ-ʾ** (Z **x/ġ-z-ʾ**; Hob89 216 **ġ-d-ʾ**) to fold up, to bind (AlfH 43; AvidH 33; RivSh 141; = סוֹבֵב, הִקִּיף, כִּתֵּר„ PolG) [MacD 93 **xādé** fold up < Ar خدع?].

כדא (OA חדא) f. **xḏa/xıdda** one (NT); אלד כדא כמא וכמא **ʾıllıd xḏa kma ukma** How much more so; cf. כא.

כדאדה v. אכדאדה

כדאם צנאמה (Ar) sg./pl. **xadām ṣanāme** pagan(s), idol worshipper(s) (BaBin 123).

כדאסר, כדיאסר (OA חד עסר, חֲדֵיסַר) **xadeʾsar** eleven.

כדארא 1, ג'דארא (< כ-ד-ר) v.n. **xḏāra** (Z **x/ġzāra**) peddling in villages (a common Jewish occupation); **gōra gēzılwa lxzāra** Her husband used to be a peddler; go hunting (Socin 162).

כדארא 2 (< כ-ד-ר; cf. OA הֲדוֹרָא/OS ܚܕܘܪܐ) m. **xaḏāra** peddler.

כדומא, ג'דומא (< כ-ד-מ) m. **x/ġadōma** servant (NT5 397); pl. כַּדוֹמֵי **xadōme** (RivSh 268).

כ-ד-י (OA חדי) **x-ḏ-y** to rejoice; IV to make someone rejoice (NT, BT, AvidH 65).

כדייא (OA חדייא) m. **xıḏya** (Z **xızya**) breast, tit; pl. כדיואתא **xıḏyıwāṯa** (Z **xız-**; cf. PolG) (NT+).

כדיותא (OA חֲדוּתָא) f. **xıḏyūṯa** (Z **xız-**) joy (NT, BT; PolG).

כ-ד-מ, ג'-ד-מ (Ar) **x/ġ-d-m** to serve, worship; IV to enslave, employ (NT5 385) (NT+).

כדמה, ג'ודמה (Ar) f. **xıdme, ġudme** service (NT+).

כדמותא (Ar) f. **xıddamūṯa** servitude, maid job (NT5 402; SaLH 149).

כדמתא (Ar) f. **xıddamta** servant maid; pl. כדמיאתא **xıddamyāṯa** (cf. PolG) (NT+).

כדמתכר, כזמתכר (Ar-K/P) **xıd/zmatkar** servant (=H מְשָׁרֵת, BT2).

כ-ד-ר 1, ג'-ד-ר (OA חדר/הדר/OS ܚܕܪ) **x/ġ-ḏ/d-r** (Z **x/ġ-z-r**; Hob89 216 **ġ-d-r**) to prowl about (RivSh 145; AvidH 50), peddle; encircle, protect: **ʾē mıṣwa xazra qāmox** May this mitzvah (act of charity) protect you (against evil); seize: כאדרבו כרבא **xāḏırbu karba** They will be seized by anger; be infected, swollen: **ʾaqle xzırra uqam** qatʾila His foot became infected/swollen and was amputated; xizyawāsi ġzirru My breasts became infected (SaAC 31); IV to turn away (vt); to distribute, circulate (NT5 383); מכדר אלי באלא maxdir ʾilli bāla Pay attention to me (NT5 399); cf. כדארא.

כ-ד-ר 2 II (Ar) x-d-r to veil, envelope oneself (NT2, BT1).

כדר (OA חדר) prep. xadir (Z xazir) around, near, next to; tu xazri Sit next to me.

כדרואן (< כדר) xadirwān around; ארבא כדרואנה ʾarba xadirwāne round about it; la xa xazrax uxazirwānax all alone by yourself (PolG) (NT+).

כה v. תכית

כוא, אכוא, (ל)שכווא, כו, כו-לא (K/IrAr xū; cf. OA כו word of emphasis, SokBA 555?) (i)xwa (NT5 382), (la)šxwa (BaBin165; SaAC2), xō, xu-lá (BaBin 152), xúlla, ma-xúna (=H הֲיִתָּכֵן, PolG), well then, after all, so, indeed, really? (=H -הֲ, Ruth 1:11, 13); xula dunye kalwe xila 'Has the world been eaten by dogs? Is this the end of the world? Why the haste? ; אאהת כוא מרה מוהל ובהן איות ʾāhit xwa mare muhil ubihen-īwit (cf. MeAl 188, n. 61; RivSh 235); cf. לכוא; לא 2 [cf. Blanc 150: xō(b) ... to imply speaker's hope or conviction].

כואגֿא (Ar< P) m. xwāja lord, master, Mr. (Merchant) So-and-So, mainly in folktales about Kurds: — ʿali Mr. Ali (Socin 159; cf. Blanc, 151); pl. xwājāye (SaLH 161); cf. חוגֿא.

כואזגין (K) inv. xwāzgin demanding a bride as reward, responding to the rules (PolU 104).

כואזגינותא (K) xwāzginūta fulfillment of rules: having a bride as a reward (PolU 104).

כואזינותא (K) xwāzinūta wishing; šʾiśle risted - He shook the rope of wanting (to enter the house), he rang the bell (PolU 382).

כואי (< P joy?) xwāyi care: latla - uxudāni She doesn't have any care (SaAC 14).

כואנא (OA אַכְוָאנָא < P xwān) f. xwāna table (round and short legged) for baking while sitting on the floor.

כוארא, כוורתא (OA חיוארא/OS ܚܶܘܳܪܳܐ ,חִיוָרְתִּי) adj. xwāra, xwarta white; xwāra x-talga white as snow, very white.

כווארותא, כוארותא (< כוארא) f. xwarūta whiteness; dairy food; snow: ʾarʾa kulla pišla xwarūsa the entire area became covered with snow.

כוארזא (K < P خـواهر زاده) m. xwārza nephew (PolU 293).

כוארנאיא, כוארניתא (< כוארא) adj. xwārnāya, -nēta whitish.

כוארסתי, כווריסתי (K/P?) xwāristi corn aftergrowth (=H סָפִיחַ, BT3; BaBin 48).

כואת, כות v. אכואת

כובא (K xum) m. xūba liquid blue used to dye mourning clothes; xūba brēši Woe to me!

כובאט (Ar) xubāṭ struggle, painful beseeching (NT); cf. כ-ב-ט.

כודאני (K) xudāni good care, sponsorship, adoption (cf. RivP 210; PolG); ʾ-w-z - to take care (of a person); cf. ביכודן.

כודה דזיכוא נאסכת (K) xude dizzexwa nāskit God knows His thieves (PolU 418).

כודידא (K God-given) xudēda male name.

כודרישא v. כאייה

כווה (OA חִיוּוֵי, SokPA 197/חִיוְיֵי ,חִיוְיֵ, M. Jastrow 452/חִיוְיָא, SokBA 425/OS ܚܶܘܝܳܐ/Mand היויא) m. xuwwe snake; cf. כוויתא; pl. כְּווַאוֵי xuwwāwe (BT4, D), xuwwāta (Sa83c 18, Am); כְּוַאוַאסַא =xiwwāwāsa (?) (RivSh. 168); xūwiwāsa (PolG) (NT+) [Mutz 237 xiwa, pl. -e].

כוורא (OA חבורא Habor River) m. xawōra river (=H נָהָר, BT4, Z; cf, BaBin 143; RivSh 242); pl. xawōre (PolU 362); cf. נהרא, כזלא רעולא,.

כווזי (K) interj. xwazī, xuzzī (+PolG) Would that! One wishes (=H לוּ, BT4).

כ-ו-י 1 IV (OA/OS חוי show, mention) vi/vt x-w-y to appear, to seem, to show up; to show; gmaxwēwa ʾille d- He looked like he...muxwēle ʾilla She doesn't look well, She has lost weight (lit., It shows on her) (cf. PolU 391)[1: מוכויינה muxūyanne He showed me (f.); 3: מכוולילה máxwūlile Show him (you, pl.) to me!]; cf. כ-ז-י.

כ-ו-י 2 (OA חבי hide) x-w-y only in ḥisse xwēle/xūya He has a hoarse voice; lost his voice [cf. OA חסי נחבי/OS ܡܰܚܶܐ ܚܣܐ to lower one's voice, SokBA 400].

כוידנכה (< K saltier?) f. x(i)wēdanke travel or shepherd's food-bag (RivSh 242; PolG).

כויאני (K) **xuyāni** relatives, people of the house (Segal #31).
כויצא (OA/OS חביצא m. dish of flour, honey, and oil) f. **xwīṣa** crushed bread pieces soaked in hot butter and sprinkled with sugar [cf. SokBA 401 האי חביצא דאית ביה פירורין כזית a h. dish which has olive sized bread pieces].
כווית(א) (< כווה) f. **xuwwīṯa** sharp-tongued, poisonous, 'snake'-like woman.
כוכא (Ar خوخ peach; OS ܚܘܚܐ/OA חָחָא, חָאחָא plum) f. **xōxa** peach; pl. **xōxe**.
כוכותא v. ככותא
כ-ו-כ-צ׳ III (Ar خوض absorb) **x-o-x-ẓ** to soak (vt) (PolU 279) [1: **mxōxıẓ-**].
כול, כולון v. א-כ-ל
כולא 1 (OA/OS חֲבְלָא) **xōla** rope; **zılle xōla basır dōla** the rope followed the bucket (both fell in the well: One loss followed another; also: Wife has to follow husband where ever he goes; cf. PolU 362); pl. **xōle**; cf. כוולתא.
כולא 2 v. כוא
כֻולְדָא (OA/OS חוּלְדָּא mole) **xulda** chameleon (=H תִּנְשֶׁמֶת, BT3, D).
כוולי-בסרו (K) **xwalli-bsaro** (you) miserable one (lit. ashes on the head) (PolU 110).
כולם-כולם (< K **xulīn** boiling, outburst?) **xulım- xulım** commotion, tumult (due to abnormal birth) (PolU 371).
כולמא v. כלמא
כולאצי, כלאצי (K < Ar) f. **xülāṣi** salvation (NT, BT).
כולקא (Ar) **xulqa** character, bad temperament; גאודי כולקא אליהון **g'ōḏi xulqa 'ıllēhun** They get angry at them (NT).
כולקתא, כוליאקתא (Ar) f. **xul(yā)qıta** creation, existence (=H הַיְקוּם, BT1), pl. כוליאקתיאתא **xulyāqıtyāṯa** (NT2).
כוולתא (< כולא) f. **xawılta** necklace (PolU 42); cf. ריך.
כומרתא (OA/OS חוּמַרְתָּא) f. **xumırṯa** bead; **-tıt šınsa** a magical bead put on one's chest to keep him in deep sleep (PolU 110); pl. **xumre** (PolG) (OA/OS pl. חומרי).
כֻון, כוון (K/P?) **x/kwan** (?) would that, one wishes (NT2; NTU3 1a) [MacD 127: **kwān**].
כונא v. כוא
כונוקתא (< כ-נ-ק) f. **xunuqta** throat (PolG).
כֻונְכָאר (K/P) **xunkar** magnate (=H נָגִיד).

כונכארי (K/P roal [weight]) **xunkāri** large weight unit, about 14 kg [=4 מניא; cf. MeAl 183; Jaba-Justi 316 on قنطار].
כונאו, כונאב, כונף (K) m. **xunaf** (Z), **xunav/w** (NT), dew.
כ-ו-פ II (Ar) **x-w-f** to fear, to shake (PolG).
כוף (Ar) m. **xōf** fear (NT).
כופאנא (< כוף) adj. m. **xōfāna** frightening, awesome (NT).
כופארי, כופארא, כפארתי (K < Ar غفر; cf. OA/OS כּוּפְרָא compensation) **xufāri, xufāra** (BaBin 151; PolG), **xfārati** ransom (=H כֹּפֶר, BT2), atonement; cf. ג׳-פ-ר.
כפו v. כופו
כ-ו-צ (OA חבץ) **x-w-ṣ** mix bread pieces in hot butter; cf. כויצא.
כ-ו-ר (OA חבר/חוור) **x-w-r** to become white; **xōra pāsox/'ıllox** May you be proud, fortunate (AvidH 22);**'ēni kxōri** I suffer greatly (from pain); IV to make white; **'ilāha māxurra 'ıllox** May God make you fortunate; **ṣıfır muxūra** polished copper. cf. כ-י-מ, כוארא
כורא (< OA/OS חַבְרָא) **xōra, xūra** (BT2, Arodh), friend, associate; the other; כוד גלות בש יקורא מכורה **kud gālūṯ bıš yaqūra mxōre** Each exile (being) more oppressive than the other; כא טלא כורה **xa ṯla xōre** one to another; cf. אוכינא; like (prep.): **xōr dē brāta lēs ulag bāre** There is none like this girl and there will never be; v. כור-צודרא; כוורתא 1; pl. c. **xūrāṯa, xūrawāṯa, xūrāne** (NT+).
כֻורָאדֵי (< K?) pl./f. (?) **xurāḏe** kind of leek (=H חָצִיר, BT4, D).
כורגא (OA חורגא) m. **xurga** step-son, half brother.
כורגתא (OA חורגתא) f. **xurıgṯa** step-daughter; half sister.
כורגניאתא (K < Ar خُرج travel bag +גנתא bag?) pl. **xurjınyāṯa** (money) bags (PolU 213); cf. גזינה.
כורדא (IrAr < P) m. **xurda** small change; cf. פארה דקיקה; **xúrda-frūš** haberdasher (PolG).
כוורו (K) adv. **xwarrū** purely, almost entirely: **'e gubta xwarru mıšxa-la** This cheese is very rich with butter.

כורט(ותא) v. כורת(ותא)

כורטמנתא (OS ܚܘܪܛܡܢܬܐ) f. **xurṭmanta** a chickpea; pl. **xurṭmāne** [MacD 106 **xāriṭmāntā** pea; no origin given; but v. Brockelmann 256].

כורמא (P) m. **xurma** a fine kind of soft dates [Khan 585 **xurma** dates, K].

כורסאני (P-Ar) inv. **xurasāni** superior kind of carpet (PolU 317).

כור-צודרא (< כורא+צודרא) m. **xōr-ṣudra** underpants (euph.); cf. שרואלא.

כורט, כורית, כורת (K) inv. ⁺**xurt, xurıt** (+NT), aggressive, violent (NT+).

כוורתא 1, כורתתא (OA/OS חַבְרְתָא) f. **xawırta, xūratta**, friend; other of equal status; placenta (=H שִׁלְיָה; pl. **xawıryāta, xūrāta**; cf. כורא.

כוורתא 2 v. כוארא

כורטותא, כורתותא (< כורת) f. ⁺**xurtuta** force, violence; **bxurtūta** by force, reluctantly.

כוש (IrAr < K/P) inv. **xōš** good (precedes noun): **xōš-nāša-le** He is a good person (cf. Blanc 151].

כושאבה (K/P) f. **xōšāve** sweet fruit drink.

כוושי (K/P) **xwaši** comfort living, good life; pl. **xwašīyat** (=H מַעֲדַנִּים, BT1). NT+

כושיבא (OA/OS חד בשבא) m. **xu/ošēba** Sunday (NT+) [KHAN 585 **xušába**].

כושכוכה (K little sister) f. **xıškōke** young Kurdish female villager (selling produce).

כושכושתא (< כ-ש-כ-ש) **xušxušta** rattling sound.

כזאלא v. ג'זאלא

כזאנה (Ar) f. **xazāne** closet, storage room.

ג'-ז-ד-ג, כ-ז-ד-כ, כ-ז-ד-ג III (< ?) **x/ġ-z-d-g/k** to be bereft, harmed (NT2); to mistreat [NT5 384) [cf. MacD 168 **xuzdāgā** misfortune].

כזורא (OA/OS חזירא/Mand היזורא) m. **xızūra** wild pig, boar; cf. בראזא, כ-נ-ז-ר.

ג'-ז-י, כ-ז-י (OA חזי) **x/ġ-z-y** to see; **la xzēle bıgyāne** He didn't feel up to it; **xzēlebe** he foresaw him [1: **xzē-** ; **xızyannu** They saw me, f. (NT); 2: **xāze; xā(za)x**; 3:**xzi** (Z, m.; but Hob89 182:f), **xze** (Z, f.); **xzūn** (NT, pl.), **xzāwun** (Z, pl..); IV to show; be seen (rare: לְמַכְזוֹיֵי AvidH 47; מוּכְזֵילוּ RivSh 180; Hob89 220); cf. כ-ו-י.

כזי, ג'זי (< כ-ז-י) **x/ġz/i** as if (PolG).

כזינא, כזינה (Ar) f. **xızēna, xazīne** treasure; pl. כזיניאתא **xızenyāta** (NT5 392) (NT+).

כזיתא, ג'זיתא (< כ-ז-י) n. act. **x/ġzēta** sight, seeing (PolGr 33).

כזלא (< Ar غسل wash?) m. **xızla** rivulet (PolU145); cf. כוורא, רעולא, גלל; pl. **xızle** (PolU 362).

כזמא (K) m. **xızma** relative by marriage; **pıšlu xızme** intermarried (=H הִתְחַתְּנוּ, BT1, D).

כזמאיי (K) **xızmāye** relation by marriage (NT).

כזם-וכוין (K) **xızm-u-xwīn** relatives by mariage (PolU 386).

כזמתא (Ar) f. **xzamta** nose-ring; pl. כזמיאתא **xzamyāta**. NT+ [Khan 585 **xizma**].

כ-ז-נ, ג'-ז-נ (Ar) **x/ġ-z-n** to store; cf. מכזן (NT+).

כזנא (IrAr [Jastrow 1990b:343]) f. **xızna** fine linen fabric; cf. גאפון.

כטא (Ar; cf. OA חֶטְאָה/OS ܚܛܗܐ) f. **xaṭa** sin; pl. **xaṭāye/-he/-ʾe** (NT+); cf. כ-ט-י.

כטאיא, כטיתא (OA חַטָּיָא) adj. **xaṭāya, xaṭēta** sinner. NT+

כ-ט-ב (Ar) **x-ṭ-b** to preach (in mosque), give a speech; to betroth, marry off (cf. PolG).

כטבה (Ar) f. **xıṭbe** betrothal (PolG).

כטה (OA חִיטֵּי/OS ܚܛܐ) f./pl? **xıṭṭe** wheat; **xıṭṭe mıyanta** soft wheat dish (eaten in winter on Sabbath); v. מיאנא **xıṭṭe mūsıli** wheat dish with saffron; כטיתא **xıṭṭıta** a grain of wheat [cf. OA חִיטְּתָא; Mand חטיתא; Khan 585 **xiṭṭe** wheat; **xiṭṭa**, sg., f. grain of wheat].

כְּטַא כַּר (Ar-K) **xaṭa-kar** sinner; pl. כטהכרה **xaṭa(h)kare** sinners (=H חַטָּאִים, BT1); **p-y-š** - be guilty (=H נֶאֱשַׁם, PolG).

כ-ט-י (OA/OS/Ar) **x-ṭ-y** to sin, to err; IV to cause to sin (RivSh 121; PolG) (NT+).

כטיתא, כֶּטִיתָא (OA חטיתא) f. **x(ı)ṭīta** sin, wrong doing (NT5 402; PolG)[cf. MacD 97 **xṭītā**].

כ-ט-ר 1 (OA/OS חטר strike) **x-ṭ-r** to fall hard full length; hit hard to the ground: ואל אראה כטירן **uʾıl ʾarʾa xṭīrın** was hit hard to the ground (BaBin 132; cf. PolG); cf. כאטורא.

כ-ט-ר 2 (Ar) **x-ṭ-r** to occur, be possible; לג גכטרא מאידה **lag gxaṭra mʾīde** He cannot afford it (NT).

כטרא (OA חוטרא) m./f. **xıṭra** rod (NT).

כייאטא, כייטתא (OA/OS חַיָּיטָא/Ar خيّاط) **xayāṭa, xayaṭṭa** tailor, seamstress; cf. כ-י-ט.

כייאל (Ar) **xıyāl** fantasy; **ʾ-w-ḏ xıyāl** to imagine, fantasize (NT5 388).

כייפתא, כיאפא (< כ-י-פ) **xayāpa, xayapta** washer (of the dead before burial).

כיארא (Ar) f. **xıyyāra** cucumber; pl. **xıyyāre**.

כיארוכה (K< Ar) f. **xıyārōke** amulet case in shape of thin cucumber.

כיבו (< יוכבד) p.n.f. **xēvo** Jochebed (hypo.).

כיבנתא, כיבאנא (< כיביה) adj. **xēvāna, -anta** seasonal (fruit).

כיבת (K < Ar خيمة) **xıvat** (canvas, military) tent; pl. **xīvatat** (PolU 35, 40).

כיג׳כא (K) m. **xıčaka** line scratched on floor.

כי-ג׳נגא (< תכית+ג׳נגא) m. **xe-čanga** armpit.

כיביה, כיויה (K?) **xēv/we** season (Sa83c 22, Am); cf. כיבאנא

כיוכא (< כ-י-כ) m. **xıyyōka** itch.

כיותא (OA/OS חַיּוּתָא raw state, being alive) f. **xayūṯa** the state of lying-in, time of birth; **mıtla bxayūsa** She died while giving birth.

כיז v. כיס

כ-י-ט (OA חיט) **x-y-ṭ** to sew; IV to have a suit/dress sewed by a tailor/seamstress.

כ-י-י (OA/OS חיי) **x-y-y** to live, come back to life; IV to revive, to sustain [1: **xyē**; 2: **xāye** (sg./pl.); 3: **xyi/xyē**; 4: **maxyōye** (NT+).

כייתא, כֵיתַא (OA חַיְיתָא midwife) f. **xayēṯa, xēṯa** (BT3, D; BaBin 32), lying-in woman (= H יוֹלֶדֶת, BT3, D); pl. **xayāṯa** (=H חָיוֹת, BT2, Arodh).

כ-י-כ (OA חכך/OS حك) vt/vi **x-y-k** to scratch, to itch; cf. כיוכא.

כיל- v. א-כ-ל

כילא (OA/OS חילא) m. **xēla** strength (=H חַיִל, BT; POLG); v. נ-כ-ל (NT+).

כילייא (K) f. **xēlīya** veil (=H מַסְוֶה, BT2); pl. **xēlīyat**.

כילפתא (OA חִלְפְּתָא, M. Jastrow 472; חִילָפָא, SokBA 430) f. **xīlapta** willow (branches used for the sukkah).

כ-י-מ (OA חמם) vi **x-y-m** to become warm (NT5 409); cf. ש-כ-נ, כ-מ-כ-מ, כמא [MacD 90].

כימא (Ar) f. **xēma** tent; pl. **xēmāṯa** (Z; PolG), כֵימַאמֵי **xēmāme** (AvidH 64) (NT+).

כ-י-נ (Ar) **x-y-n** to betray; cf. כאיין.

כינא, כין, כן, כית, כת, כיתא (OA א(ת)אחרינ) m./f./pl. (Z) **xēna, xı/en, xēta, xı/et** other; **xa ḥāxām xēta** another teacher (MeAl 178); כינא ג׳ו **ču xēna** no one else ; pl.(NT) כינה **xēne**. v. 2 שאתא, לילה, כא, כארא, בומכת, אוכינא (NT+).

כיס, כיז (K< Arm) m. **xīs/z** (cf. RivSh 163; PolG) [MacD 97 **xīz(ā)** small sand, dust].

כ-י-פ (OA/OS חפף wash the hair) vi/vt **x-y-p** to bathe, wash oneself (NT+).

כיפזאני (K) inv. **xefzāni** magician (PolU 195).

כיר (Ar) **ᐩxēr** benevolence, affluence; **xāzıt - mınna** May it benefit you; **ʾalpa xēre xāzıt ba** Enjoy her very much! (PolU 129); **pāsox pāsıt — īla** You bring good news (PolG); pl. כיריה **ᐩxēre**; **xēr-u-xērāt** all kind of favors (PolU 236).

כיר נסי (< Ar-K نسيه by credit?) **xēr nıssi** How good! (PolU 351).

כירתא, כירתותא (< ג׳ירא 2) **xīrıta, xīratūṯa** zeal, energy (cf. PolG); cf. בי-כירת.

כ-י-ש III (K/Ar?) vi **x-y-š** to slide or move while sitting on the floor; crawl (=H זָחַל) ; cf. כשכשוכה; IV to move (vt).

כישתא v. כשתא

כית(א) v. כינא, תכית

כייתא v. כֵיתַא

ככינא v. כא

ככותא, כוכותא (OA חיכוכא?) **xükūṯa** (tax imposed due to) provocation (PolU 38), revolt. NT+

ככמא (< כא+כמא) **xakma** some, several, kind of (cf. PolG); partly אקלאתיה ככמא פרזלא וככמא כ׳ספא **ʾaqlāṯe xakma prızla uxakma xıspa** his feet (were) partly iron and partly clay; cf. כפג׳א (NT+).

כ-פ-ר-כ, כ-כ-פ-ר III (< כ-פ-ר) **x-k-p-r** to dig, do a little digging (PolG, PolUL 402); **x-p-r-k** dig around, unearth; דהבה וחיואניה גמכפרכילה **dahbe uḥēwāne gımxaprıkīle** beasts and animals unearth it (= buried body) (NTU4).

כל- v. א-כ-ל

כ-ל-א 1 (Ar خلع) vt/vi **x-l-ʾ** to sprain (NT+).

כ-ל-א 2 (<כלאתא) **x-l-ʾ** to grant gifts (NT5 396; Zaken 389 [RivSh 271 קים כַלֵילֵי **qım xālēle**].

כלא 1 (OA חִילָּא/OS خلا dust, grit) **xılla**, only in **xa – mıṭra** light rain (lit., a dust rain).

כלא 2 (Ar) **xala** deserted area; **mʾarʾıd xala-le**

ʾisya He is famished; cf. כ-ל-י 2.
כלאץ (Ar) adv. **xalāṣ** completely (PolU 264).
כלאצי v. כולאצי
כלאקא, כאלק (< כ-ל-ק) m. **xalāqa** (Z; PolG), **xālıq** (NT), the Creator, God
כלאקה (< K/P/T **x/qālīče** small carpet) pl. **xalāqe** (small?) carpets (PolG).
כלאתא (Ar خلعة) f. **xıleʾta** gift; pl. אֶכְלֶיאֶיְתַא כְלֶיתְיַיתַא, **xıleʾ(t)yāṯa** (=H מָנוֹת, PolG).
כ-ל-ו (OA/OS חלב) **x-l-w** to milk.
כלוא, כליא (OA/OS חַלְבָא) **xalwa , xılya** (PolU 207: ChNA; cf. Mutzafi 301), milk; cf. משכא.
כלויא (Ar خال/OS ܚܠܐ) m. **xalōya** maternal uncle; pl. **xalowāṯa**; cf. כלתא, כאלו. NT+[Mutz 236 **xalōna**
כלול, כלולייא, כלולאיי(K < OS/OA חֲלִיל hollow) **xılol, xılōlīya, xılōlāyi** cavern, hollow. NT+
כלולא v. הלולא
כלונתא (< כאתא 1) f. **xalunta** sister (NT2, and only once) [cf. Mutz 236 **xalunta**].
כ-ל-י 1 (OA/OS חלי) **x-l-y** to be sweet; to please; VI to sweeten; בדושא מכלילא **bdūša maxlēla** It should be sweetened with honey (NT5 408).
כ-ל-י 2 (Ar) **x-l-y** to be empty; **bēsa xlēle mınnox** The house feels empty without you; IV to leave without **ʾilāha la maxlēlox mınne** May God not leave you without him, May he be well!
כליא, כליתא (OA/OS חֲלְיָא/< כ-ל-י 1, p.p.) **xılya, xlīṯa** sweet; pleasant; **dımme xılya** He is pleasant, sweet; **xılya x-šākar/dūša** very sweet (child); v. כלוא.
כליונכא (< כליא) m. **xılyōnka** sweet little boy; cf. כליתונכה.
כליותא (< כליא) f. **xılyūṯa** sweetness, pleasantness; **b-** joyfully (NT5 409).
כלימא, כלמתא (OA חלימא) **xlīma, xlımta** thick, robust (cf. PolG).
כלימותא (OA חלימותא) f. **xlīmūṯa** thickness (cf. PolG).
כליפותא (< כ-ל-פ 2) **xlīfūṯa** disobedience (=H סָרָה, BT5).
כליצא, כלצתא (< כ-ל-צ, p.p.) **xlīṣa, xlīṣta** finished; consumed; fugitive (=H פָּלִיט, BT1).
כליקא (< כ-ל-ק, p.p.) m. **xlīqa** creature.
כליתונכה (< כליתא) f, **xlīṯōnke** sweet girl; cf. כליונכא.
כלכאלה (K/Ar) pl. **xalxāle** anklets.
כ-ל-כ-ל III (OA חלחל) **x-l-x-l** to be consumptive, weak.
כ-ל-ל II2 (OA/OS חלל) **x-l-l** to wash, clean (NT+).
כ-ל-מ 1 (OA/OS חלם close together, be well, healthy) **x-l-m** to be thick, fat, robust, healthy looking; IV to make fat; to harden (vt)(NT5 395).
כ-ל-מ 2 (OA חלם) **x-l-m** to dream; IV to tell a dream (PolG).
כלמא, כולמא(OA/OS חֶלְמָא) m. **xı/ulma** dream (BT1, D; RivSh 261; PolG); **xılmi mpıqle** my dream came true; **xılmox šālōm** May your dream be of peace; **xılmox baṭīla** May your (bad) dream be of no consequence.
כלמאנא (OA חוּלְמָנָא/OS ܫܘܠܡܢܐ) m. **xılmāna** strength, power; often as hendiadys: **ʾilāha yāwıllox xēla uxılmāna** May God grant you strength and energy. NT+
כלמתא (K< Ar خدمة) f. **xılmıta** work, task, service, affair; pl. כלמתיאתא **xılmıtyāṯa**. NT+
כ-ל-פ 1 II (OA/OS חלף) **x-l-p** to exchange, to substitute (cf. PolG).
כ-ל-פ 2 I/II (Ar) **x-l-f** to deviate; disobey (NT, BT, PolG).
כלפונא (< כ-ל-פ 1) m. **xılpōna** substitute (=H תְּמוּרָה, BT3).
כ-ל-צ (Ar/OA) vt/vi **x-l-ṣ** to escape; to be redeemed; to finish; to be on verge of dying (Z); **xlıṣlan mıġzaz** We closed a deal, reached an agreement; - **m**-to get rid of; II (NT, Am)/IV (Z) to rescue; v. מכלצאנא (NT+).
כלציתא (< כ-ל-צ) f. **xlaṣīṯa** end, final point (cf. PolG; PolU 84); **xlaṣis dunye** end of the world (PolU 270)
כ-ל-ק 1 (Ar) vi/vt **x-l-q** (God:) to create; come into being: **sulṭan bdaʿūsa xlıqle** The sultan was born thanks to a prayer (PolU 2) (NT+).
כ-ל-ק 2 v. ג'-ל-ק
כלקיתא (< כ-ל-ק) f. **xlaqīṯa** creation (PolG).
כלתא (OS/Ar; v. כלויא) f. **xalta** maternal aunt; **xalto** auntie, Mrs. (vocative); pl. **xaltāṯa**.
כמא (OA/OS חומא) **xımma** heat; cf. כ-י-מ (NT+).

כ-מ-א (OA/OS חמע) **x-m-ʾ** to be leavened (NT5 410); IV to leaven (vt); cf. כמירא (NT+).

כמאטא (OS ܡܚܛܐ; OA מַחְטָא, f.) f. **xmāṭa** needle; **xmāṭıd kutla** straight pin; pl. **xmāṭe** [Khan 585 **xmaʾa**].

כמארא (OA/OS חֲמָרָא) m. **xmāra** donkey; **xmāra yarīxa** leapfrog (game); cf. כמרתא (NT+).

כמארג׳י (Ar-T) m. **xam(m)ārči** wine dealer (PolG).

כמאתא 1 (OA/OS חֲמָתָא, חמאתא) f. **xmāta** mother-in-law.

כמאתא 2 v. כמתא

כמוטאנא, כמוטנתא, כמוטו (< כמוטה) adj. **xmōṭāna** (m.), **-anta** (f.), **xmōṭo** (m./f.), snotty.

כמוטה (Ar مخاط) pl. **xmōṭe** snot, nasal mucus (cf. PolG); **mšīlu xmōṭox** Wipe your nose!

כמוצא, כמוצתא (OA חמוצא) adj. **xamūṣa, xamuṣta** sour; cf. כמצתא.

כמוצותא, כמצותא (< כמוצא) **xamuṣūta, xımṣūta** sourness.

כמותא (< כמתא) f. **xamūta** maidenhood. NT+

כמיאנא (OS ܚܡܝܢܐ/ܚܡܐ/OA חֲמָא, חֲמוּ-) m. **xımyāna** father-in-law.

כמימא, כממתא (OA/OS חַמִּימָא) adj. **xamīma, xamımta** hot (NT); cf. שכינא.

כמימותא (OA/OS חַמִּימוּתָא) f. **xamīmūta** heat (NT).

כמירא (OA/OS חמירא) **xmīra** yeast, leaven (=H חָמֵץ, BT2); **qṭāʾıd xmīra** (period of) cessation of leaven (=Passover)(PolU 421); cf. כ-מ-א.

כ-מ-כ-מ III (OS ܚܡܚܡ) **x-m-x-m** to keep warm; simmer; restore (health) (PolU 111); to spoil (food due to heat); cf. כ-י-מ.

כ-מ-ל II (K) **x-m-l** to adorn (bride, room; cf. PolG); כָּאלוֹ מְכוֹמַלְתָּא **kālo mxōmalta** adorned bride (=H כַּלָּה כְּלוּלָה, AvidH).

כ-מ-צ (OA/OS חמץ) **x-m-ṣ** be sour; IV make sour; אכואתד כמירא דגמכמצלה לישא **ʾıxwāṭıd xmīra dgmaxmıṣle lēša** as leaven which makes dough sour (NT4 164); cf. כ-מ-א.

כמצא, כמצתא (< כ-מ-צ) **xımṣa** (Arodh), **xamıṣta** (Z), sour soup with dumplings eaten on Sabbath Eve; **xamıṣta kūvi** a special kind of sour soup with meat and poached eggs.

כמרא (OA/OS חמרא) **⁺xamra** wine; cf. כמארג׳י. NT+

כמרותא (< כמארא) f. **xmarūta** stupidity.

כמרתא (OA/OS חֲמָרְתָּא; v. כמארא) f. **xmarta** she-ass; pl. **xmaryāta** (cf. PolG) (NT+).

כמשא (OA/OS חַמְשָׁא) m./f. **xamša** five; cf. כאמש; **xamša upalge** quick, sloppy job; **mṣōlēle xamša upalge** He prayed fast, skipping a lot (NT+).

כמשאסר (OS ܚܡܫܥܣܪ; OA חֲמֵשׁ עֲשַׂר) **xamšaʾsar**.

כמשושב (OA/OS חמשא בְּשַׁבָּא) **xamšōšıb** (Z), **xamšūšıb** (BT1, Am), Thursday.

כמשי (OA חמשי) **xamši** fifty; pl. כמשיואתא **xamšıyawāta** (?) groups of fifty persons (NT2) (NT+).

כמשמא, כמשא אמאייה (OA חמש מאה) **xammıšma, xamša ʾımmāye**, five-hundred.

כמתא 1 (< OS ܚܡܬܐ virgo pubescens, Brock. 238) f. **xamta** maiden, young woman; pl. כמאתא **xamāta**; cf. בראתא בוכר, (NT+).

כמתא 2 (OA חמתא) f. **xımta** heat, temperature (NT5 409; NT6 136) [MacD 102: **ximtā**].

כנאקא (< כ-נ-ק) **xnāqa** strangulation, choking.

כנג׳י v. כפג׳א

כנג̇ר (K/P) m. **xanjar** dagger; pl. **xanjāre**.

כנדק, כנדקוקא (< Ar خندق moat) m. **xandaq** moat (PolU 65), **xandaqōqa** basement-house (of very poor people).

כ-נ-ז (Ar خنس/خنث hide/fold) **x-n-z** to gird, to hem, tuck up a garment (NT+).

כ-נ-ז-ר III (Ar خنزير pig) **x-n-z-r** to threaten, to snort like a pig (RivSh 231); cf. כזורא.

כני- (< אכני) **-axni** we (attached pron. with a.p., e.g., קבלכני **qabl-axni** we accept); cf. -כ-.

כניקה (Ar) pl. **xanīqe** bars of yoke (=H מוטות, BT3).

כ-נ-ק (OA/OS חנק; Ar خنق) vt/vi **x-n-q** to choke; cf. כונוקתא מכנקתא, (NT+).

כסה (OA חַסָּא/OS ܚܣܬܐ; pl. ܚܣܐ/Ar خس < Ak **xassū**) f./pl. **xasse** lettuce; **xa rēša xasse** one head of lettuce.

כסילא, כסלתא (OA חסילא) p.p. **xsīla, xsılta** weaned. NT+

כ-ס-ל (OA חסל) vt **x-s-l** to wean (cf. PolG).

כ-ס-פ (Ar) **x-s-f** to be pressed in, dented, cracked (land)(cf. PolG: **ʾarʾa xsıfta** בְּקוּעָה).

כספא (OA חַסְפָּא/OS سَرْطا) m. **xıspa** clay, pottery (NT+).

כספה (Ar) f. **xasfe** shrinkage, wasting away (=H פְּחֶתֶת, BT3); cf. כ-ס-פ.

כ-ס-ר (Ar) **x-s-r** to lose, forfeit; IV to cause loss (NT+).

כַּסְתַּא (P) **xasta** sick, infirm (RivSh 182).

כסתא-כאנא (IrAr< P/T) f. **xasta-xāna** hospital.

כפאקא (< כ-פ-ק 1) **xpāqa** bosom, lap; cf. כאנא.

כפארא (OA חפרא) m. **xapāra** grave-digger.

כפג̇א, כנג̇י (< כא+K **pič** bit) **xapča** (Z, BaBin 135), **xanči** (AvidH; RivSh 155) a bit, a few, some, awhile; **-xıt** soon, about to (Hob89 182; PolG); cf. ככמא. [MacD 92, 103:**xa(d)čā, xančā/ī, xa pyāšā**; Mutz 236 **xánči**].

כפו, כופו (H/OA חופה) f. **xüppo** bride's veil.

כפורא (K/Ar غفير guard, soldier) m. **xafūra** (?) comrade, buddy (BaBin 101).

כ-פ-י (OA/OS חפי cover/Ar خفي hide) **x-p/f-y** to be obscure (NT).

כפיאיא, כפייתא (OS ܚܦܝܐ) adj. **xıpyāya, xıpyēta** barefoot.

כפיאת, כאפאיית, כופייאת (Ar) pl. **xa/ufāyat** mysteries.

כפיותא (< כ-פ-י) f. **xıpyūta** darkness, obscurity (NT).

כפיפא, כפפתא (Ar) adj./adv. **xafīfa, xafıfta** light, diligent, pale (tea); **garma xafīfe** She is sweet (lit., her bones [are] light); **ʾīze xafıfta** He is diligent, quick; **qu -** Get up quickly, right away! (PolU 445); Cf. יקורא.

כפיפותא, כפיפתותא (< כפיפא) f. **xafīf(at)ūta** ease, lightness (BaBin 132; PolG).

כ-פ-כ-ר III (K) **x-f-k-r** to trap (BaBin 162).

כפכתא (K< Ar فخّ) **xaffıkta** snare, trap (for birds); pl. **xaffıkyāta** (BaBin 131).

כ-פ-ל (Ar غفل) **x-f-l** to sleep lightly (cf. PolG), fall asleep unaware while sitting; **xfila la xfāla** half asleep.

כפלתי v. ז'ג'פלתי

כ-פ-פ II2 (Ar) vt/vi **x-f-f** to become or make lighter; decrease; belittle: **gımxaffıf ʾıbbe** He doesn't show him respect; **mxuffıle bʾēn baxte** He became less respected by his wife.

כ-פ-ק 1, כ-ב-ק, II (OA/OS חבק+OS ܚܒܩ embrace) **x-p-q, x-b-q** (+PolG), to hug, embrace; cf. כפאקא (NT+).

כ-פ-ק 2, ח-פ-ק (Ar خفق; cf. OA חפק choke?) **x/ḥ-f-q** to be stirred, excited (NT); **xfīqıd jinne** ravaged by demons (=H לְחוּמֵי רֶשֶׁף, BT5).

כ-פ-ר 1 (OA/OS חפר) **x-p-r** to dig (NT+).

כ-פ-ר 2 v. ג'-פ-ר

כ-פ-ר-כ v. כ-כ-פ-ר

כפרתא 1 (< כ-פ-ר 1) f. **xıpparta** excavation, mine (cf. PolG).

כפרתא 2 (< כ-פ-ר 1) n. act. **xparta** digging (PolGr 33).

כצא (Ar) **xıṣṣa** particularity; **bıd - dīde** by his own right (Polu 287).

כצוא (Ar castration) f. **xıṣwa** dishonest charity (pun on מצוה).

כצוצי (Ar) **xıṣūṣi** special, private service; purposely.

כ-צ-י (Ar) **x-ṣ-y** to castrate.

כציא (< כ-צ-י) p.p. **xısya** castrated, eunuch (= H סריס, NT5 394); v. גאויש.

כצלתא (Ar) f. **xaṣlıta** quality, feature; pl. כצלאתא **xaṣlāta** (NT).

כ-צ-ב v. ג'-צ-ב

כ-צ-ד v. ג'-צ-ד

כ-ר-א (< rare OA רחע [=H רחץ, Ar رحض] ?) **x-r-ʾ** to scrape, rub and clean thoroughly with water (body, floor: SaAC 8); cf. כרואתא [Fassberg 288-90]

כראבי (K < Ar) inv. **xırābi** desolate, ruined (=H בֹּהוּ, BT1) (NT+).

כר(א)בותא (< כראבי) f. **xırabūta** (cf. PolG).

כרא-בסתה (K) ⁺**xırra-baste** island, dry area in a river).

כַּרַאג̇, כְּרֵיג̇ (Ar/P خراج, خرج tax tribute; cf. OA כראגא/אַכְרָגָא/הֲלָךְ; SokBA568) m. **xara/ıj** levy (=H סֵבֶל, PolG; מֶכֶס, BT4, D); due punishment (PolU 158); usually in pl. כְּרַג̇את, כראג̇יה, כרג̇ה **xar(ā)je, xarjāt** taxes, tributes (as vassals); כַּרְג̇י כַּרוֹג̇י **xarje xarōje** very many taxes (RivSh 272).

כראיא, כריתא (OA אחריא) adj. **xarāya, xarēta** last (NT+).

כראיה (OA אחרין) adv. **x(a/ı)rāye** later (cf.

PolG); בֵּיכְרָאיֵי ,ביכראייה (NT2, AvidH 24; RivSh 179, 266), **bexarāye** in the end.

כראכת-לבא (< כ-ר-כ) v.n. **xrāxıt-lıbba** mercy (PolGr 88).

כרארא (< ?) f. ⁺**xarāra** big container or basket used by porters (PolU 87, 236).

כראשא, כראשכר (OA חרשא) **xarāša, xarāškar** magician, craftsman; pl. **xaraškare** (=H חַרְטֻמִּים, BT2); cf. כרשה, כשופכר (NT+).

כ-ר-ב-ט III (Ar) **x-r-b-ṭ** to entangle (?) (PolG).

כ-ר-ב-ק III (K) vt/vi **x-r-b-q** be or become entangled (BaBin 120; PolG); גו כתויה מכורבקתא **go kıtwe mxurbaqta** entangled among thorns (NTU4 150a).

כ-ר-ב-ש III v. ב-ר-כ-ש

כ-ר-ג-ל v. ג-ר-כ-ל

כ-ר-גֿ 1 (Ar خرج go out/حراج auction?) vi **x-r-j** to sell; **ʾanya qāpūtat la xrıjlu** These overcoats did not sell well (remained unsold); to spend, buy things (for a holiday) (PolU 421; PolG).

כ-ר-גֿ 2 (OA/OS חרט/חרק?) **x-r-č** to gnash teeth; to lock well (door) (cf. MeAl 182; PolG).

כרגֿייה (Ar) pl. **xarjīye** jewelry or embroidery made of little coins.

כ-ר-גֿ-מ III (IrAr **x-r-m-š**) **x-r-č-m** to scratch in order to injure.

כ-ר-ד-א (< כ-ד-א) **x-r-d̠-ʾ** (Z **x-r-z-ʾ**) to be entangled.

כרדלה (OA/OS חַרְדְּלָא) f. **xardalle** mustard.

כ-ר-ו (OA/OS חרב) vi **x-r-w** to be ruined; be bad, evil; spoiled, out of order; to faint (cf. PolG); **xāru bēsıd bābe** Damn, how great it is! (lit. May his father's house be ruined) (PolU 151) IV (vt) to destroy, break, spoil; make evil. NT+

כרואתא (< כ-ר-א) f. **xaroʾta** rough bathing sponge (to scrap tough dirt); pl. **xaroʾyāt̠a**.

כר-ומר (K) ⁺**xırr-u-mırr** odds and ends (PolU).

כרווע (Ar) **xarwaᶜ** castor; used only in **dehn xarwaᶜ** castor oil.

כרופא v. כריפא

כרושא (OS ܚܪܘܫܐ) **xarū/ōša** (?) throat [NT5 405) [cf. MAcD **xārūšā**].

כרותא v. כריוא

כ-ר-ז, ג'-ר-ז (OA/OS חרז/Ar خرز) **x/ġ-r-z** to string (beads); to arrange (=H עָרַךְ, BT2); to pierce (=H דָּקַר, BT4; cf. BaBin 103].

כ-ר-ט, כ-ר-ס (OA חרט) **x-r-ṭ/s** to gnash (teeth in anger) (NT); to press together; lock (zipper); pull tight (belt, string); cf. כ- 2 ר-גֿ (NT+) [Mutz 238 **xrs**]

כ-ר-י (OA חרי) **x-r-y** to defecate; **xrēle ʾıllu** He is much smarter than they are (said in irony); **xrēlu go qōru** They went to hell, they 'croaked' (PolU 304); cf. אכרה.

כְּרֵיגֿ v. כַּרַאגֿ

כריוא, כרותא (< כ-ר-ו) p.p. **xrīwa, xrūta** ruined, bad, evil; fainted; spoiled (taste), broken.

כריוותא (< כריוא) f. **xrīwūt̠a** evilness, evil doing.

כרינא (onomat) **xırrēna** race, chase (PolU 5).

כרינתא (< כ-ר-כ-ר) **xırrēnta** snore (PolU 110).

כריפא, כרופא (OA/OS חריפא) **xarīpa** (NT), **xarūpa** (Z), sharp (sword); pungent (food); torrential (river) (NT3).

כריש (< תכית+רישא) prep. **xarēš, xerēš** (+PolG), under the head (=H מְרַאֲשׁוֹת, BT1).

כ-ר-כ (OA/OS חרך) **x-r-x** to be singed; mostly in metaphor: **lıbbi xrıxle ʾıbbe** I felt sorry for him (cf. Pol 111); cf. כראכת לבא.

כרכא, כרכה (K) adj. ⁺**xırraka, -ke** loose, warn out (faucet fixure, screw, etc.).

כרכאצא (< כאצא ?) m. **xırxāṣa** sash, belt, girdle.

כרכיתכה, כרכיטכה (< ר-כ-ט ?) f. ⁺**xırxītke** restlessness, rush, impulse (AmU2 6a).

כרכץ (< כאצא?) adv. (ʾıl) ⁺**xırxaṣ** (Z < **xırxat̠**? cf. PolG **xırxas**) inside out; the reverse surface of textile; wrong side/way; v. קשטץ [cf. MacD 286 ܚܪܟܬ **xerxat** upside down; inside out].

כ-ר-כ-צ III (< OA חריץ) vt **x-r-x-ṣ** to scratch, to groove (NT2).

כ-ר-כ-ר III (Ar/K) ⁺**x-r-x-r** to snore; to have pity (=H נִכְמְרוּ, PolG); cf. כרינתא, כרכרתא.

כרכריתא (OA חרחורא) f. **xarxarīt̠a** fever, delirium (=H חַרְחֻר, BT5).

כרכרתא (< כ-ר-כ-ר) f. ⁺**xırxırta** snoring (cf. PolG); **ʾ-w-z** – to snore (SaAC 22).

כ-ר-מ (OA חרם/Ar خرم) **⁺x-r-m** to pierce (=H חָרוּם, BT3).
כ-ר-נ-א III (< ?) **x-r-n-ʾ** to be rolled in a blanket (for fun and game).
כרנופה (K < Ar?/OA/OS חֲרוּבָא < Ak **xarūb/pu**) pl. **⁺xırnūfe** fresh carob fruit.
כ-ר-ס 1 v. כ-ר-ט
כ-ר-ס 1 (Ar) **x-r-s** to become mute (ZU 72a).
כרסא, כרסה (Ar) adj. **xarsa, xarse** mute, dumb (RivSh 182).
כ-ר-ע (Ar be languid) **x-r-ᶜ** to be scared, frightened.
כ-ר-פ 1 IV (OA/OS חרף) vt **x-r-p** to sharpen (**skīna máxrıpla** BaBin 154); cf. כריפא.
כ-ר-פ 2 (< כ-ר-פ 1?) vi **x-r-p** to fit well (cover of a box).
כרפינא (K/onomat?) **xarpēna** speeding sounds and movments of floating on river (PolU 8).
כ-ר-ק v. ג'-ר-ק
כרש (K) **xırš** barren tree; cf. כרשי.
כ-ר-ש (OA/OS חרש) **x-r-š** to practice divination (=H עוֹנֵן, BT3).
כרשה, לִיכְשֵׁי (OA/OS חֲרָשֵׁי) pl. **xırše, lıxše** (+PolG), incantations, sorcery (NT5 407); cf. כראשא.
כרשי (< כרש; cf. OA חירשא plant) **xırši** barrenness of trees (NT3).
כ-ר-ת-נ III (< כורת?) **x-r-t-n** to oppress (=H הוֹנָה, BT3, D).
כשבונא (OA/OS חוּשְׁבָּנָא; but M. Jastrow 441 also חֶשְׁבּוֹנָא, Targ.) m. **xıš/žbōna** account, calculation, plan; בכשבונו **bxıšbōnu** They assumed (NT5 387); **la qam mēsınna bxıšbōna** I didn't take her into account.
כשבייה (Ar) f. **xašabīye** wooden shack.
כ-ש-ב-נ III (< כשבונא) **x-š/ž-b-n** to calculate, to make account (with) (NT5 387; Segal #94).
כ-ש-ו (OA/OS חשב) **x-š-w** to think; **xšu** Come to think of it, actually (SaAC 1, 12); II/IV to calculate (cf. Pol 111) (NT+).
כשויתא (< כ-ש-ו; cf. OA חשיבותא) f. **xšawīṯa** thought, intention.
כשוכא, כשוכתא (OS ܚܫܘܟܐ dark; +OA/OS חשׁיכא) adj. **xašūka, xašukta** dark, dim (eyesight) (NT+).
כשוף, כְּשׁוּפִים (H כשוף, כשופים) **xıššūf** (BaBin 90), **xıšūfīm** witchcraft; **mare-xıšūfat** sorcerers (PolU 385).
כשופכר (H-P) m./f. **xıšūfkar** witch, diviner (=H מְכַשֵּׁפָה, BT2; יִדְּעוֹנִי, BT3); pl. **xıšūfkare** (=H מְכַשְּׁפִים, BT2); cf. כראשא.
כשים (K < Ar غشيم) inv. **xašim** simpleton, naïve.
כשימותא (< כשים) f. **xašīmūṯa** naïvité, ignorance.
כ-ש-כ 1 (OA/OS חשך) **x-š-k** to grow dark; **ʾēna xšīke** She is a miser; **dunye xšıkla bʾēne** He became depressed; IV darken vi/vt (NT+).
כ-ש-כ 2 (OS ܚܫܚ) **x-š-x** to be (religiously) proper: **lak xāšıx la ṣēmıt** It is not proper for you not to fast (on Yom Kippur) (NT+).
כשכא (OS ܚܫܘܟܐ) **xıška** darkness; **xıške xašūke** totally dark places (NT+).
כשכאנא, כשכנתא (< כשכא) adj. **xıškāna, xıškanta** dark, dimly lighted (cf. PolG).
כשכאשה (K **xırxāš**) pl. **xıšxāše** dry carobs; cf. כרנופה.
כ-ש-כ-ש III (Ar) **x-š-x-š** to rattle; cf. כושכושתא.
כשכשוכה (< כ-י-ש) f. **xıšxıššōke** 'slider', a lazy woman who does most of her house chores by just sliding on her rear end.
כשכתא (OA חֲשֵׁכְתָּא) f. **xšakta** dusk (Avin78 93).
כשלא (OA/OS חשל to forge; to crush?) **xıšla** hot ashes (BaBin 154).
כ-ש-מ IV (K/P) **x-š-m** to feel alienated (daughter-in-law who after a quarrel goes back to live temporarily with her parents).
כשרה (K < OS ܚܫܠܬܐ) pl. **xıšre** jewels (NT) [cf. Mutz 239 **xšılta~šxılta**; Khan 585 **xšilta**].
כשתא, כִּישְׁתָא (P خشت) **xıšta** lance (=H חֲנִית, PolG) [cf. MacD 108 **xišt** small spear].
כת v. כינא
כתאיא, כתיתא (OA תחתאה) adj. **xtāya, xtēṯa** lower.
כתואתא v. כאתא 1
כתותא (< כאתא 2) **xaṯūṯa** (Z **xasūsa**) newness; mostly in **xāsa mxasūse** brand new.
כתימא, כתמתא (< כ-ת-מ) p.p. sealed, closed (NT); brimful, loaded (Z).
כתירא 1 (< כ-ת-ר) p.p. **xtīra** selected (NT3).

כתירא 2 (< ?) m. **xatīra** torch (=H לַפִּיד, BT1).

כ-ת-מ (OA/OS חתם to seal) vi/vt **x-t-m** to seal, to end (NT5 411); to obscure (NT2); to overfill or be overfull (Z); cf. כתימא.

כתם, כתמא (Ar خَتم/OA/OS חָתְמָא) **xıtım, xıtma** seal, signet (NT3; Zaken 391; PolG).

כתמיתא (< כ-ת-מ; cf. OA חֲתָמוּתָא, חֲתִימוּתָא) **xtamīṯa** signature (PolG).

כ-ת-נ II (OA/OS חתן) **x-t-n** to intermarry (=H הִתְחַתֵּן, BT1; BaBin 66); cf. כזמא.

כתנא (OA/OS חַתְנָא) m. **xıtna** bridegroom; son-in-law; pl. **xıtnawāṯa** (BT1; PolG); **xıtne** (SaLH)(OA pl. חַתְנֵי, חַתְנְוָותָא, SokBA 463).

כתנותא (< כתנא) n. abst. **xıtnūṯa** matrimony; **naqša bxıtnūsox lōšıtta** May you wear it at your wedding.

כ-ת-ר (Ar اختار) **x-t-r** to select; כתריה בגיאניה **xtırre bıgyāne** He bragged, praised himself (NT).

כ-ת-ת II (< כתותא; cf. OA/OS חדת, pa. 'to promulgate new ruling) **x-ṯ-ṯ** (Z **x-s-s**) to renew, make like new (cf. Hob89 220; PolG).

כתתא v. כאתא 2

ל(1)

ל (OA/OS לָמַד) **lāmad** (Z **lāmas**) the 12th letter of the Hebrew alphabet; **tlāṯi** thirty.

-ל (OA/OS/Mand) **l-** to, by; כיליתן לארייה **xīlētın l'arye** You were eaten by lions (NT2); **sāwun rrāv [< l+rāv]-u-nēčir** Go hunting (PolU 3);v. אל.

לא 1, לאה, לָאת, לג (OA/OS/Mand) **la, la'/h** (pausal or emphasis), **lat** [< **la+d**?] (RivSh 211, 214, 215, 223, 237; cf. לָאת גִדֵישִׁיוַוא **lat gıdēšīwa**, לאת גֵיטַרְכַנַך **lat gṭarkannax**, לָאת וֵילַא **lat wēla**, PolG; **lat kī'ın** PolUR 22); **lag** [<**la+g**] (before a.p.), no; **lēwa/e** she/he is not; **lēwu** they are not; **lēwax** we are not, etc. **la(-)piš** no more (left); **la...la** neither... nor; **ula xa'** not even one (was left); **la 'ixāla ula štāya** without food or drink (PolG); **la-bāš** (adj.) no-good, inferior (people) (SaLH 150); **la-baxta/gōra** unmarried, single; **la-gwāra** unmarried (PolU 351a); **la harē** no use, no response (lit., no yes) (PolU 423); **la hē ula la'** absolute nothing (SaAC 21); **xšūli la-hāwıt zīla** I thought lest you had gone (PolG); may be attached to next word: להאוילו **la-hāwēlu**; למצך **la-mṣax**; v. ולא 1.

לא 2 (< לא1) **la** assertive particle: **la ḥakōmıt kullu ḥēwānē-le 'arya** After all the lion is the king of all animals (Avin78 94); **la faqīr hādax-īle** Certainly the poor are (=behave) like that (PolU 433); **la mıtli** I have indeed (almsot) died (PolU 16); v. כוא.

לא 3 v. אילא

-לא 1 (OA לה) **-la** she, it (f.) (subject pron. with p.p.: פלטלא **plıṭ-la** she went out); her, it (object pron.: קבלכלא **qablax-la** we accept it); מרה לא, מרילה **mırrē-la(h)** he said to her; קבולא צלותי **qbul-la ṣlōṯi** Accept {it} my prayer! (NT+).

לא(-) 2 v. אילא

ל(א)אסא (< ל-א-ס chew?) **l'āsa** being aware, knowing; only with **la**: **zılle la-l'āsi** (PolG **lá-lāsi**) He went without my knowledge.

לאבד (Ar) adv. **lābıd** certainly, inevitably (NT).

לאוונטא (*IrAr< T< IT) **lāwanṭa** lavender, after-shave lotion, perfume.

לאוין (OA-H) pl. **lāwīn** prohibitions, the Thou- shall-nots: אל לאוין תורה לא אוריתן **'ıl lāwīn (d)tōra la 'ōrētın** Do not violate Torah's prohibitions (BaBin 69).

לאזם (Ar) inv. **lāzım** (It's) necessary; one has to (cf. PolG); cf. ל-ז-מ (NT+).

לאיה-לאיה (AzT) Lullaby! Go to sleep! (soothing lullaby sounds); cf. האיה-האיה [MacD 148].

לַא-יַאלַא (< לא+יאלא) **la-yāla** childless (=H עֲרִירִי, BT1, D).

ליכון v. לא יכון

איל v. לאיל

לאינא, אלינא (OA/OS לְגִינָא bottle, flask) f. **l'īna, 'līna** large and deep jar, used for storage of food or drinks; **-t xamra** jar of wine (PolG); pl. **l'īne**.

לאייק, לאיק (K< Ar) inv. **lāyıq** worthy; בלאיקי **blāyıqi** properly; cf. לייאקא (NT+).

-לאל (OA -ל) prep. **lāl-** to, by (virtue of), through (NT); cf. אל ; בילי לאלוך **bēli lālox** between me and you (NT); בילה לאליהון **bēle lālēhun** between him and them (NT5 408)[cf. MacD 149: **lālī** I myself; by me].

ל-א-ל-א III (OA/OS לעג>לגלג deride; stammer, SokBA 619; SokPA 277; or< לאלא?) **l-'-l-'** to stutter.

לאלא, לאלו, לאלותא, לאלה (< K) **lāla, lālo, lālōta** (m.); **lāle** (f.) stutterer.

ליאמא v. לאמא

לאן (Ar) conj. **lı'an** for, because (NT).

ל-א-ס (OA עלס, אלס, לעס; SokBA 136) **l-'-s** to chew; v. לאאסא (NT+).

לאסתא (< ל-א-ס) f. **l'asta** chewing.

לאסתיכ (IrAr/T< E) **lāstik** elastic rubber string.

לא עזב ולא יעזוב (H) **lō 'āzāv walō ya'azōv** (God) has not forsaken and will not forsake!

לא v. לאת

להתא v. לאתא

לַאתֶכְתַא (K **lat/lehtik** section of land marked for plowing on a certain day) **latekṯa** turn of the plow (=H מַעֲנָה, PolG:I Sam 14:14.)

עלאתריכ v. לאתריכ

לבא (OA) m. **lıbba** heart, mind; בלביה **blıbbe** as he liked; בלביהון **blıbbēhun** they intended to; לביה אימה אילה **lıbbe(h) 'ımmāh-īle** He cares about her; אודלו דלא לביה **'udlu**

dla lıbbe(h) They acted against his will (cf. Pol108: **la lıbbax** against your wish); **lıbbox-íle** as you wish, fine (Socin 161); הולילה ליבא **hullēle lıbba** He gave him courage; לא האויה ליבוך כסלי **la hāwe lıbbox kısli** Don't worry about me; לביה גפאייש **lıbbe gpāyıš** He will be sad, angry; ג'מריה לבא **ġmırre lıbba** She fainted; לבא סכניה She calmed down; לא רמליה בלביה **la rımle blıbbe** He did not brag; יאקדלו לבוה **yāqıdlu lıbbuh** They feel pity [cf. MeAl 177]; **lıbbe *rımle/šqılle/mqōlıᶜle** He felt nauseated; **ḥmılle rıš lıbbi** (The food) caused me heartburn; **lıbbe kımle mınna** He doesn't like her anymore; **lıbbe *mlēle** He became very sad; **kıs lıbbi** I think, assume (SaAC 9); **lıbbe psīxa** He is generous, likes to spend money ('his heart open'); **lıbbe bassima** happy, content; **lıbbe zılle ʾıl** He felt like having (certain food; cf. RivSh 139); **lıbbe š-qrāya** He likes studying (PolU 289); **lıbbe pıšle kısla** He became worried about her (cf. RivSh 224: **lıbbe pıšle ʾıbba**); **kīʾēla blıbba** He knows it by heart; **lıbbe qteʾle** He was terrified; **blıbba bassīma** Use it in good health; **mār ʾay dlıbbox** Say what is on your mind; **bxa lıbba** united, harmonious (marriage); pl. לבוואתא **lıbbawāṯa** (NT5 400; cf. AlfH 91: לְבֶוָסָא **lıbbıwāsa**); לביה **lıbbe** (NT5 391, 399); לְבָאבֵי **lıbbābe** (AvidH 7; PolG).

לבינה, נוין (K) pl. **lıvīne** (Z; PolG), **nıwīn** (NT), bedding items, bed-clothes; נפילא לנוין **npīla lnıwīn** bed ridden.

ל-ב-כ (Ar) **l-b-k** to be too busy, entangled.

לבכתא (K< Ar لُبّ) f. **lıbbıkṯa** kernel, grain; a bit; pl. **lıbbıkyāṯa** (=H חַרְצַנִּים, BT; PolG).

ב-י-ל v. ל-ב-ל

ל-ב-ש (< Ar pick up?) **l-b-š** to cling to (child to an adult): **xzi māṯo lbıšle ʾıbbi** Look, how he clings to me (doesn't leave me alone)!

לא v. לג

לגלג (K/P/T< Ar لقلق) m. **laglag** stork; cf. חגי לגלג.

לג לעומר (H) **lag laᶜōmer** the 33rd day of the counting of Omer (a Jewish Holiday) [cf. Mutz. 209 **laġlaᶜómır**].

לגן (K/T/P لگن baking pan, dish for washing hands; cf. OA לְקָנָא basin, bowl/OS لـحمنا < Gr λεκανη) m. **lagan** large serving dish; cf. לאינא?

לגוגך (K) inv. **lajūjık** rash, impetuous (NT); cf. לוזך.

נ-ג-כ v. ל-ג-כ

ל-ג-מ (Ar) **l-j-m** to harness; cf. ליאמא, לג'אבא.

לג'אבא, לג'אוו (K) m. **lı/aġāva** (Z; PolG), **lıġāw** (NT), bridle; cf. ל-ג-מ, ליאמא.

ל-ג'-ב II (< לג'אבא) **l-ġ-v** to bridle.

לג'ווּתא (Ar) f. **laġwıta** mania, excessive interest.

לג'ם (Ar mine) m. **laġam** cave (PolU 87); cf. קונברא

ל-ד-ג' (Ar) **l-d-ġ** to sting; to insult.

לדתא, לצתא (Ar) f. **laḏḏıta, lazzıta** (Z), joy.

לה- 1, ליה- (OA) **-leh** he (subject pron. with p.p.): **xzē-le** He saw; מוסקנה (NT) **musq-an-ne [‹ -le]** He brought me up; him, it (m.) (object pron.: **qāṭıl-le** He kills him; **kīʾē-le** He knows it; **máxwu-li-le** Show him to me!

לה-2 v. אילה

להבדיל (H) **lahavdīn** (Z) not to mention holy things with secular ones; keep them apart.

ל-ה-ג (IrAr be eager/OA לחך lick?) **l-h-g** to eat voraciously, to lick up (=H לָחַךְ, BT4); cf. ל-כ-כ [Garbell 287/MacD 149: **l-k-x** lick].

להווגיתא (Ar) f. **lahwajīṯa** excessive heat.

להום (Ar لهب?) m. **lıhom** blaze, oven's heat [= PolG: **tehım** = חמימות ??].

ל-ה-י (< *l-h-w< OA להב) vi **l-h-y** shine, gleam; cf. להום, להתא, להווגיתא, להיבה, פ-ל-ה-י? NT+

להיבה (Ar) f. **lahībe** flame; pl. להיבתיאתא **lahībıtyāṯa**. NT+

להתא, לַאתַא, לַאְתַא (< ל-ה-י/OA להט?) f. **lahta, laʾta** (BaBin 111), **lāta** (RivSh 280), candle's flame.

לו- (OA להון) **-lu** they (subject pron. with p.p. or predicate: **ysıq-lu** They went up; קליוילו **qlīwe-lu** They are clean); them (object pron.: **malpī-lu** They teach them); cf. אהנון.

לוו (Ar) adv. **law** therefore (NT).

לואתא (OA/OS לוֹעָא jaw) f. **loʾta** chewing gum.

לוביא (Ar/P/T; OA רוביא) f. **lobya** green beans.

לובנא, לובנתא (Ar لَبِنَة، لبْن; OA לְבֵינְתָא; OS ܠܒܢܬܐ; Mand ליבתא) f. **lubna, lubınta** brick; pl. לונה **lūne** (NT1; NT5 404), **lubne** (Z) (OA לְיבְנֵי, OS ܠܒܢܐ [cf. MacD 144 **lyūnā**].

לוושא (T/P لواش) m. **lawōša** kind of long big bread (PolU 429).

לוזינא (Ar/P) f. **lōzīna** almomd cake.

לוזך (K) inv. **luzık** hasty, rash (NT); cf. לזי, לגוגך.

לוח (H) **lūwaḥ** tablet (of gemstone; of the heart); pl. לוחות **lūḥōṯ** the Tablets (of the Covenant) (BT5) (NT+).

לוחא (Ar لَوح; cf. OA לַוְחָא, לוּחָא m. wooden plank) **lōḥa** board (NT, f.); bar (of soap) (Z, m.).

לוי, ליואיא (H לֵוִי/OA לֵיוָאָה/OS ܠܘܝܐ) **lēwi, lēwāya** Levite, Levi (used as p.n. as well); pl. ליואיה **lēwāye**.

לוין, לוון, לון, לו אן (Ar) adv. **law-ı/u/an** (not) even (NT; cf. לָווּן **lawun**=H אֲפִלּוּ, AvidH 17).

לויתן (H) m. **liwyāṯān** Leviathan; mythic fish to be eaten by the righteous ones in the world to come (NT+).

ל-ו-כ (OA לְבַךְ hold fast) **l-w-x** to be dirty, sticky [cf. Mutz. 210]

-לוך (OA לך) **-lox** you (m.sg. subject pron. with p.p.): **šqıl-lox** you took; optional ethical dative: **qū-lox** Get up! Object pron. with a.p.:**našqā-lox** She kisses you; cf. אאהת 1.

לוכמא (Ar) m. **lukma** fist; pl. **lukme**.

לוכנדא v. לוקנטא

לוכס (IrAr< En) **luks** Lux, gas mantle lantern.

לולב (H) m. **lūlav/f** the lulav (palm branch).

לולו-יאקות (Ar) **lūl(u)-(u)yāqut** diamond (cf. PolG: **lūl** אבן חן לבנה כמו זכוכית).

ל-ו-ל-ח III (< לוחא) **l-ō-l-ḥ** to soak laundry in soapy water.

לולייא (K/T/P tube, spout) f. **lūlīya** sink, laver (PolG) [MacD **lūlā, lūlika** pipe].

לומן, לומאנה (K لومه< Ar blame) adv. **lawman, láwmāne** because of this, therefore, that is why (=H לָכֵן, בַּעֲבוּר זֶה, PolG).

לומלא (OA/Mand מַמְלָא, OS ܡܡܠܠܐ speech) m. **lumla** speech, utterance; ability to speak, usually in hendiadys: **(d)la lumla ula lišāna** very quiet person (cf. PolG; PolU 373).

לונא v. לובנא

לוונדייה (K) **lawandīye** dance song (PolU 439).

לוקמא (Ar) m. **luqma** mouthful.

לוקנטא, לוכנדא (IrAr/T< It) f. **lōqanṭa** (Z), **lōkanda** (PolG), restaurant; pl. **lōqanṭat**.

לורד (T< En) m. **lōrd** lord, wealthy person (cf. PolU 85)

לורי (Ar< En) **lōri** truck, lorry.

ל-ו-ש (OA/OS/Mand לבש) **l-w-š** to wear, put on (the phylacteries); IV to dress someone, to cover; למלווושה **lmalwōše** to dress him (NT5 397).

לושתא (OA לבשתא) f. **lwašta** garment, clothing.

לותכתא (K) f. **lōtıkta** kick (in the air out of joy), leap, dance; pl. **lōtıkyāṯa**.

לזי, לזיתא (K) f. **laz(z)i, lazzīta** haste, rush; **blazzi** hastily, quickly; **ma lazzīla ʾıllox** Why are you in a hurry; **mın lazzīte** being in a hurry, he...; cf. לוזך, ל-י-ז. NT+

ל-ז-ם (Ar) **l-z-m** to oblige, impose; cf. לאזם.

לח (Ar) adv./inv. **laḥḥ** exact(ly) related: **xalōya** - exact maternal uncle (SaAC 18).

לחיים טובים (H) **lahayyīm ṭōvīm** Bless you! (May your sneeze be 'for good life') (RivPr #94); cf. תיר בז'י.

לחמד ללאה v. חמדלא

לחיפא (K< Ar) m. **lıḥēfa** quilt.

ל-ח-ם (Ar) **l-ḥ-m** to fit well in place (vi); IV to solder, to set well in place (vt); to hit the target (PolU 385).

ל-ח-ק IV (Ar) **l-ḥ-q** to have sufficient time (AvidH 46, 68; NTU4 161a); cf. מ-ד-ו.

לטומא (< ל-ט-ם) m. **laṭōma** slap (RivSh 241); cf. רשומא.

ל-ט-י (Ar لطي/لطا settle down, shelter oneself) **l-ṭ-y** to sleep comfortably, cozily (PolG).

לטיף (Ar) **laṭīf** nice: מא לטיף אילו כליקה דכלקלוך **ma laṭīf-īlu xlīqe dxlıqlox** How beautiful are the creatures you have created! (NTU4 157b

ל-ט-כ (Ar) **l-ṭ-x** to stick (vi), be attached (=H דָּבַק, BT1, Ruth 1:14; NT; פָּגַע ב-, PolG); IV to attach (VT) (לְמַלְטוֹכֵי = לְחַבָּרָא, AvidH 7).

ל-ט-ם (Ar) **l-ṭ-m** to slap (oneself) as a sign of grief (cf. MeAl 190; PolG).

-לי (OA) **-li** I (subject pron. with p.p.): פלטלי **plıṭ-li** I went out; דאבנה לי **dıbnē-li** That I built; me (object pron.): **qāṭıl-li** He kills me; **qṭul-li** Kill me! מכוולילה **máxwū-li-le** Show him to me!

ליאל (< אאלא) adv. **lē'al** that side, beyond, further (=H הָלְאָה, BT1).

ליאמא, לאמא (OA/OS לוּגְמָא jaw; Mand cheek > K **lāme**) m. **lı'ma** (NT), **ˈlāma** (Z; RivSh 218 לָאמָא), jaw (NT), meat of cattle's head, cheek (Z); pl. **ˈlamāme** (Z); cf. ל-ג-ם, לוקמא, לג'אבא [MacD 145 **lāmā** bridle, jaw].

ליאפא (< ל-י-פ) **layāpa** learner, one who learns to do things fast.

לייאקא (Ar) f. **lıyāqa** worth, value (BaBin 136); cf. לאיק.

ליב- (OA לא אית ב-) **lēb-** being unable: **lēbi ṣēmın** I am unable to fast; **lēbu 'ıllan** They can't overpower us; cf. איב-.

ל-י-ג̇ (Ar لجّ) **l-y-j** to beseech (=H פָּצַר, BT1, D).

ליו- v. לא

ליואיא v. לוי

ליואן (Ar< P) m. **līwan** ante-chamber, hall (cf. PolG).

ל-י-ז IV (< לזי) vi/vt **l-y-z** to hasten (NT+).

ליזא (< ל-י-ז) m. **līza** diligent (BaBin 151).

ל-י-ט I/II (OA/OS לוט) **l-y-ṭ** to curse (NT5 388, 399).

ליטא, מליטא (OA לִיטָא) **līṭa, mılīṭa** (?) accursed (NT5 402; BaBin 152).

ל-י-כ (H > JAB > IrAr) **l-y-x** to go away, leave quietly (cryptic); **lōx mqabıl ra'ıš** Go away before he (=a little child) notices; [cf. JAB (Ben-Jacob 95): **līx mın hōn** Leave here quietly; IrAr: **lāx, ylīx** to leave in a hurry, beat it; cf. Blanc 145].

ליכא v. איכא

לכון, לא יכון ליכון (Ar) **la-ykun** (NT, BT, AvidH 28), **lakun** (Z), lest (NT+).

-ליכון, -לוכון, (OA לכון) **-lēxun** (NT), **-lōxun** (Z), you (c. pl. subject pron. with p.p.**šqıl-lē/ōxun** You took); you (c. pl. object pron. **šāqıl-lē/ōxun** He takes you).

לילה, ליליה, לילי (OA/OS/Mand לֵילְיָא< absolute לֵילֵי) m. **lēle** night; אד ליליה **'ad lēle** (Z **'ızlal**) tonight; פלגד לילה **palgıd/d lēle** (Z **palgızlal**) midnight; כּוּד ליל **kudlel** every night (RivSh 274; Z **kuzlel**); **lēl šabsa** Sabbath Eve; **lēl 'ırōta**, Friday Eve; **lēl šašše** the night before Brith Milah; **lēlxın, lalxın/t** last night (cf. PolG); **xa-lal-xın** another night, tomorrow night (Socin 161); pl. לילואתא **lēlıwāta**; but v. **'arbi yōme u'arbi lēle** (!) forty days and forty nights (BT5) OA pl. לֵילָוֵי, לֵילָוָתָא [Mutz 2000b 298, n. 6].

ליל-הודא (OA יהודה + לֵילְיָא) **lēl hūza** (Z) the demon of Judea (SaLH 140)

לילייה (Ar) f. **lēlīye** the night celebrations before the wedding day; **lēlīyıd dugle** a rehearsal two nights before the wedding day.

ל-י-מ 1 (Ar لمّ) **l-y-m** to hem, tuck in, press together (cf. Pol 108; PolG); cf. ל-מ-ל-מ.

ל-י-מ 2 IV (Ar لوم) **l-y-m** to blame, reproach: **nāše gmalīmīlan** people blame us (for this) (cf. PolU 273).

לִים (< לימשתיה) m. **līm** clay, etc., carried to the shore by torrential waves: מאטו איביה מצאליה ליבא דיליה גריקא מוך לים דילי גבאן בחרי **māṭo 'ībe mṣāle lıbba dīle ġrīqa mux līm dīle gıvān baḥre** How can a heart sunken like the clay at the sea shore pray (ZU 73b)?

לימונא (Ar لَيمون; OA לֵימְנָא) f. **laymūna**; pl. **laymūne**

לימשתיה (K) f. **līmıšte** torrential wave: גתיא כדא לימשתיה אלד או דפתאר וגמכלליה **gıtya xda - 'ıllıd 'aw daftar ugımxallılāle** A torrential wave comes and washes that book (NTU4 162a); cf. לים.

ליס (K) m. **līs** roosting place (usually a bar).

ל-י-ס (< ליס) **l-y-s** to roost; **kısyāsa glēsi rēše barbar 'āṣırta** Chicken roost on it towards the evening.

ל-י-פ 1, י-ל-פ (OA/OS ילף ,אלף) **l-y-p** I [1: **lıp-**; 2: **lāyıp lēp-** (but NT ילפ- **yalp-** ~ ליפ- **lēp-**); 3: **lōp**; 4: **lyāpa**] to learn; **y-l-p** IV [1: **mōlıp-**; 2/3: **mālıp**; 4: **malōpe**] to teach, to accustom (NT+) [cf. Mutz 240 **ylp**].

ל-י-פ 2 (Ar لفّ) **l-y-f** to wrap around (PolG).

ליפא, לפתא (< ל-י-פ, p.p.) adj. **līpa, lıpta** educated, accustomed.

לירא (זהב) (T< Libra) m. **līra (zahab)** gold coin; pl. **līre (zahab)** (cf. PolU 431.

ל-י-ש (OA/OS/Mand לוש) **l-y-š** to knead (NT5 409) (NT+).

לישא (OA/OS לֵישָׁא, לֵיישָׁא) m. **lēša** dough.

לישאנא, לשאנא (OA/OS/Mand לִישָּׁנָא, לישאנא)

m. li/īšāna (NT5 384) tongue, language, speech; nation; līšāne yarīxa impudent, one who answers back; līšān qōdēš the Holy Tongue (Hebrew); lišāna dēni/lišān hozāye our/Jewish Neo-Aramaic [=Khan 373 lišānit targum/nošan/atxa w-atxa].

לישתא (< ל-י-ש) f. layašta kneading woman.

לית, ליתן (OA -לית , לָא אִית) lēt (Z lēs), lē/ītun (Z lēsın; AvidH 53 לֵיתֵין), there is not; תליה(י)ל lıtle (NT), latle (Z) He doesn't have; לתוא lı/atwa (Z laswa) There was not; laswāle He didn't have; laswābe He was unable; cf. -ליב, אית.

-לך (OA) -lax you (f. sg. subject pron. with p.p., e.g.: šqıl-lax You took; you (f. sg. object pron. with a.p.: nāšiq-lax He kisses you; ethical dative: qū-lax Get (you) up (NT+).

לך 1, לכא 1 v. אכא

לך 2 v. -ג

לכא 2 (Ar< K/P لك million) m. lıkka large number, plenty; pl. lıkke, lıkkawāta; šōʾi lıkke a huge amount [cf. Blanc 156].

לכווא, לאכוא (< לא+כוא) adv. laxwa otherwise, lest (BaBin 131; NTU2 40b; PolG).

לכון v. ליכון

ל-כ-ז (Ar) l-k-z nudge, push with elbow, fist; to pinch (NT5 394; NTU4 159b); cf. נ-ג-ז.

ל-כ-כ 1 (OS ܠܚܟ/ܠܚܟ/OA לחך lick?) l-k-x to eat secretly, to hide something for oneself.

ל-כ-כ 2 (Ar لك lac, resin) l-k-k to secure, seal well (PolU 353).

לכמא (OA/OS לחמא) laxma bread; wēlu xīle laxma umılxa ʾımmıd xauxıt They have eaten bread and salt together (=They are close friends); laxma raqīqa/qrīča thin crunchy bread; laxmıd ʾēda unleavened bread (other than matzah) for Passover (NT+) [Khan 573 lixma].

ל-כ-ש (OA לחש) l-x-š to whisper (NT5 394)); mutter incantation (RivSh138); cf. -ת-ל-כ-ש.

לכשא (OA לִיחְשָׁא) lıxša whisper; v. כרשא (NT+).

לכתמא (OA על אחת כמה וכמה) adv. láxatma (Z láxasma) How much more so (=H אַף כִּי, BT5); v. כדא, כמא, על אחת כמה וכמה.

ללאא (< OA עלעא/OS ܠܠܥܐ rib?) m. lılʾa slice of fruit; pl. lılʾe.

למא סבב (< סבב) lma sabab For what reason? Why? (NT).

למאמה v. ליאמא

למיש (AzT?) lamīš thorough (bath); v. חמם.

ל-מ-ל-מ (< ל-י-מ 1) vt l-m-l-m to gather, collect.

למנדי (< לא+מנדי) la-mındi nothing; בלמנדי bla-mındi for nothing, free of charge; cf. גמנדי (NT).

למפא (IrAr< It) f. ⁺lampa kerosene lamp.

-למצ v. מ-צ-י

-לן (OA) -lan we (subject pron with p.p.): כזילן xzē-lan we saw; us (object pron with a.p. and imperative): qāṭıl-lan; He kills us; אגרושלן ıgruš-lan Draw us! (NT+).

לנגא (P) langa lame (NTU2 79b); cf. ערגא.

לנדהאיא, לנדהיתא (< K?) m. landıhāya, -hēta, giant, huge person; cf. חמבשאיא.

לסאן (Ar) lisān language, speech (NT).

לעאבא, לעבאנא, לעבנתא, לעבנתא (< לעבה) adj. laᶜāba, laᶜabta (PolG), lıᶜbāna, lıᶜbanta (Z), 'actor', insincere, pretender.

לעבה (Ar) pl. lıᶜbe games, acts of pretense (cf. PolU 406)

ל-ע-ב-ט III (OA/Ar lbṭ) l-ᶜ-b-ṭ to wiggle, be restless, very eager and anxious; mluᶜbıṭle ṭāla He is 'dying' to have her.

ל-ע-ו-ש III (Ar?) l-ᶜ-w-š to annoy, torment.

ל-ע-ט (OA לעט/Ar لطع) l-ᶜ-ṭ to lick up [MacD l-ṭ-ᶜ/l-ᶜ-ṭ; Mutz. 210 ltᶜ].

ל-ע-ל-ע III (Ar لألأ) l-ᶜ-l-ᶜ to glitter, shine.

לעלי (Ar) laᶜli ruby (NT3).

ל-ע-נ II (Ar) l-ᶜ-n to curse (NT); cf. מלוענא.

ל-ע-פ-צ III (Ar لفظ?) l-ᶜ-f-ṣ to disobey, to move freely; lēbe mlaᶜfıṣ mqāme He doesn't dare to do any thing at his presence (out of fear).

לעשתון (Ar لا عشت) laᶜaštūn (I wish) I didn't live (after those days, they were so good!), a nostalgic word common in women's speech.

לעתיד לבוא (H) leᶜātīd lāvō in the world to come (NT).

לפא 1 (K) m. ⁺lappa (small)lump; pıšle xa ⁺lappa He became scared, withdrawn; paw, handroll (PolG; PolU 115); pl. ⁺lappāpe palms, hands (PolU 383) [MacD150 tiny weight; handful].

לפא 2 (Ar) f. **laffa** roll of paper, etc.

לפאחא (Ar?) f. **lıffāḥa** modern scarf for men.

לפיכא (Ar لَبْخه) f. ⁺**lappīxa** thick paste, mess.

ל-פ-ל-פ III (< IrAr **lblb** be smooth talker?) **l-p-l-p** to importune, try hard to sell merchandise to a client at a cheap price: **qam mlaplıpla ʾıbbe** He praised it to him; מְלַפְּלוֹפִּי =H תחנוני, AvidH; הִתְחַנֵּן, PolG).

לפץ' (Ar) m. **lafaẓ, lavẓ** pronunciation, utterance; cf. ל-ע-פ-צ (NT+).

לקא (< Ar/OA lick?) m. **laqqa** a bite of food; **mxi xa laqqa** Have a bite!

ל-ק-ט 1 (OA/OS לקט) **l-q-ṭ** to glean, to pick up (flowers, things, children); cf. מלקט, מלקטתא; לקיטא (NT+).

ל-ק-ט 2 II (< ל-ק-ט 1) **l-q-ṭ** to gossip, slander, gather rumors (Z; PolG); cf. מלקטו

לקטא (OA) m. **lıqṭa** gleaning; picking up.

ל-ק-ט-נ III (< נוקטא?) **l-q-ṭ-n** to be spotted ; v. מלוקטנא.

ל-ק-י (OA/H לקי) **l-q-y** to suffer (due to a religious offence), to perish (=H נִסְפָּה, BT1, D; PolG; לָקָה AvidH 37; AlfH 47); II to cause suffering (RivSh 175).

לקיטא (< ל-ק-ט) adv. **lqīṭa** diligently, neatly.

ל-ק-ל-ק III (Ar) **l-q-l-q** to rattle, be shaky (= H: דפקו שערי רחמים לפתוח; BaBin 153; PolG).

ל-ק-פ (Ar catch) **l-q-f** to sew in coarse stiches, to hem with pins.

לקפכה (< ל-ק-פ) f. **laqafke** coarse stich.

לשא (K) f. (Z)/m.(NT) **lašša** (human) body, flesh (cf. NT5 397 =m.; Pol 108/PolG=f.).

לשון ארמי (H) **lāšōn ʾarammī** Aramaic language (NT3).

לשון הרע (H) **lāšon hārāᶜ** evil tongue, slander (cf. ZU 73a).

לשון קודש (H) **lāšon qōdeš** the holy tongue, Hebrew; v. לישאנא.

לשכווא v. כוא

לת v. לא 1

לתוא v. לית

לתיך (< תכית) adv. **ltēx** down, downward.

מ (m)

מ, ם (H) **mēm pašūṭa/saṯūma** (Z **sas-**) the open (= non final position)/closed (= final position) mem letter; **ʾarbi** forty.

-מ 1 v. מן 1

-מ 2 (T) **m-** indicates a 'doublet' (=the real noun but with its first consonant replaced with **m-**) to indicate 'all kinds of, and the like', e.g., **julle-mulle** all kinds of clothes; **pılda-mılda** hair residue, and the like; **pīrakat-mīrakat** old women and the like (PolU 58).

-מ 3 (OA) **m-, ma-** the initial particle of the derivational conjugations forms: **mbāqır** he asks; **mšādır** Send! **mbōšılle** He cooked; **mbāšōle** cooking; occasionally omitted: בַּקְרַךְ·**(m)baqrax** (RivSh 274) We shall ask; **maʾmır** he builds; **mtufsır** was interpreted.

מא, מה, מהא (OA מָאן, מָא, מָה) **mā, māha** (+NT), what; what for: **ʿōha mā pısrā-le** What is this meat for ? (PolG); **ma la mırri ṭālox** Didn't I tell you? (PolG); מהילא **mahīla** (NT)/**mayla** (Z) what is it? (MeAl 184, n.49); מא שפירא אילה **mā šapīra-īle** How beautiful is ...! (NT3); מא רנג **mā rang** How? מא עגב **ma ʿajab** How come (I wonder)? ...מא אד...האדך **mā ʾaḏ...hādax**... Just as...so... מאד **mād/t** whatever; מנד מאד **mınnıd mād** due to, out of; **mālox** What is wrong with you? (MeAl 190); cf. מו.

מָאבְּיָינָא (< א-ב-י 2) m. **mʾabyāna** consumption (lit. swelling) (=H שַׁחֶפֶת, BT3, D); cf. גזגזיתא.

מא-ביני, מא בין (Ar) **mā-bayni/bēn** between, among (BT2, Arodh); cf. נאביאן.

מאבת v. ב-י-ת

מאגה (K) f. **māče** kiss (babytalk).

מאג'ב v. א-כ-פ

מאד v. מא

מאדה (< Ar مؤدّى task, meaning?) f. **maʾadde** fact, matter (PolG).

מאדייא (< H מדי) m. **māḏāya** Mede (NT2).

מאדים (H) m. **maʾdīm** the planet Mars (NT2).

מאדם, מדאם (Ar ما دام) adv. **mādām** as long as (BaBin 14; PolG); cf. ד-י-מ.

מאהר v. ה-י-ר

מאוביא, מאוביתא (< א-ב-י 2) p.p. **mʾubya, mʾōbēṯa** swollen; **mʾubyıd kıpna** swollen due to hunger (=H מְזֵי רָעָב, BT5); rheumatic.

מאוד, מאודה v. א-ו-ד

מאולפא, מאולפתא (< א-ל-פ 2) p.p. **mʾulfa, mʾōlafta** blessed, good natured (child).

מאוסתא (< ?) f. **maʾusta** stomach ache, indigestion.

מאורארא, מאוראררתא (< א-ר-א-ר) p.p. **mʾurʾıra, mʾurʾarta** pampered, spoiled child.

מאזורא (< ?) m. **⁺māzōra** bar, pole, large stick.

מאזתא v. מזתא

מאזד, מאזית v. ז-י-ד

מאחל v. ח-י-ל

מאחר v. ח-י-ר

מאטו(ף), מָא טוב, מוטו, מֵטוֹב (< מא+1 טוף) **māṭo(f/v)** (RivSh 278-9; PolG), **mōṭo** (BT2, Arodh) how? what sort? [MacD 165 **mōṭū**; Mutz 212 < OA מה טב/טיב; OS ܡܐ ܛܒ].

מאטרסגל (IrAr< En) m. **māṭırsígıl** motorcycle.

מאיא 1, מאייה, מַאיֵי (OA/OS/Mand מַיָּא; -מֵימֵי) pl. **⁺māya, ⁺māye** (+NT; BT2, D, Arodh; RivSh 176; Hob85 227; SaLH), water;**-ıd ʾēne bızlu** He worked very hard (lit., the water of his eyes spilled); He lost his composure (PolU 268); **zılle rıš** —; He went to the river (euph. for relieving oneself); **rēš** — (start of a) strong current (PolU 363); **mundēle b-** He sold way below its value (PolU 11), waste (PolU 305); v. מיאנא [Khan 574 **maʿe**].

מאיא 2, מיאיא (OA/OS מְעַיָּיא) m. **me/ıʾya** bowel (cf. PolG); pl. מאיואתא **meʾyawāṯa** (NT5 389), **mēʾewāṯa** (Ruth 1:11) (OA pl. מעיוני!, SokBA 694: 2#מעיינא); cf. מילאכה.

מאינאנא (< א-י-נ) **maʾināna** helper (=H עֵזֶר, BT1, Am; cf. RivSh 273).

מאיסתא v. מזתא

מאיקאנא (< א-י-ק) m. **maʾiqāna** besieger, foe (NT4; NT5 402; BT2).

מאיר (H) p.n. **mīʾır** Meir; cf. מירו.

מאכת v. כ-י-ת

מאל 1 (K< Ar) m. **māl** property, wealth, house; **māl-mīrat, māl-wēran** Damned be your house; **hāwıt ž-māle ṣālıḥa** May you be of a prosperous home (cf. PolU 246); v. צ-ל-ח.

מאל 2 v. א-מ-ר 1
מאל 3 v. מא
מאלא/ה* (OA/OS מַעְלָא; -מַעְלֵי entrance, eve of) **māla/e** attested only once in יומד מאלד אידא **yōmıd m(ʾ)ālıd ʾēḏa** Eve of Holiday (NT5 407); cf. י-א-ל ; ארותא [Mutz 211 **maʿlēla** Eve (of Sabbath or Holiday); pl. **maʿlelawe**; MacD188 eve of fast].
מַאלְכְוַא, מַאלֶיכְוֵי (K) m. **mālıxwa/e** landlord, chief (=H נָשִׂיא, BT1, D; PolG); pl. מַאלְכְווַאנֵי **mālıxwāne** (=H נוֹגְשִׂים, BT1, D); מליכואיי **malıxwāye** (= H שוטרים, BaBin 24; PolG).
מאלם v. ל-י-מ 2
מאלף v. ל-י-פ
מאם כולם (K) ⁺**mām xulam** Sir, (Uncle is) your servant (PolU 141).
מאמו (K) m. **māmo** Uncle (used by young people addressing a paternal uncle or any old person)[Khan 574 **māma**].
מאמור (Ar) m. **maʾmur** order, command (NT); commander, officer (Z).
מאמראנא (< א-מ-ר 2) m. **maʾımrāna** builder.
מאסק v. י-ס-ק
מאסתא v. מזתא
מא עלינא (Ar) **mā ʿalēna** It's not our business
מאפק v. נ-פ-ק
מאר (< א-מ-ר) **mār** (that is to) say, let us say; quote (a saying:) (PolG).
מארא (OA מָרְיָא, מָרֵי-/מארי; pl. מָרָוָותָא, מָרֵי) **māra** owner; מארי **māri** my Master; מרה ג'ירא **mare-ġira** zealot; מארד עולם **mārıd ʿōlām** Master of the World; מארד שמה **mārıd šımme** Master of Heaven; בכתא מריה עאקל **baxta mare ʿāqıl** intelligent woman; מרה גורא **mare gōra** married (woman); מרה ג̆רמכתא **mare čarmıkṯa** uncircumcised (=H עָרֵל, BT); מרה פסחא **mare pısha** the host of the Passover Seder (vs. פסחאיא an invited guest at the Seder); **mare mā wētın** What is on you mind? What is your decision? (PolU 292); pl. מרואתא **marawāṯa**; מא גנאפא מאל טלא מרואתה **ma gnāfeʾ māl ṯla marawāṯe** How useful is wealth for his owner (on death)? Cf. מרתא.
מארמאצי(כא) (K snake-fish) m. **mārmāṣī(ka)** eel (cf. PolU 263).
מאשלא (Ar ما شاء الله What God wanted) ⁺**māšalla** amulet stuck on the forehead of small children; how fortunate! (said on great wealth, beauty, etc); cf. הלא-הלא.
מאשה (K/P) pl. **māše** cow peas, a kind of green cheap lentils (eaten by the poor).
מאת v. מא
מאתא 1 (OA/OS מאתא, מָתָא < Ak **mātu**, f. town) f. **māṯa** (Z **māsa**) village (Z), city, inhabited place (NT; BT, D); pl. מתואתא **maṯwāṯa** (OA pl. מָתְוָתָא) (NT+).
מאתא 2 (< ?) f. **maʾta** redness or pimple in the eye; cf. כאלו [MacD189 **mʿtʾ** grape; pimple].
מאתאיא (< מאתא 1) m. **māṯāya** villager.
מאתה, אמתיה (OA מָאתֵי, מָאתַן; OS/Mand מאתין) **māṯe, ʾımmāṯe** (?), two hundred (NT2); v. אמא.
מ-ב-א v. נ-ו-א
מבאוא (< מן אאוא?) adv. **mbāwa** (?) hence, the reason that (NT2; NT5 389; NT6 134).
מבאקי (Ar) **mabāqi** residue, the rest of (NT+).
מבהדלאנא, מבהדלניתא (< ב-ה-ד-ל)n.ag. **mbahdılāna, -nīṯa** confusing person (PolGr 43).
מבוהדלא, מבוהדלתא (< ב-ה-ד-ל) p.p. **mbúhdıla, mbuhdalta** mixed-up, dissolute.
מבול (H) **mabbūl** the biblical flood (NT); **mıbbūl mıššāmāyim** torrential rain (cf. PolU 362).
מבולקנא, מבולקנתא (< ב-ל-ק-נ) p.p. **mvúlqına, -anta** spotted (sheep) (=H טָלוּא, BT1).
מבוניא, מבוניתא (< ב-נ-י) p.p. **mbunya, mbōnēṯa** selected, chosen, cleared.
מבורבזא, מבורבזתא (< ב-ר-ב-ז) p.p. **mbúrbıza, mburbazta** scattered, spread.
מבורכא, מבורכתא (< ב-ר-כ) p.p. **mburxa. mbōraxta** blessed (for people only); **-d ʾilāha** blessed by God, very gifted; wedded, married; v. מברוכה; בריכא.
מבותה (< ב-י-ת) f. **mabōṯe** (Z **mabōse**) Sabbath-food cooked overnight; pl. **mabōṯat** (SaLH 148).
מביין (Ar) inv. **mbayyın** obvious (NT).
מַבִירְיַינַא (< ב-ר-י) m. **mabıryāna** creator (=H מְחוֹלֵל, BT5, D).
מבכרא (Ar) f. **mabxara** censer, fire pan (=H מַחְתָּה, BT3, D) ; pl. מַבְכַּרְיַיאתַא (BT4, D).
מבנוכה v. בנוכה
מבסמאנא (< ב-ס-מ) m. **mbasmāna** healer (=H רוֹפֵא, BT2).

מבקראנא (< ב-ק-ר) m. **mbaqrāna** inquisitive.

מברד (IrAr, Ar) m. ⁺**mabrad** file, rasp; pl. ⁺**mabrāde** cf. ב-ר-ד.

מברוכה (< ב-ר-כ) v.n. **mbarōxe** reciting the seven blessings in a Jewish wedding; wedding; marriage (NT+).

מבשלניתא (< ב-ש-ל) n. ag. f. **mbašlanīṯa** cook (PolGr 43); cf. מטבכג׳י.

מגדלי בלורית (H) pl. **mıgaddılē bılōrīṯ** those who dress their hair in Gentile (Roman) fashion (NT2).

מגוביא, מגוביתא (< ג-ב-י) p.p. **mgubya. mgōbēṯa** chosen, selected.

מגומבלא, מגומבלתא (< ג-מ-ב-ל) p.p. **mgumbıla, mgumbalta** rounded, ball-shaped

מגלא, מגרא (OA/OS מַגְּלָא; מַגָּלְתָא) m. **magla, magra** sickle (=H חֶרְמֵשׁ, BT); cf. שאלוכה.

מגלה, מגילה (H; cf. OA מגילתא) f. **maǧılla** the scroll of the Book of Esther; **ʾēḏ maǧılla** the Purim Holiday.

מגרתי (K?) adv. **magırti** as if, so to speak.

מגׄא (Ar/IrAr rain) inv. **mıjja** soaking-wet.

מגׄאל (Ar) **mıjāl** life extent; time; respite; conjugal period (=H עוֹנָה, BT2, Arodh); מגׄאלד קטאפא **-ıd qṭafa** (grape) harvest time (Sa83c 16, Am); pl. מַגָ׳אלֵי **majāle** (BaBin 151) (NT+).

מגׄאן (Ar) **majān** (in) vain, falsly (NT).

מגׄבור (Ar) inv. **majbūr** reluctant; cf. ג׳-ב-ר.

מגׄבורותא (< מגׄבור) **majburūṯa** reluctance (cf. PolG).

מגׄוגׄא (< מגׄא) m. **mıjjōja** over soaked soap-bar.

מגׄוככא (< ג׳-כ-כ) p.p. **mčukkıka** armed.

מגׄורמסא, מגׄורמסתא (< ג׳-ר-מ-ס) p.p. **mčurmısa, -masta,** withered (=H נִדָּף, BT3).

מגׄיד v. גׄיד

מגׄידי(יא) (Ar) **majīdi(ya)** a Turkish (Ottoman) silver coin (PolU 8); pl. **majīdīye**.

מגׄכ (K?) **mıččık** only in **ṣurṭıd** — insolent.

מגׄלס (Ar) **ma/ıjlıs** council (BaBin 123; Zaken 392; PolU 123).

מ-ג׳-מ-ג׳ III (< 0A מצמץ?) ⁺**m-č-m-č** to eat tiny pieces of meat off the bone, to lick, to suck (a breast) (PolU 326).

מגׄמע (Ar) m. **majmaᶜ** gathering (of water)(=H מִקְוֶה, BT1).

מגׄססאנא (< ג׳-ס-ס) m. **mjassısāna** spy (=H מְרַגֵּל, BT1).

מגׄרכאנא (< ג׳-ר-כ) m. **mačırxāna** sharpener (of knives), forger of tools (=H לוֹטֵשׁ, BT1).

מגׄרייה (Ar) f. **majrīye** incident, event (NT).

מג׳אצא (IrAr/K < P **maqāze** < Fr magasin < Ar مخزن) f. department store [cf. Blanc 157].

מג׳ארא (Ar) ⁺**mıǧāra** cave; pl. מְגַרֵי ⁺**mıǧāre** (RivSh 274); cf. מערה.

מג׳בינה v. ג׳בינה

מג׳דאדה v. אכדאדה

מג׳ובה v. א-כ-פ

מג׳זן v. מכזן

מג׳לקתא (< ג׳-ל-ק) f. **maǧlaqta** rim (=H מִסְגֶּרֶת, BT2).

מג׳נטיס (Ar< Gr) m. **maǧnatīs** magnet.

מג׳רב v. מוג׳רב

מג׳רפתא (Ar ladle) f. **maǧrafta** fire pan (=H מַחְתָּה, BT3); oar (v. ג׳-ר-פ); pl. מַגְ׳רַפְיַיאתַא **maǧrapyāṯa** (=H מְנַקִּיּוֹת, BT4, D).

מדא (Ar) f. **mıdda** time, while: **zılla mıdda go palga xa yarxa** A month went by meanwhile.

מדארא (Ar) f. ⁺**mıdāra** huge millstone rotated by mule.

מדארתא (< ד-א-ר) f. **madʾarta** (return to one's) previous position (PolU 158); vomit.

מדבח (Ar; OA/OS מַדְבְּחָא) m. **maḏbaḥ** (Z ⁺**mazbaḥ**) altar; pl. מדבאחה **maḏbāḥe** (NT+).

מדבראנא (< ד-ב-ר; cf. OA/OS/Mand מְדַבְּרָנָא leader) m. **mdabrāna** provider, bread-winner.

מדג׳אדה, מדג׳ז v. אכדאדה

מ-ד-ו (Ar مدي) **m-d-w** to have sufficient time to do something (מְדוּלֵי **mıdūle** = H הספיק, AvidH 4; PolG); לא מודוליה מפולטלה **la mudūle mpōlıṭle** He didn't take it out in time (NT5 407); **la madwıt gōrıt** May you die before marriage [cf. MacD 158].

מדוגמגא (< ד-ג-מ-ג) **mdugmıga** stout, full-bodied (PolUL 385).

מדוויה (Ar/H?) **madwe/mdawōye** (?) hardship, pain (NT2).

מדוור, מִידַוִיר (Ar) inv. ⁺**mıdawwır** round (cf.PolG).

מְדוֹעֵי v. צ-י-ע

מדיאנאיא (H) **mıḏyānāya** Midianite (NT, BT).

מדירא v. מצירא

מדיתא (OA/Mand מדינְתא; OS ܡܕܝܢܬܐ) f. **mḏīta**

city (NT); pl. מדניאתא **md̲ınyāt̲a** (NT5 385, 392); cf. באז'ר.

מדומדמא, מדומדמתא (ד-מ-ד-מ 2) p.p. **mdumdıma, -damta**, bleeding., wounded (PolU 40).

מדעי (Ar) m. **mıddaʿi** the prosecuted; cf. דאעי.

מדפונייה (K< Ar) f. **madfūnīye** tomato soup with meat dumplings (usually a Sabbath dish; cf. Judeo-Spanish **dafīna**).

מדריאנא (< ד-ר-י) m. **mdaryāna** scatterer, maker (?) (NT2).

מדריש, מדרֶש (OS) adv. **mıdreš** moreover, once again, before, already, well then (NT; NT5 385, 407, 409; PolG [cf. Garbell 319].

מדרש, ביתד מדרש (H) m. **(bēt̲d) mıdraš** house of study; small synagogue (Z); pl. (באתד) מדרשות/.מדראשה **(bātıd) mıdrāšōt̲/mıdrāše**; מִדְרַשֵׁי אִלָּיֶא **mıdrāše ʾılāye** Heavenly schools (RivSh 200) (NT+).

מדת הדין (H) **middat̲ haddīn** the (Divine) measure of (severe) judgment (NT).

מדת רחמים (H) **middat̲ raḥamīm** the (Divine) measure of merciful judgment.

מה, מהא v. מא

מהגויה (< ה-ג'-י) v.n. **mhajōye** vocalization, pronunciation.

מוהל v. מהול

מוהור v. מהור

מהימן (H-OA) inv. **mhēman** loyal, honest.

מהינה (K) f. **mahīne** mare, steed (Pol 108); cf. סוסה; pl. **mahīnāt̲a** (PolU 430), **mahīne** (PolU 12), **mahīnat** (PolG) [Khan 574 **mahinta**; pl. **mahinye**].

מהלכאנא (< ה-ל-כ) m. **mahılkāna** destroyer (=H מַשְׁחִית, BT2).

מ-ה-ר 1 I (NT)/IV (Z) (Ar < P) **m-h-r** to stamp (NT5 403), to seal, to sign (AlfH 67); cf. מוהור. (NT+).

מ-ה-ר 2 v. ה-י-ר

מרהום v. מחרום, מהרום

מהתי (K?) **mahati** mating (animals); **ʾ-w-z** - to encourage a male animal to mount the female for breeding purpose (PolU 64).

מו, מוד (< מא) **mu(d), mo(d)** Does...? (=H -הֲ, BT/PolG; ?... כלום); because; מו לא, מולא **mu la** Isn't? Why not? (NT5 383) מיאאוא **m(u)-yāʾāwa** Did she know? מיאאינא **m(u)-yāʾēna** How do I know? (NT2) [cf. IrAr **mā, mū**; MacD 161].

מואאבה (K **mo** 'slope' +**āve** 'water') f. **mōʾāve** water current (down a slope/result of flood?) (PolU 301).

מואבאיה (H) pl. **moʾavāye** Moabites (NT, BT).

מואתקא (< א-ת-ק) p.p. **muʾtıqa** long stored (food) (=H נוֹשָׁן, BT3).

מוגא (Ar) m. **mōja** (sea) wave; pl. מוגה **mōje** food sent as gifts to friends on Purim (=H מנות, NT5 404) (NT+).

מוג'ב (Ar) **mūjıb** according to; manner; situation; **bıd dō** — in this condition (PolG).

-מוג'ב v. א-כ-פ

מוג'רב, מוג'רוב, מג'רב (Ar) m. **muġrūb, maġrab** (PolU 16), west (=H יָמָּה, BT4); cf. מערב.

מודה (H) inv. **mōd̲e** thankful: פשליה מודה **pıšle mōd̲e** He thanked (God)(NT2); גְפֵישַׁך מוֹדֶה **gpēšax mōd̲e** We are grateful (AvidH 68).

מודור (Ar مدير) m. **múdur** principal, manager (PolU 151).

מוהור, מהור (Ar< P) m. **mühor** seal, imprint; cf. מ-ה-ר (NT+).

מוהל, מהול, מוהלת(א) (Ar/K) **mühül, mohlıta, mohlat** (+Z; POLG; PolU 105), respite; **halli** — Give me a break! Dont rush me! (NT+).

-מוהר v. ה-י-ר

מוז (Ar; cf. OA/OS מוֹזָא < P **mōz**) **mūz** banana; v. כבושא

-מוז/מוזונה, מוזונה v. ו-ז/ד-נ

מוזונה v. ו-ד-נ

מוזיקא (K/Ar/T < E) f. **mōzīqa** harmonica, wind musical instrument; v. מרואדא. pl. מוזיקת **mōzīqat** (BaBin 121)/**mōzīqe** (PolG).

מוזכה (< K hornet?) **mōzıke** the damned thing (SaAC 3).

מוזלין (T< E) **mōzlīn** muslin (a fine fabric originally made in Mosul).

מוחב, מוחיב, מוחוב (Ar) m. **muḥūb** lover (NT); cf. מחיבאנא.

מחובה v. מוחבה

מוחיבא, מוחבתא (< ח-י-ב) p.p. **muḥība, mōḥabta** beloved, dear friend (=H יָדִיד, BT5) (NT+).

מוחכם, מוחכום (Ar) inv. **muḥküm** solid, done well; thorough(ly).

מוחסן (Ar) inv. **müḥsın** beautiful (Pol 108), good looking (SaAC).

מוחסנותא (< מוחסן) **muḥsınūṯa** beauty (SaAC)

מוחצרתא (<ח-צ׳-ר) f. **muḥẓarta** cult prostitute (=H קְדֵשָׁה, BT).

מחתרגי v. מוחתגי

וטן v. מוטן

מוטרבאיא, מוטרביתא (K < Ar مطرب) **muṭırbāya, -bēṯa**, (Gypsy) musician; beggar.

מוך, מַך, מוכואת, מכואת (< אך) prep. **muxwāṯ**, **maxwāṯ** (NT5 409), **múxus** (PolG), **mux, max** (BT2, Arodh; AvidH 11; AvidH 11).

מוכא (OA/OS מוּחָא) m. **mōxa** brain; **ʾaxla mōxe** Let him have it, die by it (a stolen thing, etc., said reluctantly) (NT+).

מוכור v. מוכרוה

מוכל- v. א-כ-ל

מוכר- v. א-כ-ר, כ-ר-ו

מוכרא (< ?) **mukra** heap (of stones) (Sa83c 30, Am) [MacD 163 heap of stones].

מוכרוה, מוכור, מכרו, מִיכְּרוֹ (< מכרוה) m. **mükro(h), mukur** (BT3, D; BaBin 39, 47; PolG), abomination (=H תּוֹעֵבָה, BT1, BT2; פִּגּוּל/שִׁקּוּץ, BT3); pl. **mukrūhāt**.

מוֹכְרוֹהֻתָא (< מוכרוה) **mokrohūṯa** abomination (PolG)

מוכתר (Ar) m. **muxtar** Mukhtar; Jewish official in charge of vital statistics; his title follows his proper name: Sasson Mukhtar.

מוכתרותא (< מוכתר) f. **muxtarūṯa** the office of the mukhtar.

מולא v. מו

מולאיי (Ar) **mawlāyi** My Master (=God) in יא רבי ומולאיי **ya rabbi umawlāyi** O God (NT5 382).

מוולוד (< Ar) **mawlūd** offspring; birthday celebration; **ʾ-w-z** - celebrate birthday (PolU 82); pl. **mawlūde** (=H תּוֹלְדוֹת, BT).

מומאתא (OA מוֹמָתָא, sg. f./pl.) f. sg./pl. **mōmāṯa** oath(s) אֵיהַא מוֹמָתָא וֵילָא **ʾēha mōmāṯa wēla** this oath was (= H הַשְּׁבוּעָה היתה, PolG); — **ʿısye** strict oaths; cf. י-מ-י (NT+).

מונה (Ar) f/pl.? **mūne** mud, slime; only in **gwīla bmūne** (You) wretched (lit. soiled with slime)! Cf. סיאנא.

מוני (K) inv. **mōni** too serious, unfriendly.

מונשקתא (< נ-ש-ק) f. **munšaqta** kiss (NT; cf. Mutzafi 317 **manšuqta**); cf. נשוקתא.

מוס (Ar) **mūs** razor blade.

מוסק- v. י-ס-ק

מועגזאת (Ar) pl. **muʿjizāt** hardships (NT2).

מוערפה v. מעריפתא

מופרק (K < Ar مُفرَغ) **mufraq** metal (Zaken 389), steel (PolG).

מופתי (Ar) n. **mufti** Mufti (PolU 109)

מוצח- V. צ-י-ח

מוצל (Ar) **mōṣıl** Mosul; Assyria (=H אַשּׁוּר, BT, NT).

מוצלח (Ar) inv. **muṣlıḥ** peaceful, benefactor, good (person) (PolU 245).

מוצלנאיה (< מוצל) pl. **mōṣılnāye** residents of Mosul ; the Assyrians (=H אַשּׁוּרִים, BT1).

מוצמט, מזמוט (Ar مُصْمَت 'massive, solid, not hollow') inv. **muṣmıṭ** (Z), **mazmūṭ** (NT), solid, full (grain), of good quality [cf. Mutz 242 ***zmt** 'to fill or be full'; ***zmita** 'full'].

מוצת- v. צ-י-ת

מוקבלא (< ק-ב-ל) p.p. **muqbıla** parallel (=H מַקְבִּיל, BT2).

מוקדר (Ar) **muqdar** approximate amount, (right) measure; **basır xa** - after some time/distance (cf. PolG); pl. מוקדארה **muqdāre** (NT5 410).

מוקרא (OS yolk; OA brain) m. **muqra** yolk.

מוקש, מוקשכא (H snare) m. **mōqēš, mōqēška** gentile holiday (pejor.); cf. ג׳יצא (NT+).

מוראד, מר(א)ד (Ar) m. **murād** (NT), **mırad** (Z), wish, will (Pol 108); במוראד **bmurād** willingly, contently; pl. **mırāde**; **ḥaṣli mırādox** May your wishes come true! **mırad lıbbı pışlu ʾāhet** You have become (the object of) my desires (PolG).

מוּרַאן (K?) **murān** death, massacre (?) (RivSh 231).

מורויש (K **mırj**) **murwiš** spelt wheat, a kind of wheat (=H כֻּסֶּמֶת, BT2).

מורמאנא (K?) **mormāna** odd whatever (PolU 80); cf. **ʾāpōra**.

מושה v. משה

מושכ- v. ש-כ-כ

מושלמאנא, מושלמנתא (< ש-ל-ם) **mušılmāna, -manta** Muslim [cf. Khan 567 **bšilmāna**].

מושלמנותא (< ש-ל-מ) f. **mušılmanūṯa** Islam.

מושראבה (Ar) pl. **mušrābe** drinks (NT5 409).

מושרוק, משרק (Ar) m. **mušruq, mıšrıq** east;

kṭawīla mın mušruq umın muġrub It is worth s great deal (lit. 'from east and west') (PolU 102).

מושתק v. משתאק

מותא (OA/OS) m. **mōṯa** (Z **mōsa**) death; **mıtle mōs ʾilāha** He died a natural death.

מותאנא (OA/OS) **mōṯāna** pestilence (=H דֶּבֶר, BT4); נפליה מותאנא **npılle mōṯāna** a pestilence broke out (NT+).

מותו- v. י-ת-ו

מותוע (K < Ar مطيع 'obedient'?) **mutuʿ** rule, control; v. בר 2.

מותי- V. א-ת-י

מותכא (K < Ar) m. **mūtaka** weakling, lifeless.

מז (K < Ar) inv. **mız(z)** tart, sourish.

מזא 1 (K/P/T/Ar) m. **mazza** appetizers taken with alcohol drinks; pl. **-e** (PolU 221).

מזא 2 v. מזתא

מ-ז-א (OA מזג) **m-z-ʾ** to offer libation (=H הִסִּיךְ, BT1).

מזאאה (< מ-ז-א) v.n. **mzāʾa** libation (=H נֶסֶךְ, BT1).

מזאזא (< ?) **mızāza** (Z) builder's plum line(?).

מזאח (Ar) m. **mızāḥ** jest, frivolity (NT+).

מזאכא (< ?) f. **mızāxa** mill box, grain bag.

מזאנא, מזנתא (< מזתא) adj. **mızzāna, -anta** hairy (=H שָׂעִר, PolG).

מזבנאנא, מזבננתא (OA/OS מְזַבְּנָנָא) **mzabnāna, -anta** seller; cf. זואנא, ז-ב-נ.

מזגפתה (K) **mızgafte** mosque (PolG).

מזג'ן v. מכזן

מזד (Ar مزاد) m. **mızad** public sale, auction.

מזה v. מזתא

מזודה (< ז-י-ד) **mazōde** increasing; breed (=H תַּרְבּוּת, BT4).

מזוזה (H) f. **mazūza** mezuzah (an amulet on the doorpost of Jewish homes); pl. מְזוּזֵי **mazūze** (BT2, D) (NT+).

מזונות (H) pl. **mazōnōṯ** (Z **-s**) cooked dishes (on which one has to recite בורא מיני מזונות) ; cf. העץ, האדמה.

מזחף v. זחף

מזידא (OS) f. **mzīḏa** (Z **mzīza**) dry leather bag made of whole goat skin [cf. Maclean 166; Khan 575 **mzila** container made of skin].

מזייתיה (< ?) **mızyıte** (?) with **ʾ-w-ḏ** =to gather the choice fruits in a vinyard (BaBin 41).

מזיקין, מזיקין (H) pl. **mazzīqīm/n** demonic injurers (NT2).

מזל (H; OA מַזָּלָא) m. **mazzāl** luck; גורא עני מזל דידיה כריוא **gōra ʿāni mazzāl dīde xrīwa** Poor man has bad luck (BaBin 50); pl. מזלות **mazzālōṯ** (NT3; BT1, Am); מזאליה **mazzāle** (NT2; BaBin 108).

מזמוט v. מוצמט

מִזְרַח (H) **mızraḥ** east (=H קֵדְמָה, BT1, D; RivSh 271); cf. שרקי.

מזתא, מסתא, מאיסתא, מאסתא, מְאזְתָּא (OS ܡܙܬܐ; OA מַזְיָא < OA מְעַזְיָא [goat] hair?, SokBA 652) f. **mız/sta** (Z; PolG), **mʾısta** (NT), **mʾızta** (AvidH 27) a hair; גטאנתא עולם לכדא מאסתא **gṭaʾnıtta ʿōlām lxḏa mʾısta** Thou carry the world by a hair (NTU4 157b); **mıstıt lıbbe qṭēʾla** He was very scared; pl. **mızze** (cf. OS ܡܙܐ); **kīʾın kma mızze ʾīs bšırme** I know how many hairs he has on his buttocks = I know him very well; cf. מזאנא, בולא [Khan 575 **mista**, pl. **mise, mistanye**].

מז'א 1 (K **mij**) m. **mıžža** fog; **mıžž-u-morān** thick fog.

מז'א 2 (K **mej**) **mažža** brain (cf. PolG); cf. מוכא.

מז'ג'ולתא (< ש-ג'-ל) f. **mıžġulta** preoccupation, obsession.

מז'ג'יר, מג'יר (Ar) adv. **mıžġēr, mġēr** except, besides.

מז'ולאנכא (K) m. **mıžžūlánka** eyebrow; pl. מִיגֻ'ולַנְכַּאת **mıžžūlánkat** (=H גַּבּוֹת, BT3, D).

מז'מז'א (Ar مشمش) f. **mıžmıžža** apricot; pl. **mıžmıžže**.

מז'ניד, מז'נו v. ז'נו

מחאמי (Ar) m. **mıḥāmi** lawyer; good speaker; cf. אבוקאט.

מחאפה (Ar محافة) f. **maḥāfe** canopy; cf. חופה.

מחארבג'י (Ar-T) **maḥarbači** fighter, bully (PolU 409).

מחבוב(א), מחבובתא (Ar)**maḥbūb(a), maḥbubta,** beloved (PolG); **-tıt lıbbi** My love (PolG).

מחג'ג'אנא, מחג'ג'נתא (< ח-ג'-ג') n.ag. **mḥajjıjāna, -anta** quarrelsome, complainer.

מחג'ר (IrAr/JAB) m. **mḥajjır** banister.

מחוא (Ar) f. **mıḥwa** shelter, refuge, resting

place; דוכד מחואייה **dūkıd mıḥwāye** his shelter (NT5 394); **latli mıḥwa mqāme** I don't have any rest because of him; pl. מחואיה **mıḥwāye** (NT+).

מחוביה, מוחבה, מחבה (Ar) **müḥübbe** love; cf. חבה.

מחושיא, מחושיתא (< ח-ש-י) p.p. **mḥušya, mḥōšēṯa** stuffed (NT+).

מחותא (OA מחוותא) f. **maḥūṯa** the indicator for reading from the Torah Scroll.

מחטא (Ar) f. **maḥaṭṭa** (train) station.

מ-ח-י (Ar/H) **m-ḥ-y** to be wiped out; **māḥe šımme** May his name be obliterated; cf. ימח שמו וזכרו; IV(Z; RivSh 206)/ I(NT3) to wipe out (NT+).

מחיבאנא, מחיבנתא (< ח-י-ב) n.ag. **maḥībāna, -anta** lover; cf. מוחיב (NT+).

ברוך מחייה המתים .v מחייה המתים

מחילה (H) **maḥīla** Forgive me, Sorry!

מחכיאנא, מחכיינתא (< ח-כ-י) n.ag. **maḥkıyāna, -anta** smooth talker, story teller.

מחכיתא (< ח-כ-י) f. **maḥkēṯa** (Z; PolG), **mḥakēṯa** (AvidH 6) tale, story, issue; **-lēs** no argument (PolU 29; pl. מַחְכֵּייָתַא **maḥkıyāṯa** (=H שְׁנִינָה, BT5, D).

מחכמא, מחכמה (Ar) f. **maḥkama/e** trial, court; cf. חאכם; kingdom (=H מַמְלָכָה, BT5; PolG); cf. חכומא; ח-כ-מ; pl. **maḥkamat**.

מחלב (Ar) m. **maḥlab** amulet-necklace made of beads, ambergris, and the dried fruits of prunus mahaleb.

מחלה (Ar) f. **maḥalle** neighborhood; pl. **maḥallat** (but RivSh 145: מַחַלִי **maḥalli**) ; **-ıt hozāye** the Jewish neighborhood.

מחנאנא (< ח-נ-נ) n.ag. **mḥannāna** gracious (=H חַנּוּן, BT2); מרחמנא ומחננא **mraḥmāna umḥannāna** merciful and gracious (=H רחום וחנון, NT5 398).

מחס (K< Ar محاس) m. **maḥas** currycomb, horse grooming; **mxēle sūse bıd maḥas** He groomed the horse (Socin 162); cf. מוחתגי.

מחפורא, מכפורא (K) m. **maḥfūra** (Z, PolG), **max-** (Socin 161), fluffy floor carpet; pl. **maḥfūre** [cf. MacD 161: **mahpūr** carpet of the best sort; Jaba-Justi 391: **meh/xfūr**; Khan 574 **maxforta** carpet].

מחצול (Ar) m. **maḥṣul** profit, income (NT+).

מחצראנא (< ח-צ-ר) n.ag. m. **mḥaṣrāna** besieger (NT+).

מחצ̇ר (Ar) m. **maḥẓar** meeting, assembly; destiny, fate (NT); מחצ̇ר כיר **maḥẓar xēr**, מעדר כ̇יל **maʿḍar xēl** (ZU 72b), defending council; אודלא מחצ̇ר **ʾuḏla maḥẓar** She pleaded (her case); v. כימא.

מחצ̇רכירותא (Ar) f. **maḥẓarxērūṯa** benevolent presence (BaBin 154); מעדר כ̇ילותא **maʿḍar xēlūṯa** recommendation (ZU 73b).

מחרוז (Ar) **maḥrūz** cautious (PolG); cf. ח-ר-ז.

מחרום, מהרום(א) (Ar) **maḥ/hrūm** indigent, deprived person (=H דָּל, AvidH 49, 70); pl. מח/הרומין **maḥ/hrūmīn** (NT4; NT5 404).

מח/הרומותא (< מחרום) **maḥ/hrūmūṯa** indigence; pl. מהרומאתא **mahrūmāṯa** deprivations (AmU2 2b,10a).

מחשמו, מחשמה (< ימח שמו) f. **maḥšamo/e** a curse; a woman who curses a lot; accursed woman.

מחתרגי, מוחתגי(P مهتر > K **meytar** coacher?) **maḥtarči** (PolU 125), **muḥtači** (PolU 3), groom (of horses); cf. מעתרכאנה.

מטאלא (K< OA shelter) f. **mıṭāla** shield (=H מָגֵן, BT1; צִנָּה, PolG: IKg 10:16); pl. מִטַאלֶי **mıṭāle** (RivSh 245).

מטבך (Ar) m. **maṭbax** kitchen; pl. **maṭbāxe**.

מטבכגי (Ar-T) **maṭbaxči** cook; pl. **-čīyat**.

מטבכייה (Ar) f. **maṭbaxīye** big cooking pot; pl. **maṭbaxīyat**.

מטה (H) f. **mıṭṭa** bier, casket.

מטווה (< מ-ט-י) f. **mıṭūwe** (low) level; **ʿēba-le ... maṭya ldē mıṭūwe** It is a shame (for her) to reach such an (inferior) level (Pol 109).

מטויא, מטוויתא (< ט-ו-י; cf. OA מְטַוֵּי, adj. roasted) p.p. **mṭūya , mṭōwēṯa** roasted.

מטולקא, מטולקתא (< ט-ל-ק) p.p. **mṭulqa, mṭōlaqta** divorced (NT+).

מטומג̇א (< ט-מ-ג̇) p.p.m. **mṭumǵa** sealed (PolG).

מטומיא, מטומיתא (< ט-מ-י) p.p. **mṭumya, mṭōmēṯa** polluted, ritually unclean; cf. טומיא.

מטומעא (< ט-מ-ע) p.p.m. **mṭumʿa** plaited (=H זָהָב שָׁחוּט, PolG: 1Kg 10:16).

מ-ט-י (OA/OS/Mand) vi **m-ṭ-y** to arrive, reach an end; to be overcome, overtaken (with fear)(NT3); מִיטֶלָאבֻו **mıṭēlābu** It overtook him (=H הִדְבִּיקֻתְהוּ, PolG:Jdg 20:42); to ripen (Z); מטה ועדא **mṭe waᶜda** time has come (NT); **mṭēla mınne** He reached his limit, became angry; IV to bring to an end (NT3), to help someone to arrive; **mamṭīlan lbēsa** Take us home.

מטיע (Ar) inv. **mıṭīᶜ** obedient (NT).

מטלביה (Ar) f. **maṭlabe** request; pl. מטלביאתא **maṭlabyāṯa** (NT5 398); **maṭlabat** (PolG).

מת-מרים v. מט-מרים

מטנזא (Ar/P) f. **maṭnaza** mockery, ridicule (BaBin121).

מטפיינתא (< ט-פ-י) n.ag. f. **mṭapyanēṯa** baking woman (=sticks loaves on oven's walls).

מ-ט-ר IV (OA) **m-ṭ-r** to send rain (=H הִמְטִיר, BT1).

מטרא (OA/OS/Mand) **mıṭra** rain; **k-w-š/ʾ-ṯ-y mıṭra** = to rain; pl. **mıṭrāre** (BT3) (NT+). [Khan 575, pl. **miṭrāne**].

מטראקא (Ar مطرقة; cf. OA/OS/Mand מַטְּרְקָא goad, prodding stick) **mıṭraqa** hammer (NT2).

מטרייה (cf. Ar ممطر/منطر < OA מנטר; cf. OA מטריי protector demons; מַטַּרְתָא safekeping/Mand מאטאראיא purgatory demons/OS ܡܛܪܐ watchman) f. **maṭ(ṭ)arīye** coat (NT2) (Avishur1989 139; Fraenkel 51f.)[cf. Mengozzi 262 **maṭāriyā** robe?]

מטרלוז (IrAr< Fr mitrailleuse) **matrallōz** machine gun.

מטרטמאנא, מטרטמנתא (< ט-ר-ט-מ)n.ag. **mṭarṭımāna, -anta,** complainer, rival (=H מְרִיבִים, PolG).

מטרן (Ar< Gr) **maṭran** archbishop (PolU 286).

מי- (< **mēṯi** 'Bring'?) **me-** precedes imperative: **me-halli** Give me!

מ-י-א (< Ar ميع to flow?) vt/vi **m-y-ʾ** to quiver like a liquid, to churn, be unstable: **kšaʾšēna, gmēʾēna, latli pışta nıšāma** I shake, I quiver, I have no soul left (PolU 114); **baḥḥar šʾıšla, meʾla** the sea shook and quivered (PolU 129; cf. Mutzafi 301 churn); thrive or make thrive: **lag mēʾāwa ṭalōhun** They didn't do well; **kan ʾilāha la māyeʾla/ mīʾāle** If God doesn't bring about success (there will not be one) (PolG); .

מיאיא v. מאיא 2

מייאנא, מיינתא (< מאיא 1?) adj. **mıyāna, -anta** moist, liquidy, soft; **xıṭṭe mıyanta** soft wheat dish (somewhat liquidy).

מיאסא (< מ-י-ס) **myāsa** measure, measuring (NT2).

מ-י-ג̇ (Ar ميج sap) vi **m-y-j** to melt, soak (soap, dried milk); cf. מגוגא, מיג̇ו.

מיג̇ו (< מ-י-ג̇) f. **mējo** wooden bowl used for softening dried milk balls for מצ̇ירא.

מ-י-ד (Ar مدّ) vt **m-y-d** to stretch (NT3).

מיידאן, מידן (Ar) m. **maydan** town square, open space; pl. מיידאנה **maydāne** (NT+).

מידאנכה (< מיידאן) f. **maydānke** patio, yard.

מידו (JAB) f. **mēdo** Sabbath or Holiday set table or plate containing bread and salt. **ṭabaqtıd mēdo** tablecloth; cf. מיזא [cf. Blanc 157].

מיהואני (K) **mehwāni** feast, hospitality.

מיוצא (< מ-י-צ) m. **mayōṣa** baby, suckling (NT+).

מיזא (K/IrAr< Sp) f. **mēza** table; cf. מידו, ספרא שולחן,; pl. **mēze** [cf. Blanc 157-8].

מ-י-כ (OS ܡܚܚ) vt **m-x-x** to smell; cf. מ-כ-מ-, ר-י-כ כ.

מיכא ,מֵיכָּאֵן v. איכא

מיכו (< H מיכאל) p.n. **mīxo** Michael, Mikey.

מִיכְּוָאיֵי (Ar) f. **mıkwāye** burn, cauterization (=H מִכְוָה, BT3, D).

מיכותכה (K) f. **mēkutke** mallet, large wooden hammer; cf. דנגא; pl. **mēkutkat.**

מיכרו v. מוכרוה

מ-י-ל IV (< מילא) **m-y-l** to dye with blue color (PolU 24) [2:(**julle**) **gmamīlax-lu**].

מי-לא v. מא

מילא (OA ink) m. **mīla** liquid blue dye.

מילאכה (K **mēlak** liver) pl. **melāke** bowels; **nāve u- qızlu** He had much pity (for someone) (cf. PolG, PolU 373); cf. מאיא 2.

מילאנא, מילנתא (< מילא) adj. **mīlāna, -anta** blue (Z), green (NT) [MacD 173 blue, green; Krotkoff 129].

מילה v. גזארא 1, ברית מילה, אות מילה

מים אחרונים חובה (H) ⁺**māyim ʾaḥaronīm ḥōva** with **p-y-š** to become very poor; cf. על הארץ ועל המזון.

מַיִם חַיִּים (H) **māyim ḥayyīm** fresh running water (BT3, D).

מימונכה (K) f. **maymunke** monkey; pl. **maymunkat** (cf. PolG)

מימורה (< א-מ-ר II) v.n. only as hendiadys with אימארא: **ʾimāra umēmōre** a lot of arguing (cf. PolG).

מימי (< ?) inv. **mīmi** well, OK, You are all better now (talking to a baby).

מֵינְכָאנָא (< נ-י-כ) **mēnxāna** spotter, spectator (=H צֹפֶה, PolG); cf. קלאויז.

מינכתא (< נ-י-כ) **mēnaxta** look, glance (cf. PolG).

מ-י-ס (< Ar مس touch, feel?) **m-y-s** to measure (NT2).

מיפוכתא (< ?) **mēpuxta** dates syrup [MacD 214 **n/mépüxtā** treacle, molasses].

מ-י-צ (OA/OS מצץ) vt **m-y-ṣ** to suck; IV to nurse (vt) (RivSh 158); cf. ממצאנא, מיוצא.

מ-י-ר (OA/OS מרר) ⁺**m-y-r** to be bitter; IV embitter, make bitter, sadden (מומירכלוך **mumīraxlox** =H עכרתנו You saddened us, NT5 402; ⁺**mōmırre** = H הֵמַר, Ruth 1:20); cf. מיירתא, מרירא.

מירא (K< Ar) m. **mīra** emir, lord, wealthy person; pl. **mīre**.

מיראתא, מירת (K< Ar ميراث) **mīrāta, mīrat** unclaimed inheritance; miserable, good for nothing; common in curses with **p-y-š** to be dispossessed; **ppēša mīrat** (the land) shall be forsaken (=H תֵּעָזֵב, BT3); pl. (**māl-**) **mīrātin** (PolU 317); v. מאל (NT+).

מירגיה, מירגא (K **mirk**/P **marġ**/OA/OS **margā**/Ar **marj**) f. **mērge, mērga** (+NT, PolU 326, SokBA 703), oasis, meadow; cf. פיש-מירגה; pl. **mērgat** (but RivSh 288 מִירְגַסָא **mırj/gāsa?**) (NT+).

מירו (< מאיר) p.n. **mīro** Meir (hypo.).

מירי (K **mere** harm/**muru** beads to ward off evil eye) **mēri** evil ghost, harmful demon (NT1).

מירכא (K) m. **mērıka** guy, fellow.

מירכאני (K) inv./adv. **mērıkānī** (woman dressed in) men's style (Socin 164).

מירת v. מיראתא

מיירתא (< מ-י-ר) f. ⁺**myarta** bitterness (BaBin 115).

מירתאנא, מירתנתא (< י-ר-ת) n.ag. **mayrıṯāna, -anta** inheritor, nearest relative (=H שְׁאֵר, BT4,D).

מירתתא (< י-ר-ת) f. **mayraṯṯa** (Z -asta) possession, inheritance (=H מוֹרָשָׁה, BT1).

מירתותא (< מיראתא) f. **mīratūṯa** (dis)inheritance (with **ʾ-z-l**) (PolU 233).

מִישָׁארֶי (K< Ar 'saw'/'behive') pl. **mišāre** stings, pins (=H שְׂכִּים, BT4, D).

מי שברך (H) **mī-šabbērax** a traditional Hebrew blessing; **ʾ-w-ḏ** - to recite this blessing.

מישומא (Ar مشؤوم unlucky) m. **mīšūma** wretched, the damned thing [cf. MacD 174].

מ-י-ת (OA) **m-y-ṯ/t** (Z **m-y-s/t**) to die [1: **mıt-**; 2: **māyıṯ**; 3:**mōṯ**; 4:**myaṯa**]; **mıtle mōs ʾilāha** He died a natural death; IV to put to death, kill; cause much hardship [1: **mōmıṯ**; 2/3: **māmıṯ**; 4: **mamōṯe**] (NT+).

מיתא, מתתא (OA) p.p. **mīṯa** (Z **mīsa**), **mıṯṯa** dead; pl. מיתה **mīṯe**, מיתאנה **mīṯāne** (NT3).

מיתה משונה/חטופה (H) **mīṯa mašunna/ ḥaṭūfa** unnatural death.

מיתותא (OA/OS) f. **mīṯūṯa** death, act of dying (RivSh 228).

מיתכא, מיתכה (מיתא) adj. **mīṯaka, -ke** looks like dead, of poor energy (PolU 64); cf. מותכא.

מיתר (IrAr/K/T< En) m. **mētar** meter; cf. יארדא.

מיתרו (IrAr?)**mitro** kind of fabric (PolU 422).

מך v. מוך

מכא v. אכא

מכבה (Ar?) f. **mıkabbe** large and heavy basket used to cover food to keep it from cats, etc. [MacD 163, 173 **mūkabā, mīkabé**].

מכביני v. מג'בינה

מכגין v. אכגן

מכואת v. מוך

מכדאדה, מכדד v. אכדאדה

מכובראנא (< כ-ו-ב-ר) m. ⁺**mkōbırāna** muezzin, announcer of the hour of Muslim prayer (PolU 255).

מכובלא, מכובלתא (< כ-ב-ל) p.p. **mxubla, mxōbalta** leper, grimy.

מכוזדגא, מכוזדגתא (< כ-ז-ד-ג-א) p.p. **mxuzdıga, -agta** bereft, suffered a misfortune (NT3).

מכוכ (Ar) m. **makkuk** weaver's shuttle.

מכולה v. א-כ-ל

מכונייה (AnAr?) f. **mıkkōnīye** adept (housewife), often in hendiadys with מעדלה

mʿaddale.

מכוניותא (< מכונייה) f. mıkkōnıyūṯa quality of being a good housewife (Pol 108; PolG).

מכורכא, מכורכתא (< כ-ר-כ) p.p. mkurxa, mkōraxta shrouded; common in curses: (May you be) shrouded!

מכושרא, מכושרתא (< כ-ו-ש-ר) p.p. mkūšıra, mkōšarta koshered (meat: washed of blood).

מכות (מצרים/מרדות) (H) makkōṯ (mıṣrāyim/ mardūṯ) the biblical plagues of Egypt; common in curses: xōl makkōs mıṣrāyim Eat the plagues! makkōs mardūs hāwe ʾılla May the plagues be upon her! Cf. עשר מכות.

מכזן, מג'זן, מזגן (Ar) m. max/ġzan, mazġan cf. PolG), treasure house (NT3); storage room; pl. maġzāne (AvidH 41), mazġāne store (cities)(=H עָרֵי מִסְכְּנוֹת, BT2); cf. מג'אצא (NT+).

מ-כ-י (OA/OS מחא/מחי, strike, protest) m-x-y to beat, strike; play (musical instrument); to mark (NT3); qam māxēli He hit me; mxēlu ʾıllan They have informed (the authorities) about us, betrayed us; mxēle ʾılla He embezzled, took advantage of the situation; qundare mxēlu lʾaqli The shoes pressed hard on my feet; qam maxēlu lpāsi He returned them [=the gifts] to me (an act of grave insult); mxēle (xabre) ʾıbbi He insulted/criticized me, made fun of me (BaBin 115; SaAC 18); mxēle l/bʾurxa He hit the road (cf. PolG; SaAC 19).

מכינא (Ar< It) f. makīna machine (cf. PolG); makīn-xyāṭa sewing machine; makīn-(dyāqid) pısra meat mincer.

מכינאנא v. כינאנא

מככאלא (OA/OS מַכְחָלָא) m. mıkxāla kohl stick for eye painting (PolU 253).

מכלוט (Ar) m. maxlūṭ mixed, impure (= כִּלְאַיִם, BT3).

מכלוק (Ar) m. maxlūq creature; pl. מכלוקאת maxlūqāt (NT); מַכְלוּקֵי maxlūqe (AvidH 71).

מכליאנא, מכליאניתא (< כ-ל-י) n.ag. maxılyāna, -nīṯa sweetener (PolG).

מכלצאנא (< כ-ל-צ) n.ag. mxalṣāna (NT), maxıl- (Z), redeemer (=H גּוֹאֵל, BT3; PolG).

מכלתא (OS ܡܚܠܬܐ; OA/Mand מַהוֹלְתָא < Ak maxxaltu) f. fine sieve; pl. maxılyāṯa; cf. ארבאלא; נ-כ-ל.

מכנקתא (P < Ar; cf. Ak maxnaqu sling, noose?) f. maxnaqta necklace (lit., choker); ring (=H טַבַּעַת, BT4, D); pl. maxnaqyāṯa.

מ-כ-ס v. כ-י-ס 2

מכסב (Ar) m. maksab earning (PolG).

מכרואנא, מכרונתא (< כ-ר-ו) n.ag. maxırwāna, -anta destroyer; spoiler (NT+).

מכרו v. מוכרוה

מכרוה (Ar) inv. makrūh detested, odious (NT).

מכרור (Ar) m. a very refined arrack.

מכשואנא (< כ-ש-ו) n.ag. mxašwāna thoughtful (NT).

מכתב (K< Ar) m. maktab (public) school; v. דאנא.

מכתבג'י (Ar-T) m. maktabči teacher (PolU 151).

מכתווא (OS ܡܟܬܘܒܐ) f. maxtūwa awl; v. כתוא?

מלא 1 (K/P< Ar مَولَى) m. malla mullah, Muslim functionary; pl. mallāye (PolU 21).

מלא 2 (< OS ܡܠܐ) mılla string; pl. מְלָאלֵי (=H נִימִין, AvidH 8)[MacD180 miltā].

מלא 3 (K) mıl(l)a high hill (PolU 6).

מלאזם (Ar) mlāzım adherent, orthodox (NT).

מלאטא (< JAB) f. mıllāṭa pacifier; milk bottle (SaAC 18); v. מצאצא.

מלאך, מלאכא, מלאאכא (H-OA) mal(ʾ)ax, malʾāxa (c.) angel, a very good person; pl. מלאכים, מלאכין מלאכינה, מַלְאַכֵי, מלאאכה malʾāxe (NT5 405; RivSh 195), malʾaxīne (AlfM 19; PolU 308), malʾāxīm/n; מלאכה דשינה, מלאאכית שינה malʾāxıt/s šēna angels of peace (NT5 387); malāxıd šēna hāwe ʾımmox May the angels of peace be with you! banya malāxīn dšabsa (I swear) by these Sabbath' angels! kavos malaxīne honor (worthy) of angels (PolU 438).

מלאך פלוני ,מלאךהמוות (H; cf. OA מלאך מוֹתָא) malʿax hammāweṯ, malʾax pılōni Angel of Death, certain angel (euph.); cf. מלכלמות.

מלאכי השרת (H) malʾāxe haššārēṯ ministering angels (NT+).

מלאכות (H) pl. malāxōṯ jobs forbidden on Sabbath (BaBin 80).

מלבאנותא (K) f. malavānūṯa the skill of swimming; cf. מלואנא.

מלבן (Ar; cf. OA מַלְבְּנָא) m. malban mould for bricks.

מלבס (Ar) mlabıs Jordan almond(s); pl.

- **se/-sat** (cf. PolG).
מלדום (IrAr) m.⁺**maldūm** dish of tomatoes, eggplant and meat.
מלואנא (K) **malıwāna** sailor; רישד מלואנה **rēšid malıwāne** captain (=H רַב הַמַּלָּחִים, NT6 133).
מלוכא, מלוכתא (< מלכא 1) adj. **malūxa, maluxta** salty.
מלוכה, מלוקה (K **melū**) pl. **mılōke, malōqe** (Ruth 2:7) harvested sheaves (=H קָצִיר/עֹמֶר, BT3); cf. מלכא 3.
מלול (Ar مَلول weary) inv. **mallul** sorrowful, painful (= H דַּוָּי, Sa83c 20, Am).
מלוענא, מלוענתא (< ל-ע-נ) p.p. **mluʿna, mlōʾanta** cursed, accursed (NT5 399).
מלוקטנא (< ל-ק-ט-נ) p.p. **mluqṭına** spotted (sheep) (=H טָלוּא/בָּרֹד/עָקֹד, BT1).
מלחם (K< Ar) m. **malḥam** ointment; **malḥame slimāni** miraculous ointment (FT); pl. **malḥāme** (PolU 140).
מ-ל-י 1 (OA/OS/Mand be full, fill, complete) vt/vi ⁺**m-l-y** to fill; be filled (cf. PolG).
מ-ל-י 2 (< מ-ל-י 1) **m-l-y** to be sufficient; **mlēle tēran** It was sufficient for us; גמליוליני **gmālewaleni** It would be enough for us (=H דַּיֵּנוּ, AlfH 50); ולא גמאליה ד- **ula gmāle d-** (As if) it wasn't enough that...(NT2); לג מאלי **lag māle** It is not enough; **lak malya tēr kullan** It (f.) is/will not be enough for all of us; מאלה **mmāle (‹ bmāle)** It will be enough.
מליא, מליתא/ מליצה (< מ-ל-י 1) p.p. ⁺**mılya,** ⁺**mlīṯa/ mlīṣa** (AlfH 69) full, filled (NT+).
מליון (IrAr/T< E) **mılyon** million; pl. **-ne** (PolU 267).
מליזאנא, מליזנתא (< ל-י-ז) n.ag. **malīzāna, -anta** rash, diligent, able to catch up (=H קְשׁוּרִים, BT1).
מליטא v. ליטא
מ-ל-כ 1 I/IV (Ar) **m-l-k** to acquire, to inherit; ארץ ישראל ממלכיתון...**mamlıkētun** You shall inherit the land of Israel (RivSh 186; cf. NT5 405); VI to install as king (NT+).
מ-ל-כ 2 IV (OA/OS מלח) **m-l-x** to salt (BaBin 22).
מלך (H) m. **mēlex** king (title David, Solomon, Messiah); מלך מלכי המלכים (ממ"ה) **mēlex malxē hammılāxīm** King of kings (=God) (NT).
מלכ 1, מִלְכִינִי (Ar مِلك; cf. OA/OS מוּלְכָּנָא < Ar مُلك) m. **mılk** (Z), **mılkīni** (BT3, D; AvidH 67; NT5 386) estate, possessions.
מלכ 2 (Ar) m. **malık** king (Z); cf. חכומא, שולטאנא, מלכא 2; מלכתא
מלכא 1 (OA/OS מלחא) f. **mılxa** salt; v. לכמא.
מלכא 2 (OA/OS/Mand) **malka** king (rare: NT3; SaLH); cf. שולטאנא, חכומא.
מלכא 3 (*K< Ar 'royal'?) inv. **malaká** choice, ripe (fruits) (PolU 418); v. פגא; cf. מלוכה.
מלכה (H) f.p.n. **malka** Malka.
מַלְכַּת שַׁבָא (H) **málka(t) šáva** Queen of Sheba (RivSh 262, 266; Z).
מלכלמות (Ar) m. **malkılmot** Angel of Death, evil person; cf. מלאך המות; pl. **malkılmōte** aggressive people, bullies (PolU 409).
מלכתא (< מלכ 2/OA מַלְכְּתָא) f. **malıkṯa** queen.
מלפאנא, מלפנתא (< ל-י-פ) n.ag. **malpāna, -anta** teacher, instructor.
מלץ (K **melisi**) inv. **mallıṣ** crouched down, motionless (chicken, child before falling asleep).
מַלְקוּת (H) **malqūṯ** punishment of lashes (BT5, D); v. בלא 2.
מלקט (Ar) m. **malqaṭ** pincers (to move burning coals); pl. **malqāṭe** (=H מַלְקָחַיִם, BT2; cf. Segal #127); cf. מלקטתא.
מלקטו, מלקטניתא (< ל-ק-ט) f. **mlaqṭo, mlaqṭanīṯa** gossip, newsmonger.
מלקטתא (< מלקט) f. **malqaṭṭa** tiny spoon; small pincers; pl. **malqaṭyāṯa** (SaLH 161).
מלשינוכה (H מלשין) f. **malšīnōke** newsmonger; smooth talker
מלשינותא, מלשינתותא (H) f. **malšīn(at)ūṯa** newsmongering; smooth talking.
מלתא, מִלַּתֵּי (K/P/T< Ar< OA word) f. **mıllıta** (Z), **mıllate** (AvidH 59)[Nakano 1970 198: **millíʾta**] nation, ethnic group; cf. 1 אמתא; pl. **mıllıtyāṯa**.
מלתיך v. תכית
מלתקא (Ar) **mıltaqa** (hazardous) encounter (NT5 385; NTU4 164b).
ממא (K **meme** breast, food) m. **mamma** bread, food (baby talk); cf. עם [Mutz 211

mamona breast].

ממאנה (< ממא) f. **mammāne** nursling, little girl (SaNR).

ממון קורח (H) **mamōn qōraḥ** the wealth of Korach; legendary wealth.

ממזר (H; cf. OA ממזירא, ממזירתא) ⁺**mamzēr** bastard (NT+).

מַמֶיתְלַאנַא (< מ-ת-ל) n.ag. **mametlāna** bard, one who recites proverbs (=H מוֹשֵׁל, BT4, D].

ממכאנה (K) pl. **mamkāne** breasts (PolU 207: ChNA).

ממלחא (Ar) f. **mamlaḥa** salt dish.

ממנון (Ar) inv. **mamnūun** grateful; **ʾāya rāba-la mamnūn mınnox** She is very grateful to you (cf. RivSh 261; PolG).

ממצאנא, ממצנתא, ממצניתא (< מ-י-צ) n.ag. **mamṣāna** nursing person, pedagogue (NT3); **-anta** (RivSh 156), **-anīta** (PolG), nursing woman; **mamṣanīs gurge** a mighty woman (lit., nurses wolves); pl. **mamṣāne** (=H מֵינִיקוֹת, עָלוֹת, BT1), ממצניאתא **mamṣanyāta** (RivSh 156) [Cf. Mutz 214 **mamiṣanta: -ṣāne**].

ממראאנא, ממראנתא (< מ-ר-א) n.ag. **mamırʾāna, -anta** painful, causing pain (BT3).

מן 1, מנד (OA/OS/Mand) **mın(nıd)** from, (more) than, out of, things such as (NT5 408); with (RivSh119, 121; BT2, Arodh; AvidH 49); because of (sin); for the sake of (NT3); on (the left/right side); if, as soon as: **mın yāʾe, rēšēni pqāṭéʾle** As soon as he knows (of this), he will cut our heads off (PolG); **mınne umıgyāne/ mınne ʾılle** by itself, instinctively; מד **mad** from this; v. אכא

מן 2, מן וסלוה, מנסלווה, מָנָסַלְוֵי (H-OA מָנָא וּסַלְוֵי) **man, man- (w)asalwe** (NT5 386; AvidH 42) manna and quails; delicacies (NT3); cf. אראורא; קטאאה.

מן 3, מאן, מני, מאני (OA/OS/Mand מַאן, מן; + OA מאן הוא > מַנּוּ; מאן היא > מַנִּי, SokBA 712) **man** (NT), **mani** (+NT, Z), who? he who.

מ-נ-א (OA מנע) **m-n-ʾ** to prevent.

מנאגׄא (Ar) **mınāja** seclusion, confidential talk with God (NT2).

מנארא (Ar) f. ⁺**mın(n)āra** minaret; pl. **-re** (PolU 232).

מנגנא (IrAr/P/K< OA< Gr) **mangana** device, primitive machine [MacD screw press].

מנגׄלונכה (K) f. **manjalonke** small copper pot.

מַנְגִׁנִיקִי (Ar< Gr) **manjınīqe** ballista (RivSh 141).

מנגׄר v. מנשר

מ-נ-ד-ר III (< מנדורתא) **m-n-d-r** to smooth the roof with a roller (before rain).

מנדורתא, מנדרונה (K/P?) f. **mandurta, -darūne** (PolG), stone roller for smoothing mud roofs against leaking ; cf. מדארא [MacD 182 **mandrültā**< K; Krotkoff 127-28, 134].

מנדי (OA מִידָּא, מִידִּי/Mand מינדא) **mındi** thing; **xa-mındi** something; למנדי **lamındi** (NT)/**čımındi** (Z) nothing; v. שמא; pl. מנדייה **mındīye** (NT) (OA pl. מִידָּאנֵי, מִידֵּי; cf. אוואיה [cf. Mutz 213 **mındixe** 'things'; **mındixāne** 'valuable things, necessities'].

מנדייאנא (< נ-ד-י) n.ag. **mandyāna** archer, shooter (NT4).

מנה (K< Ar) f. **mıne** wish, desire; גאודי מנה **gʾōdi mıne** They wish (NT); cf. מניכר.

מנהג (H) **mınhāġ** religious custom; pl. מנהגים **mınhāġīm** (= H חֻקִּים, BT) (NT+).

מנהרתא (< נ-ה-ר) f. **manharta** kindling, fire (BaBin 152).

מנוחה (H) f. **manūḥa** resting place, in **manūḥāse/a bganʿēzın** May his/her resting place be in Paradise (Z), said after mentioning the name of a deceased person.

מנוקדא, מנוקדתא (< נ-ק-ד) p.p. **mnuqda, mnōqadta** (Z **mnuqz-**)meat made kosher by removing the tallow.

מנורה (H) f. **manōra** lampstand (BT2, D, Arodh).

-נושא v. מנוש

מנזל (Ar) m. **manzal** inn, house, settlement (NT); room (=H חֶדֶר, BT1; קֻבָּה, BT4, D); dark storage room (Z); pl. **manzāle** (=H קִנִּים, BT1); luck (< H מזל) (PolG).

מנזלונכא (< מנזל) m. **manzalonka** small dark room.

מנחה (H) **mınḥa** the afternoon prayer.

מנטיק (Ar) **manṭiq** logic, faculty of speech (NT2).

מני v. מן 3

מ-נ-י (OA/OS) **m-n-y** to count (NT+).

מניא (OA/OS מַנְיָא mane) m. **manya** large weight unit (about 3 1/2 kg, or 1/4 of כונכארי; PolU 438 = 9 וקייא) [but MacD 183 = a pound; Jaba-Justi 316 = 12 וקייא].

מניאנא, מנין (OA/OS/H) m. **mınyāna, mınyan** number (BaBin 8); דלא מניאנא **dla-mınyāna** numerous; cf. עדד (NT+).

מניכר (K) inv. **mnēkar** desirous, eager (cf. PolU 19); cf. מנה.

מנמנוכת (< מן+ K -**kat**, dim.) pl. **mınmınnōkat** little portions of food, snacks, 'little from this and little from that'.

מ-נ-ס v. ו-נ-ס

מנסלווה v. מן 2

מנפעא (Ar) f. **manfaᶜa** benefit; cf. נ-פ-א (NT+).

מנקדאנא v. נקדאנא

מנקל (Ar) m. **manqal** brazier; pl. **manqāle**.

מנשה, נשה, נשוכא (H) p.n. m. **manašše, našše, naššōka** (hypo.) Manasseh.

מנשר, מנגר (Ar) m. **manšar** (Z), **mančar** (Hob89 184); pl. **manšāre**.

מנתא (K< Ar) f. **mınta** favor, kindness; דרילה מנתא אליני **drēle mınta ʾıllēni** He did us a favor (NT), He made us feel obliged (Z); לתליה מנתא מנוך **latle mınta mınnox** He doesn't feel obliged by you (NTU4 163a; PolG); **qbılle/ṭʾınne mınta mınnu** He was grateful to them; **šıkır umınta mınnox** Thanks and gratitude to You (PolU 114); **mınte ʾıl gyāne** Let him keep his gift; pl. **mıntāṯa**.

מסאסא (OA) m. **massāsa** ox-goad (NT2).

מסאתא (OS ܡܣܐܬܐ/OA מַסַּחְתָּא) f. **mıs(s)āṯa** scales (cf. PolG).

מסהבאנא, מסהבנתא (< סהבה) n.ag. **msahvāna, -anta** awesome, scary (=H נוֹרָא, BT5); cf. סהבאנא.

מסוגר, מן סוגר (Ar مزوكر/امسوكر insured< It **sicurtá**) adv. **m-/mın-sōgar** for sure, surely (cf. PolG).

מסולטא (< ס-ל-ט) p.p.m. **msulṭa** one in tight control (PolU 365).

מסטרא (IrAr) f. **masṭara** ruler, satraight edge; clipping of clothe.

מ-ס-י (OA/OS מְשִׁי to wash, primarily face, hands, etc., soak, rub < Ak **mesū**, SokBA 690; Greenfield 1991: 594; rather than מסי melt, flow, drip/ SokPA 320; SokBA 690 to condense) **m-s-y** to wash (NT: body/clothes; Z: only clothes; cf. PolG).

מסינא (K/P) f. **massīna** bronze jar with spout used for ritual hand-washing (נטילה) (Z); drinking jar (NT5 394); **massīn qahwa** coffee pot (PolU 290); pl. **-e** (PolG).

מ-ס-כ (Ar) **m-s-x** to become messy (food); IV to make messy, abuse (food).

מסכ, מסך (Ar) m. **mısk** musk, perfume (NT+).

מסכא (OS ܡܣܚܐ) m. **masxa** fire-pan, scoop, little shovel (=H יָעֶה, BT2; מַחְתָּה, BT3, D).

מסכין, מסכינא (OA/OS מִסְכֵּינָא poor/Ar مسكين humble < Ak **muškēnu** poor) **mískin** (Z, inv.), **mıskēna** (NT), humble, poor; good kid (Z); cf. מסכיתא; pl. מסכינה **mıskēne** (NT5 408) [Khan 575 **miskena** poor].

מסכינותא (< מסכין; cf. OA/OS מִסְכֵּינוּתָא) f. **mıskinūṯa** poverty (=H עֳנִי, BT1, D; OA עַנְיָא, AvidH 16).

מסכיתא (< מסכינא) f. **mıskēta** (?) deprived, impoverished (NT3).

מסכן (Ar) m. **maskan** residence, residing place; pl. **maskāne** (NT+).

מסלא v. מתלא

מסלוקא (Ar) f. **maslōqa** wheat-and-meat ball soup spiced with much saffron (for Sabbath).

מסנד (Ar) **masnad** sill (=H מִסְעָד, PolG); pl. **masnāde** (=H אֲדָנִים, BT2); leaning pads (AmU2 5a).

מספלניתא (< ס-פ-ל) n.ag.f. **msaflanīṯa** a female that tends to miscarry.

מסק- v. י-ס-ק

מסקלאנא, מסקלאניתא (< ס-ק-ל) n. ag. **masıqlāna, -nīṯa** dandy, coquette (PolGr 43).

מסראגא (Ar) f. **mısrāja** lampstand; cf. מנורה.

מסרבס v. מצרבס

מסרקא (OA/OS מַסְרְקָא, מַסּוּרְקָא) m. **masırqa** comb.

מסתא 1 (K/P ماست; cf. OA/Mand מַסּוּתָא/OS ܡܣܛܐ/ ܡܣܬܐ curdled milk < √ מסי condense; SokBA 671) f. **masta** yoghurt.

מסתא 2 v. מזתא

מסתוג̆בא (< ס-ת-ו-ג̆-ב) p.p. mıstūjıba guilty, condemned (NT5 391; PolG).
מסתור (Ar) inv. mastūr modest (woman).
מסתחאק (< Ar) inv. mıstaḥaq deserving, worthy (Sa83c 24, Am).
מסתכה (Ar< Gr) f. mıstakke mastic, resin (NT+).
מעאהדא (Ar معاهدة) f. maᶜāhada pact (PolU 3).
מעבוד (Ar) maᶜbud idol, god; pl. מעבודת/מעבודין maᶜbūdat/maᶜbūdīn (NT2), maᶜbūde (Z); maᶜbūde nuxrāye idolatry (cf. PolG).
מעג̆ון (Ar) m. maᶜjūn tomato sauce.
מעג̆זאתה (Ar) f. maᶜjızāte hardship (=H תְּלָאָה, BT2).
מעדדנתא (< מעדודה) n.ag.f. mᶜaddıdanta wailing woman; pl. מעדדנייאתא/מעדדאני mᶜaddıdanyāṯa (Sa83c 34, Am)/mᶜaddıdāne (ibid. Z).
מעדה 1 (Ar) f. maᶜde stomach.
מעדה 2 (< Ar equipment?) f. maᶜadde fact, matter, business (PolG); cf. עדה.
מעדודה (< ע-ד-ד) v.n. mᶜaddōde eulogy, lamentation (=H מִסְפֵּד, BT1).
מעדלה (Ar) f. mᶜaddale orderly housewife; v. מכונייה.
מעדר כ̇לותא v. מחצ̇רכירותא
מעובה v. ע-י-ב
מעוגנת (H) f. mı/aᶜuggeneṯ deserted wife (cf. PolU 351a); anything not being used for a long time (Z); pl. mıᶜugganōṯ (Ruth 1:13).
מעוז, מעוזי (< Ar) m. mıᶜūz, mıᶜūzi, necessary stuff (Zaken 389), shortage (PolG); cf. ע-י-ז.
מעוזזא, מעוזזתא (< ע-ז-ז) p.p. mᶜuzzıza, mᶜuzzazta esteemed, dear (=H נִכְבָּד, BT1).
מעולמא (< ע-ל-מ) p.p.m. mᶜulma tamed (calf); la-mᶜulma untamed, wild (Sa83c 26, Am).
מעזול (Ar) inv. maᶜzūl deprived (NT).
מעזייאנה (< ע-ז-י) pl. mᶜazyāne eulogizing (women) (NTU4 152b, 165a); cf. מעדדנתא.
מעיין 1 (Ar معاون) inv. mᶜayyın helper (NT).
מעיין 2 (Ar) adv. maᶜayyēn certainly, surely.
מעיירא (Ar) maᶜyara disgrace (NT).
מעימל (AnAr< Ar معامل) m. mᶜēmıl client.
מעישא (Ar) f. mıᶜīša livelihood, food (PolU 204); cf. מעש, ע-י-ש.
מעלום (Ar) adv. maᶜlūm It is well known, obvious (NT+).
מעלופיית (Ar) pl. maᶜlūfīyat fattened ship (=H כָּרִים, BT5); cf. ע-ל-פ.
מעלם (Ar) m. maᶜallım teacher, rabbi; maᶜallım murdax Rabbi Murdakh; pl. maᶜalmīne (PolU 21) [cf. Khan 574]
מעלק-מטלק (Ar) inv. naᶜallıq-maṭallıq hanging attached-detached, hanging-loose, having to make a rather difficult choice (PolU 315).
מעמד (H) maᶜamaḏ (at the) presence (of) (NT3).
מעמלתא (Ar) f. mıᶜamlıta business, trade, transaction (NT+).
מעמראנא, מעמרנתא (< ע-מ-ר) n.ag. mᶜamrāna, -anta bossy, complainer.
מעמר באשי (< ע-מ-ר) inv. maᶜmar bāši 'big boss', chief complainer.
מענה, מענאייה (Ar) f. maᶜne, maᶜnāye meaning; v. בי-מענה; n-p-q mmaᶜne to be exceptional, wonderful; pl. מעאנייה/מענתיאתא maᶜānīye (NT2)/maᶜnıtyāṯa (NT3) commentaries.
מַעַפ̇ (Ar) maᶜaf pardon (= H הֲנָחָה, PolG: Esth 2:18; PolU 1); cf. טורכן טלק.
מעצרא (Ar; cf. OA/OS מַעְצְרָא, מַעֲצַרְתָּא) f. maᶜṣara oil or wine press.
מעקול (Ar) m./f. reasonable (NT); noble, aristocrat; pl. maᶜqūle (=H אֲצִילִים, BT2).
מעקולותא (< מעקול) maᶜqulūṯa nobleness (PolG).
מַעֲרַב (H; cf. OA/OS מערבא) maᶜarav west (=H יָמָּה, BT1, D; RivSh 156, 271; ZU 72a); cf. מוג̆'רב.
מערגא (P/Ar معرك 'campain'?) m. maᶜraga horse race, 'joy ride' on a horse (PolU 65).
מערה (H) f. mıᶜāra the Cave of Machpelah (BT1); cf. מג̆'ארא.
מערטו (< ע-ר-ט) m./f. mᶜarṭo loud farter (pejor.); cf. מפשיו.
מעריפתא, מוערפה (K< Ar) f. maᶜrīfıta, moᶜrıfe (PolG), good manners, courtesy; mare-maᶜrīfıta courteous.
מעש (Ar) m. maᶜaš income, salary of an

official; pl. **māʿaše** (cf. RivSh 158; PolG); cf. ע-י-ש, מעישא
מעשה (H) **maʿase** (Jewish) folktale (non Jewish: PolU 44); מעשה עגל - **ʿēgel** the biblical golden calf case (NT); pl. **maʿasīyōṯ/maʿasat**; מעשים (טובים/רעים) **maʿasīm (ṭōvīm/rāʿīm)** (good/bad) deeds.
מעשר (H) **maʿásser** (Z, BT) tithe (NT3:m./f.); pl. מעשרות **maʿsarōṯ** (?)(BaBin 25).
מעתרכאנה (T **mehterhane** military band< P مهتر governor, groom) **maʿtarxāne** (wedding) band (Socin 160); cf. מחתרגי.
מפוצנא, מפוצנתא (< פ-צ-נ) p.p. **mpuṣna, mpōṣanta** glorious, praiseworthy (NT+).
מפחלאנא (< פ-ח-ל) n.ag. **mfaḥlāna** forgiving (God) (=H נוֹשֵׂא עָווֹן, BT2).
מפטיר (H) m. **máftir** the last reader in Torah.
מ-פ-כ v. נ-פ-כ
מ-פ-ל v. נ-פ-ל
מפלס (Ar) inv. **miflis** penniless, flat broke.
מפסה (Ar?) f. **mifse** skimmer, flat strainer.
מ-פ-צ v. נ-פ-צ
מ-פ-ק v. נ-פ-ק
מפקתא (< נ-פ-ק) f. **mpaqta** exit, starting point; pl. **mpaqyāṯa** (=H מוֹצָאִים, BT4).
מפר (Ar مفر) m. **mifar** escape (NT+).
מפרח (Ar) inv. **mifarraḥ** enjoyable, gladdening (spacious yard) (PolU 320).
מפרקאנא (< פ-ר-ק) m. **mparqāna** savior (=H מוֹשִׁיעַ, AvidH 54).
מפרש (Ar) m. **mafraš** carpet (BaBin 106, 116), bedspread (Z); pl. **mafrāše**.
מפשיו (< פ-ש-י) m./f. **mpašyo** silent farter (pejor.); cf. מערטו
מפתכר (Ar) inv. **miftixir** fine, praiseworthy (NT2).
מצאצא (Ar) f. **maṣṣāṣa** rubber nipple (SaAC 18); cf. מלאטא.
מצה (H) f. **máṣṣa** matzah; pl. מַצּוֹיֵי **máṣṣōye** (AvidH46), מִצּוֹיֵי **míṣṣōye** (AlfH 23).
מצוה, מִצְוַוא (H מִצְוָה; OA מִצְוָא, מִצְוְתָא SokBA 698) f. **miṣwa** religious duty; act of charity; pl. מצואיה, מִצְוַיֵי, מצוות **miṣwāye, miṣwōṯ** (OA pl. מִצְוָתָא); often as hendiadys: **miṣwāye-ṣadāqe** acts of charity, good deeds; v. כצוא.
מצוראנא (< צ-ו-ר) n.ag. **mṣōrāna** photographer (PolG)
מצורע (H) **miṣurrāʿ** leper (pejor.); often with רע: **rāʿ-miṣurrāʿ** evil-leper.
מצחף (Ar) m. **maṣḥaf** (non-Jewish) book (NT5 395); cf. חמש. pl. **maṣḥāfe**.
מ-צ-י (OA/OS/Mand < Ak **maṣū**) **m-ṣ-y** to be able [2: גמצי/ גמצה **gimṣe/i**, למצן **lamṣin**; but once לא גמאצית **la gmāṣit**, Sa83c 26, Am] (NT+).
מצכרא (Ar) f. **maṣxara** mockery (NTU4 165a).
מצלחא (Ar) f. **maṣlaḥa** interest, welfare (NT+).
מצעראנא, מצערנתא (< צ-ע-ר) n.ag. **mṣaʿrāna, -anta** 'foul mouth', one who curses a lot (NT+).
מצר (Ar) **miṣṣir** Egypt (NT+).
מצראיא, מצריתא (OA) **miṣrāya, -ēṯa** Egyptian; pl. מצראיה **miṣrāye** (NT+).
מצרף (Ar) m. **maṣraf** expense (cf. PolG); pl. **-rāfe**; cf. צ-ר-פ 2.
מצרבץ, מסרבץ (< צ-ר-ב-ס) m. **⁺misarbis** spinning wheel, reel.
מצ̈בטא (Ar) f. **maẓbaṭa** procès-verbal (PolU 388).
מצ̈בוט, מַדְבּוּט (Ar) inv. **maẓbūṭ** exact, determined (=H נָכוֹן, BT1); certain, correct; **ʾil** - certainly, for sure (cf. PolG).
מצ̈בח v. מדבח
מצ̈בטא (Ar) f. **maẓbaṭa** plan, protocol (PolU 77).
מצ̈ירא, מדירא (Ar) f. **⁺maẓīra** soup made of dried sour milk and wheat balls (eaten during the Jewish mourning days of 1st-8th of Ab in Z, and in Shavuot in Am; cf. Amedi 62).
מצ̈רא (Ar) f. **miẓarra** harm (Pol 109), **muẓurra** (PolG).
מקאבל (Ar) inv. **miqābil** compared to, versus, against (NT+).
מקאבר, מקבארה (Ar) pl. **maqābir, maqbāre** graves, cemetery (NT); cf. קורא.
מקבל v. קבל
מקבלנתא (< ק-ב-ל) n.ag.f. **mqablanta** midwife (BT2, Am); pl. **mqablanyāṯa**; cf. קבאלא גדכה 3, [Mutz 240 **maydilanta**; cf. OA מוֹלְדָא; OS ܡܘܠܕܢܝܬܐ].
מקדושה (< ק-ד-ש) **mqadōše** engagement,

betrothal; reciting the קדוש over wine.

מקדר (Ar) m. **maqaddır** tragic accident (cf. Pol 108), ordained decree.

מקדשאנא (< ק-ד-ש) n.ag. **mqadšāna** one who recites the קדוש over wine.

מקובל (H) m. **miqubbāl** pious holy man, cabbalist; pl. **miqubbālīm** (MeAl 175).

מקודשא, מקודשתא (< ק-ד-ש) p.p. **mqudša, mqōdašta** holy; engaged (to be married).

מקווא (IrAr) m. **miqawwa** corrugated cardboard.

מִקְוֶה (H) water source (BT3, D; BaBin 28); v. טבילה.

מקוטמנא, מקוטמנתא (< ק-ט-מ-נ) p.p. **mqúṭmına, -ánta** unlucky (MeAl 187), damned, accursed (SaAC 17).

מקומא (< ק-ו-מ) a.p.f. **mqōma** possible; לא גמקומא **la gımqōma** It is impossible (NT); cf. ב-ר-י.

מקוקרא, מקוקרתא (< ק-ו-ק-ר) p.p. **mqūqıra** (cf. PolG), **mqōqarta**, hollow.

מקחבאנא (ק-ח-ב) n.ag. **mqaḥbāna,** adulterer.

מקטנה (Ar) f. **mqaṭṭane** waist coat with cotton filling; pl. **mqaṭṭanat** (cf. PolU 417).

מקטרג (H< Gr) inv. **mıqaṭrēǧ** accuser (NT).

מקיים (Ar) **mqayyam** surviver, existing (NT).

מקלאא (< OA קלע) **mıqlāʾa** projectile, sling (NT).

מקלה (Ar) f. **maqle** frying pan.

מקעאדיה (Ar) pl. **maqʿāde** sitting places (of nobility), divans (AmU2 5b).

מקץ (Ar) m. **maqqaṣ** scissors; cf. ק-י-צ.

מקצד (Ar) m. **maqṣad** goal, purpose (PolU 7).

מקרויה (< ק-ר-י) v.n. **maqrōye** study readying (PolU 285).

מקריאנא (< ק-ר-י) n.ag. **maqıryāna** teacher, lector; cf. מעלם, מלפאנא.

-מר v. א-מ-ר

מ-ר-א, מ-ר-י (OA/OS מרע) **m-r-ʾ/y** to feel pain, to ache; לבי גמארי **lıbbi gmāre** (BaBin 141; cf. Sa83c 20, Z);My heart aches; IV to cause pain; **lıbbi qam mamreʾle** He caused me heartache, he saddened me.

מרא (Ar مَرّ ; OA מָרָא/OS ܡܪܐ < Ak **marru**) m. +**marra** spade, hoe.

מראא (OA/OS מַרְעָא illness) m. **marʾa** pain.

מראד v. מוראד

מראותא (< מ-ר-א) f. **marʾūṯa** aching, pain; מראותא דוויקנא **marʾūṯa dwīqınna** I was seized by pain, illness (Sa83 c 22, Am).

מראיאנא (< ר-א-י) n.ag. **marʾıyāna** shepherd (NT3); cf. שבאנא.

מרא-מר (K?) adv. +**mırra**-+**mır** full session with all due pomposity (PolU 6).

מראקא (Ar) f. +**marāqa** soup (cf. PolG).

מרו(ה) (Ar) +**mıra/ār(e)** bitter food (AmU2 5a; PolU 265).

מראתא, מריאתא (OA מריעתא) f. **mareʾṯa** aching, sick (NT3); cf. מרואא.

מרבא (Ar) +**mırabba** jam, jelly.

מרבע (Ar) **mırabbaʿ** square (=H רָבוּעַ, BT2).

מרגא (IrAr) f. +**marga** garbanzo and rice soup.

מרגלא (OS< Ar مرجل) m. **marıgla** caldron); pl. **-e** (= דּוּדִים, PolG).

מ-ר-ג̀ (< OA/OS מרס rub?) vi/vt +**m-r-č** to crush (=H רָמַס, רִטֵּשׁ, PolG); be crushed; cf. מריג̀א (NT+).

מרג̀ (ומרג̀) (onomat) +**mırč(-u-mırč)** sounds of kissing (PolU 38); of baby's sucking (PolU 319).

מרג̇אנה (Ar< Gr; cf. OA/OS מרגניתא, מורגנא coral) p.n.f. **mırjāne** Margaret.

מרג̀ואתא (< מ-ר-ג̀) +**mırčoʾta** crushed bread with hot butter (PolU 427); cf. פרג̀ואתא.

מרג̇וחא (Ar) f. +**marjōḥa** swing (for children).

מ-ר-ג̇-ח III (Ar) **m-r-j-ḥ** to swing; cf. ז-נ-ז-ק.

מרד 1 (IrAr< P man) inv. **mard** generous, one who likes to spend money on others.

מרד 2 v. מוראד

מרדכי (H) p.n. **mordaxay, mordax, mordax-xāye** (=May Mordax live!) Mordecai.

מרה v. מארא

מרהום (Ar) inv. +**marhūm** proper, elevated (NTU4 158b by error מהרום?).

מרואא (< מ-ר-א) adj. m. **marūʾa** painful; v. מראתא.

מרואדא, מרודתא (AnAr) f. +**mırwāda** (cf. PolG), +**mırwadta** earring (NT3); pl. מרואדה +**mırwāde**; **-dıd mōzīqa** 'musical' earings, with three little bells attached (NT+).

מרואחא (Ar; cf. OA מַרְוַחְתָּא fan) f. ⁺**mırwāḥa** fan; cf. ר-ו-ח.

מרווה, מרוות, מרוותא (Ar) f. ⁺**mırūwe,** ⁺**mırwat** (cf. PolG), ⁺**mürwıta** manlihood, sense of honor, generosity (Pol 108), consideration (Segal #89); במרווה **bmırūwe** I beg you, kindly (NT3); v. -בי מרוות.

מרור, מָרוֹר (H) m. ⁺**māror, marur** (AvidH 55) bitter herb (eaten on Passover night)(NT+).

מרות(א) (K **mirūz**) m. **mırrut(a)** (sullen) face; **mırrūte mšuršıṭa** morose, one in a bad mood.

מרזא (P) **marza** river bank, seashore (NT); cf. גבאן.

מרזדגתא, מַרְזַגְתָא (< ר-ז-ד-ג) f. **mrazdagta, marzagta** (PolG) set, fitting, campaign (=H מַעֲרָכָה, BT2; PolG:I Sam 4:2).

מרזיבא, מרזיוא (OS ܡܪܙܒܐ; OA מַרְזֵיבָא, מרזאבא; Ar مرزاب) m. **marzīva** (Z), **marzīwa** (NTU4 152b), waterspout; torrential rain; pl. **marzīv/we** [cf. Blanc 156-7: **mezrīb**].

מרחמאנא, רַחְמָנָא (< ר-ח-מ/OS ܡܪܚܡܢܐ) m. **(m)raḥmāna** (RivSh 186, 209) merciful; common in **ʾilāha mraḥmāna** God is merciful!(NT+).

מרתבה v. מַרְטַבֵּי

מ-ר-י v. מ-ר-א

מריגא, מרגתא (< מ-ר-ג) p.p. ⁺**mrīča,** ⁺**mrıčta** (NTU4 164a) weakling; one with crushed testes (BT3).

מרים, מרי, מרו (H) p.n.f. **mıryam, mıre, mıro** Miriam, Mary; **mıryam** ⁺ᶜ**ızra** (Ar عذراء) Virgin Mary; cf. מת-מרים.

מרימויה (K?) f. **marimōye** mourning period (7 days); **zılle lmarimōye** He went to pay his condolences.

מרי-מרוך (< א-מ-ר) **mırri-mırrox** (hostile) argument ('I said-you said').

מרירא, מרירתא/מַרִיתָא (OA/OS מרירא bitter, cruel) adj. ⁺**marīra,** ⁺**marırta** (NT5 404), ⁺**marıtta** (Ruth 1:20; PolG), bitter (NT+).

מרירותא, מרירתותא (OA) f. **marīr(at)ūṯa** (NT+).

מרכב (Ar; cf. OA/OS מַרְכַּבְתָּא) m. (Z)/f. (NT) ⁺**markab** ship; pl. **markābe** (cf. PolG); cf. ספינא, גמייא.

מרם (Ar) m. ⁺**maram** desire.

מ-ר-מ-ר III (< מ-י-ר) vt ⁺**m-r-m-r** to embitter (=H מֵרֵר, BT2, D); vi to growl, be enraged: אך אריא גמרמר ʾ**ıx** ʾ**arya gmarmır** He growls like a lion (NTU4 159b).

מרמר (Ar/T< Gr; cf. OA מַרְמְרָא) m. ⁺**marmar** marble; pl. מרמארה **marmāre** (NT3) (NT+).

מרעז (Ar<OA מר(ע) עיזי) **mar**ᶜ**az** cloth made of fine goat-wool.

מרפיג' (K/P 'coiled snake') m. ⁺**marpīč** rubber hose.

מרצע (Ar) inv. **mraṣṣa**ᶜ inlaid (NT3); cf. ר-צ-ע.

מ-ר-ק (OA) vt **m-r-q** to clean, polish (BT3).

מרק (K/T< Ar 'anxiety') m. ⁺**maraq** curiosity, desire, obsession (PolG; PolU 7).

מרקאאנא (< ר-ק-א) n. ag. m. **mraq**ʾ**āna** shoe repairman (PolGr 43)

מרקלי (K/T) inv. ⁺**maraqli** curious, interested (cf. PolU 286).

מררתא (OA/OS מְרָרְתָּא) f. ⁺**mararta** gall bladder, bile.

מרשא (OA מָרֵישָׁא beam/OS ܡܪܫܐ pestle, mortar?) m. ⁺**marsha** flintstone slab; pl. ⁺**marše**; cf. פרשא.

מרתא 1 (OA/OS/Ar) f. **marta** woman; אאיא מרתית גורילא ʾ**āya martıt gōrēla** She is a married woman (NT); cf. מארא.

מרתא 2 v. מרירא

מרתבה, מַרְטַבֵּי (Ar) f. ⁺**martabe** (high) rank (NT), position (BT1, D).

מרתכתא (< ר-ת-כ) f. ⁺**marṯaxta** (Z -**saxta**) sweet boiled mixture (=H מִרְקַחַת, BT2).

מרתוכא (AzT) **martōxa** huge loaf (PolU 428) [cf. Macd 200 **mirtūxā** cake< AzT].

מרתפע (Ar) **mırtıfı**ᶜ loud (voice) (NT2).

משאיה (Ar?) **mıššāye** shoes, slippers (sg. **mıššēṯa**) (cf. PolG) [cf. MacD 202].

משבכ (Ar) **mšabbak** checkered (=H תַּשְׁבֵּץ, BT20; שְׂבָכָה (PolG).; cf. ש-ב-כ.

משג'לתא (< ש-ג'-ל) f. **mıšġılta** occupation, business (NT3).

משה (רבינו) (H) **mōše/a (rabbēnu)** Moses our master; **b—** (I swear) by Moses! (NT+).

משויא, משויתא (< ש-ו-י) p.p. **mšūya, mšōwē**t**a** spread with carpet (place), made up (bed).

משולהמא, משולהמתא (< ש-ל-ה-מ) p.p. **mšúlhıma, -amta** glutton, starved.

משומד (H; cf. OA מְשַׁעְמְדָא apostate, SokBA 716) **mašúmma**d (Z +-z) apostate; any raging fitful person; cf. ש-מ-ד.

משוורא (Ar) f. **mašwara** advice, offer; משוורא סריתא - **srīta** plot, evil council (NT5 394); cf. שירתא, ש-ו-ר, שיר ומשאורת.

משולקנא, משולקנתא (< ש-ל-ק-נ) p.p. **mšúlqına, -anta** spotted (sheep) (=H עָקֹד/ נָקֹד, BT1).

משומשקא (< ש-מ-ש-ק) **mšúmšıqa: qōma** - willowy body (PolG).

משורשטא, משורשטתא (< ש-ר-ש-ט) p.p. **mšúršıṭa, -aṭta** drawn (face), dragging, hung (rope).

משותתא (< ש-ת-ת) p.p. **mšúttıta** (m.), **mšuttatta** (f.), dispersed, exiled (NT+).

משטאכא (OA משטחא) m. **mıšṭāxa** smooth floor for sorting the grapes.

מ-ש-י 1 (OA) **m-š-y** to wipe, clean (Pol 108).

מ-ש-י 2 IV (OA משהי?) **m-š-y** to wait (NT2).

משיח, מְשִׁיחַ, מלך משיח, משיח ברד דדויד/יוסף/ אפרים (H; cf. OA/OS מְשִׁיחָא; v. אישו) **(mēlex) māšīyaḥ, mišīyaḥ** (RivSh 201), **(brıd ddāwid/yōsef/ʾefrāyim)** (King) Messiah (son of David/ Joseph/Ephraim) (NT3) (NT+).

משיחא v. אישו

מַשֵׁיכְדָאנָא (ש-כ-ד) n.ag. **mašēxdāna** herald (=H מְבַשֵּׂר, PolG).

משינא (onomat) **mıššēna** rustle (PolU 5).

משיתא v. משאייה

מ-ש-כ (OA/OS משח) **m-š-x** to anoint, rub with oil.

משכא 1 (OA/OS משחא oil, fat) m. **mıšxa** butter, milk fat. (vs. דהנא **dehna** meat fat) (NT+).

משכא 2 ((OA מַשְׁכָּא, OS ܡܫܟܐ hide) m. **maška** sheepskin used as milk container [Garbell **miška** skin].

מִשְׁכַּב זָכוֹר (H) **mıškav zaxu/or** pederasty (BT5, D).

משכלולכה (< K?) f. **mašxalulke** lizard, mole (=H חֹלֶד/לְטָאָה, BT3).

משכן (H; cf. OA/OS מַשְׁכְּנָא tent) m. **mıškan** the biblical tabernacle.

משל (H) m. **māšāl** parable, (for) example; cf. מתלא; pl. משלות **mašalōt**.

משלכאנא, משלכנתא (< ש-ל-כ) n.ag. **mšalxāna, -anta** robber, one who charges high prices.

משלטכאנא, משלטכנתא (< ש-ל-ט-כ) n.ag. **mšalṭıxāna, -anta** usurper.

משמע (Ar) **mšammaᶜ** raincoat.

מְשַׁמֵר, משאמיר (K **mišemr** deserted< OS ܫܡܪ to dismiss, forsake) inv. **mısāmır** unfaithful (in sexual relations), desereter (NT3).

משמרה (H) f. +**mıšmāra** watch, group-reading of biblical portions on Sabbath in memory of a deceased person during the first year.

מ-ש-מ-ש III (OA) **m-š-m-š** to feel, grope, fondle caress (cf. Pol 108; PolG).

מ-ש-נ (< משנא) **m-š-n** to whet [3: **mšunne** Whet it!] (PolG).

משנא (OS ܡܫܢܐ<OA שנן) **mıšna** whetstone; **čōʾa x-mıšna** as smooth as whetstone; cf. מ-ש-נ.

משנה (H) **mıšna** Mishna (book of Jewish Law); cf. ששה סדרי משנה (NT+).

מִשְׁנֵה תּוֹרָה (H) **mısnē-tōrā** a copy of Torah (?) (BT5, D).

משניתא (< ש-נ-י 1) f. **mšanē**t**a** change of place, sojourn (=H מַסָּע, BT); pl. **mšanyā**t**a**.

משעל (Ar) m. **mıšᶜal** torch; pl. משעאלה **mıšᶜāle** (NT).

משפקאנא (< ש-פ-ק) n.ag. **mšafqāna** gracious, merciful (=H חַנּוּן, AvidH 61).

משקעאנא (< ש-ק-ע) n.ag. **mšaqᶜāna** cobbler.

משקץ (Ar iron arrowhead) **mašqaṣ** circumcision clamp.

משתאק, מושתק (Ar) inv. **mı/ušta/āq** yearning, desirous (cf. PolG) (NT+).

משתהוייה (< ש-ת-ה-י) v.n. **mıštıhōye** appetite (NT5 409).

משתהיב (< Ar هيب?) inv. **mıštahib** awesome (NT2).

משתרף (Ar) inv. **mıštarıf** noble, superior (NT2).

מִתָּא 1 (Ar متعه) f. **mıta** merchandise (BaBin 45) [cf. MacD 207 **matᶜa**].

מתא 2 v. אתא
מתואתא v. מאתא
מתוגׄא (< ת-ו-גׄ) p.p. **mtūja** crowned.
מתכאפל (Ar) inv. **mıtakāfıl** liable, guarantor (NT2).
מתככאנא (< ת-כ-כ) n.ag. **mtakkıkāna** a stick with which the string-tie is inserted into traditional trousers; v. תכתא.
מתכראנא, מתכרנתא (< ת-כ-ר) n.ag. **matxırāna, -anta** reminder (BT4).
מ-ת-ל (OA/Ar) **m-ṯ-l** to liken; to tell parables (NT).
מתלא (OA/OS מַתְלָא/Ar مَثَل) m. **maṯala** (Z **masala**) like, likeness, example (NT).
מתלה, מתלוכה (< K< Ar) f. **maṯale, matle** (BT4), **maṯalōke** parable; cf. משל; pl. **matlāt** (BT4).
מתלתין (Ar) **mṯallaṯīn** things made of three parts (NT2).
מתמדן (Ar) inv. **mımaddın** refined, cultured.
מת-מרים (OS ܡܪܬ ܡܪܝܡ) +**mat-mıryam** St. Mary; over-pamperd girl (worshiped by her parents); cf. אישו.
מתן בוכרא (H מתנה) **mattān buxra** gift given to the firstborn (SaAC 16).
מתפסראנא (< ת-פ-ס-ר) n.ag. **mtafsırāna** interpreter, translator (NT+).
מתקל (Ar; cf. OA/OS מַתְקָלָא) m. **mıṯqal** (Z **mısqal**) weight, carat; shekel (BT2, D); **bıd mısqal uᶜıyar** by weight and measure (Zaken 391).
מתרגם (H; cf. OA/OS מְתַרְגְּמָנָא) m. **mıtargem** the Translator, Onkelos (NT2); cf. תלגמן.

נ (n)

נ, ן (H) **nūn kafūfa/pašūṭa** bent (=non-final)/stretched (final) nun; **xamši** fifty.

-נ- (OA) **-ın-/-an-** me (m./f. object pron.: מפולטנה **mpulṭ-ın/-an-ne** He took me out); cf. -ינא, -אנא.

-ן 1 (OA) **-an** our (possessive pron.); cf. -יני (NT+).

-ן 2 (< ?) **-ın** an optional suffixed 'nunation' of the imperative or passive: **kōš/kōš-ın** Come down! מירן/מיר **mīr/mīr-ın** was said (NT+).

-נא/-נ (K) **na-** un-, not; cf. -נא, נכווש, נצך שהרזא.

נא-ובת (K) **na-wabıt** Let it not be (that...): **na-wabıt ṭam'ıttu** In no way you should taste them (PolU 15).

נאבה v. הנאויה.

נאב-ונישן (K) adv. **(b)nāv-u-nīšan** very explicitly (lit. by name and sign) (SaAC 20).

נאברכה (K? OA/OS נִבְרָא web or fiber of a date palm?) f. **nābarke** (fruit) basket (cf. PolU 437).

נאבייאן, נוויאן (K) prep.**nāvıyān** (Z), **nawyān** (NT), between, among, amidst.

נאבין (Ar مـــــا بين) prep. **nābēn** between; **nābēn(ēn)i unābēnox** between me and you; **zılla nābēne xa šāta** A year later (PolG).

נאבנג'י (K) inv. **nāvınji** average, intermediate (cf. PolG); pl. נאונג'ין **nawınjīn** average ones (NTU4 154b); **nāvınjiyat** people of middle income (PolU 59).

נאבת (Ar) m. **nābat** rock candy.

נ-א-ה I/IV (OA/OS נגה to break of dawn) vi **n-'-h** to light, to dawn (NT2; NTU2 40a); cf. באנהה, נאהתא.

נאהתא (< נ-א-ה; cf. OA/OS נַגְהָא daybreak) f. **n'ahta** dawn (NT); cf. באנהה.

נא-וביד (K) **ná-wabıd** let it not be, lest, in no way (MeAl 183, n. 44)(FT).

נאזה (K/T) p.n.f. **nāze** (Coy, Graceful).

נאזכ (K/P) inv. **nāzık** lean, tender, weak.

נאטורא (OA/OS) m. **nāṭōra** guard, watchman.

נאטורותא (< נאטורא) **nāṭōrūṯa** working as guard.

נאטרבאן (OA-K) **nāṭırvan** care-taker of vineyard (BaBin 164).

נאטרואנותא (< נאטרבאן) **nāṭırwānūṯa** work as care-taker (PolG).

נאיא, ניתא (Ar نيّ) adj. **nāya, nēṯa** raw, not cooked enough (=H נָא, BT2; BaBin 63).

נאכם (P) inv. **nākam** compliant (NT).

נאכאמי, נכאמיה, נאכמותא, נכמותא (P) f. **nakāmi/-e nakamūṯa** disconcertedness (NT5 402); shame (PolG); גרשן נאכאמי **garšın nakāmi** I comply, yield.

נאלנאלתא (K/P/T **nāl** 'lamentation') f. **nālnālta** (sounds of aching, suffering (PolU 325) [cf. MacD 214 **nālānāl**].

נאמוס (Ar< Gr) m. **nāmus** proper behavior; **mare nāmus** responsible, conscientious; v. בי-נאמוס; pl. נַאמֻוסֵי **nāmūse** (RivSh 235).

נ-א-ס (OA נעץ/נגס?) vt/vi **n-'-s** to sting (BaBin 141; RivSh 120; PolG); **qam nā'ısle xuwwe** He was stung by a snake; cf. נ-ג-ז; be insulted: **hakan 'amrīle xa xabra, gnā'ıs** If one tells him anything, he gets insulted (NT+) [MacD 208 **nā'iṣ/nā'iṣ** sting, bite; Garbell 290 **n-y-s** bite (one's) finger].

נאסתא (< נ-א-ס) f. **n'asta** sting (by snake, etc.).

נאעורא 1 (Ar) f. **nā'ōra** water wheel.

נאעורא 2 (< נ-ע-ר) m. **nā'ōra** brayer, jack-ass.

נא-עלג' (K-Ar) inv. **na-'ılaj** (one with) no-cure, no-choice (Pol 109; PolG), essential (PolGr 229).

נא-עלג'ותא (< נא-עלג') **na-'ılajūṯa** lack of choice, helplessness (cf. PolG).

נאפא (K/P soft skin) f. **nāfa** nap, soft hair (cf. PolU 299).

נאקושא (OS) m. **nāqōša** [PolG **naqōša**] church sounding-board, gong.

נאקץ (Ar) inv. **nāqıṣ** deficient (NTU2 40a).

נ-א-ר (< ?) **n-'-r** be spoiled, offensive (child).

נאשא (OA אינאשא, אִינָשָׁא; OS ܐܢܫܐ) m. **nāša** person; **palgıd nāša** weakling; pl. **nāše; nāš gyāna/xāuxıt** relative(s) (lit., of self/each other (=H מוֹדָע, Ruth 2:1) (NT+).

נא-שהרזא (K) inv. **na-šahraza** simpleton,

not-smart (NT+).

נאשותא (< נאשא) f. **nāšūṯa** good human relations.

נאתא v. נהתא

נאתפה (K/Ar نتف pluck?) f. **nātıfe** bandage that 'sucks' excessive milk from the (ailing) breast (SaAC 21).

נ-ב-א v. נ-ו-א

נבה (K) **nabbe** Yes, Sir (PolU 223).

נבואא, נבווא (OA/OS/Mand מַבּוּעָא) m. **nabōʾa, nabōwa** spring of water (NT); cf. נ-ו-א.

נבואה, נָבוּאָה, נוואה (H; OA נְבִיאוּתָא) f. **navūʾa, nawūʾa** (NTU4 161a), prophecy, divine spirit, vision (H רוּחַ/מַרְאָה/מַחֲזֶה, BT4; חָזוֹן, AvidH 52); cf. נבווה, נויותא.

נבווה (Ar) f. **nıbūwe** prophecy (NT); cf. נבואה, נויותא.

נבז אמיר (Ar نفس امير) **navz ʾamīr** choosy, selective, finicky (PolG).

נ-ב-י II (OA/OS נבי, pa./Ar نبّي) **n-b-y** to prophesy; speak (God) (= H דִּבֶּר, PolG: 2Kg 9:36)(NT+).

נביא, נָבִי (H; OA נְבִייָא) m. **nāvi** prophet (RivSh 272); cf. נויא; pl. נביאים**navīʾīm** [Khan 576 **nābi** (< JAB?); pl. **neb/vīʾīm, nevīʾe**].

נביאה (H) f. **navīʾa** prophetess (BT2) [cf. Mutz 216 **nıwyelta**].

נבייה, נבייתא(Ar) f. **nabīye, nabīyēṯa** prophetess; cf. נויא [MacD 209 **nwītā**].

נבילה (H) f. **navēla** (unkosher) dead body of animal (BT3).

נבין v. לבינה

נ-ב-ל (י-ב-ל ,ב-י-ל) IV (OA יבל) **n-b-l (b-y-l, y-b-l)** to lead away, carry away; **taxmīne qam nablīle uqam mēsēle** His thoughts shook him; cf. א-ז-ל; **lag nablın ulag mēsın** I froze, I didn't know what to do (PolG); **ʾe skīna la gnabla** This knife doesn't cut well; [1:**m/n/lōbıl**; 2/3:**m/n/lābıl** (Z), **mnābıl (< bn-), m/n/lōbıl** (NT); 4: **m/n/labōle**](NT+).

נ-ב-ש (Ar نفش) **n-b-š** to card (wool, cotton).

נגאחא (H) m. **nagāḥa** goring (ox) (=H נַגָּח, BT2, Am).

נגבא v. ז'נגבא

נגום (< נגון/K?) m. **nıgum** pattern (PolU 53).

נגון (H/JAB) m. **nıgun, nıgūn** melody.

נ-ג-ז (< OA נגז/OS نمو peck?) **n-g-z** to bite with lips, to eat a morsel (not interchangeable with נ-א-ס); to bite the lip when hearing surprising or bad news (cf. PolG); to push by elbow (PolG; < ל-כ-ז?).

נגזא (< נ-ג-ז) m. **nagza** a bite, a mouthful.

נ-ג-ל (< OS ܢܓܠ clear away) **n-g-l** to tidy, put things away; cf. נ-ק-ל?

נג'א (OA נתשא?) m. **nıč(č)a** piece (of meat)(=H נֵתַח, PolG); **ḥaqqe ʾōzīle nıččé-nıčče** He deserves to be cut to small pieces; cf. נ-ג'-נ-ג'.

נג'ארא (Ar نجّار; OA/OS נַגָּרָא) m. **ᐩnajāra** carpenter; craftsman (=H חָרָשׁ, BT2); cf. נ-ג'-ר [Khan 576 **nagāra**!].

נג'ארותא (< נג'ארא) **najārūṯa** carpentry (PolG).

נג'דא, נז'דא (K < Ar fight, rescue) f. **nıj/žda** gang, troupe; pl. נג'דאתא**nıjdāṯa** (NT+).

נגהאן, נג'הו (P/K?) adv. **nagahān, najıhu** (?) unawares, suddenly (NTU4 162b; RivSh 188); cf. ז'נגבא.

נג'ו 1 (K) **na-ču** not any (good): **naču nāša-le** He is not a good person; **na-ču šūla-le** It is a bad affair.

נג'ו 2 (< נסים) p.n.m. **nıččo** Nissim (hypo.).

נ-ג'-ו (Ar √نجو to escape, get away) **n-j-w** to snatch, tear away and escape (NT+) [cf. Garbell 286 **j-n-v** < K/T?; MacD. 54 **jānū** to seize, snatch < Ar جنا pluck/OS ܓܢܒ steal?].

נג'וכא (K **lāčik**) m. **nıččōka** white linen for covering head and face [MacD 148 **lāčigā**].

נְגְ'וֹתָא (< נ-ג'-ו) **nıjōṯa** (?) snatched animal body (=H טֶרֶף, PolG:Gen 49:9). (!)

נ-ג'-ח (Ar) **n-j-ḥ** to pass an exam, do well in studies.

נג'יוא, נג'ותא (< נ-ג'-ו) p.p. **njīwa, njūta** snatched, unkosher animal body torn by beasts (=H טְרֵפָה, BT3); cf. טְרֵיפָה.

נ-ג'-כ, ל-ג'-כ II (< נג'וכא) **n/l-č-k** to cover head and face with scarf.

נ-ג'-ל (OA נתש ל-/נשל) vt/vi **n-č-l** to uproot, unplug, pull out (RivSh 142); **lıbbi nčılle mkıpna** I am famished (cf. PolG)[MacD 214].

נ-ג'-נ-ג' III (< נג'א) **n-č-n-č** to cut meat to small pieces.

נ-ג'-ר (Ar) **ᐩn-j-r** to saw; **njāra** (vn) craft (=H חֲרֹשֶׁת, BT2); cf. נג'ארא (NT+).

נְדָבָה (H) f. **nıḏāva** voluntary sacrifice; pl. נְדָבוֹת **nıḏāvōṯ** (BT3, D); cf. סכייה.

נדביכה (H-K?) f. **nıdvīke** deserted, unloved wife (living on charity).

נ-ד-י, נ-י-ד (OA/OS נדי, af. to cast, sprinkle) **n-d-y** (Z), **n-y-d** (PolG:D), to leap, jump; IV to throw away, cast, miscarry; cf. ט-ר-ח; **mandi ʾızox** Have some food ('cast your hand'); **mundēle gāve** He started walking; **mandīle dūkıd ʾāza ʾīzox** Get rid of it, throw it as far as you can! **mandax gyānan kıs** We beg the help of, throw ourselves at the feet of (PolU 421); **mandax rēše** We'll attack him (PolU 78).

נדימה (P < Ar boon companion) **nadīme** boon: **rwēle bıt saʿāde u-** He grew up with luxury and boon [perhaps error for **naʿīme**; cf. נעמה].

נ-ד-מ (Ar) **n-d-m** to regret; — **baṯr-** to feel sorry after (someone is gone) (PolG); **ndımli lʿāqıli** I changed my mind (NT+).

נ-ד-ר, נ-צ-ר (OA/OS/H נדר) **n-ḏ-r** (Z **ˈn-z-r**) to vow, promise (PolU 248).

נדר (H) m. **nēḏer** (Z **ˈnēzer**) vow; **bala ˈnēzer** not vowing, I don't promise; pl. **nıḏārīm** (BT3).

נדרא (OA) m. **nıḏra** (Z **ˈnızra**) vow; בכול נדרי **bkunˈnızre** (I swear) by All the Vows (a solemn prayer of Yom Kippur) (NT+).

נ-ה-ב (Ar) **n-h-b** to rob, plunder.

נהגא, נהגונכא (K/P **nahang** crocodle) m. **nahga, nahgōnka** 'big-ish', large (young person, cattle).

נ-ה-ג' (Ar) **n-ḥ-j** to pant.

נהואתא (< נ-ה-י) pl. **nehwāṯa** groans (sg. **nehwa?**) (NT5 392, 397; Sa83c 34, Am).

נ-ה-י (OA) **n-h-y** to groan, to yearn (NT+).

נהיא, נהיתא (< נ-ה-י) p.p. **nıhya, nhīṯa** groaning, weary (=H יָגֵעַ, BT5).

נהין (K?) **nahīn** extreme measure (?) (AmU2 6a) **b- darūṯa** (?) extreme vigor (?): אן צלומיה דצלמי אליכון בנהין דרותא the oppressors who oppress you with utmost vigor (Sa83c 20, Am).

נהירא , נהרתא (OA) p.p. **nhīra, nhırta** lighted (candle).

נהליכה (K?) pl. **nahlīke** beds, mats (?): שוייאתה ונהליכה משוייה **šūyāṯe u- mšūye** his beds and mats (?) put up (AmU2 4b).

נ-ה-ר (OA/OS/Mand) **n-h-r** to light (vi), be radiant (face of beautiful woman or spiritual man); **gnahra mux šrāʾa** She shines like a candle= very pretty (PolU 284); IV to light (vt).

נהרא, ניהרא (OA/OS/Mand נַהֲרָא) m. **nehra** river (NT, AvidH 23); cf. שטא, כוורא; laundry (Z); **ʾuzla nehra** she did the laundry [cf. Mutz 215]; pl. נהרה **nehre** (NT), נהרואתא**nehrawāṯa** (RivSh 175; NT6: 134; PolG) (OA נהרוותא) [Khan 576 **nehera** (!) 'washing (clothes)', K(!)].

נהראיא, נהריתא (< נהרא) **nehrāya, -ēṯa,** laundry person (?) (PolU 49).

נ-ה-ש (< Ar bite) **n-h-š** to tear off (PolG).

נהתא, נאתא (< OS pl. **ʾeḏnā[ha]ṯā?**) **nahaṯa/ nahṯa** ? (NT3), **nāṯa** (Z **nāsa**); **y-h-w-l** - be attentive (PolG); pl. נהתיאתא, נתיאתא **nahaṯyāta** (NT4), **na/ıṯyāṯa** [Mengozzi 281: **n(h)āṯa**, pl. **nhāṯyāṯā**; Garbell 322 **ˈnahala, ˈn(a)halta**; pl. **ˈnahalye**; MacD 219 **nāṯā, nāšā, nāwīya**; pl. **n(h)aṯyāṯā**; Krotkoff 131; Hoberman 1985 228; Mutz 216 **nḥāla**; Khan 576 **naḥāla**].

נ-ו-א, נ-ב-א, מ-ב-א (OA/OS נבע) **n-w-ʾ, n-v/b-ʾ** (NT6 136), **m-b-ʾ** (PolGr 175), to ooze, to bloom (NT6 136), to start growing (beard) ; cf. נבואא (NT+).

נואאה (< נ-ו-א) pl. **nawāʾe** springing (water) (=H מַיִם חַיִּים, BT1).

נואגא, נוגתא (K **nevi**/P **nawāda**[!]) **nawāga** grandson, **nawagta** granddaughter; pl. **nawāgīn(e)** (NT+). [MacD 210 **nāwigā**].

נובא (Ar) f. **nōba** shift, watch; pl. **nōbe** (NT+).[Khan 576 **nobta**].

נובדר (K) m. **nobadar** vigilant, night guard (cf. PolU 365).

נֻוּבַּרִייֶ (K) **nūbarīye** new and choice fruits (of the season) (=H בִּכּוּרִים, BT4, D).

נוהאלא (K) m. **nohāla** valley (=H גַּיְא, PolG).

נווא (< OS?) m. **nuwwa** some type of spinach [MacD 211ܢܘܼܐ = **nūwā** < OS branch, sprout, sucker, shoot].

נוובת (K) adv. **nawabıt** in no way, you may not (PolU 96).

נ-ו-ז (< OS ܢܘܙ to disturb?) **n-w-z** to scold (cf. PolG) [Garbell 322 **nwazta** rebuke].

נוזנוזתא (K نیزه نیز) **nuznuzta** weak moaning (of dying people), yelping (cf. PolG; PolU

14).
נוזתא (< נ-ו-ז) f. **nwazta** scolding, fear (=H מִגְעֶרֶת, BT5).
נוח (H) p.n.m. **nūwaḥ** Noah.
נוט (< ?) m. **nōṭ** rage (?); **nōṭ-īle go ʾēne** He is raging, seething.
נוביא, נבייא, נווייא, נויא (OA) **nūya** (Z), **nuvya** (Sa83c 20, Am), **nw/vīya** (NT), prophet [MacD 209:**nwīya**; Garbell 322 **niwya**].
נאבייאן v. נווייאן
נויותא (OA נביותא) f. **nūyūta** (?)(NT); cf. נבואה, נבווה.
נ-ו-כ (OA/OS נבח) **n-w-x** to bark; to croak: **nuxle** 'he barked', pejor. pun with **nıxle** he rested, passed away.
נ(ו)כראיא, נ(ו)כריתא (OA נוכראָה, OS ܢܘܟܪܝܐ) **nu/ıxrāya**, **nu/ıxrēta** stranger, foreign(er), non-Jew (RivSh 195; =H גֵּר, PolG).
נוכריותא (< נוכראיא) f. **nuxrayūta** foreign country; alienation; cf. ג'ריבותא (NT+).
נוולתא (OS/OA נַוְלָא) f. **nawılta** horizontal loom [Mutz 236 **xanūla** (= **xa nūla** 'a loom'??)].
נומא, נומאנא (OS) **nōma, nōmāna** deep sleep (RivSh 115) (=H תַּרְדֵּמָה, BT1, Am); cf. שנתא נ-מ-נ-מ, טוטרמא,.
נומרא 1 ((Ar) f. **⁺numra** number (of a house) (PolU 317), figure.
נומרא 2 v. נמרא
נונה-נווה (< ניאו?) f. **nūne-⁺nawwe** a woman who whimpers a lot.
נ-ו-נ-ו III (v. ניאו) **⁺n-o-n-o** to meow; **wēla ⁺mnōnōye mux qaṭūsa** She is whining like a cat.
נוניתא (OA/OS/MAnd נוּנָא) f. **nunīta** fish; pl. **nunyāta, nūne** (Segal #47) (OA נוּנִין).
נוע, נועא (Ar) m. **nōᶜ(a)** kind, sort; בּגו נוע **bču nōᶜ** in no way; pl. נועה **nōᶜe**.
נוקבא, נקבא (OA נוּקְבָּא, OS ܢܘܩܒܐ; Mand ניקבא) m. **nu/ıqba** hole, cavity; **nuqbıd širma** anus; pl. **nuqbābe** (cf. PolGr 52); cf. נ-ק-ב.
נוקוא, נקוא, נוקבא, נִיקְוָתָא, נ(ו)קותא (OA נִיקְבְתָא, נוּקְבְתָא/OS ܢܘܩܒܬܐ, ܢܩܒܐ) **nüqwa, nüqva** (NT; BT1, AM), **nüq(q)ūta** (Z, PolG), female [cf. Mutz 216 **nıqwelta**].
נוקטא (Ar) f. **nuqṭa** spot; garrison; **nuqṭa-ḥarfe** spelling, vocalization; pl. נוקטי-נוקטי **nuqṭé-nuqṭe** spotted; cf. מלוקטנא.
נוקצאני, נוקצותא (K< Ar) f. **nuqṣāni, nuqṣūta** (PolG), shortage (NT+).
נוקרא (Ar) m. **nuqra** silver, precious metal (RivSh 264).
נורא 1 (OA/OS/Mand, m./f.) m. **nūra**; f. **⁺nūra** (Gz73 81), fire (NT+).
נורא 2 (OA/OS < Ak **nāmaru**) m. **nōra** mirror.
נוראיא (< נורא 1) **nūrāya** a gentile who lights fire for Jews on Sabbath (= Yiddish שבת-גוי).
נֻורִייַא (< לוליא pipe shaped?) **nūrīya** rolled-up (tortilla kind of) bread (?); **ʾıṣra nūriyıt laxma** = H עֶשָׂרָה לֶחֶם, PolG:1Kg 14; PolU 35).
נוש (K/P) m. **nōš** (elixier of) life; **ṣaḥḥa unōš** For good health!
נושא (OS ܢܦܫܐ) f. **nōša** self; **b/mnōše, b/mnōš(ıd) gyāne** by himself, he alone (cf. RivSh 272 מְנוֹשֶׁת גַאנֵי); אִבְנוֹשֵׁי **ıbnōše** He (shall be) apart (=H בָּדָד, BT3, D).
נשוקתא v. נושקתא
נסבתא v. נזבתא
נזים (K **nizm** low, inferior?) inv. **nızım** (?) inferior (metal) (?) (NT2).
נזיר, נַאזִיר (H; cf. OA/OS נזירא) **⁺nazīr** Nazirite, consecrate person; pl. **⁺nazīrīm** (BT3).
נ-ז-ע (Ar be in agony?) **n-z-ᶜ** to cry and sigh (BaBin 111).
נ-ז-ר (H/OA) **⁺n-z-r** to abstain from (BT3; BaBin 58).
נחום, נחו (H) p.n.m. **nāḥum, nıḥo** Nahum.
נחיד (Ar نحيد) **naḥīd** polished stone (NT).
נחמה (H) f. **nıḥāma** consolation; הולילה נחמה **hullēle nıḥāma** He consoled him (NT).
נחמיה (H) p.n. **naḥamya** Nehemiah.
נחס (K < Ar) inv. **naḥs** unpleasant, troublesome.
נ-ח-ק, נ-ק-ח (OS ܢܩܚ to peck?) **n-ḥ-q** (Z; PolG), **n-q-ḥ** (BT4, D), to touch; **- lnūra** to touch fire = end of Sabbath (PolU 435) [MacD 217 **n-q-x** < OS to bruise slightly; Segal #68: perhaps Ar **l-ḥ-q** reach].
נחקאנא, נחקנתא (K-Ar) adj. **naḥaqqāna, -anta** unjust, guilty, wicked (=H רָשָׁע, BT4, D; PolG); cf. חקאנא.
נחת (H) **naḥaṯ** (Z **naḥas**) ease of mind (PolG).
נטארא (< נ-ט-ר) m. **naṭāra** guardian, guard;

cf. נאטורא (NT+).

נטילה, נטילת ידים (H) **naṭīla, naṭīlaṯ yāḏāyim** ritual hand washing before eating; **ʾ-w-ḏ naṭīla** to wash hands in this ritual.

נ-ט-ל 1 (Ar to bath in aromatic water) **n-ṭ-l** to become wet, moist (clothes from dew, fog).

נ-ט-ל 2 I/II (H-OA) **n-ṭ-l** to wash hands (cf. PolU 306); cf. נטילה.

נ-ט-פ (OA/OS) **n-ṭ-p** to drip (NT2, NT5 402).

נ-ט-ר (OA/OS/Mand) **n-ṭ-r** to keep, to guard; **ʾilāha nāṭırrox** May God keep you=Thank you (said by an older person to a young person); to watch, wait: **ntırri hīl duqlāla šınsa** I waited until she fell asleep (PolG).

נטרתא (< נ-ט-ר) f. **nṭarta** obeying (laws) (=H מִשְׁמֶרֶת, BT1).

ניאו (onomat.) **⁺nyā/aw** meow (PolU 339).

ניאכא (OA/OS נְיָחָא) v.n. **nyāxa** resting.

ניארה v. נייר

ניב השתי ניב מאיי (K) adv. **nīv hıšti, nıv māyi** (rescued) half dead, half alive (PolU 375).

ניבישכ (K) **nīvīšk** fresh, sweet butter.

ניג'יר (K < P نخچیر > OA נחשיר) m. **nēčīr** hunting game (NT+).

ניג'ירבאן (K < P > OA נחשירכן) m. **nēčīr-vān** hunter.

נ-י-ד v. נ-ד-י

נידה (H) f. **nıdda** menstruating woman; אִבְּנִידָא **ıbnıdda** at (time of) menstruation (=H דָּוָה, BT3, D).

נייה (Ar) f. **nīye** (evil) intention (NT+).

ניזיכד (K) adv. **nēzīkıd** about; **nēzıkıd ʾımma nāše** about a hundred people (cf. PolU 4).

נ-י-כ (OA נ-י-ח) **n-y-x** to rest, to calm; to die (euph.); נכלא גיאניה **nıxla gyāne(h)** He passed away; **nıxle mın gyāne** He (finally) died (rested from his suffering); **nıxle brıxle** He disencumbered himself (of certain responsibility); IV to give respite, to relieve; **ʾilāha mānıxle** May God rest his soul; to look, rest eyes upon [NT1: **mʾōnıx-**; 2/3: **mʾēnıx**; 4: **mʾēnōxe**; Z 1: **mōnıx-**; 2/3: **mēnıx**; 4: **mēnōxe, manoxe**]; cf. מינכתא (Hob89 218; MeAl 180, n. 27; PolGr 157, D).

ניך (< ניכא/onomat) **nixxx** sound and movment of animal dropping down to rest or mate (PolU 63).

ניכא, נכתא (OA/OS נִיחָא) p.p., adj. adv. **nīxa, nıxta** calm, rested; dead (euph.); **nīxa brīxa** disencumbered; **rīxa nīxa** pleasing fragrance (=H רֵיחַ נִיחוֹחַ, BT2); softly (PolG); **xāye nīxe** comfortable life (Cf. PolUL 274)(NT+).

ניכותא (OA/OS ניחותא) f. **nīxūṯa** rest, calm (=H מְנוּחָה, PolG); בניכותא **b-** calmly (NT+).

ניכתא (OA/OS נְיָחְתָא) f. **nyaxta** rest (from someone's annoyance).

נ-י-מ (OA) **n-y-m** to doze (cf. PolG); cf. נ-מ-נ-מ.

נימויי (IrAr **nūmāyi**) lemon-yellow (NT3).

נינואייה (H) pl. **nīnwāye** Ninevites (NT6 135).

ניני (< תרניני) **nīni** dance (baby talk); cf. ר-ק-ד.

ניסן (H) **nīsan** The Hebrew month of Nissan (April); (beginning of) spring; **bēbūn nīsan** cyclamen; cf. אדר.

ניפַּקְתָּא (< נ-פ-ק; cf. OA מַפַּקְתָּא excrement) f. **nıpaqta** excrement (H צֵאָה, BT5, D).

נייר (K/P no-friend) **nayar** enemy (cf. PolU 141); pl. **nayāre** (PolU 379).

נירא (OA) m. **nīra** yoke (NT+).

נירגזא, נרגזא (K/P/T; OA נרקיס; Mand נארגיס < Gr) m. **nergıza** narcissus, marigold.

נירווא (< Ak **nērebu** entrance) **nērwa** Kurdish town with an old Jewish community (NT1)

ניריג, ניריא (K/P) m. **nērıg, nērīya** stag, he-goat; pl. **nērīye/-yat** (BT1; PolG).

נ-י-ש-נ III (< נישן) **n-ī-š-n** to mark out (=H תֵּאָה, BT4; cf. PolG)[1: **mnīšın-**; 2/3: **mnēšın**; 4: **lımnīšōne**].

נישן, נישנקא (K/P < OS ܢܫܢܐ) m. sign, engagement ring [cf. Blanc 158]; **drēlu - ʾılla** She is engaged [Blanc **nēšan** be betrothed] (NT+).

נאכאמיה v. נכאמי

נ-כ-ב (Ar) **n-k-b** to hurt, annoy; **lıbbi qam nākıble** (My child) is pestering me.

נכופא, נכופתא (OS) adj. **naxōpa, naxupta** shy.

נכווש (K/P) inv. **naxwaš** sick, unhealthy (NT5 409); untasty (Z); pl. **naxwašīn** patients (NT).

נכוושותא (< נכווש) f. **naxwašūṯa** sickness (NT); hard times (Z); pl. נכושיאתא **naxwašyāṯa** (NT, BT5, D; RivSh 274).

נכילא, נכלתא (OA נְהִילָא) p.p. **nxīla, nxılta**

sifted; exhausted (energy).

נכיפא, נכפתא (< נ-כ-פ)p.p. **nxīpa, nxıpta** ashamed.

נכירא (OA/OS נחירא nostril) m. **naxīra** nose; cf. פוקא (NT+).

נ-כ-ל (OS ܢܚܠ/Ar نخل) **n-x-l** to sieve; cf. מכלתא; become thin, weak: אנכלה כיליהון **nxılle xēlēhun** Their strength has waned (cf. PolG); IV to cause exhaustion (NT5 385); כילי מונכל **xēli munxıl** They exhausted my strength (BaBin 115).

נכלא (K) m. **nıkkıla** beak; pl. **nıkkılāle**.

נכמותא v. נאכאמי

נ-כ-נ-כ 1 III (OA נאק?) **n-k-n-k** to whimper.

נ-כ-נ-כ 2 III (< מ-כ-מ-כ?) **n-x-n-x** to mumble threats, to breathe heavily on one's neck.

נכנכתא (< נ-כ-נ-כ 2) f. **nıxnıxta** overt hostility.

נ-כ-פ (OS) **n-x-p** to be shy, modest; **nxıple bıgyāne** He felt embarrassed (NT+).

נכפותא (OS) f. **nıxpūṯa** shyness, modesty (NT+).

נ-כ-ר (Ar) ⁺**n-k-r** to deny: **nkīrīle pāre dēni** He denied (having) our money (as a loan)(=H כִּחֵשׁ/כִּחֵד, BT1); cf. ע-נ-כ-ר.

נמיר (K no-man) inv. **namēr** impotent.

נ-מ-נ-מ III (OA) **n-m-n-m** to slumber, have a light sleep (sitting) (cf. PolG); cf. נ-י-מ.

נמרא, נומרא (OA/OS נִמְרָא) m. **nümra** leopard, tiger (NT) [cf. Mutz 216 **nımra**]; cf. פלנג.

נמרדי (K/P) **na-mardi** no-valor, usually: – **la** **ʾ-w-z** do it without any delay or hesitation (PolU 6, 227).

ננא (K. **mamm**?) m. **nanna** baby's breast (?)(baby talk); cf. גֿגֿא.

ננכא (OA/OS ננחא mint < Ak **nanixu**, SokBA 756) m. **nanxa** fresh mint; cf. נענע [MacD 215 **nānā, ninxā**].

נס (H) m./f. **nēs** miracle (cf. PolU 299; 319); pl. **nıssīm**; cf. נסים.

נסאבא (Ar) **nasāba** familial relation (PolG).

נסבתא, נזבתא (Ar نسبة) f. **nıs/zbıta** occasion, case, issue, circumstance; pl. נזבתיאתא **nızbıtyāṯa** (NT).

נסים, נסו, נגֿכו (H) p.n.m. **nıssim, nısso, nıčko** (hypo.) Nissim.

נסלא (Ar) m. **nısla** progeny, descendants (NT).

נעאמא (Ar) f. **nıʿāma** ostrich; also p.n.f.; cf. ברת נעאמא.

נ-ע-ד v. ס-ע-ד

נעה (< ?) pl. **naʿʿe** raisins (baby talk); cf. יבשתתא.

נ-ע-ל II (Ar) **n-ʿ-l** to shoe (horse, donkey) (RivP II 212); to marry off (pejor. of gentile marriage); cf. פ-ר-ת-מ [Mutz 215].

נעלא (Ar) m. **naʿla** horseshoe; pl. **naʿle** (PolU 223)

נעלג̇י (Ar-T) m. **naʿalči** horseshoer.

נעלה (Ar لعنة) f. **naʿle** curse; **naʿle lbābe uyımme** a curse upon his father and mother! (cf. PolU 408).

נעלתא (Ar) f. **naʿalta** plain slipper, sole; pl. **naʿāle**.

נעם (Ar) **naʿam** Yes, Indeed (NT); Here I am (=H הִנֵּנִי, BT1).

נ-ע-מ (Ar) **n-ʿ-m** to bestow (NT).

נעמה, נעמתא (Ar) f. **nıʿme, nıʿmıta** life of ease, amenity; בנעמתי **bnıʿmıti** (I swear) by my benevolence (NT, RivSh 190); cf. נדימה.

נ-ע-נ-ע III (Ar عنعن?) **n-ʿ-n-ʿ** to moan (child); to mildly refuse (PolG).

נענע (Ar) **naʿnaʿ** mint (candy); v. קורצא; cf. ננכא.

נ-ע-ר (Ar/OA) **n-ʿ-r** to bray.

נ-פ-א, נ-פ-י (Ar نفع) **n-f-ʾ, n-f-y** (+NT; cf. BaBin 142 גנאפי **gnāfe**; נפייאלו **nafyālu**, Sa83c 4o, Am), to be useful; ולא גנפאא האדך **ula gnafʾa hādax** It is improper; cf. נפע מנפע, נפאתא,.

נפאתא (< נ-פ-א) f. **nfaʾta** benefit (BaBin 136).

נפטנגא (K) m. **naftanga** loins (=H מָתְנַיִם/חֲלָצַיִם, BT1).

נפטר (H) inv. **nıftar** deceased; פשליה נפטר **pıšle nıftar** He passed away (NT2) [cf. Mutz 216/ Khan 576 **niftār ġ-d-r** 'to pass away'.

נפיר (Ar) m. **nafīr** trumpet (NT); cf. בוקד נפירא

נפיר-עאם (Ar) **nafīr-ʿām** general alarm or call to arms (PolU 200).

נ-פ-כ, מ-פ-כ (OA/OS נפח) **n/m-p-x** to blow (air with lips); exaggerate a story, to swell; נְפַכַא **npāxa** swelling (=H שַׁחֶפֶת, BT5, D).

נ-פ-ל, מ-פ-ל (OA) **n/m-p-l** to fall, befall; **mpılle basri** He followed me, dragged after me; נאפל בקדאלוך **nāpıl bıqḏālox** You will be responsible for him; נאפל מקדאלוך **nāpıl mıqḏālox** You will be exempt from being responsible for him; גנאפל אילא חלא **gnāpıl ʾılla ḥılla** It necessitates taking the hallah from it (NT5 410); **mpılla bʾīze/ṭāle** He was lucky, had a great opportunity; - **bʾızwa** It came up by lot;- **go lıbbe** It occurred to him;- **qam-/b-lıbbe** He fell in love with her; He liked it; **-e darba** There was an opportunity; **qētan - lqısra** The bow of the shoelace slipped into a double knot; **-u lxauxıt** They are angry at each other; - **xē xēle** aged prematurely (PolG); **-e nābēn** He interceded between; IV cause to fall, drop down; **mampılla mın bratūṯa** He deflowers her (PolU 365) (NT+).

נפלה (< Ar نفل clover?) f. **nafale** the thickness of standing crops, grass, carpets); cf. נאפא.

נפלתא (< נ-פ-ל) n.act. **npalta** (kind of) falling (RivP 209).

נפס, נפסא (Ar) m. **nafas, nafsa** (RivSh 111), inhalation, breath; soul, person, individual; pl. **nafāse** (PolU 72); נפוסה **nafūse** (counted) persons (BT5).

נפע (Ar) **nafaᶜ** benefit, use; cf. מנפעא, נ-פ-א.

נ-פ-צ, מ-פ-צ (OA/OS) **n/m-p-ṣ** to beat rugs, shake off (clothes, etc.) (Pol 109; AlfH 87).

נ-פ-ק, מ-פ-ק (OA/OS נפק) **n/m-p-q** (cf. PolG) to go out; **mpıqle mdalaq dīda** He handled her well (v. דלק) ;**-e (m)wājıb dīda** He fulfilled his duty towards her; **-e mḥaqqu** He worsted them; **-a mʾīzi** It is out of my hands; **-a mmaᶜne** It is exaggerated, extraordinary; **bōzēna ma dnapqa bʾīzi** I'll do whatever I can; IV (פ-י-ק **p-y-q**) to take out; **gmāpıq xabra mgo xabra** He is loquacious; **la gmāpıqla gyāne bē xaʾ** He doesn't want to get involved in this; **māpıq šarṭ** He fulfills the condition (PolU 104) [1: **mōpıq-**; 2/3: **māpıq**; 4: **mapōqe**] (Z; NT3); cf. פ-ל-ט; v. צורתא.

נפקא (Ar) f. **nafaqa** alimony, expenses; מסואתיני בדברא ראבא ונפקא **masuʾıttēni bdabra rāba u —** May You satiate us with much sustenance and money to spend (NTU4 165a) (NT+).

נפקתא (Ar نَفَقَة; cf. OA נִפְקְתָא expenses) f. **nafqıta** consumption, ability to consume: **lā kēxıl ⁺rāba, nafqıte zurta-la** He doesn't eat much, his consumption is small; cf. ניפקתא.

נ-פ-ר (Ar) **⁺n-f-r** to blow the nose.

נפר (Ar) **nafar** m. (per) person; pl. **nafāre**.

נפתלי, נפתו (H) p.n.m. **naftāli, nıfto** Naphtali.

נצאיא, נציתא (< נ-צ-י) **naṣāya, naṣēṯa** quarrelsome.

נ-צ-ו (OA נצב) **n-ṣ-w** to plant, hammer in, pitch (tent) (NT+).

נצוצא, נצותא (OA/OS/Mand מַצּוּתָא) f. **naṣūṯa** (+Z/PolG **naṣūṣa**) war, fight; pl. נצואתא **naṣwāṯa** (NT+).

נ-צ-ח (Ar) **n-ṣ-ḥ** to advise (NT+).

נ-צ-י (OA/OS) **n-ṣ-y** to fight, to wage war; IV to make someone fight (RivSh 207) (NT+).

נציב (Ar) m. **naṣīb** luck, lot, opportunity (cf. PolG); **yā nāṣīb** lottery (NT+).

נציחתא (Ar-P) f. **naṣīḥıta** advice; cf. שירתא.

נצאך, נְצַאך (K-T) inv. **naṣax** sick, patient; cf. צאך; **p-y-š** - be sick (=H חָלָה, PolG); -pl. נְצַאכִינֵי **nıṣāxīne** (AvidH 68).

נצכותא (< נצך) f. **naṣaxūṯa** sickness.

נ-צ-ל (Ar) **n-ṣ-l** to drip (water from hanging wet clothes; cf. PolG); cf. צ-נ-צ-ל.

נצרתא (Ar-P) f. **nıṣrıta** winning quality, charisma (PolU 8), victory (PolU 247).

נ-צ-ר 1 (Ar) **n-ẓ-r** to glance; **ʾēne nẓırra ʾılli** His eye caught a glance of me; **ʾēni lē(wa) nẓırta ʾılle** I have never seen him; **ʾēnox lag naẓra bču nāša** You will not see any human being (PolG).

נ-צ-ר 2 v. נ-ד-ר

נקאשא, נקשתא (< נ-ק-ש) **naqāša, naqašta** embroiderer.

נ-ק-ב (Ar; OA/OS נקב) vt/vi **n-q-b** to pierce; **qam nāqıblu nasyāsi** He gave me a headache; to have holes in: **jēbābi nqıblu** My pockets have holes in them (cf. Zaken 388); cf. נוקבא.

נקבא v. נוקבא

נ-ק-ב-ר III (< נ-ק-ב) **⁺n-q-b-r** to poke about, dig out.

נ-ק-ד (OA/OS נקד to clean) **n-q-ḏ** (Z **n-q-z**) to become thin, lean (cf. PolG); II (< OA נקז?) to pick the tallow and sinews out of meat (to make it kosher) [MacD 217 **n-q-d** be thin; **n-q-z** to peck; Garbell 290 **n-q-l** to grow thin].

נקדאנא, מנקדאנא, (מ)נקדנתא (< נ-ק-ד) a.p.

(m)naqd̲āna, -d̲anta one who picks the tallow and sinews from meat (to make it kosher).
נקדי (Ar) **nıqdi** (pay in) cash.
נקוא, נקותא v. נוקוא
נקוצא, נקוצתא (< נ-ק-צ) adj. **naqōṣa, naquṣta** lacking; minus: מאתיה נקוץ כא **māt̲e naqōṣ xa** two hundred minus one (NT4) (NT+).
נקוצותא (< נקוצא) f. **naqōṣūt̲a** shortage, lessening.
נקותא v. נוקוא
נ-ק-ז v. נ-ק-ד
נ-ק-ח v. נ-ח-ק
נ-ק-ט (Ar) vi **n-q-ṭ** to drip; **dımma gnāqıṭwa nın ʾēne** Blood was dripping from his eyes=He was very furious (BaBin 136); IV to drop, drip (vt): **gmanqıṭaxwa xalwa go pımme** We used to drip milk into his mouth (SaAc 9).
נ-ק-י (OA/OS) **n-q-y** to be pure, innocent; II/IV to make pure (BT4).
נקייא, נקיתא (< נ-ק-י) p.p. **nıqya, nqīt̲a** pure, innocent, honest (=H נָקִי, BT,PolG) (NT+).
נקידא, נקדתא (OA נקידא clean, pure) adj. **naqīd̲a, naqıd̲ta** (Z **naqīza, naqız/sta**) thin, lean; cf. נ-ק-ד.
נ-ק-ל (Ar) **n-q-l** to carry away things (short distances, back and forth); cf. נ-ג-ל?
נקלא (Ar) f. **naqla** recurrent time; **xa naqla** once; **naqıl tre** second time; pl. **naqle**.
נ-ק-מ (OA) **n-q-m** to take revenge.
נקמתא, נקמה (H) f. **naqamta, naqāma** (NT5 396) vengeance, torture; pl. נְקַמִיתְיָתַא **naqāmıtyāt̲a** (=H שְׁפָטִים, BT2, Am), נקמות **naqāmōt̲** ; cf. אנתקאם.
נ-ק-נ-ק (IrAr **n-g-n-g**) **n-q-n-q** to eat small amounts, to have a bite, a snack.
נ-ק-צ (Ar) **n-q-ṣ** to lessen (vi); IV to lessen (vt) (NT+).
נ-ק-ר (OA/OS) **n-q-r** to peck; to engrave (=H פִּתַּח/חָרַת, BT2; נקירא **nqīra** = חָרוּץ, AlfH 49); **pāse nqırta** one with pock-marked face.
נ-ק-ש (OA/Ar) **n-q-š** to hurt, touch; ולא נאקש אל כיפה פרזלא **ula nāqıš ʾıl kēpe prızla** Let no iron touch any stones; שמשא נקשא אלוהון **šımša naqša ʾıllēhun** Sun will affect them (NT5 409); **naqša ʾıllox** May this (happy occasion) happen to you too (lit. touch you; said in weddings to an unmarried person); **naqša ltamāmati** May you bring this to a successful end; to embroider (Z); IV to wish, foretell good news (by analogy of present to future; cf. PolG) (NT+).
נקשא (< נ-ק-ש) m. **naqša** (**naqıš-**) ornament, embroidery; example model (Segall #132); **naqši brēšu drīle** Let them suffer like me! (BaBin 113); **naqši brēšax** May you have what I have (PolG).
נרא (< K/P male camel?) m. **ˀnırra** strong and stocky man.
נראא (OA נרגא) m. **narʾa** axe (NT+).
נרגזא v. נירגזא
נשא (K **nišāy** flour-milk dish) choice flour (=H סֹלֶת, BT), rice soup cream.
נשאיא, נשיתא (< נ-ש-י)n. ag. **našāya, našēt̲a** forgetful.
נשאמא v. נשמה
נשוקתא, נוּשְׁקְתַא (OA נושקתא, נשיקתא; OS ܢܘܫܩܬܐ) f. **našuqta, nušıqta** (RivSh 195); cf. מונשקתא; pl. נשוקיאתא **našuqyāt̲a**.
נ-ש-ט (OA/OS) **n-š-ṭ** to skin; to scrape (=H הִפְשִׁיט/הִקְצִיעַ, BT3; cf. BaBin 127).
נ-ש-י (OA/OS) **n-š-y** to forget; IV to make someone forget (=H נַשֵּׁה, BT1; PolG) (NT+).
נשיא, נָאשִׂיא (H) m. **nāsī** biblical tribal chief (BT); pl. נשיאים **nasīʾīm**.
נשכוואר, נשכור (P) **nıšxwar** uneaten, unconsumed residue (NT3; NTU4 165b).
נשמה, נשאמא (H; OA נִישְׁמְתָא) f. **nıšāma** soul; **nıšāme dʾırra** He regained his strength; pl. נשאמה **nıšāme/**
נשמות **nıšāmōt̲** (NT5 405) [cf. Khan 576].
נ-ש-פ (Ar; OA to blow) **n-š-f** to dry up (vi); IV to dry up (Vt) (NT+).
נ-ש-ק (OA/OS/Mand) **n-š-q** to kiss; IV only in **nšāqa umanšōqe** kissing and the like (PolU 202). NT+
נשרא (OA/OS/Mand) m. **ˀnıšra** eagle; pl. **-e** (PolG) (NT+).
נהתא v. נתיאתא
נ-ת-נ (Ar) **n-t-n** to stink (NT+).
נ-ת-ר (OA) **n-t̲-r** (Z **n-s-r**) to fall off (leaves, fruits); IV to cause fruits, leaves to fall off by shaking the tree; to shed tears (BaBin 114; MeAl 190; PolG).

ס (s)

ס (H) **sāmax** the 15th letter in the Hebrew alphabet; **ʾıšti** sixty.

סאבק (Ar) inv. **sābıq** early (fruit) (NT3); cf. בוכרא.

סאוא, סאוונא (OA/OS/Mand סבא, סאבא) **sāwa** (NT, PolG:D, Am), **sāwōna** (Z), old man, grandfather; pl. סָאוֵי **sāwe** (=H זְקֵנִים, PolG:D), **sāwōne** (Z); cf. ס-ו-י, סותא, סוויא, סיבותא, באבא [Khan **sona**].

סאוון v. א-ז-ל

סאטורא (OS/Ar) m. **sāṭōra** butcher's knife, cleaver; pl. **sāṭōre**.

סאכו (K/IrAr < It **sago** < L) f. **sāko** jacket (European style); pl. **sākōyat, -ye** (PolG).

סאלא (OA סלא) **sāla** basket, tray (AvidH 5).

ס-א-ל-כ III (< Ar صعلك be a beggar?) **s-ʾ-l-k** to suffer: דאים רחמיה מאילאהא גטאלב דלא מסאלך **dāyim raḥme mʾilāha gṭālıb dla msaʾlık** He always asks mercy from God so that he will not suffer (AmU2 5a); become a beggar: טלד לא מסאלכת ופישת מסכינא **tlad la msaᶜlıkıt upēšıt mıskīna** so that you don't become a beggar and destitute (NTU4 160a); to torture (child:mother, by pestering) (Z).

סאמא, סַהְמָא (OA/OS סַמָּא) m. **sāma** (Z), **sahma** (AvidH 59), poison, rage; מפולטלו סאמוה ברישה **mpōlıṭlu sāmuh brēše** They poured out their wrath on him (=took their vengeance on him); cf. ס-מ-מ, סאמיתא (NT+).

סאמאנא, סאמנתא (< סאמא) adj. **sāmāna, sāmanta** poisonous, furious (cf. PolG); cf. ס-מ-מ.

סאמיתא, סַהְמִיתָא (< סאמא) **sāmīta** (Z), **sahmīta** (BT5, D; BaBin 40), rage (=H אַף, חָרוֹן, BT); **mın -te** out of his rage (PolG).

סאנאהי, סהנאיי (K/P) inv. **sanāhi** (NT), **sahnāyi** (Z, PolG). easy(ly).

סאעא, סעא, צעא (Ar) f. **sāᶜa** (NT) **ṣaᶜᶜa** (Z, BaBin 10), time, moment; hour; watch, clock (Z); סאעא זאורתא **sāᶜa zʾurta** a little while; **ṣaᶜᶜa naquṣta** troubling time; **ṣaᶜᶜa xafıfta** Have an easy time! pl. סעאתא **saᶜāṯa** (NT 5 407), **ṣaᶜᶜe** (Z, PolG); cf. שאתא 1 [Khan 580 **saᶜa(ta)**].

סאעג'י (IrAr) m. **sāᶜači** watchmaker, watch repairing shop.

סאקא (Ar) f. **sāqa** leg; leg-warmer; pl. סָאקֵי **sāqe** (Bt5, D), **sāqāqe** (Z); cf. שאקא.

סארא, סיארא (OA סערא) m. **seʾra** goat (coarse) hair; cf. כז'א.

סארג'א v. צארג'א

סארטלאנא (OA/OS סרטנא) m. **sārıṭlāna** crab [MacD 231 **serṭānā, serṭlānā**].

ס-ב-ב II2 (Ar) **s-b-b** to cause, to bring about (=H הִתְגָּרָה, גָּמַל, PolG:Gen 50:15; 2Kg 14:10).

סבב (Ar) m. **sabab** reason, cause; בסבב **bsabab** because of, for the sake of; so that; מסבב **msabab** due to; למא סבב **lma sabab** Why? For what reason? cf. סבה (NT+)..

סבג'י (Ar/P; v. זְבַגָא) **sabaji** black shell (NT3).

סבה, סבתא (H/Ar سَبَّة) f. **sıbbe** (PolG), **sıbbıta** (Zaken 392; **sıbbıttıt-**, PolG)), cause (of); cf. סבב; **bsıbbıtox** thanks to you, due to you.

ס-ב-ח, צ-ב-ח II (Ar) **s/ṣ-b-ḥ** to sing hymns, to praise (NT+).

סבט, צבט (< K< P سبد 'box, chest'?) **⁺sabat** chicken's chest (meat) (PolU 296); cf. סוסה.

סבכאטר, ספכאטר (< K < Ar سبب+خاطر?) **sab/pxāṭır** for the sake of (cf. PolG); cf. סבב.

סבלסורכת (< K?) pl. **savlasurkat** youngsters?, thugs? (PolU 155).

סבעי סבעיני (IrAr) **sabᶜe-sabᶜēni** centipede.

סבתא v. סבה

סבתו, ספתו (Ar سبت) p.n.m. **sab/pto** (given to males born on Saturday); cf. שבתא, שמביכו.

ס-ג'-ד, ס-ת-ג'/ד, ס-י-ג', ס-ג'-ד (Ar سجد; cf. OA/OS

סגד) s-j-d (Z), s-d/t-j, s-j-j, s-y-j (NT, PolG) to bow down, to worship (NT+).

סגלי (P/T < Ar) sıjıli registration; ʾ-w-z - to register (marriage) (PolU 39).

סדה (Ar سُدّة seat) f. sıdde pulpit (in synagogue) [cf. Garbell 330 sitta pulpit].

סדודא (< Ar سدّاد) m. sıddōda stopper (ShKC 123).

ס-ד-ר (H/OA) s-d-r to arrange, to set (NT2).

סה v. א-ז-ל 1

ס-ה-ב, ס-ה-ו I/II (< סהבה) s-h-v (Z), s-h-w (Hob89 219) to fear (AlfH 91; BaBin 2,6).

סהבאיא, סהביתא (< סהבה) adj. (yāla) sahvāya, (yalta) sahvēṯa infant (child); pl. (yalunke) sahvāye (BaBin 114).

סהבאנא, סהבניתא, סהאנא, סהוניתא (< סהבה) adj. sahvāna , -ēsa (Z), sahwāna, -ēṯa (NT5 389) awesome, terrifying.

סהבה, סהוה (K sehev, saw < P sahim) f. sahve (Z, PolG), sahwe (NT; RivSh 160), terror, awe; pl. סַהְוֵי אוּרְוֵי sahwe ʾurwe great fears (AvidH 31)[cf. סאמיתא; MacD 221 saham terror; Garbell 329 sahm fear, dread].

ס-ה-ד (OA/OS/Mand סהד, שהד) s-h-ḏ to testify; כו אימי דסהדליה אלד כוריה בדוגלא ku ʾēmi dshıḏle ʾıllıd xōre bdugla Whoever testifies against his fellow falsely; IV make someone testify (Z, but = I in RivSh 185), testify (against) (=H עָנָה, PolG: Ruth 1:21).

סהדא (OA/OS/Mand סָהֲדָא, שהדא) m. sahḏa (Z sahza) witness (NT+).

סהדותא (OA/OS Mand סָהֲדוּתָא, שהדותא) f. sahḏūṯa testimony (Z, PolG sahzūsa) ;; ṣandūqıd sahḏūṯa the Ark of Testimony (NT, BT) (NT+).

סהואנא v. סהבאנא

סהוה v. סהבה

ס-ה-י (Ar) s-h-y to err, be distracted (NT); to wonder (BaBin 152).

סהיותא (< ס-ה-י) f. sehyūṯa error, negligence (NT5 382, 406).

סהל, סהיל (Ar) inv. sahıl facil; לא דאוקלא סהיל la dāwıqla sahıl He should not belittle it (NT).

סהלא (Ar سِهْل) m. sehla sand ; cf. כיס [MacD 226 sīlā /sēlā 'sand' < OS sēlā 'seaweed'?].

ס-ה-מ II (Ar) s-h-m to apportion, grant (=H זָבַל/זָבַד, BT1).

סהמא 1 (Ar) m. portion, lot; pl. sahme (NT+).

סהמא 2 v. סאמא

סהמיתא v. סאמיתא

סהנאי v. סאנאהי

סהרא, סיהרא (OA סִיהֲרָא; OS ܣܗܪܐ) m. sehra (+Z, PolG: šımšıd sehra) moon; month (NT):(סהריה) בסהרד טלאהא bsehrıd ṯlāha (sehre) on the third month; cf. ירכא.

סיהראנה, סיראנה, סהראנה (K < Ar سيران 'walk') f. sehrāne, sērāne communal procession and picnic in the country side (during Passover or Succoth Holidays) (Sa83c 38, Am; PolG).

סוא (Ar) sawa similar, equal; וכולו וילו בסוא ukullu wēlu bsawa and all of them were similar, of equal quality (NT+).

ס-ו-א (OA שבע/ס) s-w-ʾ to be satiated; la sōʾıttu xāyox May you not live long; IV to satiate, to fill (NTU4 165a; Segal #11).

סואא (OA שָׂבְעָא, שׂוֹבְעָא) m. sūʾa abundance, plenty to eat (=H שָׂבָע, BT1).

סואנה (< ?) swāne roof edge; pl. swanāne [MacD 222 swīnā 'edge of roof, rim'].

סואתא (<ס-ו-א) f. swaʾta satiety, satisfaction; וכאזכליה סואתן uxazaxle swaʾtan So that we may look at him to our satisfaction; xōl swaʾtox Eat your fill! [Khan 580 swāta].

סובא v. תּובא

סוגר v. מסוגר

סוג̇ (T) m. sūj fault (RivSh 259; PolG); ʾēha brēla bsūj dīdi This happened because of me; לא סוג̇ ולא סבב la sūj ula sabab for no reason at all (BaBin 123).

סודרא v. צודרא

ס-ו-י, ס-י-ו (OA/OS/Mand סאב) s-w-y (Z), s-y-w (NT/Z) to become old (=H זָקֵן, PolG), worn out (=H בָּלָה, BT1); cf. סאוא [1:-אִסְוֵי swē- (PolG)/sū- (PolU 9); 2: סיוי sēwi (NT2)]. (NT+)..

סויאא, סויאתא (< ס-ו-א) p.p. swīʾa, sweʾta satiated, full [Khan 580 siwya, swita].

סוויא (< סאוא) m. sawōya grandfather (cf. PolG); v. סאוא, סותא.

סוכה (H) f. sukka booth, sukkah; pl. sukkat [Khan 580 sukke Festival od Succoth].

סולטן (Ar) m. sulṭan king, sultan; cf. שולטן, חכומא.

סולטנותא (< שולטן) f. **sulṭanūṯa** sultanship (PolU 149); cf. שולטנותא.
סולתא (< OS זבלתא*?) f. **sulta** dunghill (=H אַשְׁפֹּת, AvidH 49; NTU4 164b); cf. כאבלתא [MacD 222 **sūlā** <OS **zbl'**?].
סון v. א-ז-ל
סוני דת, שונא דת (H) adj. **sōni daṯ** hateful of (Jewish) religion.
סון ישראל v. שונאי ישראל
סוניכא, סוניכה (H שונא) adj. **sonīka, sōnīke** hateful.
סונקיא [= סונקאנא?](OS ܣܘܢܩܢܐ) **sunqāya** (?) (=**sunqāna**) need, necessity (NTU4 160b).
סוסה, סוסי, סֻוסַא, סוסתא (OA/OS/Mand סוּסְיָא, m.; סוּסְתָא, f.) m. **sūse** (Z), **sūsa** (PolG:D), horse; chicken breast-bone (which 'looks' like riding seat; cf. סבט); **susta** (NT, f.), mare; **sūs-bırqa/pōxa** very fast horse ('lightning/wind horse') (PolU 110); cf. מהינה.; pl. סוסואתא, סֻוסַוָותַא **susawāṯa** (cf. Riv. Sh 276) (NT+) [Khan 580 **susa, suse**].
סיסנה v. סוסן והלאלת
ספתא v. סופואתא
סוף העולם (H) **sōf haʿōlām** the edge of the earth; זלה מסוף העולם ועד סופו (the sound) echoed all over the world (NT2; NT5 383).
סופיר (H) **sōfēr** scribe; pl. סופירה **sōfēre** (NT).
ס-ו-ק II (Ar) **s-w-q** go to the market, to shop.
סוק, סוקון v. י-ס-ק
סוקאלי, סקאלי, סקאלייא (< ס-ק-ל) m. **sa/uqāli(ya)** finery (=H עֲדִי, BT2), jewel, adornment; pl. **suqāliyat/suqāle** (= H עֲדָיִים, AvidH 22).
סור, סִיר, צור (Ar سِرّ) m. ⁺**sur, sır** secret (MeAl 188); pl. **ṣurre** (cf. PolG).
סוראיא, סוּרַיַא, סוריתא (OS Syrian) **sōrāya, sur-** (PolG:D), **sōrēṯa** [Gz73 84: **ṣoráya, ṣorésa**], Christian; uncircumcised (=H עָרֵל, BT3, D); קיסר כפורא וסוראיא **qēsar - usōrāya** infidel and uncircumcised Caesar (BaBin 139); pl. **sōrāye, surāye** (סֻורַאיֶי, PolG).
סורדאר (< סור) inv. **surdār** mystery-revealer (God) (NTU4 157b).
סוריותא, סורות, סורית (< OS) **sōrayūṯa, suruṯ** (Z **surus**), **sūreṯ** Christianity, Christian Neo-Aramaic, Christendom (SaLH), Christian territory (PolU 286).

סורכה, צורכה (K< P سرخچه) f. ⁺**sōrake** measles.
סורמא, סרמא (T/K) m. **sürma** silky cloth embroidered with silver threads.
סותא 1 (K **sūt** trap < Ar سُدّ) f. **sūta** dam.
סותא 2 (OA/OS סבתא) f. **sōta** grandmother; old woman (NT); אתואליה כא ימא קוי סותא **ʾıṯwāle xa yımma qawi sōta** He had a mother (who was) very old; **sōta-sawōya** grandparents; v. סותנתא, תותו; כאכא [Khan 580 **sota**, pl. **sawāle**].
סותלי (< ?) **sutli** strong wool yarn (PolG).
סותנתא (< סותא 2) f. **sōtınta** old woman; pl. **sōtınyāṯa**.
סזגונא v. ססגונא
סחנאייה, צחנאייה (K < Ar صحن) f. **ṣ/sahnāye** plate, dish; pl. **ṣ/ṣahnāyat**.
סחאר(א) (Ar) **saḥār(a)** magician (NT+).
סחיון v. ציון
ס-ח-ר (Ar) **s-ḥ-r** to practice sorcery, devination (=H נִחֵשׁ, BT1).
סחר (Ar) m. **sıḥır** sorcery, magic; pl. **sıḥre**, צִיחְרֵי **ṣiḥre** (?) (PolF:D).
סחראיי (P < Ar صحراء) f. **saḥrāye** desert (NT); cf. ברייא.
סחר-בנד (K) inv. **sıḥır-band** enchanted (PolU 165).
סחרכר (Ar-K) m. **sıḥırkar** magician; pl. **sıḥırkare** (=H אוֹבוֹת, BT3); cf. סחארא, כשופכר, כראשא.
סתויר v. סטויר
ס-ט-י (OA/OS ס-ט-י deviate) **s-ṭ-y** be conceited.
סטיא, סטיתא (< ס-ט-י) p.p. **sıṭya, sṭīṯa** conceited.
סטלה, צטלה (P/Ar < L **situla**) f. ⁺**satle** bucket.
ס-ט-מ, צ-ט-מ (Ar صدم bang, strike/OA סטם seal?) ⁺**s-t-m** to be ruined, only with ה-ג'-מ as hendiadys: **bēsu hjımle-stımle** their house is 'ruined', they have one bad luck after another; cf. צ-נ-ד-מ [cf. Mutz 228 **ṣṭm**].
אסטמבול v.סטמבול
סטמיה (< צדמה?) **saṭme**, ⁺**satme** terror, fear (=H בעתה, AmU2 4b).
סטרא v. צטרא
סטרא אחרא (H-OA) f. **sıṭra (ʾa)ḥara** evil spirit; **sıṭra-ḥara ʾurra go qalwe** evil spirit entered his body; mad, raging woman.
סי v. א-ז-ל

סיאאה z (OA סייגא) m. **syāʾa/e** fence(s)(NT; ZU 72b); cf. טאן.

סיאגא (v. ס-ג-ד) vn **syāja** bow, worship (NT).

סיאדא (< ס-י-ד) vn **syāda** plugging, stopping up.

סיאנא (OA סיין/סוון) m. **syāna** mire; **ʾıtlu mūne usyāna** They are very poor (have only mud and mud); cf. מונה, טינא.

סיאסי (Ar) **sıyāsi** moderation, diplomacy; **muḥkēla ʾımma b —** He spoke with her in moderation (PolG); cf. סיאסת.

סיאסת (Ar-P) **sıyāsat** expediency; סיאסת אביני מטועלו **sıyāsat ʾıbbēni mṭōʿıllu** They played expediency games with us (NTU4 148b).

סיבוכה (K little apple) f. **sīvōke** swelling (resulting from a blow), wound, bruise (=H חַבּוּרָה, BT1).

סיבותא (OA/OS/Mand סיבותא) f. **sēvūṯa** (Z, PolG, NT+) old age; v. סאוס, סותא.

סיבייא (K **sewi** يتيم الام) m. **sēvīya** one orphaned of mother: **yāla pıšle yatūma u-** The child became orphaned of father and mother (PolU 211).

סיבכ (SA سَيْبَك) m. **sībak** a cane tied to baby's penis to enable him to urinate through a hole in the crib into a pot.

סֵי גוּהָאת (K) **sē-guhat** pitchfork, trident (=H שְׁלֹשׁ קִלְּשׁוֹן, PolG:1S13:21).

ס-י-ג v. ס-ג-ד

סיג׳וק(א) (T) m. **sījōq(a)** sausage (made of dry and very spiced meat).

ס-י-ד (Ar سدّ) **s-y-d** to block (wells, etc.) (NT+).

סייד, סיידא (Ar) m. **sayyıd, sayda** Mister, Sir (used with Muslim functionary)(PolU 255).

סייד אל פאצ׳ל (Ar) **sayyıd al-fāẓıl** the Merritorious (epithet of Moses)(NT2).

סידארא (IrAr) f. **sīdāra** urban Iraqi cap [< P/Gr **cidaris**/H כֶּתֶר (Persian) King's headdress?; v. JSS 44 (1999): 40].

סיהרא v. סהרא

ס-י-ו v. ס-ו-י

סיואנא (K) f. **sīwāna** umbrella; cf. שמסייא.

סיון (H) **sīwan** the month of Sivan (June).

סִיחְתָא v. צחתא

סיטא, ציטא (OS) m. ⁺**sīṭa** span (=H זֶרֶת, BT2); very short distance; 'shorty'; pl. **sīṭe** (PolG).

סי-טבקי (K) inv. **sē-ṭabaqi** of three decks (=H שְׁלִישִׁים, BT1); three-story (house).

סיכה (Ar/P سيخ 'spit'?) **sīxe** feverish shudder (Pol 110).

סיכורא (K) m. **sīxurra** porcupine('s) needle; sty in the eye.

ס-י-ל (H סלל commit lewdness; M. Jastrow 995) **s-y-l** fuck (common in vulgar curses).

סילאח v. צליח

סִילְמוֹאְתָה v.

ס-י-מ (Ar سأم) **s-y-m** to hate, detest, be angry; **sımle mınna** He hated her, became tired of her; VI to make angry (NT5 396), to hate: מוסימנו **musīmınnu** They hated me (Sa83c 16, Am).

סים (P/K/T silver string, wire of any metal) m. **sīm** wire fence [cf. Khan 580 **sehma** silver].

סימא 1, סמתא (< ס-י-מ) p.p. **sīma, sımta** hateful, angry (NT+).

סימא 2 v. סמא

סִימַלְתָא (OS ܣܒܠܬܐ/OA סולמא) **simalta** ladder (= H סֻלָּם, PolG [D]); cf. גראדה.

סימן (H < Gr) m. **sīmān** mark; pl. סימנים סימאנים, **sīmānīm** (NT; RivSh 147).

סימן טוב, סימנטוב (H) p.n.m. **sīmánṭof** 'Good Omen' **čīmo** (hypo).

סימרכה (K/P سيمرغ) f. **sīmarxe** a legendary eagle that serves as a mighty 'airplane' in Jewish-Kurdish folktales; eagle (PolG).

סינורא (K/T < Gr) **sīnōra** border (RivSh 171, 197) [cf. MacD 228].

סינידיום v. תִינידיום

סינמא (IrAr < E) f. **sīnama** cinema, movie.

סיסייארי (K < P سيسالك wagtail) f. **sīsıyyāri** a kind of large bird; stork (=H חֲסִידָה, BT3).

סיסנא (K; cf. OA/OS סוֹסַאן < P **sōsan** › Ar سوسن) m. **sīsına** lily; **sūsın-u-halālat** various flowers; סיסנה **sīsıne** p.n.f. Susan (NT+).

סיפא (OA) m. **sēpa** sword; v. ג-ר-ש; pendant-charm shaped as sword with engraved Hebrew letters against evil spirits (NT+).

סיפכא (< K?) **sīpaka** fine, elegant person; pl.

sīpakat (Pol 110; PolG); cf. גנדאיא, תרלאל.

סי-צאלא (K) inv. **sē-ṣāla** a three-year-old (=H מְשֻׁלָּשׁ, BT1).

ס-י-ר, צ-י-ר II (Ar) ⁺**s-y-r** to saunter, walk for pleasure; זלה למציורה גאוד גנתיה **zılle lmṣayōre gāwıd gınte(h)** He went to stroll inside his garden (NT5 402).

סיר v. סור

סירא v. י-ס-ר

סיראנה v. סהראנה

סירכתא (< K) **sīrıkta** garlic; cf. תומא.

סירמואי v. סרניאא

סכאכה v. סכתא

סכאנא, סכונא (< ס-כ-נ) m. **sakā/ōna** resident, dweller (NT+).

סכווא, סוכוא (OS ܣܘܟܘܐ) m. **sı/üxwa** clear blue sky, fine weather (cf. PolG) [Khan **sixwa**].

סכופא (< ס-כ-פ) m. **saxōpa** flour jar (which is inverted to pour the flour out); **sōm saxōpa** false ('inverted, upside down') fast.

ס-כ-ט (Ar) **s-x-ṭ** to detest (NT).

ס-כ-י 1 (OA/OS סחי wash onself, bathe) **s-x-y** to swim, bathe in a river (only) (Z); IV to wash the body (NT) (NT+).

ס-כ-י 2 (Ar) **s-x-y** to bestow, be generous; **hāl mā dsāxe lıbbox** Give as much as your heart is generously inclined; cf. סכייה.

סכי (Ar) inv. **saxi** generous (=H נָדִיב, BT2).

סכייה (Ar) f. **saxīye** free will or thanksgiving offering (=H נְדִיבִים עֲדָבָה/תּוֹדָה, BT3, PolG).

סכינא 1 (OA/OS סַכִּינָא) f. **skīna** (Z), **sikkína** (Gz73 84), knife; pl. **skīne, sikkíne** (Gz); **skīn šaḥīṭa** ritual slaughtering knife [Khan 580 **skita**, pl. **skinye**].

סכינא 2, סכנתא (< ס-כ-נ) p.p. **skīna, skınta** dweller; calm; **lıbbe skīna** his mind at ease (PolG).

סכלא (OA) adj. ignorant, infant (?) (NT4).

ס-כ-נ (Ar) **s-k-n** to dwell; calm down (vi); IV to let reside, restore, install.

סכנה (H) f. **sakkāna** danger (BaBin 24).

ס-כ-פ (OA/OS סחף) **s-x-p/f** to fall on the face; turn upside down (PolG; SaAC 3); cf. סכופא.

ס-כ-ר, צ-כ-ר (Ar) ⁺**s-k-r** (cf. PolG) to be drunk; IV to intoxicate, to intentionally let someone drink a lot (NT+).

סכרא 1 (Ar) m. ⁺**sıkra** intoxication.

סכרא 2, סכרה, צעכרא (Ar?) f. ⁺**sa(ᶜ)karra(ḥ), sakkáraḥ** (PolG), anguish; **ṣaᶜkarrıd lıbbu turra/tūla** They calmed down, their anguish subsided (cf. PolG).

סכתא (OA/OS/Mand סִיכְּתָא < Ak **sikkātu**) f. **sıkta** peg; pl. סכיאתא **sıkyāta** (NT); **sıkkāke** (Z) (OA pl. סִיכֵּי) [Khan 580 **sikta**, pl. **sikke**].

סכתג'י (T) m. **saxtači** plotter, false accuser.

סכתר (T 'fuck off') **sıktır** a must dispersion; - **qahwasi** the third coffee after which all divan's guests have to leave (PolU 60).

סל (Ar) m. **sıl** tuberculosis.

סלאלתא (Ar) f. **sılālıta** offsprings, dynasty (NT5 385).

סלאמה (Ar) f. **salāme** peace, wellness; pl. סלאמתייה **salāmatīye** (NT)/סְלַמִיתְיַתַא **sılāmıtyāta** (=H שְׁלָמִים, BT3, D).

סלאמתי, צלאמתי (K < Ar سلامة) ⁺**slāmatī** good health (cf. PolG); **ʾāzētun bıslāmatī** Bon Voyage! May you go safely!

ס-ל-ב (Ar) **s-l-b** to plunder (=H בָּזַז, BT1).

סלוגתי (K/Ar **sālık**?) pl. **saluġte** current news (RivSh 262) [cf. MacD 265 **ṣāliġ**].

סלוה (Ar) pl. **salwe** quails (NT3); cf. קטאאה, מן 2.

ס-ל-ט, צ-ל-ט II (Ar) **s/ṣ-l-ṭ** to set up as a ruler (NT+).

סלטנה (Ar) f. **salṭane** royalty (PolU 102), luxurious living (PolU 8).

ס-ל-י II (Ar) **s-l-y** to console, to entertain (NT); cf. תסל.

סליחות (H) pl. ⁺**salīḥōt** penitential hymns; **yarxıd** - the month of Ellul (SaAC 12); pl. of pl. ⁺**salīḥōsat**.

סלים (Ar) inv. **salīm** well, one in good health; פלטלו סלים ובסימה **plıṭlu salim ubassīme** They came out alive and well (NT); **ṣāx-salīm** alive and well (Z, PolG); pl. סלימין **salīmīn**.

סליקתא (Ar) f. **salīqıta** disposition (PolU 344).

סלכ (IrAr < En) m. **sılk** rayon (artificial silk).

ס-ל-מ (Ar) **s-l-m** to come out safe; סלמלו מן מותא **slımlu mın mōta** They were safe from death (NT5 384); II to greet, welcome; to deliver (RiVSh 245); cf. ת-ס-ל-מ (NT+).

סלעא (Ar) f. **sılᶜa** merchandise (NT).

ס-ל-פ II (Ar) **s-l-f** to deduct interest (=H הִשִּׁיךְ, BT5).

סלף (Ar) **salaf** interest on loan (=H נֶשֶׁךְ, BT2).

סלקא (OA) m. **sılqa** beet; **ṭarpı(d) sılqe** beet's green leaves (used in soups) (cf. PolG) [Khan 580 **silqa** beetroot, K < Ar].

סלשיר (Ar-K?) m. **sallašir** deep basket; cf. טבק.

סמא, סימא, צמא (K) m. ⁺**sımma** hoof (=H פַּרְסָה, BT2); pl. **ṣımmāme** (BT5).

סמאוי (Ar) inv. **samawi** sky-blue (=H תְּכֵלֶת, BT2).

סמאור (P/K/T < R) **samāwar** samovar.

סמאכא 1, אֶסְמַאכַא (< ס-מ-כ) vn **smāxa** becoming pregnant, pregnancy (=H הֵרָיוֹן, PolG).

סמאכא 2 (JAB < H-OA סְמָכָא authority, basis) **sımmāxa** Rabbinical authorization to be a שוחט; cf. סמכא.

סמאל (H) **sammā'ēl** Sammael, Angel of Death (NT); cf. מלכלמות.

סמאעא (Ar) f. **sammāᶜa** stethoscope (PolU 300).

סמבילה (K) pl. **sımbēle** mustache(s) [Khan 580 **simbla**].

סם המות, סמאמות (H) **sam-(h)ammāweṯ** deadly poison (Sa83c 18, Am; AmU2 10a).

סמוך (H) **sāmux** the Biblical section read before the מפטיר.

סמוקא, סמוקתא (OA סוּמָּקָא, סוּמַּקְתִּי; OS ܣܘܡܩܐ, ܣܘܡܩܬܐ) adj. **smōqa, smuqta** red; **smōqa ᶜılōqa** very healthy (red-radiating); **'aw -** blood (PolG) (NT+).

סמוקה (< סמוקא) pl. **smōqe** sumac (acid spice).

סמוקנאיא, סמוקניתא (< סמוקא) adj. **smoqnāya, -nēṯa** reddish (RivSh 243; PolG).

סמורה v. באיה סמורה

ס-מ-ח 1 II (Ar) **s-m-ḥ** to forgive, permit.

ס-מ-ח 2 II (< IsH שמח?) **s-m-ḥ** rejoice (PolG).

ס-מ-ט (< Ar scald?) **s-m-ṭ** to scrub and clean dishes; **māyıd smāṭa** greasy water.

ס-מ-י (OA/OS/Mand) **s-m-y** to become blind (arch.); cf. ש-ת-ה-ר, ע-מ-י.

סמיד, סֶמִית (Ar/P/OA/OS סְמִידָא < Ak **samīdu**) **semīd/t** (PolG) semolina, fine wheat flour (=H סֹלֶת, BT1, D).

סמידייה (< סמיד) f. **sımmēdīye** dish made of fine flour.

סמיכא v. איאלא

ס-מ-כ (OA/OS סמך support, prop up) **s-m-x** to lean on, uphold (NT); be pregnant (Z, PolG:D); IV to impregnate; cf. א-ב-י 2.

סמכא (OS) **samxa** (leaning) wall or fence (of stones) (AmU2 4b, 5b).

סמכתא (< ס-מ-כ) p.p. **smıxta** pregnant; pl. **smīxe**.(RivSh 143).

ס-מ-מ II (OA) **s-m-m** to poison (vt); become very angry (vi)(SaLH 149; PolG); cf. סאמא.

סממנה (H סממנים?) **sammımāne** (?) exempla, typical savory anecdotes; טלד מחאככני סממנה מרירה מנד שעבוד דמצראיה **ṭlad mḥakaxni — marīre mınnıd šıᶜbūḏ dmıṣrāye** so that we may tell bitter exempla of the enslavement by the Egyptians (NT5 411).

סמסאר (Ar) m. **sımsār** broker (PolG).

סמסארותא (< סמסאר) **sımsārūṯa** brokerage (PolG).

ס-מ-ק (OA/OS/Mand) **s-m-q** to become red; IV to become or make red, to blush, expose to shame (NT+).

סמקא (< ס-מ-ק) m. **sımqa** the red part of meat.

סמרתא (< ?) f. **sımmarta** edge (?), known only as **sımmartıd xāṣa** the edge of the spine near the anus (=H קֻבָּה, anus, vulva, BT4)[< OS ܣܢܩܐ fishing line; spout? cf. MacD 266].

סנאא (OA) m. **san'a, sanā'a** enemy; pl. סנאה, סנאאה, **san'e, sanā'e** (NT).

סנאדא (< ס-נ-ד) m. **sanāda** supporter (=H סוֹמֵךְ, AvidH 67).

סנגׄאק(א) (K/T/Ar) m. **sınjāq(a)** banner (NT, BT).

סנגיתק (K) **sıngıtāq** stonewall (RivSh 157).

ס-נ-ד (Ar) **s-n-d** to support (NT+).

סנד (Ar) m. **sanad** promissory note; pl. **sanāde**.

סנדלתא v. צנדלתא

סנדוק v. צנדוק

סנדן (Ar) m. **sından** anvil; pl. **sındāne**.

סנה v. אלווסנא

סנהדרין (H < Gr) **san(h)aḏrīn** Sanhedrin (NT+).

סנחיריב (H) p.n. **sanḥēriv** Sennacherib (NT3).

סנטא v. צנתא

ס-נ-י, שׂ-נ-י (BT5, D), (OA/OS) **s-n-y** to hate; IV to make hateful (NT+).

סניותא (OA) f. **sanyūṯa** hate.

סניכ, סנך (K?) **sınnik** blight, mildew (=H יֵרָקוֹן, BT5; NTU4 165b); cf. זנכ. [Krotkoff 123 agricultural pest]

סניקא, סנקתא (< ס-נ-ק) p.p. **snīqa, snıqta**

needy; - u'īqa one in tight situation (PolG) (NT+).

סניקותא (< סניקא) **sniqūta** need, necessity (Pol 110).

סנסארא (< ?) m. **sınsāra** spine.

ס-נ-ק (OA) **s-n-q** to need; לא סניק דפקדכלו **la sniq dpaqdaxlu** It isn't necessary to check them (NT407); IV to make needy: **'ilāha la masnıqlōxun** May God never make you needy!(NT+).

סנסלתא (Ar) f. **sınsılta** offsprings; cf. נסלא.

סססא (K **sist** 'fresh, tender') **sıssa** the soft part of seeds such as pumpkin's.

סזגונא, ססגונא (OA) m. **sıs/zgōna** an unknown animal (=H תַּחַשׁ = dolphin?, BT).

סםקה (K **seska**) pl. **sısqe** tiny pieces of deep fried fat, used as stuffing.

סעא, סעאתא v. סאעא

סעאדה (Ar) f. **sa'āde** happiness, luxury (NT+).

סעארה, שְׂעֺרֵי (OA שְׂעָרֵי) **⁺sa'āre** barley (cf. PolG); סערתא **⁺sa'arta** a barley grain; eye-cataract.

ס-ע-ד (Ar) vt/vi **s-'-d** to be happy, successful; **'aya s'ıdla-n'ıdla** She became quite happy with her life; **'ilāha sā'ıdlox** May God help you (said to someone in distress; cf. PolG).

סְעוֹדָה, סעודא, סַעוּדָא (NT3)(H; cf. OA סְעוֹדְתָא) f. **sı'ōda** (Z **sı'ōza**), **sa'ūd/da** (RivSh 190), Jewish festive meal (=H כֵּרָה, PolG); **- dmīse** a meal in the memory of the deceased (PolU 307); - **rēš yarxa/rēš šāta** meal in memory of the deceased one month/a year after one's death (Amedi 70); v. תפלים; pl. **sı'ōdat** (MeAl 188) [Mutz 232 **sa'ōda**; Khan 580 **sa/o'oda**].

סעידא, סעדתא (< ס-ע-ד) p.p. **s'īda, s'ıdta** happy (SaAC 20).

סער (Ar) m. **sı'ır** price (cf. PolG); cf. חקא.

סערתא v. סעארה

ספארה v. ספר

ספאתא v. ספתא

ספדיתא (OA בי סדיא; סַדְיָא [< אסדיא*]; אִיסָדָא; ; פסדיות [< בי סדיות]; OS ܣܘܣܦܐ; cf. Ar وسادة) f. **spadīta** pillow, bolster; pl. **spadyāta** (cf. PolG; but RivSh 265 סִפַּתִי = **sıppāti** ?) [Khan 580 **sawila** pillow].

ספהי(ן) (K) inv. handsome. good, noble; pl. ספהייה **spahīye** (NT2) (NT+).

ספהי(נ)אתותא, סְפַהְיַתִי (< ספהי) f. **spahi(n)yātūta, spahyati** (Am) beauty (PolG), majesty (=H הוֹד, BT4)), praise (H=תְּהִלָּה, AvidH 54, 70).

ספו (< ספתא) m./f. **sıppo** person with large (and ugly) lips.

ספואתא v. ספתא

ספויא (< ס-פ-י) m. **sapōya** snack, wrap sandwich; ישראל כא ספויילו **yisrā'ēl xa sapōyīlu** Israel is just a snack for me (said by Pharaoh); **sapōyıd kālo** bride's wrap (filled with fried eggs, tasted by the bride and then by her unmarried friends for good luck).

ספטא v. צפטא

ס-פ-י (OA to apportion food; cf. H מספוא fodder) **s-p-y** to pour (food), fill (bags) by hands (PolU 252); II to deliver (to enemy); to deliver one's soul, to die (PolG); to entrust (NT).

ספיל (Ar) inv. **safīl** very needy, lowly (NT; cf. Mengozzi 287 'miserable'); miscarrying (=H מְשַׁכֵּלָה, BT2); **'-w-d safil** to bereave (BT3, D); cf. ס-פ-ל.

ספינא (Ar; cf. OA/OS ספינתא) f. **safīna** boat, (Noah's) ark (=H תֵּבָה, BT1); pl. **safīnat** (PolU 312). cf. גמיא, מרכב, פאפור.

ספינדארא (K 'poplar') m. **spindāra** poplar, cedar (=H אֶרֶז, BT3; PolG); v. סרטאיא.

ספיסא, ספסתא (< ס-פ-ס) p.p. **spīsa, spısta** rotten.

ספיקא, ספקתא (< ס-פ-ק) p.p. **spīqa, spıqta** empty; often as hendiadys: **spīqa srīqa** very empty.

סְפִיקוּתָא (< ספיקא) f. **spīqūta** emptiness, in vain (=H לָרִיק, BT3, D).

ספירתו (IrAr < It) m. **spirto** medicinal spirit.

ספכאטר v. סבכאטר

ס-פ-ל II (< ספיל) **s-f-l** to bereave (=H שִׁכֵּל/ שָׁכַל, BT1; PolG).

ספלי (IrAr) inv. **sıfli** inferior person.

ס-פ-ס (< Gr?) **s-p-s** to rot, stink (=H הִבְאִישׁ, BT2; NT5 390) [Garbell 291; MacD 229].

ספסתכה (v. ספיסא) f. **spıstake** messy woman (SaAC 19).

ס-פ-ק (OS) **s-p-q** to be empty; II to empty; cf. ס-ר-ק (NT+).

ס-פ-ר 1 I/II (OS/OA/Mand סבר think, conclude) **s-p-r** to expect, hope (NT, BT; =H שִׂבֵּר, Ruth

1:12)); cf. ספרתא.

ס-פ-ר 2 II (Ar) **s-f-r** to travel; cf. ספר 2.

ספר 1 (H) m. **sēfır** (Bible) book: ספרד שופטים **sıfrıd šōfṭīm** Book of Judges (NT); cf. (תורה) ספר חמש,,.

ספר 2, ספאר (Ar) m. **safar** journey; אאזל אבד ספאר **ʾāzıl ʾıbbıd safar** He travels (NT5 408); הם אוד אילה בספר **ham ʾōd -īle bsafar** also one who is amidst a journey (ibid.); pl. ספארה **safāre**; אודן ספארה **ʾōd̲ın safāre** I travel (a lot).

ספרא, צפרא (Ar صَفرة /T **sofra**) f./m.? **⁺sa/ıfra** table (NT3; NTU4 163a; PolG:m.), leather mat used as table during travel; cf. מיזא שולחן,,; **-ṭām u-ṭām** (magical) table of many superior delicacies (PolU 317).

ספר-בלכ (T **sefer berlik**) **safar bılıık** Turkish mobilization during First World War.

ספרגלא (OS/OA אספרגלא) m. **sparıgla** quince.

ספרג׳י, צפרג׳י (< ספרא) **⁺sıfrači** waiter (Gz).

ספר-טאס (T/IrAr) m. **sıfır-ṭās** lunch/travel box (with 3-4 dishes fastened on top of each other).

ספרתא (OA סברתא) f. **sparta** hope, expectation (BT; = H תִּקְוָה, Ruth 1:12; PolG).

סיפר/ספר (תורה) (H) m. **sēfar (⁺tōra)** the scroll of the Pentateuch; pl. ספרי תורה/תורות **sıfrē ⁺tōra/⁺tōrōt̲** (NT, BaBin 145), **sēfar-⁺tōrat** (Z).

ספתא (OA) f. **sıpt̲a** lip; shore; **sıpse ʾwīzāle** He showed disapproval (by stretching, 'making', the lower lip); **xa sıpsa zwaʾta** a piece of bread (PolG); pl. /ספואתא/סִיפְוָותָא שפאתא/סופאתא **süppāṭa, sıpwāt̲a** (NT5 389; RivSh 97; ZU 73a) (OA סיפוותא, שִׂיפְתָתָא) [Khan 580] **spāla**].

ס-פ-ת-ח III (Ar) **s-f-t-ḥ** to have the first sale in the morning; **hēš lēwın msuftıḥa** I haven't done any business yet.

סקאטא (IrAr?) m. **saqqāṭa** animal interior parts: bowels, liver, lungs, heart.

סקאלי, סקאלייא v. סוקאלי

סקופתא, אִיסְקֻופְתָא (OA איסקופתא/כופתא; OS ܐܣܩܘܦܬܐ <Ak **askuppatu**) f. **(ʾı)squpt̲a** doorpost (=H מַשְׁקוֹף, BT2); pl. **squpyāt̲a**.

ס-ק-ט, צ-ק-ט (Ar) vi **s-q-ṭ** to squat; to fail an exam; stay behind a grade; drop, fall (cf. PolG), land (fly on food).

סקט, צקט, סקטוכא, סקטוכה (Ar-K) **⁺saqat** (inv.), **saqaṭōka** (m.), **saqaṭōke** (f.) a cripple; handicapped (cf. PolG); cf. פלונכא.

סקילא, סקלתא (< ס-ק-ל) adj. **sqīla, sqılta** beautiful (NT+).

סקילותא (< סקילא)f. **sqīlūt̲a** beauty (RivSh 181).

ס-ק-ל (OA/OS/Mand סקל polish, adorn **s-q-l** to become beautiful (cf. PolG); IV (Z/PolG)/ II (NT) to make beautiful (NT5 394); cf. סוקאלי.

סקלה v. י-ס-ק

סר (K) m. **sır(r)** freezing, severe cold; cf. סראריייה, ס-ר-ר.

סר-אבראז (K) adv. **sar-avrāz** up the hill (PolU 63); v. סרנשיף.

סראדא (OA סְרָדָא/OS ܣܪܕܐ) f. **sırrād̲a** (Z **sırrāza**) coarse sieve (BaBin 103); cf. מכלתא; ס-ר-ד.

סראסת (< סר-ראסת*) (P) **sar-rast** straight ahead, direct (route) (NT2; NTU4 151b; PolG).

סראריייה (K) **sarrārīye** vicious cold; cf. סר.

סרבא (K?) **sarva** propriety: **lēwe bsarva dīda** He is not suitable for her (she deserves a better one).

סרבור (K) m. **sarbor** traumatic experience, misfortune: **⁺rāba sarbōre-lu ʾısye brēša** She has many misfortunes; adventure (Pol 110; PolG); cf. סרהאתיכה.

ס-ר-ג II (OA) **s-r-g** to saddle (NT); cf. קורטאנא.

סרגבא (K?) **sarıgva** sudden; **b-** suddenly, ahead of time (PolU 24); cf. ז׳נגבא.

סרגרדאן (P) inv. **sargardān** restless, wanderer (NT).

ס-ר-ד (< סראדא) **s-r-d̲** to sieve with coarse sieve.

סר-דוולת (K/P) **sar-dawlat** lucky, brings luck (PolU 409).

סרדכתא (P/K) f. **sardıkt̲a** molten idol (=H מַסֵּכָה, BT, סֶמֶל ,פֶּסֶל, PolG); covering, curtain (=H פָּרֹכֶת, BT2, Am); pl. סַרְדְכְיָיתָא (=H אֲשֵׁרִים, PolG)

סרדר (P سردار high oficer) **sardar** chief, head of tribe (=H שַׂר, BT); pl. שַׂרְדַארֵי (BT5, D).

ס-ר-ד-ר III (< סרדר) **s-r-d-r** to prevail (=H שָׂרָה, BT1) (NT+).

סרהאתיכה (K) f. **sarhātīke** anecdote, personal incident (cf. PolU 152); cf. סרבור, מעשה.

סרובר (K) **sar-u-bar** preparations, arrangements in advance.

סרוכאני v. סרכאני

סרוקולוך (K) **sar-u-qullox** ugly face (pejor.); **lēbi xāzınne sar-u-qullox dīde** I cannot look at his face!

סרח, סֶרַח (H) p.n. f. **Seraḥ** Serah (RivSh 150).

ס-ר-ט (OA) vi/vt **s-r-ṭ** to cut, slash, bruise.

סרטא (OA) m. **sırṭa** incise, gash (=H שֶׂרֶט, BT3).

סרטאיא (K main branch) m. **sarṭāya** the main and best part of the poplar tree (used for construction and furniture).

סרה-סריאני (K-Ar سر سيران) **sare-seryāni** at the crossroads (=H פֶּתַח עֵינַיִם, BT1).

ס-ר-י (OA/OS/Mand) **s-r-y** to be bad, evil; IV to make evil, to spoil (=H הֵרַע, AvidH 27; PolG) (NT, BT); cf. כ-ר-ו.

סריא, סריתא (< ס-ר-י) p.p. **sırya, srīṯa** evil, bad, sinner (NT, BT).

סריותא (< סריא) f. **sıryūṯa** evilness (NT5 395).

סריכא, סרכתא (< ס-ר-כ) p.p. **srīxa, srıxta** fresh, aggressive, vicious (BaBin 123); **xasse srıxta** coarse lettuce (watered too much).

סריקא, סרקתא (OA/OS) p.p. **srīqa, srıqta** combed (hair); empty (rare); v. ספיקא.

סרי-רא, סר-רה (K) **sarē-ra** start of a road (PolU 15); **dōs sar-re** trail to main road (PolU 258).

ס-ר-כ (OA סרח decay) **s-r-x** to act as powerful, be like an animal; **srıxle-klūle** he has become like a mad dog, aggressive and ill-mannered; cf. צ-ר-ע (NT+) [MacD 267 سرخ be mad or energetic < OS سرخ inflame?]

סרוכאני, סרכהאני, סַרְכַּאנִי, סרכאני (K) **sarek(h)āni, sarukāni, sarkāni** springhead (NT4); water source (=H מִקְוֶה, BT1, Am); spring (=H מַעְיָן, BT3, D).

סרכיתא (< ס-ר-כ) f. **sarraxīṯa** animal-like aggression; cf. כלויתא.

סרכולא, סרכולה (K) **sarkōla** (m.), **-le** (f.), (one) without headdress, bare-headed.

סרכרינכה (< K/P?) f. **sarkarrīnke** wild beast that is assumed to eat man's head'.

סר-לא-הוא (K-Ar?) **sar-la-hawa** light-headed, confused (cf. PolU 237).

סרמוטא (OA סמרטוטא) m. **sırmōṭa** rag.

ס-ר-מ-ט III (< OA מרט) **s-r-m-ṭ** to become a rag, to tear (vi) (=H נִמְרַט, BT3).

סרמייאן (K/P?) m. **sarmiyan** person in charge, leader (Pol 110; PolG).

סרמרגיה (P) f. **sar-merge** on death-bed, on verge of dying (NT).

סרניאא, סִרְנוֹאְתָא, סִירְמוֹאְתָא (P?) **sarnī'a** (m., NT), **sırn/mo'ta** (f., BaBin 162; PolG), grape skin; דלא גטאויה כא סרניאד אנויה **dla gṭāwe xa sırnī'ıd 'ınwe** He is not worth anything ('has the value of a grape skin'); pl. סִירְמוֹאֵי **sırmō'e** grape stones (=H חַרְצַנִּים, BT4, D).

סרנסר (K) **saransar** whole (month, etc.) (PolU 41),

סרנשיף (K) **sarnıšīf** downhill (PolU 63); v. סר-אבראז.

ס-ר-ס-פ III (< ס-ר-פ?) **⁺s-r-s-p** to 'empty' (a store) (=buy without paying), to sup it up (PolU 214); cf. צ-פ-צ-פ.

סרספיאת (< K white head?) pl. **sarspiyat** (?) old women: **baxtāsa** — (Sa83c 36, Am).

סר-עסכר (K) **sar-ʿaskar** chief of army (=H שַׂר צָבָא, BT1).

ס-ר-פ (OS/OA שרף gulp down) **s-r-p** sup up, slurp; IV to feed soup (=H הִלְעִיט, BT1).

סר-פראז (P) inv. **sar-fırāz** proud (PolU 437).

סרפש (< ?) **sarfaš** foot support, inside sole.

ס-ר-ק 1 (OA/OS/Mand) **s-r-q** to comb.

ס-ר-ק 2 (OA/OS) **s-r-q** to become empty; II to empty (NT5 410), to pour, to cast (=H הֶעֱרָה/שָׁפַךְ/יָצַק, BT3; נִצֵּל, AvidH); cf. ס-פ-ק.

ס-ר-ר II2 (<סר) vi **s-r-r** to freeze; **msurırri mqarsa** I froze from (being exposed to) cold.

סר-ראסת* v. סראסת

סר-רש (K 'black-head') inv. **sar-raš** unreliable (human:in sexual relations) (PolU 265).

סרשויה (K) f. **sasršōye** toilet, bathing section.

סרתיכה (K) f. **sartīke** top cream, sweet butter.

סרתירא (P) m. **sar-tīra** arrow-head (NT).

סרתישתה (K) f. **sar-tēšte** light breakfast (before main breakfast) (cf. PolU 124).

סתא, סתה (< ?) f. **sıtta/e** large stone mortar [cf. PolG; Garbell 330 **sitta** stone mortar].

ס-ת-ג̇ v. ס-ג̇-ד

ס-ת-ה-ל III (Ar استأهل) **s-t-h-l** to deserve, be worthy of [1: **mıstōhıl**; 2: **mıstāhıl-**] (NT+).

סתוא (OA/OS/Mand) m. **sıṯwa** (Z **sıswa**) winter.

סת-ו-ג̇-ב III (Ar) **st-w-j-b** to condemn oneself (cf. PolG); cf. ו-ג̇-ב, מסתוג̇בא.

סְתֵיוִיר, אסתיויר, אסתיור, צטויר, סטויר, סתויר (K) ***stawir** (Z), **(ı)stēwir** (NT3; AvidH 49) barren woman; cf. עאקרא.

סתונא v. אסתונא

סתירא, סתירתא (< ס-ת-ר) p.p. **stīra, stırta** modest (BaBin 104).

סת-אל-בלאד (Ar) f. **sıtt-ıl-blād** Baghdad, Mistress of all cities (PolU 90).

סת-ע-ב-ר III (Ar) **st-ʾ-b-r** to contemplate, consider (NT).

ס-ת-ר (OA/Ar) vt/vi **s-t-r** to cover or be covered (for modesty) (PolU 20); **ʾilāha stırre ʾılle** God covered his nakedness (RivSh 119) provide shelter (NT+).

סתר (Ar) **sıtır** decently clothed (PolG); privacy (SaAC 23).

סתרא (Ar ستر veil, cover/OA סִתְרָא secret) m. **sıtra** curtain, cover; genitals: סתרד כורוך לא גאליתן **sıtrıd xōrox la gālētın** Do not uncover your fellow's (wife's) genitals; Do not commit adultery (NT+).

ע (ᶜ)

ע (H) **ᶜāyin** the Hebrew letter 'Ayin; **šōʾi** seventy.

עאבורא (< Ar عبر to cross) m. **ᶜabōra** current, stream (NT3); cf. עברא 1 [cf. MacD 234 **(ᶜ)būrā** 'ford'].

עאגורא v. אאגורא

עאדה (Ar) f. **ᶜāde** habit, custom (=H תְּעוּדָה, Ruth 4:7); menstrual period (=H אֹרַח נָשִׁים, BT1); **baxta ᶜade** plain woman (PolG); pl. **ᶜādat** (NT+).

עאדתי (< עאדה) inv. **ᶜādati** plain, regular (PolU 129).

עאדל (Ar) inv. **ᶜādıl** honest (NT+).

עאווז (Ar) **ᶜawaz** shortage, scarcity, need; pl. עאווזת, עאווזה, עוויזת **ᶜawāze/ᶜawazat** (NT), **ᶜawēzat** (BaBin 64); cf. ע-י-ז.

עאלאיא, עאלַא (K **ala** < Ar علاية/عَلَم?) f. **ᶜālāya** (Z), **ᶜāla** (D) flag, banner (=H נֵס, BT4, D); pl. **ᶜālāyat**; cf. עלם 2.

עאלם 1 (Ar) m. **ᶜālam** world; כולא עאלם **kulla ᶜālam** all world, each and every one; **ᶜālam dar ᶜalam** all the masses, multitudes; הל עאלם **hal ᶜālam** forever; cf. דונייה, אבד 2 עולם,. (NT+).

עאלם 2 (Ar) **ᶜālım** learned person; pl. **ᶜālımīn** (NT+).

עאלם 3 v. עלם 2

עאנא (IrAr) f. **ᶜāna** Ana, a small Iraqi coin.

עאניכא v. עניכא

עאסא v. אאסא

עאעה (K?< P ققّه children's excrement) pl. **ᶜāᶜe** 'kaka' (baby talk); cf. גוגה.

עאעו (< עאעה) **ᶜāᶜo** child who soils its pants; cf. גוגו.

עאצרתא, עאצר (Ar عصر) **ᶜāṣırta** (Z), **ᶜāṣır** (BT1, Am; RivSh 124), evening, late afternoon; pl. **ᶜāṣıryāṯa** (BaBin 11).

עאקל 1 (Ar) inv. **ᶜāqıl** wise, smart.

עאקל 2, עקל (Ar عقل) m. **ᶜāqıl** (Z, NT), **ᶜaqıl** (+NT), reason, mind, knowledge (=H דַּעַת, BT1); מעקל דידה **mᶜaqıl dīde** on his own initiative; **mār ta ᶜāqılox** Imagine! (Pol 105); **ᶜaqıl did šımšon mınne ıšqılla** She confounded Samson (RivSh 220); **ᶜāqıle ⁺rāba qṭeʾle ʾılla** He liked her very much (PolG); **ᶜāqıla pıšle bıd do qōma spahin** She kept thinking of that beautiful body (PolG); cf. עקלותא, בי-עאקל; v. ק-ט-א (NT+).

עאקל-מנד (Ar-P) inv. **ᶜāqıl-mand** wise,smart (PolU 77).

עאקרא, עאקרה (Ar) f. **ᶜāqıra/e** barren woman (NT3); cf. סתויר.

עאשר v. אשר

עבאדא 1 (< ע-ב-ד) m. **ᶜabāda** worshipper; pl. עבדין, עבאד **ᶜabād(īn)** (?) (NT2).

עבאדא 2 (< ע-ב-ד) v.n. **ᶜbāda** worship (NT+).

ע-ב-ד (Ar) **ᶜ-b-d** to worship; cf. כ-ד-ם (NT+).

עבד (Ar) **ᶜabd** Negro (slave) (PolG).

עבדה (Ar) f. **ᶜabde** Negress.

עבדאלא (K < Ar servant of God) m. **ᶜabdāla** simple honest man (SaNR); cf. עבד(א)ל.

עבד(א)ל, עבדלא (K-Ar) p.n.m. **ᶜabdal, ⁺ᶜabdalla** Abdul, Abdalla; cf. עובדיה.

עבודה זרה, ע"ז (H) **ᶜavōḏa** (Z **ᶜavōza**) **⁺zāra** idol worship (NT+).

עבודת פרעה (H) **ʾavōzas parᶜo** hard labor (Z).

ע-ב-י v. א-ב-י 2

עבייה (Ar) f. **ᶜabayye** cloak, mantle (=H אַדֶּרֶת, BT1).

עביק (Ar) m. **ᶜabīq** perfume (NT3); cf. ע-ב-ק.

עבירה (H) f. **⁺ᶜavēra** transgression; pl. עבירות **ᶜavērōṯ** (ZU 72b) (NT+).

ע-ב-ק (Ar) **ᶜ-b-q** to be suffused with smoke, smell; choke (crying) (PolG); cf. עביק (NT+).

עברא 1 (< Ar عبر cross?) f. **⁺ᶜabra** raft, barge made of logs tied over inflated shipskins; cf. עאבורא [cf. K **ḥabra** barque, Jaba-Justi 140; H עֲבָרָה raft, 2 Sam 19:19; OA ארבא 'boat']; pl. **⁺ᶜabre**.

עברא 2 (Ar) f. **ᶜıbra** warning (NT5 386).

עבראיא, עבריתא (H) **ᶜıvrāya, ᶜıvrēṯa** a Hebrew (RivSh 140) fellow Jew (Z, cryptic for **hōḏāya**); pl. עִבְרַיֵא (!) **ᶜıbrāye** (?) (RivSh 136).

עגאלא (IrAr < Ar عقال) f. **ᶜagāla** rope ring put over head scarf; cf. אקאלא

עגונה (H) **ᶜagūna** deserted wife (NT); cf.

מעוגנת.

עגיד (Ar عقيد officer) m. **ᶜagid** nobleman, hero, knight; pl. **ᶜagide** (=H פָּרָשִׁים, BT1).

עגל (H) **ᶜēġıl** Golden Calf (NT; Sa83c 18, Am).

עג'אלא v. הגעלה

עגֿאלא (Ar) f. **ᶜajāla** carriage; pl. עֲגַאלֵי **ᶜajāle** (=H עֲגָלוֹת, BT1, D; cf. RivSh 149).

ע-גֿ-ב II (Ar) **ᶜ-j-b** to wonder, to be amazed; cf. א-גֿ-ב (NT+).

עגֿב (Ar) m. **ᶜajab** wonder; **ma ᶜajab** How come (I wonder)?!; **p-y-š b-** to be in incredibly bad condition; pl. עגֿאבה, עגֿבי/ואתא **ᶜajābe, ᶜajaby/wāṯa** (NT), **ᶜajabāṯa** (AvidH 68).

עגֿגֿ (Ar) m. **ᶜıjaj** swirling or raised dust; smoke (=H קִיטוֹר, BT1, D); cf. תוז.

עגֿו v. עוגֿו

עגֿובכא, עגֿובכה(Ar-K) adj. **ᶜıjūbka, -ke**, eccentric, peculiar, queer (person).

ע-גֿ-ז (Ar) **ᶜ-j-z** to be weary; - **mın** be sick/tired of; - **mın rōḥāyi** I am tired of my life (PolU 365); IV to exhaust someone; **⁺rāba qam maᶜjızaxlox** We troubled you too much; excuse us (NT+).

עגֿם (Ar) **ᶜajam** Persia, Elam (=H עֵילָם, BT1).

עגֿמאיא, עגֿמיתא (< עגֿם) **ᶜajamāya, -mēṯa,** Persian person, Iranian.

ע-גֿ-ן (Ar) **ᶜ-j-n** to knead (NT5 410); cf. ל-י-ש.

עגֿנא (Ar) f. **ᶜıjna** batch or bowl of dough (=H עֲרִיסָה, BT4) (NT+).

ע-גֿ-ק (< Ar عجق to confuse?) **ᶜ-j-q** to be elated, excited; **⁺rāba ᶜjıqle ⁾ıbba** He was very delighted to see her (cf. Zaken 390; PolG).

עדא (Ar) m. **ᶜıdda** working tool, equipment; pl. **ᶜıdde** (Zaken 387).

עדאב, עודאב (Ar) m. **ᶜaḏāb** (Z **ᶜazāb**), **ᶜuḏāb** (NT), suffering.

ע-ד-ב II (Ar) **ᶜ-ḏ-b** (Z **ᶜ-z-b**) to torture, punish, trouble (NT+).

עדב/פ (< IrAr?) m. **ᶜıdab/p** pus.

ע-ד-ד II2 (Ar) **ᶜ-d-d** to lament, eulogize (NT+).

עדד (Ar) m. **ᶜadad** number, numerical value; detailing; דלא עדד **dla ᶜadad** numerous, numberless; cf. מניאנא.

עדים (H) pl. **ᶜēḏīm** (Z **ᶜēzīm**) witnesses (in Jewish marriage contract); cf. סהדא.

ע-ד-ל II (Ar) **ᶜ-d-l** to straighten, to flatten (NT+).

ע-ד-מ (Ar) vi/vt **ᶜ-d-m** to destroy, abuse; to be destroyed, abused (NT+).

עדרא v. מרים

עהד v. אהד

עואוה v. עויא

עואן (K < Ar) **ᶜawān** enemy (NTU 153b); hostility (NT2) [cf. Mutz 193 **ᶜoynāna** <H עוין].

עואנגֿותא (< עואן) f. **ᶜawānčūṯa** hostility, slander.

עובא (Ar عُبّ/OA עוּבָּא/חוּבָּא) m. **ᶜubba** bosom, breast pocket (RivSh 266).

עובדיה (H) p.n.m. **⁺ᶜavazya** (Z) Obadiah (SaAC 15); cf. עבדאל.

עוגב, עוגיב (< עויא+גיבא) adv. **ᶜōgıb** inside, inwardly.

עוגֿא (Ar عوج bend; عُجّة omelet?) f. **ᶜujja** hunch; thick mess.

עגֿו, עוגֿו (< עוגֿא) inv. **ᶜüjjo** hunchbacked.

ע-ו-ד II (Ar) **ᶜ-w-d** to accustom (NT2).

עון, עוון (H) f. **ᶜāwōn** iniquity (BT1); v. קדאלא; misery, suffering: **ᶜāwōn-īle, hallūle xapča ⁾ixāla** He is (in) misery, give him some food; pl. עוונות **ᶜawōnōṯ** (NT+).

עוויזת v. עאווז

עוטמא v. עטמא

ע-ו-י (Ar/OA) **ᶜ-w-y** to bark, whine; scream (pejor.); complain.

עויא, לעויא (OA גו, לגו) **(l)ᶜōya** inside; **go ᶜōya** inside the room (RivSh 134); cf. עוגב; pl. **ᶜawāwe** indoors (NT+) [cf. Khan 573 **lóᵓa**].

עוינכה (Ar-K) f. **ᶜıwīnke** monocle, eyeglasses. pl. **ᶜıwīnkat**.

עוירא, עוורתא (< ע-ו-ר) p.p. **ᶜwīra, ᶜwırta** cross-eyed; cf. בעויר.

עולבא (OS/Ar sack, box) f. **ᶜulba** bushel (=H אֵיפָה, BT; cf. Segal #140); pl. **ᶜulbe**.

עולבכתא (K < עולבא) f. **ᶜulbıkṯa** (wooden) basket (=H תֵּבָה, BT2); pl. **ᶜulbıkyāṯa**.

עולה (H) **ᶜōla** (biblical) burnt offering (BT3).

עולייא, עוֹלִיתָא (Ar) f. **ᶜōlīya** (Z), **ᶜōlīṯa** (RivPr 210), upper floor, attic, loft.

עולם, עוֹלָא (H) f. **ᶜōlām** (Z), **ᶜōla** (RivSh 181-2; but 282 עוֹלָם, f.), world; a lot: **⁾ixāl ᶜōlām wēle go bēṯu** They have a lot of food in their house; often as hendiadys: **dunye uᶜōlām** great many (people) (cf. BaBin 119); עולם הבא **ᶜōlām habba** the world to come (cf. PolU 290); עולם השפל **ᶜōlām haššēfel** the nether world; עולם כמנהגו נוהג **ᶜōlām kıminhāġō nōhēġ** the world (nature) follows its natural course; cf. עאלם, דונייה; v. אסתאדא.

עומבר v. עמבר, ענבר

עומקה (Ar/OA) pl. **ᶜumqe** deep seas, the abyss (NT).

עומר1, עמר (Ar) m. **⁺ᶜümır** age, lifetime; דלא עמרד ה' **dla ᶜımrıd ʾilāha** (die) untimely, unnaturally (NT5 394, 402); cf. מותא.

עומר 2 v. לג לעומר

עון, עוון (Ar) **ᶜawn** help , assistance (NT).

ע-ו-נ II (< עואן) **ᶜ-w-n** to be hostile; to inform on someone (NT); cf. ע-י-נ 2.

עונא (K **qūn**) **ᶜūna** buttocks, anus (baby talk, or for rhyming: **ʾaw gdāwıq nūne, ktarya ᶜūne** He who catches fish, his buttocks get wet (Segal #47); cf. שרמא.

עֻונְבַּרֵי v. עמבר 1

עונה (H) f. **ᶜōna** conjugal right (BT2).

ע-ו-ק II (Ar) **ᶜ-w-q** to delay; be delayed (NT+).

עוקגא (IrAr) f. **ᶜuqča** heel of shoe; cf. כעבייה.

ע-ו-ר (Ar) vi **ᶜ-w-r** to become cross-eyed; twisted (place) (PolG); cf. עוירא, בעויר.

עורבן (IrAr pl. of **ᶜurbī** 'tribal man') f. **ᶜórban** tribe, tribal unit of housholds (PolU 6); pl. **ᶜorbanat/-ne** (PolU 71).

עורדא (Ar عُرضة 'target') **ᶜorda** war cry by raiders: Give back loot or else... (PolU 54).

עורטיתא (ע-ר-ט >) f. **ᶜurṭīṯa** wind (with sound), fart; v. פושיתא; pl. **ᶜurṭyāṯa**; - **bšırme la ḥmıllu** He was over elated (PolU 369) [Garbell 339 **⁺wirtila**].

עורכ (K **ʾūr** stomach) **ᶜūrık** used only in **qalya** - fried meat of cheap parts (stomach, etc.) bought only by the poor.

עזאזל (H) **ᶜazāzēl** (biblical) Azazel (BT3).

עזאיא (Ar) f. **ᶜazāya** mourning, lamentation; **d-w-q ᶜazāya** to lament, have mourning session (RivSh 222); cf. שין 2, ע-ז-י, מעזייאנה.

עזה v. עזתא

עז וגאל, עז וגל (Ar) **ᶜazz(a)-wa-jal** (?) May (God) be glorified (NT2, NT5 382).

ע-ז-ז II2 (Ar) **ᶜ-z-z** to show respect. NT+

ע-ז-י II (Ar) **ᶜ-z-y** to console, eulogize; cf. עזאיא.

עזיז, עזיזא (Ar) p.n. **ᶜaziz** (m.), **ᶜazīza** (f.), dear.

עזיזא, עזזתא (Ar) adj. **ᶜazīza, ᶜazızta** dear, precious; **ᶜazıztıt lıbba** sweetheart (PolG); pl. עזיזין **ᶜazīzīn**; cf. אעז (NT+).

עזיזותא (< עזיזא) f. **ᶜazīzūṯa** dearness (RivSh 190).

עזימה (Ar) f. **ᶜazīme** banquet, dinner party.

ע-ז-מ (Ar) **ᶜ-z-m** to invite to a banquet; to recite an incantation (**ʾıl** over, upon).

עזרא, עזרו, עאזו (H) p.n.m. **⁺ᶜızra,⁺ᶜızro, ⁺ᶜāzo** Ezra (regular and hypo. forms).

עזרה (H) **ᶜazāra** the Azarah chamber (NT3).

עזתא, עזה (Ar) **ᶜızzıta, ᶜızze** honor, glory (NT+).

עטאייתא (Ar) f. **ᶜaṭāyıta** generous favor, gift, help (PolU 122).

עטארא (Ar) m. **ᶜaṭāra** shopkeeper.

עטארותא (< עטארא) f. **ᶜaṭārūṯa** shop keeping.

עטילא v. בטילא

ע-ט-ל (Ar) vi **ᶜ-ṭ-l** to be delayed, stop (working); **mıṭra ᶜṭılle** The rain stopped; II to delay (vt), keep idle; cf. ע-נ-ט-ל (NT+).

עטמא, עוטמא (OA אטמא, עטמא) f. **ᶜüṭma** thigh; pl. **ᶜüṭmāṯa** (OA אטמהתא, אטמי).

עיאל, עילתא (Ar) **ᶜıyal, ᶜıyalıta** (RivSh 126, 149) children, family; cf. עיל; v. איאלא (NT+).

עיאנא 1 (< ע-י-נ 1) v.n. **ᶜyāna** help (=H עֵזֶר, BT1).

עיאנא 2 (< ע-י-נ 1) m. **ᶜayāna** helper (God) · (BaBin 131).

עיאנא 3 (< ע-י-נ 2) **ᶜayāna** sharpshooter (PolG).

עיאר (Ar) m. **⁺ᶜıyar** weight, measure (=H הִין, BT3, D); pl. **⁺ᶜıyāre**.

ע-י-ב II (Ar) **ᶜ-y-b** to mock, make fun of (cf. PolG) [1:**mōᶜıb**-2/3:**māᶜıb**; 4:**maᶜobe**].

עיבא (Ar) m. **ᶜēba** blemish, disgrace, shameful (act, report); nakedness (=H עֶרְוָה, BT); **nqıble jēbox, mpıqle ᶜēbox** When your pocket has holes, your disgrace is out.

עיבור (H) m. **⁺ᶜıbbur** intercalation, calendar; א-ו-ד עיבור **ʾ-w-ḏ** - to prepare the calendar; ריזד עיבור **rēzıd** - the calculation of the calendar (NT+).

ע-י-ג̆ (Ar?) **⁺ᶜ-y-č** to smear (syrop), to stick

(on one's gums).

עיגז (< Ar عاجز) inv. ᶜējız not feeling well (PolU 318).

עיגזותא (< עיגז) ᶜējızūṯa discomfort (PolU 348).

עידאנא v. אידאנא

עיון (Ar) pl. ᶜıyūn (spiritual) eyes, vision (NT2).

ע-י-ז (Ar عوز) ᶜ-y-z to lack, be missing; **ma gᶜāyızlōxun** What do you need? II/IV **ʾilāha la mᶜāyızlōxun** May God cause you no shortage; cf. עאווז (NT+).

עיל (Ar) **ᶜēl** (tribal Arab) populace (PolU 56).

עילתא v. עיאל

ע-י-נ 1 (< Ar عون) **ᶜ-y-n** to help (God:man); **ʾilāha ᶜāyın** God willing; **ṣurte la qam ᶜēnāle** He felt shy (PolG); cf. א-י-נ (NT+).

ע-י-נ 2 (< ע-ו-נ) **ᶜ-y-n** to target, aim (gun) (PolG); cf. עיאנא 3; II to (maliciously) eye, to lurk (NT); (< OA) to inspect, see (NT5 384).

עין (Ar) adv. **ᶜayn** exactly; **ʾāya ᶜayn mux yımma-la** She is exactly like her mother; **ḥıkkōsa bᶜayna** (He told) the (same) story {itself} exactly (PolU 254).

עין יפה (H) **ᶜēn yāfa** grace; **b** – graciously, pleasingly (PolU 293).

עיינתא (< ע-י-נ 1) f. **ᶜıyanta** help (BaBin 121; **bıd ᶜıyantıt ʾīlāha** By God's help (PolG).

ע-י-פ (Ar) **ᶜ-y-f** to be in despair; **ᶜıfle mın gyāne** He gave up on his life (Avin78, 93).

עיקו v. איקו

עירוב (H) m. **ᶜēruv/f** eruv (a Sabbath law).

ע-י-ש (Ar) **ᶜ-y-š** to live, make a living; IV to provide a living, support (cf. PolG); cf. מעש.

עייש, עיש (Ar) m. **ᶜīš** (Z), **ᶜayš** (NT2; NTU4 163a; Hob89 183), livelihood, way of life (Pol 105); **ᶜīš ʾīqa** poverty (Avin78 93).

עכאברה v. אכאברה

ע-כ-ס (Ar inverse) **ᶜ-k-s** to be cross; **ᶜkısle mınnan** He became angry with us.

על אחת כמה וכמה ,על אכ"ו (H) **ʾal ʾaḥaṯ kammā wëxammā** How much more so (NT); cf.לכתמא.

עלאפא (Ar) m. **ᶜalāfa** seller of grains.

עלאתריכ ,לאתריכ (IrAr/AnAr < E) **(ᶜa)latrīk** electric light.

על באב אלה (Ar) **ʾal bāb ⁺ʾalla** destitute, very poor (PolU 420).

עלג̇ (Ar) m. **ᶜı/alaj** remedy, solution; **la ʾuzlan ču ᶜalaj mınna** We didn't manage to trick her (Socin 163); -? Any solution? (PolU 123).

על דרך הפשט/הדרש (H) **ᶜal dērex hammidrāš/happēšāṭ** according to a homiletical/literal interpretation (NT).

עלה (Ar) f. **ᶜılle** illness, grief; pl. **ᶜıllıtyāṯa**.

על הארץ ועל המזון (H) **ᶜala-ʾāreṣ uᶜala-mmazōn** with **p-y-š** to be very poor, be left with nothing; cf. מים אחרונים חובה.

עלו-עלו (K) m. **ᶜalo-ᶜalo** turkey; pl. **ᶜalō-ᶜalōyat**.

עלוג̇ה (IrAr < P آلوچه) pl. **ᶜallūje** small yellow plums (Hob89 182).

עלווסנא v. אלווסנא

עלוקא, עלוקתא (< ע-ל-ק) adj. **ᶜılōqa, ᶜıluqta** radiating, healthy (person); v. סמוקא.

עלוקתא (< OA עקל to curve?) **ᶜaluqta** winding (road): אורכא פלמתא ועלוקתא **ʾurxa ⁺plımta u** — curved and winding road (NTU4 159a).

ע-ל-י II (Ar) vt **ᶜ-l-y** to fly way up; מעאלתו אך כיפא גו מקלאא **mᶜālıttu ʾıx kēpa go mıqlāʾa** You fly them up as a stone by a projectile (NT5 388); carry up and away.

עליו השלום, ע"ה (H) **ᶜalāwa haššālom** peace be upon him (said about deceased Rabbis).

עליכאנא, עליכנתא (< עלכ) adj. **ᶜıllēkāna, -kanta**, viscous, 'chewy'.

עליכם שלום v. שלום עליכם

עליק, עֲלִיקָא (Ar) m. **ᶜaliq(a)**, fodder (hanging on animal's neck) (=H מִסְפּוֹא, BT1; RivSh 130); pl. **ᶜalīqe** (Socin 162).

עלכ (Ar) m. **ᶜılık** chewing gum; cf. מסתכה.

ע-ל-מ (Ar) **ᶜ-l-m** to know, learn, find out, be expert; IV to inform, let know; cf. מעלם (NT+).

עלם 1 (Ar) m. **ᶜılm** knowledge, learning, wisdom (NT).

עלם 2, עאלם (Ar) **ᶜalam** flag, banner (=H נֵס, BT4; cf. עאלאיא.

עלמודא (IrAr < It **alla moda**) adv. **ᶜalmōda** (woman dressed) in European style (vs. traditional Kurdish).

ע-ל-ע-ל III (Ar عنعن sigh, moan?) **ᶜ-l-ᶜ-l** to

torment (someone by not doing what is expected), to give someone a hard time (child moaning and nagging his mother).

עלעליתא (< ע-ל-ע-ל) f. **ᶜalᶜalīṯa** torment (=H תַּשְׁנִיק, AlfH 61), pester.

ע-ל-פ II (Ar) **ᶜ-l-f** to be healthy, robust; מְיְעֻולְפֵי (=H בְּרִיאִים, PolG); cf. מעלופיית.

ע-ל-ק (Ar علق catch) **ᶜ-l-q** to (search and) find; **la ᶜlıqle bʾīzan čımındi** We didn't find any bargain, to earn (Avin78 93); to touch (Hob89 215; PolG); to meet: **ᶜlıqle bxa naša** He met a person (by chance)(cf. Pol 105); to hit a target; to be kindled; **ʾanya ṣīwe la gᶜalqi** These pieces of wood aren't catching fire; to become pregnant (SaAC 20: **basır zılla, ʾāna har jēda ᶜliqli** After she died, I soon became pregnant); II kindle, start fire (cf. א-ל-ק): **máᶜlıqla šrāʾa** Light the lamp! Cf. ת-ע-ל-ק.

עלקוש (Ar القوش/H אלקוש?) **ᶜálquš** Alqush, a village north of Mosul, a reputed site of the shrine of **nāḥum ᶜalqušnāya**, the Biblical prophet Nahum the Elqoshite, which was visited by the Kurdish Jews every Shavuoth.

עלש v. בלש

עם (< ?) **ᶜamm** food, eat (baby talk); cf. אממ.

עמא (Ar) **ᶜama** blindness (a curse said in anger on seeing someone stumble over something).

ע-מ/נ-ב-ר III (< עמבר 1) **⁺ᶜ-m/n-b-r** to store (=H חָמֵשׁ, צָבַר, BT1; כָּמַס, BT5).

עמבר 1, עומבר (Ar عَنبر) m. **⁺ᶜümbar** storage, large pile; pl. עמבארה, עֻונְבָּרֵי, עַמְבָּרֵי **ᶜüm/nbāre** (=H אֲסָמִים, BT5, D), **ᶜambāre** (AvidH 41).

עמבר 2 v. ענבר

עמדייא (K **ᶜamēdi** < Ar عَمـــادِيَه) **ᶜamıdya** Amadiya, (an old Kurdish town with an old Jewish community mentioned already by Benjamin of Tudela, ca. 11th century).

עמדנאיא, עמדניתא (< עמדייא) **ᶜamıdnāya, -nēṯa** one from Amadiya.

עמרצא, עם הארץ (H) **ᶜamma-ʾāreṣ** (Z), **ᶜamaarıṣ** (Hob89 185). **ᶜammareṣa** (Br93 246) boor, unlearned person.

עמוד השחר (H) **ʾammūḏ haššāḥar** dawn (=H הַשַּׁחַר, BT1).

עמוד ענן (H) **ᶜammūḏ ᶜānān** the (biblical) Pillar of Clouds (RivSh 177); cf. אסתונא.

עמום (Ar) f. **ᶜümūm** entire (city) (PolU 148).

עמונאיא, עמוניתא (H) **ᶜammōnāya, -ēṯa** Ammonite (NT, BT); beggar, miser (Z).

עמוקא, עמוקתא (H-OA עמוק deep; dark color; cf. OA עַמֵּק to deepen; to make darker) adj. **ᶜamūqa, ᶜamuqta** dark (tea, liquid); deep (=H עָמֹק, BT3, D); cf. גמואא, ע-מ-ק.

ע-מ-י (Ar) **ᶜ-m-y** to be blind, unaware, fool.

עמיא, עמיתא (< ע-מ-י) p.p. **ᶜımya, ᶜmīṯa** fool, unaware, indiscriminate.

עמידה (H) f. **ᶜamīḏa** (Z **ᶜamīza**) Amida prayer (SaLH 147).

ע-מ-ל II (Ar) **ᶜ-m-l** to trade, negotiate (NT+).

עמ(א)ל (Ar) m. **ᶜama/āl** deed, business; often as hendiadys: **šūlu uᶜamālu pıšle ʾāwa** That became their constant occupation (PolU 3); pl. עמאלה **ᶜamāle** (NT+).

עמלייא (Ar) f. **ᶜamalīya** (modern) surgery; **ᶜuzle** - He had a surgery.

עמלק, מן זרע עמלק (H) p.n. **ᶜamālēq, mın zēraᶜ ᶜamalēq** descendant of Amalek, Amalekite, a vicious person.

עמנואל, עמו (H) p.n.m. **ᶜımmānūʾēl, ᶜammo** (hypo.) Emmanuel, Manuel.

ע-מ-ק (< עמיקא) **ᶜ-m-q** to become dark (tea).

ע-מ-ר II (Ar أمـــر) **⁺ᶜ-m-r** to boss someone around; **la ⁺mᶜamrıt ʾılli** Don't boss me around (cf. א-מ-ר 2); to care, show concern; לא פיש מעאמרבו **la pīš mᶜāmırbu** He (God) doesn't care about them anymore (NT5 396).

עמר v. עומר 1, אמר

עמרצא v. עם הארץ

ע-מ-ש (Ar be blear-eyed; restore?) **ᶜ-m-š** to prosper, be materially content.

ען, ענד, עינד (Ar) prep.**ᶜan(nıd), ᶜınnıd** (+NT), about, regarding; **ʾurri ᶜanne** I forgave him, I yielded to his will.

ענאבה (Ar انياب 'fangs'?) pl. **ᶜınnābe** teeth(?) of an old she-ass) (PolU 431).

ענאייתא (Ar) f. **ᶜınāyıta** care, interest (NT+).

ע-נ-ב-ר v. ע-מ-ב-ר

ענבר, עמבר, עומבר (Ar) m. **ʾan/mbar, ᶜumbar**, ambergris, amber perfume; pl. מסכו עומבארה **mısk-u-ᶜumbāre** (AmU2 2b) (NT+).

ענגליזי v. אנגליזי

ענגאצה v. אנגאצה

ענג'יל v. אנג'יל

ע-נ-ת v. ע-נ-ד
ענו, עֲנָיו (H) m. ᶜānāw humble (BT4).
ענווה (H) ᶜanāwa humility (AmU2 5b).
ע-נ-ט-ל III (< ע-ט-ל) ᶜ-n-ṭ-l to be delayed, hampered (sarc.).
עני (H) ᶜāni poor person; pl. עניים ᶜaniyīm (NT+).
ענייד (< Ar عناد) ᶜınyad mutual resistance: **mpıllu l-** they (brothers) became against each other (PolU 172); cf. ענתותא, ע-נ-ת.
עניות (H; cf. OA עֲנִיוּתָא) f. ᶜınyūṯ (Z ᶜınyūs; +PolG: ᶜanyūṯ) poverty (=H עֳנִי, BT1); cf. דקדוקין.
עניכה, עניכא (H-K) ᶜānīka (m.), ᶜanīke (f.), poor, wretched; **ᶜānīka dgo mıdraš** very poor (lit. a poor man who [has to live] in school/synagogue).
עני מעונה (H) ᶜāni mıᶜunne very poor.
עניאן, ענין (H) ᶜınyān issue, matter (NT); בד ענין **bıd** — seriously (BaBin 163; NTU4 184).
ע-נ-כ-ר III (Ar انكار denial) vi ᶜ-n-k-r to be obstinate, to refuse (=H מֵאֵן, BT1; cf. PolG); cf. נ-כ-ר, ר-כ-ר 2.
עֲנָנֵי כָּבוֹד, ענני כבוד (H) pl. ᶜanane kāvōḏ the clouds of divine Glory (NT, RivSh 164).
ענס וגנס (Ar أنس وجن) ᶜıns-u-jıns humans or demons, usually said about a desolate place that has no sign of life of any kind (cf. Br93 199); **la ᶜıns ula jıns** neither...nor (PolG).
ענסאן v. אנסאן
ענפרם (IrAr/P ʾ/ʾāfarīm/n) ᶜanfarım bravo! — **ṯālox** Bravo to you! (PolU 245).
ענקא (Ar عُنق/OA עונקא) m. ᶜanqa neck (?), only in **ᶜanqe turre** He is totally exhausted (lit., his neck has broken); cf. קדלא.
ענקצתי (K < Ar عن قصد) adv. ᶜanqaṣti on purpose, with malicious intent (=H בְּזָדוֹן, BT5).
ע-נ-ד, ע-נ-ת II (Ar عند) vt ᶜ-n-t/d to refuse, oppose (NT; Sa83c 26, Am; PolG); cf. ענייד.
ענתותא (< ע-נ-ת) ᶜınatūṯa coercion (NT2); דלא ענתותא **dla** —voluntarily (NTU4 149a).
עסכר v. אסכר
עסכרייא (Ar) f. ᶜaskarīya military service (SaAC 8)

עסלי (Ar) inv. ᶜasli brown, honey-colored.
עסר v. עאצרתא
עפו (Ar) ᶜafu amnesty; ʾ-w-ḏ ᶜafu to pardon (prisoner) (MeAl 181).
ע-פ-י (Ar) ᶜ-f-y to forgive, yield, show mercy.
ע-פ-נ (Ar) ᶜ-f-n to become moldy, rotten.
עפצא (OS/OA עפצא, אפצא; Ar عفص) m. ᶜapṣa gallnut.; pl. ᶜapṣe.
עפריכה (K-Ar?) ᶜafrīke some kind of fish; pl. ᶜafrīkat (PolU 263, 434).
עצא (Ar) m. ᶜaṣṣa stick, cane; pl. ᶜaṣṣāye.
ע-צ-י (Ar) ᶜ-ṣ-y to rebel, be difficult; be stuck, delayed (Z); **ᶜṣēle bqanāne** He felt totally at a loss (NT+).
עציא, עציתא (< ע-צ-י) p.p. ᶜıṣya, ᶜṣīṯa fortified; difficult; rebellious; strict (oath) (PolG) (NT+).
עציותא (< עציא) f. ᶜıṣyūṯa rebellion, crime (=H פֶּשַׁע, BT1).
עצל, עציל (K < Ar اصل) m. ᶜaṣıl (good) origin; v. בי-עצל; the main thing: עַצִיל פְּלְכַאנַא ᶜaṣıl **pılxāna** the main thing is working, having a job (RivPr 212).
עצלאיא, עצליתא (< עצל) ᶜaṣlāya. -ēṯa of good quality, kind, noble, citizen (=H אֶזְרָח, BT2); בנונד עצלאייה **bnōnıd ᶜaṣlāye** decent people.
עצלאיותא (< עצלאיא) n. abst. ᶜaṣlāyūṯa decency (PolUR 47).
עצמות (H bones) ᶜaṣamōṯ (Z -ōs) difficult, rigid person; cf. עצעוץ.
עצעוץ (Ar) m. ᶜaṣᶜuṣ tail bone (=H עָצֶה, BT3); difficult person; cf. עצמות.
ע-צ-ר (Ar/OA עצר/אצר) ᶜ-ṣ-r to squeeze, press (grapes), wring (NT+).
עצים, אעצים (Ar) inv. ᶜazīm, ıᶜzīm (?) (NT2), numerous, great (NT+).
ע-צ-מ (Ar) ᶜ-z-m to increase; II glorify (NT+).
עצמת (Ar) ᶜazamat (?) multitudes; **ᶜazamat nāše** throngs of people (NT2).
עקאב (Ar) ᶜıqāb punishment, bitter end (NT).
עקאר (Ar) ᶜaqār estates, farms.
ע-ק-ד (Ar) ᶜ-q-d to congeal, freeze: **xızyawāsa ᶜqıdlu** Her breasts were too hard (to nurse); were full, firm (=H נכונו, AvidH 37).
עקושא, עקושתא (OA אֲקוּשָׁא, עקושא hard; OS ܥܩܘܫܐ erection of penis; SokBA 160) adj. ᶜaqūša, ᶜaqušta thick (liquid, soup), humorless (talk, person); cf. ע-ק-ש [cf.

Garbell 311 **yaqūša**].

עקידה (דיצחק) (H) f. **ᶜaqēḏa (dyıṣḥaq)** the Binding (of Isaac) (NT3).

עקיקי, עקיקא (Ar) **ᶜaqīqi/a** carnelian (pearl) (NT3).

עקל v. עאקל 2

עקלותא (< עאקל 2) **ᶜaqlūṯa** cleverness; cf. -בי עקלותא (NT+).

ע-ק-ש (OA אקש become hard < *עקש) **ᶜ-q-š** to become thick (soup, liquid); cf. עקושא (NT+) [cf. MacD 19 **āqiš/qāʾiš** 'freeze, be cold' (food, person)].

ערבאב (Ar/K?) inv. **ᶜarbāb** smart, intelligent (PolU 122).

ערביתא, ערבאיא (Ar) **ᶜarabāya, -bēṯa** an Arab, Ishmaelite (BT1; RivSh 140).

ערבאנא (Ar) f. **ᶜarabāna** carriage (pulled by horse); pl. **ᶜarabānat** (cf. PolG); cf. ערבייה.

ערבה, עראבא (H) f. **⁺ᶜarāva** willow (used for לולב); **lēl** - the vigilant night of the seventh day of Succoth (= ליל הושענא רבא; Amedi 55).

ערבי (Ar) **ᶜárabi** Arabic (language) (SaAC 17).

ערבייה (Ar) f. **ᶜarabīye** carriage; pl. **ᶜarabīyat** (PolG); cf. ערבאנא.

ערביסתאן (K/P) **ᶜarabistān** Arabia (PolU 55).

ערבית (H) f. **ᶜarviṯ** the daily evening prayer.

ערב רב, ערברב, עֵרֶב רַאב (H) **⁺ᶜēriv-rav** the mixed multitudes; the riffraff (=H אֲסַפְסוּף, BT4) (NT+).

ע-ר-ג̇ II (Ar) **ᶜ-r-j** to limp (=H יָקַע/צָלַע, BT1).

ערגא, ערג̇ה (< ע-ר-ג̇) **ᶜarja** (m.), **ᶜarje** (f.) lame (=H פִּסֵּחַ/נָתוּק, BT3; cf. PolG).

ערדכן (K?) **ᶜardaxan** junk storage room.

ערודין, עראדין (Ar اراض?) **ᶜarō/āḏın** Aradhin (village west of Amidya, with a very small Jewish community).

עֶרְוַוה (H) **ᶜırwa** nakedness, genitals (BT3, D).

ערז (K < Ar عرض) m. **ᶜarz** honor, repute; only in **ᶜarza qam tāwırre** He blasphemed her dignity (by curses, etc.); cf. בי-ערז.

ע-ר-ט (OS; cf. Ar ضرط) **ᶜ-r-ṭ** to break wind (with sound); cf. מערטו/עורטיתא/פ-ש-י [MacD 244, 288 **ᶜ-r-ṭ/r-ᶜ-ṭ** 'pedere cum sonito'].

ע-ר-י II (Ar عرو bond) **ᶜ-r-y** to solder (PolG).

עארישה, ערישה (< Ar?) **ᶜarīše** branches (?), huts (?): אבד עארישה דידה מועלקכלוך **ʾıbbıd ᶜarīše dīde muᶜlıqaxlox** At his (=Satan's) branches you hanged us (NTU4 164a).

ערמותא v. ארמותא

ערנווא v. ארנווא

ערקין, ערקי (Ar عرق; T/K **rākī**) m. **ᶜaraqin** (Z; PolG), **ᶜaraqi** (NT5 409), arrack, raki; pl. **ᶜaraqīne** (PolU 221).

ערש (Ar) **ᶜarš** the Divine throne (NT).

ע-ש-י II (Ar) **ᶜ-š-y** to eat supper (Hob89 217).

עשיר (H) **ᶜāšīr** wealthy (NT); cf. אתירא.

עשירתא (K < Ar) f. **ᶜašīrıta** tribe, clan, people (=H קהל, NT5 401); pl. עשירתיאתא, עשרייאתא, **ᶜašīrıtyāṯa**, **ᶜašrıyāṯa** (AmU2 5a).

ע-ש-ק (Ar) **ᶜ-š-q** to be in love, desire (=H חָשַׁק, BT1); פיכיה...אהנון אילו עשקלו **fēke...ʾahnun ʾıllu ᶜšıqlu** They desired the fruits (AmU1 79a); **ᶜšıqlu lxāuxıt** They fell in love; **ᶜšıqle ʾılla** He desired her (NT+).

עשק (Ar) m. **ᶜıšq** passion, (ardor of) love, desire (=H תְּשׁוּקָה, BT1); cf. הבינותא.

עשקוייכא (< עשק) **ᶜıšqōyīka** philanderer, dandy.

ע-ש-ר II (Ar) **ᶜ-š-r** to tithe (=H עִשֵּׂר, BT1); cf. מעשר.

עשר אאית, עשראיית, עַשְׁרַאיַאת (Ar) **ᶜaš(ı)r-(ʾ)āyāt** the Ten Commandments (NT).

עשרת הדברות, עֲשֶׂר דִּבְּרוֹת (H) **ᶜēser dıbrōṯ** (RivSh 186), **⁺ᶜasēres haddıbrōs** (Z) the Ten Commandments.

עשרים וארבע (H) **ᶜısrim wıʾarbaᶜ** the Twenty Four (Books of the Jewish Bible) (NT3).

עשר מכות (H) **ᶜeser makkōṯ** the ten plagues (of Egypt)(NT); used as a curse after one farts (RivPr #94); **— hāwe go lıbbe** May the Ten Plagues strike his heart; cf. מכות מצרים.

עתו (< K **qito**; cf. קותא) m. **ᶜıto** little one, tiny fellow (=baby, toddler) (baby talk).

עָתִיד (H) **ᶜāṯīḏ** expecting, awaiting (BT5, D).

עתמאת (Ar) **ᶜatamāt** deep darkness (NT).

ע-ת-ר (Ar) **ᶜ-ṯ-r** to stumble, trip (NT); IV to cause one to stumble (NTU4 183a).

פ, פּ (p)

פ, ף (H) pē kafūfa/pašūṭa non-final/final (bent, stretched) Pe; ⁺tmāne eighty.

פאוה v. ה-ו-י

פאטכתא (K) f. pāṭıkta back of the neck; pl. pāṭıkyāta.

פאי-דוס (K/T be inactive, stop work) ⁺pāy dōs Put down arms, war is over! (PolU 142).

פאכא, פכתא (OS ﻓﻘﺤﺔ) adj. pāxa , paxta bland, lacking salt; cf. פכיהא.

פאכית(א) (T/K/IrAr < E) f. ⁺pākēt(a) packet of cigarettes; pl. ⁺pākētat.

פאלא 1 (OS ﻓﺠﻼ; OA פּוּגְלָא) m. peʾla radish [AK puglu; Ar fu/ijl; Mutz 217 pella; Khan 577 pela].

פאלא 2, פלא (K pēl) m. peʾla (Z), pa/ella (?) (NT2) wave; pl. peʾle (Z), פַּלֵּי, פלה palle (NT5 387, AvidH 53).

פאלא 3 (OA פעלא) m. paʾla manual laborer.

פאלבן (K < P پهلوان) m. ⁺palavan acrobat, tightrope walker (cf. PolG).

פאלבנותא (< פאלבן) n. abst. ⁺palavanūta acrobatics.

פאלותא (< פאלא 3) paʾlūta manual labor.

פאלטו (T/IrAr < Fr paletot) pālṭo (women's) overcoat.

פאפא, פאפר-פרנג (T/IrAr) ⁺pāpa, ⁺pāpır(i) ⁺fırrang Pope (of the Franks) (PolU 38); cf. באבא.

פאפור (K/AnAr< Ar بابور < It vapore) m. ⁺pāpur ship, steamship; pl. ⁺pāpūre (MeAl 190).

פאצכובי (K wild sheep) m. pāṣkūvi deer; pl. פַּצְכּוּבִיֵּיאת paṣkūvīyat (=H אַיָּל, PolG).

פאקז' (K) inv. pāqıž clean; cf. פ-ק-ז'; v. פיס.

פארא (T) m. pāra coin; pāra xwāra ta yōma kōma (Save) a white (silver) coin for a black day (hard times); pl. pāre money; pāre daqīqe small change.

פארגא (P) f. ⁺parča segment of textile, cotton or linen cloth; pl. ⁺parče.

פארזונ(כא) (K filter bag)m. ⁺pārzun(ka) woven back-bag in which Kurdish women carry their babies while working.

פארז, פארס (K/P پرهیز; > OA פרהז to avoid) pārız/s diet, abstinence; d-w-q - to be on a diet (SaAC 13, 21); cf. פ-ר-ז.

פאשא (T) m. ⁺pāša nobleman, pasha; pl. פאשאיה pāšāye (NT, Z, RivSh 279), פַּשַׁוַת pāšawāt (RivSh 277).

פאשבא v. ברא-פאשבא

פאשבי(נ)כה (K) f. pāšıvī(n)ke back yard (PolU 13).

פאשיבה (K) f. ⁺pāšīve late night meal.

פאשיזינכה (K) pāš(y)ızīnke back bag, travel bag (PolU 111, 224, 227); cf. כורג̇ניאתא.

פאשפאשכי (K)pāšpāški backwards (PolU 217).

פאשרוז'(ותא) (K) pāšrōž(ūta) end of days, the days-to-come; pl. פאשרווזאתא -žawāta. (NT2, NT5 394, RivSh 276).

פאתא (OA) f. pata (Z pāsa) face, surface; פאתא בפאתא pāta bpāta face to face (NT3); pāse kumta embarassed; v. פ-י-, כ-ו-ר, אימי מ; pl. patwāta cheeks (Pol 109).

פג̇ולכתא (K?) f. pıččōlıkta small bundle, swaddling clothes, diaper; pl. -yāta.

פ-ג̇-ל (K?) vt/vi ⁺p-č-l to make or be messy, sticky; cf. פג̇ליסכה [cf. MacD 251: be crooked, perverse < pātil to twist?].

פדומא (OA פְּדאמא < P padām) m. pıddōma stopper, plug [cf. Ar فدام mouth cover; MacD 254 pandām dam (no source given); K pāldān shove].

פהנא (K) m. pehna kick; m-x-y - to kick; mxēle - ldawılte He kicked his own fortune (PolG).

פ-ה-ר II (OS) p-h-r to yawn.

פואאנא, פואנתא (< פואה) pōʾāna, -ʾanta humorist.

פואה (OS ﻓﻮﻫﺎ enjoyment?) pl. humorous anecdotes.

פוג̇ (K/T) inv. pūč empty inside (nut); kulla gēza ʾıl pūč All (this) results in nothing (PolG).

פוג̇א-שולת (K) pūča-šōlat silly activity, foolish affair.

פּוּגְיֵיתוּתָא (< פוג̇) pučyātūta vanity, nothingness (=H תֹּהוּ, הֶבֶל, PolG).

פודרא (K/IrAr It) ⁺podra talc powder.

פוזא (K nose, face) ⁺pōza 'sour face'; face (and

upper body) (Pol 109; PolG; PolU 375).

פוטיפר (< H?) p.n.m. pōṭipar Potiphar (name of a legendary king) (PolU 384).

פוכא (OA פוחא) **pōxa** (Z), **pūxa** (BT1, Am), wind, air (Pol 109); cf. פ-כ-פ-כ, פ-י-כ.

פויא v. ה-ו-י

פוכתא (OS ܦܘܟܬܐ) f. **pukta** belch, hiccup; pl. **pukyāta**.

פול (K/P/IrAr) **pūl** postage stamp [Khan 577 **pūla** coin, piece].

פולא (< פול) **pūla** coin, money, in: **la pāra ula** - not any kind of money (PolU 229).

פולאד, פולאת (P/Ar) **pōlad/t** (Z -z/s) steel, very strong: **ʾāwa ʾalās pōlas-īlu ʾılle** He has tireless feet; **ṣurtıd pōlaz** shameless.

פוליס (IrAr/T/K En) **⁺pōlīs** police(man); pl. **⁺pōlīṣe** (PolU 294), **⁺pōlīṣat** (PolU 294).

פולכא (K P پول) m. **pūlaka** fish-scale; pl. **pūlakat** (=H קַשְׂקֶשֶׂת, BT3, Z, D); cf. פלסא.

פומא v. פמא

פוסטא (IrAr/T < It) **⁺posta** post, mail; **qınyānıd** - mail carrier mule

פוסטצ'י (T) **⁺postači** mailman.

פופלין (IrAr < En) m. **poplīn** poplin.

פוצאני, פַּצְנִיֵי (K) f. **puṣāni** (Z, BT2), **paṣnīye** (=H שֶׁבַח, הַלֵּל AvidH 54, 68), praise, hymn.

פוקא (OS) m. **pōqa** nostril; pl. **pōqāqe** (cf. PolG) [Khan 577 **poqa** nose].

פוקראתא (OS vertebra) pl. **puqrāta** tonsils; **puqrase mpıllu** He has tonsillitis.

פורא (K) m. **pōra** wild rooster (PolU 3); cf. דיכלא פורא.

פוראאיא, פוראיתא (OA פרע) **purʾāya, purʾēta** uncovered, mostly in hendyadis: **šulxāya-purʾāya** very poor (naked uncovered).

פורענות (H) **purʿānūt** tribulation (NT).

פורתא (K) f. **purta** animal's shed, hair, fur (cf. PolU 373)

פוש (K) m. **pūš** straw, dry grass; **pūš-u-palaš** all kinds of straw (PolU 19, 436).

פושייא (K/P) f. **pōšīya** turban, head scarf [Khan 577 **poši** veil].

פושתכה, פושתכ(א) (K/IrAr queer) **puštak(a), -ke** lout, bad character (PolU 343).

פותא (K) **pūta** care **la ʾuzle-ba ču pūta** He didn't take care of her, didn't show any interest in her.

פותאנא, פותנתא (< פוג'/K **pūt** weak, discolored?) **pūtāna, pūtanta** rotten, porous inside.

פותינה (IrAr < Fr **bottines**) pl. **pōtıne** boots; cf. גזמה, פצטאלה.

פזמון (H) m. **pızmon** Hebrew hymn for Sabbath and Holiday; pl. **pızmōne** (MeAl 188).

פזרוכה (K) f. **pızrūke** cold wind and heavy rain, storm (cf. PolG).

פז'גוז'א v. פשכא 2

פ-ז'-ד-ג III (K?) **p-ž-d-g** to tear to pieces, destroy something for lack of care.

פטוכא 1, פטוכתא (< פ-ט-כ) adj. **pṭōxa, pṭuxta** wide, broad [Khan 576 **paṭūxa**].

פטוכא 2 (< פ-ט-כ) **paṭōxa** cake of dried manure (used as fuel by the poor).

פטירא (OA) **paṭīra** unleavened bread (NT3; BT2; PolG); but Z only pl. **paṭīre**; v. אידא 2 [cf. Khan 576 **paṭīre**].

פ-ט-כ (OA בטח be at ease/Ar فطح be broad, flat) **p-ṭ-x** to lie flat, sit broadly; II to make flat, spread over (=H רוֹקַע, AvidH 66).

פטכות(א), פוטכות(א) (< פ-ט-כ) f. **pı/üṭxūt(a)** width (cf. PolG) (NT+).

פטריכ (T< Gr) **paṭrık** patriarch (cf. PolU 286).

פיאיא, פיינא (K) **⁺payāya** (Z, RivSh 176), **payāna** (NT5 396), pedestrian, foot soldier (=H רַגְלִי, BT4) (NT+).

פיאלא (K/T < P پیاله < Gr) f. **p(ı)yāla** drinking glass [cf. Garbel 325 **⁺pyala** goblet, tumbler, m.; Khan 577 cup, phial].

פייא-סבכ (K) inv. **⁺paya-sıvık** light-footed, energized (PolU 112).

פִּיַא-רֵיכֵי (K) f. **⁺payā-rēke** pedestrian road (cf. PolU 13); pl. פִּיַא-רֵיכַאת **payā-rēkat** (=H מְסִלּוֹת, PolG).

פיב(א), פיוא (K) adv. **pēv(a)** (Z), **pēwa** (NT5 399), onwards, thereafter; **matta upēva. mıdyo pıf/pēva** (PolG), from now on; **mtam upēva** from there on (NT+).

פיבו (< K measured?) inv. **pīvo** shallow (river in the summer).

פיגוהרכאנה (K) **pēguhırkāne** bartering of sisters for marriage.

פיג'ין (< ?) **pējın** faint sound, echo; v. חס.

פיצ'כה (K **pēček** winding) f. **pēčake** whirlpool (in a river).

פיצ'כתא (K) **pēčıkta** swaddled baby (PolU 79).

פ-י-ד 1 II (< פיידא) **p-y-d** to be available, exist.

פ-י-ד 2 (< Ar فات ?) **p-y-d** to pass: **ʾırōtıd pıdla** past Friday; cross (river) (PolG:D).

פיידא (P) inv. **payda** available, existent; **p-y-š payda** to be available (NT).

פיוכא, פיוכתא (< פ-י-כ) **payūxa, payuxta** airy, cool (NTU4 161b); cf. פוכא.

פ-י-כ (OA פוח) **p-y-x** to become cooler; **dunye pıxla** The weather (world) cooled down; טלד פיכא כמתא דיהון **t̲lad pēxa xımta dōhun** So that their heat cools off (NT5 409); **lıbbe pıxle** He felt happy, his wish was satisfied; IV to cool (vt), to air; make one's heart happy: **gōr ḥayya, lıbbi māpıxle** Marry early, make me happy! (cf. PolG).

פיכוארין (K) m. **pēxwārin** condiment, any food added to bread.

פיכולה (< K/P barefoot?) pl. **pēkōle** foot soldiers (Sa83c 18, Am).

פילא (K?) **pēla** kind of fabric (PolU 214).

פילבתא (K) f. **pēlavta** slipper; **-ox plımta** (He never said to him:) Your shoe is crooked (= the slightest of criticism) (PolU 275); pl. **pēlāve** (cf. Ruth 4:7-8; PolG) [Khan 577 **perāw**; pl. **perāve**].

פילוסוף (H < Gr) **pīlōsōf** (?) philosopher (NT).

פִּינְגָבֵי (K) **pingāve** footsteps (RivSh 129); cf. גאבה.

פינחס, פינחוס, פינו (H) p.n.m. **pinḥas** (Z), **pinḥos** (NT5 406), **pīno** (hypo.) Phineas.

פינשכ (K?) inv. **penšak** leading (mule) (PolU 84); cf. פהנא ?

פיס, פיסכא, פיסכה (K) **pīs** (inv.), **pīsaka** (m.), **pīsake** (f.), filthy; **pīse pāqıž** dirty-clean (sarcastic of filthy woman who 'cleans' one mess by creating another); v. פ-ק-ז', פאקז'

פיסא (< P) **pēsa** small copper coin (PolU 307).

פסמיר v. פיס אמירה

פייסגל (IrAr < En) m. ⁺**pāysıgıl** bicycle.

פ-י-ק 1 v. נ-פ-ק

פ-י-ק 2 (OA פקק to block) **p-y-q** to become still; cf. פיקא.

פיקא (OS) **pī/ēqa** dumb, still (NT).

פיקה (< נ-פ-ק?) pl. **pīqe** soft/noisy excrement.

פיקו (< פיקה) **pīqo** little soiler (endearing term for baby).

פיקייע (<H/OA פקיח smart?) **pēqīyaᶜ** only with **ṣurtıd pēqīyaᶜ** shameless face, impudent.

פירה, פירכה (K) f. **pīre, pīrake** old woman; pl. **pīrakat** (PolU 58), **pīrat** (PolU 324); cf. דאפירכה.

פירוזא (P) **pīrōza** turquoise (NT3; H נֹפֶךְ, BT2, D).

פירוס (K < P پیروز favored by fortune) inv. **pīros** safe (to eat) unpoisioned (PolU 193).

פִּירְזִכְּתָא (< פ-ר-ז-א) f. **pırzıkt̲a** skin rash, scar (lit. bread crust); pl. פִּירְזִכְּיַיאתָא (=H צָרֶבֶת/ סַפַּחַת, BT3, D).

פ-י-ש (OA) **p-y-š** to remain over, stay; become, be; פשלה נפטר **pıšle nıfṭar** He passed away; פשלה מודה **pıšle mōd̲e** He thanked, was grateful; to happen: פשלא אד תקלה אלד ישראל **pıšla ʾad̲ taqqāla ʾıllıd yısrāʾēl** That mishap occurred to Israel; פשלא בצראכא She began shouting; לביה גפאייש **lıbbe gpāyıš** He feels insulted, angry, sad (cf. PolG); **la pēšınwa š-dunye basır mōse** (I wish) I did not survive him (PolU 435); v. לבא; IV to leave a residue (PolG: Exod. 12:10) (NT+).

פיש (< פ-י-ש) **pīš** (there is/are) still (cf. NT5 385, 406), already (PolG); לא, לפיש פיש **la-pīš** (there is/are) no more; never again.

פישגאב (K front eyed) inv. **pēščāv** vigilant, alert, energetic (PolU 115); cf. גארגאב.

פישייה (K) adv. **pēšīye** towards, ahead.

פישכש (K/P) n/inv **pēškıš** great gift (PolU 246); good-looking (PolU 307).

פישמאלכה (K) f. **pēšmālke** apron for adults.

פיש-מירגה (K) f. **pēš-mērge** oasis; cf. מירגיה.

פִּישְׁרַא (< פסרא meat?) **pišra** (?) stalk, stem (=H גִּבְעֹל; PolG:Ex 9:31; perhaps error for פִּשְׁתָּה ?); cf. גוזכתא.

פישת-ראצת (< K **pišt-rāst** straight back? cf. Ar ظهر) adv. **pēšt rāṣt** surely, clearly (PolG).

פיתותכא (K **pıtık** small) m. **petutka** remnant.

פ-כ-א II (OS ܦܥܐ) **p-k-ʾ** to belch, have hiccup; cf. פוכתא.

פכא (< פקכא?) m. (embroidered) **paxxa** flower, bud).

פ-כ-ה (OS; OA פכה) **p-k-h** to be weak (tea), dull (color, taste), go numb (heart) (=H פָּג, BT1).

פכיהא, פכיהתא (< פ-כ-ה) adj. **pakīha, pakehta** not sour enough (soup); weak (tea), dull (color); cf. פאכא.

פ-כ-פ-כ III (< פוכא?) **p-x-p-x** to swell, be too ripe, be too mushy.

פלא 1 (K **pel**) ⁺**palla** live coal; pl. ⁺**palle** (cf. PolG); cf. פ-ל-ה-י.

פלא 2 (K **pel** piece) m. **pılla** a bit, dash (of salt, pepper).

פלא 3 v. פאלא 2

פ-ל-א, פ-ל-י I/II (OA פלג/פלע) **p-l-ʾ** (Z, PolG), **p-l-y** (RivSh 170-71), to divide, share; cf. פלגא.

פלאא (< פ-ל-א) **pılʾa** small (=half?) stick; only with **qaṭīʾa-pılʾe**; v. קטיאא.

פלאכא, פלכתא (OA פלחא) **plāxa, plaxta** worker, bread winner; cf. פ-ל-כ.

פלגא, פלגה (OA) m. **palga/e** half, middle; **tūle go palga** He sat in the middle; פלגד לילי **palgıd lēle** (Z **palgızlal**; pl. **palgızlāle**) midnight; **palgıd yōm** noon; כא ופלגה **xa upalge(h)** one and a half; **šātá palgé** a year and half (PolG); v. כמשא; **palgıd-nāša** weak person, weakling; **zılla xa ṣaʿʿa go palga** Meanwhile an hour had passed (cf. RivSh 246); **xsāra umaḥṣul lpalga** loss and profit split in half (PolU 311); pl. **palgāge** (NT+). [Khan 577 **pilga**].

פלגאיא, פלגיתא (OA) adj. **palgāya, palgēṯa** medium, intermediate, one in the middle [Khan 577 **pilgāwa**].

פלגותא (OA) f. **palgūṯa** middle, center; **palgūs baḥḥar** in the middle of the ocean (=H בְּלֶב יָם, BT2; MeAl 190).

פלדא-מלדא (K?) **pılda-mılda** residue of hair or wool, dirt.

פלדין (K?) **paladīn** mad, confused (PolU350).

פ-ל-ה-י III (< פלא+ל-ה-י 1) ⁺**p-l-h-y** to glow, radiate (a person) (cf. PolG).

פלוך, פולוך (K **pelixī**) inv. brittle.

פלוני (H) m. **palōni** angel of death (euph.); strong aggressive person; v. מלאך.

פלונכא, פלונכה (K?) **pallunka, -ke** (f.) cripple, one with twisted spine; cf. סקט.

פ-ל-ט (OA) **p-l-ṭ** to get out (NT); cf. נ-פ-ק; פלטלה מכברה **plıṭle mxabre** He disobeyed his word; פאלט מחקה **pālıṭ mḥaqqe** He will fulfill, execute; פאלט בפאתיה **pālıṭ bpāṯe** He will disobey him; II to issue (vt); take or bring out (NT, BT1, Am; BT2, Arodh; Hob89 218).

פ-ל-י (OAS) **p-l-y** to pick lice from hair.

פלימא, פלמתא (< פ-ל-מ) adj. **plīma, plımta** crooked, twisted, dishonest.

פלימותא (< פלימא) f. ⁺**plīmūṯa** crookedness, injustice (=H עָוֶל, BT3; בְּלִיַּעַל, PolG) (NT+).

פ-ל-כ (OA פלח) **p-l-x** to work, earn a living; IV to employ; cf. פלאכא.

פלכאנא (OA פולחנא) m. **pılxāna** work, job.

פ-ל-מ (OA) ⁺**p-l-m** vt/vi to twist or be twisted; to deviate, to violate (law, BaBin 124); II to bend, twist (Hob 89 218) (NT+).

פלנג (K/P) ⁺**pılıng** tiger; pl. ⁺**pılınge** (PolG).

פ-ל-ע-ז III (< H לעז?) **p-l-ʿ-z** to mock, make fun of (an elder) (BaBin 133; Sa83c 20, Am).

פלש v. פוש

פלשקא (IrAr < K **pelišt** ruin) inv. **palašqa** delapidated, ruined.

פלשתאיא, פלשתנאיא (< H) **pılıšt(ın)āya** Philistine (NT+).

פמא, פומא, פימא, כִימַא, כמא (OA פומא) m. **pı/ümma, kımma** (RivP 211; PolU 207: ChNA), mouth; פמד סיפא **pımmıd sēpa** sword's edge; **qam daryālan go pımmıd nāše** She made us the talk of the town; **bxa pımma** unanimously (MeAl 191); pl. **pı/um(m)āme** (PolG) [cf. Khan 577 **pimma**, pl. **pimmāne**; cf. OA פּוּמָנֵי].

פמפא (IrAr < En) ⁺**pampa** pump.

פנגא (IrAr **panka**) f. ⁺**panga** electric fan.

פנג' (IrAr **banj**) ⁺**panč** anesthetic, narcotic (PolU 239).

פנג'א (K/P) m. ⁺**panja** claw; handful; פַּנְגַ'א שִׁיר **panja-šır** cancer (lion's claw), skin disease (=H חֶרֶס, BT5, D); cancer; v. בחס.

פנג'רוכה (< פנג'רייה) f. **panjarōke** open wound, 'little window' (=H פֶּצַע, BT2, Arodh).

פנג'רייה, פנג'ריכה (K) f. **panjarīye, -rīke** (dim., PolU 149), window; pl. **panjarīyat.**

פנדאן (K/IrAr < En?) ⁺**pandān** fountain (pen); v. קלם פנדאן; פדומא (?).

פ-נ-ד-צ III (K?) **p-n-d-ṣ** to lie down, settle down (said indignantly to hyperactive child): **mpandıṣ lxa dūka** Settle down somewhere (already, you jerk)!

פנזיף (< IrAr **banzīn**) ⁺**panzīf** benzine, gas.

פנזיפכאנא (IrAr) f. ⁺**panzīf-xana** gas station.

פנטרון, פנטלון (IrAr/T < It) m. ⁺**pantárun, pintálon** (Gz73 82), European style pants;

v. שרוול.

פני (K **peni**; cf. OA פְּנָיָא evening) ⁺**panni** shady hidden spot (SaAC 12); pl. פְּנַיָּאת ⁺**panīyat** discolored spots (H בֶּהָרוֹת, BT3, D) (NT+). [cf. MacD 254 **pānyā** shade, shadow < OS evening, lit. turning].

פנים בפנים (H) adv. **pānim bappānim** face to face, very intimately.

פ-ס-א (OA פסע) **p-s-ʾ** to step (in prayer) (cf. RivSh 257).

פסואתא (< פ-ס-א) f. **pasoʾta** step, pace, footstep; pl. פסואה, פסואיאתא **pasōʾe, pasoʾyāṯa** (NT+).

פסוק, פאסוק (H) m. **pāsuq** biblical verse; pl. פסוקי, פסוקים **pasūqe, pasūqim** (NT+).

פ-ס-ח II (H) **p-s-ḥ** to celebrate the Passover Seder as a guest (AvidH 16; AlfH 26; PolG).

פסחא (OA פִּסְחָא; OS فصحا) m. **pısḥa** Passover; v. אידא 2.

פסחאיא, פסחיתא (< פסחא) m. **pısḥāya, -ḥēṯa** guest at Passover Seder.

פסילא, פסלתא (< פ-ס-ל) p.p. **psīla, psılta** unfit.

פסכוית (IrAr < En) **pıskıwīt** biscuit, cookie.

פ-ס-ל (H-OA) **p-s-l** to be or declare unfit (for religious use).

פסל מיכה (H) **pısıl mıxa** lifeless, dummy (like biblical 'Micah's idol').

פסמיר (K son of emir) m. **pısmir** prince, nobleman; pl. פיס אמירה **pīs ʾamīre** (NT4), **pısmīre** (Z).

פ-צ-נ v. פ-ס-נ

פסטפור, פספורט (T < It) ⁺**passaport,** ⁺**pastapor** passport.

פ-ס-פ-ס v. פ-צ-פ-צ 2

פסרא, פִּצְרָא (OA/OS/Mand בשׂרא, ביסרא) m. **pısra, pıṣra** ? (RivSh 245), flesh, meat; **pısra (u)dımma** flesh and blood (human beings); **pısra mnuqza** meat from which the unkosher fat has been removed; **pısır kāke** gums; pl. **pısrāre** meat dishes (cf. PolG; SaAC 20) (NT+)

פסראנא, פסרנתא (< פסרא) **pısrāna, -anta** fleshy.

פסתא 1 (< OS towel?) **pasta** used only in **rīxıd pasta** smell of burning cloth [cf. MacD 255 burning rag or cloth].

פסתא 2 (K **beste**) f. **pasta** a type of Kurdish song [cf. IrAr **pasta** a kind of Iraqi folk song or verse].

פסתא 3 (< K**bestin** to tie) f. **pısta** a tied linen bag tied suspended from a hook used as strainer for preparation of soft cheese.

פעולות (H) **peʿullōṯ** foolish action(s).

פפה (K **pey**) pl. **pappe** feet (mostly baby talk); cf. אקלא.

פפוכ, פפוכה, פפוכתא (K) f. **pappuk(e/ta)** cuckoo (symbol of sorrow in Kurdish folklore); kite, hawk (=H אַיָּה, דָאָה, BT5).

פפוכא, פפוכה/פפוכתא (K) adj. **pappūka, -ūke/-ukta** pitiful; **-ıt xmāra** the poor donkey; pl. **pappūkin** (PolG).

פפץ (T) m. **papaṣ** the king of cards.

פצטאלה (K < Ar بسطار) pl. **pıṣṭāle** (military, farming) boots; cf. פותינה.

פצטווה (K **berstu**) f. **pıṣṭūwe** collar of garment [PolG **pıstūwe**].

פ-צ-י (OA) **p-ṣ-y** to rescue (NTU2 40a).

פאצכובי v. פַּצְכֻּבִּיִּאת

פצמם (K) m. **pıṣmam** cousin,nephew (PolU 1).

פ-ס-נ II, פ-צ-נ (K/P) **p-ṣ-n, p-s-n** (+PolG), to praise (NT+).

פוצאני v. פַּצְנֵיי

פ-צ-פ-צ 1 III (OA נפץ shake off?) **p-ṣ-p-ṣ** to rip off, cause financial loss.

פ-צ-פ-צ 2, פ-ס-פ-ס III (onomat.) **p-ṣ/s-p-ṣ/s** to whisper, murmur [cf. Oraham 409 **pṣpṣ** murmur, hiss].

פצריכ (K?) **paṣrik** grimy rag; pl. **paṣrōke** (PolU 240).

פ-צ-ר-כ III (K?) **p-ṣ-r-k** to become a rag.

פ-ק-א (OA/OS פקע) vt/vi **p-q-ʾ** to split, explode; **pqeʾle mqaḥrīte** He almost died from his excessive grieving; cf. פ-ר-ק-א [Mutz 217 **pʿq~pḥq**].

פקאאד כישה (< פ-ק-א) m. **pqāʾıd xēše** humorist, joker (lit. one who splits -?).

פ-ק-ד (OS) **p-q-ḏ** to examine, check (NT5 406)[MacD 190 visit, look at].

פַּקֶאְתָא (< בקא?) f. **paqeʾta** frog (AvidH 36).

פקואתא 1 (< פ-ק-א) **paqoʾta** only in **xıṭṭe paqoʾta** cracked wheat dish.

פקואתא 2 (=קואתא?) f. **paqoʾta** spider [cf. H פקעת coil of threads?].

פקוסכה (K **pākusk** < OA פקועא) f. **paquske** winter cherry; pl. **paquskat** (=H רְבִיבִים, BT5).

פ-ק-ז' II (< פאקז') vt **p-q-ž** to cleanse (PolU 4).

פקיכא, פקכתא (< פ-ק-כ) p.p. **pqīxa, pqıxta** flowering, blooming; **range pqīxa** looking well (after illness).

פקיעו (< פ-ק-א) inv. **paqīʿo** one with injured eye.

פ-ק-כ (OS ܦܩܚ) **p-q-x** to blossom, sprout; IV to cause to grow (=H הִצְמִיחַ, BT1; NT5 393).

פקכא (OS) m. **pıqxa** plant, sprout (=H צֶמַח, BT1); pl. **pıqxe**.

פקפקושכה (K) f. **paqpaqoške** bubble, balloon, percussion cap.

פר (onomat) **pırrr** bird's take off or landing (PolU 18); cf. בר.

פ-ר-א (OA/OS פרע) **p-r-ʾ** to repay, retribute (NT, BT, arch.).

פרא, פרונכא (K/P) **parra** (m.), **parrōnke** (f.), feather; leaf of thin paper (for cigarette, short letter), little note (PolU 366) (NT+).

פראא (< K/OA?) m. **parʾa** (earth saturation after first/last) rain (=H יוֹרֶה/מַלְקוֹשׁ, BT5); **ʾo mıtra sēle rābıd rāba, parʾa bnāpıl** It has been raining so much, bringing much saturation (?) [cf. K **pele** first appreciable rain of autumn sufficient for ploughing to begin (Wahby-Edmonds 103); cf. פרדא 1.

פראאת הוויאתא (< פ-ר-א) m. **parāʾıt hawūyāṯa** the Benefactor (God) (NT5 391).

פראו, פראותא (< פ-ר-א) f. **parʾo, parʾūṯa** retribution (NTU4 164b; NT5 388, 402).

פראטא (OA/OS portion, tearing) v.n. **prāṭa** hard work; **ʾez-praṭile** Holiday of Hard Labor = Passover, pun with **paṭire** unleavened bread; cf. פרטיתא.

פראשא 1 (OA) ⁺**parāša** horseman, knight (NT).

פראשא 2 (< פ-ר-ש) ⁺**parāša** a little bird that spreads its wings while sitting (according to local folklore, when asked: **parāša , dıqın qāša kmaʾīla** Spreading-bird, how long is the priest's beard? it spreads its wings as an answer).

פרגנדא (P) inv. **parganda** vagabond, disorderly; cf. גירו; pl. **pargandat** odds and ends, remains (in store) (PolU 422).

פרג̆ואתא (< פרזואתא?) f. **pırčoʾta** crushed dumplings mixed with oil; cf. מרג̆ואתא.

פ-ר-ג̆-כ, פ-ר-ג̆-מ III (K?) **p-r-č-k** (Z), **p-r-č-m** (NT), to pluck (feathers; v. פרא; cf. PolG); pinch off, shave smooth (=H מָלַק/קָרַח, BT3, D); v. פרג̆מתא [Garbell 290 crumble].

פ-ר-ג̆-ב/פ III (K?) **p-r-č-v/f** to sit down, settle down (said indignantly to a hyperactive child); cf. פ-נ-ד-צ.

פרג̆ייה v. פרג̆ייה

פ-ר-ג̆-מ v. פ-ר-ג̆-כ

פרג̆ומכתא, פרג̆מתא (K/T) f. **parčamta** (NT), **parčumıkṯa** (Z), forelock; top branch (PolU 31) [Khan 577 **pirča** a hair].

פרדא 1, פרדאיה (K/P) f. **parda, pardāye** (PolG) curtain (=H פָּרֹכֶת/יְרִיעָה, BT2; כַּפֹּרֶת, BT3); פרדא דאינאנה **parda dʾēnāne** curtain of clouds (NT5 404); **- qamēsa/xarēēsa** first/last rain (?); cf. פראא; pl. **pardāṯa**.

פרדא 2 (< ?) **pırda** sole, foot surface (?); only in **la gyātu rıš pırdıd ʾaqle** He is hyperactive [cf. MacD 256 web-footed].

פרדך (K/IrAr) **pardax** drinking glass.

פ-ר-ה, פ-ר-י' (OA) **p-r-h/y** to be abundant, overflow (NT); cf. פ-ר-ה.

פַּרְוַואזַא (P) m. **parwāza** bolt, cross-beam; cf. פשתואנא.

פ-ר-ה-ל III (< פ-ר-ת-כ+ה-ל-ה-ל) **p-r-h-l** to crumble.

פרואר, פִּרְוָור (P پروار nourishment?) **parwār** (?)(NT), **fırwar** (PolG), divine command, utterance (=H פִּי-ה', PolG); **ʾ-w-ḏ -** to command; to follow (God's) orders.

פרוכה (< K **perūk** fine object) pl./f. **parrōke** textiles, cloth, mixed merchandise (PolG).

פָּרוֹכֶת (H) **parōxeṯ** the curtain of tabernacle (BT3, D); cf. פרדא.

פרונכה v. פרא

פ-ר-ז (P **p-r-h-z** > OA פרהז) **p-r-z** to keep away from (evil), protect (God:people against ailments, evil); keep clean and well (clothes); cf. פארז [Garbell 290 **p-h-r-z**]

פ-ר-ז-א III (OS ܦܪܙܠ piece or crust of bread; Ar فرزعه bundle of fodder) **p-r-z-ʾ** to cut bread to small pieces; cf. פירזכתא, פרזואתא.

פרזואה, פרזואיאתא (< פ-ר-ז-א) pl. **pırzōʾe, pırzoʾyāṯa** (PolG), bread crumbs.

פרזואתא (< פ-ר-ז-א) f. **pırzoʾta** dish made of small pieces of bread soaked with hot butter.

פרזלא (OA/OS פַּרְזְלָא) m. **prızla** iron; **prızla**

qarīra la dēqētın Don't hammer cold iron; pl. **prızle** (Zaken 391), **prızlāle** (PolGr 52).

פ-ר-ט (OA/OS split, tear) vt/vi **p-r-ṭ** to tear apart; to fuck (in very vulgar curses); to 'croak' (cf. PolU 304); - **mkıpna** to starve.

פרטאנא (OS ܦܪܛܐܢܐ) m. **parṭe'na** flea [cf. Mutz 217 **partı'nta**]

פרטיתא (< פ-ר-ט) **parraṭīṯa** (Z, PolG: -**ṭīṣa**) excruciating work (PolG); cf. פראטא.

פ-ר-ת/ט-מ III (K **petirme** graft) ***p-r-t-m*** to graft (sarcastic about Gentile wedding): **qāša qam *partımlu lxauxıt*** The priest married (grafted) them to each other [cf. MacD 189 **p-ṭ-r-m** to graft, vaccinate]; cf. נ-ע-ל.

פ-ר-י v. פ-ר-ה

פריהא (< פ-ר-ה) p.p. **prīha** common, abundant (NT).

פרייא (K/P) f. **parīya** a fairy; pl. **parīyat** (PolU 19).

פריס (P/K **ṣanam perest** idolatrous) **parēs** only in **ṣanam parēs** evil, angry, unpleasant person (< idol worshipper).

פרישא (< פ-ר-ש) p.p. **prīša** secluded (NT).

פרישותא, פרשיתא (< פרישא) f. **prīšūṯa**, **prašīṯa** (AvidH 30), seclusion.

פ-ר-כ 1 (OA פרח) **p-r-x** to fly; VI to let fly, send free (a bird) (NT, BT1, Am; RivSh 262).

פ-ר-כ 2 (OS) **p-r-x** to rub (oil) (=H בָּלַל, BT2).

פ-ר-כ 3 II (< פ-ר-ק) **p-r-k** to break off (business partners): **'āni šırīke wēlu bale mpōrıklu** They were partners, but they broke off.

פרכתא, פרכה (K **pir** bridge) f. **parrıkṯa**, **parrıke** (PolG:D), little bridge connecting two roofs or on a brook.

פ-ר-מ (OA/OS פרם chop) **p-r-m** to cut open; dishevel (=H פָּרַם/פָּרַע, BT3, D).

פרמא (< פ-ר-מ) m. **pırma** large slice (of melon, watermelon, etc.).

פרנסה (H) f. **parnāsa** income, livelihood; also a common family name in Z (< OA פרנסא communal leader?)

פ-ר-ס (OA/OS/Mand פרס) vt/vi **p-r-s** to spread; to pitch (tent) (=H נָטָה, BT1).

פרסנאיא, פרסניתא (OA פרסאה/OS ܦܪܣܝܐ) Persian person; cf. עג'מאיא.

פ-ר-פ-א III (OS ܦܪܦܐ) **p-r-p-'** to rinse, wash (dishes, mouth).

פרפוטה (< פ-ר-פ--ט) pl. **pırpōṭe** tatters (PolG).

פ-ר-פ-ט 1 III (< פ-ר-ט) **p-r-p-ṭ** to tear to pieces (vi/vt), wear out (clothes); cf. פרפוטה.

פ-ר-פ-ט 2 III (OA פרפר/K flutter, convolute) **p-r-p-ṭ** to agonize, to 'die' for: **mpurpıṭle ṭāla** He has been dying to marry/have her (cf. PolG) [Mutz 219 ***prpr*** to agonize]

פרפישכ (< פרפרושכה?) inv.**pırpīšek** diligent.

פרפכינה (OS/OA פרפחינא) f. **parpaxīne** purslane [cf. Ar فرفخ; P پربهان].

פ-ר-פ-ס III (< פ-ר-ס) **p-r-p-s** to separate or cut into tiny pieces, spread on larger area.

פ-ר-פ-ש III (< פ-ר-ש) vi **p-r-p-š** to break up, stop fighting (AMU2 10a)

פ-ר-פ-ר III (OA crumble; move in agony) ***p-r-p-r*** to have a noisy diarrhea; cf. פ-ר-פ-ט.

פרפרושכה (K پرپوشك) f. **parparrōške** butterfly; cf. פרפישכ, גְּפגפיסכה

פרצווה (K **parsū**) f. **paraṣūwe** rib cage (=H צֶלַע, BT1, Am); **'āna lag masyanna rıš - dgyāni** I was trying to ignore it (pain) (SaAC 5) [PolG: -**wa**; pl. -**we**]

פ-ר-צ-נ III (< פרצנה) **p-r-ṣ-n** to separate the seeds of pommegranates (PolU 338).

פרצנתא (OS/OA) f. **pırṣınta** kernel, grain; pimple, abcess, scurf (=H נֶתֶק, BT3, D); pl. פרצנה **pırṣıne**; **p- dxmīra** granules of leavened bread (NT5 406); **p- dmaqōze** malignant growth (abcess of burning).

פ-ר-ק (OA) **p-r-q** to desist, to let off; פרוק מני **prōq mınni** Let me (destroy them); **šuqli pruqli** Leave me alone; **balax pruqla mınni** Let me off of your trouble, Go away! (PolU 267); to tear apart (stich); **bala dīde prıqla mınnan** We got rid of him (lit., his trouble); II to redeem, to free, to atone (NT5 386; AvidH 67, 69); IV to separate (people fighting, wrestlers; cf. PolG); cf. פ-ר-כ 3; מפרקאנא.

פ-ר-ק-א III (OS ܦܪܩܐ) vi/vt **p-r-q-'** to crack, peel (plaster, dry skin) (PolG).

פ-ר-ש (OA) vi/vt **p-r-š** to split, be separated; to interpret (MeAl 178); IV to separate (vt) [Ruth 1:17 **mafrıš** (!)=H יַפְרִיד] (NT+).

פרשא (< פ-ר-ש) **parša** (?) estate, plot (NT2).

פרשאנא (< פ-ר-ש) n.ag. **paršāna** explicator; **paršān kōda ukulyāsa** the Explicator of liver and kidneys (=God) (PolU 299).

פרשה (H) f. **⁺parāša** weekly segment of Torah; pl. פרשיות **parašīyōṯ**, **⁺parāše** (NT+).

פרשיתא v. פרישותא

פ-ר-ש-ק III (< OS ܦܫܩ interpret?) to stretch (feet), straighten, smooth (wrinkles) (NT+).

פרת (H/Ar) **pırat** (BT1, Am), **⁺firat** (BT1, Z) Euphrates.

פרתא (< OS/OA bran; SokBA 941) f. **parta** sawdust (PolG).

פרתווה (K **pertew** ray?) f. **pırtuwwe** shed hair (of dogs, cats).

פ-ר-ת-כ 1 III (OS ܦܪܬ) vi/vt **p-r-t-x** to break into bits (=H פָּתַת, BT3), to crumble (NT+).

פ-ר-ת-כ 2 III (K) **p-r-t-k** to snatch (pieces of bread from a loaf).

פרתכא (< פ-ר-ת-כ 1) m. **pırtxa** crumb; pl. פרתכה **pırtxe** (NT5 406).

פרתכתא (< פ-ר-ת-כ 2) f. **pırtıkṯa** tiny piece, a bit.

פ-ר-ת-מ v. פ-ר-ט-מ

פ-ר-ת-פ, פ-ר-ד-ב III (< K?) **p-r-t-f** (NT), **p-r-d-v** (PolG), to cast, throw [cf. Garbell 290 **p-r-t-f** throw].

פרתקאלא (IrAr/T) f. **pırtıqāla** orange; cf. תרנגא.

פ-ש-א (OS ܦܫܪ) **p-š-ʾ** to be come lukewarm.

פשה (K) f. **piše** cat, pussy (baby talk); **piše-piše** calling a cat to come out; cf. קאטא.

פשואא, פשואתא (OS ܦܫܘܪܐ) **pašūʾa, pašoʾta** lukewarm; cf. פ-ש-א

פשורכא, פשורכה (< פ-ש-ר) f. **pašūrka, -e** funny, lighthearted person.

פ-ש-ח (< OA/OS break, tear, detach?) **p-š-ḥ** to wide open (woman: her legs obscenely).

פ-ש-ט (OA) **p-š-ṭ** to stretch (hand, foot) (NT+).

פשט (H) **pıšāṭ, píššaṭ** expanded Neo-Aramaic Bible commentary (NT2); cf. שרח, תפסיר.

פ-ש-ט-ר III (< פ-ש-ט) **p-š-ṭ-r** to stretch, extend.

פ-ש-י II (OA expand, blow up) **p-š-y** to break wind noiselessly; v. ע-ר-ט, מפשיו. [cf. Ar فسّي].

פשיכה-פשאנה (K) f. **pıšīke-pıšāne** milkweed flying seed.

פשיקא, פשוקא, פשקתא (< פ-ש-ק) p.p./adj. **pšīqa/pašūqa pšıqta** joyful (NT5 399; NTU4 152b).

פ-ש-כ 1 II (v. פשכא 2) **p-š-k** to sprout (=H הֵצִיץ, BT4).

פשכא 1 (K portion) **piška** small portion of meat placed over full plate of rice or wheat (cf, PolU 410) [=Khan **piška** sufficiency?]

פשכא 2, פז'גושתא (K **piškuš** button; flower) **piška** sprout, flower (=H נֵץ, BT1); **pižgušta** button (PolG); nipple; pl. **pižgōže** clasps (=H קְרָסִים, BT2; cf. BaBin 121).

פשכולתא (K/P) **pıškulta** little dung ball of sheep; pl. **pıškule** [cf. Garbell 316 **kušpulta**].

פשכורה, בשכורה (< ?) f. **pıškūre** (Z), **bıškūre** (PolG), ceiling [but MacD 305 only **škūrī** (!); perhaps from original ***bēṯ-škūre** ?].

פשלויש (< K/T **bāš-šāwīš** good servant ?) **pašlawīš** waiter (PolG).

פ-ש-מ II (K/P) **p-š-m** regret, feel sorry (NT).

פשפושא (< פ-ש-פ-ש) m. rag; torn, worn out cloth.

פ-ש-פ-ש III (OS ܦܫ be worn; cf. OA פשפש rub?) vi/vt **p-š-p-š** to make or become rags; cf. פשפושא; to break, crash (=H מָחַץ, BT4); fall apart (NT5 389; BaBin 112; RivSh 251)[cf. PolG: נהיה לחתיכות; Garbell 290 rub between the fingers; MacD 192 dissolve, reduce to pulp].

פ-ש-ק (OS make easy, plain) **p-š-q** to be glad, joyful (cf. PolG); cf. פ-ר-ש-ק (NT+) [cf. MacD 260 to stretch, stand upright].

פשק (K?) inv. **pıšq** unimportant, trifle (thing).

פ-ש-ר (OS/OA) **p-š-r** to melt (vi); IV to melt (vt); chew the cud (=H גָּרַר, BT3); v. פשורכה.

פשתואנא, פשתכא (K/P) **pıštawāna, pıštaka** bolt, cross-beam, bar (=H בְּרִיחַ, BT2; דֶּלֶת, PolG).

פשתא-מאזו (K) **pišta-māzo** tenderloin, beef undercut.

פש(ת)בא (K) **piš(t)va** back (euph.), anus; v. ברבא (PolU 71).

פשת-ופשת (K) adv. **pišt-u-pišt** (horse)the

door; **dunye psıxla** There is relief (from making a u-turn, reversing itself.

פישת-ראצת v. פשת-ראסת

פתא (IrAr **putta** < P **pat** soft fine hair?) **pıtta** type of fine silk fabric; **kurtak pıtta** robe made of this fabric (SaAC 9).

פתאנא v. בדאנא

פתואתא v. פאתא

פתולתא (OA פתילתא) f. **pṯulta** (Z **psulta**) wick; chicken-breast meat; pl. **pṯulyāṯa**.

פתחון-פה (H) **piṯhōn pe** pretext, excuse (NT).

פ-ת-כ (OA פתח) vi/vt **p-ṯ-x** (Z **p-s-x**; Hob89 221/RivSh 141/182 **p-t-x**) to open; **darga psıxle** the door opened; **psuxle darga** Open long rain; lit. the world opened); **psıxla ʾıllōhun** Their (economical) situation improved.

פ-ת-ל (OA) **p-t-l** to twist (threads); cf. פ-ת-ל.

פתלא (OA/OS) m. **petla** a spin of the spindle; **gmaxya** - She strikes the spindle for a spin.

פתפותא, פתפאתא (< פ-ת-פ-ת) **pıtpōta** (Z), **patpāta** (Am, Br93 115), worn-out cloth, rag (Z), handkerchief (Am).

פ-ת-פ-ת III (H-OA פתפת; M. Jastrow 1255) **p-t-p-t** to fall apart, shred.

פ, פּ (f)

פאבריקא (Ar<Sp) f. **fābrīqa** factory.

פאיס (Ar فـــايض interest, usury) **fāyıs** tax (PolG).

פאלא 1 (<?) m. **fāla** (large) piece, layer (of meat); pl. **fāle** sheets of paper (Br48 317).

פאל(א) 2 (K<Ar) m. **fāl(a)** fortune, omen; v. פתאח אל פאל.

פאנוזא(K<Ar<Gr) f. ***fānōza** lantern (cf. PolG).

פאנירא (T/K/IrAr<EN) **fānēra** flannel (undershirt); v. צודרא.

פאפא (p astonishing?) inv. **fāfa** simpleton, slightly retarded person.

פאפון (IrAr) m. **fāfōn** aluminum (dish).

פאצוליא (Ar<L) f. **fāṣōlya** beans.

פארגון (IrAr<E) m. **fārgōn** wagon, train car.

פג׳א, פג׳כה (Ar) f. **fıjja, fıjjíke** unripe fruit, especially mellon; pl. **-íkat** (PolU 418).

פהו v. אפרים

פהומא, פהומתא (<פ-ה-מ) **fahōma, fahumta** intelligent (cf. PolG).

פהומותא (<פהומא) f. **fahōmū<u>t</u>a** intelligence, wisdom (=H חָכְמָה, BT2); cf. חוכמה.

פהים (Ar) adj. **fáhim** intelligent (PolGr 36).

פ-ה-מ (Ar) **f-h-m** to understand; IV to explain, make one understand (NT+).

פִיהוֹם, פהם, פוהום (Ar فَهم) m. **fühom, fıhım** (PolG) understanding (=H תְּבוּנָה, BT2).

פכר, פוכור (Ar) m. **fukur, fıkır** thought, opinion, reflection; א-ו-ד פוכור **ʾ-w-<u>d</u> fukur** to be concerned, worry, reflect (NT+).

פועאליה v. פעלה

פוקל עאדה (Ar) adv. **fōq-ıl-ʿāde** (being wise) above the norm, extra-ordinarily (PolU 3).

פוקיר, פוקר (Ar) **fuqır** poverty (NT).

פורג׳א (Ar) **furja** delightful-to-look-at (NT3); cf. פ-ר-ג׳.

פ-ח-ל II (Ar) to forgive, pardon; **xāya mfaḥlālu <u>t</u>ālox** She will willingly give her life for you (PolG); cf. פיחל חלאל.

פחלא (Ar) m. **faḥla** male of domestic animals.

פחש (Ar) **faḥıš** disgrace, abomination; crude, obscene (inv.); cf. פשחתיאתא.(NT+).

פטארא (<פ-ט-ר) vn **fṭāra** eating breakfast; **fṭār ṣōma** fast breaking meal (SaAC 6).

פ-ט-מ (Ar) **f-ṭ-m** to be weaned (=H נִגְמַל, BT1, D); cf. כ-ס-ל.

פטנא v. פתנא

פ-ט-ס (Ar) vt/vi **f-ṭ-s** to suffocate (while sleeping).

פ-ט-פ-ט III (IrAr make a sucking noise) **f-ṭ-f-ṭ** to smoke a cigarette hastily.

פ-ט-ר (Ar) **f-ṭ-r** eat breakfast, break a fast PolG); cf. פטארא; IV to help one to break the fast (**qam maftırāli ʾāya**, SaAC 7).

פיארא, פיירתא (<פ-י-ר) **fayāra, fayarta** flier, flying bird (RivP 211).

פיג׳-ופאג׳כת (K?) pl. **fīč-u-fāčkat** trinkets, silly toys, useless things.

פיידא (Ar) **fayda** use, benefit.

פייה, פייתא (<Ar فئة detachment?) **fīye, fıyyıta** volume, position, value (?) **la kīʾın mayla fıyyıte** I don't know what position/volume he/it holds (=H איזה מקום הוא תופס, PolG); **ʾe mıtaʾ fīye dīda ʾēha-la** This merchandise -its value is this (PolU 400).

פ-י-ח (Ar) vt **f-y-ḥ** to spread in the air (fragrance; cf. PolG) (NT+).

פיחל חלאל (K-Ar فحيل) inv. **fēḥıl ḥalāl** (May one be) totally forgiven! (said after mentioning a deceased one); cf. פ-ח-ל.(PolG)

פ-י-כ (Ar فكّ) vi **f-y-k** to be detached, to come off: גרמיה בד פרשי ופיכי מן לשה **garme bıd parši ufēki mın lašše** His bones will be separated and detached from his flesh (NT5 389); IV to release: מופכלא נוניתא יונה אלד יושא **mōfıkla nunī<u>t</u>a yōna ʾıllıd yōša** The fish released Jonah over the dry land (NT6 135).

פיכא (K<Ar فاكهة) m. **fēka** fruit; **fēkıd kāsa** fruit of the womb, children; pl. **fēke,** פיקיה **fēqe** (Sa83c 22, Am)[Khan 568 **fekye**].

פיל (Ar) m. **fīl** elephant; v. כאכא (NT+).

פיס (K/T<Fez, Morocco) **fēs** felt hat with

tassle, fez, tarboosh.

פ-י-ר (K/Ar فرّ) vi **f-y-r** to fly, run fast, disappear; flee (sleep); IV to fly (vt), throw far away; cut off (head by executioner's sword)(FT) (NT+).

פירסא (K brave<Ar فارس knight) inv. **fērısa** mighty person; pl. פֵּירְסֵי **fērıse** (RivSh 245).

פישכא (K<T) m. **fīšaka** bullet, cartridge; pl. **fīšakat, fīšake** (Zaken 390).

פ-י-ת (Ar) **f-y-t** to pass, slip away, drop off (vi); IV to pass (vt), let go: מופתלוך **mōfıtlox**/ פתלא מאידוך **fıtla m'īdox** You missed (the opportunity) (NT+).

פיתא (<?) inv. **fīta** large, huge, big-ish; **xa fīta** (or **-tıd**) **gōra** a huge person (cf. PolG).

פ-כ-פ-כ III (Ar فكه to jest) **f-k-f-k** to banter; cf. פ-ק-פ-ק.

פ-כ-ר II, ת-פ-כ-ר III, פ-י-כ-ר III (Ar) **f-k-r / t-f-k-r** (Z), **f-ē-k-r** (NT5 386, AvidH 69) to reflect, contemplate [2/3: **mfākır** (Z), **mfēkır** (NT); 4: **mfakōre** (Z), מפיכורה **mfēkōre** NTU 151b].

פלאנא, (כס)פלאנ(כס), ביבאנ(כס) (Ar-K; cf. OS/OA פְּלָן) inv. **flān(a)** so-and-so; **flānkas (bēvankas), flāna nāša(/baxta, nāše)** certain man(/woman/ people); (=H פְּלוֹנִי אַלְמוֹנִי, Ruth 4:1); **flān bēvan** this and that (job) (PolU 80); פלאנא כצייה **flāna xısye** certain eunochs (NT5 394); **flānkaso/-e** Mr./Mrs. So-and-So! Husband!/Wife! (NT+).

פלחנאיה (Ar) pl. **fallahnāye** peasants (Hob89 183).

פלישא, פלשתא (<פ-ל-ש) p.p. **flīša, flıšta** exhausted.

פליתא (Ar فالت) m. **falīta** dissolute (cf. PolG; but Segal #62 **palīta**, by error?); cf. פ-ל-ת.

פלכ (Ar) m. **falak** (wheel of) fortune, fate; pl. פלאכיה **falāke**/ אפלאך **'aflāk**; v. גּרכא, באלא באבה-פלאכה, (NT+).

פ-ל-ס (IrAr to shell beans or peas) **f-l-s** to mash (dates after removing their stones).

פלסא (Ar) m. **fılsa** penny; pl. פלסה **fılse** fish scales (NT); cf. פולכא (NT+).

פ-ל-ע-ג III (Ar فلج+عوج have palsy+be crooked?) **f-l-ʿ-j** to be twisted and ridiculous.

פלפלא (Ar) m. **fılfıla** pepper; **fılfıle kōme/smōqe** black/red peppers.

פלק (Ar) m. **falaq** stick with rope used to tie the feet for beating (used in Jewish school for offences against the teachers).

פלקא (Ar) m. **fılqa** (one half of) split log.

פ-ל-ש (Ar unfold; IrAr demolish) vi/vt **f-l-š** be exhausted; to exhaust someone (cf. PolG).

פ-ל-ת (Ar) **f-l-t** to slip away (**m'īz** from the hand of; cf. PolG); to recover: **lak falta** She will not recover (from clutches of a malignant disease); **flıtlan-ba** we have lost it; to have intercourse (**'ıl** with), be licentious; cf. פליתא; IV to let go, to free.

פנא (Ar) **fana** annihilation; אודלו פנא **'udlu fana** They annihilated (NT5 403); cf. פ-נ-י.

פנ[א]ייה (<פ-נ-י) **fanāye** mortals (NTU4 150b).

פנג̇כתא (K) f. **fınjıkta** kick, jump; pl. **fınjıkyāta**.

פנדא (K/Ar) **fında** candle (NT).

פ-נ-ד-ש, ש-נ-ד-פ III (Ar?) **f-n-d-š** (Z), **š-n-d-f** (BT3, D; =H נָתַץ, פָּרַץ, הָרַס, PolG:D), to destroy, to ruin [Garbell 292 **š-n-d-f** upset, confuse].

פנדשתא (<פ-נ-ד-ש) f. **fandašta** breach (=H פֶּרֶץ, BT1).

פנה (Ar) pl. **fanne** arts (of war) (PolU 173), tricks (PolU 406).

פ-נ-י (Ar) **f-n-y** to perish, be destroyed (=H גָּוַע, BT; cf. PolG); IV to annihilate; cf. פנא.

פנר (K<T<R<Gr **fanarion**) **fanar** lantern (Socin 161, 162); cf. פאנוזא.

פ-נ-ש II (<Ar?) **f-n-š** to fire, let go (PolG).

פסאדותא (<פ-ס-ד) f. **fasādūta** corruption.

פסד (K<Ar فاسد) inv. **fasad** corrupted person.

פ-ס-ח II (<Ar deliver safely?) **f-s-ḥ** to lead (=H הִנְחָה, PolG [1Kg 10:26]).

פ-ס-ד (Ar) **f-s-d** to spoil, corrupt (NT2).

פ-ס-פ-ס III (Ar?) **f-s-f-s** to hesitate (in business), to miss a bargain.

פסתאנא (IrAr/T/P) m. **fıstāna** full length gown (for women and children); פסתאנכא

fıstānka women's shirt [cf. En fustian <L type of cloth made of cotton].

פסתאקא (Ar < P > Gr > L; cf. OS/OA פִּיסְתְּקָא) f. fıstāqa pistachio; fıstaq šāmi cashew nuts; fistaq al-ʿabīd peanuts.

פ-ע-ל (Ar) f-ʿ-l to act lewdly (לְפְעַלָא אִבַּא lıfʿāla ʾıbba =H לְרִבְעָה, BT3, D); cf. -בי פעול; to accomplish (God for men, NT5 400).

פעלה, פעאלה, פועאליה (Ar) pl. fıʿle (Z, cf. PolG), fūʿāle (NT) (evil) deeds.

פצא (Ar) m. fıṣṣa piece, segment (of כותילה) ; stone of ring; kull wēlu xē -ıd ʾasıqse They are all under his control (PolU 293)

פצח, פציח(א) (Ar) fısaḥ, faṣīḥ(a) eloquent, clear voice (NT).

פ-צ-ל II (Ar) f-ṣ-l to cut out, make to measure (Socin 159; to peel (=H פִּצֵּל, BT1, D); to cut into design (=H קִצֵּץ, BT2, D).

פצל (Ar) fısal cutting out, body shape; quota (=H תֹּכֶן, BT2, D; PolG).

פצלא (Ar) m. fasla chapter; segment of פרשה (i.e. שני, שלישי, etc.) q-ṭ-ʾ - to cut an agreement, sign a deal (PolU 128).

פצ̇א (Ar) faza relief, respite (NT3); space; פצ̇א דדונייה faza ddunye world space (NT6 134).

פ-צ̇-ל I/IV f-z-l to grant, endow (NT).

פצ̇לא (Ar) fazla act of kindness, grace (NT).

פקא, פק(ל)ושכא (K feqe<Ar فقيه) m. faqqa, faqqōška, faqlōška, Muslim clergy; pl. faqyāne (PolGr 51); -(l)ōškat (PolU 21, 254).

פקד, פקט (Ar) faqad, faqaṭ only, however (=H אַךְ/רַק, BT1; BaBin 127).

פקושכא v. פקא

פקיר(א) (Ar) inv. faqīr(a) poor (person); pl. פקירין/-ם faqīrīn/m (NT5 408; BaBin 48, 49), faqīre (AvidH 10), faqir (PolG); cf. עניכא.

פקיר וז'אר (K) faqīr-u-žār the poor and the destitute.

פקירושכא, פקירושכה (<פקיר) faqīroška, -ke, a poor person (PolU 408).

פקירתותא (<פקיר) f. faqīratūṯa poverty (cf. PolG); cf. עניות.

פקלושכת v. פקא

פ-ק-ס (Ar) f-q-s to break (an egg); beʾta fqısta egg fried suny side up; be swollen/ cracked (feet) (BT5).

פ-ק-פ-ק III (Ar) f-q-f-q feel elated (cf. PolU 129, 369); cf. פ-כ-פ-כ.

פראיץ' v. פרץ'

פראג'יה (Ar) f. farāje recovery; נכוושותד פראג'יה naxwašūṯıd farāje recoverable disease (NT).

פ-ר-ג̇ 1 II (Ar) f-r-j to view for pleasure (a procession, ceremony); cf. פורג̇א; to dispel (grief); ʾilāha mfārıjla ʾıllox May God ease your affliction (MeAl 188-9) (NT+).

פ-ר-ג̇ 2 II (<פרג̇א) f-r-č to brush (PolG)

פרג̇א (T/K<E) f. fırča brush.

פַּרַגְיֵיה (K<Ar) f. farajīye, para- (PolG), shirt (=H כְּתֹנֶת, BT1, D); cf. צודרא; coat (=H מְעִיל, BT2, D; PolG); cf. סאכו [Garbell 306 faraji].

פרדא (Ar) f. ˙farda bale, full bag; pl. ˙farde (PolU 251).

פ-ר-ה, פ-ר-י (Ar فره bring forth fine children/ فري to fabricate) f-r-h/y to be fertile, abundant; frōhun zōdun be fertile and increase (=H פְּרוּ וּרְבוּ, BT1; נַבֻוְאַה פְּרֵיהְתַא =H חָזוֹן נִפְרָץ, PolG); II/IV to make fertile (=H הִפְרָה, BT1; PolG); cf. פ-ר-י.

פרהאן (Ar ?) fırhān abundance (?): לתלך כולאצי ופרהאן latlax xulāṣi u- You don't have salvation and abundance (?) (NTU4 184b).

פרוג̇כא (Ar-K) m. farrūjka young chicken.

פרור (K فرو) fıror curdled butter (PolU 427).

פרואר v. פְּרְוָור

פ-ר-ז II (Ar) f-r-z to keep away, separate (NT5 407); cf. פ-ר-ז.

פרזן (<פ-ר-ז) m. farzan distinction (in battle), rescue, (God's) help (PolU 287).

פ-ר-ח (Ar) f-r-ḥ to rejoice (NT; BT2, D; RivSh 152, 195; AvidH 10; PolG; PolU 307); scare, startle or be scared (Z only).

פרחא, פַּרְחִיְיֵה (Ar) f. farḥa, farḥīye joy, celebration (=H שִׂמְחָה, BT1/BT5, D; PolG).

פ-ר-י v. פ-ר-ה

פריהא (<פ-ר-ה) p.p. frīha abundant (NT).

פריחא, פרחתא (<פ-ר-ח) p.p. frīḥa, frıḥta glad (NT); frightened (Z).

פריכה (K) f. fırike green ear of corn (=H בִּכּוּרִים/אָבִיב, BT2; PolG) [Garbell 306

farik].

פ-ר-כ (Ar) **f-r-k** to husk (corn), rub or crush between fingers.

פרכא (Ar chick) m. **farxa** chick; cub (=H גּוֹזָל/גּוּר, BT5; PolG).

פרמן (<Ar<T) m. **fırman** order, decree; pl. **fırmāne** (=H [שֶׁפֶר] אִמְרֵי, BT1; cf. PolG).

פ-ר-מ-נ III (<פרמן) **f-r-m-n** to order, issue a decree (=H גָּזַר, AlfH 37; BaBin 62, 125).

פרנא (Ar/T/K; OA פורני<It/L) f. ⁺**fırna** baker's oven, bakery; **laxmıd fırna** baker's bread.

פרנג (P/OS) ⁺**fırrang** (Z) the Franks, Christian Europe; v. פאפא; Edom (NT5 381).

פרנגאיה (<פרנג) pl. **frangāye** Edomites (NT; BaBin 124); - טורת **ṭūrıt** - Mount Seir (= H הר שעיר, NTU4 155b).

פרנגסטאן (<פרנג) **fırrangıstān** The Frank (Christian/European) camp (PolU 91).

פ-ר-נ-ח III (Ar?) **f-r-n-ḥ** to lie down relaxed.

פרנייה (<פרנא) f. **farnīye** thick bread with egg-yolk and sesame spread on its top (Br93 276; ShKC 137).

פרנתייה (<?) **farantīye** (?) a gold coin (NT2; AmU2 4b).

פרסנג (P) m. **farsang** distance measure (12,000 cubits); pl. **farsange** (NT+).

פרסתא (Ar-P فرصت) f. **fırısta** occasion (PolG).

פרפורי (Ar<K/P **fağfūrī**) m. **farfūri** fine porcelain, china [cf. Khan 568 **faxfurta** plate; pl. **faxfurye**].

פ-ר-פ-ט III (Ar) **f-r-f-ṭ** to waste money heedlessly.

פ-ר-פ-ש III (Ar) **f-r-f-š** to refresh oneself, be revived (by eating fruits after heavy meal).

פ-ר-צ' (Ar) **f-r-ẓ** to impose, enjoin (NT).

פרץ' (Ar) **farẓ** precept, (religious) duty (cf. PolG); pl. פראיץ' **farāyız̤** (NT3).

פ-ר-ק (Ar) ⁺**f-r-q** to distinguish, recognize, be able to see; **pıšle sāwōna, lak fārıq** He has aged; he doesn't see well (cf. PolG); מא פריקלי יומא אוהא **ma frıqle yōma ʾōha** How is this day different (BaBin 116); ימא יושא פריקילי **yāma yōša friqīle** He separated between the dry land and the sea (RivSh 199).

פרק (Ar) m. ⁺**farq** difference.

פרקותא (<פרק) f. ⁺**farqūṯa** distinction, discrimination; redemption (=H פְּדוּת, PolG).

פרקסיני (K **ferāq** vessle+**sēni** tray) f. **faraqsēni** large flat tray; cf. צינייא.

פרר (K<Ar فرّار) m. **fırar** fugitive, runaway.

פ-ר-ש II (Ar) ⁺**f-r-š** to cover (floor with carpets), pave (with slates of stone); כֵּיפִּית אִימְפָרוֹשֵׁי **kēpıt ımfarōše** paving stones (=H אַבְנֵי מַשְׂכִּית, BT3, D); v. פ-ר-ש.

פרשא (Ar) m. ⁺**farša** slate (of gold, stone), flintstone; stone (cf. PolG) cf. מרשא **marša**.

פשארי (P<Ar) **fıšāri** vanity, wickedness (=H אָוֶן, BT4); pl. פֶּשַׁרִיֵּיאת **fıšāriyat** (=H הֲבָלִים, BT5, D).

פשחתיאתא (Ar فاحشات) pl. **fašḥıtyāṯa** abominations (NT); cf. פחש.

פ-ש-ת-כ III (<K?) vi/vt **f-š-t-k** to escape, slip through; deliver, give birth (animals, or people, pejorative).

פתאח אל פאל (Ar) **fattāḥ ıl-fāl** fortune teller.

פתויה, פתווה (Ar) f. **fatwe** religious instruction (NT); חכמים לא הולו פתויה **ḥāxāmim la hullu fatwe** The Rabbis didn't instruct (about this) (NT5 406, 410); cf. הלכה.

פ-ת-ח (Ar) **f-t-ḥ** to be wide open (wound).

פ-ת-ל (Ar) vt/vi **f-t-l** to twist; to dance while energetically turning and twisting; cf. פ-ת-ל.

פטנא, פתנא (Ar) f. **fıtna** (NT), **fıṭna** (Z), plot (=H תואנה, NT5 394); quarrel; **ḥajji fıṭna** quarrelsome person.

פתקה (Ar) f. **fatqe** (medical) rupture, hernia, (malignant) growth.

פתרא (K<Ar/IrAr) f. **fıtra** grain measure (1/4 bushel, about 7 kg); biblical omer (BT2).

פ-ת-ש II (Ar) **f-t-š** to search, explore (NT+).

צ(ṣ)

צ, ץ (H) ṣad **kafūfa/pašūṭa** bent (=non final)/stretched (final) **ṣade**; **ʾıčʾi** ninety.

צאבון (Ar < L/Gr) m. **ṣābun** soap; cf. לוחא מגוגא,; pl. **ṣābūne**; **-ıt rīxa** perfumed soaps (PolG).

צאג'לם v. צאך

צאדא (Ar ساده < P) inv. **ṣāda** plain, undiluted.

צאדק (Ar) **ṣādıq** truthful, honest; pl. צאדקין **ṣādıqīn** (NT).

צאך, צאג'לם (K < T) inv. **ṣāx**, **ṣāğlam** wholesome, unbroken; alive, well; **wēlu ṣāx-salīm** They are alive and well; **pıšle ṣāx** He came back to life; **hāwıt ṣāx ubassīma** Be well! (PolG); cf. נצך.

צאכותא (< צאך) f. **ṣāxūṯa** well-being, life, lifetime (RivSh 228); cf. נצכותא.

צאלח (Ar) inv. **ṣālıḥ** sincere, righteous (also m.p.n.); כמילו שפירה וצאלח שואאלוך **kmaylu šapīre uṣālıḥ šoʾālox** How nice and right are your deeds; pl. צאלחין **ṣālıḥīn** (NT) rigeteous people; צָאלִיחֵי **ṣālıḥe** (AvidH 52).

צאלחא (Ar) f.p.n. **ṣālḥa** Salha; cf. צ-ל-ח, צאלח.

צאפוייה (Ar صفّايه) f. **ṣāfōye** metal strainer (cf. PolG); cf. צפיא 2; pl. **ṣāfōyat**.

צאפון v. צפון

צאר (K cold) inv. **ṣār** tasteless; v. טאמצאר.

צארגא, סארגא (P ساروج quicklime?) **ṣārıja** kind of (entrance to?) a valley (?) (PolU 84).

צארות v. צרות

צארותא (< צר-עין?) f. **ṣārūṯa** grudge; **b-** grudgingly, not wholeheartedly.

צבאג'א (Ar) m. **ṣabāğa** dyer; cf. צ-ו-א.

צבאג'ותא (< צבאג'א) **ṣabāğūṯa** dying (SaAC 21).

צובאח v. צבאח

צ-ב-ג', ס-ב-ג' (Ar) **ṣ-b-ğ**, **ⁿs-b-ğ** (RivSh 142), to dye, dip in liquid color.

צבואתא (OS ܨܒܥܐ; OA אצבעתא, אוצבעתא; Mand עצבא) f. **ṣaboʾta** finger, toe; **ṣīta-ṣaboʾta** shorty, little person; pl. **ṣubʾāṯa** (cf. PolG) (OA אַצְבְּעָתָא; OS ܨܒܥܬܐ [Khan 586 **zbuʾta**].

צ-ב-ח 1 II (Ar) **ṣ-b-ḥ** to rise early (=H הִשְׁכִּים, BT).

צ-ב-ח 2 v. ס-ב-ח

צבט v. סבט

צ-ב-י II (< Ar) **ṣ-b-y** be rewarded by raising/having good children: **ʾilāha mṣabēlox** May you enjoy your family.

צבי (Ar youth/H deer) p.n.m. **ṣabi** Sebi.

צביחא (Ar fresh, pretty) p.n.f. Sabiha.

צבייא, צבי (Ar) m./f. **ṣabīya** , **ṣabbi**, tender: **yāla** - tender child(PolU 210); **brāta** - very young girl (PolU 244); **gumlonka ṣabbi** camel with tender meat; cf. צבי.

צ-ב-ר I/II (Ar) **ṣ-b-r** to be patient, content; be in control of oneself (=H הִתְאַפֵּק, BT1); not to be bored, relax (Z); לבי אבוך גמצבראנא **lıbbi ʾıbbox gımṣabrāna** I calm my heart with Thee (BaBin 136) (NT+).

צבר 1 (K < Ar) m. **ṣabır** patience, contentment (Zaken 390); **ṣabran ʾıḏlal bāṯe ʾıbbox** Tonight we'll enjoy your company (PolG); **ṣabri qam mēsıtte** You entertained me, kept me from being bored [Khan 582 **ṣburta**].

צבר 2 (Ar aloe) m. **ṣabır** wormwood (=H לַעֲנָה, BT5); v. צורא.

צברייה (< צבר 1) p.n.f. **ṣabrīya** Sabriya.

צג'אר (Ar) **ṣığar** belittling, disrespect (NT).

צ-ד-א, צ-ד-י II (Ar صدع) **ṣ-d-ʾ/y** to harm, cause pain (NT); violate, rape (=H עִנָּה, BT; PolG).

צדאקא 1, צדקת (H צַדֶּקֶת) f. **ṣaddāqa** (Z, NT5 393; SaAC 15, PolU 400), **ṣaddeqeṯ**(+NT), righteous female (=H אֵשֶׁת חַיִל, Ruth 3:11); v. צדיק; pl. צדאקת **ṣaddāqat** (NT3, Z) [cf. Mutz 227 **ṣaddáqet**].

צדאקא 2, צדקה (H/Ar) f. **ṣadāqa** charity, merit (=H צְדָקָה, BT1); pl. צדאקיה **ṣadāqe** mostly in hendiadys: **mıṣwāye-ṣadāqe** acts of charity.

צדגם (T?) adv. **ṣıddıgım** sulkingly.

צדיק (H) **ṣaddīq** righteous, quiet, gentle (PolU 245); **ṣáddiq** p.n.f.; או צדיק משה **ʾaw ṣaddīq mōše** The righteous Moses (NT3); צדיק גמור **ṣaddīq gāmūr** perfect righteous (NT); pl. צדיקים **ṣaddīqīm**; **ṣaddīqe** (MeAl 188; RivSh 190); v. רשע, צדאקא 1.

צדיקא (Ar) p.n.f. **ṣadīqa** (Friend).

צ-ד-ל (OA צ-ד-י+ל) **ṣ-d-l** to fear; **ṣádlēle** He feared; לא גצדלה **la gṣadle** He does not fear; לא צדליכון **la ṣadlēxun** Do (pl.) not fear! לא צדואלו **la ṣadwālu** They would not care (NT5 385); **ṣadlu** They are worried (that...); **ṣadli ʾāse mıṭra** I am afraid it will rain; **la ṣadlox** Don't worry! (NT+).

צדמה (Ar) f. **ṣadme** shock, upset (NTU3 1b); v. סטמיה.

צ-ד-ק (OA/Ar) **ṣ-d-q** to become upright (BaBin 57); II/IV to accept or declare as just (NT, BT5, D); to prove one's innocence (=H הִצְטַדֵּק, BT1, D).

צדק (H) **ṣēdeq** justice (NT2).

צדקה v. צדאקא 2

צדקותא (OA/Ar) f. **ṣıdqūṯa** righteousness; cf. רשעותא; **ṣadaqūṯa** friendship (AmU2 5b).

צדרא, סַדְרַא (Ar) m. **˙sadra** breast, front; דארי אידוה לצדרוה **dāre ʾıḏuh lṣadruh** They greet (lit. put their hands on their chest)(NT); pl. **ṣadrāre** (=H חָזוֹת, BT3) (NT+).

צדרייא, צדרייה (Ar) f. **ṣadrīya/e** waistcoat, apron; cf. צודרא.

צהוא, צ-ה-י, צהיא v. צחוא, צ-ח-י, צחיא

ציון v. צהיון

צ-ה-ל (OA) **ṣ-h-l** to neigh (horse) (NT2); to be cheerful (voice) (AmU2 5a).

צ-ו-א (OA צבע) **ṣ-w-ʾ** to dye, color (with henna); cf. צ-ב-ג'.

צוב (Ar/OS) prep. **ṣōb** near, by; אאזך בצוביהון **ʾāzax bṣōbēhun** We shall go near them (NT5 409).

צובאאתא v. צבואתא

צובאח (Ar) **ṣubāḥ** morning (NT); pl. **ṣabāḥe** (SaNR 330); cf. בנוכה.

צובאחייה (K < Ar) f. **ṣubāḥīye** festive wedding-breakfast (Br93 142).

צובוג' (Ar) m. **ṣubuġ** color, shoe polish.

צווד, צוואד, סַוַואט, צְוַואט, צְוַאות (Ar سـواد) **˙sawad/t** (herds of) sheep, cattle (=H מִקְנֶה, BT; PolG).

צודאע (Ar headache) **ṣudāᶜ** pain; danger, affliction (NT); מרכב פשלא בצודאע קוי **markab pıšla bṣudāᶜ qawi** The ship was in great danger (NT2); (=H תַּשְׁנִיק, AvidH 52).

צודרא, סודרא (Ar صُدْرَة bodice, camisole; cf. OA צְדְרָא) f. **˙sudra** shirt, tunic (=H כְּתֹנֶת, BT1); סֻודֶיר כִּיתַּאן **˙sudır kıttan** linen shirt (=H מִדּוֹ בַד, BT3, D); **˙sudır fānēra** flannel undershirt; **xōr-˙sudra** underpants; pl. סֻודְרַ(א)תַא **˙sudrāṯa** loincloths (=H חֲגוֹרֹת, BT1; כֻּתֳּנוֹת, BT2, D; PolG); cf. צדרא, צדרייא [Khan 582 **ṣidra**].

צוואנא (Ar صـوّان flintstone; cf. OA צוּנָּמָא hard rock?) adj. **ṣuwwāna, -anta,** sharp-edged (flintstone) [PolG: **suwānā** <K سوهان file].

צוחביה (Ar) f. **ṣuḥbe** banquet, party, meeting of friends (NT2, NT5 392).

צ-ו-י (Ar) **ṣ-w-y** to become hard, petrified.

צויא, צויתא (> צ-ו-י) p.p. **ṣūya, ṣwīṯa** hardened, dry (skin).

צולח (Ar) m. **ṣulḥ** peace, reconciliation; **ʾuzlu ṣulḥ** they made peace, surrendered (=H הִשְׁלִים, BT5).

צולתא (K **sol**/OA סולייס < L **solea** sole) f. **ṣawılta** shoe, slipper (NT2); pl. צוליה **ṣōle** (NT4) [cf. MAcD 263].

צומא (OA) m. **ṣōma** a fast; צומא רווא//עזיזא/ דכל נדרי **ṣōma ruwwa/ᶜazīza/dkunnızre** Yom Kippur (Great/of Zion/Precious/Kol-Nidre Fast); צום חזינה/צום אורוה/סחיון **ṣōm ḥazīne (Z)/ṣōm ˙sıḥyon ʾurwa** (Amedi 63) the Ninth of Ab Fast (Mourning-/Great Zion- Fast); cf. תענית.

צוערתא, צְעוּרְתַא (OS ܨܘܚܪܐ) f. **ṣuᶜırta** (NT), **ṣıᶜurta** (BT1, D; PolG) curse; pl. צועראתא **ṣuᶜrāṯa**; cf. צ-ע-ר [Khan 574 **maṣᶜorta**].

צופא (T **sofa** hall < Ar صُفَّـة stone bench) m. **ṣūpa** the inner hall in the house, used in winter as a living room; ante-room; room (PolG); v. ברבאנכה.

צופיכא (Ar-K) **ṣōfīka** Sufi, ascetic (PolU 82)

צוציתא (OA/OS curled hair) f. **ṣuṣīṯa** braid; pl. **ṣuṣyāṯa** (NT+).

צוצנתא (OS ܨܘܨܢ southern wood?) f. **ṣuṣṣanta** medlar, azarole (Ar زعرور); pl. **ṣuṣṣāne**.

צ-ו-ר II (Ar) **ṣ-w-r** to take or draw a picture [p.p.: **mṣūra, mṣōwarta,** PolG] ; cf. מצוראנא.

צור v. סור

צורא, צוּרַה (Ar سَوره intoxication?) **ṣūra** poison (=H רוש/ראש, BT5); וצביר בצוראbṣūra

uṣabır with poison and venom (BaBin 115); צוּרָא מִירָאן ṣūra mırān death poison (RivSh 231).
צורכה v. סורכה
צורך גדול/קטן (H) ṣōre(x) gāḏōl/qāṭān small/large need (euph. by men for urination/defecation) [cf. יתוית צורך yatwıt ṣōrex BaBin 29].
צורר (מצורר) (H) ṣōrēr (mısurrar) (most evil) trouble-maker.
צורתא (OA/Ar) f. ṣurta face; photo, picture (Z); image (=H צֶלֶם, BT1, Am); ṣurte qwīsa (he is) insolent (RivSh 255); muqwēle ṣurte He behaved insolently; v. פיקייע, מגג; pl. צוּרִיַיאתַא ṣuryāṯa (=H כְּרֻבִים); mapōqıd ṣuryāsa taking pictures; cf. צ-ו-ר (NT+).
צורת-חאל (K < Ar) ṣūrat ḥāl shape, form, way, condition; bču — in no way; bxa — in some way; bēma — In what way? (cf. PolG)!
צות, צוט (Ar) m. ṣōt voice; pl. ṣōte shrieks; d-r-y - to shriek (SaAC 12) cf. חס, קאלא.
צחו-סווה (K-Ar صح + سوء الضن) ṣaḥḥ-u-suwwe finding out if someone is OK (PolU 428).
צחוא, צהוא (OA צחותא, צחיא) m. ṣeḥwa (NT3); ṣehwa (Z), thirst; cf. סכווא, צחיותא.
צ-ח-י, צ-ה-י (OA צחי) ṣ-ḥ-y (NT5 411), ṣ-h-y (Z, PolG), to be thirsty.
צחיא, צהיתא, צהיא (<צ-ח-י) p.p. ṣeḥya (NT3), ṣehya (+NT, Z), ṣhīṯa (Z, f.), thirsty [Hoberman 1985 227; Khan 582 ṣiḥya].
צחיותא (OA) f. ṣeḥyūṯa thirst (NT3); cf. צחוא.
צחיחא (H-OA) ṣaḥīḥa bright (NT3), clear (voice) (NT2).
צחנאיה v. סחנאיה
צחתא, צחת, צחא, סִיחְחַא (K < Ar) f. ṣa/ıḥḥı(ta) health, vigor (= H און, PolG); ṣaḥḥıtox bassımta Bravo, well done! dōqıt-ba ṣaḥḥıta/ṣaḥḥat hōyālox May it be for health and strength (said after eating/ bathing); ṣaḥḥıte dʾırra He recovered.
צטאפא (< גאפא?) ṣṭāpa two handfuls: čange uṣṭāpe his handful (/wing) and two handfuls (/hand strike)? (PolG).
צטויר v. סתויר
צטלה v. סטלה
צ-ט-מ v. ס-ט-מ
צטפא (OA סטף) m. ṣıṭpa crack, hole (NT3).
צטרא, סטרא (IrAr) f. ʿṣaṭra slap (PolU 321).

צ-י-ב (Ar) ṣ-y-b to hit the target (AmU2 10a).
צ-י-ד (OA/Ar) ṣ-y-ḏ/d to hunt (=H צָד, BT1).
צידא, צַיַאדַא (OA/Ar) ṣēḏa, ṣyāda (BT3, D), hunt, game (=H צַיִד, BT1, BT3); cf. ניג׳יר.
ציוא (OS/OA ציבא firewood) m. ṣīwa tree, wood; חגיאתא דציוא ḥajyāṯa dṣīwa wooden utensils (NT5 410), pl. ṣīwe; cf. דארא, אילאנא.
ציואיא (< ציוא) m. ṣīwāya wood-cutter (cf. Avin78 93; PolG).
ציון, צהיון, סחיון (H) p.n.m. ṣıyyon Zion (person); cf. גונא; ṣıhyon, sıḥyon Zion (land) (SaLH; Amedi 63 thirst by mistake).
ציורתא (OA צירתא; OS ܨܝܪܬܐ) f. ṣīwarta door socket (NT+).
צ-י-ח (Ar صح ـل?) ṣ-y-ḥ to have free time, opportunity: la kṣāyılan ʾıdyo ʾāzax ltāma We don't have time today to go there; lak ṣāyıḥwālu They didn't have time; la ṣıḥlēlan tımmal We didn't have time yesterday; IV to visit, call on: ʾınkan ṣāyıḥli bāsın maṣīḥınnox If I have free time, I'll come and visit you (cf. BaBin 164; Hob89 219; PolG); to examine (=H בִּקֵּר/ בִּקֹּרֶת, BT3), (women) check (pockets of men) (PolU 27) [cf. K ṣaḥ kirin to revise].
צִיחְרֵי v. סחר
צייחה (Ar?) pl.(+f.?) ṣayīḥe crushed wheat.
ציטא v. סיטא
צילאחי v. סילאחי
צ-י-מ (OA) ṣ-y-m to fast; cf. צומא. NT +
צימא, צמתא (< צ-י-מ) p.p. ṣīma, ṣımta fasting.
צ-י-נ (OA צנן) ṣ-y-n to have chills, stinging pain (in teeth): kāki ṣınnu My teeth are numbed (after drinking cold water); to be discolored, rot: bır ḥalya la kṣāyın, bale tūma kṣāyın Fresh anise does not rot, but garlic does [MacD 262 to burn, be angry].
ציניא (Ar) f. ṣēnīya large, round metal plate, serving tray (cf. PolG); pl. ṣēnīyat (=H קְעָרוֹת, BT2); cf. פרקסיני [Khan 580 sinya].
ציצית (H) f. ṣīṣiṯ (Z ṣīṣis, ṣīṣi) prayer-shawl; pl. ציציות ṣīṣīyōṯ (NT), ṣīṣīyat (Z).
ציצרכא (K/OS ܨܪܨܘܪܐ; OA צרצרא) m. ṣīṣırka cricket; cf. גיגרכא.
צ-י-ר v. ס-י-ר
צ-י-ת IV (OA) ṣ-y-ṯ (Z ṣ-y-s/ṣ) to listen [1:mōṣıṯ-; 2/3:māṣıṯ; 4:maṣōṯe) (NT+).
צ-כ-ר v. ס-כ-ר

צ-ל-ו (OA צלב) ṣ-l-w to crucify, to hang (NT+).
צלאבה (Ar) f. ṣalābe gallows (NT5 400, 403).
צלאמתי v. סלאמתי
צלותא, צְלוֹצָא (OA) f. ṣlōṯa, ṣlōṣa (RivSh 120), prayer; pl. צלואתא ṣlawāṯa, צלויאתא ṣloyāsa (PolG) (NT+).
צ-ל-ח 1 (Ar سلح) ṣ-l-ḥ to arm (NT).
צ-ל-ח 2 (Ar/H/OA) ṣ-l-ḥ to be appropriate; II to make up; reconcile (vt/vi; cf. PolG); I/IV to be or make successful (BT1, AvidH 65, AlfH 73 NT); šūla dōhun ṣlıḥle bīzu Their task was successful (Zaken 389); ʾilāha ṣālıḥla ʾurxox/hōya ʾurxox ṣlıḥta Have a good journey! (cf. PolG); cf. צאלח מאל.
צ-ל-ט v. ס-ל-ט
צ-ל-י 1 II (OA) ṣ-l-y to pray (=H הֶעְתִּיר, PolG). NT+
צ-ל-י 2 (OA) ṣ-l-y to pitch (a tent), to erect, install (a trap) (BaBin 86; PolG).
צליב v. כאגו-צליב
צליוא (< צ-ל-ו) p.p. ṣlīwa crucified, hung; Jesus: bıṣlīwa ḥayya By living Christ (imititation of Christian speakers).
צליח, סילאח (Ar) ṣalīḥ (NT), silāḥ (Z, PolG), weapon; pl. צליחה, סִילַאחֵי ṣalīḥe (NT5 386), silāḥe (RivSh 234).
צליחא, צלחתא (< צ-ל-ח 2) p.p. ṣlīḥa, ṣlıḥta successful; common in blessings:har hāwıt ṣlīḥa May you be always successful!
צ-ל-כ (OA צלח) vt/vi ṣ-l-x to split, crack (NT+).
צלכא (OA צלחא) m. ṣılxa a crack; pl. ṣılxe.
צ-ל-כ-נ III (< צ-ל-כ) vt ṣ-l-x-n to split.
צלכתא (< K sellek basket?) f. ṣallıkṯa basket?, container? (PolU 264).
צמא v. סמא
צמבלועא (Ar?) m. ṣamballōʿa icicle, hanging ice from roof's edge.
צמירא (< צ-מ-ר) p.p. ṣmīra congested (nose), naxīre ṣmīra one with nasal speech.
צ-מ-ר (OA/OS retain flow) vi/vt ṣ-m-r be congested; to fill (space), block (NT2).
צנאא (Ar صانع) m. ṣanʾa craftsman (NT); cf. צנעתכר.
צנאתא (K/P < Ar صناعة) f. ṣaneʾta craft, skill; mare-ṣaneʾta craftsman; pl. ṣaneʿıtyāṯa (BT1), ṣanʾāṯa (PolGr 53) (NT+) [Khan 582 ṣinʿata, sg.]
צנדוק(א), סנדוק (Ar/P/OS) m. ṣandūq(a), sanduq box, chest; the Ark; cf. ארון; sanduq zamāra phonograph (singing box) (NT+).
צנדל (Ar < L/Gr) ṣandal sandal wood (NT3).
צנדלתא, סנדלתא (Ar/OA סנדלא < L/Gr) f. ⁺ṣandalta a sandal; pl. ⁺sandāle.
צ-נ-ד-מ III (Ar صدم hurt, bang) ṣ-n-d-m to have or cause severe headache (due to noise, banging, etc.)(cf. PolG); גגלה ומצונדמלה gıjle umṣundımle he felt dizzy and had a banging headache; v. ס-ט-מ.
צ-נ-ד-ר III [?](< Ar استنظر?) ṣ-n-d-r to wait a long time (PolG).
צנורתא (OS) f. ṣınnurta knitting needle; cf. כושתא.
צנטא v. צנתא
צנם (Ar) m. ṣanam idol, statue, image; v. פריס; pl. ṣanāme (=H אֱלִילִים, BT3; פְּסִילִים, BT5); pl. צנאמיה ṣanāme; ṣānāmıd šımša sun idols (=H חַמָּנִים, BT3) (NT+).
צ-נ-ע 1 (Ar) ṣ-n-ʿ to make, shape (idols) (NT).
צ-נ-ע 2 (H-OA) ṣ-n-ʿ to be modest (NT3).
צנעתא (< צ-נ-ע 2) p.p. f. ṣnıʿta modest (NT3).
צנעתכר (Ar-P) ṣanʿatkar craftsman (cf. PolG); cf. צנאא.
צ-נ-צ-ל III (Ar نصل drop) ṣ-n-ṣ-l to drip (slowly), drain out (= H נִמְצָה [דָמוֹ], BT3, D).
צנתא, צנטא, סנטא (< Ar صامت?) inv. ⁺santa withdrawn (person), calm; ʾaw yōma xawōra ⁺santa wēle That day the river was calm (safe to cross); stillness (PolG).
צעא v. סאעא
צעבא (Ar) adj. ṣaʿba difficult, harsh (NT).
צעבה (Ar) f. ṣaʿbe difficulty (NT5 385).
צ-ע-ד (Ar go up) ṣ-ʿ-d with mʾīḏa (from hand) to afford (to pay) (NTU4 161b).
צוערתא v. צעורתא
צעכרה v. סכרא 2
צ-ע-ר II (OA) ṣ-ʿ-r to curse, revile, call names.
צער (H) f. ṣāʿar sorrow, suffering (NT5 397; RivSh 127); איהא צער בטאנכלא ʾēha ṣāʿar bṭaʾnaxla We will bear this (f.) sorrow (BaBin 135); ⁺rāba ṣāʿar xzēla ʾēne He suffered a lot (his eye saw much sorrow);

lax bixāla ṣaʿar ʾıbbe We are grieved about him (eat grief) (Hob89 184).

צפארא (Ar) m. **ṣafāra** coppersmith (cf. RivSh. 280 סַפָּרַא); cf. צפר 2.

צפארה (OS/OA צַפְּרָא; pl. צִיפְּרָנֵי/ܨܦܪ̈ܐ) sg./pl. (?) **ṣpāre** morning(s) (ChNA), only in: **ʾēwa smōqa bıspāre, šqōl xāṭora uysa lgāre** Red cloud in the morning(s), start fixing your roof (it will rain soon) (Sabar78).

צפון, צאפון (H; cf. OA ציפונא) **ṣāfon** north (BT5; PolU 321) (NT+).

צפורתא (OA) f. **ṣıppurta** bird (NT2).

צ-פ-ט II (IrAr) **ṣ-f-ṭ** to stack, line up (books, etc.) (cf. PolG).

צפטא, ספטא (IrAr; cf. OA/OS סַפְטָא < P **safad** box, basket?) f. **ṣafṭa, ⁺safta** pack (of papers, bills).

צ-פ-י (Ar صفي) **ṣ-p-y** to be pure, clear; II to purify, clarify; **mṣupya, mṣupēṯa** pure (=H מַכֹּלֶת [חִטִּים], כָּתִית, PolG:1 kg 5:25) (NT+).

צפיא 1, צפיתא (< צ-פ-י) p.p. **ṣıpya, ṣpīṯa** pure, clear; תובּיה צפיתא **tōbe ṣpīṯa** wholehearted repentance (NT5 381); **ṣpīya** guiltless (=H נָקִי, BT2, Arodh); **blıbba ṣıpya** with clear conscience, without worry (NT+).

צפיא 2 (< צ-פ-י) m. **ṣapya** strainer, filter bag (thick woven bag to let extra liquid drip out very slowly; cf. PolG).; cooler; cf. צאפויה [Mutz 228 **ṣapyo**, f.]

צפיותא (< צ-פ-י) f. **ṣıpyūṯa** purity, clarity, innocence (NT+).

צפירא (Ar) f. **ṣafīra** whistle.

צ-פ-נ (Ar) **ṣ-f-n** gaze, brood, muse (cf. PolG).

צ-פ-צ-פ 1 III (OA be pressed?) **ṣ-p-ṣ-p** to rob, to overcharge; cf. ס-ר-ס-פ.

צ-פ-צ-פ 2 III (H-OA) **ṣ-f-ṣ-f** to chirp (only in RivSh 183).

צ-פ-ר (Ar) **ṣ-f-r** to whistle; cf. **צפירא.**

צפר 1, צִיפֶּיר (Ar) m. **ṣıfır** copper (cf. PolG); pl. **ṣıfre** cooper items (Zaken 391); cf. צפארא.

צפר 2 (Ar) m. **ṣıfır** zero.

צפרא, צפרג׳ v. ספרג׳, ספרא

צפרתא (Ar bile, hunger?) f. **ṣıfrıta** strength, patience; appetite; **mare-ṣıfrıta** healthy, one with good appetite/digestion.

צ-ק-ט v. ס-ק-ט

צראפא (Ar صرّاف/OS/OA צַרָּפָא) **ṣarrāfa** money changer; cf. צ-ר-פ 2.

צ/ס-ר-ב-ס III (IrAr **srbs**) **⁺s-r-b-s** to reel (yarn out of wool); cf. מצרבס; to loiter, get entangled; **gımṣarbıs go ʾaqlāsi** He (my little son) clings to me.

צרועא, צרועתא (< צ-ר-ע) adj. **ṣarūʿa, ṣaruʿta** stale, rotten (nuts, seeds).

צרופא (< צ-ר-פ 1) m. **ṣırrōpa** frost-bite.

צרות, צארות (H) pl./sg. **ṣārōt/ṯ** trouble(s), affliction(s): **[xzēli] xa - bıd hwāya dīdox** I had such a trouble at birthing you (SaAC 21; RivSh 130).

צ-ר-י (OA) **ṣ-r-y** to slit, tear (flesh), cut open (watermelon) (cf. Pol 110; PolG).

צריעא, צרעתא (< צ-ר-ע) p.p. **ṣrīʿa, ṣrıʿta**, crazed.

צ-ר-כ (Ar/OA) **ṣ-r-x** to call, scream, anounce; IV to proclaim (NT) (NT+).

צרכתא (< צ-ר-כ) f. **ṣraxta** scream, shout (=H זְעָקָה/צְעָקָה, BT1); pl. צרכיאתא **ṣraxyāṯa** (NT5 397; BaBin 10).

צ-ר-ע (Ar صُرِعَ be epileptic; v. ס-ר-כ) **ṣ-r-ʿ** go mad, become weird, stupid; stale; cf. צרועא צריעא,.

צר-עין (H) inv. **ṣarʿāyın** stingy, envious; also **ṣar-ʿāyinka** (m.), **ṣar-ʿayınke** (f.); cf. צארותא.

צ-ר-פ 1 II (OA to burn, shrivel) **ṣ-r-p** to have frost-bite; v. צרופא [MacD 267 be pungent].

צ-ר-פ 2 II (Ar) **ṣ-r-f** to exchange bills by coins, to cash; **la gımṣarfa ṭālan** It does not pay for us (to do it); IV to spend money (cf. RivSh 198; RivPr 210); cf. צראפא, מצרף.

צתרא v. סתרא

צ̇(ẓ)

צ̇אבט (Ar) ẓābıṭ officer; pl.-ṭān officials (=H שׁוֹטְרִים, BT5);-ṭat (PolU 36); cf. צ̇מבאט.

צ̇אד v. זאד

צ̇אהר (Ar) ẓāhır evident; בצ̇אהר bẓāhır openly, publicly (NT2).

צ̇איע v. צ̇-י-ע

צ̇אלם (Ar) inv. ẓālım oppressor, wicked.

צ̇באנא v. זבאנא

צ̇-ב-ח v. ד̇-ב-ח

צ̇ביחא, צ̇ניחתא v. ד̇ביחא

צ̇-ב-ט, ד-ב-ט (Ar) ẓ-b-ṭ, ⁺z-b-ṭ (BT5, D; PolG), hold tight, overpower (RivSh 216); v. ת-ב-ת.

צ̇-ה-ר (Ar) ẓ-h-r to shine, to dawn, appear (sun, God) (NT5 383); illuminate (difficult words); IV to show, reveal (NT).

צ̇ולום, דִילְים (Ar) m. ẓulum, ⁺d̲ılım (BT, D) oppression, corruption (=H עֹשֶׁק/חָמָס, BT).

צ̇ופא v. זופא

צ̇-י-ע, ד-י-ע (Ar) ẓ/⁺d̲-y-ᶜ (cf. PolG; Hob89 216 ḍ-y-ᶜ) to disappear, be lost; לג צ̇איע lag ẓāyıᶜ Nothing is hidden (from Him); zılle ẓāyıᶜ It was wasted, in vain [1: ẓaᶜ - (Z, SaLH 145), ⁺d̲eᶜ- (RivP 102 דֵיעְתַּלָא)]; IV lose, annihilate (=H אִבֵּד, PolG) [4: מַדוֹעֵי maḍōᶜe] (NT+).

צ̇יעתא (< צ̇-י-ע) f. ẓyaᶜta (BT3), ẓēᶜıta (BT2), loss (=H אֲבֵדָה, BT).

צ̇-י-ף II (Ar) ẓ-y-f to host (a banquet) (NT5 392).

צ̇יקתא, דיקתא (Ar) f. ẓēqıta, ⁺dīqıtta (!) (PolG) affliction (BaBin 150).

צ̇לומא, זַלוֹמַא (< צ̇-ל-מ) m. ẓ/⁺d̲alōma oppressor (BaBin 136).

צ̇-ל-מ, ד-ל-מ (Ar) vt/vi ẓ-l-m, ⁺d̲-l-m (D), to oppress (=H עָשַׁק, BT3); be deprived: ẓlımli, latli čuxa māʾınni I have been deprived; I don't have any body to help me.

צ̇לעום v. זלעום

צ̇מבאט (< Ar ضبّاط) ẓımbāṭ officer; pl. -āṭat (PolU 302); cf. צ̇אבט

צ̇-מ-ב-ר v. ז-מ-ב-ר

צ̇-נ-ג-ר v. ז-נ-ג-ר 2

צ̇עיף (Ar) inv. ẓaᶜif weak, frail; תולאתא רככתא וצ̇עיף tōleʾṯa rakıxta uẓaᶜif a soft and weak (worm) (NT+).

צ̇עיפא, צ̇עפתא (Ar) n. ẓaᶜīfa, ẓaᶜıfta weakling; ביני קויא לצ̇עיפא bēni qūya lẓaᶜīfa between the strong and the weak one.

צ̇עיפונכא, צ̇עיפונכה (< צ̇עיף) ẓaᶜīfonka (m.), -ke (f.), very frail, thin person.

צ̇עיפתותא (< צ̇עיף) f. ẓaᶜifatūṯa weakness.

צ̇-ע-פ (Ar) ẓ-ᶜ-f to become weak; IV to make weak.

צ̇רא v. זרא

צ̇-ר-ב, ד-ר-ב II (Ar) ẓ-r-b, ⁺d̲-r-b (D), to afflict (=H נָגַף, נֶגַע, BT; PolG) (cf. NT5 382).

צ̇רבאבא (K < Ar ضرّ poligamy) m. ẓırbāba stepfather; cf. ארתא, בך-באבא.

צ̇רביגכה v. זרביגכה

צ̇רבא, דְרְבָא, צ̇רביה (Ar) ẓarba/e blow, plague; pl. ẓarbıtyāṯa (=H נְגָעִים, מַכּוֹת, מַגֵּפוֹת, BT; PolG).

צ̇רצ̌כונכא (K) m. ẓırčkonka farter, show-off weakling (PolU 34)

צ̇רצ̌נג (K fart sound?) ẓırčang only in: - musyāle mınna He exhausted her sexually (PolU 261).

צ̇רדאבה v. זרדאבה

צ̇-ר-ד-ב v. ז-ר-ד-ב

צ̇רדיתא v. זרדיתא

צ̇רור (Ar) ẓarūr necessity (NT).

צ̇-ר-ט (Ar to fart) ẓ-r-ṭ to lie shamelessly, tell obvious lies; cf. ע-ר-ט.

צ̇רטא (< צ̇-ר-ט) m. ẓırṭa shameless lie; pl. ẓırṭe.

צ̇רטאנא, צ̇רטנתא (< צ̇רטא) ẓırṭāna, -anta shameless liar.

צ̇רנה v. זרנה

צ̇רניך v. זרניך

צ̇רקתא v. זרקתא

צ̇רף (Ar) m. ẓarf envelope; pl. ẓarfe.

צ̇-ר-ר II2 (Ar) ẓ-r-r to harm, cause damage.

צ̇רר (Ar) m. ẓarar harm , damage.

ק (q)

ק (H) **qōf** the Hebrew letter qof; **ʾımma** hundred.

-ק v. -ג

קאבל (Ar) inv. **qābıl** worthy, capable (NT3).

קאגׄא (< K?) f. **qāča** wedding chamber, tent (?) (PolU 64).

קאגׄכה (K) f. **qāčıke** resin used as chewing gum.

קאדר (Ar) inv. **qādır** capable, deserving (NT3).

קאורמא (K/Ar < T) f. **ᐩqāwırma** salted meat.

קאזא (K/P/T) **qāza** goose; pl. **qāze**.

קאזא-קלמבאזא (K **kez**) f. **qāza-qalımbāza** beetle.

קאזוך (K/T/IrAr) m. **qāzox** scaffold, impalement pole; cf. ק-ו-ז-ג'.

קאטא, קטותא (OS < L) **qāṭa** (m.), **qaṭūṯa** (f.), cat; pl. **qāṭe** (m., rare), **qaṭwāṯa** (f., c.) [cf. Mutz 220 **qāṭū** , f.; pl. **qaṭwe**; Khan **qaṭṭu**, pl. **qaṭṭwe**].

קאידא (T < Ar) f. **qāyda** right (size), one's measure; **ʾıl qāyda** at proper measure.

קאיא, קאיכתא (K < T) f. **qāya, qāyıkṯa** small boat, little barge (PolU 215, 216).

קאים (K < Ar) inv. **qāyım** extant, everlasting (NT); strong, enduring, solid (Z; PolG).

קאימקם (Ar) m. **qāymaqam** local governor.

קאיש (K/T) **qāyıš** (modern) belt; cf. כרכאצא.

קאישאנא, קאישנתא (< קאיש), **qāyıšāna, -anta** elastic, stretchable; cf. עליכאנא.

קאלא (OA קלא, קאלא) m. **qāla** voice, sound; pl. **qāle** (NT+).

קאל-מגׄאל (Ar) **qāl-mıjāl** harrassing sound (by dog at thieves)(PolU 116); **ʾ-w-z** - make such sounds (ibid).

קאמא (Ar) **qāma** stature, body; cf. קומא (NT+).

קאמא-קאמא (< קם) adv. **qāmá-qāma** (move forward) gradually, first few and then many [Khan 578 **qāma** in the front, in the open].

קאנא (OA/OS קרנא) f. **qāna** horn; pl. **qanāne**; —**šṭıllūle** He was astonished (MeAl 192).

קאנה-קוגׄה (< קאנא+קוגׄא) **qāne-qōče** shoulders (a game: children sit on shoulders of adults and 'gore' each other; cf. PolG).

קאן וגׄאן (K/P?) **qān-u-jān** (beat someone) to the pulp (lit. body and soul?) (PolU 348).

קאנון (Ar < Gr) **qānun** law, rule.

קאנע (Ar)m. **qānıᶜ** content person; pl. קאנעין **qānıᶜīn** (NT); cf. קניעא, ק-נ-ע.

קאנקינה, קאלקינה (OA קנקנא vessel?) pl. **qān/laqīne** old broken vessels [cf. JAB **qalāqīl** things not used anymore].

קאעא (Ar/OS) **qāᶜa** raven, crow; **qāᶜa(-qırra)** miser; cf. קרא, קרגא (NT+).

קאפא (< ?) **qāpa** case, box [cf. MacD 282 lid].

קאפויא (< ק-פ-י 2) m. **qāfōya** driftwood; cf. קפיא.

קאפות (T/K < Fr capot) f. **qāput** felt overcoat (PolU 20).

קאצא (IrAr < It cassa) f. **qāṣa** vault, safe, coffer.

קאצוד (K < Ar) m. **qāṣud** messenger, delegate; pl. קָאסוּדֵי **qās/ṣūde** (RivSh 263, 273).

קאצ(ו)דותא (< קאצוד) f. **qāṣūdūṯa** mission (NT+).

קאצ̇י (Ar) m. **qāẓi** qadi, Muslim judge.

קאצ̇יותא (< קאצ̇י) f. **qāẓıyūṯa** office of qadi (NT).

קאקאני (< P. خاقاني-royal?) **qāqāni** a type of large real estate aquisition (PolU 289).

קאקבה (OS ܩܩܒܐ /OA קַכְּבָא, m. jar, pot < Gr κακκαβη) f. **qāqıbe** large pot, caldron (SaAC 11); pl. **qāqıbat** (Zaken 388; PolG).

קארוגׄכא (K?) m. **qārūčka** small clay bowl.

קארון v. הארון

קאשא (OS/OA קַשָּׁא < קשישא elder) m. **qāša** Christian priest; pl. **qāše**, **qāšyāne** (PolGr 51).

קאתי (Kqa < Ar قط) adv. **qāti** Surely, Isn't...?! (begins a yes/no rhetorical qustion(PolU 3).

קאתל (Ar) **qātıl** murderer, hostile person. NT+

קאתרגׄאיא (T/K) m. **qātırčāya** muleteer, trader.

קאתרגׄותא (< קאתרגׄאיא) n. abs. **qātırčūṯa** trading (PolU 246).

קבא (T) inv. **qaba** haughty, aloof (puffed up).

קבאחא (Ar) f. **qabāḥa** shameful act (cf. PolG).

קבאלא 1 (Ar) f. **qabāla** contract, commission.

קבאלא 2 (Ar?) f. **qabbāla** cupboard, recess in the wall serving as cupboard.

קבאלא 3 (Ar قابلة) f. **qabāla** midwife; pl. קבאלת **qabālat** (NT); cf. מקבלנתא.

קבי v. קי

קבילא 1, קבלתא (< ק-ב-ל) p.p. **qbīla. qbılta** acceptable, agreeable, respected (NT5 393).

קבילא 2 (Ar tribe) f. **qabīla** gang; אודי קבילא אילה **ʾōḏi qabīla ʾılle** They gang up against him (NT); tribal clan (PolU 351).

ק-ב-ל (OA/Ar) **q-b-l** to accept, agree; receive, serve as midwife (=H יִלְּדָה, BT2 Am); cf. מקבלנתא; to let: **bāžūr lēle la qbılu ʾēne šaxni** Troubling thoughts of the night did not let him fall asleep (PolG); IV make someone agree: **ṭāpe bxāse ...hīl maqbılla** He should pester his sister till he makes her agree (PolU 364); cf. PolG) (NT+).

קבל, מקבל (Ar) prep. **(m)qabıl** before; cf. קם.

קבלה (H) f. **qabbāla** Kabbala, mysticism.

ק-ב-צ̇ (Ar) **q-b-ẓ** to catch, arrest (NT2).

קבצא (Ar) f. **qabẓa** hand's breadth (=H טֹפַח/טֶפַח BT2, PolG); pl. קבציה **qabẓe** (NT5 407).

קבקאבה (Ar) pl. **qabqābe** wooden logs, bathing shoes (sg. **qabqabta**).

קגג', קגך (K < T) **qačax/ġ** smuggler; pl. **qačāġe**.

קגג'ותא (< קגג') f. **qačaġūṯa** smuggling.

קגין v. אכגין

קגלא (IrAr/T) **qıčla** police station, jail [Khan 578 **qišla**].

ק-ג-מ (AnAr) **q-č-m** to chat (cf. PolU 281).

ק-ג-פ (< ?) ⁺**q-č-p** to be totally exhausted (cf. PolG)[cf. MacD 278 to wring the neck].

ק-ג̇-ק-ג̇ III (K to crow) **q-j-q-j** to talk too loud.

קד(א) v. קדרא 1

קדא (< ק-ד-ד) m. **qı/adda** (short) log (cf. PolG); cf. קדו.

קדאלא (OA) f. **qḏāla** (Z **qzāla**) neck; **pıšle bıqzāli** I am stuck with it; כטיתיני בקדאלוך **xṭīṯēni bıqḏālox** May you suffer for our iniquity (our sin on your neck); **ʿāwōn dīdox bıqzāli** May I suffer for your iniquity (said by mother to son); **ʿāwōn dīdi bdārınna bıqzālox** I'll make you guilty of my suffering (PolU 238); **bıtwār qzāle** unfortunately (PolU 424); pl. **qḏalāle** (NT+).

קדאמה (Ar) pl. **qadāme** feet; **qadāmi turru** My feet are hurting (from much walking).

קדאג'א (T/P) **qadaġa** decree, warning (NT2).

ק-ד-ד II2 (OA/OS/Ar) **q-d-d** to cut (firewood, etc.) into small pieces (cf. PolU 381).

קדו (< קדא?) **qaddo** short and stocky person.

קדוחא (< ק-ד-ח 1) m. **qadōḥa** igniter; **kepa qadōḥa** flintstone, igniter.

קדומה (< ק-ד-מ) adv. **qadōme** tomorrow; יומד קדומה **yōmıd qadōme** in the future, in the days to come (NT; RivSh 191, 277) [Khan 577 **qadóme**].

קדוש, קידוש (H) m. **qıddūš** wine; **qıddūš dyıbšāṯa** raisin wine; kidush, blessing over wine (NT5 411); **ʾuzle qıddūš** He recited (made) the kidush.

קדושה, קְדֻשָּׁא (H) f. **qadušša** sanctity (AvidH 34); בקדושה וטהרה **bqadušša uṭahāra** in sanctity and purity.

קודשתא v. קודשתא

ק-ד-ח 1 (Ar قدح/OA/OS קדח blaze up) **q-d-ḥ** to strike fire, ignite, flare (=H קָדַח, BT5; הִתְלַקַּח, PolG); rub (magical feathers to have a long distance call); cf. קדוחא.

ק-ד-ח 2 (< ק-ד-ח 1?) **q-d-ḥ** to wander, go far away in search of something: **kulla dunye qdīḥāli ula ʿlıqle bʾīzi** I searched for it everywhere, but didn't find it.

ק-ד-י v. ק-צ-י

קדידא (Ar) m. **qadīda** hard, frozen, pickled.

קדילא (OA קלידא < Gr) m. **qḏīla** (Z **qzīla**) key; pl. **qḏīle**.

קדים (Ar) inv. **qadīm** ancient; קדים זמאן **qadīm(u) zamān** ancient times (NT+).

קדיפא (K < Ar قطيفة) f. **qadīfa** velvet cloth.

קדיש (H) m. **qaddīš** kadish, memorial prayer.

קְדֵישָׁא (H) f. **qadēša** prostitute (BT1, D).

קדכא v. קתכא

קדלאלה v. קדאלא

ק-ד-מ II (OA/Ar) **q-d-m** to proceed, to offer, bring forward; get up early (NT5 394) (NT+).

קדם (Ar) **qadam** foot; pl. **qadāme** (cf. PolG).

קדנגא (K?) f. **qadanga** public restroom.

קדר II (Ar) **q-d-r** to measure (NT5 410), estimate, try on (clothes); show respect.

קדרא 1, קדר, קדא (Ar) m. **qadra, qadır, qadda**

size; זאורא קדר זאורותה (He blessed) younger one according to his young age; אד קדרא עולם נאשה **ʾad qadra ʿōlam nāše** such a large number of people; **qadır ḥāli** according to my ability, as much as I can afford; cf. אסקדא אוקד„; honor: **d-w-q qadır** to show respect; **t-w-r qadır** to insult; **bqadır** honorably; cf. עזתא; pl. **qadāre** measures (=H שְׁעָרִים, BT1).

קדרא 2 (OA קידרא pot, potful of food) f. **qıdra** (Z **qızra**) cooked food (cf. NT5 409); pl. **qıdrāṯa** (PolG).

ק-ד-ש II (Ar) **q-d-š** to sanctify, betroth (NT+).

קהוא, קהווה/קהויה (Ar) f. **qahwa** (Z), **qahwe** (NT), coffee, coffee-house; alcoholic drink (?)(NT5 409); pl. **qahwe** (PolG).

קהואי (< קהוא) inv. **qahwāyi** brown; pink (?).

קהוא-כאנא (IrAr/T) **qahwa-xāna** coffeehouse.

ק(ה)ואנא (IrAr **qawāna**) f. **qa(h)wāna** phonograph record.

קהוא-גאג׳(ה) (K جاغ chamber) **qahwa-jāğ(e)** coffeehouse (on river bank) (PolU 232).

קהוגי (Ar-T) m. **qahwači** coffehouse owner; butler in divan (NT); pl. **qahwačiyat** [שַׂר הַמַּשְׁקִים, BT1).

ק-ה-י v. ק-ח-י

קהל (H) m. **qahal** (Jewish) congregation, synagogue audience; pl. קהלות ישראל **qıhıllōṯ ⁺yısrāʾēl** Jewish communities.

קהתי v. קחתי

קהרא v. קחרא

קו v. ק-י-מ

ק-ו-א (OA ק-ו-ע/*קבע) **q-w-ʾ** to drain, become waterless (?); only in **baloʾtox qōʾa** May your throat dry up (?)!; cf. קוואא [cf. OA קועא windpipe, neck; MacD 268 **q-b-ʾ, q-w-ʾ, q-b-ʿ** collect water; pour out < OS مضا; H יִקָּווּ הַמַּיִם, Gen1:9].

קוא קוא קוא (onomat.) **qwa qwa** frog sounds, quack, croak (PolUL 243).

קווּאדא (Ar) **qawwāda** procuress (Segal #38).

קואזא (Ar قوّاس archer) m. **qawwāza** police, guard (RivSh 159); pl. **qawwāze**.

ק(ה)ואנא v. קואנא

קואתא, קותא (OS ܩܘܬܐ) f. **qoʾta, qōta** spider; cf. קנקותא.

קובא (Ar قبّة; cf. OA/OS קוּבְתָּא) f. **qubba** chamber (=H קֻבָּה, BT4) (NT+).

קוגא (T/K horn) m. **qōča** goring; **m-x-y qōče** to gore; -, **qōčıka** (hollow, twisted) log, piece of wood (PolU 108); cf. קורמא 1.

קוגאנא (< קוגא) **qōčāna** wont to gore (bull).

קוגאנה (< קוגא) f./pl.? **qōčāne** goring game; cf. קאנה-קוגה.

קודא 1 (OA) **qōda** clay bowl; **xa qōda masta** a bowl of yoghurt (PolU 257); **qōdıd garme** (the frail) human body.

קודא 2 (OS) m. **qōḏa** (Z **qōẓa**) fetters, pillory; cf. ק-ו-צ׳ [MacD 271].

קודרתא (Ar) f. **qudrıta** (Divine) omnipotence (=H אֶצְבַּע אֱלֹהִים, BT2; יַד ה׳, BT4, D); urge, ability, wish to act (PolG) (NT+).

קודש (H) **qōdeš** holiness, shrine; Jerusalem (SaLH 147); pl. **qadašīm** (BT2).

קודשא (OA) m. **qudša** holy abode.

קודשתא, קדושתא (OS ܡܩܕܫܐ amulet earring) f. **qüdüšta** small section of bunch of grapes (cf. קודשתא Sa83c 16, Am); pl. קדושיאתא **qüdüšyāṯa** (BaBin 42) [Mutz 222 **qulašta**].

קוואא (< ק-ו-א?) m. **qawōʾa** hollow gourd used as cup or bowl [cf. MacD 268 **qawā** mug].

קוותא (K< Ar) f. **quwwıta** power, strength; - **hāwēlox** May you have strength (said to a laboring person) (Amedi 73) (NT+). [Khan 578 **qiwta**].

ק-ו-ז-ג׳ III (IrAr) **⁺q-ō-z-ğ** to impale (=H הוֹקִיעַ, BT4); cf. קאזוך.

קוטא (K **quz** < Ar/P كُس?) m. **qūṭa** vagina; cf. בנדובא, גיגלכא [MacD 272 **qūṭā** womb].

קוטיפא (OA קְטוּפָא/OS ܩܛܘܦܐ) m. **quṭēfa** cluster (of grapes, dates; cf. ק-ט-פ 1 (NT+).

קטמא v. קוטמא

קוטנאסכת (K?) pl. **quṭnāskat** blue beads.

ק-ו-י (< Ar) **q-w-y** become strong, harsh; IV to strengthen, make difficult, be strict; **muqwēle ṣurte** He acted boldly (NT+).

קוִי (Ar) adv. **qawi** very, much: טלא הודאייה פשלא קוי שהיאנא וכדיותא **ṭla ḥoḏāye pıšla qawi šahyāna uxıdyūṯa** The Jews have much celebration and joy (NT5 403); בד קוִי קוִי **bıd qawi qawi** very much (=H בְּמְאֹד מְאֹד, AvidH 27; cf. RivSh 196; BT1, Am, D; PolG); v. קי.

קויא, קוויא, קוּבְיֵי, קְבִיָא, קויתא (< ק-ו-י) p.p. **qūya** (Z, NT), **quwya** (+NT)**quvya**, pl. **quvye** (AvidH 70), **qwīṯa**, f.,strong, harsh, difficult; **ṣurte qwīsa** impudent; NT+ [Khan 578 **qiwya, quya**].

קויאתי (< קויא) f. **quyati** (?) strictness; בקויאתי **bqūyati** severly, strictly; ליתן אילוה פקאדא בקויאתי **līṯn ʾilluh pqāḏa bqūyāti** One does not have to check them strictly (NT5 406).

קויותא (< קויא) f. **qūyūṯa** strength (=H חֹזֶק, BT2; קֶרִי, BT3, D) [AvidH 71 קֻוְיוּסָא **quw/vyūsa**].

קול 1 (H) interj. **qōl** silence! (lit. voice, an admonition against talking during prayer).

קול 2 (Ar) m. **qōl** (oral) agreement, condition; **ʾuzli qōl ʾımme** I made a condition with him; **qōli-qōlox basır gıšra** Let's agree to meet behind the bridge (Socin 164); pl. קוֹלֵי **qōle** rules (=H מִשְׁפָּטִים, AlfH 33).

קול- v. ק-י-מ

קולאאא, קולאאה (OS ܩܘܠܥܐ/OA קָלָא clod; sling stone) m. **qulāʾa** lump (of cheese) (Z); pl. קולאה (!) **qulāʾe** sling-stones, clods of earth.

קולבא (OS) m. **qulba** bracelet (=H אֶצְעָדָה/ צָמִיד, BT4); pl. **qulbe** (cf. PolG)

קולזום, קולוזום v. קלזם

קוליא (OS ܩܘܠܐ leg, limb < Gr) m. **qulya** large bone; thigh (=H שׁוֹק, BT3, D; BT4, D); cf. עטמא [Garbell 328].

קולנגא (K) m. **qulınga** road runner, crane. **xafīfa x-qulınga** quick as a crane.

קולוניא (IrAr < E) **qōlōnya** eau de cologne.

קולפא v. קופלא

קולקולתא 1 (K **qulqul**) f. **qulqulta** door's lock, bar; door's peeping hole (?).

קולקולתא 2 (< גורגורתא?) f. **qulqulta** throat (cf. PolU 40); soul; **rōḥāye wēla go** — He loves her very much; His soul is enmeshed in hers.

קום (Ar) m. **qōm** (Z), **qawm** (BT2, Arodh; AvidH 20, 30), nation, people (NT+).

ק-ו-מ II (Ar) **q-w-m** be possible, occur (NT); have sudden bad weather (Z); cf. ק-י-מ.

קומא (<OA קומתא f. body?) m. **qōma** stature, posture (including of snake, RivPr II 211); cf. קאמא; **bqōma** ⁺**rōmāna** proudly (=H קוֹמְמִיּוּת, BT3, D); **bārux-xabba bo qōma** Welcome! (SaNR).

קומארה (Ar) pl. only ⁺**qumāre** gambling games (cf. PolG).

קומארג׳י (IrAr) m./f. **qumārči** gambler; pl. **qumārčīyat**.

קומברא (Ar/T/K) f. **qumbara** bomb, mine; v. קונברא [Khan 578 **qumbla** bomb].

קומנדר (Ar/T < E) m. ⁺**qomandar** commander.

קומש (T/K/Ar) m. **qumaš** cloth, imported fabric (for suits); pl. קומאשיה **qumāše** (NT+).

קונאג׳ v. קונך

קונא-קחבה (K) **qūna-qaḥbe** prostitute's arse, free-for-all place.

קונברא (< קומברא) **qunbara** cavity, tunnel, mine; cf. לגֿם; pl. קונבריה **qunbare** (NT).

קונגֿכה (K **qūnjik** little arse) f. **qūnjıke** hiding place in a cave (PolUL 391).

קונדהה (K) f. **qūndahe** prostitute (lit., arse-giver); **— unīve** (You) prostitute and half, super mischiecvous (cf. PolU 126); v. שרמא.

קונדרג׳י (T) m./f. **qundarči** shoemaker.

קונדרתא (K/T < Gr) f. **qundarta** (modern) shoe; pl. **qundare** (Z), **kun-** (PolG); cf. פילבתא.

קונך (K < T **konak**) m. **qōnax** inn (= H מָלוֹן, BT1).; pl. **qunāġe** (=H מַסְעִים, BT2, Arodh).

קונסור (IrAr < E) m. ⁺**qunsor** consul.

קוסורי (K < Ar قصّر) **qusūri** shortcoming; **la š-w-q/ʾ-w-z** - to provide good care (cf. PolG); cf. תקסיר(י).

קופא (OA collectio box<Ak **quppu**) m. **qūpa** wicker basket; pl. **qūpe**.

קופגֿא (T) f. **qopča** button; pl. **qopče**.

קופיא (T < It) **qōpya** copying pencil.

קולפא, קופלא (Ar قُفل/OA/OS קוּפְלָא) m. **qufla** (Z), **qulfa** (NT) lock; cf. ק-פ-ל 2.

קופלתא (Ar) f. **qufılta** buttonhole; cf. ק-פ-ל.

קופת עריכה (H) **quppa(ṯ) ʿarīxa** welfare fund.

קוצרייא (Ar) f. **quṣrīya** chamber pot; cf. קעאדה.

ק-ו-צ̇ II (< קוצ̇א 2) **q-w-ẓ** to chain, fetter; יסירא ומקוצ̇א **ysīra umqūẓa** chained and fettered (BaBin 136).

קוצ̇א v. קודא 2

קצ̇רקוט v. קוצ̇ורקוט

קוקא (OS) **qōqa** clay pot; **mbōšılle ṯlōxe go qōqa** He cooked lentils in a pot (a jocose translation of דצ"ך עד"ש באח"ב, the acronym of the ten plagues in the Passover's Haggadah).

ק-ו-ק-ב, ק-ב-ק-ב III (< Ar قبقب bray?) **q-ō/b-q-b** to keep awake (talkative guest who stays late): **qam qōqıblan hīl palgızlal** He kept us awake till midninght [Cf. MacD **mqapqip** to cluck < OS].

ק-ו-ק-ר, ק-ר-ק-ר III, ק-ו-ר II(OA קרר bore/Ar قور) ⁺**q-ō/r-q-r**, ⁺**q-w-r** to hollow out, pull out; אֵינֵי קָאם קַרְקִרִילוּ **ʾēne qam qarqırīlu** They pulled his eyes out (RivSh 226); cf. מקוקרא [1/2/3: **mqōqır**; cf. PolG] [=Khan 578 **qawqor** deep, low place, K].

קוקתא (OS) f. **quqta** large jar; pl. **quqyāṯa** (cf. PolU 309)

ק-ו-ר 1 (OA קבר) **q-w-r** to bury; to outwit: **qam qāwırre bṣāxūse** He buried him alive, he proved to be superior to him (NT+).

ק-ו-ר 2 v. ק-ו-ק-ר

קור (< Ar قور) inv. **qōr** thin, emaciated (PolG).

קורא 1 (OA קברא) m. **qōra** grave; **go qōr bābe/ ʾıxre lqōre** to hell with him; pl. קוראתא **qōrāṯa** cemetery (NT+).

קורא 2 (< ?) m. **qūra** sack, bag; pl. **qurāṯa** (RivSh 129, 130).

קורא 3, קורונא(K < T قـوروق unripe; cf. כמתא) m. **qurra, qurrōna** lad (PolU 207: ChNA).

קורבן v. קרבן

קורגה (K?) f. ⁺**qurrage** somewhat old (she-ass) (PolU 428).

קורדאיא, קורדיתא (OS/OA קַרְדְוָיָא) **qurd̠āya, qurd̠ēṯa** Kurd (Arodh); cf. כורדינאיא.

קֻורְזֻום, קֻורְזֻם v. קלזם

קורטאנא (K) m. **qurṭāna** saddle; cf. ס-ר-ג.

קורי (IrAr < P) f. ⁺**qōri** teapot; pl. **qōrīyat** [Khan 578 **qori, qorya** bowl, pan].

קורמא 1, קורמכתא (OS < Gr) m. ⁺**qurma, qurmıkṯa** (thick and twisted) log, firewood; main part of neck, truck (PolU 113).

קורמא 2 (< קורמא 1?) m. ⁺**qurma** ear ridge (cf. PolG), concha (=H תְּנוּךְ אֹזֶן, BT2).

קורמא-ביקא (< קורמא1+ביקא) **qurma-bīqa** (Z ⁺**qurma-zīqa**) tea-drinking party held on snow days at school (lit. log [for fire]-bottle [to drink from] (Br93 339).

קורמז (Ar/K/P) m. **qurmız** crimson, kermes, red dyestuff (NT+).

קורניתא (OA קרנא; Ar قُرنه) f. ⁺**qurnīṯa** corner; pl. **qurnyāṯa** (=H כְּסָלִים, BT3, D); cf. דפנא (NT+).

קורנפל(א) (Ar) m. **qurınfıl(a)** clove, carnation [v. Br93 88-89]; a kind of nosering.

קורען (K/JAB < Ar) m. **qurʿan** the Koran.

קורצא (Ar disk) **qurṣa** disk, coin: **xa qurṣıt dehwa** a golden coin (but PolG: 'Handvoll'); **qurṣıd naʿnaʿ** mint candy (in disk shape); cf. ק-ר-צ 1?

קורקורינכה (< קורי) f.⁺**qorqorīnke** small teapot.

ק(ו)שטניתא (OA) f. **qüšṭanīṯa** bow (NT, Sa83c 24, Am); pl. קושטניאתא **qušṭanyāṯa** (NT); cf. קשטרון.

קושיא, קושיה (H) f. **qušya** difficult question (NT).

קושמן (< קושן?) **qōšman** horse race (?), military exercises (?) (PolU 353).

קושן (T/P) m. **qōšan** hosts (of heaven); pl. **qōšāne** (=H צְבָא [הַשָּׁמַיִם],BT1); cf. ק-ש-נ (NT).

קות (Ar) m. **qūt** foodstuff (=H מִחְיָה, AlfH 67).

קותא 1, קותה (K < P **kūtāh**) **qutta** (m.), **qutte** (f.), short person; cf. עתו.

קותא 2 (< קוותא?) **qōta** only in the greeting **qōta (hā)wēlox** Welcome back! Response is: **raḥme lbābox-yımmox** (cf. PolU 430).

קותא 3 v. קואתא

קותייא (K **qutī**/IrAr **qūṭiya** <T **kutu**) f. **qōtīya** small tin box (PolU 36);-**ıd bırmuṭ** snuff box.

קזא 1 (T) f. **qızza** the queen in cards.

קזא 2 v. קצא

קזאזא (Ar) m. **qazāza** glazier, craftsman (=H חוֹשֵׁב, BT2).

קזאנה (Ar/K < T) f. ⁺**qa/ızāne** pot; pl. ⁺**qazānat** (cf. Zaken 388; PolG); cf. קרא-קזאן.

קזלקוט, קזרקות (SA قـزلقـرد < T red maggot [in your nose] > Go to hell) ⁺**qızzıl/rqōt** (smell/taste of) hell! (PolU 14), disgusting, awful!

ק-ח-ב II (Ar) **q-ḥ-b** to prostitute oneself (Segall #35) (NT+).

קחבא, קחבה, קחבכה (Ar) f. **qaḥba/e, qaḥbıke** prostitute; pl. **qaḥbıkat**; cf. זונה, ברדאיי.

קטוא (< ?) m. **qaṭwa** darning hook (used for repair); cf. כושתא [cf. MacD 276].
קטוטו (H קטטה) **qaṭōṭo** quarrelsome woman.
קטונא (< ק-ט-נ) m. **qıṭṭōna** mildew (Z); garbage, dunghill (NT).
קטותא, קטואתא v. קאטא
קטיאא (OA קטיעא) m. **qaṭīʾa** stick; **qaṭīʾa-pılʾe** stick game, using a long stick to bat a short one); pl. **qaṭīʾe** (cf. PolG).
קטירא (OA קטר be arched?) m. **qṭīra** handful (=H קֹמֶץ/חֹפֶן, BT3; cf. PolG).
ק-ט-ל (OA/OS/Mand) **q-ṭ-l** to kill; IV to cause killing; גמקטליתון גיאניכון **gmaqṭılētun gyānēxun** You get killed (NT2) (NT+).
קטלא (OA/OS) m. **qıṭla** murder, killing; **sēle lqıṭla** He was killed (Z).
קטלנית, קטלאנית (H) **qaṭlānīṯ** husband killer (one whose husbands die prematurely) (NT2); cf. קלועא.
קטמא, קוטמא, קיטמא (OA) m. **qüṭma** ash; nothing of substance; — **brēši** Alas, bad news; — **brēšox** May you mourn [Khan 578 **qaṭma**]
קטמאנא (OA ash-colored) m. **qıṭmāna** sheer nothing (is left); absolutely worth nothing.
ק-ט-מ-נ III (< OA קטם turn into ash) vt/vi **q-ṭ-m-n** to suffer or cause great loss (lit., be in ashes, to mourn), become unlucky.
ק-ט-נ II (Ar) **q-ṭ-n** become musty, mouldy (food); cf. קטונא.
קַטְעִי (Ar) inv. **qaṭʿi** absolute, forever (sale as slave) (BaBin 80).
קטעיין (Ar) adv. **qaṭʿīyan** absolutely (not)(BaBin 119).
ק-ט-פ 1 (Ar) **q-ṭ-f** to pick, pluck (fruits, flowers); cf. קוטיפא.
ק-ט-פ 2 (OA) **q-ṭ-p** to pick up at one go; gather (grapes)(=H בָּצַר, BT3); **qṭīpāle šınse** He slept just enough, had a quick nap.
ק-ט-ק-ט III (< ק-ט-א) **q-ṭ-q-ṭ** to mince, cut small.
ק-ט-ר v. ק-ת-ר
קטרא (OS ܟܐܦܐ rock/OA קְתָרִין bowlders) m. ***qaṭra** rock; — **mjōbāna** echo, echoing rock; impudent (one who talks back); pl. **qaṭrāre, qaṭre** (=H צורים, BT4, סְלָעִים, PolG) (NT+).
קי, קוי, קבי (< קוי) interr. **qay, qawi** (cf. MeAl 184), **qavi** (Hob89 182), why? (cf. PolG) **qay qūya** Why so! (said when one doesn't want to answer a 'why?' question)

קחבותא (< קחבא) f. **qaḥbūṯa** prostitution, adultery (NT+).
קחורא, קחורתא (< ק-ח-ר) adj. **qaḥūra, qaḥurta** sad (cf. PolG)
ק-ח-ט (Ar) vt/vi **q-ḥ-ṭ** be very thirsty; cf. קחתי; **dunye qḥīṭāle** he looked all over (PolU 5).
ק-ח-י, ק-ה-י (OA/OS קהי) **q-ḥ/h-y** (teeth) be set on edge; (knife) become dull; IV to set on edge (AvidH מַקְחִי=H הַקְהֵה; cf. PolG).
קחפא (Ar skull)) m. **qaḥfa** clay flower pot, potsherd; ugly woman.
ק-ח-ר (IrAr **q-h/ḥ-r** subdue) **q-ḥ-r** to grieve; IV to upset, cause grieve (NT+).
קחרא, קחריתא (IrAr **qahra**) f. **qaḥra, qaḥrīta** worry, grief; **mıtle mqaḥrīte** He died out of grief; **mqaḥır brone** out of grief for his son; **šqaḥra xwa ʾavet baḥra** out of grief, I threw myself in the river (SaAC 21) [RivSh 224 קַהְרָא; 259 קַחְרָא **qah/ḥra**].
קחתי, קהתי (K < Ar قحط) f. **qaḥ/hti** dearth, thirst, desolate land (=H תֹּהוּ/צִמָּאוֹן, BT5); זחמי וקהתי **zaḥme uqahti** hardship and scarcity (BaBin 106); cf. ק-ח-ט.
קט (Ar) **qaṭ** (not) at all (with emphasis); perchance? (opens a question; cf. H כלום; NT) [AvidH 34 הַקַד **haqad**=H -הֲ].
ק-ט-א (OA קטע) vt/vi **q-ṭ-ʾ** to cut, to hew; to reduce, deduct; to stop; to shorten; to spoil (milk); - **tıxub** cross border (PolU 286); **ma qqāṭeʾ ʿāqılox** What do you think? What have you decided; **ʿāqıli la qṭeʾle ʿılla** I didn't like her; **qqāṭeʾ qam gyāne** He shows off, brags; **ʾilāha qāṭeʾla mgēb mōsox** May God consider this (misfortune) instead of your death; - **qāla** to silence or be silent; **qṭōʾ qālox** Shut up! IV to mince; to branch (NT4); **qam maqṭıʾāle ʿāqıle** She convinced him (NT+).
קטאא (OA קטעא) m. **qıṭʾa** segment, section, piece; pl. **qıṭʾe** [but AvidH 24 קִטְאָאֵי **qıṭʾāʾe**]. NT+
קטאאה (Ar قطا sand-grouse). sg./pl. **qaṭāʾa/e** quail(s) (=H שְׂלָו, BT2); cf. מן 2.
קטאונכא (< קטאא) m. **qıṭʾōnka** tiny piece.
קטאלא, קטלתא (OA) **qaṭāla, qaṭalta** killer.
קטאפא (< ק-ט-פ) m. **qṭāpa** vintage (=H בָּצִיר, BT3); cf. רִיפְּצָא.

[MacD 272 **qawī/qay** why; very].

קייאמא (OA) **qayyāma** eternity, ever; **la gdā'ır hil qayyāma** He will never come back (said after a long wait); cf. קיים.

קיאמתא, קיימה (K < Ar) f. **qyāmıta, qıyyēme** resurrection; ability to stand (=H תְּקוּמָה, BT3, D); great uproar, torrential rain.

קיאצא (< ק-י-צ) **qayāṣa** shearer (=H גּוֹזֵז, PolG).

ק-י-ג̇ (< ק-י-צ?) ⁺**q-y-č** to cut a slice of meat; to amputate; **pappūka, 'aqle qam qēčila** poor thing, his foot was amputated; to pick (fruit) [Hob89 221); cf. ג̇-י-ג̇ 2 [cf. MacD 278 **qéčī** scissors].

קיג̇ור (K **qojōr**) inv. ⁺**qīčor** something very salty, used only in **malūxa x-qīčor**.

קיג̇כ (K yellow, green) **qīčık** dark red dye.

ק-י-ד 1 II (Ar) **q-y-d** to write down (accounts, lists); be strict.

ק-י-ד 2 v. י-ק-ד

קידתא (< י-ק-ד) f. **qyad̲ta** (Z **qyazta**) burn (=H כְּוִיָּה, BT2; צָרֶבֶת, BT3).

קיטא (OA) m. **qēṭa** summer; **qēṭa bābıd faqīrīn-īle** Summer is father of the poor.

קילך (K?) adv. **qēlax** a little; קילך קילך **qēlax-qēlax** little by little; יאן ראבא יאן קילך **yān rāba yān qēlax** Be it much or little (NT5 408) [cf. MacD 278 **qēlaġ/x** little < K(?); Mengozzi 302: **qaylāx** a little < K].

ק-י-מ (OA) **q-y-m** to get up; be erect (penis); be fulfilled (blessing, curse); קמלה צמלה **qimle ṣımle** He began fasting, fasted; קמלו אל פאתוך **qımlu 'il pātox** They rebelled against you; סאעה קמתילא **sā'e qımtēla** He is in luck; **qımle bsēfar-tōra** He had an aliya; **qımle ž-gyāne** He stood up; recovered, became alert (MeAl 183); **qqēmıwa ugyatwīwa mızġas blıššāna bassīma** They got along very well (PolG)[3: **qū(lox)**; קומון **qūmun** (NT3); **qūn, qū(lōxun)**]; IV to practice (precepts); to appoint, to establish a (ruler); to raise (children) (BaBin 131) [1: **mōqım**; 2/3: **māqım**; 4: **maqōme**]. NT+

קים v. קם, קימה

קיים, קַיָּאם (H-OA) m. **qayyām** everlasting, eternal (NT); live (God) (=H חַי, BT4); cf. קייאמא.

קימא 1 (K) m. **qīma** minced fat for stuffing.

קימא 2 (< ק-י-מ) p.p. **qīma** erect (Segal #58); awake, up.

קימה, קימתא, -קים (Ar) f. **qīme, qīmıta, qīm-** value, at the price of; importance (cf. PolG).

קיימה v. קיאמתא

קימך (K < T) m. **qēmax** sweet clotted butter.

קיימתא (< ק-י-מ) n. act. **qyamta** (kind of) rising.

קיסונכא (< OS ܩܝܣܐ wood) m.**qaysunka** bobbin.

קיסי (K < T) f. **qaysi** dried apricots.

קיסר (H < L) m. **qēsar** Roman ruler (NT).

קיע (< H כיח phlegm/Ar قيح puss?) **qīya'** filth(y); **jullox pışlu qīya'** Your clothes have become filthy, disgusting; cf. כך.

ק-י-צ (OA קצץ) **q-y-ṣ** to shear; cf. מקץ קיאצא,; **'ırbıd qyāṣa** sheep ready to be sheared (metaphor for Jewish people) (RivSh 202; NTU4 150b); be pinched (fingers in the door); - **(roḥāyıd) gyāna** to exert onself, work very hard (SaAC 1; cf. PolG).

ק-י-ר 1 (OA קרר) **q-y-r** to become cold; **bqāyırrox** You'll catch cold; **qarri** I feel cold; **qırra b'ēni** It lost its value for me; IV to cool (vt); cf. קרתא, קרירא.

ק-י-ר 2 II (Ar) ⁺**q-y-r** to tar, seal with pitch; cf. קירא.

ק-י-ר 3 (Ar قرّ) **q-y-r** to confess; be conviced (NT); cf. ק-ר-ר.

קירא (OA <Ak **qīru** > Gr/L) f. ⁺**qīra** tar, pitch; v. אירא; **kōma x-qīra** pitch black, real ugly; **zılle bqīra ubqalāla** went to hell; v. קללה, דבוקאנא.

קיתן (K/IrAr < T) m. **qētan** lacing string.

קלאא (Ar قلعة) f. **qal'a** fortress; pl. קלאאתא **qal'āt̲a** (NT); קַלַיֵי **qalāye** (RivSh 143).

קְלַאוִיז (T **kılavuz** leader of a file) **qı/alawiz** watchman (= H צֹפֶה, PolG); cf. מינכאנא.

קלאייה (< ק-ל-י?) **qlāya/e** (?) roasting (?): only once in **qırbōnıt** - roasting sacrifices (=H תמידים ומוספים) (NTU4 149b).

קלאיי (< קלה 1) ⁺**qalāyi** raw tin(=H בְּדִיל, BT4).

קלאמא (Ar قلم/OA קולמוס < Gr/L) **qalāma** pencil; engraving tool (=H חֶרֶט, BT2); cf. קלמי, קלם פנדאן.

קלאתכת (K< Ar قلي fry, roast) pl. **qalātkat** parched grains (=H קָלִי, BT3; Ruth 2:14).

ק-ל-ב (Ar) II **q-l-b** to turn over, change course; change for worse (weather); **qlıble range** His appearance changed (for worse) **qlıble ʾılli** He betrayed me, reversed our agreement; IV to pour (cooked food from pot to plate), to serve (cooked dish); v. ת-נ-י.

קלב (Ar/K/T/P) inv. **qalb** counterfeit, false insincere.

ק-ל-ב-ז III (< ק-ל-ב) **q-l-b-z** to roll over (cf. PolG).

קלבתא (< ק-ל-ב) f. **qlabta** upheaval (=H הֲפֵכָה, BT1); pl. **qlabyāṯa** treasons (=H תַּהְפּוּכוֹת, BT5).

קלה 1 (K < T **kalay**/Ar قلعي; cf. OA קִילְיָא alkali, potash) f. **qıle** white tin, pewter; cf. קלאיי.

קלה 2 (K **qele** crow) f. **qılle** hawk (SaLH)[cf. MacD 279].

קלה-דלה (Ar قلّة ذلّة) **qılle-dılle** scarcity, abject conditions; **qam marūyāle brōna b-** She raised her son in sheer scarcity.

ק-ל-ו (< ?) **q-l-w** to become clean; to be atoned (sin)(NT5 406); II to clean; cf. קליוא (NT+). [< MacD 279 **qāl** pure, unalloyed metal < T? Mutz 221 **qalwa** <OS ܡܟܠܒܐ mold > *order > cleanliness?].

קלווא (OS < Ar قالب) m. **qalwa** mould, matrix; image (=H צֶלֶם, BT1), body: **sāṭān ʾurre go qalwe** Satan entered his body (PolG).

קלולא, קלולתא (OS; cf. OA קְלִיל) adj. **qalūla, qalulta** light, quick, simple (NT)[cf. Khan 577].

קלונכא (K) m. **qalunka** smoking pipe.

קלו-קלו (K? cf. כלורא) f. **qılo-qılo** bagel-shaped pastry; pl. **qılo-qılōyat**.

קלועא, קלועתא (< ק-ל-ע) **qalōʿa, qaluʿta** one (husband or wife) whose disposition causes death to the spouse (PolU 353); cf. קטלנית.

קלותא v. קליוא

קלזם, קולזום, קוּלְזֻּום, קוּרְזֵּום, קֻלְזַם, קוּרְזֶם (Ar < Gr?) **qülzüm, qılzam, qurzım,** reed (NT; BT4, D; AvidH 53; PolG); cf. בחרד קלזם, קלאמא, קרם.

ק-ל-ט-י III (OA קלט?) **q-l-ṭ-y** to pine, to be lovesick (Pol 108) [=MacD 195 **mqalṭī** to curdle; be inflamed (heart)].

ק-ל-י 1 (OA burn, roast, destroy/Ar) **q-l-y** to fry, roast (seeds); cf. מקלה, קלאתכת.

ק-ל-י 2 (Ar depart, rise in the air (bird)) **q-l-y** to become rare, disappear (from the market); **qlēle mrıš pōxıd dunye** It is not obtainable anymore [=MacD 195 run fast].

קליא 1 (< ק-ל-י 1) m. **qalya** fried and heavily salted meat (preserved for winter) [Khan 577 **qalya** fat of a sheep's tail]..

קליא 2 , קליתא (< ק-ל-י 1) p.p. **qılya, qlīṯa** fried; **laxma** - crunchy thin bread; cf. קריגא.

קליוא, קלותא (< ק-ל-ו) p.p. **qlīwa, qlūta** clean (NT+).

קליוותא (< קליוא) **qlīwūṯa** neatness, cleanliness.

קלייה (< AnAr?) f. **qalīye** saffron soup.

קליל (Ar; cf. OA/OS קליל קליל little by little) adj. **qalīl** few: **qalīl dyōmāṯa** a few days (NT3); pl. קלילין **qalīlīn** (her merits are) few (NT3).

קליסרכה (K) f. **qalīserke** sauteed spiced meat.

קלכתא (K **qalik** turtle's shell) f. **qalıkṯa** sheath (=H נָדָן, PolG, PolUL 401).

קללה (H) f. **qalāla** used only in **zılle (bqīra u)bqalāla** He went to hell (what do I care).

קלמא (OS; OA קַלְמְתָא) f. **qalma** louse; pl. קלמיה **qalme** NT+ [Khan 577 **qamla**, f.].

קלם טרש (K vet's knife) **qalam ṭırraš** fine razor, accurate cutting tool (PolU 336, 365).

קלמי (Ar/P; cf. קלאמא) inv. **qalamí** slim, pencil-like (PolU 15).

קלם פנדאן (K < IrAr?) **qalam ⁺panmdān** fountain pen; v. פנדאן, קלאמא.

קלס (K) inv. **qals** stingy.

ק-ל-ע (Ar drive away) **q-l-ʿ** to go away, go to hell (cf. PolG); to cause harm by casting the evil eye: **qam qalʿīlu barxe deni** (People) caused our lambs to die; cf. קלועא; IV in **lıbbe mqō/ūlıʿle** He felt disgusted (MeAl 180).

ק-ל-פ II **q-l-p** to peel (NT+).

קלפא ((OA/OS קְלָפְתָא) m. **qalpa** peel; pl. **qalpe**.

קלפוגכא (< קלפא) m. **qalpučka** tiny shell

(such as of the acorn (PolU 317)
קלפכתא (< קלפא) f. **qalpıkta** bark, shell of dry fruits; pl. **qalpıkyata** (=H פְּצָלוֹת, BT1).
קם 1, קָם/ קִים, קאמ-, מקם מן (OA) **qam ~ qım** (RivSh 115, 121, 269, 270), **qām-, mqam mın** before, in front of , ahead of; compared to (PolU 229) לקאמן **lqāman** in the following; קאמיהון קאמיהון **qāmēhun-qāmēhun** (was moving constantly) ahead of them; מקם האדך **mqam hādax** (NT5 407), **mqam dē-xa** (Z), because of this.
קם 2 (ק-י-מ/ קם 1?) **qam**, a conversive particle used with a.p. to convey past tense: **qam našqāle** She kissed him vs. **našqāle** She kisses/will kiss him; **qam xazyāli xmarta** the she-ass saw me (BT4).
קמא (< קי+מא) **qammā** why?; cf. טלא 1.
קמאיא, קמיתא (OA) adj. **qamāya, qamēta** first, previous, early, ancient; pl. **qamāye** (NT+) [Khan 578 **qmaʾel**].
קמאייה (< קמאיא) adv. **qamāye** first, before, days of yore; **bıd qamāye** in the beginning (=H בְּרֵאשִׁית, BT1); **ʾıl qamāye dīde** towards him (=H לִקְרָאתוֹ, BT1); **mın qamāye** since immemorial times (=H מֵעוֹלָם, BT1) (NT+).
קְמַאיֻותַא (< קמאיא) f. **qamāyūta** fore (cf. PolG).
קמארא (IrAr< It) **qamāra** sedan car, taxi.
קמג'ור (K) m. **qamčur** tax imposed on sheep based on their number.
קמג'י, קאמג'י (T) **qa/āmči** whip (cf. PolU 236); pl. **qamčīyat**.
ק-מ-ט (OA) vt/vi **q-m-ṭ** to shrink, squeeze hard; II to harden (heart) (=H אִמֵּץ,BT5); cf. ק-ר-מ-ט.
ק-מ-י (< ?) **q-m-y** to scorch (as by iron).
קמיותא, קַמַיֻותַא (< קמאיא) f. **qamayūta** prior state, beginning (NT5 409); towards (=H לִקְרַאת, BT2, D).
קְמִיטוּתָא (< ק-מ-ט) f. **qmīṭūta** hardening (=H חֹזֶק יָד, AvidH 22).
קמיסא, קמסתא (< ק-מ-ס) p.p. **qmīsa, qmısta** very clean; often as hendiadys: **qlīwa-qmīsa**.
קמיתא v. קמאיא
ק-מ-כ II (קמכא; OA √ קמח to dress hides with flour; OS to make flour) **q-m-x** to be sprinkled with flour, to taste flour-like.
קמכא (OA קמחא) m. **qamxa** flour; cf. ק-מ-כ.
ק-מ-ס (Ar to plunge in water/OA קימץ to scrape off with bent fingers?) to be very clean (clothes); cf. קמיסא.
קמצא (OA) m. **qamṣa** locust; pl. **qamṣe**.
קמרי (Ar) **qamari** an Ottoman coin; pl. **qamariye** (PolU 420).
קנא 1, קנתא (OA nest, cluster, family) f. **qınna** (Z), **qınta** (+NT), nest; v. דבורא; pl. **qınnāne**.
קנא 2 (OS ܩܢܐ) f. **qınna** the kernel or meat of nuts; pl. **qınne**; cf. ק-נ-נ [cf. Mutz 221]
קנאה (H) **qınʾa** envy; cf. כין; pl. קְנָאוֹת (BT4,D).
קנאנה v. קאנא
קנארא (Ar) m. **qınnāra** butcher's hook.
קנד (K/P/Ar) m. **qand**, usually **šākar qand**, rock or loaf of sugar.
קנדג' (IrAr < P **qand āb**?) **qandaġ**, or **čāyi qandaġ**, very weak tea, hot water and sugar (for sick people).
קנדהארי (K) adj. **qındıhāri** wheat of superior quality.
קנדילא (Ar/OA < L candle) f. **qandēla** hanging oil lamp; cf. למפא, פאנוזא, שמעא.
קנדלייה (K < Ar?) f. **qandalīye** large clay jar, glazed only inside, with narrow base and mouth but wide belly (cf. PolU 427).
קנדרושכא (K? cf. P **kandaruš** dwarf, hillock) m. **qındırōška** tiny-round one (endearing term for toddlers) (SaNR).
קנויז (AzT) m. **qanawiz/s** fine silk cloth (SaAc 9) [MacD 281 **qānāwūz**].
קנטר (Ar) m. **qınṭar** kantar (large weight unit), talent (=H כִּכָּר, BT2; חֹמֶר שְׂעוֹרִים, BT3, D); huge amount; pl. **qınṭāre**.
קניא (OA) m. **qanya** cane, stalk; **-ıt qōma** spine (PolG); **b- rēšan kēse grāʾa** We are very strong/smart (our head can be shaved by a cane) (PolU 4) (NT+).
קניאנא (OA/OS קניינא property, livestock) m. **qınyāna** riding animal; house animal; pl. **qınyāne** (=H בְּעִיר, BT1).
קנין (H) m. **qınyan** possession (NT3); **d-w-q - ta xawxıt** to sign an agreement (PolU 351).
קַנִינַא (Ar) m. **qanīna** flask, chalice (RivSh 127)

קניעא, קנעתא (< ק-נ-ע) p.p. **qnīʿa, qnıʿta** content, modest; cf. קאנע.

ק-נ-נ II (< קנא 2) **q-n-n** to make or become crispy (roasted snack seeds).

ק-נ-ע (Ar) **q-n-ʿ** to be satisfied with little;IV to convince, make one content (NT+).

קנפא (IrAr/T/K < It/Sp/Fr) m. **qanapa** padded bench; pl. **qanapat**.

קַנְקוּתַא (< ?) f. **qanqūṯa** (?) spider (RivSh 256); cf. פקואתא 1, קואתא.

ק-נ-ק-ח III (Ar قنح thirst) **q-n-q-ḥ** be very thirsty, drink to the last drop.

קסטא 1 v. קצתא

קסטא 2 (Ar قسط) m. **qısṭa** portion, allotment.

קסטור (K) m. **qasṭor** velvety textile for women's overcoat.

ק-ס-מ 1 (OA/Ar) **q-s-m** to divine (NT); to swear, promise (RivSh 238).

ק-ס-מ 2 (Ar) **q-s-m** to divide (NT5, 407).

קסמא (Ar) m. **qısma** part, section; lot, portion (PolG) (NT+).

קפאטמא (T) f. **qappāṭma** kept mistress.

קפאנא (P/T/K < Ar قبّان) f. **qappāna** scale beam.

קפו (< ?) **qıppo** spider's web, fleecy dirt; **duqle qıppo** It is covered with sooty lint.

ק-פ-ח (Ar قحف wash, sweeep away?) **q-f-ḥ** to drink to the last drop; cf. ק-נ-ק-ח.

ק-פ-ט (IrAr fill up) **q-p-ṭ** to cover well, seal; fill up (an empty ship) (PolU 309).

קפטן (Ar < E) **qapṭan** captain; pl. **qapṭāne** (PolU 309).

ק-פ-י 1 II (OS) **q-p-y** to collect, pick up things (such as firewood), search and find (BaBin 152, 154), to procure (PolG) [MacD 282 catch in hand or mouth, much used by dogs].

ק-פ-י 2 (Ar; OA/OS) **q-f-y** to surface at river's bank (drowned people, logs), to anchor.

קפיא (OA/OS קוּפְיָא) m. **qapya** dry branch, floating wood (PolG); cf. קאפויא [=MacD 283 **qāpyū** long pole used to gather fruits or honey]; cf. ק-פ-י 1.

קפילא, קפלתא (< ק-פ-ל 2) p.p. **qfīla, qfılta** inhibited, fearful.

קפך, קפג' (K< T) m. **qapax/ġ** cover (of pots, cans); pl. **qapāġe** (cf. PolG).

ק-פ-ל 1 (OA) **q-p-l** to fold (arms) (NT).

ק-פ-ל 2 (Ar lock) **q-f-l** to lock, button; to be inhibited, fearful; cf. קפילא; קופלא.

קפלא (OS/Ar/K) f. **qıfla** (Z) group (of birds, travelers); pl. קפלאתא **qıflāṯa**. (NT+)

קפלאיא (< קפלא) m. **qıflāya** traveler (with a group, caravan) (NT).

קפץ (Ar; cf. OA קפצא/OS ܩܦܨܐ birdcage) m. **qafaṣ** chicken coop, cage (BaBin 159).

קפץ, קפץ' (Ar قبض/قفص) inv. **qafẓ/ṣ** constipated; **pıšle qafṣ** He has become constipated.

קפרא (Ar) **qafra** desolate (NT3); עודאבד קפרא **ʿuḏābıd** - suffering of desolation (AmU2 5a).

קפראנא (K **kaper**) f. **qaprāna** booth, stall.

קפתא (< ?) f. **qafta** bunch (of plants), nosegay; pl. **qaftıkyāṯa** (PolU 24)

קץ (H) m. **qēṣ** end of days, Messianic times: קץ משיח הייא מכוילליני **qēṣ māšīyaḥ hayya maxwēleni** Show us soon the Messianic Times (BaBin 7) (NT+).

קצאבא, קצאפא (< Ar قصاب; OA/OS **qaṣṣāvā**) m. **qaṣāba** (Z), **qaṣāpa** (NT), butcher; **qaṣṣāb bāši** royal/chief butcher (PolUR 59).

קצאבותא (< קצאבא) f. **qaṣābūṯa** butchership.

קצבא (Ar; cf. OA קַשְׁבָא) **qaṣba** palm-tree (NT3); a date (Z); v. דארא [Khan 578 **qaṣpa**].

קצבכאנא (Ar-T) f. **qaṣabxāna** slaughter-house (=H טֶבַח, BaBin 118).

ק-צ-ד (Ar) **q-ṣ-d** to intend, aspire (NT); to have intercourse (euph.) (RivP 212).

קצד (Ar) m. **qaṣd** aim, intention; לא אודואלי קצד **la ʾuḏwāli qaṣd** I had not expected; **ʾuzli qaṣdıd ʾilāha** I did God's will (PolU 33) NT+

קצה (Ar) f, **qıṣṣe** cutting (clothes) (PolU 80).

קצור 1, קצודי (K < Ar) **qıṣūr(i)** laxity, shortcoming; **la gōzi ču qıṣūr** They do all they can, they save no effort.

קצור 2 (IrAr) m. **qıṣur** change (left after buying something); **la hullēli ču qıṣur** He didn't give me any change.

קציפא, קצפתא (< ק-צ-פ) p.p. **qṣīfa, qṣıfta** damned (but also used jocously)(cf. PolG).

ק-צ-פ, ק-ר-צ-פ III (Ar) **q-ṣ-f, q-r-ṣ-f** to die/or kill untimely (cf. PolG) (used mostly in curses); v. קציפא.

קצצתא (OA piece of wood) f. **qıṣaṣta** lump of sugar; pl. **qıṣaṣyāṯa**.

ק-צ-ק-צ III (OA קצץ; IrAr **gṣgṣ**) **q-ṣ-q-ṣ** to snick, cut up; cf. מקץ, ק-י-צ; be afflicted: **nıšāmə mquṣqıṣla** his soul was in pain (PolU 330).

קצרא (Ar < L) m. **qaṣra** castle; pl. קצריה **qaṣrə** (NT5 383); - **uquṣūrkat** all kind of castles; קצרארה **qaṣrārə** (BaBin 103, Z; PolG); קצראניה **qaṣrānə** (Sa83c 39, Am).

קצתא, קסתא, קסטא (P/K < Ar) f. ⁺**qıṣta** story, affair; **mā qıṣta-la** What is happening? **qıṣṣıt** prep. about (PolG); pl. קצתיאתא קצתה, **qıṣtyāṯa, qıṣtə** (NT+) [Khan 578 **quṣta**].

קצ̇א, קזא (Ar قضاء) **qaẓ/za** district (PolU 123).

ק-צ̇-י, ק-ד-י (Ar) vt/vi **q-ẓ-y, q-ḍ-y** (BT5, D; AvidH 42; Hob89 221), to provide (need), fulfill wish; be taken care of (need); **qẓēlu ʾēza** They managed to provide for the holiday; **la qazya** (This is) impossible (PolG); - **gyāna d-** prepare oneself to (PolG). NT+

קזלקוט v. קצ̇ל/רקוט

קקא (< ?) m. **qaqqa** walnut (baby talk); cf. גוזא.

קקואנא, קקואנתא (OS < Ak **qaqabānu**) f. **qaqwān(t)a**. red-legged partridge [cf. OA קקואי name of an unclean bird; קקתא, קקא pelican].

קקרא (< OA ככרא talent, heavy weight?) ⁺**qaqra** very important, learned person.

קרא (<קרגא/T **qara** black) ⁺**qırra** crow, miser; v. קאעא.

קראא (OA קרא, קרעא) m. **qarʾa** zucchini, squash; pl. **qarʾe** (=H קִשּׁוּאִים, BT4); cf. קראתא.

קראדא (K worn out) **qarrāda** strip of loose threads at the edge of carpets or woven materials.

קרז'אנא, קרז'נתא (< קרא) adj. ⁺**qırrıžāna, -anta,** pitch black (PolU 277).

קרא-טפא (T black hill) **qara ṭappa** hell, far-away place.

קראיא 1 (< ק-ר-י) vn **qrāya** reading, studying; call or singing of a bird (PolU 344).

קראיא 2, קריתא (< ק-ר-י) **qarāya, qarēṯa** one who reads, reader, learned person (BaBin 104); **pıšla xa qarēsa, ḥāxām xōra les** She became a learned woman, no sage like her (PolU 310); v. כתאוא 2.

קרא-קזאן (K/T) **qará-⁺qazān** cooking pot (PolU 17)

קראר v. קרר

קראתא, קריאתא, קריתא(< קראא) f. **qareʾṯa, qarēṯa**, pumpkin, gourd (cf. NT6 136); **qareʾṯıd māya** turtle [cf. MacD 284 **qrā, qarāyā** tortoise; no source given].

קרבאלך (K/IrAr < T) ⁺**qarabālax** throng, noise (cf. PolG); **ḥajji** - Mr. Noise, agitator.

קרבן, קורבן, קרבון (H/Ar > K/P) m. ⁺**qurban, qurbon** (+NT3; BT2, Arodh), sacrifice; common in women's speech with their sons or dear ones: **pēšan qurbānox** May I become in lieu of you (if anything bad might happen to you); **pıšle ⁺qurbānox** He passed away; **qurbān ʾilāha** (May I be His) sacrifice, God (common epithet for God) (cf. PolU 373); pl. קוּרבַּנֵי/קוּרְבּוֹנֵי **qurbā/ōne** (RivSh 173); **qurbānōṯ** (=H עוֹלוֹת, BT1, Z).

קרגא, קרגה (< K/T/P **qirğu** merlin?) adj. ⁺**qırrıga, -e** miser, miserable (=crow?); cf. קאעא; pl. ⁺**qırrıgat** [=MacD 284 **qerğā** crow, small falcon?].

ק-ר-ג̇ (< ק-ר-ט/Ar قرش nibble, crunch) **q-r-č** to crunch; cf. קריג̇א.

קרג̇איא, קרג̇יתא (K < T) **qaračāya, -čēṯa** gypsy, beggar (BaBin 115); pl. **qaračāye** (=H זַמְזְמִים, BT5).

ק-ר-פ-ג̇ v. ק-ר-ג̇-פ

ק-ר-ד-כ (< OS صرص broken skull?) **q-r-d-x** to smash [cf. MacD 196 make noise; Khan 557 be shuttered].

ק-ר-ו (OA קרב) **q-r-w** to come near; IV to bring near; to offer (sacrifice) (NT+).

קרוא (OA קורבא) **qırwa** near(ness); לקרוא דידה **lqırwa dīde** near it; דילו קרוא אילה **dīlu qırwa ʾılle** Who are close to him (NT); קרוילה **qırwēle** He is near (NT5

401); קרויה **qırwe** near (adj. pl.: Sa83c 34, Am).
קרואוה (pl. of קרוא)adv. **qırwāwe** around, about (temporal and spatial) (cf. Gz73 83).
קרוג̇כא (< Ar-K?) m. **qaručka** small clay bowl.
קרוטא (< ?) m. **qırrōṭa** cartlilage, esophagus [cf. MacD 284 **qarūč/ṭa**].
קרופא (< ק-ר-פ 1?) **qırrōpa** old stooping man.
קרוש (T/Ar) m. **qıruš** small Turkish coin; biblical coin (=H גֵּרָה, BT2); pl. **qırūše**.
קרושתא (< OA קרש) f. **qırušta** engraved spot, crusted surface; pl. **qırušyāṯa** (=H נְקֻדּוֹת [הַכָּסֶף], AvidH 41); cf. גז'נז'ה.
ק-ר-ז' (< קרז') vi **q-r-ž** (**rēš**-upon) crowd (PolU 281).
קרז' (< K?) **qırrıž** pile,heap; **p-y-š** - to pile (vi), to crowd (PolU 289).
ק-ר-ט (OA) **q-r-ṭ** to crunch, bite; cf. ק-ר-ג̇.
קרטאלא (OS/Ar < Gr; cf. OA קרטליתא small basket) m. **qırṭāla** huge basket.
ק-ר-ת-נ III (< קורטאנא), ק-ר-ט-נ **⁺q-r-t-n** to saddle (=H חָבַשׁ, BT, PolG); cf. ס-ר-ג.
ק-ר-י (OA) **q-r-y** to call, read, study; **qrēle qāme** He tried to convince him; קריאנא תלביס אלה **qaryāna talbīs ᵓılle** I will (falsely) plot against him; to invite to a festive meal (Socin 161)[3: **qrūn** (NT5 404), **qrāwun** (Z)]; IV to teach (reading); to ask one to read; read aloud; v. קראיא, מקרויה, מקריאנא (NT+).
קרי (H) **⁺qēri** nocturnal emission of semen (BaBin 30)(=H מִקְרֵה-לָיְלָה, BT5) (NT+).
קריאתא v. קראתא, קריתא 1
קריג̇א (< ק-ר-ג̇) p.p. **qrīča** crunchy (bread) (cf. PolU 331).
קריוא, קרותא (OA/OS קריבא) adj. **qarīwa, qarūta** close, near; **qarīwi** My fellow (Christian) (used by Jews when talking to a Christian): **qarīwi matte** My dear Matthew!
קריון, אקריון (< ק-ר-ו) adv. **(ı)qrīwın** soon (NT2).
קריסכתא (K **čirusk**) f. **qrīsıkṯa** spark; pl. **qrīsıkyāṯa**.
קריעת ים סוף (H) **qırīᶜaṯ yām sūf** (biblical) Splitting of Red sea (NT2).
קרירא, קרתא/קררתא (OA) adj. **qarīra, qarırta, qarıtta** (cf. PolG) cold; food or drink served cold (NT5 410); cf. ק-י-ר קרתא,.
קריר דארואח (Ar) **qarīr dᵓarwāḥ** the serene souls (?) (NT2).
קריתא 1 (OA) f. **qarīṯa** wooden beam; pl. קְרַיַּאתַא **qaryāṯa** (=H בְּרִיחִים/קְרָסִים, BT2, D) (NT+). [Khan 578 **qārita** beam, pl. **qarye**].
קריתא 2 (< ק-ר-י) f. **qarēṯa** banquet by invitation.
קריתא 3 v. קראתא
ק-ר-כ (OA/OS קרח be bald) **q-r-x** to fade, turn pale; cf. ק-ר-ק-כ [cf. Mutz 22].
ק-ר-מ 1 (< OA/OS form a film/crust) **q-r-m** be covered (with ashes) or colored (as mourning sign); used mostly in curses in women talk: **qarmat-ṣabġat** May you wear mourning colored clothes; **qrımli-ṣbıġli** How great is my loss; cf. קרמתא; to cover with skin (only in RivSh 112)[MacD 285 cover].
ק-ר-מ 2 (K freeze, contort) **⁺q-r-m** to become stiff from sitting or standing too long.
קרם, קֻרַאם (K **qeram‹qalam**) m. **⁺qı/urram** reed (Z)(=H סוּף, BT; PolG); v. קלזם.
ק-ר-מ-ז III (< קורמז) **q-r-m-z** to turn brownish, well done (fried food).
ק-ר-מ-ט III (OS < ק-מ-ט) vt/vi **q-r-m-ṭ** to wrinkle; be sad (face) (PolG).
ק-ר-מ-כ III (OA קמח pulverize) vt/vi **q-r-m-x** to smash; be smashed, crushed; cf. קמכא.
קרמתא 1 (< ק-ר-מ 1) f. **qaramta** cover, tablecloth of the Seder plate (Br93 284).
קרמתא 2 (< ק-ר-מ 1?) f. **qaramta** pastry filled with dates and fried till having red-brown color; beautiful maiden with such color; pl. **qaramyāṯa**.
קרנאצא (Ar قرناس fore or top) **⁺qırnāṣ** top:**gūnīye ⁺mılye hīl -u** bags full to their rim (PolU 383).
ק-ר-נ-צ III (< ?) **q-r-n-ṣ** to crouch [=MacD 196 **mqarniz**].
קרסיסכא, קרסיסכה (< K?) adj. **qarasiska, -ke,** cute (child) (SaAC 23
ק-ר-פ 1 (K **qerpol** heap) **q-r-p** to heap, to jam, to crowd (PolU 8); v. קרופא, ק-ר-ק-פ

ק-ר-פ 2 (< Ar peel?) ⁺q-r-f to wrench (Pol 109), to pinch off (=H מָלַק, BT3, D); **lıbbi ⁺qrıfle mızdoʾsa** I was very frightened.

ק-ר-פ-ג̇, ק-ר-ג̇-פ III (< ?) **q-r-p-č, q-r-č-p** to overwhelm (a bird in order to catch it); to snatch (PolU 345); to make love violently.

ק-ר-פ-צ III (Ar) **q-r-f-ṣ** to squat (with hands around legs).

ק-ר-צ 1 (OA/Ar) vt **q-r-ṣ** to pinch (Segal #56); to freeze (vi); cf. קורצא?

ק-ר-צ 2 (Ar قرص) **q-r-ṣ** to freeze, benumb.

ק-ר-צ-פ v. ק-צ-פ

קרקודא (K) **qarqōda** skeleton, thin person.

קרקול (K/T sentry) m. **qaraqōl** head of **nıžda** robbers band (PolU 428).

ק-ר-ק-כ III (< ק-ר-כ) **q-r-q-x** to clear; **ʾıqır šımme mqurqıxle** It dawned (bottom of sky cleared).

קרקנדאיא (< ?) m. **qarqındāya** atheist, hedonist [cf. Macd **qarqandā** stubborn, pugnacious].

ק-ר-ק-פ III (< ק-ר-פ 1) **q-r-q-p** to overcrowd, become a burden (a guest); become old and bent; cf. קרופא [MacD 196 to butt; be old].

קרקפתא (OA) f. **qarqıpta** skull; pl. **qarqıpyāta** (cf. PolGr 55)

ק-ר-ק-ר 1 III (OA/Ar) ⁺**q-r-q-r** to argue, shout.

ק-ר-ק-ר 2 v. ק-ו-ק-ר

קרקרתא (< ק-ר-ק-ר 1) f. **qırqırta** clamor, loud arguments (PolU 353).

ק-ר-ק-ש III (< OA קשקש?) **q-r-q-š** to shout, quarrel (NT2); cf. ק-ג̇-ק-ג̇.

קרקש (K < T having black eyebrow?) **qaraqaš** well-built, strong (?) (mule) (PolU 113).

קרקשא (< ק-ר-ק-ש) m. **qarqaša** a quarrel, shouting (NT2; NTU4 159b); pl. קַרְקַשֵׁי **qarqāše** tremors (=H זעזועים, RivSh 282).

קראר, קרר (Ar) m. ⁺**qıra/ār** decision (Z; PolU 1); confession, admission (NT); cf. ק-י-ר.

ק-ר-ש II (AnAr < T **karıšmak**) **q-r-š** to show interest, get involved; **la gımqarši ʾıbbe** They (=his children) don't take care of him (cf. PolG).

קרשא ((OA/OS קַשָּׁא) m. **qırša** straw (cf. PolG).

קרתא (OA) f. **qarta** cold weather; **mxēla-le qarta** He caught cold; cf. קרירא, ק-י-ר [Khan 578 **qarda**].

ק-ר-ת-נ v. ק-ר-ט-נ

ק-ש-ט 1 (Ar) **q-š-ṭ** to strip, remove extra fat.

ק-ש-ט 2 (OA הקשיט) **q-š-ṭ** to prepare, arrange (NT5 403).

קושטניתא v. קשטניתא

קשטת, קשטץ (< OS ܩܘܫܛܬܐ) adv. **qıšṭaṣ** (Z < **qıštat**?) obverse, the 'right' or printed surface of a cloth or dress; v. כרכץ.

קשטרון (< OA קשתא דמרן?) m. **qešṭaron** rainbow [=Macd 287 **qaštī māran** bow of our Lord).

ק-ש-י (H-OA) IV **q-š-y** to argue, ask difficult questions (NT); cf. קושיה.

קשיא, קשיתא (< ק-ש-י) adj. **qıšya, qšīta** difficult, unhappy (child).

ק-ש-מ-ר III (IrAr) **q-š-m-r** to poke fun at.

קשמר III (IrAr) inv. **qašmar** shameless.

קשמרותא (< קשמר) f. **qašmarūta** shamelessness.

קשמשא (P) f. **qıšmıšša** tiny raisin; pl. **qıšmıšše**.

ק-ש-נ II (< קושן) **q-š-n** to throng (=H צָבָא, BT4).

ק-ש-ע (Ar) **q-š-ʿ** go away, clear off (PolU 23, 90); cf. ש-ק-ע.

ק-ש-פ (Ar) vi **q-š-f** be crusty, dry (SaAC 13).

קשקולנכת (K?) pl. **qašqulankat** smelling salts to awaken a fainted/'dead' person (PolU 58).

קשקלאעא (< ?) **qašqıllāʿa** old and weird person.

קשתא, קֶ/קִישְׁתַא (OA) f. **qašta** (Z), **qe/ısta** (PolG), bow; cf. קשטרון, קושטניתא; pl. קֶישְׁיַאתַא **qešyāta** (PolG).

קתכא, קטכא, קדכא (< Ar قدح) **qatxa** (Z), **qaṭxa** (AvidH 62), **qadxa** (RivSh 192), cup; pl. **qatxe** (=H קְשָׂוֹת, BT2)[MacD 276 **qathā** glass, bowl, **qāṭıxtā** wooden bowl].

קתל (Ar) m. **qıtıl** murder, bloodshed (RivSh 217).

קתרא (OA) m. **qıṯra** (Z **qısra**) knot; bundle **-ıt pāre** purse; plot (=H קֶשֶׁר, PolG: 2Kg 11:14); pl. **qıṯrāre**.

ק-ת-ר, ק-ט-ר (?) (OA/OS ק-ת-ר*, ק-ט-ר) **q-ṯ-r** (Z **q-s-r**) , **q-ṭ-r** (only in RivSh 134), to tie; to produce (almonds) (=H גָּמַל {שְׁקֵדִים}, BT4, D) (NT+).

ר (r)

ר (H) **rōš, rēš** the Hebrew letter Resh; **tarteʾma** two hundred.

ראב (K راڤ) ⁺**rāv**, always in hendiadys: ⁺**rāv-u-nēčir** hunting, chase (PolU 3)

ראבא (OA רַבָּא) adj./adv. ⁺**rāba** great, a lot, many; -לא וילי בראבא ד **la wēle brāba d-** It was not long since...; גורא ראבא **gōra rāba** a great man (NT3); very: **xa baxta ⁺rāba sqıl̄ta** a very beautiful woman (Z);⁺**rābıd-⁺rāba** at the utmost (cf. PolG); very many/much; ראבה שנה **rābe šınne** many years (NT; =H רַבִּים, BT1); ראבה ראבה **rābe rābe** many many, great many (NT3); cf. רבתא, רורוא, בשרב [Hob 91 61-62; Khan 579 **rāba** much, very].

ראדא (OS ܪܛܝܐ) adj. **reʾda** fresh, tender; used only with **šeʾde reʾde** fresh green almonds.

ראדיו (IrAr < E) m. ⁺**rādıyo** radio.

ראהיבן (K/P) **rāhivan** road-guard (PolU 25).

ראוא (OA רַעֲוָא will) m. **reʾwa** zest; used only as hendiadys with טמאא: **gmaḥke btımʾa ureʾwa** He tells (stories) with much relish and zest; **la šqılle ču ṭımʾa ureʾwa mın ʾixāli** He didnt relish my food at all (PolG).

ראובן (H) p.n.m. ⁺**rūven** Reuben.

ראודנא v. רְאוֹדָנָא

ראוייא, ראיא, (Ar) f. **rāwīya, rāya** (?) water skin-bag (PolU 25).

ראולא 1, ראולתא (< ר-א-ל) **rıʾōla** (m.), **rıʾulta** (f., BaBin 10;=H חֲרָדָה, PolG) shivering (NT+).

ראולא 2 v. רעולא

ראזואן (P/K) m. ⁺**rāzwan** gardener, vine-dresser (NT+).

ראחתא (P/K) f. **rāḥıta** rest, calm; cf. רחת.

ר-א-י (OA רעי) vt **r-ʾ-y** to graze, look for food (PolG); IV to shepherd (cf. PolG); **ʾīwanta ugurga mızġaz grāʾe** Wolf and ewe grazing together (=very peaceful) (PolU 143) (NT+).

ראיי, ראי (Ar رأي) m. ⁺**rāy(i)** counsel, plan (Pol 110); **drēlu rāyi ʾılle** They advised him (cf. PolG); cf. ר-י-י, ראייכאר, תגביר (NT+).

ראידא, ראדתא (OS ܪܛܝܐ) adj. **raʾīda** (Z **raʾīza**), **raʾıdta**, fresh, tender (vegetable, fruit, flower; cf. PolG)(=H רַעֲנָן, BT5); cf. ראדא.

ראיה (H) ⁺**raʾāya, rāya**, analogy, example, evidence; **šqıllox/ʾāzıllox ⁺rāya mın dēha** Use this as an example! (cf. AlfM 3).

רַאייכַאר (P) **rāykar** counselor (=H יוֹעֵץ, PolG).

ר-א-ל (OA רעל) vi **r-ʾ-l** to shake, quiver; take care very devotedly: **yımme ⁺rāba graʾlāwa ʾımme** His mother cared for him a lot (PolG); IV vt to shake (=H הֶחֱרִיד, PolG)(NT+).

ראלא (OS ܪܥܠܐ) m. **reʾla** shivering; cf. ראולא.

ראסת 1, ראצט (K/P) ⁺**rāst** right (hand), straight (way), correct, honest (person); pl. ראסתין **rāstīn** (=H יְשָׁרִים, BT4).[PolG: רַאצַאט **rāṣaṭ**].

ראסתה (K/P) f./adv. ⁺**rāste** (on) the right (hand)(cf. PolG); cf. גַּפֵּה, ימה.

ראסתותא, רַצְטוּתָא (< ראסת) f. **rastūta** honesty, what is upright (=H הַיָּשָׁר, BT2; יָשָׁר, PolG).

ראעותא (< רע) f. **rāʿūta** evilness, malice.

ראעיבן (Ar-K) m. **rāʿīvan** shepherd (PolU 292)

ראעכו, ראעכה (< רע) **rāʿıko** (m.), **rāʿıke** (f.), little evil person.

ראעתא (Ar رعيّة) f. **rāʿıta** flock, protected group.

ראפא (< Ar رف?) f. ⁺**rāpa** shelf, ledge [cf. MacD 295 **rāpā**, but Garbell 328 **rafta**].

ראצט v. ראסת

ר-א-ש (OA/OS/Mand רגש) **r-ʾ-š** to notice, wake up (as a result of noise, etc.); **la - lıgyāne** He was unaware (Socin 162); IV make aware, draw attention of: **la marʿıšet ʾıbbēni ḥakōma** Dont draw kings attention to us (PolG) (NT+).

ראש בית דין (H) m. **rōš bēt dīn** chief judge (in Jewish court) (RivP 210).

ראש השנה (H) m. ⁺**rōšāna** Jewish New Year.

ראתא (OA/OS) f. **rāta** (Z ⁺**rāsa**) lung(s).

ראתב (Ar) m. ⁺**rātıb** equistarian gear (PolU 7).

רב (H) m. **rāv, rıbbi** Rabbi; pl. רבנים, רבנין **rabbānīm/n** (MeAl190); cf. רבי 1.

רב אל סמאואת (Ar) **rab ıl-samāwāt** Master

of Heavens (NTU3 1a).

רבא, רובא (OA רִיבַּבְתָּא; cf. רוּבָּא large amount; OS ܪܘܒܐ) **⁺rübba** myriad; pl. רבה רבואתא **rıbbe rıbbawāṯa** a huge number, countless (cf. PolG: **rubwāsa**; RivSh 195 רובי רבאבות **rubbe rıvāvōṯ**; OA -רִיבֵּי, ריבואתא).

רבאבא (Ar) f. **⁺rabbāba** rebab, a fiddle; **rabbābıd qaysa** braggart (wooden fiddle).

רב אל עאלמין, רבל עאלמין (Ar) **rabb-ıl-ᶜālamīn** Master of the world (NT); cf. רבון העולם.

רבולא (< OS p.n. Bishop Rabula?) **rabūla** big shot, important figure: **pıšle xa rabūla** He has become a big shot.

רבון העולם/העולמים (H) m. **rıbbōn hāᶜōlām(īm)** (NT), **rıbbōne šılle-ᶜōlām(im)** (PolU 9), Master of the World (God); cf. רב אל עאלמין.

רבותא (OA רְבוּתָא) f. **⁺rabūṯa** greatness, high position; maturity (PolG) (NT+).

רבותי (H) **rabbōṯay** My Masters, Gentlemen (NT; Ruth 4:2).

רבי 1 (H) **⁺rıbbi** Rabbi (title of ancient Jewish sages); v. חכם [Garbell 328 **ribbi** m./f.].

רבי 2 (Ar) **⁺rabbi** My God, please God; v. יא; common in blessings and curses: **⁺rabbi māṭıt bısılāmati** May you arrive in peace; cf. מולאיי.

רביכותא v. רויכותא

רבית (H) **rıbbıṯ** usury, accrued interest (BT3; BaBin 79).

רבנה, רבנו, רבנא (K slave, orphan < OS monk) **⁺rabbana/o** m., **⁺rabbane** f. destitute, you poor one (PolU 119; PolU 209)

רבנתא (< רבנא) f. **⁺rabbanta** nun, sister of mercy; pl. **⁺rabbanyāṯa**.

רבקה (H) p.n.f. **⁺rıfqa** Rebecca [MacD 295 **rapqā**].

רבתא, רַפְתָא, רַפְצָא (OA) adj. f. **⁺rabṯa**, **rapṯa** (BT1, D), **rapṣa** (AvidH 52) great, big, old; cf. ראבא, רורוא (NT+).

רג'א (Ar) **rıja** plea (BaBin 126; ZU73b; PolG); cf. ר-ג'-י, ארג'ו.

רג'אל (Ar) **rıjāl** (strong) men (NT2).

ר-ג'-י II (Ar) **r-j-y** beg, supplicate; גמרג'ינא מנוך **gmarjēna mınnox** I beg you (NT5 382).

רג'ינא (< IrAr? < L queen?) p.n.f. **rajīna** Regina.

ר-ג'-ם (Ar) **⁺r-j-m** to kill by stoning (=H רָגַם/ סָקַל, BT; PolG; NT).

ר-ד-י II (< Ar increase flock?) **r-d-y** to sire (pejor.).

רהין (Ar) **rahın** pawn, security, pledge (=H עֵרָבוֹן, BT1).

ר-ה-מ v. ר-י-מ 2

ר-ה-נ II (< רהין) **r-h-n** to pawn, pledge.

רואה (OA רַבְעֵי*) **rō'e** three years ago; v. תלתה שתקה, [cf. OS ܐܫܬܩܕܡ four years hence; Mutz 232 **talódel** three years ago].

רובא, רובואתא v. רבא

רוביכא (K) m. **rūvīka** fox (=H שָׁפָן, BT3/5!); pl. **rūvīkat** (cf. PolG).

רובע, רִיבֵּיע, רֻובְּעָא/רֻובְּאַא (Ar; OA רִיבְעָא) m. **rübıᶜ**, **rubᶜ/'a** (BT3, BT4, D).

רובר (K < P رودبار) **rōbar** (Socin 163), **rūbar** (PolG), brook, river; pl. **rūbāre** (PolG) [Khan **rubār**579].

רוגזא (OA-H) **ruġza** anger (NT2; NT6 135) [cf. Mengozzi 307 **ruġzā**].

רוג'מא (Ar) m. **rujma** hail of stones (NT2).

רודאנא, רְאוֹדָנָא (< OA רעד) f. **rōḏāna** (Z **rōzāna**), **r'ōdāna** (=H חַלְחָלָה, AvidH) earthquake [cf. MacD 290 **rōdānā**; Garbell 328 **⁺rotana**; Mutz 224 **⁺rotāna** < OA רתת **rtt** tremble; but OS ܙܘܥܐ].

רורוא v. רווא

ר-ו-ח IV (Ar) **r-w-ḥ** to fan, ventilate (cf. PolG), hover (=H רִחֵף, BT1, Am); cf. מרואחא.

רוחאיא, רוּחָאיָא (Ar روح) f. **rō/ūḥāya** spirit (of life) (AvidH 69); **-ye fırra** He almost died (out of fear); **-ye d'ırra** He recovered (cf. PolG); **la gyāwınna brōḥāyi** I love her very much (PolU 110); cf. נשמה

רוחאנייא (Ar) f. **rōḥānīya** minor soul; usually in **rōḥāye zılla, - pıšla** his (major) soul has gone, (only) his minor soul remained (= he was on the verge of dying) (PolU 104).

רוחאניית (Ar) pl. **rūḥānīyat** divine spirits, angels (NT2).

רוחבאלא (Ar?) m. **ruḥbāla** a gold coin in neclace.

רוח הקודש (H) f. **rūwaḥ haqqōdeš** the Holy Spirit (NT+).

רוח רעה (H) f. **ruwwa(ḥ) rāᶜa** evil spirit; **ruwwa rāᶜa 'urra go qalwe** He acted insanely (evil spirit entered his body) (PolU

378).

רוטא (Ar [Dozy] روط) m. **rōṭa** log (PolU 421).

ר-ו-י (OA רבי) ⁺**r-w-y** to grow, become big; כומד כיתיה וילה גראוה **kumıd kēṯe wēle grāwe** It is becoming bigger and bigge גפאייש קאלד שופר ברואיא **gpāyıš qālıd šōfar bırwāya** The sound of the horn was becoming louder and louder; IV to raise (children), make big, exalt, exaggerate; **gmarwēla gyāne** He brags (=H הִתְנַשֵּׂא/הִשְׂתָּרֵר, BT4) [1:**murwē-**, **múrūya** (m./f.), **murwēṯa** (f.)] (NT+).

רויכא, רוכתא, רוויכתא (OA רויחא) p.p. **rwīxa, ruxta** (Z)/**rwıxta** (NT4), wide, spacious; **behna rwīxa** patience; **behne rwīxa** patient.

רויכותא, רביכותא (OA רויחותא) f. **rwīxūṯa, rvīxūṯa** (+NT), spaciousness, vacant place; **xyēlu bıt naḥas ubıt** - They lived with peace of mind and comfort (PolG).

ר-ו-כ (OA רוח) **r-w-x** to become wide, spacious; - **ʾıllu** They became rich; **lag rōxa hīl la ʾēqa** (Ones situation) doesnt improve until it worsens; IV to widen; **ʾilāha maruxla ʾıllox** May God make you prosper! (NT+).

רוכא (OA/OS רוּחָא/רְווּחָא) f. ⁺**rōxa** rheumatism, swelling [cf. MacD **rūxā**; Garbell 328 **rōxa**].

רוככא (OA/OS רוּכָּכָא softness) m. **rukxa** breast meat of chicken.

רוכצא, רוקצא (Ar) f. **rux/qṣa** permit, permission.

רומאיא (OA רוֹמָאָה) m. **rōmāya** Roman, Greek (BaBin 135).

רומאנא 1, רומנתא (OS ܪܘܡܢܐ) adj. ⁺**rō/ūmāna** (cf. PolG),**-anta**, high, tall, superior; איניה רומנתא **ʾēne -anta** ambitious, aspiring (NT+).

רומאנא 2 (< רומאנא 1?) m. ⁺**rōmāna** childrens fever caused by the new (=high?) moon; **duqle mrōmāna** he has this type of fever.

רומחא (Ar/OA) f. ⁺**rumḥa** spear, lance (NT+).

רומנותא (< רומאנא) f. **rōmanūṯa** loftiness, height (NT+).

רומתא (OS ܪܘܡܬܐ/ܪܘܡܬܐ) f. **rumta** hill; pl. רומיאתא **rumyāṯa** (NT).

רוון v. תכת

רוצה לומר (H) **rōṣé lōmár** that is to say (NT).

רוקה (OA/OS רוּקָא) pl. **rōqe** saliva, spittle; sg. (rare): **ruqta** (BaBin 30); cf. ר-י-ק [Khan 579 **roqe**].

רוקצא v. רוכצא

רורא (K **rūrik**) m. ⁺**rūra** laurel-bay, oleander.

רורוא, רררא, רווא, אורוא (OA רברבא/OS ܪܘܪܒܐ) m. **rūrwa** (NT), **ruwwa** (Z), **ʾurwa** (BT1, Am; AvidH 25; RivSh 136, 262) great, big, large; pl. **ruwwe** big; **ruwwāne** magnates (cf. OA רַבְרְבָנֵי nobles) (=H נְשִׂיאִים, BT2); commanders (PolG); אֲרְוַאנֵי **ʾurwāne** (RivSh 270; Sa83c 24, Am); cf. ראבא [Khan 579 **ruwwa**, f. **rubta, rabta** big; **ruwwāne** important people].

רורוותא, רררוותא, רררונותא (< רברבותא) f. **rūrwūṯa** (NT), **rūrwanūṯa** (NT5 392), greatness, maturity.

רושתא (OS ܪܘܦܫܐ < Ak **rapaštu**) f. **rušta** shovel; pl. **rušyāṯa** [cf. Ar رفش; Krotkoff 126-27].

רות (K) inv. **rūt** unclothed, poor; plain.

רוותותא, רותותא (< ?) f. **rawtūṯa** (?) difference, discrimination: ולא האוה בו רותותא (רוותותא) ביני רורוה לזאורה יאן ביני אתירא למסכינא **la hāwe-bu rawtūṯa bēni rūrwe lzᶜōre yān bēni ʾatīra lmıskīna** They should not discriminate between young and old, or between rich and poor (NT2).

רזא (OS ܪܘܙܐ/ܪܘܙܐ/Ar رز; cf. OA אֲרוּזָא) m. ⁺**rızza** rice; - **xamūṣa** sour rice (dish); - **bkısēsa** rice with chicken.

רזאלה (K/T < Ar رذالة) f. ⁺**razāle** ill treatment, misery; cf. ר-ז-ל, רזיל, רזילתותא.

ר-ז-ג-ר III (K **rēzger** plan) ⁺**r-z-g-r** to prepare (for a journey) (cf. PolG).

ר-ז-ד-ג III, ר-ז-כ, ר-ז-ג II (P رزدق line) ⁺**r-z-d-g** (Z; PolG), **r-z-k** (BT3, D), **r-z-g** (RivSh 239; PolG) arrange, set (=H עָרַךְ, BT); cf. ר-ז-ג-ר, ריזא.

רזדגתא, רַזְדַּכְתָּא (< ר-ז-ד-ג) f. ⁺**razdag/kta** set, row (=H מַעֲרֶכֶת, BT3; PolG); pl. ⁺**razdag/kyāṯa**.

רזואנגי, רזואנא (K) ⁺**razwānči, -āna** (PolG), gardener, vine-dresser.

רזיל (T/K < Ar رذيل) inv. ⁺**razil** miser; cf. רזאלה.

רזילתותא (< רזיל) f. **razīlatūṯa** poverty, misery.

ר-ז-ל II (Ar رذل) vt/vi ⁺**r-z-l** to abuse, or be

abused, to illtreat (Segal #107; PolU 245).

רז"ל (H)= רבותינו זכרונם לברכה **rabbōṯēnu zixrōnām livrāxā** our masters of blessed memory (NT).

ר-ז-ק IV (Ar) **r-z-q** to grant, provide (God:livelihood) (=H פִּרְנֵס, AvidH 67) (NT+).

רזק, רסק (Ar) m. **rıziq, rısq** [NT], provision, livelihood, lot; pl. ארזאק **ʾarzāq** (NT2).

רחום וחנון (H) **rāḥūm weḥannūn** merciful and compassionate (God) (NT2).

רחוקא, רחוקתא (OA רַחִיקָא) adj./adv. **raḥūqa, raḥuqta** [but Gz73 84 **raxúqa, raxúqta**] distant, far; far away (=H הַרְחֵק, BT1).

רחים (Ar) inv. **raḥim** merciful (God); **lıbbe** – compassionate (cf. PolG) (NT+).

רחל, רחלו (H) **rāḥel, raḥlo,** Rachel; cf. גֹחו. [MacD 292 **rāxīl**].

ר-ח-מ I/II (H/Ar/OA) **⁺r-ḥ-m** to have mercy; cf. מרחמאנא (NT+).

רחמא (Ar) p.n.f. **raḥma** Rahma.

רחמה, רחמתא (Ar/OA) f. **raḥme, raḥmıta** (+NT2), mercy; **braḥme** Bless you! said after sneezing; response: —**lbābox-yımmox** (Amedi 72; Segal #100); **ʾ-z-l qam -t ʾilāha** to pass away (PolU 243); pl. רחמתיאתא **raḥmıtyāṯa** (=H רַחֲמִים, BT; PolG) (NT+).

רחמים (H) p.n.m. **raḥamim** Rahamim; cf. חמו.

רחמנא v. מרחמנא

רחמנותא (OA) f. **raḥmānūṯa** mercy (NT5 400).

ר-ח-ק (OA) **r-ḥ-q** to go far, stay away; IV to remove, put at distance; cf. רחוקא (NT+).

רחקא, רקא (< ר-ח-ק; OA רוחקא) adv. **raḥqa, raqqa** (NT2), far, afar; - **mınnox/maxxa** May it be far from you/from here (said when mentioning an ailment) (SaAC 1, 8, 9); מרקא **mrıqqa** from afar [MacD 296: **mrixqā, rıqqa**].

רחת (K < Ar) inv./adv. **raḥat** calm, relaxed; **blıbba** - in peace of mind (cf.PolG); **tu raḥat** Sit quietly; **lēwe raḥat** He is not well; cf. ראחתא.

רחתותא (< רחת) f. **raḥatūṯa** serenity (PolG).

רטובא (Ar) f. humidity; deep water (=H תְּהוֹם, BT5, D).

רטל(א) (Ar/OS < Gr **litra**) m. **rıṭl(a)** rotl, large weight or dry measure (cf. PolG).

רטרוטא (< ר-ט-ר-ט) m. **rıṭrōṭa** cartilage; feeble person; pl. **rıṭrōṭe**.

ר-ט-ר-ט III (OA רטט/רתת) **r-ṭ-r-ṭ** be feeble, cartilage-like [cf. Mutz 224]

ר-י-א (OA רעע) vt/vi **r-y-ʾ** to pulverize, crush [1: **reʾ-**; 2: **rayeʾ**; 3: **rōʾ**; 4: **ryāʾa**] (NT+).

ריאא, ריאתא (< ר-י-א) p.p. **rīʾa, reʾta** pulverized.

ריאוא v. ראוא

ריבאזא, ריווסא (K < P/Ar **rībās**) m. **rēvāsa** (Z), **rēwōsa** (Arodh), rhubarb; cf. יאמיצא.

ר-י-ג̇ (Ar رج/روج) vi **r-y-j** to crawl (baby, insect), creep (NT+). [cf. MacD 292].

ר-י-ד (< OA רעד?) vi **r-y-ḏ** (NT, BT4, D; Z **r-y-z**) to budge, move a little (=H מָשׁ, BT4); **ryāzıd sıppāsa** utterance of her lips (=H מִבְטָא שְׂפָתַיִם, BT4); IV to move a little (vt); cf. רודאנא [Garbell 291 **r-y-t**; not in MacD].

ר-י-ז IV (< ריזא) vt **r-y-z** to set in rows (NT).

ריזא (K) m. **rēza** row, order; pl. ריזי **rēze** (NT+).

ריחאנא, רחאנא (Ar) **ri/aḥāna** sweet basil; **qōmıt rıḥāna/mux šıtlıt** - (woman with a) good looking body (PolG) (NT+).

ריחאנה (Ar) p.n.f. **rıḥāne** [cf. MacD 292].

ר-י-י II (<ראיי) **r-y-y** to rule over; רַאי בִּימְרַאיְיֵתִין **rāy bımrāyētın** (=H מָשׁוֹל תִּמְשֹׁל, BT1, D); deal shrewdly (=H הִתְחַכֵּם, BT2, D; AvidH 28; PolG).

ר-י-כ IV (OA ריח) vt **⁺r-y-x** to sniff, smell (NT, BT1, D; AvidH 59; Hob89 219); cf. מ-י-כ.

ריך (K) m. **⁺rīx** cattles dung; **xawıltıd rīx** necklace made of dung (worn by crazed or humiliated person) (PolU 42).

ריכא (OA ריחא) m. **rīxa** (Z), **rēxa** (Hob89 185), fragrance, smell; ש-ק-ל ריכא **š-q-l rīxa** to sniff; **ṣābun rīxa** perfumed soap.

רֵילָא (OS/K?) **rēla** brook; cf. רעולא; lowland (= H שְׁפֵלָה, PolG:1Kg 10:27) [MacD 293 **rélā** < K wood, silva].

ר-י-מ 1, י-ר-מ (OA) **⁺r-y-m, y-r-m** (+NT), to rise, be lifted [1:-ירמ/-רמ **(y)rım**; 2 ראים **rāyım**]; IV to raise, to lift [cf. MacD 288 **rāyim/yārim/ʾārim**].

ר-י-מ 2, ר-ה-מ (Ar) **r-y-m** (NT), **r-h-m** (Z), to be desirable, fitting; לא רמלה בלביה **la rımle blıbbe** He didnt like him (NT2); **la**

⁺rhımla ṭalēni We didnt have an opportunity; cf. מרם.

רימא 1 (K/Ar?) p.n.f. rīma Rima.

רימא 2, רמתא (< ר-י-מ 1) p.p. ⁺rīma, ⁺rımta elevated, gone-up.

רימא 3 (K/P rīm) m. ⁺rēma pus; darfıd rēma sheepskin (full) of pus=ugly and fat woman.

רִימּוֹנִייֶה (H-Ar) f. rımmōnīye pommegranate-shaped ornament, especially those used for decorating the Torah scroll box (=H רִמּוֹן, BT2, D; Br93 255); cf. ארמותא.

רימתא (< ר-י-מ) n. act. ryamta (kind of) rising, getting up; v. יתותא (PolG).

ר-י-ס 1, ר-י-צ I (Z), IV (NT) (OA רסס) ⁺r-y-s to sprinkle (=H זָרַק, הִזָּה, BT, PolG).

ר-י-ס 2 (< רסתא?) r-y-s chicken: to rest on bar.

ריסא, רסתא (< ר-י-ס 2) p.p.⁺rīsa, rısta crunchy bread or matzah softened with water.

ריספי (K) m. rēspi elder, old; clans head (NT, BT, FT); pl. ריספייה (NY3), -yāne (PolU 45, 291); cf. סאוא, זקן.

רִיפְּצָא (< ?) rıpṣa vintage (=H בָּצִיר, BT3, D); cf. קטאפא [MacD 295 ripsā sowing watered ground < OS rps beat, kick?]

רִיצּוּם v. רסום

ר-י-ק (OA רקק) r-y-q to spit; cf. רוקה (NT+).

רירא (OA/OS/Mand) m. ⁺rīra mucus, drivel.

ריש 1 (P) m. rīš plumage; rīš-ennaᶜām soft (ostrich) feathers (Pol 110; PolG); disguise (PolU 165); v. רישא-ריש; cf. פרא.

רישא, ריש 2, רש, -ש/ -ז' (OA) m./prep. rēš, rıš/ž, š-/ž- (K) head, beginning; on, over; מרישי mrēši from over me; לרישי lrēši (I welcome you) very gladly; qımle žgyāne He stood up (PolG); go ᵓēnan urıš rēšan (We welcome you) very gladly (BaBin 137); rıž rēše over his head (MeAl 192); pıšla rēši I am stuck with it (=merchandise); muᶜṭıllox rēši You have been delayed because of me; breš dızmıne ashes (euph.); cf. קטמא; ריש יאמא rēš yāma sea-shore; ריש סיהרא rēš sehra (Z — yarxa) new month; רישד שאתא rēšıd šāta beginning of a year; death anniversary; reš šātıd ᵓesukka end of Sukkot (SaAC 7); reš-šātox brıxta Happy new year (said at the end of Passover/ Sukkot! Cf. Mutz 223 rēš šāta = אסרו חג); v. -ראש השנה; reš tmanya the eighth day after ones death (Br93 201); rēše wīša stubborn (his head dry); rēše ruwwa arrogant (his head big); rēše šaxīna hot-tempered, too enthusiastic; ᵓāxıl rēšox May (what you stole) eat your head; May you die with it; rēšan mnōšan-īle We are independent; rēše la-gbēle They hate him (PolU 388); v. מאיא, מדרש, כריש, כאייה, ז'כפלתי; pl. רישוואתא rēšawāṯa (RivSh 120) (NT+).

רישאיא (OS) m. rēšāya the head of the family, chief (NT2).

רישא-ריש (< ריש 1) rīš-a-rīš disguised by magic (young woman in shape of gazelle, or eagle) (PolU 165).

רישבר (K?) rēšbar (fruit?) grocer (PolU 366).

ריש כזיא (רישא+כזיא) m. rēš xızya nipple (head of breast) (SaAC 12).

רישכאסא v. אשכאתא

ריש-מאל(א) (OS) rēš-māl(a) the capital fund, total wealth.

רכא (K rike) f. rakka birdcage (cf. PolG)

רכאוא (OA רכבא) m. rakāwa rider, horseman; cf. פראשא (NT+).

רכאוותא (< רכאוא) rakawūṯa riding (PolU 226).

רכאנא, רכנתא (< רכי) adj. rıkkāna, -anta, obstinate (PolG).

ר-כ-ו (OA רכב) r-k-w to ride; IV to help one ride, put on (ones shoulders, etc.).

רְכָּווּתַא (< ר-כ-ו) f. rkawūṯa riding, ride (=H מֶרְכָּב, BT3, D).

ר-כ-ט (OA/OS/Mand רהט) r-x-ṭ to run (NT); cf. א-ר-ק; IV to bring fast (NT).

רכטה v. רכתה

רכי (K/P) f. ⁺rıkki reluctance; ברכי brıkki reluctantly; d-w-q - to be obstinate, to fret (NT+).[MacD 296 riqī (!) fretting]

רכיבה (Ar ركاب) pl. rıkēbe stirrups (Socin 162).

רכיכא, רככתא (OA רַכִּיךְ) adj. rakīxa, rakıxta soft, tender (NT+).

רכיכותא (OA) f. rakīxūṯa softness, weakness (=H מֹרֶךְ, BT3, D).

ר-כ-כ 1 (OA) r-k-x to become soft; IV to make soft (NT+).

ר-כ-כ 2 II (< רכי) ⁺r-k-k to be obstinate (cf. PolG; [4: mrakkōke]).

ר-כ-נ (Ar quiet/OS sink/OA bend over) vi **⁺r-k-n** to settle down (sediments) [=MacD 293 **r-x-n**].

ר-כ-ש (OA רחש) **r-x-š** to teem, creep (=H רָמַשׂ/שָׁרַץ, BT1).

רכשא, רכש (OA ריחשא) m. **rıxša** (NT), **rıxš** (BT) insect(s) (=H רֶמֶשׂ, BT1); property (?)(=H רְכוּשׁ, BT1/BT4, D); pl. רִיכְשַׁאת **rıxšat** (PolG).

רכת/טה (K/P رخت) trappings, equipment) pl. **raxt/ṭe** bandoleer, usually: **-u-fīšakat** (SaAC 19) [MacD 292 trappings of horse].

רמאל (Ar) m. **rammāl** geomancer; pl. /רמאלין רמילין **rammā/ēlin** geomancer (NT); cf. רמל.

רמאשה v. בירמאשה

רמבו-טופ (T?) adv. **⁺rımb-u-ṭōp** (with) much clamor of celebration (PolU 41); cf. טופ.

ר-מ-ז (H/OA) **r-m-z** to hint, gesticulate (NT2; NT5 394; AvidH 9); cf. רמז.

רמז (H) **remez** allusion (NT2).

ר-מ-י (OA/OS/Mand cast) **r-m-y** to lay (hen:eggs, Z); to overlay (=H צִפָּה, PolG: I Kg 10:18) [cf. MacD 293: to cast in a mould, fill up a hollow].

רמל (Ar) m. **ramal** geomancy; **m-x-y b-** to perform geomancy, fortune-telling (PolU 89); cf. רמאל.

רנג (P) **⁺rang** [PolG רַאנַג **ranag** =H מַרְאֶה] color, shade, look; מא רנג **ma rang** How? (NT2); pl. רנגה **⁺range**; רנגה רנגה **rangé-range** various shades (of colors, meanings) (NT3)(NT+).

ר-נ-ג-נ III (< רנג) **r-n-g-n** to color (BaBin 71).

רנדה (K) f. **⁺rande** beautiful (smooth) girl (SaLH 332); cf. ס-ק-ל [cf. MacD 294].

ר-נ-ד-ש III (< רנדש) **⁺r-n-d-š** to scrape by plane.

רנדש (P shavings/K) f. **⁺randaš** a plane.

רנייה (K) f. **ranīye** avalanche, snow mass (Segal #67).

רסום, רסומה, רִיצֻומֵי, רִיצֻום, רסומת (Ar) **⁺rısūm(e), -mat,** law(s), rule(s) (=H /חֹק חֻקּוֹת, BT1, D; PolG), documents (PolU 365); cf. ר-ס-מ.

רסוקתא (AzT?) f. **rasuqta** necklace; pl. רסוקיאתא **rasuqyāṯa** (NT) [cf. MacD 294].

ר-ס-מ, ר-צ-מ (Ar) **⁺r-s-m** to engrave, inscribe (NT); to decree, proscribe: רסמלוך ליאמא **rsımlox lyāma** You ordered the sea... (NT5 388); to draw, paint (Z); cf. רסום.

ר-ס-נ v. ר-צ-נ

ר-ס-ק v. ר-ז-ק

רסתא (K; cf. OA ריתא cord, belt) f. **rısta** thick rope (used by loggers); pl. **rıstyāṯa**; רַסְתִּכְיָאסָא **rastıkyāsa** (=H עֲבוֹתִים, AvidH 65).

רע (H) inv. **⁺rāᶜ** evil; **baxta/nāše ⁺rāᶜ** bad woman/people; but **ʾēna/rūwwa(ḥ) ⁺rāᶜa** evil eye/spirit; v. ראעכו.

רע מצורע (H) inv. **rāᶜ mısurrāᶜ** very evil, morally ugly person.

רעולא (OS فُحلا) **raᶜōla** rivulet (NT5 396; Sa83c 24, Am); pl. רעוליה **raᶜōle** (NT); רְאוֹלָאת **raʾōlat** (BT3, D).

רפאל, רפו (H) p.n.m. **⁺rafāʾel, ⁺rafo** (hypo.) Rafael, Rafi

רְפוּאָה (H) f. **rafūʾa** healing (RivSh 274); **šınsıt šēna udeʾsıt rafūʾa** (May God grant you) a peaceful sleep and healthy sweat.

ר-פ-י 1 (OA/OS/Mand) **⁺r-p-y** to be set free against (dog, evil person), to attack: ראפיה אבד ולאת ונהבילא **rāpe ʾıbbıd walāt unahbīla** They attack a city and plunder it (Sa83c 18, Am); II to dispatch (NT: מראפי, RivSh 216:אמרופילי); IV to let go; send adrift (RivSh 155), to deliver: ירושלים מרפתא באידיני **yarušlayim marpıtta bʾıḏēni** May You deliver Jerusalem in our hands (RivSh 201); to set against: מרפתו באכדאדה **marpıttu bʾıxdāḏe** You set them against each other (NT5 388); **murpēle pōxa** to blow wind (euph.), fart (RivP #94) (NT+).

ר-פ-י 2 (OA) **r-p-y** to be loose, weak; IV to make loose, weak (NT+).

רפיא, רפיתא (< ר-פ-י 2) p.p. **rıpya, rpīṯa** loose, slack; weakling; **rıpyıt ʾaqlāṯa** one with disabled feet (=H נְכֵה רַגְלַיִם, PolG:2 S 9:3).

רפיותא (OA/OS רפיותא) f. **rıpyūṯa** weakness.

רפכת (K ريحين herbu) pl. **rappıkat** flowers, blossoms (PolU 9).

ר-פ-ר-פ III (OA/OS) **⁺r-p-r-p** to hover (bird) (=H רִחֵף, BT5); cf. ה-ב-ב; become loose, shaky: אסתונד שמי מרופרפלו **ʾıstūnıd šımme mruprıplu** The pillars of heaven became

loose (RivSh 180).
רפתא, רפצא v. רבתא
רצאצי (< רצץ) inv. rıṣāṣī lead color, gray.
רצוא (P رسوا) inv. rıṣwa disgraced (Pol 110; PolG 'schande').
רַצְטֻוּתָא v. ראסתותא
ר-צ-כ v. ר-ת-כ
ר-צ-מ v. ר-ס-מ
ר-צ-ן, ר-ס-ן II (Ar رصن consolidate?) vi/vt ⁺r-s-n to keep cooking (rice, etc.) till the water evaporates and the dish becomes solid.
ר-צ-ע II (Ar) r-ṣ-ᶜ to inlay (NT3); cf. מרצע.
רצץ, רצאץ (Ar) m. rıṣaṣ lead; **yaqūra x-rıṣaṣ** very heavy (heavy as lead) (NT+).
רצ̇א, ריצ̇א, רוצ̇א (Ar) m. **rıẓa, rüẓa** (+NT), will, wish; ריצ̇איוך **rıẓāyox** (May it be) Your will (NT3); האוה רוצ̇א **hāwe rüẓa** May it be (Your) will (NT2) (NT+).
ר-צ̇-י (Ar) ⁺**r-ẓ-y** be satisfied; **la wēle ⁺rizya mın pısır lašši** He wasnt satisfied with my flesh (PolG); IV pay debts (PolU 1) (NT+).
רק (K) inv. ⁺**raq** rigid, stiff, obstinate.
רקא 1 v. רחקא
רקא 2 (K رق turtle) **raqqa dīd māya** frog; pl. **-e** (PolG; PolUL 251); cf. בקא.
ר-ק-א II (OA/OS רקע) **r-q-ᵓ** to patch.
רקאתא (< ר-ק-א; OA רוּקְעֲתָא piece of cloth) f. **raqaᵓta** patch; pl. **raqāᵓe**.
ר-ק-ד (OA/OS/Mand) **r-q-d̲**(Z **r-q-z**) to dance.
רקאדא 1 (< **r-q-d̲**) v.n. dance, dancing.
רקאדא 2, רקדתא (< ר-ק-ד) n. ag. **raqād̲a, raqad̲ta** dancer, one who dances well.
רקיקא, רקקתא (OA) adj. **raqīqa, raqıqta** thin (inanimate objects: bread, paper, etc.).
רקם (Ar) m. ⁺**raqam** (serial) number.
ר-ק-ק (OA) **r-q-q** to become thin; II to hammer out (sheets of metal) (=H רִקֵּעַ, BT2), to thin.
רקרקתא (onomat.) f. ⁺**raqraqta** din (PolU 232).
ררוא v. רורוא
ררוותא, ררונותא v. רורוותא
רש 1 v. ריישא

רש 2 (K) inv. **raš** black (PolG); cf. כומא.
רשאיי (K blackness) **raššāyi** silhouette,image (PolU 38, 299).
רשאשא (Ar) f. **rıššāša** machinegun.
רשומא (< ר-ש-ם; OA רוּשְׁמָא/רְשׁוּם mark, seal impression) m. **rašōma** vertical hand used as cursing sign; a blow with open hand on top of the head (to indicate disdain, disapproval; cf. PolG); pl. **rašōme** (RivSh 226; 240) [cf. MacD 291 **rušmā** sign of the cross].
רשות (H) **rašut̲** permission (Ruth 4:8, add.).
ר-ש-ם (OA) ⁺**r-š-m** to vertically hold an open hand against someones face as a sign of curse (by quarreling women); cf. רשומא.
רשע (H) m. ⁺**rāšāᶜ** wicked; רשע (ד)פרעה **rāšāᶜ (d)parᶜo** the wicked Pharaoh (NT3); אד רשע עמלק/עמלק רשע **ᵓad̲ rāšāᶜ ᶜamālēq/ᶜamālēq rāšāᶜ** the wicked Amalek (NT3); רשע גמור **rāšāᶜ gāmūr** absolute wicked; pl. רשעים ⁺**rāšāᶜīm** (Z, NT5 382).
ר-ש-ע (H-OA) ⁺**r-š-ᶜ** to scheme against (=H הֵזִיד, BT2); IV to lust, to cause to lust (=H זָנָה/הִזְנָה, BT2) [cf. Garbell 291 ⁺**r-š-ᶜ-y**].
רשעה, רשעא, רשאעא, רשעתא(H) f. **rıšᶜa** (Z [cf. Mutz 223]), **rašāᶜa** (+NT), wicked; **rašāᶜta** adulteress (=H נוֹאֶפֶת, BT3).
רשעותא (OA) f. **rıšᶜūt̲a** wickedness, depravity (H זִמָּה, BT3, D), adultery (=H זְנוּת, BT4; זְנוּנִים, PolG:2Kg 9:22).
רשרשינקא (K?) **rašrašinqa** noisemaker for Purim (Am, Br93 351).
רשתה ניתא (K) f. **rıšte nēt̲a** raw macaroni, little lumps of dough (Am, Br93 241).
רתוכה (< ר-ת-כ) adj. pl. **rat̲ūxe** (Z **rasūxe**) boiling hot (water) (NT5 409).
ר-ת-כ, ר-צ-כ (OA רתח) **r-t̲-x** (Z/PolG ⁺**r-s-x**) to boil (vi), to bubble; - **go lıbba** to be attractive, appealing for marital relations (PolG); IV to boil (vt), blend (=H רָקַח, BT2).
רתכא (OA ריתחא anger<boiling) m. **rıt̲xa** (Z ⁺**rısxa**) boiling; **qlıble ⁺rısxa** (dish) has boiled enough.

ש (š)

ש (H) **šīn (sīn)**; **ṭıllatma** (Z **ṭıllasma**) three hundred.

-ש v. רישא

שאבאשה (K/P) ⁺**šābāše** pl. wedding gifts, musicians money.

שאבלוט (K/P) m. **šāballuṭ** chestnut (=H לוֹט, BT1); cf. בלוטא.

שאגרדא (T/K < P) **šāgırda** apprentice; pl. **-e** (PolU 320).

שאדא, שיאדא (OS ܫܓܕܐ < OA pl. שִׁיגְדֵי) m. **šeʾda** (Z **šeʾza**) almond tree (=H לוּז, BT1); cf. בושאדא; pl. **šeʾde** fresh almonds (=H שְׁקֵדִים, BT4); **šeʾze-reʾze** green fresh almonds; **bšeʾze ušākar** (raise) with luxury (PolU 110).

שאה (P) **šāh** shah, king (PolU 38).

שאויש v. גאוישא

שאול, שָׁאוּל (H) p.n.m. **šāʾ/wul** Saul (RivSh 230).

שְׁאוֹל (H) **šıʾōl** Sheol, hell (=H שְׁאוֹל, BT5, D).

שאולא (OS ܫܥܠܐ) m. **šıʾōla** cough; cf. ש-א-ל.

שַׁאכַא v. שַׁכַא

שאכר 1 (Ar<P>OA/OS שכר/ شكر; SokBA 1145) m. **šākar** sugar; **- kalla** sugar loaf (< IrAr); בשאכר יאן בדושא **bšākar yān bdūša** with sugar or honey (NT5 408); **xabrox bqaṭʾanne bšākar** Ill cut your word with sugar (said as an apology for interrupting someones speech); cf. שכרוכא.

שאכר 2 (Ar) inv. ⁺**šākır** grateful; pl. שאכרין **šākırīn** grateful people (NT2) (NT+).

ש-א-ל (OS ܫܥܠ) **š-ʾ-l** to cough; cf. שאולא.

שאלא (K/P/Ar) f. **šāla** fabric shawl used by men as belt; cf. שלמא

שאלה (H) f. **šıʾēla** question (NT2).

שאלוכה (K) f. **šālōke** sickle (=H חֶרְמֵשׁ, BT5, D).

שאלן, שָׁאלָאן (K **šale** I hope < Ar ان شاء الله?) **šālan** (AvidH 5, 8) one wishes, would that: שאלן ה'ד עאלמין פארא טלאתוך אך שואלוך **šālan ʾilāhıd ʿālmīn pāreʾ ṭlāṯox ʾıx šuʾālox** May God of the Universe reward you as your deeds (NT5 402); cf. אישלא.

שאם (Ar) **šām** Damascus, Syria; **šām-u-šıngar** far away places.

שאמא (Ar; OA שומא) f. **šāma** beauty mark, mole.

שאמה-קאזא (< K?) **šāmē-qāza** safe, peaceful (PolU 143).

שאמנאיא (< שאם) **šāmnāya** of Damascus (BT1); **xmarta šāmēsa** fast she-ass (PolU 429).

שׂאן v. ז'אן

שאנס (K < Fr) ⁺**šāns** good luck.

שאפא v. שהפזא

שַׁאפִילֵיל (Ar خـشـاف الليل) **šāfıllēl** bat (=H עֲטַלֵּף, BT3, D).

שאפרא, ששפרא, שהפרא (P) m. **šāparra, šah/š-** wing feather, wing (=H כָּנָף, BT1, Am); tree branch (NT2); fin (=H סְנַפִּיר, BT3, D) (NT+).

שאקא (OA) f. **šāqa** leg; cf. סאקא; pl. שקאניה **šaqāne** (NT) (NT+).

שאקאנא, שאקנתא (< שאקא) adj. **šāqāna, šāqanta** leggy, tall person.

ש-א-ר (OA/OS/Mand שגר heat up) **š-ʾ-r** to start fire, kindle (vi); be enraptured, fired (audience by a good singer); IV to kindle, heat (oven).

שָׁארַא (< P شـهـر) **šāra** town, multitude (RivP 211).

ש-א-ש (OA/OS שגש disturb, upset) vt/vi **š-ʾ-š** to shake; to rock a cradle; **šʾıšle rēše** He shook his head in disbelief (cf. PolG); **kšaʾša gyāna** She walks like a peacock (flaunting her beauty); **dunye kšaʾša bale la kxarwa** The world shakes but doesnt get destroyed.

שאש (K) inv. **šāš** confused, troubled.

שאשתא (< ש-א-ש) f. **šʾašta** rock, waving (=H תְּנוּפָה, BT2).

שאתא 1, שיאתא (OA שָׁעְתָא) f. **šeʾṯa** hour, time (NT); = Z **šēsa** (?), used only in **qurra mār šēsa** damned thing (said when trying to rememer a word) (PolU 19); v. זאיא ; cf. סאעא.

שאתא 2, שנא (OA שתא) f. **šāta, šınna** year; שאתא כיתא **šāta xēta** (NT5 411) / **xa šat-xít** (Z)/next year, another year; cf. רישא, אשת, כושת, שתקה; **šōʾa kıtte šınna** (!) seven singular years (cf. PolU 145); pl. שנה

šınne; šınne-dāne immemorial times.

שאתא 3 (OA/OS אִישָׁתָא, איששאתא fire, fever < Ak išātu fire, inflammation; Mand עשׁאתא) f. šāṯa (Z šāsa) fever [Khan 581 šāla, f.].

שבא (K) m. šıv(v)a thin branch, stick (PolU 113); pl. šıv(v)e.

שבאבה (Ar) f. šabābe flute (NT); cf. בלורה.

שבאביכה (< שבאכא) f. šabābīke little window (PolG)

שבאכא (Ar) f. šıb(b)āka (fishing) net; window (PolG); pl. שבאכי šıbāke windows (BaBin 149; RivP 210); cf. שבאביכה..

שבאנא, שובאן, שב'אן, שוואן, שִׁיבָאנָא / שִׁיוָאנָא. (K) šıvāna (Z), šıv/wāna (RivSh 231-32), šüvān, šüwān (+NT2) shepherd; šıvanta (f.) (=H רוֹעָה, BT1) [Khan 582 šwān].

ש-ב-ד II (OA/OS שפד) š-b-ḏ (Z š-b-z) to skewer; cf. שבודא.

שבה (Ar) f. šabbe alum.

ש-ב-ה, ש-פ-ה, ש-פ-י, ש-ב-י II (Ar شبه) š-b/p-h (NT), š-p-y (Z, +NT), š-b-y (BT4, D; Hob89 219), to resemble, to liken; cf. תשאביה.

שבהתא (Ar) f. šıbıhta resemblance (NT2), likeness (=H דְּמוּת, BT1, Am); cf. שבי.

שבודא (OA/OS שפודא) šabūḏa (Z, PolG šabūza) skewer; pl. שבודה šabūḏe (NT5 409) (NT+).

שבועה (H) f. šavū'a oath; די ימילי בשבועה dı ymīli bšavū'a Swear to me by oath! (NT+).

שָׁבוּעוֹת (H) šavō/ū'ōṯ Feast of Weeks (BT4, D); v. אידא 2, שוואא.

שבוקא (OS) m. šabūqa, rod, ply branch (used for punishment; =H שׁוֹט, PolG); scepter (=H שֵׁבֶט, BT1); pl. šabūqe (PolG); שבוקד אנואר šabūqıd 'anwār rods of fire (NT5 383).

שבט 1 (H) šēveṯ tribe (of Israel); pl. שבטים šıvāṯīm; cf. שוטא (NT+).

שבט 2 (H) m. šavaṭ month of Shevat.

ש-ב-י v. ש-ב-ה

שבי (Ar شبه) m. šıbi gold-like, worthless metal [MacD 298 šıbe brass, copper].

ש-ב-כ II (Ar) š-b-k to make net-work (=H שָׂבָךְ, BT2); cf. משבכ, שבאכא.

שבככאן (Ar-K) m. šabakvan fisherman (by net-casting) (PolU 320).

שבככאנותא (< שבככאן) f. šıbakvānūṯa fishing, fishery (by net-casting).

שבלתא v. שובלתא

שבת, שַׁבָּת (H) šı/abbāṯ Sabbath; mostly in the greeting (Z): šabbā(s) šālōm Have a Sabbath of peace; and its response šabbā-šālōm ṭo(v)-(u) mavōrāx Have a Sabbath of peace and blessing; v. בלא 2.

שבתא, שַׁבְתָא, שפתא (OA) f. ša/ıbṯa (RivSh 198; Z šab/psa) Sabbath, Saturday; week: בימא יומא מן שבתא bēma yōma mın šabṯa Which day of the week? v. יקורתא; pl. שַׁבָּתָא, שובאתא, שבאתא ša/ubāṯa (BT3, RivSh199, Avin78 95; PolG); šabawása (Nakano 1970 202).

שבתאי, שבו (H) p.n.m šabbáṯay, šabbo (hypo) Sabbatay; cf. סבתו, שמביכו.

שגא (< ?) šagga penis (Am), in npılle baṯır šaggıd gyāne followed his own whim.

שגדא v. שכדא

שג'יל, ז'ג'יל (Ar) š/žağil day-worker; pl. šağīle (PolGr 36).

ש-ג'-ל, ז'-ג'-ל, ג'-ג'-ל (Ar) š/ž-ğ-l to work, be busy, to occupy oneself (b- with); IV to employ; - gyāne keep himself busy (Pol 109); be late, occupied (Hob89 218).

שדאנא, שדנתא (OS) adj. šıḏāna (Z šızāna), šıḏanta mad, bedeviled (=H מְתְעַתֵּעַ, PolG); cf. ש-י-ד-ן, שידא; šıḏāna-ṣrī'a complete idiot.

שדאנותא (< שדאנא) f. šıḏānūṯa madness.

שדה (Ar) f. šidde hardship (NT5 385).

ש-ד-י (OA spin, cast) š-ḏ-y (Z š-z-y) to unstich (vi), fall apart (BaBin115).

שדי (H) m. šadday Shadday, the Almighty; an amulet (Z); cf. שדייכא, שם שדי; pl. šaddayīyat amulets (Z) (NT+).

שדיד (Ar) šadīd severe (punishment)(NT; RivSh 154)).

שדייכא (< שדי) m. šaddayīka silver amulet with the name שדי engraved on it; pl. šaddyīkat.

שדים, שדין, שֵׁדִים (H) šēḏīm/n, šıḏīm(?) (RivSh 199), demons (NT3) (=H שְׂעִירִים, BT3, D; שֵׁדִים, BT5); cf. גנא, שידא [Khan 581 šedime].

ש-ד-ר II (OA) š-d-r to send (NT+).

שהארא, שהרתא (OS vigilant) ša/ıhāra, -arta blind; pl. שַׁהְרָאנֵי, שָׁהָארֵי šahāre (cf. PolG), šaḥrāne (AvidSh 64, 68); cf. ש-ח-ה-ר.

שהוותא (Ar) f. šaḥwıta desire, appetite; pl. šaḥwıtyāṯa; cf. ש-ח-ה-י.

ש-ה-י (< שהיאנא) š-h-y to celebrate, be cheerful.

שהיאנא (K/P royal ?) f. šaḥyāna celebration, feast for all (Z, NT5 403, RivSh 148); **shaḥyāna pıšla go danya xurāsa** These friends became joyful (Zaken 389).

שהיאנאתותא (< שהיאנא) šaḥyānātūṯa joy of celebration (PolG).

שהכול (H) šākōl the blessing over drinking water.

ש(ה)מיזא (K? cf. מז) šaḥmīza sour drink [Br93 103, 280].

שהפזא, שאפא (< K šāp seasonal flood?) šaḥpıza, šāpa trail (PolU 131); cf. שופא.

שהפרא v. שאפרא

שהראנא v. שהארא

שַׁהֲרוּתָא (< שהארא) šaharūṯa (night) blindness (=H סַנְוֵרִים, Polg, D:2 Kg 6:18; cf. שפכורותא).

שהרזא (K) inv. šaḥraza smart, expert; cf. נא-שהרזא (NT+).

ש-ה-ר-ז III (K) š-h-r-z to be smart, familiar.

שהרירה (< שהארא/OA-OS zahrū/īrā ?) pl. šaḥrīre rays of lights: קט גכאזיתון מנדי שהרירה ברישד טורא Do you see any rays of lights on top of the mountain ? (=H אור צץ, NTU4 151b).

שהריסתאן (K/P) šaḥristān large city (PolU 90); large crowd in a wedding (PolU 60).

שוא 1 (H?) adv. šwa for no reason: ʾawa šwa zılle He just went (having no special reason; cf. PolG).

שוא 2, אשוא (OA שבע) f. (ı)šwa(ʾ) seven (NT); cf. שואמא.

שואא, שווא (OA שבעא) m./f. šōʾa , šawwa (Hob89 183), seven; week; šōʾá-ʾımmāye seven hundred (BT); cf. שואמא; שׁוֹאֲגָא šōʾaga (D)/ xa-ušōʾa (Z) sevenfold (BT3); cf. שבתא, שוואא (NT+).

שואאלא v. שולא

שואוא, שוותא, שְׁיוֹתָא (OA שיבבא/OS ܫܒܒܐ) šwāwa, šwōta (f.), neighbor (=H שָׁכֵן, שְׁכֵנָה, BT2; PolG); cf. גירן [Mutz 231 šwāwa, šwafta (!)]

שואוותא (OA שיבבותא) f. neighborhood (SaNR).

שואי (OA שבעין) šōʾi seventy; שואי כארה šōʾi kāre (NT)/ šōʾiga (Z)/ šōʾi gāhe (BABin 151) despite, although (NT+).

שואלא v. שולא

שואמא, שוואמא (OA שבע מאה) š(o)waʾma seven hundred; v. שואא [MacD 299 šōwamā].

שואסר, שוואסר, אשואסר (OA שבע עסר) š(o)waʾsar (BT1 247), ʾıšwaʾsar (PolU 250), seventeen [Khan 581 šoʾa-sar].

שובא (K) šōva furrow (BaBin 49); cf. תאכא; ʾ-w-ḏ- to clean a garden of all its vegetations (PolU 347).

שובאן, שוואן v. שבאנא

שובאתא v. שבתא

שובבים (H) pl. šōvāvīm a fast of three continuous days before ראש השנה.

שובלתא, שבולתא (OA שבלתא, שׁוּבַּלְתָּא) f. šübülṯa ear of corn; pl. šuble (OA pl. שׁוּבְלֵי).

שובראתא (< ?) pl. šubrāṯa bracelets (NT2; Br93 128).

שוד, שות (< OA שבוק ד- ?) šud/t Let...! שוד פלטי šud palṭi Let them go out! שׁוּת כָּאזֵי Let him find! (=H יִרְאֶה, BT1; RivSh 235); שוד מיתין šud mēṯın; Let me die, May I die! (cf. PolG) שוד שויקיואלה šud šwīqīwāle (NT, =Z šud hāwēwa`šwīqa dōhun) He should have left them; štāwe (‹ šud hāwe) Let it be (so); its o.k.

שודה (< שכדא?) šōḏe (Z šōze) joy (Br93 145); v. בישודה [cf. MacD 301].

שוואא (OA שבועא) m šawōʾa seven (years) (=H שָׁבוּעַ, BT1= Gen 29:27); seven days, a week (BT3); pl. שְׁוּאוֹתָא šawōʾō/āṯa (?) (=H שָׁבוּעוֹת, BT, D) [MacD 298 seven weeks...].

שוחד (H) m. šōḥaḏ(Z šōḥaz/s) bribe (BT2).

שוחט (H) m. šōḥēṭ ritual slaughterer (cf. PolU 391); pl. šōḥaṭīm; ṣlōṯıd - the early prayer-shift of slaughterers; cf. שחיטה.

שוטא, שווטא (OA שבטא) m. šūṭa (Z), šıwṭa (NT), tribe; cf. שבט; pl. שוטה, שׁוּטְי šūṭe, šüwṭe (AvidH 53); cf. גויא.

ש-ו-י II (OA make into) š-w-y (dūka) to spread carpets, bedding on floor (Socin 161; PolG); cf. שויתא, משויא (NT+).

שוין, לשוינד, שוינותא (K < P stān) prep. šwīn, lšwīnıd, šwīnūṯ(a) (PolU 31), in place of, instead of (=H תַּחַת, BT) [RivSh 203 שׁוּנִת šūnıt; PolG: אֶשְׁוִין]; cf. גיבא (NT+).

שוינואר (K < שוין) šwīnwār inheritor,

replacement, residue (NTU4 150a).

שויתא (< ש-ו-י; cf. OA תשויתא bed/שויתא comfort, relaxation?) f. **šwīṯa** bedding, bed (=H יָצוּעַ/מִשְׁכָּב/מִטָּה, BT1; עוֹנָה, BT2); pl. שוייאתא **šūyāṯa** (AmU2 4b; PolG) (NT+).

שולא , שואלא (Ar شغل/OS ܫܘܥܠܐ) **šūla** (Z), **šuʾ(ā)la** (?) (NT1), work, deed, affair, case; לתלוך שואלא אביהון **latlox šuʾ(ā)la ʾıbbēhun** Dont worry about them (NTU4 162a); **latlox šūla** Dont worry (PolU 21); pl. שׁוּאלֵי, שֻׁאַלֶי, שואלה שוואלה, **šo/uʾ(ā)le** (Z, NT; BT1, D; PolG); cf. עמל. [MacD 301 **šu(ġ)lā, šūlā**; Mengozzi 311 **šula, šuʾlē**].

שולחן, שלחן (H) **šulḥan** table (NT, BT2; Avin78 94; BaBin 122); **šulḥan ʾavrāham ʾāvīnu hāwe šulḥan dīdox** May your table be as (abundant) as that of our ancestor Abraham; cf. ספרא, מיזא, מידו.

שולטאנא (OA) m. **šulṭāna** king (NT; RivSh 184)); cf. סולטן, מלך, מלכא, חכומא [Khan 582].

שולטנותא (OA) **šulṭanūṯa** kingship (NT).

שולטנתא (OA) f. **šulṭanta** queen (NT5 394); cf. מלכתא, חכומתא.

שולכאיא, שולכיתא (< ש-ל-כ) adj. **šulxāya, -xēṯa** naked, poor (having no clothes to wear); cf. פוראאיא, אאהופ [Khan 581 **šlixa, šluxa**].

שולפא v. שלפא

שומאאתא (< ש-מ-א) pl. **šumʾāṯa** rumors (PolG).

שומר ישראל (H) **šōmēr yisrāʾēl** Guardian of Israel (=Elijah, RivSh 273).

שונא דת (H) **sōní-dāṯ** (Z **-dās**) one who hates (Jewish) religion.

שונאי ישראל (H) pl. **sōn(ʾe)-yisrāʾēl** enemies of Jews, "Jews" in quoting a Gentile curse (Z, RivSh 211, 231); **sōn-yisrāʾēl hāwe bḥāli** May the enemies of Israel be in my condition (said by very sick woman when asked how she is); — **hāwe hādax ẓaʿif uqhīre** May the enemies of Israel be so weak and greiving (PolU 391); **barmınnān** — plain awful, horrible (PolU 282).

שונשלתא v. שנשלתא

שופא (OS mark) **šōpa** location, indication, reference (NT2).

שופאע (Ar) **šufāʿ** recommendation (NT).

שופולא v. שפולא

שופיר (T/K/SyAr < Fr) m. ***šōfēr** (assistant) driver, chauffeur.

שופר (H) m. ***šōfar** horn, shofar; **b-** (I swear) by the shofar; cf. תקיעה; pl. שופארה **šōfāre** (BaBin 154).

שופרא (OA) m. **šupra** beauty (AmU2 5a).

ש-ו-ק (OA שבק) **š-w-q** to leave (behind); שוקלה כאיה אבד חאצרין **šuqle xāye ʾıbbıd** [Z **ta**] **ḥāẓırīn** He passed away (lit., left life for the present [audience]); to let (cf. שוד); טלמא אשוקלן דזלו ישראל **ṭlamā ıšwıqlan dzıllu yisrāʾēl** Why did we let Israel leave; to let live; **šuqla ldūka** Forget it, you wouldnt believe this (lit., leave it in its place) (Avin78 94).

שוקא 1 (OA) m. **šūqa** market; pl. **šūqāne** (PolG) (NT+).

שוקא 2 v. גוקא

ש-ו-ר II (Ar) ***š-w-r** to seek advise, consult: — **bıt/ʾımmıt xauxét** They consulted each other (Zaken 389; PolG).

שורא (OA) m. **šūra** (city) wall; pl. שוראנה **šūrāne** (cf. RivSh 276) (NT+).

שורבא (K/P) f. **šorba** (rice) soup; cf. מראקא.

שורוב, שרוב (K < Ar) m. **šu/ırūb** sweet drink; pl. **šurūbat** (PolU 311); cf. שרבת.

שורטא, שורטי (Ar) **šurṭa/i** policeman.

שור-שור-שור (onomat.) **šor-šor-šor** sound of running water from a jar, etc. (PolU 121).

ש(ו)רשורכה, ש(ו)רשורתא (< ש-ר-ש-ר) f. ***šüršürke, -ta** profuse water/sweat/blood drops (PolU 103, 121); cf. שרשורא.

שושא, שֵׁישַׁא, שוּשַׁא (Ar/T/K < P > OA שִׁישָׁא, SokBA 1141) **šīša šūša, šēša** glass bottle, glass work (=H בַּקְבֻּק, PolG; RivSh 265).

שושלתא (OA; cf. שנשלתא) **šōšalta** silver or gold chain-ornament; pl. **šušlāṯa** [Br93 128].

שושמה, ששמה (OA שו(מ)שמא) pl. **šušme** sesames; v. ג-ל-פ.

שושמנתא (< שושמה?) f. **šušmanta** livers lobe (=H יֹתֶרֶת, BT2/3).

שושנה, שושה (H) p.n.f. **šōšanna, šōše** (hypo.), Shoshana, Susannah, Suzie (SaLH 139).

שושתר (P) **šuštar** (ancient) Susa (NT3).

שות v. שוד

שותפה (H) pl. **šuttāfe** (Let us be) partners, (mostly in crypto-Jewish); cf. חצי.

שחאטא v. שכאטא

שחיטה (H) f. **šaḥīṭa** ritual slaughtering (cf.

PolU 391); cf. הלכה.

שחיר v. ז'חר

שְׁחָקִים (H) šıḥāqīm the heavens (BT5, D).

שחרית (H) f. šaḥriṯ Jewish morning prayer.

שטא (Ar) m. šaṭṭa river, stream (NT3; BT1, Am); cf. כוורא, נהרא.

ש-ט-ח (OA/OS שטח to spread out) š-ṭ-ḥ to lie down, stretch oneself on the ground or bed; IV to spread (vt), stretch, put to bed (Pol 108); cf. ש-ר-ט-ח, ש-ט-כ.

ש-ט-י (OA/OS/Mand שוט fly, move around) š-ṭ-y to swim (NT), sail (boat), roam, shoot (a star) (=H דָּרַךְ, BT4).

שטיפא (< ש-ט-פ) šaṭifa(?) current, flow (NT2).

ש-ט-כ (OA שטח) š-ṭ-x hang clothes to dry (cf. PolG), to spread out (quails on the ground) (=H שָׁטַח, BT4), to lay open (BaBin 151); cf. ש-ט-ח [MacD 304 šāṭix spread, air clothes; IrAr šaṭiḥ flat, shallow; Ar š-ṭ-ḥ roam].

שטן (H) sāṭān Satan; cf. שייטן; - ᵓurre go qalwe Satan entered his body, became temporarily insane (cf. PolU 267); - lēwe mīsa ulag māyıs Satan is not dead and will not die (sex drive is always with us) (PolU 351a); pl. שטנים sāṭānīm (NT2) (NT+).

ש-ט-פ (OA) vt š-ṭ-f to overflow, drown; to rinse (=H שָׁטַף, BT3; NT5 410); to spill blood (RivSh 250); dımma qam šāṭıfle He was very vulgar to her (Z); cf. שטיפא (NT+).

שטפות (H שטפון) šıṭṭāfōt flood (SaAC 7); cf. טוטפות ?

שטר, שטאר (H) m. šáṭṭar (Z) document; שטר כתובה קדושין marriage contract (NT2).

שי, שין, (שיכ(ינה, (ז'י(ג (K žī) adv. (encl.) šī(n), šik(ēne), žī(g) also, too, even (Z; BT2; Ruth 1:12; 2:14; BaBin 133; Segal #60; MeAl 180, n. 29; Pol 110; PolG).

ש-י-א (OA שיע/שעע) š-y-ᵓ to whitewash, to plaster; cf. ג'-י-א (NT+).

שיאאה (< ש-י-א; OA שְׁיָעָא sealing clay) v.n. šyaᵓa house plastering.

שיאדא v. שאדא

שיבתא (Ar) f. šaybıta old age, dignity (NT2).

שידא (OA/OS/Mand) m. šēḏa demon (NT2); cf. גנא, שדים, שדאנא; v. שינא, ש-י-ד-נ.

ש-י-ד-נ III (< שדאנא) vt/vi š-ē/ī-ḏ-n (Z š-ē/ī-z-n) to become or make mad [1: mšīzın- (cf. PolG); 2/3:mšēzın; 4: mšēzōne].

שיוכייאתא (K šīv) pl. šīwıkyāṯa valleys, river-beds (NT2).

שייטן, שייטאן, שיטן (Ar) m. šayṭan (NT2; NTU4 159b), šēṭan (Z), Satan; cf. שטן.

שייטאנותא (< שייטן) šayṭānūṯa Satanism, hostility (NTU4 164a).

ש-י-כ v. ש-כ-כ

שיך (Ar) m. šēx Muslim scholar; tribal chief (pl. šexyāne, PolU 290); member of the Jewish burial society (Z); cf. חבראיא (v. Br93 191); pl. šēxyāne (PolGr 51).

שיכ, שיכינה v. שי

שיכותא, שיכתותא (< שיך) n. abst. šēx(at)ūṯa the position of the chief of tribe, sheikdom (PolU 291, 351).

שילא, שִׁילֵי, ג'יל (K < P šīra) šīla/e, čīl a drink made of steeped grapes before becoming intoxicant (≠H מִשְׁרַת/דַּם עֲנָבִים, BT1; BT4, D; BT5); cf. שרבת [cf. Ar شـيل to distill; MacD 132 čīl root, 304 šīlā red calico].

שילאבכה (K šēlū muddy+āv water?) f. šēlāvke liquid whitewash splashed on walls.

שילונא (< ?) m. šelōna a burlesque character of a Christian priest played on Passover night (Br93 290-92).

שילכתא (K?) šēlıkṯa (salvo of) bullets; pl. šēlıkyāṯa (PolGr 55, PolG); cf. שלכתא ?

ש-י-מ (OS) š-y-m to be painful (healing wound touched by accident); šīma (p.p.m.) afflicted person (NTU4 160b); IV to inflict such pain; mušılmāna mašīmāna A Muslim inflicts pain (a Jewish saying).

שין 1, שיני (K) šīn(i) mourning (RivSh 222); מן בכייא ומן שִׁינִי mın bıxya umın šīni from weeping and mourning (BaBin 154).

שין 2 v. שי

שינא, שינה (OS) f. šēna peace; לכדיותא ולשינא אאתיה אידא דיכון lxıdyūṯa ulšēna ᵓāṯe ᵓēḏa dēxun May your Holiday come for joy and peace (a greeting for approaching holiday) (NT5 411); šınsıd šēna (Have) a peaceful sleep; šēna (m)ᵓaxgıb Peace be on this side (said after mentioning demons or evil spirits) (cf. PolU 36); v. מלאך (NT+).

ש-י-פ (OA/OS/Mand שוף) vt š-y-p to rub, smear (cf. PolG).

שיפדרא (K) šīpadar(a) doorpost, threshold

(=H מְזוּזָה, BT2; מַשְׁקוֹף, PolG) [cf. MacD 305 **šīpā** doorpost].

שִׁיפַּכֵי (< ש-פ-כ) pl. **šipāxe** spermatic cords (=H שָׁפְכָה, BT5, D).

שֶׁיקֻוצִים (H) pl. **šıqqūṣīm** detestable things (=H שִׁקּוּצִים, BT5, D).

שֵׁיקִיץ v. שקץ

שירא הורכא (K) **šīra-hurka** ground rice cooked with milk and eaten on Shavuot (ShiKC).

שירה (H) **šīra** song, singing; **ʾ-m-r** - to sing, to recite (NT3); **ʾ-w-d̲** - to compose a poem (RivSh 205) [Garbell 333 **širači** singer].

שיר ומשאורת (Ar) **šīr-u-mašāwırat** discussion, councils (PolU 161); cf, שירתא.

שיר ושכר (K) **šīr-u-šakar** milk and sugar, luxury, pampering (PolU 109); cf. שאדא.

שיר(ות), שירין, ותשבחות (H) pl. **šīr(ōt̲) utišbāḥōt̲** (NT2, PolU 9), **šīrīn** (NT3), hymns, songs.

שירכ (K sap) **šīrık** sesame oil used for frying [cf. Ar سيرج].

שירתא (K < Ar شيرة) f. **šīrıta** advice, counsel (PolG); cf. ש-ו-ר, משוורא, שיר ומשאורת.

שישה (< ששה ?) pl. **šēše** boiled wheat eaten as snack by children; cf. ששה.

שישכתא (K T šiš spit) f. **šīšıkta** knitting needle; pl. **šīšıkyāta**.

שיתא 1 v. שאתא 1

שיתא 2 (< ש-ת-ת) p.p.m. **šīta** one expelled, wanderer (=H נָע, BT1).

שכ (Ar) m. **šık** doubt; cf. ש-כ-כ.

שַׁכָּא (AzT/K?) m. **šakka** young sheep; pl. שַׁאכֵי **šakke** (=H שֶׂה, כְּבָשׂוֹת, BT1, D) [cf. Garbell 332 **šakka** K f. sheep; MacD 305, 313, AzT m./f. ram/ewe three years old].

שכאטא, שחאטא (IrAr/K) f. **šıxāṭa** (Z), **šıḥḥāṭa** (Hob97 318;< SyAr), matchbox; **zıllıgıd** - match; cf. ש-כ-ט; pl. **šaḥḥāṭe** slippers (Gz73 85) [Mutz 231 **šqata**; Khan 580 **šxāṭa**].

שכאתא v. אשכאתא

שכארא v. שכרתא

שכבה (K trough) **škave** bowl, container (?): **xa - gurgur** a bowl of bulgur (PolU 427).

שכביתא (K šikeva) f. **škavēta** thin bread baked on iron sheet (like tortilla but larger); pl. **škavāye**.

שכבת זרע (H) **šıxvat̲ zēraᶜ** emission of semen (NT2; BT3).

ש-כ-ד, ש-ג'-ד II (OA/OS שחד to bribe, give a gift) **š-x/ġ-d̲** (Z **š-x-z**) to give good news (NT+).

שכדא, שג'דא (OA/OS שוחדא bribe, gift) f. **šıx/ġda** good tidings (NT+); v. שוחד; cf. ש-כ-ד, שודה.

שכווא v. כּווא

שכוונתא (OS ܩܠܡܐ louse; ܫܘܡܫܡܐ/OA שו(מ)שומנא ant) f. **šıkwanta** ant; pl. **šıkwāne** [MacD 305 **šikwānā** m.].

שכורא (OA שיחורא) m. **⁺šı/axōra** coal, charcoal; **kōma mux** — black as charcoal (PolG); cf. קירא; v. ש-כ-ר 2.

ש-כ-ט (IrAr < Ar شخط) **š-x-ṭ** to strike a match; cf. שכאטא.

שכטא (IrAr) m. **šıxṭa** line (drawn), mark.

ש-כ-י (Ar) **š-k-y** to lodge a complaint (NT+).

שכינא, שכנתא (OA שחינא) adj. **šaxīna, šaxınta** hot, warm; hot food n. (NT5 409); cf. שכוונתא; **rēše šaxīna** (he is) hot tempered (NT+).

שכינה (H) **šaxīna** Shekhinah, the Divine Presence; **b–** (I swear) by the Divine Presence (common grave oath; even Muslim Kurds swore **bdīne** – by the religion of Shekhina [cf. MacD 305-6]; **si xzi paswās** – Go to synagogue to see the open scroll of Torah (lit. Go and see the face of Shekhinah] (cf. RivSh 181); — **gnahra/glahya lgubʾēne** Shekhina shines on his forehead (said about a learned pious person) (MeAl 188; PolU 307).

שכיר(א) (K) m. **škē/ār** (natural) pile of stones, salt)(PolU 326).

שכירא 1, שכרתא (< ש-כ-ר 1) p.p. **⁺škīra, ⁺škırta** grateful, thankful.

שכירא 2, שכרתא (< ש-כ-ר 2) p.p. **⁺šxīra, ⁺šxırta** sooty, black.

שכירא (ו)כודירא (K by Gods benevolence) **š-xēra (u)xudēra** One wishes (that...) (PolG).

ש-כ-כ II2, ש-י-כ IV (Ar) **š-k-k, š-y-k** (NT), to doubt; **lıbbe mšukkıkle** (Z, PolG)= **mōšıkle** (NT) He has doubts; cf. שכ.

ש-כ-ל 1 (Ar to form) **š-k-l** to begin, start (Z; RivSh 136; MeAl 191): **škōl bıṣlōsa** Start the prayer; **škılle bīxāla** He began eating; **škıllu (bıt) msafōre** They began traveling (PolG); to befit, look well: **ʾē ṣudra**

rāba kšakla ʾıllox This shirt fits you very well (cf. NTU4 183a) **ʾāhıt kšaklıt ṯāla** You are right for her; **lak šākıllox hāwıt faqir** You dont deserve to be poor (PolG); IV to decorate (BaBin 160).

ש-כ-ל 2 IV (OA שחל) **š-x-l** to thread (beads).

שכל (Ar) m. **šikıl** shape, form; kind, variety; **ma šikıl gōra wıt** What kind of man are you? (PolG); pl. שכלה **šikle**, אשכאל **ʾaškāl** (+NT); **šıklé-šıkle, ʾaškāl-u-ʾalwān** all sorts of form and color.

שכליתא (< ש-כ-ל) **škalīṯa** beginning (PolG).

שכלתא (K **šekal**) f. **šikkalta** worn-out shoe, slipper; **la kxašwınne bšıkkalti** I think of him less than even my slipper; pl. **šıkkāle**.

ש-כ-נ (OA/OS שחן be inflamed, heat) **š-x-n** to become warm, hot; sleepy (closed eyes) (Z; PolG); be excited, carried away (Z); IV to heat, warm up (NT+).

שכנא, שְׁכְנַא (OA שחנא) m. **šıxna** boils, fever (=H שְׁחִין/קַדַּחַת, BT5; PolG) (NT+).

שכנות(א) (OS) f. **šıxnūṯ(a)** heat, warmth.

שכפתא (K) f. **škafta** cave; pl. שכפייאתא **škafyāṯa** (BaBin 149; =H צְרִחִים, PolG:1 S 13:6).

ש-כ-ר 1 (Ar) **⁺š-k-r** to thank, be grateful; **škōr ʾilāha** Thank God! (PolG).

ש-כ-ר 2 (OA/OS שחר) **⁺š-x-r** to become sooty, black; **lıbbe ⁺šxırre mınna** He doesn't love her any more; cf. כ-י-מ; IV to make black; **qam ⁺mašxırra pāse** He put him to shame; **qam ⁺mašxırre lıbbe mınna** He caused him not to love her anymore; cf. שכורא, שכרא(נא).

שכרא (OS ܫܘܚܪܐ) m. **⁺šıxra** soot; cf. שמרא.

שכראנא, שכרנתא (< שכרא) adj. **⁺šıxrāna, -anta**, sooty.

שְׁכָּרָאתִי (K-Ar) **škarāti** thanksgiving (=H הוֹדָאוֹת, AvidH 71).

שכרוכא (K-Ar) m. **šakrōka** unwrapped candy; pl. **šakrōkat**; cf. גכלית.

שכרתא, שכארא (*OA Ak **šakirru**) f. **šıxāra, šıxarta** churn, wooden bowl for chopping meat, etc. (=H מִשְׁאֶרֶת, BT5); pl. שְׁכַרְיַיאתַא **šxaryāṯa** (=H קְעָרוֹת, BT4, D) [cf. Garbell 334 **šxare** baking-trough; MacD 303 small wooden bowl].

שכתא (OS ܫܘܚܬܐ rust, tartar/ܫܘܚܬܐ skin disease; lees, feces; cf. OA שוכתא pus) f. **šıxta** dirt, grime [but Mutz 230 < OA שחת].

שכתאנא, שכתנתא (< שכתא) **šıxtāna, -anta**, dirty, grimy (NT+).

ש-כ-ת-נ III (< שכתאנא; cf. OS ܫܚܬ to rust) vt/vi **š-x-t-n** to be or make grimy.

שכתתא v. אשכאתא

שלא 1 (K < Ar) m. **šılla** crippled, lame (NT+).

שלא 2 (K) m. **šalla** Kurdish woven pants of fine wool, worn usually together with שפכתא.

שלאמא (OA) **šlāma** in **bı-** Welcome (PolU 207: ChNA); pl. **šlāme** only in the rare greeting to Christians or in nursery rhymes **bšēna ubıšlāme** Very welcome! (SaNR) [but v. Khan 581 **šlāma**, pl. **šlāme** greetings].

שלאתי (*IrAr < Ak **šillatu** vulgarity?) m. **šılāti** lout; pl. **šılātiyat**.

שלג'ם (IrAr/P>OA שַׁלְגַם turnip, SokBA 1146) **šalġam** boiled and sugared white turnips; cf. שרגומתא.

ש-ל-ה-ו III (OA שלהב?) **š-l-h-w** to languish [1: מְשׁוֹלְהוֹוְלָא **mšolhowla** (?)=H וַתֵּלַה, PolG: Gen 47:13)

ש-ל-ה-מ III (Ar لهم) **š-l-h-m** to be very hungry, gluttonous.

שלוכתא (OS ܫܠܘܟܬܐ) f. **šılluxta** slough of snakes; **xōl** - Eat slough! (said by angry mothers when asked What is there to it?).

שלום (H) **šālōm** peace; דרילה שלום איליה **drēle šālōm ʾılle** He greeted him; אילאהד ישראל בשלום גאעליכון **ʾilāhıd yisrāʾēl bšālōm jāʿıllēxun** May God of Israel make peace among you (NT5 411); **xılmox šālōm** May your dream be of peace; **wağārox šālōm** Have peaceful trips; **ʾilāha tāxırre bšālōm** May God remember him in peace (said of a person who wasnt seen for long time (Z); pl. שלומות **šalōmōṯ** only in **d-r-y** - to give regards; cf. שלאמה [Khan 581 **šalomi**].

שלום עליכם (H) **šalōm ʿalēxem** Peace be upon you!; response: **ʿalēxem šālōm** (used in folktales even by Muslims; cf. PolU 33).

שלונא (< ?) m. **šılōna** comedian in a Passover-night play (Br93 290f.).

שלוקא, שלוקתא (< ש-ל-ק) adj. **šalūqa, šaluqta** boiling hot (NT+).

שלוקאנא, שלוקנתא (< ש-ל-ק) adj. **šlōqāna, šlōqanta** one suffering from severe acne; cf. שלקו [cf. MacD 307 **šalqāna** pitted with

smallpox]; cf. ש-ל-ק-ג.
שלורא (< ?) šıllōra idiot, weirdo, duffer.
שלחן v. שולחן
ש-ל-ט-כ III (IrAr< T شلتاق false dispute) š-l-ṭ-x try to possess something by deception, covet and try to take (cf. PolG).
שליח (H) m. šālīyaḥ Rabbinical visitor; pl. שליחים šalīḥīm.
שליקא, שלקתא (OA/OS) p.p. šlīqa, šlıqta boiled; be'e šlīqe boiled eggs; cf. ש-ל-ק.
ש-ל-כ (OA שלח) š-l-x to take off (clothes, shoes); bēsıd šlīxıd pēlavta the family of unsandaled one (=H בֵּית חֲלוּץ הַנָּעַל, BT5); II to rob a traveller, to overcharge; IV to undress; cf. שולכאיא, שלוכתא, משלכאנא.
שלכתא (K)ʃ f. šıllıkṯa skull, crown of the head.
ש-ל-ל II2 (Ar) š-l-l to limp (Hob89 219).
ש-ל-מ IV (OS) š-l-m to convert to Islam; cf. מושלמאנא (NT+).
שלמא (< שאלא?) šallāma kind of fabric for women's wear (PolU 422).
שלמאקה (< ?) pl. šılmāqe tears, eye-watering (due to eye disease).
שלמה, שלו (H) šalōmo, šılo (hypo.), Solomon; שלמה המלך - hammēlex King Solomon (NT+).
שלמוכה (< K šilme weed?) f. šılmōke white-mustard leaves.
שלמים (H) pl. šılāmīm peace-offerings (BT).
שלנקא (IrAr šranqa/K širinge < E syringe] f. šalanqa shot, injection, syringe; m-x-y — to give an injection.
ש-ל-פ 1 (OA) š-l-p to be out of joint; stick out; to unsheathe; pull out (stones from the wall) (=H חָלֵץ, BT3) (NT+).
ש-ל-פ 2 II (K) š-l-f to deceive: ליליה ויומא בכובאט אילה דמשאלפליני lēle uyōma bxubāṭ-īle dımšālıflēni (Satan) is day and night trying hard to deceive us (NTU4 159a, 164a).
שלפא, שולפא (OS) m. šülpa knife-blade (=H לַהַט הַחֶרֶב, BT1; cf. PolG); שֻׁולְפֵית רֻומְחֵי šulpıt rumḥe lance-blade (RivSh 233).
שלצוטכה (K?) f. šalṣōṭke blister, canker sore.
ש-ל-ק (OA) vt/vi š-l-q to boil; to feel hot (NT+).
שלקו (< ש-ל-ק) f. šalqo smallpox, shingles; cf. שלוקאנא [MacD 307 šalqū; Krotkoff 128].
שלקינא (< ש-ל-ק) f. šalaqīna excessive heat.
ש-ל-ק-נ III (< שלוקאנא) š-l-q-n to be spotted (sheep); v. משולקנא.
ש-ל-ש-י III (OA שלשל dangle bait?) š-l-š-y to incite, set on (dogs, bees, angry person): qam mšalšēle kalba 'ıbban He set the dog against us.
ש-ל-ש-ל III (OA) š-l-š-l to drop off, pull out (=H שָׁלֹל, Ruth 2:16); cf. ש-ג-ש-ל.
שם (H) šēm Name(=God) (=H הַשֵּׁם, BT3=Lev 24:11); cf. שם המפורש; v. שם שמים, שם רע שם שדי,.
שמא (OA/OS שְׁמָא) m. šımma name; 'alpa bšımme many like him (do that); שמיה מנדי(ד) šımmēh/d-mındi anything, nothing (cf. PolG; PolU 309); -eh šūla la gōzi They dont do any work (at all) (PolU 391); d-r-y — to name; pl. שְׁמָאֵי, שמאהה, שמאיה šımmāye, -āhe, -ā'e (NT+).
ש-מ-א (OA/OS שמע) š-m-' to hear; IV to let hear; משומאנה mišum'anne He let me (f.) hear (NT3); משמאלי mašme'li Let me hear (your Torah) (NT3); to heed; mušme'la muštıqla She heeded but kept quiet (MeAl 188); אילהא לקבלי דעותי ולא מושמיאלֵי 'ilāha la-qbılle da'ūṯe ula mušme'le God didnt accept his prayer and didnt heed it (BaBin 112; cf Hob89 219).
שמאל (Ar/H) šımāl/sımōl (?) the left side (NT); דיד לַאת כִיאֵי מִן יַמִינֵי וִשְׂמָאלֵי did lat kī'e mın yamīne usimāle (RivSh 244); cf. גַּפָּה.
שמאמוכה, שמאמא (K < Ar) f. šamāmōke, šamāma, musk-melon; beautiful girl (PolU 172).
שמאתא (OA שמעתא) šme'ta fame (=H שֵׁמַע, BT4); pl. שִׁימֵאְיַיתַא (PolG).
שמביכו (K < H-OA שבת) .šambīko p.n.m. for one born on Saturday; cf. שבתאי, סבתו.
ש-מ-ב-ל III (< K šembelot chestnut?) š-m-b-l to swell: sıppāse garūse umšūmbıle His lips big and swollen (PolG).
שמד (H) šımāḏ apostasy; pl. שמדות šımāḏōṯ (NT); cf. משומד.
ש-מ-ד II (H/OA/OS) š-m-ḏ (Z *š-m-z) to be very angry, mad, behave like an apostate.
שמה, שמי (OA שמיא) m. šımme sky, heaven;

wēlu šımme m'ēl mınni u'ar'a mtēx mınni (As) Heaven is above me and earth beneath me (so I cant tell you a lie); **rēše pšımme u'aqle b'ar'a** very tall; pl. שמאההה **šımmāhe** (NT3). v. שמא (NT+).

שמה דמנדי v. שמא

שם המפורש, שֵׁם מְפוֹרָשׁ (שֶׁמֶד) (H) **(šımmıd) šēm (ham)mıfōraš, šımma-fōraš** (Z), tetragrammaton (RivSh 163, 269).

שמואל, שמו (H) p.n.m. **šamū'ēl, šammo** (hypo.), Samuel, Sam.

שמואתא (OA שְׁמוּעֲתָא) f. **šmo'ta** hearing, rumor (NT+).

שמוט

שמוכתא (OS ܫܡܘܟܬܐ) f. **ša/ımuxta** palate, roof of the mouth; **'ixāla ṭpēle bšamuxti** This food stuck to my palate; וישלא שמוכתיני **wišla šamuxtēni** Our palate is dry (BaBin 109) (cf. Mutz. 228 **šamaka**].

שמוץ (Ar شموس) inv. **šammoṣ** restive, unruly (horse) [but PolG: **šámūṭ**].

ש-מ-ח v. ס-מ-ח 2

שמטה (H; cf. OA שמיטתא) **šamıṭṭa** Sabbath year (BT3, BT5); pl. שְׁמִיטּוֹת **šamıṭṭōṯ**.

שמיה מנדי v. שמא

שמים (H) **'šāmāyi(m)** heaven; **ṣōt dīdi qam – gēzıl** My scream reached the sky/heavens (SaAC 31); cf. שמה.

שמינא, שמנתא (OA) adj. **šamīna, šamınta** fat (NT+).

שמיני עצרת (H) **šamīni ʿaṣēreṯ** the 8th day of Sukkoth.

ש-מ-כ II (< ?) **š-m-x** to become stale, lose its fine taste (cooked food not eaten in time); cf. שמוכתא [cf. MacD 203 be or make musty].

ש-מ-ן (OA) **š-m-n** to become fat; IV to make fat.

שמנא (OA/OS/Mand שומנא) m. **šımna** fat.

שמנדר (Ar) **'šamındar** beet root; cf. סלקא; pl. **'šamındāre**.

שמנדר פיר (IrAr < Fr chemin de fer) m. **šamındar fēr** train, railroad [cf. Garbell 333 **šamandafer**].

שמנותא (OA שמנינותא) f. **šımnūṯa** fatness.

ש-מ-ס II (Ar) **š-m-s** to become stale (food exposed to sun).

שמסא v. שמשא

שמסייא (Ar) f. **šamsīya** umbrella, parasol; cf. סיואנא, מטרייה.

ש-מ-ע II (Ar) **š-m-ʿ** to wax, to starch; cf. משמע.

שמעא (Ar) f. **šamʿa** wax candle, wax (=H נְכֹאת, BT1); pl. שמעה **šamʿe** candles; כולון ושתון בשמעה ושראאה **xōlun uštūn bšamʿe ušrā'e** Eat and drink with candles and lights (=H אִכלו ושתו באורה ושמחה, NT5 400) (NT+).

שמעון, שעונא (H) p.n.m. **šımʿun, šıʿūna** (hypo.) Simon.

שמע (ישראל) (H) **šamaʿ (yisrā'ēl)** a common Hebrew prayer, begins with Hear O Israel.

שמעתי (H I hear) f. **šāmaʿti** obedient (wife).

שמרא (OS) m. **šımra** soot; cf. שכרא.

שם רע (H) m. **šēm rāʿ** bad name (BaBin 69).

שמש (H) m. **šámmaš** caretaker in the synagogue (cf. MeAl 182).

שמשא, שמסא (OA) f. **šımša** sun; **'aw dla šāxın bšımšıd mbınōke, la kšāxın bšımšıd ʿāṣırta** He who doesnt get warm in the morning sun, will not get warm in the evening sun (=people dont change); **šımšıd/ -sıd sehra** moonlight (cf. PolG; PolU 360); cf. יומא, סהרא. NT+

שם שדי (H) interj. **šēm šadday** Oh God (protect me/you), said at times of sudden fear [cf. Mutz 229 **šémšadday** May God protect!].

שמשט (P **šimšād** box tree) m. **šımšaṭ** fir, accacia; pl. **šımšāṭe** (=H עֲצֵי שִׁטִּים, BT2) (NT+).

שם שמים (H) **šēm 'šāmāyim** (for) Gods sake.

ש-מ-ש-ק III (< ?) **š-m-š-q** to stroll for pleasure (NT2); to have a willowy body (PolG); v. משומשקא

שמתא (H-OA שַׁמְתָּא < שַׁמַּדְתָּא*; SokBA 1163) **šamıtta** ban, curse; v. חרם.

שנא v. שאתא

שִׂנְאָה (H) **sin'a** hatred (BT4, D); cf. ס-י-מ.

שנאנא (OA) m. **šınnāna** wooden weaving fork.

שנגא, שנגו, שנגה (K) **šanga** (m.), **šango/-ge** (f.), sweet child, playful, delicate.

שנדוכא (< K?) m. **šandōxa** pestle (used to pound meat in שכרתא).

ש-נ-ד-ל III (OA שַׁדֵּל try to convince) **š-n-d-l** to pamper, entertain.

ש-נ-ד-פ v. פ-נ-ד-ש

שנה v. שאתא 2

ש-נ-י (OA/OS change) **š-n-y** to faint; in **šnēle mgıxka** He laughed till he almost fainted;

שנילא היל מפיקלא רוחאייא **šnēla hil mpıqla rōhāya** She fainted (from sorrow) till she died (BaBin 139); cf. כ-ר-ו; II to change residence, move, depart (=H נָסַע, BT, NT).

ש-נ-ק (Ar) **š-n-q** to kill by hanging (PolG).

ש-נ-ש-ל III (< ש-ל-ש-ל) **š-n-š-l** to dangle, loosen (=H שֹׁל תָּשֹׁלּוּ, PolG:Ruth 2:16) scatter, cast.

שנשלתא (OA שילשלתא, שושילתא chain, dynasty) f. **šınšılta** large family with many kids (pejor., a bee-hive); cf. שושלתא, סנסלתא; pl. שֻׁונְשֻׁלְיַיאתַא **šunšulyāta** chains (=H רַתּוּקוֹת [זהב], PolG:1 Kg 6:21)

שנתא (OA/Mand שינתא; OS ܫܢܬܐ) f. **šınta** sleep; שנתא לאיניה לא מכילא - **l'ēne la mxēla** (NT)=**šınse la sēla** (Z; cf. PolG) He didnt (couldnt) fall asleep; **-e fırra** He has lost his need to sleep (His sleep flew away); pl. **wēla dmıxta šō'a šinyāta** She was in a very deep sleep (SaAC 22) .

שנתאנא, שנתנתא (<שנתא) adj. **šıntāna, -nta** sleepy, likes to sleep (SaAC 22).

ש-ע-ב-ד, ש-ע-ד-ב III (H) **š-ᶜ-b-d** (Z **š-ᶜ-b-z**) , **š-ᶜ-d-b** (NT5 404), to enslave (NT+).

שעבוד (H) **šıᶜbūd** slavery (NT3).

ש-ע-ו-ט III (IrAr) vi **š-ᶜ-w-ṭ** to burn with desire for a loved one (cf. PolG).

שעזרתא (Ar?) f. **⁺šaᶜzırta** coccyx; cf. גוכא.

שעטנז (H) **šaᶜatnēz** mixed material (NT3).

שעיראייה (Ar) **šaᶜīrāye** vermicelli pasta.

ש-ע-ל (Ar) **š-ᶜ-l** vi to burn, to light (NT+).

ש-ע-ק v. ש-ק-ע

שערה ערבי (K-Ar) **šıᶜre ᶜarabi** Arabic poetry.

ש-פ-א (OA שפע) **š-p-'** to descend; influence, recommend (NT); cf. ש-פ-ע.

ש-פ-ה, ש-פ-י v. ש-ב-ה

שפולא, שופולא (OA שִׁיפּוּלָא) m. **šü/ıppōla** flap, hem (cf. PolG); pl. שופולאליה **šuppōlāle** (cf. PolGr 52); **la gmāṭe l-a** She is far superior to him (He doesnt reach her hems).

שפיכא, שפכתא (< ש-פ-כ) p.p. **špīxa, špıxta** overflowing (NT+).

שפיכות דמים (H) **šıfīxūt dāmīm** bloodshed (NT).

שפיק (Ar) inv. **šafiq** tender, merciful (NT+).

שפירא, שפרתא (OA/OS/Mand) adj. **š(a)pīra, š(a)pırta** nice, good, beautiful; fair (rule)(NT; RivSh 118: שְׁפִּירַא) [Mutz 230/Khan 581 **špira**].

שפירותא (OA) f. **š(a)pīrūta** beauty (NT), pleasing (=H טוֹב, BT1, D) [Khan 581 **špirātula**].

ש-פ-כ (OA/OS/Mand) **š-p-x** vi to spill (NT), overflow (Z); cf. שִׁיפַּכִי.

שפכורותא (K/P **šav-kōr**) f. **šafkōrūta** dim sight (NT), night blindness (=H סַנְוֵרִים, BT1); cf. שהרותא.

שפכתא (K) f. **šappıkta** Kurdish woven waistcoat; v. 2 שלא.

ש-פ-ע II (Ar) **š-f-ᶜ** to intercede, plead on behalf (NT5 403); cf. ש-פ-א.

ש-פ-ק (Ar) **š-f-q** to show mercy (NT, BT).

שפקא 1, שפקתא (Ar) f. **šafaqa, šafaqta** mercy, grace; cf. שפיק.

שפקא 2 (K/IrAr < R) f. **šafqa** European hat with brim, cap.

ש-פ-ר (OA) vi **š-p-r** to please (NT); IV to better (=H הֵיטִיב, BT5).

שפרא 1 (OA) m. **šıpra** beauty (NT), tenderness (=H עֶדְנָה, BT1, D).

שפרא 2 (Ar) m. **⁺šafra** large knife; pl. **šafrāre**.

שפרזא (K) inv. **šapırza** destitute (NTU 154b).

ש-פ-ש-פ III (OS ܫܦܫܦ) vi **⁺š-p-š-p** to shuffle, drag (SaAC 23)[cf. MacD 204]

שצא (Ar) f. **šıṣṣa** fishing hook (cf. PolU 263).

שקא 1 (Ar) **šaqa** suffering (NT).

שקא 2 (Ar) m. **šaqqa** half (of slaughtered sheep), large section (cf. Avin78 94); pl. שַׁקֵי **šaqqe** strips(=H קרעים, AlfM 25); **pqı'le 'ıl dūke upıšle tre** - He split on the spot and became two sections; **qam 'āwızla šaqqé-šaqqe** He cut her into pieces (PolG).

שקא 3 v. שאקא

שקאלא (< ש-ק-ל) **šaqāla** in **šaqāla uyahāwa** (m.), **šaqalta uyahōta** (f.), trader, merchant (lit.taker-giver); v. ש-ק-ל (NT+) [Khan 582 **huwaᶜá w-šqāla** trade].

שקאמא (K) f. **šıqqāma** smack on the face.

שקאקי (K < Ar) **šaqāqí** bleeding fissure (of nipple during breast feeding) (SaAC 13).

ש-ק-י II (Ar) vi/vt **š-q-y** to toil, bother oneself; **la mšāqyat (gyānax)** Dont trouble yourself (said to a host, etc.; cf. PolG).

שקי (Ar) inv. **šaqi** one toiling, suffering (NT); cf. שקא 1.

שקיתא (OS) f. **šaqqīta** channel, water trough (=H שֹׁקֶת, BT1); pl. שַׁקְיַיאתַא **šaqyāta** (=H רְהָטִים, BT1, D) (NT+).

ש-ק-ל (OA) **š-q-l** to take; אשקלה ריכא **ʾıšqılle rīxa** He smelled (vt); שקלניה חקד **šaqlınne ḥaqqıd** I will retribute for; גשקלי וגיאוי **gšaqli ugyāwi** They argue (lit. take and give); **šqāla uyhāwa** trade, business; **lıbbi kšāqıl** I feel nauseated; **la šqılla ula hulle** He didnt respond, remained passive; **ʾilāha šqīlāle mınne** He lost his mind (God took it away from him; cf. שקלתא) (NT+).

שקלא 1 (<?) m. **šaqla** thin and long log, plank, pole (=H קֶרֶשׁ, BT2; מוֹט, BT4); stretcher, bier (made of two poles) (Br93 198; SaAC 11).

שקלא 2 (< ?) **šaqla** a kind of fish (PolU 263).

שקלאבה (K **šeql** wave+**av** water) f./pl. **šaqlāve** wave(s) reaching the shore; **-t baḥar** (=H אֲפִקֵי-יָם, PolG:2 S 22:16).

שקלתא (< ש-ק-ל) n. act. **šqalta** taking; **-tıt ʾilāha** craziness (Gods taking of ones brain; v. ש-ק-ל) (PolU 267)

ש-ק-ע, ש-ע-ק (< OA/OS sink, push in?) **š-q-ʿ**, **š-ʿ-q** (only once: PolU 250), to hit (head against the wall due to pain) (NT2); to gallop the horse away and disappear from view (Z); II to cobble, mend shoes (Z); cf. משקעאנא, ש-ק-ר-ע; שקעתא [Macd 311 run fast].

שקעתא (< ש-ק-ע) f. **ša(q)qaʿta** patch with ointment (cf. PolG); grimy rag [cf. Garbell 335 ***šqata** sticking-plaster; Mutz 231 **šqaʿta~šqaḥta** < OA שיקוע poultice < OA שַׁקַע to sink, to cover].

שקפא (Ar) f. **šaqfa** piece (of land) (PolG).

שקץ, שֵׁיקִיץ (H) **šēqıṣ** idol (NT), abomination (NT3, D); cf. שֶׁקּוּצִים.

שק"ר (H) **šīn-qōf-rōš** (!) a lie (a cryptic use by adults after telling a lie to a child to calm him down or stop his nagging); cf. דוגלא.

שקרוקתא (< ש-ק-ר-ק) f. **šaqruqta** noisemaker.

ש-ק-ר-ק III (Ar be cheerful) **š-q-r-q** to rattle.

שקשקתא (onomat.) f. **šaqšaqta** din (PolU 232).

שר (Ar) **šar(r)** evil, malice; cf. ש-ר-ר.

שראאה, שראא, שראתא (OA שְׁרָגָא < P چراغ lamp) f. **šrāʾa, šraʾta** lamp; pl. **šrāʾe** (PolG) (NT+).

שראנא, שרנתא (< שר/K **šer** quarrel) adj. **šırrāna, šırranta** quarrelsome; cf. ש-ר-ר.

שראעא (< ש-ר-ע) m. **šarāʿa** judge (NT2).

שרבדאר (Ar-P) **šarabdār** butler, cupbearer.

שרבדארותא (< שרבדאר) f. **šarabdārūṯa** (position of) cupbearing (=H מַשְׁקֶה, BT1).

ש-ר-ב-ק III (< שבוקא) **š-r-b-q** to whip, lash.

שרבת (K < Ar) **šarbat, šırūb** sweet drink; pl. שרבאתה **šarbāte** (BaBin 30); cf. שורוב.

שרגומתא (< שלג'ם) f. **šargumta** white turnip root; pl. **šargume**.

שרה (H) p.n.f. ***sara** Sarah; cf. גארוכה.

ש-ר-ו II (< שרותא) **š-r-w** to eat lunch (PolG).

שרואלא (OS شَرْوَال) m. **šırwāla** native baggy underpants; cf. כור-צודרא.

שרוב v. שורוב

שרוול (Ar/K/P **šalwār, šarwāl**; OA סרבלא leg covering) m. ***šarwal** native baggy pants; pl. ***šarwāle**; v. פנטרון, שרואלא.

שרותא (OS/OA/Mand שָׁרוּתָא meal) f. **šarūṯa** lunch, breakfast; cf. ג'דאיא [MacD 312 mid-day meal...breakfast].

ש-ר-ז 1 (*OA שזר entwine?) **š-r-z** to disentwine (woven material, a ball of yarn) [MacD 313 **šāriṣ** to collapse as a ball of string < **širṣ/za** a ball of wool or cotton unspun].

ש-ר-ז 2 (< שהרזא ?) ***š-r-z** become accustomed; **ʾīzi *šrızla** I did it offhand; **lišānox *šrızle** You speak (the new language) well.

ש-ר-ח (Ar) **š-r-ḥ** to be parched and split (throat due to too much salt) (PolU 197).

שרח, שרע (Ar) **šarḥ/ʿ** Neo-Aramaic (Biblical) translation; cf. תפסיר, פשט.

ש-ר-ט II (Ar) **š-r-ṭ** to stipulate, to bet.

שרט (Ar) m. **šarṭ** condition, covenant (=H בְּרִית, BT); pl. שרטה, שַׁרְתֵי, שרתה **šarṭe, šarte** (NT, RivSh 266); **šarṭe-u-šurūṭe** (PolU 316).

ש-ר-ט-ח III (< ש-ט-ח) **š-r-ṭ-ḥ** to lie spread (=H מֻטָּלִים, AvidH 54).

ש-ר-י (OA/OS/Mand) vt/vi **š-r-y** to dwell (NT; RivSh 190); to untie, unleash; **nūra šāre go bēsox** May your house be set on fire; to stop, alight (at an inn); to absolve (NT); to thaw (NT2); to annul the covenant (=H הֵפֵר, BT3, D); IV to install (NT); to smite with a plague: משריבו מותאנא **mašrēbu mōṯāna** He will smite them with pestilence (NT5 389); to begin (Hob89 219).

שריא, שריתא (< ש-ר-י) p.p. **šırya, šrīṯa** loose,

untied; alighted (traveller) (NT) (NT+).

שריוכא (< OS/OA סרך attach?) m. **šıryōxa** shoe-string (=H שְׂרוֹךְ, BT1; PolG) [MacD 312 **širyūxā** < Ar **šīrāk** strap of sandal].

שריטא (Ar) m. **šarīṭa** string, cord (=H מֵיתָר, BT4).

שריכא, שריכתא (Ar) **šırīka, šırıkta** partner.

שריכאתותא (< שריכא) f. **šırīkātūṯa** partnership.

שרינה (K/P) p.n.f. **šırīne** Shirine (Sweet).

שריעתא (Ar) f. **šarīᶜıta** law, religious judgment; pl. שר(י)עתיאתא **šar(i)ᶜıtyāṯa** (NT+).

שריף (Ar) inv. **šarīf** noble, glorious (NT).

ש-ר-כ II (Ar) **š-r-k** to be or make a partner; cf. שריכא (NT+).

שרכא 1 (OS/Ar bloom of life, offspring) m. **šarxa** calf (NT), calving (=H שֶׁגֶר, BT5); (animal) embryo (Z).

שרכא 2 (Ar) m. **šırka** partnership (PolU 353).

שרכייה (Ar) f. **šırkīye** partnership

שרכתא (< שרכא ?) f. **šarıxṯa** foreskin; cf. גרמכתא [MacD 312 **šariḥtā** < Ar **šarīḥa** a piece of meat].

שרמא (OS ܫܘܪܡܐ; cf. Ar سُرم) f. **šırma** anus, buttocks; **gyāwıl šırme** homosexual (lit., he gives his arse; cf. קונדהה); **kīʾın kma mızze ʾīs bšırme** I know him very well (lit., I know how many hairs are on his butt); **šırme ruxta** easily frightened person (lit., his anus [is] wide); pl. **šırmāṯa**.

שרמזאר (P **šarmsār**) abashed, ashamed (NT).

שרמזארי (P) **šarmzāri** shame, disgrace (NT).

שר-מ-ט III (Ar tear to rags?) vt/vi **š-r-m-ṭ** to entangle, be entangled.

שרס (IrAr/K < Ar شيراس [Wehr]) **šırıs** glue made of pulverized root.

ש-ר-ע (Ar) **š-r-ᶜ** to judge (justly) (NT+).

שרע 1 (Ar) **šarᶜ** religious law; judgment; **qam xālıṣle — dōhun** He finished theirjudgment (PolG); **bšarᶜi mahamad** by Muhammad's Law (PolU 21); pl. שרעיה **šarᶜe** (NT), שַׁרְעַאיֵי **šarᶜāye** (RivSh 229); cf. שריעתא (NT+).

שרע 2 v. שרח

ש-ר-פ (Ar) **š-r-f** to shine, rise (sun); appear (God) (=H זָרַח, הוֹפִיעַ, BT5); visit (by a noble person) (PolU 31).

ש-ר-פ 2 (< ?) vt/vi **⁺š-r-p** to slip or make one slip [MacD 313 fall out, slide].

שרף (Ar) m. **šaraf** honor, nobility (PolU 83).

שרפ-וטרפ (onomat/K) **šarp-u-ṭarp** sounds of beating the ground while dancing (PolU 18).

שֶׁרֶץ (H) **šērıṣ** unclean reptile, swarm (=H שֶׁרֶץ BT3, D).

שרקי, שרקאיא (Ar) adj. **šarqi, šarqāya** (+NT), eastern (wind) (NT+).

שרקינא (onomat) **šraqqēna** clatter (PolU 5).

שרקיעא (OS ܫܪܩܝܥܐ) f. **šarqīᶜa** resounding slap on the face (cf. RivSh 129); pl. **šarqīᶜe**.

שרקיתא, שַׁרַקִיתָא (< Ar شرق) **šarraqīṯa** (excessive) sun heat, radiation, sun-rise (BaBin 153; PolG).

ש-ר-ק-ע III (< שרקיעא) **š-r-q-ᶜ** to slap hard; cf. ש-ק-ע [MacD **mšarqōyē** to smack].

ש-ר-ר II (Ar) **⁺š-r-r** be hostile, threaten; cf. שר, שראנא.

שרשורא (< ש-ר-ש-ר) **⁺saršūra** rain spout (cf. PolG) [MacD 313 waterfall]; cf. שורשורכה.

ש-ר-ש-ט III (< ?) **⁺š-r-š-ṭ** to dangle, hang down; **mırrūte mšuršıṭa** angry, upset (lit., his face [is] languid); v. כ-נ-ש

ש-ר-ש-י III (OS) **š-r-š-y** to loosen, be languid וצלאן גמשרשי בתריה **waṣlan gımšarši baṯre** Our limbs languid for him (AmU2 10b).

ש-ר-ש-ר III (< ?) **⁺š-r-š-r** water: to fall with noise.

שרשרתא v. שורשורתא

שרת v. שרט

שרתא (OS ܫܪܬܐ; OA שׁוּרְתָא, שורא) f. **⁺šırṯa** (Z **⁺šırsa**) navel (NT+). [cf. Garbell 334 **šura**; Mutz 231 **⁺šūra**; H (ר)שׁ].

שש-טאייכה (K) **šaš-ṭāyīke** folded thin bread eaten with butter and honey; pl. **-kat**.

ששא (IrAr?) **šašša** popcorn, boiled wheat.

ששבין, ששבני (OA/OS שושבינא <Ak>K **šušbin**) bridegroom's best man [cf. Kaufman 94].

שש-בש (T/P/K) **šeš-bēš** backgammon.

שש-דרב (K) **šāš dárb** six-shooter (PolG).

ששה, ליל ששה (K six?) **šašše, lēl šašše** the night before the circumcision ceremony, 'Wachnacht', on which Psalms and Zohar were read to protect the mother and baby; they used to give ששא [q.v.] on the Brit night [cf. Br93 164; Garbell 333 **šašša** f.

ceremony of lighting candles on the seventh day after the birth of a boy; MacD 313 a jinn or malignant sprite, said to haunt mothers and infants].

ששה סדרי משנה (H) **šıšša sidre mišna** the six orders of Mishnah (NT3).

ששון, ששונא (H) p.n.m. **sāson, sāsōna** Sasson.

ששמה v. שושמה

ששתא (K **šāšik** turban < Ar شاشك) f. **šašta** sash, headdress (=H מִצְנֶפֶת, BT2; NT5 401) (NT+).

ששת ימי בראשית (H) **šēšet yıme bırēšīt** the six days of creation (NT).

שתאוה v. ה-ו-י, שוד.

שתאיא < ש-ת-י) vn **štāya** drinking; drink; pl. **štāye** (**rāba ʾixāle u-** many foods and drinks; PolG).

שתאנא, שתנתא (< שאתא 3) adj. **šıtāna, šıtanta** sick (with fever).

ש-ת-ה-י III (Ar) **š-t-h-y** to yearn, have appetite, desire [1:**mıštōhē-** (NT5 411); 2:**mıštāhe** (NT2); **mıštohya, mıštōhēsa** (PolG); 3: **la mıštōhētın** 4:**mıštı/ohōye** (BaBin 6; BT1).

ש-ת-ה-ר III (< שהארא) vt/vi **š-t-h-r** to blind (BT2; AlfM 27) or become blind (PolG) [1: **müštōhır-**; 2: **mıštāhır**] [cf. Mutz 229 **šhr** to be blind; **mašhır** make blind (NT+).

ש-ת-י 1 (OS/OA/Mand) **š-t-y** to drink; cf. שתאיא; to smoke (tobacco) [2: **šāte** (Z:m.Sg., pl.); **šāti** (Gz73 26:pl.; 3: שתון **štūn** (NT3; NT5 400), **štāwun** (Z)]; IV to make or let someone drink; to water (NT+).

ש-ת-י 2 IV (OA) **š-t-y** to weave, to web (RivSh 256) [cf. MacD 205 **maštī**].

שתיא, שְׁתַיָא (OA) m. **šı/atya** warp (=H שְׁתִי, BT3); spiders web (RivSh 256) [Khan 581 **šitya**].

שתי-ערב (H warp-woof) m. **šatti-ʿērıv** the cross (cryptic); cf. כאגֹו צליב.

ש-ת-ל (OA) vt/vi **š-t-l** to plant, to stick; **ʾēre štılle** His penis became erect; **qanāne štıllu gobʾēne** He was astonished (lit., horns became erect on his forehead).

שתלא (< ש-ת-ל; OA/Mand שיתלא) m. **šıtla** plant, seedling [Mutz 230 **šítıl/r** < K (< Ar?) < OA].

ש-ת-מ-ה-ר v. ת-מ-ה-ר

ש-ת-מ-ל-י III (OS) vt/vi **š-t-m-l-y** to complete, or be completed; מושתמלילה כולו וצייד אילאהא **muštımlīle kullu waṣīyıd ʾilāha** He practiced all Gods precepts (NT5 403) [cf. Mengozzi 279 to be fulfilled].

ש-ת-ן II (< שתאנא) **š-t-n** to become sick; to make sick: - **gyāna** pretend sick (PolU 112).

ש-ת-ק (OA/OS) **š-t-q** to keep silent; IV to silence; to restrain oneself from talking; v. ש-מ-א (NT+).

שתקה (OA אשתקד) adv. **šıtqe** last year; v. אשת, רואה, תלתה [cf. Kaufman 96-97; Mutz 230/Khan 581 **šítqel** (< ***šıtqed**)].

ש-ת-ת II2 (Ar) vi/vt **š-t-t** to disperse, to exile, expell; שיתא משותתא (p.p. I/II) **šīta mšutıtta** =H נָע וָנָד, BT1) (NT+).

ת, תּ (t)

ת (H) **tāu** the Hebrew letter tav; **ʾarbeʾma** four hundred.

-ת 1 v. -ד

-ת 2 v. -יתן

-ת 3 v. -אתן

תא v. טלא 1

-תא v. -לא 1

תאבור (K< T) m. **tābur** large army, battalion; a small unit (PolU 317); pl. תַאבּוּרֵי **tābūre**.

תאבות (Ar) **tābut** funeral, coffin.

תאג' v. תאנג'

תאג'ר v. תג'ר

תאזא (K) inv. **tāza** fresh (RivSh 280).

תאיא (*IrAr < En) f. **tāya** tyre .

תאכא (K) f. **tāxa** bundle (of grass); layer; belt; region; quarter of town (RivSh 145); furrow; pl. **tāxe**.

תאכם (K tool, set < T/Ar طاقم) **tāxım** cigarette-holder; set of dishes, of clothes (PolU 411).

ת-א-כ-ר III (< א-כ-ר) vi **t-ʾ-x-r** to be late, delayed (=H הִתְמַהְמֵהַּ, AvidH 47).

תאלא, תיאלא (OA/OS תעלא) m. **teʾla** fox (NT); cf. רוביכא [MacD 334 **tālā, tīlā**].

תאלאנה v. טאלאנה

תאלונא (< תאלא) **teʾlōna** little fox (NT3).

תאמא 1, תם (OA התם, תמן, תם) **tāma , tam** (mostly with affixes) there; **ltam** thither; **mın tam** thence; **tangıb/tangēba** [< **tam gēba**] that way, far away **zılle ltangıb** He went to hell; **ʾaġāti mın tangēba** dear auditor (lit. My lord, over there) (PolU 320); v. אכגב; **tamā/ōha** over there (cf. PolG) (NT+).

תאמא 2 v. טלא 1

תאנא, תינא (OA תְּינְתָא, תאינתא; pl. תְּינֵי, תאיני) **teʾna** (Z, f.), **tēna** (NT3, m.? Sa83c 17, Am, var.) fig (fruit and tree); pl. תאנה **teʾne** (cf. (PolG)[MacD 315 **tīnā**, f.].

תאנג', תאג' (K < Ar) m. **tānj, tāj** (+NT), crown; cf. ת-נ-ג'; תאנג'ת שולטאנא **tānjıt šultāna** crown of king(ship) (=H כתר מלכות, NT5 400); pl. תַאנְגַ'ת **tānjat** (=H כְּתָרֹת, PolG).

ת-א-ר (OA אתעיר) **t-ʾ-r** to awake (vi); IV to awake (vt) (NT+).

תאריך, טאריך (Ar) **t/ṭārīx** length of time, period:ʾ**ība - ʾısri šınne** It has been about twenty years (PolU 90); location signs (?) (PolU 317).

טאריסתאן v. תאריסטן

תבאלא (K?) f. **tabāla** marble (childs toy); pl. **tabāle**; **tabalāne** game of marbles.

ת-ב-ד (Mand תפת) **t-b-d/d̠** to sneeze (NT2); cf. ת-ר-ב-ז' [cf. Mand/MacD **t-p-t**; Mutz 233 **tpl**].

תבדיל הוא (Ar) **tabdīl hawa** refreshing walk, travel (for a change of air) (cf. PolU 322).

תבודא (< ת-ב-ד) **tabūd/d̠a** a sneeze, sneezing (NT2; Sa83c 18, Am).

תבירכה (K) f. **tıvīrke** turtledove (=H תּוֹר, BT).

ת-ב-ל II (OA) **t-b-l** to spice, add spices to stale food; cf. תולה, תובאלה.

ת-ב-ע (Ar) **t-b-ᶜ** to follow, trace, catch up with; insist, enforce (NT5 411) (NT+).

תבע (Ar) **tabaᶜ** following the example, likewise (NT5 409).

תברי (Ar) **tabarri** innocence; **qam mapqīle btabarri** He was declared not guilty.

תברכ (Ar) ***tabarrık** food or candy taken to a shrine to be blessed and then given to children and others (PolU 185); cf. ב-ר-כ 2.

תבשיר (K/P/Ar) m. **tabašir** chalk.

תגביר, תכביר (K < Ar **tak/dbīr**) m. **tag/kbir** advice, conspiracy (cf. PolG); pl. **tagbīre** (=H נְכָלִים, BT4), **takbīre** (RivSh158, 263).

ת-ג/כ-ב-ר III (< תגביר) vi/vt **t-g/k-b-r** to seek or give advice; to conspire; מתוגברו תכביר **mtugbırru takbir** (AlfH 61) They planned, conspired (=H יָעַץ, הִתְנַכֵּל, BT1, BT4, D).

ת-ג-ר, ת-ג'-ר II, ת-י-ג'-ר III (OA/Ar) **t-g-r** (NT), **t-j-r** (BT5, D), **t-ē-j-r** (BT1), to trade (NT), to peddle (=H סָחַר, BT1).

תג'ר, תאג'ר (Ar; cf. OA תַּגָּרָא) m. **tıjjar, tājır** merchant, trader; pl. **tıjjāre**.

תג'ארותא (< תג'ר; cf. OA תַּגָּרוּתָא) f. **tıjjārūt̠a** trade.

תהא, תחא (< K?) interj. **tıha, taḥaʾ** Alas! (=H אֲהָהּ, PolG:2 Kg 6:5)

תהדירה (Ar تحذير ?) pl. **tahd/d̠īre** warnings,

threats (NT2); cf. דהדורה.

תהום (H; cf. OA תהומא) **tıhōm** the abyss (NT, BT); pl. תְּהוֹמֵי **tıhōme** (RivSh 205), **tıhōmōt** (BT1); תהום רבה **tıhōm** ⁺**rabba** the great deep (BT1).

ת-ה-י (Ar) **t-h-y** to wander; IV to make one wander (=H הִתְעָה, BT1; PolG).

ת-ה-מ (Ar) **t-h-m** to suspect, accuse: דלא יכון בכרשה תהמילני **la ykun bxıršе tahmīlēni** Lest (they) accuse us of sorcery (NT5 407).

תהם v. להום

תהנא v. תנא 1

ת-ה-נ-י III (Ar) **t-h-n-y** to enjoy, have a good time; **wēle mtahnōye ta gyāne** He is enjoying himself; **mtuhnēle ʾıbba** ⁺**rāba** He enjoyed it a lot; [3: **mtahni** (m.),-**ne** (f.); **-nun** (pl.) PolG]; cf. ה-נ-י (NT+).

תהקת, תהקד (K? < Ar تحقيقات) adv. **tahaqqat/d** (?) certainly, truly (NT2); cf. תחקיק.

ת-ה-ש, ד-ה-ש (Ar دهش) **t-h-š** to wonder, look astonishingly at (PolG).

תהתא (< K?) m. **tahta** mattress made of pressed wool, felt.

תו- v. לו-

תו- v. יתון-

(-)תו v. י-ת-ו

תואריך, טואריך/ק (Ar) pl. ⁺**tawārīx/q** traces (?): **kıtte — lak xāzax lmāsa** We will not find any traces (of people) in the village (PolU 423); **wala — mın ʿaskar la pīšin** no one remained from the army (PolU 350).

ת-ו-ב II (Ar < OS) **t-w-b** to repent [2:**mtōba**]; cf. ת-י-ב (Segal #38).

תובא, תוביה (K < Ar) f. **tōba/e** repentance; **yā rābbi, tōbe qāmox** O God, (may my repentance (be accepted) before you; תוביה צפיתא **tōbe ṣpita** sincere repentence (NT5 381); **ʾ-w-d - /d-ʾ-r b-** to repent; cf. תשובה.

תובא כאריה, תובכאריה (Ar-K/P) pl. **tōba-kāre** repentants (NT2; NTU4 163a).

תובאלה (Ar) pl. **tubāle** spices, seasonings (NT5 408); cf. תולה, ת-ב-ל.

ת-ו-ב-כ, ת-י-ב-כ III (Ar توبيخ) **t-w/y-b-x** reproach (=H הוֹכִיחַ, BT1; NT4).

ת-ו-ג̇ v. ת-נ-ג̇

תוז, תוס (T) **tōz/s** dust; **tōz-u-ʿıjaj** dust storm.

תְוִינָא, תוונתא (< ת-ו-נ) p.p. **twīna, twınta** numb (RivP 215).

תוירא, תורתא (< ת-ו-ר) **twīra, twırta, turta** broken, humiliated; soft (eyes) (=H רַכּוֹת, BT1).

תוך, תוק (K **tox, toq** top of banner/head) **tōx, tōq** sign, miracle (NT4); outstanding(=H דגול ורם, NT5 392).

תוכום (K/P/T seed > origin, kind) m. **tuxum** type, kind:**xāzın ma - gōra-le ʾāwa** Let me see what kind of man he is (PolG); **tuxmıd ʾēš-u-ʾalam lēs go lašše** There is no trace of any sickness in his body (PolU 330).

תוכטור v. דוכתור

תוכלאנא (Ar/OA/OS) **tuklāna** trust (in God); cf. ת-כ-ל 1; promise (=H הַבְטָחָה, AvidH 24; PolG); **tuklāni ʾıbbox** In You I trust.

תוכריא v. תכוריא

תול (< Ar< En/Fr) m. **tūl** tulle (delicate fabric).

ת-ו-ל-א III, ת-ל-א II (< תולאתא; cf. OA √ תלע) **t-o/u-l-ʾ** be wormy.

תולאתא (OA תּוֹלַעְתָּא/OS **tawlıʿā**) f. **tōleʾta, tul-** (PolG), worm; pl. **tōleʾe** (Z), תוולאה **tawleʾe** (NT5 390; Amu2 5a) [Krotkoff 127].

תולה (OA תַּבְלֵי spices) pl. **tōle** coriander (=H גַּד, BT4); cf. ת-ב-ל, תובאלה [cf. Mutz 233; MacD 317].

תולת v. תִילִית

תומא (OA) m. **tūma** garlic; v. כּכתא.

תומן (P) m. **tūman** Persian gold.

ת-ו-נ (OA/OS תנב [**tnb** >**tbn**] be stiff) **t-w-n** become numb (cf. PolG); cf. תוינא [MacD 315].

תון v. י-ת-ו

תונא (OA/OS תִּיבְנָא) m. **tūna** straw.

תוס v. תוז

תוק v. תוך

ת-ו-ר (OA/OS/Mand תבר) vi/vt **t-w-r** to break; to subdue, humiliate **la tōrıt xabre** Don't go against his wish (break his word); טלד לא תאויר לבד מסכינה **tlad la tāwır lıbbıd mıskīne** So that the poor are not insulted (lit., their heart broken); **la tāwır lıbbōxun** Let not your courage falter (=H אַל יֵרַךְ לְבַבְכֶם, BT5); **ʾēne turra** He felt shy (lit., his eye broke); **turre xāṣe** He was frightened (lit., his back broke) (by bad news); **qam tōrālu garme** she broke his resistence (lit., she broke his bones); **palgızlal turre** just after midnight (NT+); cf. עצמות.

תורא 1 (OA) m. **tōra, tawra** (PolU 208: ChNA), ox; cf. תוורתא.

תורא 2 (K **tīre**) m. **tūra** twig, branch (=H שָׂרִיג, BT1; BaBin 129; NTU4 149a).

תורבא (T) f. ⁺**tōrba** large bag, package.

תורה (H) f. ⁺**tōra** the Torah; - **gmabrıqa go ʾēnu** Torah shines in their eyes (=very enlighted); Jewish studies; cf. ספר, חמש תורה, דברי תורה; (NT+).

-תורו, -תורנת v. תרה

תוריתא, תורתא (< ת-ו-ר) f. **twarīta, twarta** fracture, defeat, disaster (= H שֶׁבֶר, BT3; אֵד, BT5); pl. תווריאתא **twaryāta** (NT5 397-8).

תורכן (K/P تَرخـــان [< Mongolian]) ⁺**torxan** exemption (from tax or tribute) (PolU 1).

תוורתא (OA) f. **tawırta** cow; pl. תוראתא **tōrāta** (NT, Z), **tawıryāta** (+Z; PolGr 56-57); v. תורא 1 [Khan 583 **torta**; pl. **torye**].

תשאביה v. תֻּושַׁאבִי

תושבחין (H-OA) **tušbıḥīn** hymns (NT3); cf. שירות, תסאביח.

תפשייה v. תוושי

תותא 1 (OA) f. **tūta** (Z **tūsa**) mulberry, multree; pl. **tūte** mulberries (fruit); **tūtawāta** multrees [Khan 583 **tuwwa**, K].

תותא 2 v. י-ת-ו

תותו (< סותא 2) f. **tōto** auntie, grandma (used by youngsters addressing older woman).

תותון, תתון (T **tütün**) m. **tütün, títūn** (Socin 161) loose tobacco; cf. ברמוט.

תותיא (Ar/K/P) f. **tōtya** galvanized zinc.

תותכא (K) m. **tūtıka** small cucumber; flute (Segal #36).

תותכתא (K) f. **tōtıkta** little sweet loaf; pl. תּוּתְכִּיַּיאתָא **tōtıkyāta** (=H עֻגּוֹת, BT4, D).

תזיאנא (< K? < Ar تعـزية) **tazyāna** mourning; **mın šahyāna pıšla** - From a celebration it became a lamentation (PolU 351a) [cf. MacD 319 scourge, whip ? (no source given)].

תחאלא (OA/OS טְחָלָא/Ar طحال) f. **tıḥāla** spleen [MacD 111 **ṭāxālā**(!)].

תחבולה, תעבולא(H) **taḥ/ʿbūla** trick, wile.

תחיית המתים (H) **tıḥıyyat hammēṭīm** resurrection (NT; RivSh 183); cf. קיאמתא.

תחלי (K) **taḥli** bitterness; pl. תחלייה **taḥlīye** (AmU2 4b).

תחלישכה (K) f. **taḥlīške** bitter herbs; cf. מרור.

תחמס (< תחיית המתים) **taḥmas** (Z) known only from **hīl taḥmas qāyım** (He will not come) until Tahmas arises (=never).

תחסין/ל-כלאם (Ar) **taḥsīn/l-kalām** (They talk just) to be polite (for improving the conversation).

ת-ח-ס-נ III (Ar) **t-ḥ-s-n** to deem appropriate; usually with **la**: **la mtuḥsınna ʾaxla ʾımman** She didnt think it was proper (and felt shy) to eat with us (cf. PolG).

תחקיק (Ar) **taḥqīq** certainty, realization (NT); cf. תהקת [Khan 582 **taḥqiqāt** investigations].

תחת כנפי השכינה (H) **taḥat kanfē haššıxīna** under the (protecting) wings of the Divine Presence (NT2); cf. שכינה.

-תי v. -לי

תאלא v. תיאלא

תיאתרו (K/*IrAr/Ar < It) **tıyyātro, tīyātro** (PoG) theater, musical show (cf. PolG).

ת-י-ב (Ar/OS) **t-y-b** to repent; cf. תובה (NT+).

ת-ו-ב-כ v. ת-י-ב-כ

ת-ג-ר v. ת-י-ג'-ר

תכית v. תיך

תיכלא (K mixed, joined) m. **tēkıla** close friend; cf. ת-כ-ל 2.

ת-י-מ I (Z)/IV (Am)(OA תמם) vi/vt **t-y-m** to annihilate; be annihilated (לְמָתּוֹמֵינִי **lmatōmēēni**=H לְכַלֹּתֵנוּ, AvidH 25); to finish, end with (RivSh 136, 140).

תאנא v. תינא

תיפא (K) m./f. **tīpa** troupe, sect (NT2); branch of a river (=H רֹאשׁ, BT1, Am).

תיקא (H-OA) **tīqa** box, case of the Torah scroll (Br93 255).

תיר (K) **tēr** sufficient for; **lēbe tēran** It is not sufficient for us; **ʾībe tēr kullu** Its sufficient for all of them; cf. תיר-בז'י.

תירא (K **tūr**) m. saddle-bag.

תיר-בז'י (K)**tēr bızi** Live long enough! (said after sneezing); cf. לחיים טובים.

תירוץ (H) **tēruṣ** right answer (to difficult

question); cf. ת-ר-צ.

תירמאר (K/P) **tīramar** viper (NT4).

תישכא (K?) **tēšıka** young of animals following its mother (cf. PolG **tēška** אפרוח); pl. **-ke**.

תישתאנא (K **tešt** thing?) m. **teštāna** gift (a thing given as gift?).

תיתא (K) **tīta** forehead ornament, frontlet (=H צִיץ, BT2; BaBin 121).

תיתאלא (<?) **tītāla** dragged-on (affair).

תיתכתא (< תיתא) f. **tītıkta** fringe of scarf sitting on the forehead.

תכ תכ תכ (onomat.) **tık tık tık** sound of energetic steps (PolU 232).

תכא (< T?) m. **takka** Turkish coin, 1/21 of **līra** (PolU 432).

ת-כ-ב II (< תכוב) **t-x-b** to limit (=H הִגְבִּיל, BT2).

תכביר v. תגביר

תכברותא (< Ar) f. **takabbarūta** greatness, elevated position (PolU 159).

תכה v. תכית

תכוב (K/P < OA תחומא) m. **tıxub** boundary, domain; cf. תוכום; pl. תכובה **tıxūbe** (NT+).

תכוז (K **tekūz** perfect) inv. **takkuz** perfectionist, cautious (NT+).

תכ-ולכה (K?) pl. **takk-u-lakke** apparatus, necessary tools (PolU 350).

תכונא (OS ܛܚܘܢܐ) **txūna** wheat taken to the mill to be ground; cf. ת-כ-נ [Mutz 234 fresh flour].

תכוריא, תוכריא (< ת-כ-ר) **tüxürya** memory, remembrance (=H זֵכֶר/זִכָּרוֹן, BT; PolG); **-e bšālōm/bpaṭōxē** May his memory (be) in peace/ in manure (good/bad person).

ת-כ-י (Ar) **t-k-y** to lean, sit reclined (NT+).

תכיאיה (Ar) f. **ta/ıkyāye** guest-house (PolU 150).

כה, כית, תכה, תכית (OS ܬܚܝܬ) prep. **txēt/txe** (NT), **xēt** (+NT; Z **xēs**), **xē** (Z; but **xēsi, xēsox**, etc.), under, below; מלתיך **mıltēx** from the bottom, under (PolG); מתכית **mıtxēt** due to (NT2); v. כריש.

תכית 2 (IrAr < En) **tıkkēt** ticket; pl. **tıkkētat**.

ת-כ-כ II (Ar) **t-k-k** to thread string-tie into trousers; v. תכתא 2.

ת-כ-ל 1 (Ar/OA/OS < Ak) **t-k-l** to trust (in God); cf. תוכלאנא (NT+).

ת-כ-ל 2 (K mix) vi **t-k-l** to mix, fit, go together (foods); **čāyi la ktākıl ʾımmıd marāqa** Tea and soup dont go together; cf. תיכלא.

תכליפה (Ar) pl. **taklīfe** formalities; **y-h-w-l** – to be very courteous (PolUR 86).

תכלית (K) **taxlit** kind, sort; pl. **taxlīte** (BT4).

תכמין (Ar) m. **taxmīn** thought, devising (=H יֵצֶר, BT1).

ת-כ-מ-נ III (< תכמין) **t-x-m-n** to devise, reflect.

ת-כ-נ (OA/OS/Mand טחן) **t-x-n** to mill grain into flour (cf. Hob89 323; cf. PolG); cf. תכונא, ג-ר-ס.

ת-כ-ר (OA דכר/אידכר) **t-x-r** to remember; **ʾilāha tāxırre bšālōm** May God remember him (a deceased) in peace; IV to mention, remind (NT+).

תכת, תכתא 1 (K/P > OA טכטכא, תכתקא) m. **taxt(a)** chair, throne, wooden bed, cutting board (with legs); **taxt-u-rawan** royal coach (PolU 26) (NT+).

תכתא 2 (OA תִּיכְּתָא, SokBA 1205; M. Jastrow 1667 תִּכָּא) f. **tıkta** string-tie (for pants); pl. **tıkkāke** (OA תִּיכֵּי); cf. ת-כ-כ.

תכתבנד (P) **taxtband** luxury bed (Amu2 5a).

תכתונכא (< תכת) m. **taxtonka** footstool.

תַכְתֵי רַוַואן (P) **taxte rawān** sedan chair (=H מֶרְכָּבָה, PolG).

ת-ל-א v. ת-ו-ל-א

תלארה-בגי (K) **tıllāre-bagi** aristocrat, dandy (PolU 25).

תלביס (Ar) m. **talbīs** false charge, libel (NT2); pl. תלביסה **talbīse** (NT5 384).

תלביסאנא (< תלביס) m. **talbīsāna** plotter, libelous (NT5 401).

תלגא (OA) m. **talga** snow; **xwara x-talga** white as snow (very white); pl. **talgāge**.

ת-ל-ג-מ III (Ar ترجم) **t-l-j-m** to (orally) translate, explain; cf. תרגום, ת-פ-ס-ר.

תלגמן (Ar ترجمان) m. **tıljaman** translator, eloquent speaker (=H מֵלִיץ, BT1; נָבִיא, BT2).

תלג'ראף, תלג'ראם (T/IrAr < E) **ᵗtelgırām/f** telegram, telegraph (cf. PolU 243).

ת-ל-ת-י v. ת-ל-י

תליא (OA תליא דליבא part of the stomach) m. **talya** animal entrails (heart, liver, spleen, bowels) (=H כְּסָלִים, BT3, D); cf. ת-ל-ת-י.

תלילא, תללתא, תַלִיתָא (OS) adj. **talīla, talılta, talıtta** (BaBin 129), wet, humid; v. ת-ל-ל.

תלילותא (OS) f. **talīlūta** wetness, humidity (NT4, Z).

תליסא (OS [Brockelmann 825] ܬܠܝܣܐ) f. **tallīsa** large sack; pl. **tallīse** [cf. Ar تلّيس basket].

ת-ל-כ (OS ܬܠܟ fissure; OA תלח break) **t-l-x** (usually with **bdımma**) to bleed: **naxīri tlıxle bdımma** My nose is bleeding.

תלכא (OA תלחא piece) **tılxa** layer, pile (PolU 374); **tılxé-tılxe** several layers (PolG).

ת-ל-כ-ז III (OA/OS תכס crush, strike?) to poke, agitate fire [cf. MacD 207 **mtargiz** strike, knock; **mtarkis** snuff a candle].

ת-ל-כ-ש III (< ל-כ-ש) **t-l-x-š** to whisper to one another.

ת-ל-ל II2 (OS ܬܠܠ/OA טלל) vt/vi **t-l-l** to be or make wet; cf. תלילא.

תלמא (OS) m. **talma** large jar for carrying water from the river; **talma māxe zawırta** (When) a big jar hits a small jar (the big one breaks as well)(=oppressors eventually suffer as well) (MeAl 192).

תלמידא (OA) m. **talmīda** (Z **talmīza**) disciple; pl. תלמידים **talmīdīm** (NT3), **talmīze** (Z).

תלמיד חכם (H) m. **talmīd ḥāxām** learned Jew (PolU 288); pl. תלמידי חכמים **talmīde ḥaxāmīm** learned Jews (NT+).

תלמיד-תורה (H) m. **talmīd -ᵓtōra** educated in Jewish learning (PolU 306)

ת-ל-פ (Ar) vi/vt **t-l-f** to destroy or be destroyed (food, clothes, etc.) (BaBin 121).

תלפון (T/K/IrAr) m. **telefun** telephone.

ת-ל-פ-נ III (< תלפון) **t-l-f-n** phone; cf. כ-ב-ר.

תלתאסר (OA תְּלֵיסַר ,תלת עסר) **tıltaᵓsar** thirteen [Khan 583 ⁺**talta-sar**].

תלתה (OA תלת) **talte** (Z **talse**) two years ago; cf. רואה, שתקה [Mutz 232 **táldel**; MacD 322 the year before last, the year after next].

ת-ל-י ,ת-ל-ת-י (OA) **t-l-t-y** , **t-l-y** (+NT), to hang; cf. תליא [1: תלילו **tlēlu** (NT5 403) (=Z **mtultēlu** (cf. PolG); 3: תלולה **tlūle** (NT5 403); מתלתי **mtaltı** (NT5 396); 4: **mtaltōye** (NT5 404); **t-l-t**: **mtālit** (!), Gz73 87].

תם v. תאמא

תמא v. 1 טלא

תמאהא v. תאמא

תמאם, תמם (Ar) inv. **tama/ām** perfect; innocent; בלבא תמאם **blıbba tamam** wholeheartedly (NT+).

תמאמותא (< תמאם) **tamāmūta** innocence (=H תֹּם, BT1).

תמאמתי (K < Ar) **tamāmati** completion, final stage; remaining payment (PolU 431).

תמאנה ,טמאנה (OA תמנין) **tmāne** (NT), ⁺**tmāne** (Z), eighty (NT+).

טמאניאסר ,תמני אסר ,תמאניאסר (OA תְּמָנֵיסַר ,תמני עסר) **tmāne(-)ᵓsar** (NT), ⁺**tmāneᵓsar** (Z), eighteen (NT+).

טמבור v. תמבור

ת-מ-ה-ר III (OA תמה?) **t-m-h-r** to be shocked, to sadly wonder (BaBin 99, 101; ZU 72a), to tarry (אֲנַא וֵינַא בֵּימְתַּמְהוֹרֵי =H מִתְמַהְמֵהַּ, PolG).

תמוהא v. תאמא

תמוז (H-OA) **tammuz** the Hebrew month of Tammuz (July) (NT+).

תמל (OA) **tımmal** yesterday (NT+).

תמם v. תמאם

ת-מ-מ II2 (Ar/OA) **t-m-m** to complete; cf. ת-י-מ (NT+).

תמנא (Ar) **tamanna** salute; **š-q-l** - to salute (PolU 245).

תמניא (OA) m./f. **tmanya** eight; דתמניא ,אוד תמניא **ᵓod -, d-** the eighth; **tmanya ᵓımmāye** eight hundred (NT+).

תמר 1 (Ar ثمر) ⁽⁺⁾**tamar** fruit (NT3; Zaken 393; PolU 317); pl. תמריה **tamre** (Sa83c16, Am).

תמר 2, תמרכה (H) p.n.f. **tāmar, tāmarke** (hypo.), Tamar, Tammy.

תנא 1, תהנא (OA תננא/OS ܬܢܢܐ) m. **tınna, tehna** (+NT) smoke; תהנד נורא **tehnıd nūra** steam of fire (NT5 409); pl. תנאנה **tınnāne**.

תנא 2 (< תנה) inv. **tana** quiet, at ease; usually as hendiadys with תסל.

תנאים (H) pl. **tannāᵓim** conditions (before the wedding).

תנאנא (< תנא 1) adj. **tınnāna** smoky (=H עָשֵׁן, BT2).

תנגב ,תנגיבא v. תאמא

ת-נ-ג̇ ,ת-ג̇-נ ,ת-ו-ג̇ II; ת-נ-ג̇-י III (< תאג̇) **t-n-j, t-w-j** (+NT), **t-j-n** (NT5 405; AvidH 48), **t-n-j-y** (BT3, D), to crown; to wear headdress (=H צָנַף, BT3, D).

תנה (K< P تنهاي solitude) **tıne**: **b-** alone, by oneself, only; **tınıt** so that, only that..., just in order to: **tıne did qanᶜa** only that she would be satisfied (PolUR 49); v. תנא 2 (NT+).

תנורא 1, תַּנוּרָא (OA) m. **tanūra, tanōra** (PolG), bread oven; cf. כנונא [Khan 582 **tandura**].
תנורא 2 (Ar < P part of dress worn by dervishes > OA corselet, SokBA 1217) **⁺tannura** modern skirt.
ת-נ-ז-ל III (Ar) **t-n-z-l** to lose weight (due to illness) (SaAC 7).
ת-נ-י (OA) **t-n-y** to study, read; יתיוא בתנאיא הלכה **ytīwa bıtnāya halāxa** He was sitting studying Jewish law; II to speak, talk (NT); review, repeat study (PolG); v. תַ-נ-י.
תניתא, תְּנֵיאָתָא (OA) f. **tanēṯa, tane'ta** (BT4/5, D; Br47 323; PolG), word, written word, letter sign (Z): **la lıple xa tanēsa-ši** He didnt learn (to read) even one word/letter; argument:׳להאוילו תניתא קם ה **la-hāwēlu tanēṯa qam ʾilāha** They would not have an argument with God (NT5 383); cf. כברא; pl. תניאתא **tanyāṯa** (NT+).
ת-נ-כ II (OA אתאנח) **t-n-x** to sigh, groan (AvidH 29); cf. ח-ס-ר [cf. Mutz 233; MacD 206].
תנכ (Ar/K/P < T) m. **tanak** tin.
תנכאיה (< תנכ) f. **tanıkāye** large tin can; pl. תְּנְכַּיָיאת **-yat** (=H פַּחִים, BT4, D; cf. PolG).
תנכג׳י (T) m. **tanakči** tinsmith; pl. **tanakčīyat**.
תנכושכה (< תנכ) f. **tanakoške** little tin can or shack.
ת-נ-פ-כ III (Ar) **t-n-f-x** to be bloated from overeating.
תנת v. תנה
ת-נ-ת-נ III (OA תנן) **t-n-t-n** to fill or be filled with smoke.
תנתנא (T **tentene**) m. **tantana** lace (work).
תנתריוכ (IrAr < En) m. **tıntıryōk** tincture of iodine.
תסאביח (Ar) f.(?) **tasābīḥ** hymn (NT3); תסאביח כתתא **tasābīḥ xaṯta** new hymn (=H שירה חדשה, NT5 405); pl. תסאביח(ה), תְּצָבִיחֵי **tasabīḥ(e)** (NT2), **taṣabīhe** (AvidH 9); cf. תושבחין.
תסל, תסר (< תסלי) inv./adv. **tasal/r** secure, carefree (=H בֶּטַח, BT3; v. תנא 2) (NT+).
תסלי (Ar) **tasalli** peace of mind; בתסלי **btasalli** peacefully (NT).
תסלותא (< תסל) **tasalūṯa** serenity (NTU1 43b).
תסלים (Ar) **taslīm** benediction/incantation? (PolG); perhaps contamination with טליסם.

ת-ס-ל-מ III (Ar/K تسليم كرين) **t-s-l-m** to deliver to, hand over; cf. ס-ל-מ.
תעאלא (K< Ar) **taʿāla** the Exalted One (God) (NT2).
תעב (Ar) m. **taʿab** toil, labor (PolU 227).
תעבולא v. תחבולה
תעדא (K< Ar) **taʿadda** hostility (PolU 247).
תעה (K?) **taʿe** beating, spanking (baby talk).
תעולתא (< ת-ע-ל) f. **tı/aʿulta** game, play (cf. PolG); pl. **tıʿulyāṯa**.
תעין (Ar) **taʿ(y)īn** allotment (=H חֹק, BT1).
ת-ע-ל, ט-ע-ל (< ?) **t-ʿ-l** (Z, PolG), **ṭ-ʾ-l** (NT), to play (games); מטעלכבו **mtaʿlaxbu** we play with them (like toys) (NT5 390); **gımtāʿıl qumāre** He is a gambler (Z); **mtōʿılle brēši** He made a mockery of me(=H הִתְעַלֵּל, BT2); to let someone play (MeAl 180 , n. 30) ; cf. תעולתא [Garbell 292 **⁺t-y-l** play; Krotkoff 129-30].
ת-ע-ל-ק III (Ar) **t-ʿ-l-q** to cling, hang loose; **jērīye mtuʿlaqta** slave girl designated to an other man (=H שפחה חרופה). cf. ע-ל-ק (NT+).
תענית דיבור (H) **taʿanīṯ dıbbur** speak-fasting (a day of silence except for reading Zohar).
ת-ע-ס (Ar) **t-ʿ-s** make one blunder; תעיסילי אך שהארי **tʿisīle ʾıx bahāre** He made them blunder like blind men (PolG).
תעסיה (Ar) **taʿse** bad luck! How awful! (NT2); בתעסה **btaʿse** unfortunately (NT5 402).
ת-פ-א (Ar?) **t-f-ʾ** go away, go to hell; cf. תפו.
תפו (K **tifu**/Ar تف) **tfu** Spit on you! Fie! Phew!
תפילין, תפילים (H) **tıfıllīn/m** the tefillim phylacteries (=H טוֹטָפוֹת, BT2); v. ל-ו-ש; **b-** (I swear) by the tefillim; **sıʿōzıt** - the charity meal given on wearing the tefillim (NT+).
תפכה v. תפנג
פ-כ-ר v. ת-פ-כ-ר
ת-פ-ל II (< H תפילה prayer/תִּפְלָה folly?) **t-p-l** to pray (pejor. for Muslim prayer); v. -צ ל-י [cf. Mutz 233 **tıppol** Muslim prayer].
תפליסכה (K **tipil** finger) f. **tiflīske** snap of fingers, push with finger; **m-x-y** - to snap the fingers.
תפנג, תפכה (K/P) **tfang** (NT), **tfakke** (Z, f.), rifle; pl. תפנגיה **tfange** (NT), **tfakyāṯa** (Z).

ת-פ-נ-ק III (Ar تَفَنَّقَ indulge, live in affluence? Cf. H/OA/OS/Mand פנק) **t-f-n-q** to choke over excessive food or drink; cf. ת-נ-פ-כ.
תפסה (K **tefsi**) f. **tafse** small tray (cf. PolG).
תפסיר (Ar) m. **tafsir** (oral or written) Neo-Aramaic translation of a Hebrew text; cf. שרח; interpretation, commentary (NT); pl. תפסירה **tafsire** (NT+) [Mutz 232 **tawsir** oral trsnslation of Bible or Haggadah].
ת-פ-ס-ר III (Ar) **t-f-s-r** to explain, interpret (dream), translate (Hebrew text to Neo-Aramaic; cf. PolG); v. תרגום, ת-ל-ג׳-מ. NT+
ת-פ-ק (Ar) **t-f-q** to occur, befall, meet (by chance); לא גתפקא **la gtafqa** It is unlikely (to occur); **la tfıq-le-bu** He could not find them; בְּתַפְקִיבֵי **btafqibe** (evil things) will befall him (=H וּמְצָאוּהוּ, BT5, D); II to plot (=H קָשַׁר, 2 Kg 10:9); IV to cause the occurrence of (PolG); cf. בי-תפאקי (NT+).
תפק, תפקותא (Ar اتفاق) f. **tıfaq(ūṯa)** harmony, good relations.
תפקתא (< ת-פ-ק) f. **tfaqta** occurrence, incidence; pl. **tfaqyāṯa** things that befall someone (=H קוֹרוֹת, BT1).
תפשייה, תושי (K **tev/wši/u**) **tafšīya** (Z), **tawši** (Hob89 184), hatchet.
תפתיכ (T) **tıftık** mohair, fine soft wool; but used only in **rakīxa x-tıftık** very soft.
ת-פ-ת-פ III (< ?) **t-f-t-f** to beautify, adorn (Avin 88 260).
ת-פ-ת-ש III (Ar) **t-f-t-š** to search, investigate.
ט-צ-ד-ק, ת-צ-ד-ק III (Ar) ***t-s-d-q** to confirm, declare to be right (= הִצְדִּיק, PolG:2 S 15:4); turn to be real (a description) (PolU 330).
תצלך, טסלך (T rough) inv. **taṣlax** inappropriate, crude.
תצמה, תסמה(T تصمة girdle, strap) pl. ***tasme** shoulder straps (?), only in: -**mgo kapāne bnačlınnu** Ill pull out his straps from his shoulders (=punish severly) (PolU 173).
תקא (K **tika** prayer, demand?) **tıqqa** (?) supplication (NT2).
תקון חצות (H) **tıqqun ḥaṣoṯ** midnight prayers (Amedi 50).
תקופה 1, תקופא (H?) f. (?) **taqūfa** aggressive woman (< H תַּקִּיפָה harsh woman? cf. OA/OS תַּקִּיפָא m., תקיפתא, f.; Mengozzi 319 **taqīpa** strong < OS); cf. תקפה.
תקופה* 2 (H) attested only in תקופות שאתא **taqūfoṯ-šāta** year seasons (BaBin 25).
תקיעה (H) f. **taqīʿa** blowing the shofar; rams horn (=H יוֹבֵל, BT2); **b-** (I swear) by the shofar! Cf. שופר, ת-ק-ע.
ת-ק-ל (OA) vi/vt **t-q-l** to weigh (NT+).
תקלא (OA תִּיקְלָא) m. **tıqla** weight; **tıqle yaqūra** one who moves slowly, one not diligent.
תקלה (H) f. **taqqāla** mishap (NT2).
תקלי-תקלו (< ת-ק-ל) **taqli-taqlo** heavy, slow-moving, waddling person; cf. טפלי-טפלו.
תקנה (H) **taqqāna** solution (to a difficult issue); recovering (from serious illness).
תקסיר(י) (K< Ar تقصير) m. **taqsīr(i)** negligence; **la ʾuzleču taqsir** He didnt save any effort; **taqsīr-ḥāl** destitute, poor (PolU); cf. קוסורי.
ת-ק-ע (H) **t-q-ʿ** blow the shofar (RivSh 181).
תקפה (Ar/H?) f./pl? ***taqfe** something very sour, used only in **xamūṣa x-*taqfe** sour as —; cf. תקופה 1?
תרא v. תרה
תראא (OA תרעא) m. **tarʾa** gate, opening; pl. **tarʾāye** (PolG) (NT+). [Khan 582 **tara** door; outside].
תראצא (< ת-ר-צ) v.n. **trāṣa** cure (PolU 322).
תרארא (K) f. **trārare** plate (Hob89 184).
תראתייה (K) f./pl. **tarrātīye** moist-fresh food (PolU 15).
תרבא (OA) m. **tarba** tallow (unkosher animal fat) (=H חֵלֶב, BT); pl. **tarbābe** (BT3), **tarbe** (PolG:Am/D?)
ת-ר-ב-ז׳, ת-ר-ב-ש III(< תיר-בז׳י) **t-r-b-ž/š** to sneeze (Z; PolG)(cf. RivP#94); cf. ת-ב-ד.
תרגום (H) m. **targum** the Targum, old Aramaic translation of the Bible; **d-r-y** - to translate to (NT2); v. תפסיר, ת-ל-ג׳-מ.
תרה, תרי, תרא (OA) m. (NT), c. (Z) **tre, treʾ** (pausal/emphasis, Z), two; cf. תרתיה; כארד תרה **kārıd tre** (NT)/**zāyıd treʾ** (Z) the second time; תורו/תרו/כותרו/תורנתו/תרותניהון/תורנתיהון/ **tūru** (NT)/ **kutru** (Z, NT)/ **turıntu**/ **tırutnēhun** / **turıntēhun** (NT1) both of them both of them; **rıš kutru** / **kutırtu ʾēni** Most welcome (lit. on both of my eyes); תרווכון **tırwōxun** (AmU1 79a);

תו(ו)רותניני **türütnēni** (NT2)/ **kutrēni** (Z) both of us; **tre-tre** in pairs (=H שְׁנַיִם-שְׁנַיִם, BT1); **xa-utre'** double amount (=H מִשְׁנֶה, BT2).
תר וחשכ (K) **tarr-u-ḥıšk** fresh and dry (to eat everything undiscriminately) (PolU 384).
תרו-טולה v. טולה
תרומה (H) **⁺tarūma** (religious) offering, gift; pl. תרומות **tarūmōṯ** (BT4).
תרוונדה, טרוונדה (< P ترونده first fruits, novelties) pl.**⁺tırwande** only in hendiadys **ṭım'e** - tasty things, delicacies (PolU 287).
תרועה (H) **tarᶜūᶜa** blast of the shofar (BT3); **b-** (I swear) by the blast of the shofar! Cf. תקיעה.
תרופא, תרופתא (< OA רטיבא?) adj. **tarūpa, tarupta** fresh, wet, moist.
תרוצא, טרוסא, טרוצא (< ת-ר-צ) **⁺trōṣa** truth, truly, true (=H כֵּן, הָאֻמְנָם, BT4; NT2; NT5 402).
תרוצאנא, תרוצנתא (< תרוצא) adj. **⁺trōsāna, ⁺trōsanta**, honest, sincere.
תרוצותא, תרוצתא (< תרוצא) f. **⁺trusta, trōsūṯa** rectitude; pl. טרוסיאתא **⁺trosyāṯa** right deeds (=H צדקות, NT5 404).
תרושיבא, תרושב (OA תְּרֵי בְּשַׁבָּא) **trušēba** (NT), **trōšıb** (Z), **trūšıb** (BT1, Am), Monday [Khan 583 **trušab**].
תרז (K/T< Ar طراز) m. **tarz** form, manner; **bču tarz lēbe ᶜılla** He cant control her in any way; pl. תרזיה **tarze** (AmU1 79a).
ת-ר-ז-מ III < ?) vt/vi **t-r-z-m** to crack a bit.
תרטמתא v. טורטומתא
תרה v. תרי
ת-ר-י (OA) **t-r-y** to become wet; IV to wet, soak (VT) (RivSh 117 מִתְרֵאלֵי **mıtre'le‹ mıtrēle**) [Khan 583 **ṯ-r-y**].
תריאק v. טרייק
תריאסר, תרי אסר, תְּרֵי אֲסַר (OA תרי עסר, תריסר) **tre'sar** twelve (RivSh 272) (NT+).
תריצא ,תרצתא (< ת-ר-צ, p.p.) adj. healthy, looking well, recovered.
ת-ר-כ, ט-ר-כ (OA/Ar) **t-r-k** (Z, NT), **ṯ-r-k** (BT1, D), to desert, to neglect (NT+).
תרכא (K) m. **tarrıka** dry, lifeless (body).
תרכאיא, תרכיתא (< תרכייא) **tırkāya, tırkēṯa** Turkish person.

תרכי (K/Ar) **tırki** Turkish (language).
תרכייא (K/Ar) f. **tırkīya** Turkey (PolU 213).
תרלאל (< K?) **tarlāl** dandy: **jwanqa sīpáka u–** elegant and dandy lad (PolG).
ת-ר-מ (< תרומה; cf. H-OA תרם) **t-r-m** to offer (as donation) (=H הֵרִים, BT3).
תרמביל v. טרמביל
תרנגא, טרנגא (Ar) f. **⁺tarınja** orange; cf. פרתקאלא.
תרניני, תרנאנא (K?) **tırnāna, tırnīni** sound imitations of dance; cf. ניני; **'ēha tırnīni-la, tırnāna wēla pıšta lbasra** This is (still) the good news, the bad news is still to come" (PolU 242).
ת-ר-ס (< Ar ترس slam a door; Denizeau 61; cf. < OA תרס to oppose?) **t-r-s** to storm, enter suddenly and violently.
תרסוס (< Ar?) Tarsus (=H תרשיש) (NT6 132).
תרסי (K) inv./adv. **tırsi** stale bread (=H לֶחֶם קְלֹקֵל, BT4); **b-** (eat) bread by itself, without any condiment.
ת-ר-ע (< תרועה) **t-r-ᶜ** to blow the shofar a long blast (=H הֵרִיעַ, BT4); בד בוקיל נפירי תרעיתין **bıd bōqıl nafīre tarᶜētın** You shall blow the horns (BABin 30, 122); cf. ת-ק-ע ,ת-ר-מ.
תרעוזייא (AnAr/K) f. **⁺tırᶜōzīya** Russian cucumbers; pl. תְּרְעוֹזְיֵי **tırᶜōzīye** (=H קִשּׁוּאִים, BT4) [cf. Garbell 336 **trozita**].
ת-ר-צ, ת-ר-ס, ט-ר-צ (OA) **⁺t-r-ṣ** to heal (vi), gain weight; II to arrange, to fix; IV to heal (vt) (AlfH 73; RivSh 182).
ת-ר-ק-ל v. ד-ר-ק-ל
תְּרְקֵלְתָא v. דרקלתא
ת-ר-ת-ב III (< תרתיב) **t-r-t-b** to arrange, put in order; to create, shape (=H יָצַר, AlfM 29).
תרתיב(ה) (Ar) m. **tartib** (m.), **tartībe** (f.; PolU 8), arrangement, order; pl. **tartībe**.
תרתיה, תרתי, תרתא (OA) f. **tarte(')** two; תרתיה דבוריה **tarte dıbbōre** two bees (NT5 384); **rıš kutırtu 'ēni** Most welcome (lit., on both of my eyes); **kuturtōhun** both of them (f.) (Ruth 1:19); v. תרה.
תרתיאמא, תירתיאמה (OA תרתי מאה) **tarte'ma, tırte'ma** (BaBin 8; PolG), two hundred; cf. מאתה.
תשאביה, תשאבי, תשאבייה, תְּוֹשַׁאבִי (Ar تشابه) f.

tı/ušābi(h), tıšābiye likeness, like, image (=H דְּמוּת, BT1); pl. תשאביית **tıšābiyat** (=H צַלְמֵי-מַסֵּכוֹת, BT4); cf. ש-ב-ה.

תשובה (H) f. **tašūva** repentance; **d-ʾ-r b-** to repent (=H שָׁב, BT5); cf. תובא (NT+).

ת-ש-ו-ש III (Ar تشويش) vt/vi **t-š-w-š** to dumbfound; become stirred (=H הָמַם. Ruth 1:19; PolG).

תשושתא (< ת-ש-ו-ש) f. **tašwašta** confusion, commotion, dismay (=H מְהוּמָה/תִּמָּהוֹן, BT5).

תשתה v. טשתה

תשייא (K) f. **tašīya** spindle, distaff [cf. MUtz 232 **tašši**; Khan **tašya** spun thread].

תשמיש (H) m. **tašmiš** intercourse (BaBin 74).

תשעה באב (H) **tıšʿa bāv** mostly in **yarxıd** — the month of the fast of Ninth of Ab; cf. חזינה.

ת-ש-ק-ל III (IrAr) **t-š-q-l** to cheat, falsely accuse.

תשקלג'י (K/IrAr) m. **tašqalči** swindler, caluminator; pl. **tašqalčīyat**.

תשקלתא (K **tešqele**) f. **tašqalta** wile, false accusation; pl. תשקליאתא **tašqalyāṯa** [Khan 582 **tašqala** denunciation].

תשרי (H) **tıšri** the month of Tishri; cf. ג'ירי.

תתה (K **dast**) **tatte** hands (baby talk); cf. פפה.

תתון v. תותון

ת, תׄ (ṯ)

תבית, תביד (Ar ثابت) adv. **ṯabīt/d** (?) certainly (NT1) [cf. MacD 220 **sābit** proof; evident].

ת-ב-ת, ז-ב-ת (Ar ثبت) **ṯ-b-t** (Z **s-b-t**), **z-b-t** [< ת-ב-ד/ט-ב-צ̇?] to be established, solid, calm; II/IV to determine, establish (= H כּוֹנֵן, BT2); מתבתאנד כשבונד לבוואתא ה' **mṯabtānıd xıšbōnıd lıbbawāṯa ʾilāha** God is the assessor of thoughts of the hearts (=H תּוֹכֵן לבבות ה', NT5 400); גבאתוך ביד אורכא מזבתיתן **gavāṯox bıd ʾurxa mzabtētın** You step firmly on the road (BaBin 63).

תובא, סובא (Ar ثوب) m. **ṯōba** (Z **sōba**) bolt of fabric; **xá sōba kíttan** a bolt of linen (Socin 159) [Khan 583 **tob** roll of material].

תׄילֶית (Ar) **ṯılıṯ** (D) (Z **sılıs**; PolG **tult**!) one-third (=H שְׁלִישִׁית הַהִין, BT4).

תׄינידיום, תינד-יום (Ar) adv. **ṯēnid-yom** (Z **sēnıd-**) the day after next (Z); the next but one day: **hīl durtyom uhīl** — until the next day and the next but one day (PolG); v. דורתד-יום.

ת-מ-נ, ט-מ-נ II (Ar) **ṯ-m-n** (D), **ṭ-m-n** (Z), to estimate the value (=H הֶעֱרִיךְ, BT3); בְּמְתַמּוֹנֵי דִּידוֹך in your estimate (=H בְּעֶרְכְּךָ, BT3, D); cf. טימה.

תמן (Ar) **ṯaman** (Z **saman**) value, price (=H עֵרֶךְ, BT3).

ת-נ-י (Ar) **ṭ-n-y** (Z **s-n-y**) to turn again and again, keep changing: **dunye qqalba uksanya** The world keeps changing (its unpredictable); **qlıbli usnēli ula ṭweʾli bāš** I kept twisting and turning (in bed) and didnt sleep well (cf. PolG: **tny**].

Appendix:
An Index to Reflexes or Cognates of Jewish Babylonian Aramaic

User's Guidlines

The indexed words on the left side of each column are from Michael Sokoloff, A Dictionary of Jewish Babylonian Aramaic (forthcoming).

The words following v. on the right side of each column usually are what I presume to be reflexes or the closest cognate words of Jewish Neo-Aramaic dialects that are included in my dictionary.

As expected, many Judaic terms, and even some secular ones, are borrowed from traditional Hebrew, rather than from the equivalent Babylonian Aramaic, e.g., שלום, שטר, פשט צער, עני, עיבור, עולם, מצוה (very few exceptions, e.g., פסחא); all these are included in the Index, but in parentheses, e.g., (צערא v. צער); similarly, loan words from Arabic, e.g., (נגרא v. נגארא).

Just to satisfy the curiosity of interested scholars, in a very few cases, some very common Aramaic words are included in the index even when they do not have a reflex or a cognate in our group of dialects, and these appear in square brackets, e.g. [איתתא v. בכתא], [דיכרא v. אורזא].

When a Neo-Aramaic cognate is not sure it is followed by a question mark, e.g., ערעיתא v. צרקתא?

The index is purely for reference; full information on variant forms, meanings, and whether the word is native Aramaic or borrowed later via Persian, etc., will be found in the entries per se.

א

אב v. אָב
אבזונא v. אבזינא
אבזארא v. אַבְזָרָא
x-p-q כ̇-פ-ק v. אבק
אבריסם v. אַבְרֵישׁוֹם
čamma ג̇מא v. אַגְמָא
אנג̇אנה v. אַגָּנָא
ארא v. אַגְרָא #1
אדר v. אָדָר
אאכורא v. אהוריירא
עובא v. אוּבָּא
?נהתא v. אודנא #1
?וזא v. אווזא
kōma כ̇ומא v. אוּכָּם
1 אמתא v. אוּמְּתָא
וקייא v. אוּקְיָא
אורכא v. אורחא #1
ירכות v. אוּרְכָּא
1 א-ז-ל v. אזל #1
2 א-ז-ל v. אזל #2
אאכא, אכונא v. אֲחָא
כ̇יתא, כ̇ינא v. אחריתי, אחרינא
1 כ̇אתא v. אֲחָתָא
עטמא v. אַטְמָא
גארה v. אִיגָּרָא
אזלא v. אִיזְלָא
אייר v. אייר
כ̇ומא v. אִיכּוּם
אלווסנא v. אילווא
אילאנא v. אִילָנָא
ימא v. אִימָּא
?איונתא v. אימרתא
1 אימן v. אִימַּת
1 הי v. אין
אהנון v. אִינְּהוּ, אינון
נאשא v. אִינָשָׁא
ספדיתא v. אִיסָּדָא
סקופתא v. איסקופתא
איסר v. אִיסָּרָא #2
3 שאתא v. אישתא
אית v. אית
[בכתא v. איתתא]
כ̇ואנא v. אכואנא
איכלתא v. אכילתא
א-כ-ל v. אכל #1
אלא v. אֶלָּא
אילאהא v. אֱלָהָא
אלול v. אלול
אליתא v. אליתא
ל-א-ס v. אלס
1 ל-י-פ v. אלף
אלפא v. אלפא
אן v. אם
1 עמבר v. אַמְבָּרָא
גוזא v. אמגוזא
1 טלא v. אַמַּטּוּל
č-y-m ג̇-י-מ v. עמץ, אמץ
א-מ-ר v. אמר
אאנא v. אנא
ת-נ-כ v. אנח
אכני v. אנחנא
1 אאהת v. אַנְתְּ
2 אאהת v. אַנְתִּי
אאסא v. אָסָא
?א-ס-פ v. אסף

גיבא v. גבא #1
ג-ו-י v. גבי #1
גובתא v. גבינתא
ג-ו-ל v. גבל
ג-ו-ר v. גבר
גורא v. גברא #1
גורותא v. גברותא #1
גבארותא v. גברותא #2
גאדא v. גדא #1
גדאדא v. גדדא
גדיא v. גדיא
ג-ד-ל v. גדל #2
עויא v. גו, *גו
juhāla ג̇והאלא v. גואלקא
1 גודא v. גודא #1
2 גודא v. גודא #2
?גולתא v. גולתא
גרותא v. גורבא
ג-ז-ל v. גזל
2 ג-ז-ר v. גזר
ג-כ-כ v. גחכנא
גבארא v. גיברא
גגלא v. גיגלא
גיהנם v. גיהנם
ג-י-ר v. גייר
גלא v. גילא #1
גלדא v. גילדא
ג v. גימל
1 גנתא v. גינתא
כס v. גיסא #2
גירא v. גירא #1
גרסא v. גירסא #2
ג-ל-י v. גלי
גומלא v. גמלא
ג-נ-ו v. גנב
2 גנאוא v. גנבא #1

ספדיתא v. בי סדיא
ב-כ-י v. בכי
בכאיא v. בָּכְיָא
בכיתא v. בכיתא
ב-ל-ב-ל v. בלבל
בלוטא v. בלוטא
בלואתא v. בלועא
ב-ל-א v. בלע
בנא v. בנאה #1
ב-נ-י v. בני
בניאנא v. בניינא
?בס v. בס
בסימא v. בסים
ב-ס-מ v. בסם
?ב-ע-ב-ע v. בעבע
ב-א-י v. בעי
באקא v. בקא #1
באקא v. בקתא #1
ברונא v. ברא #1
בר-נאשה v. בר אינש-
בר-זראא v. בר זרעא #1
ברת-נעאמא v. בר נעמיתא
ורייא v. לְבַר-, בָּרָא
ברדא v. ברדא
1 ברכא v. ברחא
ב-ר-י v. ברי #1
בריכא v. ברי
?ברירא v. בריר
ב-ר-כ v. ברך
בורכתא v. ברכתא
ברקא v. ברקא #1
בראתא v. ברתא #1
ב-ש-ל v. בשל
בתר v. בתר

ג

ג-נ-ד-ר .v גנדר #1

ג-נ-י .v גני

גנונה .v גננא

גאצא .v גצא

גרן .v גראן

ג-ר-ו-נ .v גרבא #3?

ג-ר-א-ל, ג-מ-ב-ל .v גרבל?

ג-ר-ד .v גרד

גרמא .v גרמא #1

ג-ר-ס .v גרס #3

ג-ר-א .v גרע

ג-ר-פ .v גרף

ג-ר-ש .v גרש

ד

דֵיד .v ד-, די -, דיד

דבוקאנא .v דבוקא

ד-ו-ק .v דבק

ד-ב-ר .v דבר?

דברא .v דברא?

דוגלאנא, ד-ג-ל .v דגלא

דאדה, דאיה .v דדי

דהוא .v דהבא

דהינא .v דהין

ד-ה-נ .v דהן

דבא .v דובא #1

דובא .v דובא #2

דושא .v דובשא

דולא .v דוולא 1

דוכא .v דוכתא

? 1+2 ד-ו-ר .v דור #2

דורדוכנא, דורדי .v דורדיא

ד-י-ש .v דוש

גודאא judᵃ דזוד

דיוא .v דיבא #1

דיד .v דיד

דדוא .v דידבא

דייאנא, דיין .v דיינא

ד-י-ש .v דיישא

[אורזא .v דיכרא]

דלופה .v דילפא

דינר .v דינרא

דקנא .v דיקנא

דשתא .v דישתא

ת-כ-ר .v דכר

ד-נ-ד-ל, ד-ל-ד-ל .v דלי?

ד-ל-פ .v דלף

ד .v דלת

דמא .v דמא

ד-מ-ד-מ .v דמדם 1

ד-מ-י .v דמי

cf. טימה דְמֵי?

ד-מ-כ .v דמך

ד-מ-א .v דמע

דמאתא .v דמעתא

דאפא .v דפא #1

דפנא .v דפנא #2

דקננא .v דקננא

ד-י-ק .v דקק

דרגבן .v דרבנא

דראגה .v דרגא

דרום .v דרומא

דורוסת .v דרוסת

ד-ר-י .v דרי #2 1

דראאה .v דרעא

דארגין .v דרצין

ד-ר-ש .v דרש

דרוש .v דרשא

דראשא .v דרשנא

ה

אכדאדה .v הדדי

זוואדה v. זוודי
?זוואתא v. זוודתא
זוזא v. זוזא
ז-ר-ז-ע v. זוע
זבלא v. זיבלא
זיזייא v. זיזא
זונא v. זימנא
ז-כ-י v. זכי
זכאי v. זכאי
זנאיא v. זנאי
זנגֿבילא v. זנגבילא
ז-נ-י v. זני
? ז-ק-ר v. זקר
ז-ר-א v. זרע
זראא v. זרעא

ח

כ̇בושא v. חבושא
כ̇-ב-ט v. חבט
2 כ̇-ו-י v. חבי #1
כ̇ויצא v. חביצא
?כ̇-ב-ל v. חבל #1
כ̇ולא v. חבלא #2
1 כ̇-פ-ק v. ח-ב-ק
כ̇ורא v. חברא #1
כ̇א v. חד #1
כ̇ושיבא v. חד בשבא
כדאסר v. חדסר
כ̇דיותא v. חדותא, חדוא
כ̇-ד-י v. חדי
כ̇דיא v. חדיא
כ̇-ת-ת v. חדת
כ̇אתא v. חדת
2 חוקא v. חווקא
כ̇-ו-ר v. חוור

כ̇-ד-ר v. הדר #1
אאהו(ן) v. ההוא
אאהי(ן) v. ההיא
ה-ו-י v. הוי #1
הונא v. הונ-
היא v. הייא
איכא v. היכא
הלולא v. הילולא
ה-י-מ-נ v. הימן
הנדוכא v. הינדואה
אכא v. הכא
הדכא v. הכי
1 הם v. הַם
ה-נ-ד-ס v. הנדז
הנדאס v. הנדזא
ה-נ-י v. הני
אאני v. הני
הרהור v. הרהורא
אתא v. השתא

ו

ז

1 זבון v. זבונא
זמבילא v. זבילא
ז-ב-ל v. זבל
ז-ו-נ, ז-ב-נ v. זבן
זאאה v. זגא #1
ז-ה-מ v. זהם
זואא v. זוגא
זוהמא v. זוהמא

כלול v. חליל
1 כֿ-ל-מ v. חלם #1
2 כֿ-ל-מ v. חלם #2
(חלה v. חלתא #1)
כֿמיאנא v. חמא #1
כֿמימא v. חמים
כֿמימותא v. חמימותא
חמש עשֿר v. חמיסר
כֿמירא v. חמירא
כֿ-מ-כ-מ v. חמם
כֿ-מ-א v. חמע
כֿ-מ-צ v. חמץ #1
כֿמרא v. חמרא #1
כֿמארא v. חמרא #2
כֿמרתא v. חמרתא
כֿמשא v. חמשא
כֿמשאסר v. חמיסר, חמש עשֿר
כֿמשושב v. חמשא בשבא
כֿמאתא v. חֲמָתָא
(חנוכה v. חנוכתא)
(חנופה v. חנף)
כֿ-נ-ק v. חנק
(חס ושלום v. חס ל-)
כֿסה v. חסא
כֿספא v. חספא #1
כֿ-פ-י v. חפי
כֿ-י-פ v. חפף
2 כֿ-פ-ק v. חפק
כֿ-פ-ר v. חפר
ג׳-צֿ-ד v. חצד
ג׳צֿאדא v. חצדא
כֿרדלה v. חרדלא
כֿרנופה v. חרובא
כ-ר-ז v. חרז
?2 כֿ-ר-גֿ v. חרט
אכֿרה v. חרי #2

כֿטרא v. חוטרא #1
1 כֿ-ו-י v. חוי
כֿולדא v. חולדא
כֿמא v. חומא
כֿומרתא v. חומרתא
(חמש v. חומשא)
כֿורגא v. חורגא
כֿשבונא v. חושבנא
כֿ-ז-י v. חזי
כזורא v. חזירא
(חזן v. חזנא)
ח-ז-ק v. חזק
(כֿוכֿא v. חחא)
כֿ-ט-י v. חטי #1
1 כֿ-ט-ר v. חטר #1
כֿגא v. חיגא
כווה v. חיויא
כֿוארא v. חיור #1
כֿיותא v. חיותא #2
כֿטה v. חיטתא #1
כֿ-י-י v. חיי
כֿאיה v. חיי
כֿייתא v. חייתא #3
כֿילא v. חילא #1
1 כֿלא v. חילא #2
כֿלמא v. חילמא
כֿרש v. חירשא
ח v. חית
כֿ-י-כ v. חכך
כֿאלא v. חלא #2
כֿ-ל-ו v. חלב
כֿלוא v. חלבא
?חצלבאן v. חלבניתא
1 כֿ-ל-י v. חלי #1
כֿליא v. חֲלֵי
(חליק v. חליקא)

כריפא v. חריף
כ-ר-כ v. חרך
(ח-ר-מ v. חרם)
כ-ר-פ v. חרף 1
כ-ר-ג v. חרץ 2?
כאצא v. חרצא #1
כ-ר-ג v. חרק 2 #1
כרשה v. חֶרשי
כ-ש-ו v. חשב
כשוכא v. חשיך
כ-ש-כ v. חשך 1
כשכא חַשכא, חַשכתא v. חשכא
כשלא v. חשל #1+2?
כ-ת-מ v. חתם
כתם v. חתמא
כתמיתא v. חתימותא, חתמותא
כתנא v. חתנא

ט

דוקא v. טבהקא
(טבילה v. טבילותא)
ט-ב-ל v. טבל #1
טולא v. טבלא
ט-ו-א v. טבע
(טבת v. טבת)
ט-ו-י v. טובי (ל-) 2
(טוטפות v. טוטפתא?)
ט-ו-י v. ט-ו-י 1
טלא v. טולא 1
טלמתא v. טולמא
טלאשא v. טולשא
ט-י-פ v. טוף #1
טופאנא v. טופנא
טופרא v. טופרא
טורא v. טורא
תחאלא v. טחלא (!)

ת-כ-נ v. טחן (!)
טהרא v. טיהרא
טינא v. טינא
טפא v. טיפתא 1
ט-ל-ל v. טלל #1
טלניתא v. טלניתא
טלוכה v. טלפחא
ט-מ-י v. טמי
ט-מ-ר v. טמר
ט-מ-ש v. טמש
טמבור v. טנבורא
טאסה v. טסא
ט-א-י v. טעי
ט-מ-א v. טעם
טמאא v. טעמא
ט-א-נ v. טען #2
טפלא v. טפלא #1
דוקא v. טפקא
ט-ר-פ v. טרף #1
ט-ר-ק v. טרק
ט-ש-י v. ט-ש-י
טשתה v. טשתקא

י

ו-י-ש v. יבש (!)
אידא v. ידא 1
י-ד-א v. ידע
י-ה-ו-ל v. יהב
הודאיא v. יהודאה
יושא v. יובשא
(יוד v. יוד)
יומא v. יומא
יום דינא v. יומא דדינא, יום דינא
יונה v. יונא
(יונאן v. יונאה)
(אבנוס v. יונוס)

3 כוזא v. כוזתא, כוזא
ככלא v. כוחלא
כ-ו-י v. כוי
כוכא v. כוכא #2
ככותא v. כוכבא
כ-י-ל v. כול
כול- v. כולא
1. כו v. כל ד-
כוליתא v. כוליתא
כולכא v. כולכא
(כומר v. כומרא #2)
כוספא v. כוספא
כוארא v. כַּוָּרָא #3
כורכמאנא v. כורכמא
(כורסי v. כורסיא)
כשכרי v. כושקרא
כ-כ-ל v. כחל
(כ-ב-ר-ד, כברית v. כיבריתא)
1 כילא v. כיילא
כסוייא v. כיסוייא
כסתא v. כיסתא #1
1 כיפא v. כיפא #1
?גבאנה v. כיפא #2
כתאנא v. כיתנא
כאכא v. ככא #1
קאקבה v. ככבא
?קקרא v. ככרא
כלבא v. כלבא #1
כלבתא v. כלבתא #1
כלתא v. כלתא
1 כמא v. כמה
כמונא v. כמונא
כ-מ-ר v. כמר #3
?ג̆-מ-ס v. כ-מ-ש
?כרנגה v. כנגר
כנונא v. כנונא

יוקרא v. יוקרא
ירוקא v. ירוֹק, יוּרק
?יתומא v. יותא
?א-ס-פ v. יזף
(!) י-ד-ל v. ילד
ילותא v. ילדותא
1 ל-י-פ v. ילף
יאמא v. ימא
י-מ-י v. ימי
ימין v. ימינא
(יצר הרע v. יצרא)
י-ק-ד v. יקד
יקורא v. יקיר
י-ק-ר v. יקר
ירכא v. ירחא
י-ר-ק v. ירק #1
ר-י-ק v. ירק #2
ירקא v. ירקא
י-ר-ת v. ירת
י-ת-ו v. יתב
יתווא v. יתבא
יתומא v. יתם

כ

ג- v. כ-, כא
כבאבא v. כבבא
1 כודא v. כבדא
כבאזא v. כבזא
כ-ו-ש v. כבש
?גגנא v. כגנא
גד v. כד
כדונא v. כדא
?**xwa** כוא v. כו
כודנתא v. כודניא
אכואת v. כוות-
כאוא v. כוותא

1 כנשתא v. כנישתא #1
כנושתא v. כנישתא #2
כנענאיא v. כנענאה
כ-נ-ש v. כנש #1
2 כנתא v. כנתא #1
1 כנתא v. כנתא #4
?כאשייא v. כסא #1
כ-ס-כ v. כסח
כ-ס-י v. כסי
כעכא v. כעכא
(כפא v. כפא #1)
כאפא v. כפא #2
כ-פ-נ v. כפן
כפנא v. כפנא
?כפנכ v. כפניתא #2
כ-י-פ v. כפף
כ-פ-ר v. כפר
(כ̀ראג̀ v. כרגא)
1 כ-ר-י v. כרי #1
(כ-ר-ה v. כרה)
כ-ר-כ v. כרך
כרמא v. כרמא
כאסא v. כרסא
כרפסא, כרפס v. כרפסא
כיראתה v. כרתא
כ-ת-ו v. כתב
כתאוא v. כתבא
(כתובה v. כתובתא)
כאפא v. כתפא

ל

ל- v. ל-
1 לא v. לא
לובנא v. לבינתא
ל-ו-ש v. לבש
לאינא v. לגינא
ל-א-ל-א v. לוג
ליאמא v. לוגמא
(לוחא v. לווחא)
ל-י-ט v. לוט
לואתא v. לועא
ל-י-ש v. לוש
ל-כ-כ v. ל-ח-ך
לכמא v, לחמא
לבא v. ליבא
ליואיא v. ליואה
לכשא v. ליחשא
לילה v. ליליא #1
ליל-הודא v. ליליא #2
לישאנא v. לישנא
לית v. לית-
ל v. למד
איל v. לעילא
2 ל-ק-ט, 1 ל-ק-ט v. לקט
ל-ק-י v. לקי
?לקיטא v. לקיטא

מ

אמא v. מאה
3 מן v. מאן #1
מא v. מה, מאן #2
אאמן v. מאנא
נוואא v. מבועא
מגלא v. מגלא
מדבראנא v. מדברנא
מכלתא v. מהולתא
מהימן v. מהימן
(מוז v. מוזא)
מלכיני, 1 מלכ v. מולכנא
מומאתא v. מומתא
מוקרא v. מוקרא #1
מ-י-ת v. מות

מ-צ-י v. מצי #2
מ-י-ץ v. מצץ
מרא v. מרא #1
מירגיה v. מרגא
(מרג̀אנה v. מרגניתא)
(מרואחא v. מרוחתא)
מרזיבא v. מרזבא
מארא v. מריא
מרואא v. מריע
מרירא v. מריר
מ-ר-א v. מרע
מראא v. מרעא
מררתא v. מררתא
1 מרתא v. מרתא #1
מ-ש-כ v. משח #1
מ-ס-י! v. משי
משיחא v. משיח, משיחא
2 משכא v. משכא #1
1 מאתא v. מתא
מתרגם, תלג̀מן v. מתורגמנא
מתלא v. מתלא #1
(מתקל v. מתקלא)

נ

(תרנג̀א v. נארנג)
נ-ו-כ v. נבח
נ-ב-י v. נבי
נויא v. נבייא
נ-ו-א v. נבע
נאברכה? v. נבארא
נ-א-ה v. נגה #2
נאהתא v. נגהא
(נג̀ארא v. נגרא #1)
נ-ד-י v. נדי #2
נ-ד-ר v. נדר
נהירא v. נהיר
מותאנא v. מותנא
מזתא v. מזיא
(מזל v. מזלא)
כ̀מאטא v. מחטא #1
מ-כ-י v. מחי #1
מטויא v. מטוי
מ-ט-י v. מטי
מטרייה v. *מטרייא
מטראקא v. מטרקא
1 מאיא v. מיא
מנדי v. מידא
מטרא v. מיטרא
1 מלכא v. מילחא #1
1 משכא v. מישחא
מיתא v. מיתא
מיתותא v. מיתותא
מככאלא v. מכחלא
מלאך v. מלאכא
2 מ-ל-כ v. מלח
2 מ-ל-י, 1 מ-ל-י v. מלי #1
2 מלכא v. מלכא
מלכתא v. מלכתא
(ממזר v. ממזירא)
1 מן v. מן
מ-נ-י v. מני
מניא v. מניא
מניאנא v. מניינא
מ-נ-א v. מנע
מסרקא v. מסורקא
מסתא? v. מסותא #1
מסאתא v. מסחתא
מסכין v. מסכין
מזתא v. מעזיא
מאלה v. מעלי
מפקתא v. מפקתא
(מצוה v. מצותא, מצוא)

נ-ק-ב v. נקב
נ-ק-ד v. נקד #1
נ-ק-י v. נקי
נ-ק-ר v. נקר
נירגזא v. נרקס
נ-ש-ט v. נשט
נ-ש-י v. נשי #1
נ-ש-פ v. נשף #1
נ-ש-ק v. נשק
נשרא v. נשרא
(נשיא v. נשיאה)
נ-ת-ר v. נתר

ס

ס-ו-י v. סאב #1
סאוא v. סב
1 ס-פ-ר v. סבר
2 סותא v. סבתא
(ס-ג̇-ד v. סגד)
(סנדן v. סדנא 1)
ס-ה-ד v. סהד
סהדא v. סהדא
סהדותא v. סהדותא
סמוקא v. סומק
סיסנא v. סוסאן
סוסיא, סוסתא v. סוסה
1 ס-כ-י v. סחי
ס-כ-פ v. סחף
ס-ט-י v. סטי
(!) סיבותא v. סיבותא
סיון v. סיון
(סטרא אחרא v. סיטרא)
סיפא v. סייפא #1
סכתא v. סיכתא #1
סתוא v. סיתוא
(סכנה v. סכנתא)

נ-ה-ר v. נהר #1
נהרא v. נהרא #1
נוולתא v. נוולא #1
נ-י-כ v. נוח
נוכראיא v. נוכראה
נוניתא v. נונא
נוקבא v. נוקבא
נוקוא v. נוקבתא
1 נורא v. נורא #1
2 נורא v. נורא #2
(נזיר v. נזירא)
נ-ז-ר v. נזר
נכירא v. נחירא
נאטורא v. נטורא
נ-ט-ל v. נטל #2
נ-ט-פ v. נטף
נ-ט-ר v. נטר
נדר, נדרא v. נידרא
ניחא v. ניח
ניכותא v. ניחותא
ניכתא v. נייחתא
אהנון v. נינהו
ניסן v. ניסן
נירא v. נירא #1
(נשמה v. נישמתא)
נמרא v. נמרא
ננכא v. ננחא, ננהא
(נעאמא v. נעמיתא)
נ-ע-ר v. נער #1
נ-פ-כ v. נפח
נ-פ-ל v. נפל
נ-פ-צ v. נפץ
נ-פ-ק v. נפק
נפקתא v. נפקתא
נושא v. נפשא
נ-צ-י v. נצי

ת-א-ר v. עור
?ד-א-פ v. עטף
(עיבור v. עיבורא #1)
דאנא v. עידנא
אזא v. עיזא
2 ע-י-נ v. עיין
איאקא v. עייקא
אלאיא v. עילאה
(עולייא v. עיליתא #1)
?ללאא v. עילעא
אינא v. עינא #1
אנותא v. עינבתא
אקבא v. עיקבא
אקרא v. עיקרא #1
(עירוב v. עירובא)
אקוברא v. עכברא
?א-כ-ר v. עכר #2
ע-ל-י v. עלי
י-א-ל v. עלל
(עולם v. עלמא)
אמ- v. עם
עמונאיא v. עמונאה
ע-מ-י v. עמי
עמיא v. עֲמֵי
עמוקא v. עמיק
אמרא v. עמרא
(מרעז v. [ע]מרעיזי)
עני v. עֲנֵי
(עניות v. עניותא)
(ענין v. עניינא)
אינאנא v. עננא
ד-א-פ v. עפף
אפרא v. עפרא
ע-צ-ר v. עצר
א-ק-ר v. עקר
אקרוא v. עקרבא

?סלשיר v. סלא
י-ס-ק v. ס-ל-ק #1
ש-ל-ק v. סלק #2
סאמא v. סמא
ס-מ-י v. סמי
ס-מ-כ v. סמך
2 סמאכא v. סמכא
ס-מ-ק v. סמק
צנדלתא v. סנדלא
ס-נ-י v. סני
(סעודה v. סעודתא)
?צפטא v. ספטא
ס-פ-י v. ספי #1
ס-פ-ק v. ספק #2
ס-ק-ל v. סקל #2
שרואלא v. סרבלא #2
סראדא v. סרדא
?ס-ר-כ v. סרח #1
ס-ר-ט v. סרט
ס-ר-י v. סרי
סריקא v. סריק
2 ס-ר-ק v. סרק #1
1 ס-ר-ק v. סרק #2
ס-ת-ר v. סתר #1
סתרא v. סתרא #1

ע

א-ו-ד v. עבד
1 אודא v. עבדא #1
אודותא v. עבדותא
2 א-ב-י v. עבי #1
א-ו-ר v. עבר
אדוא v. עדבא
אביאנא v. עוביאנא
ע-ו-י v. עוי
עוירא v. עוירא

פ

צ

?צוב v. צוב
צ-י-ד v. צוד
צ-ו-י v. צוי #2
צומא v. צומא
צוציתא v. צוציתא #3
צורתא v. צורתא
צ-י-ת v. צות
ציוא v. ציבי
(צפון v. ציפונא)
צ-ל-ו v. צלב
צלותא v. צלותא
צ-ל-כ v. צלח #1
?צ-ל-ח v. צלח #2
2 צ-ל-י v. צלי #1
1 צ-ל-י v, צלי #2
צ-מ-ר v. צמר #2
2 צ-נ-ע v, צנע
צ-ע-ר v. צער
(צער v. צערא)
(צפארה v. צפרא)
צ-ר-י v. צרי #1
(?צ-ר-ע v. צרע)
צראפא v. צַרְפָא

ק

ג- v. קָ-, קָא
ברקול v. לקובל, לקבל, קבל
ק-ב-ל v. קבל #1
1 ק-ו-ר v. קבר
1 קורא v. קברא #1
2 ק-ד-ח, 1 ק-ד-ח v. קדח
קדאלא v. קדלא
ק-ד-מ v. קדם
ק-ד-ש v. קדש
ק-ה-י v. קהי
קובא v. קובתא
קלזם v. קולמוסא
ק-י-ם v. קום
?גומגׄא v. קומצא #1
(קומא v. קומתא)
ק v. קוף
קופא v. קופא #4
קפיא v. קופיא #1
קופלא v. קופלא
(קרבן v. קרבנא)
קורדאיא v. קורדנאה
קוטיפא v. קטופא
קטיאא v. קטיע
ק-ט-ל v. קטל
קטלא v. קטלא #1
ק-ט-מ-נ v. קטם #2
ק-ט-א v. קטע
2 ק-ט-פ v. קטף
?ק-ת-ר v. קטר #1
(קדוש v. קידושא)
2 קדרא v. קידרא
קטמא v. קיטמא
?קתרא, קטרא v. קיטרא
קיטא v. קייטא
1 קלה v. קיליא
??קימך v. קימא #1
1 קנא v. קינא #1
(קנאה v. קינא #2)
(קיסר v. קיסר)
2 ק-י-ר, קירא v. קירא #1
קאלא v. קלא #1
קולאאא v. קלא #2
2 ל-ק-ט v. קלט
1 ק-ל-י v. קלי
קליל, קילך, קלולא v. קליל
קלפכתא, קלפא v. קליפתא
קלמא v. קלמתא

ק-ל-ע? v. קלע
ק-ל-פ v. קלף
קמאיא v. קמא
קאמא-קאמא v. קמא קמא
קמכא v. קמחא
ק-ר-מ-ט v. קמט
1 קם v. קמי
ג̇-מ-ג̇? v. קמץ
כמר v. קמרא
קניא v. קניא
קניאנא v. קניינא
ק-פ-י v. קפי
(קפץ v. קפצא)
(קצאבא v. קצבא)
ק-י-צ v. קצי, קצץ
קראא, קראתא v. קרא #4
ק-ר-ו v. קרב
קורדאיא v. קרדויא
ק-ר-כ v. קרח #2
קרטאלא v. קרטליתא
ק-ר-י v. קרי #1
קראיא v. קְרָיָא
(קרי v. קריא #3)
קריוא v. קריב
2 קראיא, מקריאנא v. קריינא
1 ק-ר-מ v. קרם
קאנא v. קרנא
קרקפתא v. קרקפתא
1 ק-י-ר v. קרר
קאשא v. קשישא, קשא
קצבא v. קשבא
קשיא v. קְשֵׁי
קשתא v. קשתא
[קטרא v. קתרא]

ר

רורוא v. רברבני, רברבי, רב
ראבא v. רבא
1 רבי v. רבי
רבותא v. רבותא
ר-ו-י v. רבי #1
רבנתא, רבנא v. רַבָּנָא
(ר-ג̇-מ v. רגם)
ר-א-ש v. רגש
ר-כ-ט v. רהט
רבא v. רובא
לוביא v. רוביא
רוגזא v. רוגזא
ר-ו-כ v. רווח
רוכא v. רוכא
רחקא v. רוחקא
רויכא v. רויח
רויכותא v. רויחותא
רוככא v. רוככא
ר-י-מ v. רום
רומנותא v. רומא
רומאיא v. רומאה
(רומחא v. רומחא)
רימונייה, ארמותא v. רומנא
רוקה v. רוקא #1
רקאתא v. רוקעתא
רשומא v. רושמא
רחוקא v. רחיק
ר-ח-מ v. רחם
רחמה v. רחמי
מרחמאנא v. רחמנא
כ̇-ר-א v. (*רחע>) רחץ #2
ר-ח-ק v. רחק
ר-כ-ש v. רחש
רכשא v. רחשא #1
(רטובא v. רטב)
רבא v. ריבבתא

רבולא, ריבון v. ריבונא

(רבית v. ריביתא)

רובע v. ריבעא

[אקלא v. ריגלא]

(רוגמא v. ריגמא)

ר-י-כ v. ריח

ריכא v. ריחא

ארכה v. ריחיא

רכשא v. ריחשא

(רמז v. רימזא)

רירא v. רירא

ר v. ריש

רישאיא, רישא v. (ריש ירחא/שתא +) רישא

רישאיא v. רישנותא

רתכא v. ריתחא

ר-כ-ו v. רכב

רכיכא v. רכיך

ר-כ-כ v. רכך

ר-כ-נ v. רכן?

ר-מ-ז v. ר-מ-ז

ר-מ-י v. רמי 1#

בירמאשה v. רמשא

ר-י-ס v. רסס

ראוא v. רעוא

ר-א-י v. רעי 1#

(שבאנא v. רעיא)

[ה-ר-ה-מ v. רעם]

[גורגומתא v. רעמא]

2 ר-פ-י ,1 ר-פ-י v. רפי

רפיותא v. רפיותא

ר-ק-ד v. רקד 1#

ר-ק-א v. רקע

ר-י-ק v. רקק

(רשות v. רשותא 1#)

(רשע רשיע)

ר-ש-מ v. רשם

ר-ש-ע v. רשע

ר-ת-כ v. רתח

שׁ

שוואא v. שבועא

(ס-ב-ח v. שבח 1#)

2 שבט v. שבט

1 שבט, שוטא v. שבטא

שוואא v. שבעא

שואסר v. שְׁבַסַר

ש-ו-ק v. שבק

שבתא v. שבתא

ש-א-ר v. שגר 2#

ש-א-ש v. שגש

ש-נ-ד-ל v. שדל

ש-ד-ר v. שדר 1#

čᵃ-h-y č-ג ג-ה-י v. שהי (2+1#)

גהוא v. שהייא 1#

שובלתא v. שובלתא

שכדא v. שוחדא

ש-ט-י v. שוט

ש-ו-י v. שוי

שויתא v. שויתא

שוכתא v. שוכתא?

שולטאנא v. שולטנא

שולטנותא v. שולטנותא

שמנא v. שומנא

שושמה v. שומשמא

שכוונתא v. שומשמנא

ש-י-א v. שעי, שוע

ש-י-פ v. שוף 1#

1 שוקא v. שוקא 1#

שורא v. שורא 1#

שרתא v. שורא 2#

שושבין v. שושבינא

שנשלתא v. שושילתא

1 ש-ל-פ v. שלף #1
ש-ל-ק v. שלק
שמא v. שמא
ש-מ-ד v. שמד
שמואתא v. שמועתא
(שמטה v. שמיטתא)
ש-מ-נ v. שמן
שמנותא v. שמנינותא
ש-מ-א v. שמע
שמתא v. שמתא
ש-נ-י v. שני
ש-ע-ב-ד v. שעבד
(שעבוד v. שעבודא)
שאולא v. שעולא
č-y-ʾ ג̆-י-א v. שעע
1 שאתא v. שעתא
ש-ב-ד v. שפד
שבודא v. שפודא
שפירא v. שפיר
ש-פ-כ v. שפך
(ספיל v. שפל)
ש-פ-ר v. שפר
שאקא v. שקא
(1 ש-ת-י v. שקי #1)
č-y-q ג̆-י-ק v. שקיק
ש-ק-ל v. שקל #1
?ש-ק-ע v. שקע
שראאה v. שרגא
שרותא v. שרותא
ש-ר-י v. שרי #1
2 שאתא v. שתא
1 ש-ת-י v. שתי
(שתי-ערב v. שתיא)
ש-ת-ל v. שתל
ש-ת-ק v. שתק
שושמה v. שושמא
ש-כ-נ v. שחן
2 ש-כ-ר v. שחר #1
ש-ט-כ, ש-ט-ח v. שטח
ש-ט-פ v. שטף
(שטר v. שטרא)
?שבא v. שיבא #1
שואוא v. שיבבתא, שיבבא
שיבבותא v. שיבבותא
jıgda? ג̆גדא v. שיגדונא
שאדא v. *שיגדתא
שידא v. שידא
שכנא v. שיחנא
ש-ט-י v. שייטא #1
שנשלתא v. שילשלתא
ש v. שין
(כאכא v. שינא)
שנתא v. שינתא
č-y-ʾ ג̆-י-א, ש-י-א v. שיע
שיאאה v. שיעא
שפולא v. שיפולא
(שקץ v. שיקצא)
(שק״ר v. שיקרא)
שושא v. שישא #2
אשתא v. שיתא
אשתאסר v. שיתסר
שתלא v. שיתלא
(שכינה v. שכינתא)
1 שאכר v. שכר #1
שלג׳ם v. שלגם
č-ḥ-y? ג̆-ה-י v. (cf. שהי) שלהי
ש-ל-כ v. שלח #2
(שליח v. שליחא)
שליקא v. שליק
(שלאמא, שלום v. שלמא)
(שלמים v. שלמיא)

ת-ל-כ v. תלח
ת-ל-ת-י v. תלי
תליא v. תליא דליבא
תלמידא v. תלמידא
ת-ו-ל-א v. תלע
טלאהא v. תלתא
טלאהושב v. תלאתא בשבא
תאמא v. תמן, תם
תמוז v. תמוז
(ת-מ-מ) ת-י-מ v. תמם
תמניא v. תמניא
תמאניאסר v. תמניסר
ת-ו-נ v. תנב
ת-נ-י v. תני
1 תנא v. תננא
(תענית v. תעניתא)
(תפילין v. תפילֵי)
ט-פ-ר? v. תפר
(תקיעה v. תקיעתא)
תקופה? v. תקיף
ת-ק-ל v. תקל
(תקנה v. תקנתא)
ת-ק-ע v. תקע
תרבא v. תרבא
(תרגום v. תרגומא)
(ת-ל-גֿ-מ v. תרגם)
ת-ר-י v. תרי #2
תרה v. תרי
תריאסר v. תריסר
תרושב v. תרי בשבא
תריצא v. תריץ
תרוצותא v. תריצותא
ת-ר-כ v. תרך
ת-ר-מ v. תרם
ת-ר-ס v. תרס
תראא v. תרעא

שׂ

ס-ו-א v. שׂבע
ספתא v. שׂיפתא
[גּפה čappe v. שׂמאלא]
סעארה v. שׂערתא
ס-ר-ט v. שׂרטט
ס-ר-פ v. שׂרף #2

ת

תוירא v. תביר
תולה v. תבלא
ת-ו-ר v. תבר
תוריתא v. תברתא
(תאנגֿ v. תגא)
(תגֿר v. תגרא)
(תגֿארותא v. תגרותא)
(תהום v. תהומא)
ת-ה-י v. תהי #1
תּ v. תָו
תולאתא v. תולעתא
(תֿילית v. תולתא #1)
(סי-צאלא v. תולתא #2)
תומא v. תומא #1
1 תורא v. תורא
תוורתא v. תורתא
(תכוב v. תחומא)
תכֿית v. תחות
כֿתאיא v. תחתאה
תונא v. תיבנא
טגֿ'ארא? v. תיגרא #2
2 תכתא v. תיכתא
תאנא v. תינתא
תקלא v. תיקלא #1
(ס-פ-ל v. תכלא #1+2)
תכת v. תכתקא
תלגא v. תלגא

אגֿאסר .v תשסר

גֿירי (2 ;תשרי (1 .v תשרי čēri

ת-ר-צ .v תרץ

אגֿאא .v תשעא